AF600266

RESILIENCE *and* THE VIRTUE *of* FORTITUDE

RESILIENCE *and* THE VIRTUE *of* FORTITUDE

Aquinas in Dialogue with the Psychosocial Sciences

CRAIG STEVEN TITUS

The Catholic University of America Press
Washington, D.C.

Published with the support of the Swiss National Science Foundation.

Copyright © 2006
The Catholic University of America Press
All rights reserved
The paper used in this publication meets the minimum requirements of American National Standards for Information Science—Permanence of Paper for Printed Library Materials, ANSI Z39.48-1984.
∞

LIBRARY OF CONGRESS CATALOGING-IN-PUBLICATION DATA
Titus, Craig Steven, 1959–
Resilience and the virtue of fortitude : Aquinas in dialogue with the psychosocial sciences / Craig Steven Titus.
p. cm.
Includes bibliographical references (p.) and index.
ISBN-13: 978-0-8132-1463-4 (cloth : alk. paper)
ISBN-10: 0-8132-1463-7 (cloth : alk. paper)
1. Thomas, Aquinas, Saint, 1225?–1274. 2. Resilience (Personality trait) 3. Fortitude. I. Title.
B765.T54T53 2006
179′.9—dc22

2005032945

Contents

PART TWO. APPLICATIONS

PART THREE. FORTITUDE AND RESILIENCE TRANSCENDED

Acknowledgments

Numerous persons have contributed the intellectual support that forms the basis for this book's breadth of vision. In the first place, I owe a debt of gratitude to Fr. Servais-Théodore Pinckaers, O.P. He provides a model for doing moral theology deeply rooted in the sources of all that is good and true. Fr. Michael Sherwin, O.P., helped forge the work's final form and nuance its present content; he has done this with great intelligence and in the spirit of friendship. Mgr. Jean-Louis Bruguès, O.P., helped me wrestle with thorny methodological issues that underlie multidisciplinary dialogue about what is ever old and ever new concerning the human spirit that is faced with difficulty. Other people have also generously offered me their guidance, knowledge, and wisdom. At the risk of not justly acknowledging their unique contributions, I will simply list their names and areas of assistance: Fr. Paul Philibert, O.P. (general), Fr. Benedict Ashley, O.P. (method and moral theology), Prof. Vincent Punzo (psychology and form), Prof. Daniel Robinson (sources and form), Stefan Vanistendael (resilience and spirituality), Fr. Owen Carroll (Aquinas and Aristotle), Prof. William C. Mattison (emotions and virtue), Dr. Jorge Ferreira (resilience and psychotherapy), Prof. Stephen J. Pope (method of moral theology in dialogue with the sciences), Prof. François Ruëgg (cultural anthropology and method), Prof. Benedict Viviano, O.P. (Scripture and emotion), PD Dr. Bernard

N. Schumacher (philosophy and hope), Prof. Dominic O'Meara (Aristotle and Cicero), Prof. Meinrad Perrez (psychology of virtues, resilience, and stress), Dr. Markus Zimmerman (methods of moral theology and ethics), Dr. Michael Terranova (faith and virtue), Elise Yakuboff (proofreading), Cyril Rouiller (formatting). On a practical level, Fr. Liam Walsh, O.P., made the book possible; to him, to Fr. Benoît-Dominique de la Soujeole, O.P., the University of Fribourg, and the Albertinum I am greatly indebted. At the CUA Press, I would like to thank Dr. Gregory LaNave for his kind competence and Carol A. Kennedy for her expert copyediting. I give special thanks to my wife, Giovanna, who has contributed her realist insights and linguistic talents to the text. Together with our sons, Luca and Matteo, she has provided me with support and strength to face the difficulties of the task. With heartfelt gratitude, I see all these sources of resilience as so many reminders of God's own goodness.

Introduction

Although suffering and challenge demoralize some human beings, others cope and construct instead. Rather than grinding to a halt, certain people hurdle the obstacles or creatively maneuver around them. They even make something positive out of the negative situation. In the face of crisis, they not only survive but also thrive. Resilience capacities involve coping well with difficulty, actively resisting destructive pressures, and rebuilding positively after adversity. However, people do not exercise these capacities in equal measure. Human beings faced with similar situations end up in diverse spots. Some manage destructive life events more efficaciously. Others lose a sense of meaning or emotional stability. Certain people find a constructive outcome to the negative situation. Others become aggressive and abusive, or drug or alcohol dependent. What initiates and sustains a resilient use of human resources? What renders some individuals and groups more resilient than others? Such questions are pertinent not only for the psychosocial studies that instigated the use of the resilience concept, but also for ethical approaches.

One of this work's central theses is that ethics and moral theology can employ the resilience concept and research to heighten moral analysis at the developmental level. In so doing, ethics and moral theology need to integrate into their proper domains reflections on potential personal and social resources that are available for building character, especially in the midst of vicissitude, trial, and loss. In this perspective, I shall address the following questions: How might resilience research deepen our comprehension of the possibility and the limits of moral development? How does it enhance our understanding of fortitude and its related virtues? And can it contribute to a renewal of contemporary philosophical anthropology, virtue theory, and moral theology? While respecting diverse linguistic and conceptual idioms, I put psychosocial sciences into conversation with St. Thomas Aquinas' ethical theory and moral theology. I have chosen to revisit Thomas Aquinas' philosophical and theological ethics, since they involve an approach to a philosophy of nature- and virtue-based understanding of the person that can serve as a fruitful context for moral theory in interdisciplinary dialogue with the findings of psychological and social sciences.

To this end, I analyze pertinent psychosocial theory and data on human resilience and vulnerability. This expository investigation then leads to integrating key findings at the level of philosophical anthropology. I make a case that availing philosophical and ethical studies to such sources of fine-tuned observation enriches our understanding of the person. More than simply comparing and contrasting resilience research and Aquinas' moral theory, I enter into a philosophical discussion of the warrants for employing psychosocial studies in conceptualizations of philosophical anthropology, ethics, and moral theology. Aquinas' treatises on the virtues in general and fortitude in particular offer much to recommend themselves to such a contemporary debate. His theoretical work on the virtues is one of the most exhaustive to date, with a perennial value that is not accessed, however, without some interpretive effort. His dialogic method offers a model open to credible scientific findings and philosophical debate. Thus I employ psychosocial studies on human resilience to revitalize Aquinas' moral anthropology and to better understand the virtues associated with fortitude. Moreover, I extend this conversation to a theological dimension, in particular, to deepen moral theology from a Catholic perspective. This type of renewal of moral theology requires accessing not only the properly theological sources of Scripture and tradition, but also insights found in normative reflection and descriptive sciences, that is, in philosophical ethics and psychosocial sciences. It reflects upon the presence, action, and influence of God in human agency and society.

In chapter 1, I investigate the resilience perspective per se. Physicists have long used the term "resilience" to refer to a material's quality to resist deformation or destruction. This limited usage has inspired a more expansive approach in the psychosocial sciences, which employ it to describe the individual and social capacities to face vicissitude. The psychosocial sciences analyze human resilience as having three related facets: to cope with hardship; to resist the possible deformation of the competencies and integrity of one's community, family, and self; and to achieve a new proficiency out of the unfavorable experience. Each domain involves opportunities for positive growth, which cannot be reduced to the personal, cultural, or communal situation at hand. The three main strengths of the psychosocial resilience perspective are that it focuses on the ready resources, instead of on pathology per se; that it seeks to identify promotable patterns of coping, constancy, and construction without falling into determinism; and that it recognizes the import of life-goals without rationalistic reductionism. Resilience outcomes indicate that developmental tutors require, more often than not, growth through affective, intellectual, and spiritual trials. They involve both keeping contact with our larger goals, while grappling with intermediate ones, and remaining enrooted in personal, cultural, and communal resources.

Resilience studies thus offer input for a renewed philosophy of nature and virtue-based philosophical anthropology (chapter 2), in particular concerning the factors and processes that strengthen resilience outcomes, as well as others that weaken them. Of particular interest for us, resilience research contains both challenges and promises for the enhancement of virtue theory and moral theology (chapter 3). After introducing Aquinas' virtue-based moral theory that is rooted in a dynamic relationship of human nature, culture, and community, I then examine the way in which the psychosocial sciences' resilience findings can renew virtue theory and moral theology at the level of their underlying philosophical anthropology, in particular concerning human developmental pathways as traced through particular cultures and communities. In the light of human resilience in adversity, I then analyze Aquinas' position on moral theory and flourishing.

In the second and third parts of the book, I apply the resilience research and an anthropological vision enriched by it to the three virtue groups that confront difficulty: namely fortitude and its related virtues of initiative taking and endurance. At this point, Aquinas' experiential and realist metaphysical teaching on these virtues contributes a deeper understanding of human agency in difficult situations. Among the vast network of virtues, fortitude and its associated virtues are the most obvious dialogue partners for resilience research. Through a renewed reading of Aquinas' virtue anthropology, the rest of the book makes a rapprochement between the resilience findings and each of these virtues. I illustrate how these virtues are structurally akin to the three resilience domains. First, the exercise of each virtue confronts adversity. Second, it resists loss of acquired competencies. Third, it builds something positive out of the negative situation. I proceed with this dialogue between Thomas and resilience findings in two stages and two distinct methods.

In Part Two (chapters 4, 5, and 6), I address Aquinas' view on the acquired virtues that manage situations of danger and difficulty. This philosophical effort offers a fitting discussion partner for the psychosocial sciences, even though it outstrips them in its normative and moral competency. On the natural level, we revisit the virtues in terms of resilience research for several reasons. Particularly when one is facing hardships, it is not always personally evident which tack to take. Aquinas thus affirms that we each need to develop prudent discernment. Since the development of virtue requires time and experience, we can ask: What might we learn from the resilience outcomes to strengthen basic human capacities, promote resilience, and diminish vulnerability? At this level, I speak of moral, constructive, and resisting types of resilience in parallel with the virtues of courage, initiative, and endurance.

In Part Three (chapters 7, 8, and 9), I examine the theological dimension of these virtues and the resilience input. This level is admittedly moral theology that uses psychosocial insights, without co-opting their scientific pretensions or giving them normative status. It employs its own anthropological reflections on the meaning of these findings. This standpoint, with its scriptural, patristic, and other theological bases, involves separating the efficacy of human virtuous acts and dispositions neither from their sources in natural inclinations and capacities nor from their sources in God's constant presence and particular gifts of grace. It identifies how both human and divine sources collaborate in specific challenges and are present in the resilient results manifest in Christian virtues. At this level, I speak of a spiritual resilience, which involves the divine support offered in the midst of human agency.

PART ONE

THEORETICAL CONSIDERATIONS *of* RESILIENCE *and* VIRTUE THEORIES

1

The Resilience Perspective

Bad things can turn into good things.
HELEN (AGE 10)[1]

At every level of society, particular situations make or break the lives of children, adolescents, and adults—situations of violence, loss, indifference, and hatred. Some human beings cope well when faced with them, and others do not. Specialists call this capacity to do well in adversity "resilience." Psychosocial research has documented three types of resilience phenomena: good outcomes in the midst of high risk (coping), sustained competence under stress (constancy), and recovery from trauma (constructing).[2] In order to track these resilience phenomena, researchers have changed their perspectives and methods.[3] Moral theologians can benefit from these sciences' insights into how humans avoid pathology and develop positively.

1. Murphy 1987, 104, quoting one of her patients.

2. Cf. Consortium on the School-based Promotion of Social Competence [hereafter Consortium] 1994, 268–316, esp. 272.

3. Resilience as an approach in the human sciences has meant a triple paradigm shift: from single

Although specialists must in some way conceptualize resilience in relation to human disease, resilience is of interest beyond the context of pathology. It aids us to understand and promote the positive development occasioned by negative situations and potentially destructive challenges. The psychosocial sciences' resilience perspective has two major axes. First, it does not concentrate exclusively on human problems and pathologies. Rather, it principally focuses on the personal and communal resources on hand. Second, it seeks patterns of human coping, constancy, and constructing and ways we might promote them in the interactive context of the individual, family, and society.

Origin and Breadth of the Resilience Concept

The reality of human resilience is as old as humanity itself, even though its conceptualization in psychosocial sciences dates to the 1970s. The resilience approach attempts to unearth an aspect of human experience that medical and social sciences often have placed solely in the context of disease. The search to understand human resilience requires a shift in perspective. In order to identify the sources of human resilience, we must correct research models that overemphasize pathology. We need to look afresh at human experience.

A Brief History of Resilience: Cultural Origins and Disciplinary Lines

The human capacities to cope with adversity, resist being deformed by hardship, and construct further hardiness from the experience are as old as humankind. Their thematization, however, is a contemporary trend whose early roots are found in Anglo-American research on children and families in difficulty. Emmy Werner has been described as the mother of resilience, because of her longitudinal study of disadvantaged children and youth on the Island of Kauai.[4] One of the earlier definitions of resilience is that of Norman Garmezy (1976), who describes resilient people as having "worked well, played well, loved well and expected well."[5] According to Michael Rut-

causes to multiple cumulative dynamics, from simplistic models to complex processes, and from static studies to longitudinal investigation of interactive processes. On how the history of resilience research has seen a triple enrichment see Gore and Eckenrode 1994, 25. On the importance of such paradigm shifts for science see Kuhn 1970, and Kopfensteiner 1998, 80–88.

4. Cf. Werner and Smith 1986, 1992, and 2001.

5. Garmezy 1976.

ter (1998), an English child psychiatrist, the mental health sciences have applied the concept of resilience progressively in five steps. First, they construe it solely as an individual characteristic: what the individual did under stress. Second, resilience integrates the individual's interaction with the environment, involving also what happened before, during, and after the stress. Third, certain specialists deem it a balance of good and bad experiences. Fourth, in a medical analogy, it is seen as a type of immunization, through which we attain strengthened health by exposure to natural or induced infections. Fifth, researchers recognize that psychological challenges and a certain level of stress are useful and even necessary for human development; this focus includes emphasis on how to aid children in weathering adversities actively and successfully.[6]

The research into resilience has been international and multidisciplinary.[7] This brief history of the scientific study of resilience should mention the application of the resilience perspective to efforts to aid local communities in confronting their own difficulties, drawing as much as possible on local resources. Both developed and developing regions benefit from use of the resilience perspective.[8] Furthermore, numerous efforts to popularize the concept have also enriched medical and epidemiological models.[9] Lastly, positive psychology is the heir apparent that seeks to more comprehensively apply key insights of resilience theory and research to an ever more global perspective and therapeutic approach to human well-being and development.[10]

In the resilience research done in the human and social sciences, there are at least five interrelated groups of models: genetic models, personality models, cognitive models, developmental models, and human relationships models. Genetic models imply the search to understand how human personal and social capacities are grounded in genetic coding (as distinguished from the external and internal influences of family, society, and en-

6. Cf. Rutter 1998, 47.

7. There are numerous European (non-Anglo-American) counterparts and a host of parallel, preparatory efforts and figures. European figures in resilience research include: F. Lösel (Germany), S. Vanistendael (Belgium, Switzerland), M. Manciaux (France), B. Cyrulnik (France), M. Tousignant, (Canada), M. Perrez (Switzerland), A. Antonovsky (Israel), and so on. Some of the predecessors to resilience theory include epidemiological efforts, and risk calculations (from the insurance industry).

8. Cf. Grotberg 1995. Nongovernmental aid agencies such as the International Catholic Child Bureau, Van Leer Foundation, and so forth.

9. Cf. Vanistendael and Lecomte 2000; Cyrulnik 1998, 1999, 2001.

10. Cf. Seligman and Csikszentmihalyi 2000; Snyder and Lopez 2002; Seligman 2002; Peterson and Seligman 2004.

vironment). This approach involves sociobiology or evolutionary psychology.[11]

Personality models investigate how negative and positive outcomes can be attributable to temperamental traits and developed characters: for example, irritability or shyness, sensitivity or adaptability. This approach draws from psychoanalytical traditions and attachment theory.[12]

Cognitive models, based on developments in cognitive psychology, consider emotions as the result of the meaning a person attributes to particular interactions with the environment.[13] It seeks resilience insights based on cognitive resources, linked for example to problem-solving capacities.

Developmental models identify adaptive reactions to developmental challenges over the life span. Developmental resilience research has been characterized by variable-focused, person-focused, and pathway models.[14] In general, these approaches are rooted in developmental psychology and developmental psychopathology.[15]

The social relationships model researches how changes in important family, religious, and other social relationships either contribute to the challenges we face or help us overcome them.[16] In the pages that follow we shall identify the insights into human resilience offered by these five often overlapping models, drawing from each to the extent that it helps us grasp more deeply the role of resilience in human action.

Three Resilience Domains: Physical, Psychosocial, and Spiritual

The disciplines of physics and engineering employ the term "resilience" to refer to a material's capacity to return to its original form after being bent,

11. Its actors include: E. O. Wilson 1975 *(Sociobiology)*, Richard Dawkins 1976 *(The Selfish Gene)*, and 1995. They hypothesize that evolutionary pressures on the natural selection of genes aid their possessors to survive better in given environmental histories.

12. Some of its principal researchers are: John Bowlby 1969, 1973, 1988; Mary D. Ainsworth et al. 1978; and Jerome Kagan 1979, 1990, and 1994. Bowlby was the first to develop attachment theory, which can be considered a control-systems theory of behavior, or an evolutionary-ethological approach. Ainsworth further enriched it.

13. These studies have been mainly conducted by: Arnold 1960; Lazarus 1968, 1991a, and 1991b; Perez 1994a; McCubbin and Thompson, et al. 1998.

14. Cf. Masten and Reed 2002.

15. Cf. Piaget 1965/1932; Kohlberg 1971, 1976, 1980; Kohlberg, Lacrosse, and Ricks 1972. Its key resilience researchers are: Garmezy 1976, 1994; Rutter 1981, 1994; Masten, Best, and Garmezy 1990; Achenbach 1990; Cicchetti and Hess 1983 and Cicchetti 1990; Dale F. Hay 1988; Albert F. Osborn 1990; Jon Rolf et al. 1990; Masten and Reed 2002; Luthar 2003. Viktor Frankl 1963 can also be counted among thinkers in a developmental perspective.

16. Its principal researchers include Emmy E. Werner and Ruth S. Smith 1986, 1992, and 2001; Arnold J. Sameroff, Ronald Seifer, and C. Baldwin 1993; Michel Tousignant 1997 and 1998; Clifford Geertz 1968.

compressed, or stretched.[17] For example, after being compressed, an iron bar either returns to its original shape or does not. The iron bar's resilience is its quality to flex under pressure and return to its original form.[18] When the stress exceeds the iron bar's elastic limit, however, the bar remains bent; its resilience capacity was surpassed. Furthermore, a certain type of pressure has a "steeling" effect on metal.[19] Stretching or heating hardens metal. In sum, the literal sense of "resilience" refers to both a material's ability to resist deformation and its ability to be strengthened through contact with certain types of stress.[20]

The human sciences employ the concept of resilience to describe the physiological and psychosocial resources for facing personal and communal challenges.[21] This second type of resilience has three aspects:[22] (1) good outcomes despite actual risk, (2) resistance to destruction, and (3) positive construction.[23] It is possible not only to resist the disordering of the integrity and skills of a human person, family, or community, but also to achieve a new kind of competency, turning the negative experience into an oppor-

17. This meaning of "resilience" is the first identified in popular dictionaries. For example, *Webster's Encyclopedic Unabridged Dictionary (WEUD)* (1989) says "1. The power or ability to return to the original form, position, etc. after being bent, compressed, or stretched; elasticity"; and *Webster's New Collegiate Dictionary,* "1. The capacity of a strained body to recover its size and shape after deformation caused especially by compressive stress." *The Oxford English Dictionary* (1989) gives it as the second definition: "2. Elasticity; the power of resuming the original shape or position after compression, bending, etc.; *spec.* the energy per unit volume absorbed by a material when it is subjected to strain, or the maximum value of this when the elastic limit is not exceeded." It gives the following formula: "resilience per cubic inch in direct tension or compression may be expressed in the form $f2/2E$, where f is the intensity of stress induced and E is the modulus of elasticity" (J. A. Cormack, Definitions, Formulae and Worked Examples in Strength of Materials [London: Macdonald, 1965], iii:67).

18. Metal might nonetheless analogously have a "memory" of its minor past stresses (cf. metal fatigue and aging; or entropy—the dissipation of energy).

19. The "steeling" image of resilience has been employed by Anthony and Cohler 1987, 180; Felsman and Vaillant 1987, 305 (who quote studies done on children of schizophrenics by Bleuler 1978); Rutter 1994b, 354.

20. It should be noted that the term "resilient" has Latin roots meaning "to jump, leap or bounce back": *resiliens, resilire, re-salire.*

21. Cf. Werner and Smith 1986; Lösel and Bliesener 1990; Radke-Yarrow and Sherman 1990; Rutter 1994b.

22. Concerning this second level of meaning, *WUED* (1989) says "2. ability to recover readily from illness, depression, adversity or the like; buoyancy"; and *Webster's New Collegiate Dictionary,* "2. An ability to recover from or adjust easily to misfortune or change." *The Oxford English Dictionary* (1989) gives it as the third one: "3. *fig.* Of persons, their minds, etc.: Rising readily again after being depressed; hence cheerful, buoyant, exuberant."

23. Lösel (1992, 8) identifies three resilience phenomena, from a developmental psychopathology perspective, resilience "refers to: (1) good outcomes despite high-risk status, for example, overcoming cumulated stressors and strains; (2) sustaining competence under threat, for example, effective coping with divorce; and (3) recovering from trauma, for example, child abuse. All three phenomena may be present simultaneously in cases with multi level problems." Cf. Masten, Best, and Garmezy 1990, 2:425–44.

tunity for positive growth. The psychosocial sciences observe a resilience-effect rooted in human physiological and psychosocial capacities; they attempt to identify the various internal and external (personal and communal) factors, mechanisms, or processes that strengthen or weaken the resilience effect.[24] This second level of physiological and psychosocial resilience is of a different nature than the first. It is organic and psychic. For example, at the biological level, muscles not only perform physical labor, but also resist self-disintegration and become stronger through the effort. At cognitive, volitional, and emotional levels, likewise, we overcome challenges by solving a particular problem, as well as by resisting personal and social de-structuring. We gain something from the effort as well; we acquire understanding, problem-solving skills, self-confidence, and so forth.

A third type of resilience depends on spiritual resources. It metaphorically extends and transcends the original literal meaning of resilience, as well as its physiological and psychosocial insights. At the philosophical and theological levels, we employ skills, resist destruction, and positively construct in the face of difficulty. In order to understand spiritual resilience though, we must employ different methods of analysis. Indeed, we need to explore deeper levels of personal experience, relational assistance, and divine support. However, we can confuse the meaning and extent of insights drawn from different levels. These disciplines have different scopes and foci. The carryover of insights from the physiological and psychosocial sciences demands that we consider the limits and tentative nature of their research. In order to discern and appropriate their spiritual significance, we must evaluate an insight's import, based upon a philosophical anthropology. The difficulties of observing and evaluating spiritual resilience, though, should not deter us from seeking to understand it.

Three Aspects of Resilience: Coping, Resisting, and Constructing

A resilient act is a whole. It is not, however, understood without analyzing its three facets: coping, resisting, and constructing. In the rest of this section, I shall analyze descriptions and definitions of resilience found in the scientific literature. I have two goals. First I would like to illustrate the three dimensions of resilience: good outcomes despite risk, human resis-

24. Cf. Rutter 1994b, 373–74; Garmezy and Masten 1990; Clarke and Clarke 1992; Wilson and Gottman 1996, 204.

tance to destruction, and positive construction. The contrary dimensions involve risk, stress, and vulnerability. These facets and elements are ambiguous when taken outside of a personal and social whole, which leads to the second aim: to establish a composite definition that includes the physiological, psychosocial, and spiritual resilience of individuals and communities. Norman Garmezy's early description of resilient people, as having "worked well, played well, loved well and expected well,"[25] sets a positive goal for human living and dying. It gives wide parameters for understanding resilience research. The general and vague breadth of this definition makes it only a starting point. Nevertheless, it enables us to establish the basic meaning of resilience as "doing well in adversity." I shall formulate a more composite definition after exposing the resilience perspective and research.

Most researchers construe resilience as the individual and social capacity to cope positively with stress and adversity, as a good outcome despite risks and stress. The resilience pioneers Werner and Smith describe resilience as follows: it is the "capacity to cope effectively with the internal stresses of vulnerabilities (such as unstable patterns of autonomic reactivity, developmental imbalances, unusual sensitivities) and external stresses (such as illness, major losses, and dissolution of the family)."[26] Psychology often interprets coping as successful behavioral adaptation. Masten et al. say: "Resilience refers to the process of, capacity for, or outcome of successful adaptation despite challenging or threatening circumstances. Psychological resilience is concerned with behavioral adaptation, usually defined in terms of internal states of well-being or effective functioning in the environment or both."[27] Some researchers describe resilience as a "generally resourceful" composite

25. Garmezy 1976.

26. Werner and Smith 1986, 4. Rutter (1990, 181) uses the notion of resilience "to describe the positive pole of the ubiquitous phenomenon of individual difference in people's responses to stress and adversity."

27. Masten, Best, and Garmezy 1990, 426. There are also other researchers, in studies of strengths and weaknesses that express optimistic views about the human capacity for change and adaptation (cf. Pilling 1992, 88). On the more cautious side, Rutter (1994b, 356) says that while it used to be assumed that "because negative life events provoked or precipitated the onset of psychiatric disorder, they necessarily involved an increase in developmental discontinuities. It is now clear that this assumption is unwarranted. The biological 'norm' is neither continuity nor discontinuity, neither change nor stability (Rutter, 1994a). Both are expected and both require explanation. Depending on circumstances, negative life experiences may either accentuate preexisting psychological characteristics, be they adaptive or maladaptive, or alter them. However, the former is more common than the latter (Caspi and Moffit, 1993)." Likewise according to Sameroff and Seifer (1990, 52), developmental psychopathology assumes neither continuity (as does developmental psychology) nor discontinuity (as do the clinical psychiatrists).

of characteristics.[28] Others speak of a sense of coherence,[29] of manifest social competence—the integration of cognitive, affective, and behavioral levels,[30] or more simply of an active attempt to manage stress.[31] In spite of various disciplinary accents, coping is a universal resilience characteristic.

Second, resilience defies destructive pressures. It protects our health and skills. It resists ruptures to basic relationships. It does more than simply maintain our integrity, as if it were a static object. Indeed when we call upon our skills and resources in adversity, we must not exceed the limits of our health and strength. We need to maintain equilibrium, reestablish it, or find a new one. Rutter thus defines resilience as "the phenomenon of maintaining adaptive functioning in spite of serious risk hazards."[32] This aspect of resilience does not promote an illusion of invincibility. It does not construe resilience as an extreme competence or limit it to exceptional achievements. Instead, it underlines how we avoid failure or pathology,[33] and how we minimize or prevent negative outcomes.[34]

Third, resilience describes how strengths, resources, and skills not only enable us to cope with hardship or to defy ruin, but also to adapt positively in hardship. Resilience involves not only holding the line, but also mak-

28. Radke-Yarrow and Sherman (1990, 99), for example, say: "to show more *'umweg'* [roundabout] solutions when faced with a barrier, to be able to maintain integrated performance under stress, to be able to process simultaneously two or more competing stimuli, to be able to resist sets or illusions, to be able to both 'regress in the service of the ego' when task requirements favor such a form of adaptation and, conversely, to be able to become adaptively obsessive and even compulsive under certain other environmental presses." They attribute the origin of the notion of resilience to Lewinian, Wernerian, Murphian, and psychoanalytic concepts.

29. According to Antonovsky (1998, 8), the "sense of coherence" construct distills the core of coping and resistance resources, which are based on one's sense of comprehensibility (ability to understand situations in life), manageability (capacity to manage demands), and meaningfulness (ability to find meaning in life). Cf. McCubbin et al. 1998.

30. According to the Consortium on the School-based Promotion of Social Competence (1994, 275), "social competence [also] involves the capacity to integrate cognition, affect, and behavior to achieve specific social tasks and positive development outcomes. It comprises a set of core skills, attitudes, abilities, and feelings given functional meaning by the contexts of culture, neighborhood, and situation. Thus, social competence can be viewed in terms of 'life skills for adaptation to diverse ecologies and settings.'" Cf. Masten, Best, and Garmezy 1990, 236–56.

31. Cf. Lösel 1994, 9.

32. Rutter 1990, 209.

33. Albert F. Osborn (1990, 24) rightly points out the importance of definitions: "Decisions about the definition of competence can also result in a different concept of resilience if the focus is on avoidance of failure rather than the achievement of an exceptional level of success. When competence is defined in terms of avoidance of failure, it is usually the case that a greater proportion of vulnerable children, with respect to a given pathology, are resilient than actually develop the pathology."

34. According to E. Grotberg (1995, 7), "Resilience is a universal capacity which allows a person, group or community to prevent, minimize or overcome the damaging effects of adversity."

ing headway. Garmezy notes "the actualizing power of stressful experiences via the ameliorating force of identifiable 'protective factors.'"[35] He describes them as patterns of both positive potential and adaptive outcomes. They involve increased fitness and vigor. For Cowan et al., resilience describes "the idea that some individuals or families possess physiological strengths, psychological resourcefulness, and interpersonal skills that enable them to respond successfully to major challenges and to grow from the experience."[36] Bloom discusses growth-producing experiences in the midst of stress, and resilience as a balance of strength and stress.[37] Especially in the developmental perspective, researchers note that resilience is not a fixed attribute; indeed changes in circumstances and risks alter our resilience.[38] Murphy nonetheless describes it as a type of learned optimism about our capacity to manage problems and turn the bad experiences into something good.[39] Individual differences draw attention to how we develop resilience in the midst of suffering and adversity.[40] This facet of resilience highlights the steeling effect of trials that render us more able to master life's challenges.

Risk, Stress, and Vulnerability versus Protection, Coping, and Buffering

Although some humans do well despite their at-risk status, resilience is not absolute. No one is simply resilient. Resilience researchers seek to explain why some humans neither acquire disorders nor underdevelop when faced with a common threat. This approach draws upon but outstrips an epidemiological focus on risk, stress, and vulnerability.

35. Cf. Garmezy 1994, 10.

36. Cowan, Cowan, and Schulz 1996, 14–15.

37. According to Martin Bloom (1996, 98) resilience finds important roots in the concept of *strens* and in the salutogenic perspective: "Many years ago, Hollister (1967, 197) introduced the term *strens* to mean growth-producing experiences. It was a term that was intended to be parallel to the concept of stress. Poser and King (1975) introduced the term salutogenesis. Both these terms refer to the same important phenomenon, that there exist in nature and society many growth-promoting experiences, some of which may be intentionally introduced to target groups. [. . .] Resilient children may be hypothesized to have more *strens* than stresses. There needs to be a balance between strens and stresses." Werner and Smith (1986, 136) and Rutter (1998, 47) also use this image of balance.

38. Cf. Rutter 1990, 183–84.

39. Cf. Murphy 1987, 104.

40. Although certain resilience qualities might be based on or closely connected with predispositions, other related skills and qualities are lost or acquired, diminished or bettered. Cf. Wills et al. 1996, 108; Lösel 1994, 9.

Risk and Specific Outcomes

Risk research finds its roots in epidemiology, as well as in the calculations of commerce and insurance.[41] Epidemiological studies of risk originally attempted to document health and disease patterns and the factors associated with them. Who gets sick, who does not, and why? The question of "why" addresses issues of causality, originally the causes of mortality and physical disease. Researchers had to adapt the meaning and measure of causality and risk when they applied these concepts to mental health and illness.[42] From dichotomous definitions of risk—the ship returned to port or it did not; people developed typhoid or they did not—investigators have concerned themselves with a wider notion of outcomes: not merely the presence or absence of disease, but also issues of a disorder's duration and the number and severity of symptoms.

Psychosocial approaches have construed risk to involve both individual and social hazards, which increase negative developmental outcomes. Risk researchers identify factors that accentuate or inhibit disease and deficiency states. They also examine the underlying processes.[43] They observe that risks predispose individuals and groups to specific negative outcomes.[44] M. Rutter nonetheless resists a simplistic outlook. He observes that risks also involve the opportunity to overcome the difficulty and to develop adaptive behaviors.[45] Rutter argues first that risk factors do not produce a direct result, and second that they do not have the same high rate of effect when

41. Cf. Cowan, Cowan, and Schulz 1996, 2–3.

42. According to Judith S. Musick et al. (1987, 230), in psychiatry, the term "'risk' denotes a statistical concept indicating that a child of a parent with a major psychiatric disorder (e.g. manic-depressive illness or schizophrenia) has a greater probability of subsequently developing mental disorder than the child of a well parent. For example, 10–15% of the offspring of schizophrenic parents become schizophrenic, while 30–35% have some form of emotional disturbance."

43. The study of risk identifies factors, processes, and mechanisms that both accentuate and inhibit disease and deficiency states, and their related underlying processes. In a perspective of prevention, this research has become bipolar: on the one hand, seeking to identify what accentuates disease and disorder, i.e. vulnerability; and on the other hand, seeking the risks that may be overcome and even lead to positive adaptive behavior, i.e. resilience. Cf. Garmezy 1994, 9; cf. 9–12; Werner and Smith 1992, 3.

44. According to Cowan, Cowan, and Schulz (1996, 9): "Risks predispose individuals and populations (identifiable groups of people) to specific negative or undesirable outcomes." Concerning the statistical measuring of risk, they state: "The magnitude of risk is measured as the probability of a specific negative outcome in a population when the risk is present, compared with the probability when it is absent, or as a correlation between risk and outcomes measured as continuous rather than categorical variables."

45. Cf. Garmezy 1994, 9–12.

one factor is present alone as when two or more risk variables operate together.[46]

Risk is risk for a specific outcome, and a particular risk can be defined only in terms of an outcome. Rutter illustrates that the same variable functions differently in dissimilar circumstances. For example, shyness may be a *risk* for depression, but *neutral* concerning academic achievement, and *protective* in regard to aggression and delinquency. Thus we should not define shyness as a risk in abstraction; it is a risk only for depression. In general, "at risk" children or adults are not simply at risk, they are at risk for something.[47] Further studies suggest that strategies that work for one high-risk group will not necessarily work for a low-risk group. For example, family policies of restrictiveness—which are not pervasive in successful low-risk families—tend to function successfully in high-risk homes when there are patent risks that are understood by both parents and children.[48]

Researchers often correlate risk with stress or stressors. According to Norman Garmezy and Ann Masten, the presence of a stress stimulus event modifies our equilibrium; it has neuropsychological, cognitive, and emotional consequences, which can disrupt our adaptation.[49] Although there is a danger that such a disruption to a person's adaptation can hinder his development, it can also promote development. Indeed in the midst of crisis, we find opportunity as well as danger.[50] This ambiguity—the negative and positive potential of stress—complicates research efforts. Stress in general is difficult to quantify, contextual stress even more so, and stress-related opportunity the most.[51] Stress and risk studies nonetheless provide a basis for promoting health and resilience. They contrast positive targets for educative and social interventions. For example, better knowledge of adolescent problem behavior identifies one hurdle to overcome on the way to promoting health.[52] Furthermore, some research has gone beyond the original conceptions of risk as individual adaptation to analyze family adaptation.

46. Cf. Rutter 1990, 184; Pilling 1992, 95; Felsman and Vaillant 1987, 307.

47. In this perspective, "risk is not an accumulation of life stressors in which negative life events are associated with any manner of diseases or disorders" (Cowan, Cowan, and Schulz 1996, 10).

48. Cf. Baldwin, Baldwin, and Cole 1990, 277–79.

49. Cf. Garmezy and Masten 1990, 462–63; cited in Yule 1992, 190.

50. Cf. Felsman and Vaillant 1987, 307; Rutter 1990, 185; Werner and Smith 1992, 5.

51. Cf. Pianta, Egeland, and Sroufe 1990, 231–33.

52. Cf. Bandura 1977; Jessor and Jessor 1977; Perry and Kelder 1992; Consortium 1994, 297; Cowan, Cowan, and Schulz 1996, 33; Lazurus 1991a; Lazarus and Folkman 1984.

A Continuum of Vulnerability?

The notion of vulnerability complements that of risk. It does not constitute a statistical analysis of risk indicators, but rather an underlying process that functions only in the presence of a stressor. It increases the probability of negative outcome and becomes apparent only under the influence of a specific risk.[53] But the result is not determined beforehand. The study of vulnerabilities leads to questions such as: How can we decrease susceptibility to risk? How can we promote development and resources that diminish vulnerability?[54]

Resilience researchers have defined vulnerability as "an individual's susceptibility to a disorder";[55] "an amplifier of the probability of negative outcomes in the presence of risk." Vulnerabilities are of internal or external sorts.[56] Inner vulnerabilities include genetic predispositions or constitutional factors, as well as conditions such as low self-esteem and depression. External conditions include ineffective parenting, socio-environmental hazards, and the internal frailties of those in the surroundings. Vulnerability accounts for how the negative effects of some variables are precipitated only by a degree of risk.

Vulnerabilities spell creative potential as well. On the one hand, vulnerability can spell the occasion for positive growth. When we overcome risks or crises, we develop a further strength and reduce future vulnerability. On the other hand, what has been a resource can become a vulnerability, when pressed too far or developed in extremis. For example, a premature child's capacity to support pain can lead to not resisting dangerous limits.

Vulnerability can be understood as a non-static continuum. It is the opposite pole of protection,[57] rather than of invulnerability. During the mid-1970s, the language of "vulnerability" gave rise to that of "invulnerability" and even of "invincibility" to describe children who had managed to achieve emotional health and high competence despite adversity and stress.[58] These terms, however, were abandoned for the more relational concepts of resil-

53. Cf. Cowan, Cowan, and Schulz 1996, 11–14.

54. Cf. Petit, Lalou-Moatti, and Clervoy 1998, 3044.

55. Werner and Smith 1992.

56. Cowan, Cowan, and Schulz 1996, 14; Rutter 1994b, 373.

57. Cf. Rutter 1990, 185; Murphy and Moriarty 1976, 202–3.

58. Anthony and Cohler describe his attraction to "invulnerability" as twofold: first, since "'invulnerability' makes the point of psychological invincibility much more strikingly than the term resilience"

ience and stress-resistance.[59] Most people perform with a checkerboard of weaknesses and strengths. To view vulnerability and protection as a continuous dimension of behavior displays their extension to cognitive, volitional, and emotive phenomena. This perspective is more suggestive than viewing them as threshold phenomena. For a threshold perspective would mean that we expect either a massive breakdown in the individual's behavior from confronting a certain level of stress or stable perfection if the stress is overcome. Such threshold cutoffs are unstable grounds for judging what is healthy or acceptable, according to Radke-Yarrow.[60] However, a continuum perspective on behavior entails that we move developmentally between more and less successful adaptations to stress.

Protection, Coping, and Buffering

The triad—protection, coping, and buffering—offers counterparts to risk, stress, and vulnerability. Protective mechanisms modify our responses to stressful situations. Risk and vulnerability produce new limitations to internal equilibrium, social integration, and life-goals. They provoke obstacles to learning and expectations of negative outcomes. For example, when we fail to overcome a risk environment, we develop blockages to adaptation, learning, and hope.[61] Yet, protective processes, like a catalyst, modify our responses to risk; they counter the risk, or change our life path toward adaptation.[62]

Protection in general is more than a passive or defensive idea. It involves proactively employing our skills and stretching them in new applications. Research suggests that prevention-mediating processes reduce the impact of risk and negative chain reactions; they promote self-efficacy and self-esteem, and initiate new opportunities.[63] First, we can reduce risk by altering the risk itself. For example, we can neutralize a threat to our self-

(Anthony and Cohler 1987, xi); second, because "the ideal of invulnerability, like the idea of immortality, has haunted the human race through many and varied interpretations of mysteries appertaining to origin and extinction, to the relationship of the natural to the supernatural order, and to the apparent immunity from the disasters of illness and injury granted to certain individuals" (Anthony 1987, 41–42). He gives the examples of the Greek heroes Achilles and Hercules, the Scandinavian god Balder, and the Indian man-god Krishna.

59. Cf. Rutter 1985; Werner and Smith 1992, 4; Luthar and Zigler 1991; Masten and Garmezy 1985.

60. Cf. Radke-Yarrow and Sherman 1990, 98; Gore and Eckenrode 1994, 55–56.

61. Cf. Murphy and Moriarty 1976, 202–3.

62. Cf. Rutter 1990, 209.

63. Cf. Rutter 1994b, 373; Seligman 2002; Garmezy 1985.

image through humor. We can alter its impact by putting distance between the bad situation and ourselves. Sometimes, though, we must confront the source of risk. Second, in similar ways we can reduce negative chain reactions, such as vicious circles of coercive or anxiety-producing exchanges. Third, we can maintain self-esteem and self-efficacy through supportive personal relationships and successful task accomplishment. Finally, the way in which we handle the key turning points in life can reduce a risk trajectory to a more adaptive path.[64]

Protection pertains to an individual's genetic temperament, acquired character, communal support, and the interaction between all three. The developmental psychologists Chess and Thomas analyze protective interactions in terms of "fit." Goodness of fit entails the compatibility of an individual's temperament, character, and abilities with the demands and expectations of the social environment. Such a fit should lead to "healthy development and resiliency." Poorness of fit, however, involves demands and expectations that are excessive or incompatible with the individual's resources. A stress-producing fit can jeopardize our healthy development. We can nonetheless increase or reduce fit through felicitous or infelicitous interventions, of both external and internal sorts.[65]

Coping and adaptation are key aspects of resilience. A more detailed typology of coping operations completes the definition previously provided. First, Perrez and Reicherts identify three coping orientations: situational, representational, and evaluational.[66] Situation-oriented coping involves a person's response to the stress-inducing situation itself (by changing it, fleeing it, or putting up with it). Representation-oriented coping concerns the person's relationship to information about the situation, whereby the individual either seeks or suppresses pertinent information. Lastly, evaluation-oriented coping entails reevaluating one's goals or one's initial judgment of the situation. These specialists evaluate the adaptive adequacy of these coping processes in terms of (1) how realistically the individual perceives the relevant stressor factors; (2) how adequately he or she converts these perceptions into effective coping practices; (3) how available are ap-

64. Cf. Rutter 1990, 203–10; Maughan 1988, 214; Werner and Smith 1992, 5. There are also studies that establish a conceptual and empirical foundation for preventive intervention programs and prevention science. Cf. Coie et al. 1993, 1013–22. For pedagogical insights see Hamburg 1990. For evaluations of training programs see Masten et al. 1990, 251–53; Grotberg 1995.

65. Cf. Chess and Thomas 1992, 73.

66. Cf. Perrez and Reicherts 1992b, 29.

propriate instrumental beliefs or "behavior rules"; and (4) how effective is the coping practice in the short term, and what is its long-term relationship to well-being.[67] This evaluation of coping should recognize its social dimension. As Werner and Smith assert, optimal adaptive development entails a balance between people's capacities and their influences on the social environment.[68] This balance is dynamic: if families that adapt their behavior to cope with disadvantaged circumstances are not able to change their aspirations quickly when circumstances change, they will not be able to seize new opportunities.[69]

Specialists also describe resilience in terms of competency. Resilience competencies are multivalent. They involve personal and social levels, as well as internal and external foci. On the personal level, emotional competencies engage a person's ability to express and regulate his or her emotions. This ability is present at birth,[70] but must develop throughout an individual's emotional history. This development always occurs in the context of family and friends, social standards and cultural practices.[71] Volitional resilience competencies involve attentional processes, self-efficacy, self-worth, and an internal locus of control, as well as guarding or re-establishing emotional homeostasis and serving higher goals.[72] Intellectual resilience competencies involve problem-solving capacities, especially being able to handle cognitive complexities.[73]

On the social level, pro-social support systems reinforce personal skills.[74] First, our sense of well-being and satisfaction with family life underlie coping competencies.[75] Second, emotional and cognitive supports from others aid our efforts to manage stress and difficulty. These social supports serve to establish and practice social skills; they also compensate for deficits when they provide role models and cooperate in coping activities.[76]

Positive Stress and Stress Buffering

To define resilience in terms of those who thrive on stress is an exaggeration. Even though some humans display resilient ways to face stress, not all

67. Cf. Perrez and Reicherts 1992b, 35.
68. Cf. Werner and Smith 1986, 136.
69. Cf. Pilling 1992.
70. Cf. Durkin 1995, 296, 256, 315.
71. On the related cognitive factors, see Consortium 1994, 276; Clarke and Clarke 1992, 153.
72. Cf. Lösel 1994, 9; Rutter 1990, 206; Werner and Smith 1986, 59.
73. Cf. Reich 1995.74. Cf. Rutter 1990, 182, 189–202; Garmezy 1985.
75. Cf. Perrez 1994b, 11.
76. Cf. Clarke and Clarke 1992, 149; Lösel 1994, 9; Tousignant 1998, 67.

stresses are the same, nor are all forms of stress management. "Good stress" mobilizes and motivates people. Good stress and bad stress are two distinct neurological happenings. The brain functions differently when stress presents a positive challenge than it does when stress involves an overwhelming or demoralizing threat. The two kinds of stress parallel the operation of two distinct biological systems. When faced with good stress, the brain chemistry generates enthusiasm for a challenge. It produces a level of catecholamines—adrenaline and noradrenaline—that is proper for concentration and action. Good stress even promotes a sort of peak performance, which D. Goleman describes as "a balance point when the sympathetic nervous system is pumping (but not too much), our mood is positive, and our ability to think and react is optimal."[77]

Bad stress, however, triggers a different neurochemical response (cortisol). The amygdala, the brain's alarm, signals the alert. A lack in the prefrontal inhibitory circuitry means we let impulses run free. In this case, resilience demands that we reestablish balance between the opposing neural systems that initiate action and that inhibit it. Stress-resilient and stress-vulnerable people coordinate differently these two counterpoised tendencies. Brain imaging research demonstrates that resilient individuals start to inhibit the distress during the initial stressful event. By inhibiting the amygdala's alert, the prefrontal lobes are able to preserve clarity of thought and steady action.[78] I shall investigate the other factors of this type of self-regulation in the next section. Here it suffices to note that one type of resilience involves recovery from (bad) stress, and another, an optimized concentration and clarity in action when faced with (good) stress.

Although researchers do not fully understand how we acquire psychosocial resilience against stress and adversity, they describe the acquisition of protection as a type of stress buffering or immunity, which decreases the probability of a negative outcome in the presence of a risk.[79] Stress buffering should not be confused with conditions of low risk. A buffer variable reduces the severity of anticipated undesirable outcomes in the face of risk;

77. Goleman 1998, 89; who cites Maddi and Kobasa 1984.

78. Cf. Goleman 1998, 77–78, 88–89.

79. Rutter (1990, 186) speculates that stress buffering may happen like the adaptive changes produced through immunization to acute physical stress; for example, through electric shock, which structurally and functionally alters the neuroendocrine system, and through parachute jumping, which induces anticipatory hormone changes.

it works on the risk before, during, or after we experience it.[80] M. Rutter has observed that negative experiences can either sensitize or steel us; they can increase or decrease our vulnerability to future stressors.[81] The medical metaphor of resilience as immunity or buffering illustrates that we acquire enhanced competency through successfully managing challenges, through engaging small doses of potential risk.[82] M. Rutter employs a medical metaphor of immunization to describe how involvement with real (instead of fabricated) trials can serve to strengthen humans through active engagement in the risk. He suggests that active immunization efforts are more efficacious than facing artificial risks, or simply avoiding them. Confronting risks demands proactive construction of new competencies, rather than simply holding on to existing ones. Success, even in small trials and difficult initiatives, can thus lead to a kind of immunization to the risks involved. Through such mastery experiences, life may not become less difficult or painful, but we become more apt to live well in the midst of it because we can successfully manage the challenges.[83] Successful adaptation may mean avoiding, changing, or overcoming the difficulty rather than simply becoming accustomed to it. A warning is in order as well: just as we can acquire resilience competencies, so can we acquire contrary vulnerabilities.[84]

Researchers have described stress-buffering processes and factors in various ways,[85] such as competence or mastery,[86] and hardiness, including family hardiness.[87] This last point highlights the social nature of buffers, which can

80. For example, in the case of women who have had insecure working models of early attachment (the risk), a buffering mechanism may be a secure working model of attachment with a husband (who has secure working models), which may forge another behavioral pathway (warm and structuring relation with children), thus avoiding the potential negative outcome (repeated insecure working model of early attachment). Cf. Cohn, Silver, Cowan and Pearson 1992; Cowan, Cowan, and Schulz 1996, 14.

81. Cf. Rutter 1994b, 354.

82. In discussing the search for protective processes, Rutter (1990, 186) says: "like medicines that work, these are often of the type that tastes bad! Thus immunization does not involve direct promotion of positive physical health. To the contrary, it comprises being exposed to, and successfully coping with, a small (or modified) dose of the noxious infectious agent. Protection in this case resides not in evasion of the risk but in successful engagement with it." Cf. Cowan, Cowan, and Schulz 1996, 15 and 33; Garmezy 1985.

83. Cf. Rutter 1990, 186; Cowan, Cowan, and Schulz 1996, 15; Garmezy 1985.

84. We can acquire vulnerabilities in two ways: either cumulative adverse circumstances or developmental failures can erode existing coping skills, or we can acquire tendencies to fall prey to later stress and adversity; cf. Cowan, Cowan, and Schulz 1996, 33; Garmezy 1985; Rutter 1994b.

85. Cf. Anthony and Cohler 1987, 13.

86. Wills et al. 1996, 127; Cowan, Cowan, and Schulz 1996; Rutter 1990.

87. Cf. McCubbin et al. 1998, 54.

give a sense of control over hardship, the possibility and benefit of change, and direction in active stress management. A. Masten has suggested, however, that stress immunity is not a general quality, but rather depends on a stress response's adequacy in regard to context, circumstances, and developmental stage.[88] A buffer-related phenomenon is the "neutralizing" event, which negates or counteracts the negative impact of earlier threatening events. M. Rutter confirms this insight, adding that we may compensate for a lack in one life-domain by a relevant experience in another. For example, school and relationship sources of self-esteem and self-efficacy can serve to complement a person who has not received adequate support from home.[89]

Religious and Spiritual Resilience

Resilience research and literature rarely refer to spirituality and religion. In the next chapter, I shall explain why. As we shall see, there are methodological, cultural, and historical reasons. Here, however, I suggest that spiritual resilience stands at the intersection between applied and academic perspectives. It stands between preventing problem behaviors and promoting optimal development. Even though spiritual and religious resources are not standard psychosocial resilience research categories, they play a role in overcoming difficulty; several psychosocial studies establish a positive correlation between human well-being and religion/spirituality.[90]

First, several empirical studies indicate that religion is a positive factor. It provides protection inasmuch as religious practices facilitate coping with difficulty.[91] It conserves protective resources and helps one to build in the wake of difficulty. However, empirical research also indicates that religion can serve as a source of risk. For example, fundamentalist religious notions of fate lead to indifference about the outcome of one's actions.[92]

Second, theoretical psychology recognizes potentially positive[93] and

88. Masten (1990, 249) notes two patterns: first, an internalizing pattern of stress response (disengaged but not disruptive), which is more common to girls; and second, an externalizing pattern of stress response (disengaged but disruptive), which is more common to boys.

89. Rutter (1990, 197) furthermore points out that not all positive events are "neutralizing."

90. Cf Schumaker 1992; Hood et al. 1996; Chamberlain and Zika 1992.

91. For other empirical studies which link human well-being and religious foundations, see Post 2006 and 2002; Lösel 1994; Chamberlain and Zika 1992; Ellison et al. 1989; Garbarino and Bedard 1996, 468.

92. Andersen (1991, 375–98) has observed that girls can become indifferent to the possibilities of pregnancy, and boys to the effect of violence (such as war and gang activities).

93. Schumaker (1992, 3) presents a number of positions claiming that religion is beneficial to health,

negative[94] associations between religion and health. It illustrates a diversity of positions. Indeed, some extreme empirical, clinical, and theoretical psychosocial critiques directly address spiritual and religious teaching, resources, and practices. Nonetheless, a substantial well-reasoned middle ground maintains that religion is potentially positive. Its effects on mental and physical health depend on the content and appropriation of beliefs at personal and social levels.[95]

Semantic Issues

Numerous semantic difficulties underlie the disparity between psychosocial notions of religion and spirituality. The meaning of religion and spirituality often differs in theoretical, clinical, and experimental psychology, and sociology. The conception of religion and spirituality is important not only in searching for their relationships with resilience and health or normality and normativity, but even more fundamentally with human flourishing and happiness.

In empirical research, I have found five semantic tendencies. First, secular philosophical notions tend to override religious and spiritual ones. For example, "spiritual" and "faith" are defined solely in altruistic or humanistic terms, without reference to divinity or religion.[96] Gina O'Connell-Higgins conceives of spirituality and faith in terms of a "benevolent kingdom," a "faith

---

because it: (1) orders a chaotic world by offering cognitive structures and pacifying narratives; (2) offers hope, meaning, and purpose with a sense of emotional well-being; (3) provides a reassuring fatalism that makes suffering and pain bearable; (4) affords solutions to conflicts; (5) solves the problem of mortality through afterlife beliefs; (6) gives a sense of control through an omnipotent force; (7) establishes self-serving and other-serving moral guidelines; (8) promotes social cohesion; (9) unites people around shared understandings; and (10) provides cathartic rituals.

94. Schumaker (1992, 3–4) also claims that some types of religion are potentially detrimental to mental health, because religion can potentially: "(1) generate unhealthy levels of guilt; (2) promote self-denigration and low self-esteem by way of beliefs that devalue our fundamental nature, or aspects of our nature; (3) establish a foundation for the unhealthy repression of anger; (4) create anxiety and fear by way of beliefs in punishment for 'evil' ways; (5) impede self-direction and a sense of internal control, while acting as an obstacle to personal growth and autonomous functioning; (6) foster dependency, conformity, and suggestibility, with a resultant over-reliance on forces or groups external to oneself; (7) inhibit the expression of sexual feelings, and pave the way for sexual maladjustment; (8) encourage the view that the world is divided into camps of mutually exclusive 'saints' and 'sinners' which, in turn, increases hostility and lowers tolerance toward the 'other'; (9) instill an ill-founded paranoia concerning malevolent forces that threaten one's moral integrity; and (10) interfere with rational and critical thought."

95. Cf. Post 2006; Garbarino and Bedard 1996; Masters and Bergin 1992; Schumaker 1992; Pargament et al. 1990; Levin and Markides 1986.

96. Cf. Nye and Hay 1996, 3:145–51; Bradford 1994.

in a larger future." It is thus that she identifies two overarching resilience themes, which are more philosophical than theological: "faith in surmounting and faith in human relationships as the wellspring of overcoming."[97]

Second, there is a propensity to uncritically conceptualize religion or spirituality and related data. Thus what is said about "prayer and faith" tends to be statistically analyzed without further distinctions in religious typology. E. Werner and R. Smith's research has identified faith and prayer as one of three major sources of support for the resilient children as adults; they also note a certain correlation between mental illness and fundamentalist religion.[98]

Third, psychosocial empirical research that does explicitly focus on spirituality and religion tends to be minimalist, selective, and incomplete. This bias is due to the nature of experimental studies; in particular, their observation-based methods and statistical analysis lend themselves to reductionistic findings. For example, researchers commonly correlate attendance at a religious service with health or behavior outcomes.[99] Attendance at religious services is an inadequate experimental factor; it does not consider intention or faith considerations. However, recent studies have introduced corrective nuances; they illustrate a greater awareness of the depth and breadth of the subject. They thus render the insights on resilience and religion more valuable.[100]

Fourth, the spiritual and physical realms are often opposed in order to affirm the multidimensionality of existence. The researcher intends to ac-

97. Cf. O'Connell Higgins 1994, 171–75; Werner and Smith 1992, 207.

98. Cf. Werner and Smith 1992, 138–41, and 171–75.

99. Other empirical literature makes the following correlation between religion and health: fear of death negatively associated with religious faith; sleep disturbance negatively associated with identification of the church as a major source of support; higher self-esteem and less emotional upset (and depression) when patients reported God in control of their lives; lower levels of reported pain and greater flourishing; more favorable evaluations of coping with death of a loved one; prayer as coping response to difficulty; positive change as result of crisis; support in the face of the trauma of the death of a loved one (cf. Pargament et al. 1990, 797–98).

100. Levin and Markides (1986, 31–38) have recognized two problems in sociological studies relating religious attendance to health: (1) The multidimensionality of attending religious services relates to the multitude of reasons for attendance, which vary by gender, stage of the life cycle, generation, and/or cohort. In some research it is used as a one-dimensional operational construct. (2) Religious attendance has frequently been used in uncontrolled analyses. They suggest the need to control for social support, physical capacity, social class, and subjective religiousness. In order for health-related research to find meaningful relations concerning religious attendance (and not just statistically significant ones), they make three suggestions: (i) add variables such as subjective religiousness, belief in God, belief in an afterlife, and frequency of private prayer; (ii) control for confounding influences; (iii) consider complementary measures representing differences in religion.

knowledge that humans have a nonmaterialistic, spiritual dimension, which has a certain primacy. The danger is to compartmentalize human experience using dualistic conceptions of spiritual and physical realms.[101]

Fifth, in the name of neutrality or objectivity of empirical science, some researchers neglect or reject the possibility of religious and spiritual significance.[102] Theoretical and clinical psychologies (and experimental ones to some degree) are mixed disciplines that have religious, spiritual, and ethical presuppositions and dimensions.[103] These terms' definitions orient a good deal of how research correlates resilience, health, normativeness, and so on.

These five semantic issues highlight the challenges for considerations of religion and spirituality in empirical studies and theoretical reflections. Nonetheless, these considerations aid us to identify the resilience resources found in religion and spirituality.

"Religion" and "Spirituality"

Psychosocial specialists tend to agree that "religion"[104] is not a homogeneous or one-dimensional construct. The multifaceted nature of religious experience causes problems for analysis. Indeed, psychological research needs to address "whether" people are religious. However, it must also specify "how" they are religious.[105]

The composite notions of religiousness satisfy more readily than simple definitions. C. Y. Glock,[106] King, and Hunt have generated two of the more complete conceptions of religion;[107] in simplified form, they propose the following religious domains: belief (a person's faith—confessional or

101. Cf. Garbarino and Bedard 1996, 470.

102. This positivist methodology not only concerns a Comtean critique of religion, but it also involves to some extent empirical psychology, as well as clinical and theoretical psychology. For example, Freud is well known for associating religion and obsession neurosis. This association is not a diagnosis resulting from his psychoanalytical practice, but rather a result of his theory of religion and interpretation of culture. Cf. Watts 1997.

103. Browning (1987, 8) makes a noteworthy analysis of modern psychologies and their ethical-religious foundations. His thesis is that "significant portions of the modern psychologies, and especially the clinical psychologies, are actually instances of religio-ethical thinking. They are, in fact, mixed disciplines which contain examples of religious, ethical, and scientific languages."

104. The etymology of the word "religion" is found in the Latin *religare* (to be tied to, to fasten or bind).

105. Cf. Masters and Bergin 1992.

106. In a social psychology perspective, C. Y. Glock (1962; cited in Watts and William 1988, 10) employs a five-facet model of religion, as having theological (beliefs), ritual (practices), intellectual (knowledge), experiential (emotion), and consequential (effects) dimensions.

107. King and Hunt (1975) develop a 21-factor analysis of religiosity. A fine summary of this and other definitions of religion is found in Schumaker 1992, 4–6; cf. Hood et al. 1996.

ideological religion); intellectual (information, knowledge, and meaning concerning faith, scripture, and tradition); motivational (volition, goals, and commitment); emotional (affectivity as passive and active, implicit and explicit judgments); ritualistic and prayer (signs, symbols, and sacraments); social and cultural (community environment and interactions); experience (direct knowledge of ultimate, spiritual reality); consequential (related behavior and moral action).

This collection of interacting facets offers an extensive, even though unordered, working notion of religion. It aids in evaluating the psychosocial findings. At the theoretical level, they approach the richness of religious and spiritual phenomena. At the empirical level, however, we cannot expect definitive conclusions from psychosocial studies because of the methodological difficulties faced in observing and measuring the interrelational and relational domains of religion.[108] For these reasons experimental approaches tend make to more modest analyses.

Typologies of religious orientation provide another way to investigate "how" we appropriate religion.[109] First, one of the most useful typologies distinguishes intrinsic from extrinsic religious orientation.[110] Belief and sincere commitment guide intrinsic religious orientation, which in turn serves as a person's most fundamental source of motivation. Intrinsically motivated people internalize their beliefs and attempt to live by them regardless of the consequences. On the other hand, extrinsic religious orientation is a "utilitarian," pragmatic, and more self-centered approach. Some people thus

108. Instead of completeness, there is a modest, but helpful, constellation of variables relating religion to resilience and health. Cf. Schumaker 1992, 11.

109. Schumaker (1992, 7–9) gives an overview of typology of religious orientation:

(a) healthy / unhealthy. William James 1902 "healthy-mindedness" and the "sick soul"; Pruyser 1977 healthy versus neurotic;

(b) mature / immature. Allport 1950/1967; Batson and Ventis 1982 adding "quest" type = open minded and questioning;

(c) serious / neutralized. Adorno et al. 1950;

(d) humanistic / authoritarian. Fromm 1950;

(e) committed / consensual. Allen and Spilka 1967;

(f) functional / dysfunctional. Spilka 1989.

110. This distinction is generally attributed to Allport and Ross (1967). Over the last thirty years it has given rise to numerous discussions and changes in research parameters; some of the most important publications include: Batson and Ventis 1982; Donahue 1985; Pargament et al. 1990; Masters and Bergin 1992; Schumaker 1992; Meyer and Lausell 1996; Watts 1997. After experiencing criticism of and finding incoherencies in the original bipolar typology conceived as a continuum, Allport expounded a fourfold typology by adding *indiscriminately pro-religious* and *indiscriminately antireligious* types.

use religion to obtain status, security, self-justification, and sociability.[111]

A wide range of research supports the thesis that intrinsic religiousness and mental health positively correlate.[112] According to Schumaker, for example, intrinsic religiousness has been shown to positively correlate with seven sets of mental health criteria: "appropriate social behavior, freedom from worry and [freedom from] guilt, personal competence and control, and open-mindedness and flexibility"; while extrinsic religion has a negative relationship to them.[113] The intrinsic-extrinsic typology furthermore has served both to dispel the "uniformity myth," that all religious beliefs and practices have equal impact on psychosocial processes.[114] It also corrects oversimplified or erroneous interpretations in experimental and theoretical psychology.[115]

A second current typology analyzes the social dimension of religion and spirituality regarding their "control" and "support" functions. Researchers argue that we misconstrue the influence of religion and spirituality if these complementary social dimensions are not both utilized.[116] The "control" and "support" typology corrects narrow-sighted research.[117] Thomas and Carver use this typology to help assess religious influence upon social competence. They critique a good part of the existing research on the influence of religion as focusing almost exclusively on the control construct (described as social control theory) to the detriment of the support and motivational one.[118]

The term "spirituality," like "religion," has numerous interpretations. It is popular, even fashionable, to speak of spirituality. But it is difficult to understand. Indeed, there is no universally recognized definition, and many approaches to spirituality exist. Inasmuch as spirituality is positively associ-

111. According to research (Masters and Bergin 1992, 222), extrinsic religious orientation may take two orientations: "(1) extrinsic-social (i.e., using religion toward social gain); and (2) extrinsic-personal (i.e., using religion toward gaining comfort, security, and protection)." Donahue (1985, 416) construes extrinsic religious orientation to represent the type of religion that gives it a bad reputation.

112. They have loosely organized this research into the following two major categories: freedom from pathology and positive mental health (competent perception and expression of feelings; freedom, autonomy, and responsibility; integration and coping; self-awareness and personal growth; mature frame of orientation). Cf. Masters and Bergin 1992, 224–26; Meyer and Lausell 1996, 123–24; Donahue 1985.

113. Schumaker 1992, 15.

114. Cf. Schumaker 1992; Masters and Bergin 1992.

115. See Master and Bergin's critique (1992) of Batson and Ventis's (1982) study of religion and mental health.

116. Cf. Meyer and Lausell 1996; Thomas and Carver 1990.

117. The more popular one-sided emphasis has been on the control function of religion, which is the problem, for example, in the otherwise interesting research by R. Jessor and S. Jessor (1977).

118. Cf. Thomas and Carver 1990, 202.

ated with religion, many, if not all, of the above-mentioned comments about religion apply to spirituality as well. Nonetheless, in order to appropriate better the richness of spiritual experience, and to avoid problems in empirical and theoretical psychosocial studies, we can identify definitions and developmental perspectives on spirituality.

Meyer and Lausell propose a tripartite definition of spirituality. First, spirituality implies a belief in the existence of a higher power that provides inspiration, guidance, replenishment, and comfort. Personal experience with "a personal deity or an impersonal force" supports belief. Second, spirituality provides a cognitive framework for answering life's major questions regarding origin, identity, and relationships to others and to the world itself. Third, it involves a code for personal and collective attitude and behavior. The knowledge of and ability to uphold this code relies on surrendering to the higher power.[119] They claim that empirical studies that do not take all three of these levels into account will produce anomalies.

Developmental perspectives on spirituality (and religiousness) describe spirituality in terms of a spiritual search for meaning. Viktor Frankl, for example, interrelates spirituality with the somatic and the psychological dimensions of life.[120] He calls the spiritual quest for meaning the noetic dimension, which has roots in childhood, but primarily develops in adolescence. Reason and conscience exist in the noetic realm, through which we go beyond particular influences (including parental and societal influences) and transcend training; we thus aspire to higher levels of spiritual thought and behavior. In addition to Frankl's views, other theories address how and why spirituality develops with age. The sociobiology perspective of E. O. Wilson, for example, explains spirituality and religious practice as enhancing the gene-survival of its practitioners.[121] Religion in itself, according to Wilson, is not an absolute value, however, since not all religions have survived, for example, the Shakers (who practiced complete celibacy). Spirituality or religion has two roles in Wilson's perspective. First, it reaffirms and renews the community's moral values. Second, through early learning it subverts natural self-interests to the interests of society, which require

119. Meyer and Lausell 1996, 119.

120. According to Frankl, the somatic (physical) dimension is the instinctual level of motivation, which helps the individual and species to survive. It exists throughout life. The psychological dimension underlies the personality, which begins to form at birth and develops throughout as a result of instincts, drives, capacities, and interactions with the environment (Frankl 1967).

121. Cf. Wilson 1975, 188.

that the majority of people be "controllable." The genes that favor both the willingness to be controlled and the potential for self-sacrifice have been favored by natural selection, according to Wilson's theory.[122]

What challenges do psychology and sociology's approaches to religion and spirituality pose for theology? They often identify religion with extrinsic religious orientation and spirituality with intrinsic religious orientation, or religion with its control function and spirituality with the function of support and guidance. Spirituality is also opposed not only to religion but also to ethics. The relationship of both religion and ethics to spirituality depends on how we define and articulate religion, spirituality, and ethics.

In the midst of these challenges and nuances, how can we treat spirituality and religion in this section? First, I shall try to make apparent the coverage of the terms in the research. Terminological clarity should permit us to avoid confusing observations made on different levels. Second, I shall use religion and spirituality more or less interchangeably in my analyses, recognizing their rich domains mentioned above. This attempt to recognize the spiritual basis for religion will not out of hand favor amorphous spirituality to religion that is organized.

Spiritual Resilience

Based upon these discussions of resilience, religion, and spirituality, we can now ask: what is spiritual resilience? As a third level of resilience, spiritual resilience does not simply involve a separate domain that has no commonality with the first two. Indeed, while it relates metaphorically to the resilience of inanimate material, it has a closer relationship with the psychosocial type. It is a human reality. In order to understand spiritual resilience, we need to understand human nature and agency. Psychosocial sciences and philosophical studies aid in this regard. Yet while the spiritual-religious domain extends human experience, it is in continuity with it. To understand this type of resilience, the following chapters address the correlation of nature and grace. At present, we can say that spiritual resilience concerns the ethical, religious, and spiritual dimensions of human resilience.

Beyond the psychosocial observations of human sciences, to recognize spiritual resilience requires two changes in perspective. First, we need not merely to study the weakness of individuals and groups, but to concentrate

122. Cf. Wilson 1978, 179. Pope 1998a has judiciously critiqued Wilson's work.

on their resources, practices, and potential. This enables us to identify the strengths rooted in human spiritual character and community. These are the qualitative levels of human experience: ethical, spiritual, and religious, as well as affective, cognitive, and social. Second, we should investigate the effect of what we teach and express, which involves personal contacts, institutions, and culture. A concern for resilience-effects goes beyond a simple scrutiny of external behavior. Consequently, spiritual resilience does not concern merely those who live in "at-risk situations." It involves each human being. We all inevitably face challenges due to maturation, change, and loss, cycles of which humans continually pass throughout our lives.

We tentatively define "spiritual resilience" as the capacity, when faced with hardship and difficulty, to cope actively using religious resources, to resist the destruction of one's spiritual competencies, and to construct something positive in line with larger theological goals. This abstract definition finds more concrete expression. For example, according to the French child psychiatrist Michel Manciaux, spiritual resilience is empowered by a life-project, which serves to orient our life.[123] Empirical studies, theoretical reflections, and intervention efforts,[124] furthermore, address spiritual resilience processes in terms of meaning, motivation, hope, friendship, and caring; these realities also have both religious and secular senses.

Conclusions

Resilience's Limitations

Before I venture a composite definition of resilience, it is fitting to mention the confines of its psychosocial conceptualization. The constructive and promising nature of the resilience concept does not override it limits and dangers. Several restrictions correlate to the use of positivistic methodology. Nonetheless, correctives are possible; the next chapter will highlight them. Current research sometimes lacks a trans-situational systematic exploration of resilience and coping; this constraint is inherent to an inductive method applied to a complex reality—human individuals interacting with social groups.[125] Furthermore, the popularity of the concept of resilience consti-

123. Cf. Manciaux 1995 and 2001.

124. Cf. Meyer and Lausell 1996, 130; Garbarino and Bedard 1996, 474–75.

125. Resilience researchers often highlight the limits of resilience and coping research: cf. N. Garmezy 1990, 532.

tutes a fourfold peril. First, we can simplistically construe it as invulnerability[126] or as the idea that everyone can succeed in fame and wealth when faced with difficulty, like the so-called American dream.[127] Second, some might mistake resilience as a replacement for social change (at policy and intervention levels). Thus the question: "If some disadvantaged people have been able to develop healthily and be happy, why cannot everyone?" Facile answers do not withstand scrutiny. Third, we risk forgetting the hidden costs paid for successful survival.[128] Psychological scars often if not always accompany the resilience that individuals attain in the most difficult situations; indeed even when we integrate and accept a harsh event, it does not disappear as if it never happened; and we need also to face dangers of relapses under stress. Fourth, resilience research cannot content itself with only focusing on positive features (e.g., social competence), without also addressing the absence of negative ones (emotional and volitional disturbance).[129]

A Composite Definition of Resilience

In summary, I propose a definition of resilience with three interrelated but nonexclusive axes, which each traverse the physiological, psychosocial, and spiritual dimensions of human life and society. First, resilience is the ability to cope in adverse conditions; it endures, minimizes, or overcomes hardships. Second, it consists in resisting destructive pressures on the human person's physiological, psychosocial, and spiritual life; that is, it maintains capacities in the face of challenges, threats, and loss. Third, resilience creatively constructs and adapts after adversity; it implies recovering with maturity, confidence, and wisdom to lead a meaningful and productive life. This composite definition emphasizes not only the coping and constancy aspects of the patterns of resilience amid disadvantage, but also the constructive outcomes expressed in growth, strength, and increased adaptation in personal and social domains.

126. Cf. Felsman and Vaillant 1987, 304–11.

127. One notable version of the American dream is the Horatio Alger legend, inspired by the Unitarian minister (1834–99) who wrote numerous juvenile novels, in which the characters attain fame and wealth through practicing virtues such as honesty, diligence, and perseverance. This "American mythology" can take on an individualist flavor, that one is solely responsible for one's own progress and success. Cf. Felsman and Vaillant 1987, 304; Garmezy 1994, 13.

128. Cf. Radke-Yarrow and Sherman 1990, 114; Felsman and Vaillant 1987, 304.

129. Cf. Rutter 1994b, 359–60.

2

Resilience Input for a Virtue-Based Philosophical Anthropology

In this chapter, I investigate further the research on protective and risk processes.[1] I interpret the insights within a classic anthropological schema (temperament and emotion, cognitional and volitional processes, and familial and social contexts).[2] At the same time, I employ an overlapping division

1. Some of the studies are gender-specific. Sometimes the gender-related findings seem contradictory. For example, some of them show more disadvantage to girls than to boys in families with difficulties. (Cowan, Cowan, and Schulz 1996, 31); while others find that boys exposed to serious disorder in the family are more likely to develop emotional or behavioral disturbances (Rutter 1990, 189).

2. Although I do not outline Thomas's anthropology until chapter 3, it already serves as the basis for the division of this present section. Studies on human resilience have focused on interrelated dynamics of life that can be identified as *individual factors* (temperament, age, gender, cultural background; including volitional, cognitive, and emotional processes); *family processes* (relationships); *extra-familial processes* (concerning peers, extended family, workplace, school, and neighborhood). Cf. Hetherington and Blechman 1996, viii. One of the more complete attempts at structuring resilience findings is Stefan Vanistendael's (1995); he analyzes the resilience research-action findings as follows: social networks and unconditional acceptance; the capacity to discover some order and sense and meaning in life; a variety of skills (competencies); self-esteem; humor; contact with nature. He recognizes the importance both to care for elementary material needs and to be ready to add other undiscovered experiences to this list. Furthermore, he regroups these elements in a useful pedagogical model, the "casita." Other attempts at resilience summaries include Lösel (1994) and Grotberg (1995).

that differentiates natural characteristics from religious and spiritual ones. This meta-analysis of the resilience findings inductively identifies resources that make some difference in resilience outcomes. It offers elements for a renewed philosophy of nature and philosophical anthropology.

Temperament

Temperament: Definition and Origins

In general, "temperament" and "personality" are used to identify what differentiates human beings at the level of psychosocial makeup and activity, or mood.[3] Although definitions vary in this field, researchers generally agree that personality differences exist at an early age and that they influence development in character and social involvement. Following Allport, most psychologists concur that temperament is a dynamic organization of behavioral, attitudinal, emotional, and cognitive patterns.[4] Kagan has identified four primary temperament types: bold, timid, upbeat, and melancholic.[5] For example, by temperament some humans are more choleric than others; they must live with a propensity to be wrathful, testy, irritable, impatient, and touchy. We do this in different ways, through acquired personal strategies or skills, and more or less successfully at personal and interpersonal levels.

3. We should not confuse "personality" and "person." The former is a psychological term, while the later is theological and philosophical. I shall use "temperament" and "personality" and "personality features" interchangeably throughout this section, as do researchers such as Rutter (1990, 182).

A standard dictionary defines temperament as: "n. 1. the individual peculiarity of physical organization by which the manner of thinking, feeling, and acting of every person is permanently affected; natural disposition" (*WEUD* 1989, 1461). Ancient physiology considered temperament to be due to an individual's particular proportion of the four cardinal humors (or bodily fluids: blood, phlegm, black bile, and yellow bile), which determined physical and mental constitution.

According to Paul Ekman (1992), emotions, moods, temperaments, and emotional disorders all interrelate as a nuclear core to its derivative expressions; emotions (the various families of emotions) are the basic emotional core and are expressed in moods, temperaments, and emotional disorders. Cf. Goleman 1995, 215 and 290.

4. Cf. Allport 1937/1961; Durkin 1995, 71. A second widely accepted typology of temperament distinguishes easy, slow, and difficult temperaments: (1) "easy" infants adapt well to novel experiences, are cheerful and easily pacified when distressed; (2) "slow to warm up" infants adapt slowly, cry and fuss more, are irregular in daily routines; (3) "difficult" infants withdraw in front of novelty and have more negative moods and intense reactions, as well as irregular sleeping and eating habits (Thomas and Chess 1989; cited in Durkin 1995, 71). A third common temperament typology identifies four tendencies to interface with environmental experiences: activity, reactivity, emotionality, and sociability.

5. Kagan (1994; cited in Goleman 1995, n. 14.1) also associates patterns of brain activity with temperamental moods.

The inequality of personality qualities at an early age and throughout the life cycle poses questions about the origin of and influences on temperament. Researchers attribute some aspects of individual differences to the "raw material" (Allport 1937/1961, 33), or "inherited basis" (Buss 1992) that infants and children first bring to their interaction with the social world. The running debate concerns these questions: What is the extent of the genetic origin? What is the influence of primary caregivers? In other words, to what extent is temperament hereditary? How stable is it? And to what extent can it be changed?[6] Nondeterministic research indicates that both nature and nurture contribute something; that is, both genes and individual neuro-psycho-social factors. The latter includes influences of family, educators, media, and the surrounding environment. Most researchers recognize an interaction between endogenous attributes and environmental factors without naively distinguishing each one's contribution.[7] Moreover, they cautiously affirm that temperament qualities translate into behavior or action, which in turn further shapes the development of temperament and future behavior in the form of character.

Resilience, Temperament, and Context

Resilience researchers posit various relationships between particular temperament qualities and resilience outcomes. They analyze these qualities at different levels. First, some temperament qualities elicit positive social responses from parents, peers, teachers, and the like. These resilience-engendering personality traits include a certain culturally appropriate level of activity, sociability, and emotionality;[8] responsiveness to others and an outgoing nature;[9] flexibility and approach orientation (inasmuch as they favor effective coping);[10] attitudes such as optimism, problem-solving confi-

6. This running debate about the interaction of nature and nurture on temperament has extreme positions that attribute the developmental outcome to biological factors (temperament theorists, cf. Kagan 1994; Kagan et al. 1990) or to environmental factors (e.g., behaviorists, such as B. F. Skinner). Twin studies demonstrate the inheritability of temperamental characteristics, by showing higher correlations between monozygotic twins' temperaments than fraternal twins'. The study of stability and mutability of temperament is also rather complicated by the proximity of temperament to emerging competencies and self-organization (cf. Durkin 1995, 72–73).

7. Cf. Durkin 1995, 97, who cites Sroufe 1985.

8. Cf. Werner and Smith 1992, 192; Masten, Best, and Garmezy 1990; Garmezy 1994; Clarke and Clarke 1992, 153.

9. Cf. Booth and Booth 1997, 113.

10. Cf. Lösel 1994, 9.

dence, and perceived control;[11] autonomy, self-esteem, and a positive social orientation.[12]

Children with an "outgoing nature," for example, express a more pleasant, positive mood to their caregivers. These children tend to be quicker with a smile and laughter, or to be engaged in and maintain eye contact. They more readily join in activities and take on responsibilities. Such temperamental qualities may not only elicit positive responses from the caregiver, but also facilitate stronger attachment relationships, which in turn can be significant for one's self-image and confidence; they can particularly help us to face difficulty and challenges even from an early age. Temperament can play a more central role in certain early childhood activities, while interpersonal characteristics become more predominant in adolescence and afterward. In particular, while infants moderate stress using more constitutional factors, they count more on interpersonal interactions, such as play, later in life.[13] Indications of resilience-promoting temperamental qualities will continue to be identified as research continues.

Second, some temperament characteristics elicit negativity and aggression.[14] Such characteristics explain, in part, individual differences in risk exposure and the reasons that in the same situation people have varied experiences, some positive and others negative. For example, less interactive children may tend to be less stimulated and socialized by their caregivers, who must put more time and effort into engaging the child in visual, verbal, or play contact; such children have as a result weaker attachment bonding.[15] Clarke and Clarke hypothesize that growing up in large, chaotic, discordant families promotes temperamental irritability and lack of sociability.[16] In general Rutter notes that difficult children's temperaments can cause individual risk, since they tend to be scapegoated; for example, they attract the hostility, criticism, and irritability of a depressed parent.[17] Furthermore, aggressive or antisocial children tend also to elicit negative responses from

11. Cf. Wills 1996, 128.

12. Cf. Rutter 1990, 182; Garmezy 1985.

13. Cf. Yule 1992, 189.

14. Researchers note that underlying physiological factors can contribute to antisocial behavioral problems, such as drug and alcohol abuse (Consortium 1994, 271), as well as to depressive behavior (cf. Pope 1998a and b).

15. Cf. Spangler 1990; Bowlby 1969/1982 and 1973; Durkin 1995, 99.

16. Clarke and Clarke (1992, 153) speculate that in this situation children do "not have the opportunity to gain an understanding of social cause and effect, nor to develop planning ability or knowledge of the desirability of delayed gratification and an internal locus of control."

17. Cf. Rutter 1990, 189–202.

people outside the family: from neighbors, educators, and venders. Such behavior and responses can bring about a vicious cycle of negative experiences.[18] It can also explain further how in the same situation people have varied experiences and how concrete behavior is continuously involved in shaping such experiences.

Research demonstrates the context-specificity of resilience outcomes. The De Vries African famine study illustrates that particular temperamental characteristics put a group of children at risk in one situation, but rendered them more resilient in another. In particular, the difficult and demanding temperamental characters survived an extreme draught in Zimbabwe. Because of their persistence (in crying and demanding food), they received the scarce food that existed. The temperament that elicits negative outcomes in one situation might promote survival in another.[19] This counterintuitive insight suggests that we need to delineate resilience findings, as well as prepare for context-specific outcomes.

Researchers have also identified a variety of temperamentally risky or protective relationships that seem gender-specific.[20] Pianta, Egeland, and Sroufe have noted differences in the way in which children relate to their parents and the home environment when confronted with stress. Boys' competence and coping skills were especially linked to their relationship with their mother and home environment. Girls' competence, however, was distinguished by their mother's positive social and problem-solving characteristics. More specifically, they observed that: "'protective' environments for boys were structured, organized, emotionally supportive, and distinguished by good teaching by mothers."[21] Girls conversely did not need the same active environmental support to develop competently within a stressful household; for them, it appears as minimally important that the mothers' characteristics shield the girls, foster their independence, and be transmitted through observation and identification. Werner and Smith moreover

18. Cf. Rutter 1994b, 371–72.

19. Cf. The De Vries study on child survivors of the Zimbabwe famine (cited by Rutter 1998, 48).

20. As with a good deal of resilience research, we must employ these findings in other cultural and age contexts with care. Conflicting gender-specific findings in violent environments invite caution in extrapolating from one high-risk setting to another. Nonetheless, given that certain risks are perhaps more normal than one might think, we look to the high-risk examples as sometimes counterintuitive insights about human nature and culture, which might bear fruit in pedagogical applications. Cf. Rutter 1990, 189–202.

21. Pianta, Egeland, and Sroufe 1990, 232.

noted that for unaggressive boys in high-crime settings the tendency for shyness acts as a protective factor against delinquency and crime, while the opposite is the case for aggressive boys.[22] The identification of such a factor itself does not directly correspond to a universal psychological or sociological process for avoiding delinquency. Such a single-variable analysis leaves open questions that demand the consideration of other variables, in this case, aggressiveness. This example suggests that a temperament disposition (e.g., shyness) in one type of situation protects one boy while leaving another boy vulnerable, because of further differences in temperament (e.g., aggressiveness).

Emotions

Are human emotions disruptive and irrational? Or are they also functional and in some way rational? Theories vary. Much of contemporary culture promotes an inherited dichotomy between emotion and reason. Its proponents, both philosophers and psychological theorists, construe emotions as inherently irrational, as disruptive and maladaptive. However, other classical thinkers offer a more positive view; and some current psychological theories emphasize emotions as functional and adaptive.[23]

Emotional Judgments, Perceptions, and Social Bonding

First, according to some thinkers, emotions are judgments. They provide us ways to perceive the situation in terms of its meaning and future action. Cognitive psychologists construe attraction- or aversion-eliciting emotions to result from human perception and appraisal processes. They describe emotions as the felt tendency toward anything intuitively appraised as good or beneficial, or away from something sensed as bad or harmful.[24] The attraction and repulsion of emotion entails a judgment about the organism and the environment, or response to meaning at felt (conscious) and un-

22. Cf. Werner and Smith 1992.

23. Recent psychological theories (e.g., cognitive psychology and attachment theory) emphasize the cognitive and functional value of even negative emotions, e.g., anger, sadness, guilt, and disgust. Nonetheless, emotions are not always rational, probably because "maladaptive assumptions and excessive sensitivities" distort the appraisal of the situation according to Watts (1997, 252). Major schools of psychology have been less than generous in their study of human emotions. For example, Piaget's studies focus almost exclusively on cognitive development (cf. Durkin 1995, 20).

24. Cf. Perrez 1992.

felt (unconscious) levels.[25] On the one hand, as a type of unconscious judgment, emotions identify meaning as an instinctive, automatic, nonintellectual appraisal of the situation.[26] As conscious judgments, or a result thereof, on the other hand, emotions imply a more deliberate and conscious appreciation of meaning.

We are more or less aware of the sources of our emotions. Confronted with the suffering of refugees, we might not know why we are angry. Anger unconsciously arises from the suffering found in the situation; we empathize with others in their hunger, illness, separation from family and homeland. But we also experience a conscious level of emotional awareness when we attribute the suffering to particular historical, political, and economic causes. Rational deliberation about the situation alters the felt anger, which then no longer simply springs from general empathy, but also is generated by conscious adjudication about the source of suffering and injustice. This type of emotion is not simply a passive reaction to stimuli, even though these emotions may unfold in experiences that we encounter more as a passive than as an active subject. As emotive situations advance, our emotions constantly interrelate with preceding and consequent perceptions, thoughts, decisions, and actions.

Second, emotions alter our rational and volitional processes. They can facilitate or hinder the perception itself, as well as contiguous thoughts, judgments, and action. For example, an experience of justified anger, when moderate, can aid us in thinking through a situation. It pushes us toward a concrete corrective action. Blinding wrath, on the contrary, deforms our perception and confuses our decisions and behavior.

Emotions are stepping-stones to action. Etymologically, emotion, which comes from *motere*, involves a movement or change in the person's "action readiness"; we approach or withdraw from an object.[27] Attachment theory explains these movements. The affective appraisal process first interprets personal and environmental information. It then compares internal "set points" (established by similar or related past events) in order to select certain behaviors and prepare action. Feelings—both "positive" and "negative," pleasant and unpleasant—correlate with behavior.[28] Our appraisal process-

25. Cf. Lazarus 1991a; 1991b; Bowlby 1969; Ainsworth et al. 1978, 19.
26. Cf. Damasio 1994, 17; Wallwork 1999, 174.
27. Cf. Ekman 1992, 6:169–200.
28. Cf. Bowlby 1969; Ainsworth et al. 1978, 19.

es, including emotions, prepare and condition the resulting coping responses.[29] Furthermore, following an evolutionary psychology perspective, Daniel Goleman defines emotions as impulses to act according to plans that evolution has instilled in us. He also discusses their source in "the emotional mind," which involves a system of knowing.[30]

Third, networks of affectional support fashion emotional behavior,[31] and conversely, emotions underlie our social bonding. In particular, feelings of attachment and competency, of self-esteem and efficacy, promote emotional proficiency and social resilience. On the one hand, according to the social development model, social bonding to family and positive groups provides protection; it regulates behavior and motivates us to live by social standards.[32] Protective developmental processes, such as opportunities for participation, participation-facilitating skills, and group recognition, support social bonding.[33] Resilience research has found that substitutes can supplement the loss of primary attachment figures. Resilient adolescents, for example, overcome the risk of lost access to parental bonding through enforced attachment to an aunt or uncle, a friend, or a neighbor. However, they face danger if they bond with unresilient or destructive figures.[34] Since attachment with others brings heightened identification with their behavior, vulnerable youth multiply their risks through negative modeling.

Specific resilience research identifies the resilience-value of self-esteem, self-efficacy,[35] and confidence,[36] as well as the contrary risk related to a sense of incompetence.[37] Positive self-esteem can enable motivation and action, while negative self-images can underlie difficulties in emotional processing. When we feel worthwhile—that our actions make a difference, that our participation in a particular social setting brings added value—then our motivation and acts are more likely to withstand external and internal negative pressures. Michael Rutter finds it difficult to identify the source of self-esteem and self-efficacy; emotional processes have two bases: emotional predispositions (temperament) and acquired dispositions (conscious

29. Cf. Perrez 1994a, 347.

30. Cf. Goleman 1995, 6–8.

31. Cf. Clarke and Clarke 1992, 153.

32. Cf. Consortium 1994, 300.

33. Ibid., 301–2.

34. Tousignant (1998, 65–66, 68–69) has found that street children after the age of twelve become less adaptive once they enter into criminality.

35. Cf. Rutter (1990, 197–207) and Yule (1992, 191).

36. Cf. Lösel 1994, 9.

37. Cf. Yule 1992, 191.

and unconscious). Each feeling results from this dialogue. Researchers have furthermore found a source of felt self-esteem in each successful event. We gain this sense not only in hard-won achievements but also in minor feats. As children grow, their accomplishments in emotional management and other social experiences tend to give rise to stronger feelings of self-efficacy and higher self-esteem.[38] Such felt confidence appears to be a central component that enables resilient children and adults to cope effectively. Emmy E. Werner and Ruth S. Smith say this source of coping pertains not to a vague confidence, but rather to a confidence that we can surmount the odds, that difficulty does not spell defeat.[39]

Emotional Management Strategies

Emotional competency develops with our capacity for emotional expression and regulation. At an early age, humans express emotions. Some quickly gain competence in expressing them; others struggle with emotional composure for the rest of their lives. At the neurophysical level, emotional development relates to the supporting brain regions and synapses, which grow and wither according to emotional experience and intensity. Although emotional development continues throughout life, according to Jerome Kagan, critical stages punctuate the rest of our emotional life.[40] The abilities involved in managing our focus of attention are fundamental to emotion regulatory processes.[41] Moreover the emotional styles of primary caregivers, especially during the "formative years," leave an impact. Indeed emotional competency develops not only through an individual's ways of experiencing and expressing feelings, but also through interactions with mother, father, siblings, and peers, and with social norms and cultural practices. Both cognitive and social factors help fashion emotional behavior.[42]

38. Cf. Wills et al. 1996, 115; Wilson and Gottman 1996, 220.

39. Cf. Werner and Smith 1992, 207.

40. Cf. Kagan 1994; Goleman 1995.

41. Cf. Wilson and Gottman 1996.

42. "These factors include the encoding of relevant social cues (as in attending to others' facial expressions and to the norms of a social context); the accurate interpretation of the encoded social cues (as in perspective taking, reading intentions, and empathy); the generation of effective solutions to interpersonal problems; the realistic anticipation of consequences of, and potential obstacles to one's actions (as in delaying immediate gratification for long-term rewards and in understanding that some behaviors might have negative consequences for oneself or others); the translation of social decision into effective behavior (as in being able to approach and converse with peers and adults, showing appropriate eye contact, using an appropriate language); and the expression of a positive sense of self-efficacy (as seen in a general optimism about outcomes of one's personally initiated actions)." Consortium 1994, 276; which

Research has identified certain strategies that are effective, especially in palliating strong emotions. One strategy of regulating emotion involves "self-talk," through which an individual can soothe negative affect and focus on problem solving. Labeling emotions shifts attention away from the physiological arousal associated with the event in order to perceive it better and then cope with it. Positive uses of humor also serve as tools in managing emotions.[43] Negative "self-talk" and destructive humor, on the other hand, distract people from their particular goals and impede their performances.[44] In general, when a person faces strong affect and emotion, inadequate coping behaviors include simple passivity, self-blaming, and other-blaming.[45] In order for behavior to be adequate (responsive to our goals and criteria), we must learn to master emotions, at least to palliate the strong ones.

Research has shown that promoting feelings of self-esteem and self-efficacy is a prime strategy for resilience interventions.[46] No easy recipes exist though. Having to face age- and capacity-appropriate responsibilities and challenges can have positive effects on children and youth, including increased feelings of self-confidence, pride, a sense of meaning, and a purpose in life. On the contrary, negative emotional effects emerge when we are forced into crushing situations or left alone in the face of overwhelming tasks. Protectionist and isolationist policies can reinforce these phenomena. What effects can positive emotions have on human agency? They strengthen motivation for action instead of simple passivity or discouragement when confronted with challenges. They facilitate commitment to family, community, and one's own self.[47]

Religious Emotion

As in the case of emotion in general, personal and social input shape religious feelings.[48] Several modern thinkers establish a link between religion and emotion. Friedrich Schleiermacher (1768–1834) places the essence of religions as the feeling of absolute dependence.[49] William James's (1842–1910)

cites Dodge 1986; Dodge and Feldman 1990; Elias 1990; Kendall 1991; Jason et al. 1992; McFall 1983; Weissberg, Caplan, and Sivo 1989.

43. Cf. Berger 1997; Vanistendael and Lecomte 2000.

44. Cf. Wilson and Gottman 1996, 216.

45. Cf. Perrez 1994a.

46. Cf. Maughan 1988, 214; Werner and Smith 1992, 5, 205, and 255; Cowan, Cowan, and Schulz 1996, 32; Coie et al. 1993, 1013; Petit, Lalou-Moatti, and Clervoy 1996, 3045.

47. Cf. Tousignant 1998, 68–69.

48. Watts (1997, 246–51) investigates emotion as a model for religion.

49. See his *Addresses on Religion to Its Cultured Despisers* (orig. 1799).

psychology of religion emphasizes the biological aspect of religious emotion.[50] Rudolph Otto for his part adds a cognitive counterpart to Schleiermacher's notion of a sentiment of dependence.[51] Social constructivist views of emotion, moreover, pay special attention to emotion's social aspects, in particular to how social relationships give rise to religious emotions.[52] Gordon W. Allport's influential psychological view on religious sentiment holds that all positive sentiments involve a sort of "belief," and that specific "faith" in God carries an even warmer affection than bare "belief."[53] It can also serve several functions, including producing consequent conduct and research to discover good and truth that issue from faith.[54] According to Ralph Burhoe, religion's role in evolution and social cohesion passes through religious sentiment, which serves a selective and adaptive role in the appearance and development of human societies.[55]

This incomplete survey provides a foundation for a further typology. We can categorize attitudes and approaches toward religious emotions, and especially strong emotions, according to three main trains of thought: (1) strong emotions are a sign of strong religious life; (2) emotions need to be controlled; and (3) sensibility to emotions should be refined.[56] The first position construes strong emotions as a hallmark of robust religious life. The Hebrew Bible thus positively appraises early Israelite prophecy and dancing to ceremonial music. Christianity likewise supports emotive outpouring in the charismatic movement and in spiritual exercises and devotions.

The second position, sometimes alongside the first, emphasizes calming the emotions. The Hebrew Bible and Buddhist and Christian contemplative traditions promote this position, which nonetheless has two approaches to calming the emotions. On the one hand, we need to repress emotions. They endanger spiritual development. They tempt us toward a voluptuous style of life. According to St. Paul, the flesh seeks to override the spirit.[57]

50. See his *The Varieties of Religious Experience*, "Religion and Neurology," Lecture I, 1907, 1–26.

51. Cf. Otto 1923.

52. James R. Averill (1982) represents this view of emotion.

53. Cf. Allport 1950/1967.

54. According to Allport (1950/1967, 161; cf. 141), "a man's religion is the audacious bid he makes to bind himself to creation and to the Creator. It is his ultimate attempt to enlarge and to complete his own personality by finding the supreme context in which he rightly belongs."

55. Cf. Burhoe 1986, 469.

56. Moreover, Freud focuses more on a lack of awareness of emotions, although he has been interpreted as supporting uncontrolled expression (cf. Watts 1997, 254).

57. See St. Paul's letter to the Romans, ch. 8.

Thus, Fraser Watts and Mark Williams label Henri Suso's and John of the Cross's works as repressive approaches to the passions.[58] On the other hand, a more positive approach to calming emotions exists.[59] It holds that we need neither to repress nor necessarily to release emotions. It opposes a common notion that emotion is a kind of energy that we need to discharge. Energy models of emotions misconceive emotional states as homeostatic. Indeed, expressed feelings often increase instead of decrease the desire to express them again. Expressing emotions does not always make us feel better, nor does not doing so always make us feel worse. Psychological research has shown, for example, that anger does not normally reduce in intensity when we express it.[60]

Third, a mild ascetic perspective draws upon religions resources to refine emotions. This perspective requires a greater emotional sensitivity and awareness, instead of a simple forced-control of strong emotion.[61] The positive side of emotions illustrates that religious life can heighten emotional experiences. We can positively express joy and sorrow.[62] The goals of heightened emotional sensitivity and focused emotional expression are compatible with emotional composure and enhanced powers of concentration. A first step in educating emotional reaction involves self-observation. To name a troubling emotion can make it less troubling.[63] The purpose of religious techniques for emotional control and refinement has been to develop knowledge of and commitment to the "divine," to know and love God better. How do emotions hinder or help access to the divine? According to Watts and Williams, both religious meditation and psychotherapy can aid in obtaining

58. Cf. Watts and Williams 1988, 79–85.

59. According to Watts and Williams (1988), constructive approaches to calming the emotions include those of Augustine Baker (a seventeenth-century Benedictine monk) and Rudolf Steiner (founder of Anthroposophy).

60. Cf. Watts and Williams (1988, 83).

61. Michael Stocker and Elizabeth Hegeman (1996, 1–2) argue for the value of emotions using psychological and philosophical insights, and affirm that "An absence or deficiency of affect is a characterizing feature of many neuroses, borderline conditions, and psychoses, as well as such maladies of the spirit as meaninglessness, emptiness, ennui, *accidia*, spiritual weakness, and spiritual tiredness." Cf. Watts 1997, 255; Averill and Nunely 1992; Goleman 1995.

62. Watts (1997, 255) suggests that emotional sensitivity can enhance the religious person's awareness of God. He highlights the positive approach of Jonathan Edwards's *Religious Affections* ([1746] 1987). Watts quotes Cherry's (1966, 167) analysis of Edwards's theology of emotion: "Religious man is not one who subjects passions to the rule of reason but one whose reason is passionate and whose affection is intellectual."

63. Watts and Williams (1988, 90) offer examples from the Buddhist practice of "mindfulness" and clinical techniques for creating space to cope with problems.

a right balance of emotional distance and engagement, and of cognitive receptivity, which not only can alter the quality of attention to the divine object, but also can change the way in which it is known and loved.[64]

These nonsystematic indications of the correlation between emotion and resilience provide a foundation for our study of how we manage emotions through moral and religious capacities.

Cognitive Processes and Meaning

A large segment of resilience research focuses on cognitive processes and meaning. In the midst of vicissitude and ambivalence, we decipher information; we plan for goals; we solve problems; and we seek meaning. Cognitive and developmental psychologies are the main research protagonists in this domain. Nonetheless social psychology and the situation-behavior approach offer other important insights.

Information Management and Appraisal

Stress challenges our capacities to manage our attention and cognitive processes. Proper measure is warranted. In order to act with foresight, we need not only to receive information, but also to seek and process it. Hardships and stressors can short-circuit our thought processes. Especially when under pressure, furthermore, we need to suppress as well as collect information in order to attain our goals. Without restrictions on stimuli, we are overwhelmed and distracted. How do we use cognitive processes to interpret and overcome a quandary? Meinrad Perrez and Michael Reicherts, in a situation-behavior approach, employ stimulus-response chains to reconstruct the process of encountering stress. They observe four steps: perceptions of change, emotions, cognitions, and coping responses.[65] The initial stimulus of a micro-episode alters the subject's internal or external world. We perceive change by processing information stimuli. What we first passively receive, however, cannot be left as such. We need to muster reliable coping responses. Our emotions serve as initial judgments. We must nonetheless analyze the situation in order to evaluate the object involved and determine how to act. What are the pertinent circumstances? What similar

64. Watts and Williams 1988, 90.

65. Perrez and Reicherts (1992a, 19) base their method on the research of Lazarus 1982.

situations have we faced in the past? What alternatives exist? What consequences will come from acting or not acting? How does the present situation relate to significant goals and larger contexts of meaning? The way that we employ our cognitive (and volitional) processes to resolve difficulties serves our resilience or on the contrary renders us vulnerable.[66]

We limit resilience outcomes by either oversimplifying cognitive analyses or neglecting pertinent information and emotions.[67] According to K. Helmut Reich, we hamper our capacity to understand cognitive complexity by restricting ourselves to classical logic that posits only bivalent notions of truth. We need complementary logics and cognitive skills. Cognitively complex thinking—including analogical, dialectical, and metaphorical thinking[68] and relational and contextual reasoning—completes limited cognitive applications.[69] The ability to manage cognitive complexity favors resilience outcomes not only in academic settings, but also in everyday interactions.

Second, resilience researchers do not agree on the sources of meaning. Do we create or discover meaning? Or both? On the one hand, some researchers focus on the subjective aspect of meaning. In order to cope with stress, we attribute meaning to events.[70] We even construct shared meaning in families and other groups.[71] On the other hand, certain researchers concentrate on the objective aspect of meaning. They claim that humans have the capacity to discover meaning. Thus humans call upon the order and meaning inherent in situations, relationships, and life. We rally objective meaning to confront and overcome difficulty.[72] The resilience research and theory that places value on the subjective side emphasizes human development. It is an individual person whose understanding grows. Emphasis on the objective side posits a reality outside the individual. It assumes that we can discover external sources of meaning and goals that constitute human

66. Masten, Best, and Garmezy (1990) include "problem-solving abilities" in their summary of the protective factors. Cf. Wills et al. 1996, 110.

67. The effects of nuanced intellectual capacities, and emotional integration have been investigated in the context of teaching philosophy to children at risk (cf. Sharp and Splitter 1995) and learning "relational and contextual reasoning" (cf. Reich 1995).

68. On cognitively complex thinking, analogical thinking, and dialectical thinking, see Reich 1995, 13–14. On metaphor see McGrady 1994; Ricoeur 1981/1977.

69. "Relational and contextual reasoning" (RCR) involves ways of addressing seemingly incompatible aspects of reality; cf. Reich 1995, 14–15.

70. Cf. Lösel 1994, 9.

71. Cf. Hay 1988, 245–54.

72. Cf. Vanistendael 1995, 20–22, and Vanistendael and Lecomte 2000; cf. Post-White (1998, 281–87), who links meaning with hope.

fulfillment, well-being and happiness. I shall adjudicate this debate in the next chapter, but suggest here that at different levels both insights are true.

Third, what cognitive strategies for coping, consistency, and construction exist? I mention three here: goals, planning, and self-esteem. The integration of life goals underlies resilience efforts. However, not all goals are of equal value. Goals can range from the most all-embracing ones (well-being and happiness) to the more specific and proximate ones. Researchers have identified "planfulness and aspiration" as protective factors for goal achievement.[73] Werner and Smith's research has found a particular resilience effect when youth establish realistic educational and vocational goals by age eighteen.[74] Rutter furthermore documents the resilient effect of positive planning styles in regard to marriage (choice of spouse) and work situations. When we plan well, we avoid some risky situations.[75] Planfulness has allies in manifest cognitive competencies,[76] problem-solving skills, and self-esteem; it is rooted in a goal orientation.[77] The enemies of aspiration, however, involve under- and overprotection,[78] as well as "learned helplessness."[79]

The cognitive aspect of self-esteem promotes resilience. Resilience researchers use various terms: manifest competence and perceived efficacy,[80] a positive self-concept,[81] and self-esteem.[82] Research demonstrates that humans establish and maintain awareness of self-esteem and self-efficacy through supportive personal relationships, successful task accomplishment, and so on.[83] How does this work? On the one hand, successful task accomplishment, such as positive school experiences, can either reinforce or de-

73. Cf. Masten, Best, and Garmezy 1990; Garmezy 1994. On planfulness see Clarke and Clarke 1992, 153.

74. Cf. Werner and Smith 1986, 59.

75. Cf. Rutter 1990, 189–202, esp. 195–96.

76. Such competencies include communication competencies. Cf. Werner and Smith 1986; Lösel 1994, 9; Masten, Best, and Garmezy 1990.

77. In chapter 5, I discuss further the relationship between goals and hope; cf. Snyder et al. 1991a; Post-White 1998; Erickson, Post, and Paige 1975; Stotland 1969; Frankl 1963/1984.

78. Cf. Tousignant 1998, 69–71.

79. Cf. Seligman 1975, 38; and Murphy 1987.

80. Cf. Masten et al. 1990, 236–56; Masten, Best, and Garmezy 1990, 2:425–44; Werner and Smith 1992, 205; cf. 255.

81. Cf. Lösel 1994, 9.

82. Cf. Werner and Smith 1992, 185–86 and 205; 1986, 9; Rutter 1990, 182; Garmezy 1985.

83. According to Rutter (1990, 206), available evidence suggests that two types of experiences are most influential in the development of self-esteem and self-efficacy: "(a) secure and harmonious love relationships and (b) success in accomplishing tasks that are identified by individuals as central to their interests" (cf. Wilson and Gottman 1991).

velop self-esteem. On the other hand, the presence of relevant experiences in one domain (e.g., school) can compensate for a lack in another domain (e.g., family).[84] Although the mechanisms are not fully understood, Rutter suggests that we carry forward cognitive sets of negative and positive events, which relate to self-esteem and self-efficacy, as well as to internal working models of relationships.[85]

Constructing Social Meanings

Personal cognitive activities are not devoid of social context. In particular, the family can play an integral part in an individual's coping, constancy, and construction. In the face of difficulty, our social groups influence our adaptive appraisal, deliberation, and decision-making processes. We can illustrate the construction of social meanings in two ways. First, family members come to certain perceptions, thoughts, and decisions together. These shared family meanings reduce ambiguity and contribute to group stability and identity. Secondly, our family influences our own cognitive processes, inasmuch as each of us comprehends things through social interaction.[86] Family meanings emerge when family members interact. Shared experience and dialogue shape understanding.

Researchers speculate that family types[87] influence meaning under stress.[88] Joan Patterson and Ann Garwick hypothesize that families construct and share meanings according to three levels: the family's situational meanings, identity, and worldview.[89] These meanings undergo adaptive

84. Cf. Rutter 1990, 197 and 206–7.

85. Furthermore Rutter suggests other possibilities for later investigation: neural or neuroendocrine effects; linkages through which one type of adversity might predispose someone to another type. Cf. Rutter 1994b, 373–74; Harter 1983.

86. Peter Berger and Thomas Luckmann's classic *The Social Construction of Reality* (1966) provides theoretical grounding for the premise that social interaction creates and maintains meanings (cf. Patterson and Garwick 1998, 80–81).

87. For example, Patterson and Garwick (1998, 79–80) distinguish two family types: (1) consensus-sensitive families, which are high on coordination and closure; (2) environment-sensitive families, which are high on configuration and low on closure.

88. Cognitive factors have been present in most family stress theories. The earliest family stress model was Reuben Hill's ABCX Model: A-stressor; B-family resources; C-family's definition of stressor; X-crisis (1949; cf. the Double ABCX Model of McCubbin and Patterson, which adds the layer of perception of each element, as well as the concept of coping, and the more generalized meaning construct (cf. McCubbin et al. 1998).

89. Patterson and Garwick's (1998, 83–86) Family Adjustment and Adaptation Response (FAAR) Model (Patterson) emphasizes adjustment in terms of family and individual resilience and a salutogenic perspective. The FAAR Model differentiates two levels of family meaning: situational and global meanings. *Situational meaning* concerns the family and individual subjective meaning; *global meaning* concerns

pressures in the face of crisis, confusion, and conflict. For example, research has found that families with a medically fragile child first undergo a process of adjustment when the demands of the situation surpass their capacities. They need to adapt, to balance the demands and their capabilities. In observing the situation, they inevitably attribute meaning to the illness. They ascribe meaning at three levels. First, at the situational level, shared meanings emerge through the family adaptation process. Family members influence each other's appraisals of the situation; they may find a common definition of the crisis. The family also develops expectations about who is responsible to manage the illness. They employ internal and external resources.[90] In response to a chronically ill child, parents frequently report positive outcomes: growth and development of oneself or the family unit in response to the challenge.[91] Second, at the family identity level, they may redefine external and internal boundaries, reassign roles for family tasks, and reestablish rules and norms for interaction, in order to more effectively manage the illness. Third, concerning the family worldview, some parents modify their goals and global meanings (sense of purpose) to fit their behavioral and emotional investment in their child. Their search for the cause of the illness also influences and is influenced by their worldview, as well as by situational meanings and family identity. Further effects evolve from such a crisis. On the one hand, some families break down when members no longer agree on the purpose of their relationships. On the other, some families restructure with added strength; through shared social coping and adaptation, their unity is hardened as steel under pressure.[92]

Studies on children facing family hardships illustrate the impact of family meaning strategies on its member's cognitive processes. Michel Tousig-

---

transcending the situation, a more stable cognitive set encompassing beliefs about the family and relationship to larger community. FAAR Model comprises five dimensions: shared purpose; collectivity; framability; relativism (context); shared control (cf. 1998, 72–75).

90. Cf. Patterson and Garwick 1998, 84.

91. Cf. ibid., 75–76.

92. According to Patterson and Garwick (1998, 86), "Disastrous events shatter expectations, goals, and even world views, resulting in uncertainty and ambiguity. Individuals turn to their significant others in search of emotional comfort and an explanation for what is happening. The loss of a sense of personal control leads to joining more closely with others. Steinglass and Horan (1987) reported that families often pull together, giving up individual worldviews for a shared one. Support groups also serve this function for persons experiencing major illness." Patterson and Garwick focus on the worldview construct as being the process of relating or orienting to others, rather than being about the content of beliefs. Perhaps a preexisting synthetic worldview enhances such adaptation to chronic stress; or perhaps the nature of this stress is such that some families change their worldview.

nant finds that the perceived injustice of parental favoritism is a cumulative factor that renders already vulnerable children more so. Injustice demonstrates the dissimilarity of experience within the same family; one child receives more, and another is "under cared for." Children are inevitably nurtured differently, perhaps in terms of affection, education, or social opportunities. Given temperamental, affective, and cognitive differences, parents treat children in nonidentical ways. Such equity is more adapted than unnuanced equality. However, children interpret differently both measured diversity and outright favoritism. Nonetheless, they can find meaning even in the latter. Tousignant finds that some children recognize co-suffering as a source of coping.[93] Simply not suffering alone can give a sense of meaning; they feel solidarity with others, by realizing "the world is not hard on me alone." Tousignant finds therein the unfolding of morality, a sort of common meaning.[94] He posits that a sense of morality can render people more resilient, strangely enough in the face of injustice.

Religious Causal Attributions, Meaning, and Spiritual Resilience

How might cognitive bases of spirituality and religion enhance resilience? In general, spirituality and religion involve a worldview and direction in life, as well as purpose and criteria for action. They provide a basis for moral action and attributions of good and evil.[95] In particular, resilience research suggests that religiosity and well-being correlate through meaning.[96] Especially in trauma and difficulty, religion enhances resilient outcomes by contributing meaning and coping strategies. This correlation involves two aspects: belief's intellectual facet (information, knowledge, and meaning) and its consequence (moral aspect). However, we should not forget how the other aspects of religion and spirituality (emotion, motivation, and social dimensions) interrelate with them. What in particular does resilience research say about religious causal attributions, meaning, and spiritual resilience?

Studies suggest that the type of religious cognitive causal attribution of

93. Cf. M. Tousignant 1998.

94. Tousignant (1998, 61–72) recognizes similar findings in the study of Norma Haan (1989), namely that children who have a sense of morality are more resilient. Tousignant's analysis of moral action is limited by a Kohlbergian reductionistic identification of morality with justice; it nonetheless at least employs a conception of justice as a constitutive aspect of morality.

95. Cf. Lösel 1994; and Osborn 1994.

96. Cf. Masten and Reed 2002; Chamberlain and Zika 1992, 141 and 146.

negative or evil events predicts resilience outcomes. Such attributions sometimes overlap. We attribute the cause of the event to God (in terms of God's plan or will, anger, love or lack thereof); external causes (economic or social factors); family (its members' personalities or acts); self (temperament, character, choices); chance, and so on. For example, Joianne Shortz and Everett Worthington's study of young adults' recall of parental divorce highlights the role that religion plays in such attributions, related behavioral activities, and coping outcomes.[97] Two of their findings concern the effect of religious individuals' attributing negative events to God. First, ascribing the negative event to God's anger significantly predicted both "religious discontent" and pleading coping activities, such as "asking for miracles."[98] Secondly, attributing the events to God's plan or will was the clearest contributor to predicting spiritually based activities and positive acceptance of the events, such as "trusting God for protection and turning to God for guidance."[99] This research identifies one aspect of the relationship between an individual's "concept of God" and the resiliency of human agency.[100]

Theorists and researchers recognize that religion and spirituality serve in discovering meaning, purpose, and life goals. They emphasize differently, nonetheless, religion's role in the creation or discovery of meaning. On the one hand, they refer to religion and the inner spiritual life as "the cradle for a construction of meaning,"[101] and to faith as involving meaning making, in terms of convictional knowledge and the use of imagination.[102] They also say that individuals construct their own sense of order out of their choices, achievements, commitments, and relationships.[103] On the other hand, they affirm that we discover meaning through religious experience and practice, which give reference to spiritual order and other facets of life and the universe.[104]

How do faith development and religious-based meaning provide protective potential?[105] A spiritual belief system addresses questions of purpose

97. Shortz and Worthington 1994, 178; cf. Pargament et al. 1990.

98. Pleading activities were a general effect related not only to attribution to God's anger, but also in a lesser degree to God's will or God's lack of love, according to Shortz and Worthington (1994, 178).

99. Cf. Shortz and Worthington 1994, 178.

100. Cf. Watts and Williams 1988, 128–50.

101. Garbarino and Bedard 1996, 467.

102. O'Connell Higgins (1994, 172) uses "faith" in a more philosophical sense.

103. Cf. Baird 1985; cited in Chamberlain and Zika 1992, 146.

104. Cf. Yalom 1980; Reker and Wong 1988; cited in Chamberlain and Zika 1992, 146.

105. Cf. Lösel 1994, 8–12.

and meaning in life. It explains one's origins above and beyond name, ethnicity, family, and history. It can contribute to self-esteem; inasmuch as it affirms one's uniqueness (as creation) and purpose, and one's potential to overcome the difficulty, it confronts degrading pressures.[106] It helps people to set goals and cope with fundamental questions, especially about suffering and death. Yet religion and spirituality also have negative potential. Researchers highlight the risks that they bring to meaning and cognitive processes: closed-mindedness and identity foreclosure;[107] a sense of spiritual superiority, blind and unquestioning loyalty, and intolerance (e.g., wars, ongoing oppression, politicization of religion);[108] fundamentalist notions of fate;[109] risk for mental health;[110] and unreasonable behavioral expectations.[111]

The cognitive side of more-than-cognitive realities has been examined through developmental questions about faith, religion, and spirituality. From a dialectical perspective, Aleta Meyer and Linda Lausell argue that the open discussion of values, beliefs, and faith best promotes personal belief systems.[112] It emphasizes subjective valuation as a counterbalance for excessive stress on objective values. They claim that without such a dialectical process youth may not only "lose out on the value of hearing the viewpoints of others, they may determine that being value-free is optimal and never develop their own spirituality."[113]

Emphasis on narrative also highlights the development of resilient capacities. According to James Garbarino and Clair Bedard, a

> growing body of evidence [links] the ability to tell a coherent and *meaningful* account of one's life to the crucial variable of resilience in the face of adversity (Cohler, 1991). Indeed, this evidence offers support for the proposition that the

106. Meyer and Lausell 1996, 120.

107. Identity foreclosure "happens when an adolescent makes a commitment to a sense of self without exploring alternatives," according to Meyer and Lausell (1996, 120).

108. Meyer and Lausell 1996, 129.

109. E. Anderson speculates that a fundamentalist religious notion of fate might render a girl indifferent to the possibilities of pregnancy; cf. Anderson 1991, 375–98; found in Haggerty et al. 1994, 168.

110. In the context of specific sects, Lösel (1994, 10) has found that religious orientation may become a risk to mental health; cf. Werner and Smith 1992.

111. O'Connell Higgins (1994, 192) says that the Catholicism of 1950s in the United States has been experienced by some as promoting "nearly unattainable, thus unreasonable, behavioral expectations. Particular thorns include the [negative] virtues of infinite self-sacrifice and unreflective compliance, unfounded accusations and guilt-engendering admonitions, the tenet of original sin, and the perception of sex as sin."

112. This includes moral development. Cf. Meyer and Lausell 1996, 118; Haan 1989; Kohlberg 1976.

113. Meyer and Lausell 1996, 118.

emergence of this ability in children and youth is *the* most important foundation for resilience.[114]

This view is supported by Robert Coles (1990, 100), who finds that children, for example, not only ask questions about what is happening to them, but also want to understand why. When young people ask such questions, they call upon their experiences of religious life and spiritual values in addition to other potential explanations.

Trauma and difficulty—especially when experienced firsthand—defy the adequacy of cognitions about life's spiritual and religious dimensions. Trauma is even more disturbing for children. Garbarino and Bedard have observed that "the experience of childhood traumatization functions as a kind of 'reverse religious experience,' a process combining overwhelming arousal and overwhelming cognitions that threatens core 'meaningfulness' for the child."[115] Trauma can make evident both human vulnerability and our capacity for evil. It can shatter expectations of divine protection. Such experiences challenge meaningfulness especially for youths, because they have not yet had the time necessary to build a solid framework of meaning. They need time to develop the cognitive skills employed in making sense of such events.[116] In extreme cases such as trauma, but also in more everyday challenges, we employ cognitive processes related to experiences of religion and expressions of spirituality to cope and make sense out of life. They provide stability in both troubling and comforting changes.[117] Inasmuch as sense aids coping, the way in which we employ cognitive processes can be weighed in their resilient effects.

In lieu of a conclusion, let us simply highlight some suggestions that have surfaced from this research about how humans employ cognitive processes in reducing the impact of risk. First, we alter the riskiness of an event by altering its cognition. For example, we can neutralize or counteract the damaging alteration in our self-concept by putting the situation in its larger context, by not blaming ourselves for what is unforeseeable or for other people's failures, by pardoning self and others, and so forth.[118] Second, we

114. Garbarino and Bedard 1996, 469 (emphasis in the original).

115. Garbarino and Bedard 1996, 469; cf. 467.

116. Cf. Garbarino and Bedard1996, 471.

117. Werner and Smith (1986, 105) say that for their cohort "religion provided stability in the midst of change."

118. Rutter (1990, 197) claims that although "the concept of 'neutralizing' life events (Tennant, Bebbington, and Hurry, 1981) [. . .] postulat[es] an effect that relies on a quality that substantially negates

can cognitively alter our exposure to risk or modify our involvement in it. We can take distance from risk through the cognitive sets associated with humor or through finding alternatives such as physical distance from the situation. Furthermore, resilience support can come from the cognitive elements of religion and spirituality's capacity to aid in establishing cognitive perceptions and attributions, including in adjudicating between good and evil, and in discovering and creating meaning and goals, especially when coping with trauma and difficulty.

Volitional Processes: Attention and Competency

Can we choose to be resilient? Researchers address the volitional dimension of resilience and vulnerability in terms of: motivation, attention management and concentration competency, experiences of self-efficacy, and the ability to cope with difficulty.

Managing Attention and Motivation

First, how do humans manage attention and concentration in difficulty? Beverly J. Wilson and John M. Gottman (1996, 189–228) suggest that the human capacity to manage attention is basic to a number of risk and resilience factors. By "attentional processes" they mean a fundamental aspect of human agency: How do we direct our mind to an object? What state of consciousness accompanies this concentration?[119] Attentional processes provide a group of executive roles. They organize experience by "shuttling" between the perceptions, emotions, and cognitions.[120] This interaction is elemental to the extension, shaping, and modification of temperament and character in general. In particular, researchers have found that attention correlates to the following resilience qualities: active and social responsiveness, flexibility, both positive mood and low levels of negative emotions, feelings of self-esteem and self-efficacy,[121] mastery of basic interpersonal skills (e.g., turn

or counteracts the impact of an earlier threatening event or difficulty," not all positive events are neutralizing.

119. In this case, the term "attention" or "attentional processes" is not identical to "intention" in the technical sense of classical ethics, where it means the end of the agent (*finis operantis*). Neither is it strictly synonymous with the faculty or act of "volition" or "will" as a desire or appetite for the perceived good, nor as the efficient intending and enjoying of that good. Nonetheless, it illustrates an important aspect of volition.

120. Cf. Eysenck 1982.

121. Cf. Wilson and Gottman 1996, 190–91, and 220; Lösel 1994, 9.

taking, mutual regulation, sharing of internal states), and establishment of interpersonal relationships.

Attention affects agency according to personality type. From Ernest Wallwork's psychodynamic perspective, whether we are obsessional, hysterical, borderline, narcissistic (and so on) influences our conscious attentional processes. Such personality types also shape our interpretation of the world and our replies to it. Given the plethora of stimuli and possible interpretations, attention selectivity is inevitable. Nonetheless, we interrogate, narrow, or widen it through our sensitivity and self-directional capacities.[122]

Attentional processes manage emotion regulation, a core risk variable according to Wilson and Gottman.[123] Emotional arousal alters performance through changing our selectivity and distractibility. In general, increased attentional selectivity may result from moderate and, in some cases, high levels of arousal; it may aid active coping by focusing attention on a primary task. However, not all arousal stimuli affect performance equally. Incentive and anxiety types of arousal influence us differently. For example, high levels of "incentive arousal" increase performance on primary tasks, and do not for the most part decrease performance of subsidiary tasks. But high levels of "anxiety arousal" tend to narrow attention to the primary task to the detriment of secondary ones (by decreasing parallel cognitive processing), and may lead to greater susceptibility to distraction from internal and external events.[124]

The intensity of emotion demands two types of attention and processing. We effortlessly process some emotions, while others require exertion.[125] In the case of strong, disruptive, or distracting emotions, we must consciously focus attention away from the emotion-arousing event. The need to redirect

122. Cf. Wallwork 1999, 170–80.

123. Wilson and Gottman (1996, 193) claim that most current theories in cognitive psychology only inadequately treat the interrelation between emotions, motivation, and attention. They highlight the importance of past experience and present goals in directing attention, as well as the detrimental effect of anxiety (negative cognitions such as self-doubt and fear of failure) on performance.

124. Cf. Wilson and Gottman 1996, 194–95. The background for this theory is found in the Yerkes-Dodson law (1908), which predicts an inverted-U function between arousal and performance. This law foresees that performance is maximal with moderate levels of arousal, but lowest with very low and very high levels of arousal. This law has since been nuanced, for it has been found that different types of arousal affect performance differently.

125. Research indicates a close relationship between attention-demanding processing and physiological arousal. Physiological signs of attention include the measure of pupil diameter, heart rate, and skin conductance, all of which increase during input and processing of information; cf. Wilson and Gottman 1996, 195–97.

attention finds partial explanation in two opposite physiological abilities of the autonomic nervous system, which are a basis for attention-demanding cognitive and emotional processes and aid in reestablishing internal homeostasis. They are the sympathetic "accelerator" of the sympathetic nervous system and the vagal "brake" of the parasympathetic nervous system.[126] On the one hand, in the face of emotional stimulation and intellectual interest, the sympathetic accelerator mobilizes the body and increases the heartbeat; this self-activation prepares us to meet emergency situations (e.g., to affront or flee danger). In turn, we need to be able to calm the accelerator effect through self-soothing or emotion regulation strategies. On the other hand, the vagal brake conserves and maintains bodily resources. Since the effort of maintaining attention requires a great deal of energy, the organism seeks to decelerate and stabilize heart rate during periods of peek attention; this self-calming enables longer concentration.[127] Indeed physiological relaxation helps sustain attention and aids the arousal-lowering process.[128] In the face of high levels of anxiety, the inability to manage either of these two physiological aspects can lead to reduced attention and performance levels, heightened selectivity, and the negative effects of distractibility.[129] In general, such a double failure (increased cardiovascular reactivity and low vagal tone) may correlate with reduced resiliency, while inversely effective attention management underlies multiple resiliency strategies.

Second, the psychosocial sciences sometimes consider motivation as synonymous with volition or the human will. They thus distinguish motivational from cognitive, emotional, and temperamental sources of resilience. What are the most prevalent models of motivation? And what do the resilience studies suggest about the role of motivation in human agency?

In order to understand this resilience research, we need to differentiate two approaches to motivation: the homeostasis and growth models. The former conceptualizes humans as motivated only in order to find a balance, to fulfill a need. We eat because we feel hungry. We sleep because of fatigue. The growth-oriented framework construes motivation as a human capacity underlying our progressive growth toward an aim. We act for reasons and

126. Cf. Wilson and Gottman 1996, 195.

127. Cf. Wilson and Gottman 1996, 198–99.

128. Cf. Watts and Williams 1988, 78.

129. Attentional problems are linked to various sources, such as attention deficit hyperactive disorder (the most severe example) and intrauterine exposure to alcohol and nicotine. Wilson and Gottman (1996, 191) suggest that variability might be related to individual differences in nutrition, exposure to stress, or caregiver behaviors.

for goals. Contemporary psychology grants a central place to motivation in the individual's goal-directed agency. For example, in his humanistic psychology, Abraham H. Maslow (1908–1970) uses motivation to replace or at least integrate notions of instinct, reflexes, behavior, and stimuli-response conditioning; he thus attempts to explain human conduct, its constituent needs and goals.[130] Some research seeks to find the roots of operative resilience that we derive from the efficacy of our volition. It focuses on human motivation and its sources. It asks: how does motivation serve coping, self-conservation, and constructive competency in hardship?

Human motivation has various dimensions. Responses to the question, what moves a human being, include not only personal but also relational motivations and goals. Answers to the question, what is moved, encompass our own internal states, impulses, and resources, including our thoughts, decisions, and choices.

Human motivation involves self-control efforts that keep disruptive emotions in check, delay gratification, or stifle impulsiveness. It demands conscientious efforts to take responsibility for personal performance and social events. It also involves maintaining and being maintained by our goals and standards of life. This perspective has various names: Maslow calls it self-realization; virtue theory calls it flourishing or happiness.

Self-motivation involves harnessing cognitions, choices, and emotions behind an aim. Goal orientation is essential for paying attention, self-mastery, and even creativity. Mindfulness of goals gives the context for the self-control needed to accomplish large and small tasks. Goleman describes a successful and sustained intentional and attentional focus as a state of "flow."[131] This goal-driven state of excellence enables outstanding acts and performances, and even contributes to the development of high-quality dispositions.

On the personal level, positive self-esteem supports self-motivation and action, just as negative self-images undercut them, according to Rutter.[132] Other research indicates that feelings of self-assurance and pride, as well as a sense of purpose in life, can strengthen motivation for action and appropriate attention skills, while the contrary promote passivity, distractibility, and discouragement.[133] According to the social development model, social

130. See Maslow 1971/1987, as well as Diel 1947/1991.

131. Cf. Goleman 1998, 26, 43, 105–29.

132. Cf. Rutter 1990, 197–207; Yule 1992, 191.

133. Cf. Maughan 1988, 214.

bonding underlies a protective type of motivation. Feelings of attachment and solidarity with family and groups regulate behavior; they motivate us to live up to the group's standards.[134] Participation in social groups can promote feelings of self-worth and strengthen personal resistance to external and internal negative pressures.

Motivation, Religion, and Resilience

The spiritual and religious domain brings further light to motivation and resilience. Theoretical psychosocial science and resilience researchers have focused on the importance of religion in motivation. The two types of theoretical approaches offer distinct observations about religious motivation. The homeostatic approach affirms that activity follows a felt need. We seek a balance, a state without stimulation. In this perspective, religion is a response to human fear, anxiety, guilt, or deprivation. Religion manages these needs.[135] Although the homeostatic model of motivation usefully describes "physiological" belief and religion, we need to inquire about the adequacy of reducing religion to emotional stimuli.

A growth- or realization-oriented research relies on cognitive theories of motivation. It claims that humans seek to optimize rather than minimize stimulation. This approach explains the human desire for variety, aesthetic experience, and curiosity. In this perspective, religious activity seeks overall growth and self-realization, which involves motivational and cognitive growth. In particular, religion serves as the basic motivation, which is the human quest for meaning.[136] Nonetheless, both these perspectives highlight the motivational relevance of meaning and control, as well as mastery and self-esteem.

Resilience researchers have found that one aspect of the role of religion and spirituality in competency and motivation is the intrinsic quality of religious beliefs that reduce vulnerability to risky situations. This research distinguishes intrinsic and utilitarian bases of belief. Intrinsically religious people have a sincere belief and commitment; they thus find their most fundamental source of motivation in the principles and standards of their religion. In contrast, a utilitarian, pragmatic, or self-centered approach to religion is motivated from nonreligious operative principles, for example, the

134. Cf. Consortium 1994, 300.

135. Cf. Hood et al. 1996, 17–20.

136. V. Frankl (1963/1984) speaks of this motivation in terms of a "will to meaning."

advancement of one's own status, security, and self-justification.[137] Meyer and Lausell note that positive resilience outcomes correlate to intrinsic religious qualities such as mindfulness (of other people and of oneness with creation) or an internalized code of behavior (involving firmer control, higher maturity, and greater acceptance of personal responsibility for one's own behavior).[138] Masten, Best, and Garmezy's research suggests that religious practice (the participation in a church community and belief in a higher power) builds protective resources in the form of "competence and educational attainment."[139]

The motivational and control functions of religion offer an important typology. Religious principles and standards, parables, and narratives promote personal control and motivation. In the control function, we obey law as coming from another (from God, God's ministers and representatives, or another authority). The law is not internal to the agent except as blindly willed. We obey the law, because it is the law. In the motivational function, we internalize law. We do not simply obey it as God's command or because it is law, but we also accept it for further reasons: the common good, the kingdom of God, and so forth. Motivation and control are sometimes seen as opposing dichotomies. While distinguishable, the control and motivation functions of religion complement each other.[140]

Spiritual Competency in Coping?

Resilience research has identified religion's input on how we acquire spiritual competency through coping, according to the type of: participation the religion plays in coping; religious variables, which promote positive outcomes, and religious hope, commitment, and planfulness. According to K. I. Pargament et al., our religious beliefs affect the appraisal of and the coping with negative events in three ways.[141] First, we can involve religion, faith, or spirituality as a part of coping. A stressful event can be religious in nature, or we can appraise it as such: we can attribute the cause of an event to the plan, wrath, or uninvolvement of God. B. Spilka, P. Shaver, and L. A. Kirkpatrick claim that religious concepts highlighting orderliness, benevo-

137. Cf. Masters and Bergin 1992, 222; Donahue 1985, 416.

138. Meyer and Lausell (1996, 125–26) establish these theories from a meta-analysis of research.

139. Cf. Masten, Best, and Garmezy 1990; Haggerty et al. 1994, 168.

140. Cf. Thomas and Carver 1990, 202; D'Antonio 1983, 81–108; D'Antonio and Aldous 1983, 15–16.

141. Pargament et al. (1990, 796–7) say: "Religious appraisals, coping activities, and resources and constraints may serve a number of functions important to the resolution of problems."

lence, and justice in the universe aid us in managing negative events.[142] Religious practices and resources can help overcome negative events; for example, coping activities likewise involve religious bases; for example, prayer, confession, or support from religious people and clergy. Religious resources, motivation, or constraints operate in belief systems, norms, and congregational support. A desire for ultimate happiness or a closer relationship with God may guide coping efforts. Second, religion contributes to coping, inasmuch as religious involvement decreases the likelihood of complicating negative factors such as drug and alcohol abuse, nonmarital sexual activity, and so on. Lastly, it can be a product of a coping process; for example, because of successful events we may experience increased fervor or commitment.

Pargament et al. correlate positive coping outcomes with four religious variables.[143] The first variable is "belief in a just benevolent God." They have observed that positive coping outcomes correlate to "appraisals of events as reflective of God's will, images of a loving God, and orthodox beliefs in a just and merciful personal God." Inasmuch as the religious concepts and practices are well integrated and emphasize order in the universe and fairness in the world, they serve psychological functions regarding not only meaning, but also self-esteem and an external framework of control. On the contrary, they have found that negative coping outcomes relate to appraisals of the event as a punishment from God or as a threat, which accompanied feelings of anger and distance from God and church members. Beliefs in an angry unfair God can threaten meaningfulness, self-esteem, and control in life. A second variable is an "experience of God as a supportive partner in coping." This relationship with God is intimate, emotional, and problem focused. It involves both personal effort and recognition of limits to personal agency. It is an interactive relationship, neither simply passive nor simply active. A third variable is "involvement in religious rituals," which includes aspects of church attendance; prayer; "avoidance efforts" such as Bible reading or focus on afterlife; attempts to lead more loving, less sinful lives; support from church members and clergy. A fourth variable is the "search for spiritual and personal support through religion." Here an intrinsic spirituality is found to seek closeness with God, who secondarily is a guiding force for problem resolution. An extrinsic spirituality and utilitarian approach in

142. Cf. Spilka, Shaver, and Kirkpatrick 1985; Pargament et al. 1990, 799; Shortz and Worthington 1994, 172.

143. Cf. Pargament et al. 1990, 793, and 814–86.

contrast uses religion primarily for its usefulness in acquiring positive coping outcomes.

Religious competency (appraisal and coping) is fundamentally intertwined with the dynamics of motivation and guidance. For example, we can derive hope from a sense of competency, insofar as the experience of overcoming difficulty spawns hope for doing likewise in the future.[144] Werner and Smith claim that "the experience of the resilient children in coping with and mastering stressful life events by their actions, appeared to build immunity against 'learned helplessness,' and an attitude of 'hopefulness' instead—even in the midst of material poverty."[145] Such hope-based experiences can be shared with others.[146] Motivation, moreover, springs from the force of spiritual goals and meaning that provide guidance and support, especially when facing obstacles. Meyer and Lausell suggest that spiritual goals underlie resilience and that to become attached to them demands more than individual effort; they implicate communal and intergenerational goals and collaboration.[147]

Thomas and Carver positively correlate religious commitment and social competence,[148] in terms of increased pro-social skills such as self-esteem, social commitment, and academic achievement, and decresed tendency to develop negative attitudes and participate in activities devalued by society, such as suicide, truancy, delinquency, substance abuse, teenage pregnancy, and sexual permissiveness.[149] Moreover, religion's positive effect on social competence is illustrated through the quality of planfulness. Socially competent adolescents are characterized by their ability to plan ahead. Instead of living only in the present, they anticipate coming stages of life. They make active plans for the future concerning education, occupation, family, and so on. They also integrate religious values as goals for the future.[150] Negative effects of religion, on the contrary, include misconceived or unhealthy notions of self-sacrifice that lead to the self-abnegation within minority groups.[151]

In sum, psychosocial theory and resilience research findings enlighten human volition's role in resilient and vulnerability outcomes. The way that

144. Concerning hope, see Danieli 1994; Snyder et al. 1991a and 1991b; Seligman 1991/1998 and 1995; Breznitz 1986.

145. Werner and Smith 1986, 157; cf. Seligman 1991/1998 and 1975.

146. Cf. Werner and Smith 1992, 202–09.

147. Cf. Meyer and Lausell 1996, 125.

148. Cf. Thomas and Carver 1990, 195ff.

149. Cf. ibid., 205.

150. Cf. ibid., 212.

151. Cf. Browning 1987, 160.

volitional processes relate to resilience involves the personal dialogue between sources of stress and attentional processes; goals, self-control, and motivation; extrinsic and intrinsic motivation; and religious law, instruction, and spirit. Research suggests that we can develop volitional competencies that underlie spiritual coping, self-conservation, and positive construction. Religious coping activities offer a unique framework for dealing with the limits of personal knowledge, control, and resources. For the religiously involved, religious coping constructs offer an additional, non-repetitive source of potential resilience.[152]

Family Interactions

Finally, I shall directly address the resilience input of family relationships (in this section) and other social networks (in the next). What family dynamics operate when facing challenges to our understanding, physical health, and faith? A recourse to sociology will enrich the intercultural and experiential breadth of the study.

This search for the social context of resilience moves beyond a focus on the individual's internal sources of protection and risk, and beyond a narrow focus on the mother's influence on the child.[153] It includes the larger environment, the social world. A systems approach offers some insights into social relationships; however, it has its limits as well. We cannot simplistically translate concepts from the individual to the family or other social systems. A collective characterization is not independent of its individual members, but at the same time it is not a simple aggregate of them. We cannot simply consider families, schools, or neighborhoods resilient in terms of attribution of collective meaning or competency, as we would an individual.[154] Furthermore, psychological studies and theories attain less certainty when analyzing social dynamics than intrapersonal ones. Last, the social realm is not without its ambiguities. For example, some resilience studies demonstrate that certain people exhibit a rather antisocial resilience.[155] These challenges

152. Pargament et al. (1990, 816–18) argue that religious coping constructs can make additive (related but not redundant) contributions to nonreligious coping constructs.

153. Cf. Schaffer 1992.

154. Cf. Sagy and Antonovsky 1998, 222.

155. According to Werner and Smith (1992, 69) "career and job success was the highest priority on the agenda of the resilient men (39.1%) and women (64.7%), but the lowest priority on the agenda of their peers with problems in adolescence. Also high on the priority list of the resilient individuals were

demand a deeper analysis of the observations, empirical studies, and underlying psychosocial theories.

Family Resilience Interactions

Specialists have observed four types of family resilience interactions: (1) family fit and harmony; (2) family stress management; (3) family disruption; (4) family socioeconomic status. First, researchers have observed the effects of the family interactional styles in terms of fit and harmony. A good family fit does not necessarily mean an idyllic, picture-book family or the possession of all desirable temperament and character qualities.[156] It does mean, however, that a family establishes balanced goals that promote the well-being of its members. Protective qualities for families facing difficulty include: "family cohesion, warmth, and an absence of discord";[157] "stability and security";[158] reliable care and identification with competent roles models encouraging constructive coping;[159] "an open, supportive, and controlling educational climate [and] dosed social responsibilities and achievement demands,"[160] as well as friendship promotion among siblings.[161] The notion of family support regroups a good deal of these qualities and processes; it includes but should not be restricted to emotional support. Wills has predicted that parental support leads children "to more adaptive coping, less maladaptive coping, and development of academic and social competence."[162] His study of family support has found that families expert at coping through effective information exchange were perceived by adolescents as supportive, and promoted their competence through giving emotional affirmation (boosting the youths' sense of self-esteem and validating their feelings); through disposing of challenge- and transition-coping assistance; and through modeling useful support and communication skills (attitudes and

---

self-development and self-fulfillment (M: 34.8%; F: 38.2%). The more traditional goals of a happy marriage, children, and having a home of one's own were mentioned by only about one out of four in the group. The lowest item in priority among their life goals was close relationships with family and friends (M: 8.7%; F: 2.9%)."

156. Simply composing such a universal list would sidestep the difficulty of applicability (and verifiability) across socioeconomic and cultural environments. We are able to make only limited observations about some of the more evident resilience findings.

157. Garmezy 1985, cited in Rutter 1990, 182.

158. Cf. Booth and Booth 1997, 113.

159. Masten, Best, and Garmezy (1990), quoted by Garmezy 1994.

160. Lösel 1994, 9.

161. Cf. Dunn 1988, 233.

162. Wills et al. 1996, 117. Cf. Consortium 1994, 275.

expectations). He affirms that supportive family environments promote successful adolescent integration in larger communities and deter negative life events.[163] Thus, strongly bonded families exhibit clear standards and norms for behavior, which reduce the incidence of problem behavior. For example, this helps to diminish "precocious sexual activity, leaving school early, interpersonal violence, criminal activity, and tobacco, alcohol, or other drug use by children and adolescents."[164]

A good mother-child relationship during the first year of life is one of the key environmental factors in developmental resiliency among children at risk.[165] According to Werner and Smith, teenage girls especially find a benevolent role model in the type of competent mother, who holds a steady job and delegates household responsibilities to the daughter.[166] In high delinquency-risk environments, they also found that buffers against criminogenic stresses seemed to include the father's esteem for the mother and the mother's self-confidence, education, and maternal affection, while paternal aggressiveness and maternal permissiveness coincided with higher levels of youth criminality.[167] When the mother is unable to provide this good relationship herself, Musick et al. note the value of her enabling her child to use a "growth-enhancing alternative care-taking environment."[168] Other studies—less numerous, though growing in number—highlight the importance of the father or another male role model.[169]

Second, family support and competency underpin family stress-management styles. Researchers define "family stress" as a macro-event, as a critical life episode disturbing the homeostasis of the family.[170] Nonetheless, they emphasize differently the individual's part in coping with family stress. In a stimulus-response approach, Perrez (1994b, 7–8) identifies coping as the adaptive responses produced by an individual, in terms of perceiving a stressor, appraising it, and expressing related emotions and coping behavior.

163. Cf. Wills et al. 1996, 115–16, 127.

164. Consortium 1994, 300–301. The social development model hypothesizes the same role for standards and norms in schools and larger communities. Furthermore, Werner and Smith (1992, 185–87 and 198–200; 1986, 134–35) have found that shared values, a sense of coherence, structure, and rules in the household serve to support resilience.

165. Cf. Musick et al. 1987, 249.

166. Cf. Werner and Smith 1992, 185–86; also see Werner and Smith 1986.

167. Cf. Werner and Smith 1992, 9.

168. Cf. Musick et al. 1987, 250.

169. Cf. Werner and Smith 1992, 185–86; cf. 1986.

170. On the history of family stress analysis see Perrez 1994b, 7–8.

When family members coordinate their coping reactions, the coping effect is more efficacious. Guy Bodenmann and Meinrad Perrez (1993) illustrate how couples and families manage stress. First, inevitably one partner's stress touches the other. Someone living in a couple thus will have more exposure to stress. However, an intimate relationship also offers resources to better manage the stress together.[171] Studies of dyadic stress resolution positively correlate satisfaction of the couple and the way in which one partner communicates stress to the other.[172] Family styles of cohesiveness and adaptability correlate to coping efficacy. Not every type of dyadic management of stress is as effective as others.[173] Bodenmann and Perrez (1993) present the following theories concerning coping with risk in families. The objective intensity of stressors and the members' personal qualities (e.g., hardiness) influence family stress. Coping competence also affects family stress. In the second case, capacities to reestablish emotional homeostasis and to move forward to solve problems and achieve goals build upon one's satisfaction with family life and one's sense of well-being.[174] The style of emotional causal attribution influences the quality of emotional reactions and coping. Emotional bonding can be a possible positive result of shared stress; while when it is poorly managed, shared stress can cause emotional estrangement.[175]

Family Disruption and Socioeconomic Status

Research hypotheses and findings suggest that family disruption is detrimental to support and competence processes, and may contribute to other adverse outcomes.[176] Common sense tells us as much. However, empirical research provides needed details, according to types of disruption. Early parental loss favors vulnerability to psychiatric disorders, especially when accompanied by a serious lack of affectionate care in childhood and other direct risk variables, such as a cognitive set of helplessness and a related concept of low self-esteem.[177] Effects associated with marital conflict include a child's lower self-esteem, negative self-images, and troubled relationship with the custodial parent.[178] Unfair parental treatment of children

171. Studies document the typology of support within the couple; cf. Werner and Smith 1992; Rutter 1990, 189–202; McCubbin et al. 1998, 64.

172. Cf. Bodenmann and Perrez 1993, 3–4; Hansen 1992, 191.

173. Cf. Bodenmann and Perrez 1993, 7.

174. Cf. Perrez 1994b, 11.

175. Ibid.

176. Cf. Wills et al. 1996, 127.

177. Cf. Rutter 1990, 200.

178. Cf. Watt et al. 1990, 300.

causes imbalances to the family environment; for example, Tousignant has found parental favoritism is a cumulative factor that renders already vulnerable children more so.[179] Although seeming obvious, it has been found that good parent-child relationships can decrease risk associated with family discord.[180] An important social resource has proved to be a stable emotional relationship with at least one parent, or another adult.[181]

The family disruption experienced in divorce demonstrates more evident risks. Empirical studies correlate divorce with numerous important stressors, many of which are associated with increased risk of psychological problems for children. Parental divorce during preadolescence is additionally linked with serious difficulties involving social and parental relations, as well as scholastic and emotional adjustment.[182] For the most part, children identify feelings of distress, if not disturbance, as a result of their parents' divorce. Children's social development can be impaired; in particular, peer relations can be limited in terms of intimacy, satisfaction, reliable alliance, conflict, affection, and companionship.[183] According to Robert Emery, on the average, children function competently after divorce.[184] This competency finds its roots in numerous protective processes. Preadolescent girls tend to find support in peer friends; boys do so less than girls.[185] A good rapport with the custodial parent, furthermore, has been associated with positive self-esteem and social relations at school, while a bad rapport was associated with poorer peer relationships.[186] Indeed, nonparental substitutes and other reference persons can provide important social resources.

Other risks correlate with the family's specific socioeconomic status (SES). Yet risk cannot simply be conflated (as it sometimes is) with lower SES per se. On the one hand, evidence indicates that greater affluence and improved living conditions accompany increases in certain forms of psychosocial disorder. Young people in higher SES groups suffer a greater prevalence of suicide, an increase in crime rates, and higher incidences of drug

179. Cf. Tousignant 1998, 64.

180. According to Rutter (1990, 189–202), there are two directions of causation. Family discord can cause further problems for parent-child relationships; and negative parent-child relationships can cause further family discord. On the contrary, family harmony and good relationships can contribute to more extensive harmony and good relationships.

181. Cf. Lösel 1994, 9; Musick et al. 1987, 250; Werner and Smith 1992.

182. Cf. Watt et al. 1990, 297.

183. Cf. Watt et al. 1990, 297–8.

184. Cf. Emery 1994, 93.

185. Cf. Watt et al. 1990, 298.

186. Cf. Tousignant 1998, 64.

and alcohol problems.[187] Questions about the correlation of risk and higher or lower SES need to address the constituent components of the SES linked to actualizing or escaping from risk. Issues related to lower SES include overcrowding, inadequate nutrition, poor health care, the absence of positive role models, the compounding of anxieties;[188] while those for higher SES concern parental absence, lack of participation in meaningful household work and family activities, overprotection, overabundance (including availability of abusable substances).[189]

Family, Religion, and Spirituality

The resilience influence of family from religious and spiritual input has been found (1) to be rooted in faith and moral education and modeling; (2) to be important for marital adjustment and happiness; and (3) to correlate to a balance between the control and support functions of religion and family. First, research has widely recognized that values transfer is more effective when parents act congruently and offer a warm, supportive atmosphere at home and in church. Several studies have identified the importance not only of consistently demonstrating values, but also of discussing them in order for this transfer to occur.[190]

Second, the level of family religiosity positively correlates to marriage adjustment, understood as marital quality, satisfaction, and happiness. According to Hansen (1992, 189), in fifty years of this research "religion has consistently been identified as a factor associated with adjustment." Religion mediates adjustment through a meaning-structure, which includes a normative system with specific ideals about marital relationships.[191] Although secularization has weakened the general link between religion and family, the relationship is thought to depend on whether the family has a high or low level of religiosity. There are reasons why. Highly religious couples report higher levels of marital satisfaction and adjustment than less religious ones.[192] This correlation also occurs when comparing same-faith and interfaith marriages. Hansen explains the reports of higher satisfaction and adjustment through the greater faith-social network, and the greater con-

187. To this list, M. Rutter (1994b, 355–63) adds depressive disorders.

188. According to Rutter (1994b, 363), poverty itself is a risk factor rather than the risk mechanism, which is the family disorganization and breakup associated with poverty. Cf. Garmezy 1990, 530.

189. Cf. Consortium 1994, 270.

190. Cf. Meyer and Lausell 1996, 124; Masters and Bergin 1992.

191. Cf. Hansen 1992, 190; Berger 1967.

192. Cf. Hansen 1992.

sistency both in faith education of children and in family faith practices.[193] Mixed marriages, on the contrary, may have a secularizing effect, or be the result of lower religiosity.

Third, several factors affect the relation between the control and support functions of family and religion. The level of doctrinal certitude influences the control impact of the doctrines and related actions. When families doubt faith-based doctrines, these teachings have less of a control effect. At the same time, a cultural context that embodies such a doctrinal critique without proposing a meaningful solution leads to an even greater need for the support function of religion.[194] For example, clergy have traditionally served a caring function, which is all the more needed when families suffer from cultural disturbances (challenges to religious meaning). According to William D'Antonio and Joan Aldous, although there can be a struggle over the primacy and focus of the social control and social support functions of religion and families, the way in which family and religion collaborate in these functions strengthens each other. A separation, on the contrary, tends to weaken each of them.[195]

Interactions outside the Family

After having treated issues of relationship and resilience in terms of familial interactions, I now turn to extra-familial interactions. The overlap between these two social influences renders inevitable certain gaps on one side and repetitions on the other. Nonetheless, this section addresses resilience and risk qualities specifically associated with relationships outside the home.

Friends and Peers

Friends and peers influence us positively in numerous ways. Resilience research often makes at least fleeting reference to them.[196] Studies on the de-

193. Cf. Hansen 1992, 191.

194. Joan Aldous (1983, 63) identifies some of these difficulties as concerning conjugal love, separation, divorce, abortion, and contraception. Furthermore, hedonism and materialism have weakened the control function of religion. She has found that because of longer lives (and less contact with death), people have less of a sense of the fleetingness of life and less call upon the churches (religion and clergy) for comfort in times of grief and for aid in finding meaningfulness in loss.

195. Cf. D'Antonio and Aldous 1983, 15–16, and D'Antonio 1983, 106.

196. Cf. Bahr, Hawks and Wang 1993; Bainbridge 1992; Clarke and Clarke 1992; Dunn 1988, Meyer

velopment of friendship and friendliness include the genetic and environmental factors that interrelate in the formation of social networks. As discussed in relation to temperamental qualities, an individual's social support progresses in a dialogue between genetic and environmental factors.[197] Prosocial temperament characteristics include affability, attractiveness (physical, emotional, and psychological), sociability, outgoingness, and so on, while negative social qualities include higher levels of irritability, timidity, depression, and melancholia, and so forth.[198] Moreover, friendship networks protect against depression, while lack of such support can lead to it.

According to a study conducted in Washington, DC, highly competent youth tend to put friendships to good use. Their friendships help them to acquire a deeper understanding of themselves and to clarify their career possibilities. They share information and pool their skills. They face academic and interpersonal challenges together by drawing from each other's strengths and complementary points of view.[199] Moreover, Judy Dunn suggests that friendship mediates resilient outcomes in various difficult but normal life transitions, such as the adjustment to school.[200] Wilson and Gottman suggest that friendship networks help transform failure experiences, which frequently occur in a peer context. Friendships provide the resources needed for regulating negative arousal of moderate failure experiences and thus may lead to greater resiliency.[201] Certain studies have found that resilient women are more eager than resilient men to help friends who encounter problems. Although strongly career oriented, the women (in the study) found more sustenance through networks of social relationships that included family, friends, and coworkers.[202]

There is also a dark side to friendships. Friends and peers do not unconditionally provide a positive influence to each other. They may offer a source of risk for adolescent drug use and other forms of antisocial behavior, especially when combined with the negative modeling from drug using or delin-

---

and Lausell 1996; Rutter 1994b; Tousignant 1998; Watt et al. 1990; Werner and Smith 1992; Wills et al. 1996. However, we have not found any extensive studies on the resiliency and risks associated with friends and peers.

197. Neither genetic nor environmental factors determine the outcome of friendship development, according to Rutter (1994b, 367–68).

198. Cf. Kagan 1994.

199. Werner and Smith (1986, 104–5) refer to the studies of Hamburg and Adams 1967 and Hamburg et al. 1974.

200. Cf. Dunn 1988, 236.

201. Cf. Wilson and Gottman 1996, 216.

202. Cf. Werner and Smith 1992, 68–69.

quent peers, more general peer rejection in the elementary grades,[203] and a low level of adult support.[204] In the context of high risk, Werner and Smith have found that a fairly high proportion of resilient males acknowledged being loners, not having much interaction with friends, tending to focus on their own work, and withdrawing from others' problems.[205] Conversely, their less resilient peers depended more often on friends for emotional support in adulthood. The low levels of friendship for the resilient group and higher levels for the non-resilient suggest that certain friendship environments correlate with risk and vulnerability. This correlation does not mean that on a larger scale resilience negatively correlates with friendship. Nonetheless, the ambivalence of certain types of friendship networks indicates the need to evaluate the quality and specificity of a resilience factor (in terms of normativity, health, and happiness) and the presence of risk factors.

Caregivers and Beyond

Caregivers and adult substitutes outside the nuclear family offer resilience support that the family sometimes cannot provide. Numerous researchers show that they can instrumentally build up an individual's resilience and aid in adulthood recovery. They compensate for deficits in the family's emotional and cognitive support, and promote social competency through serving as role models.[206] A primary resilience support involves the interaction of children with a nonparental adult who supplements deficiencies in guidance, nurturance, knowledge, and even cognitive, social, and affective support.[207]

The care-giving environment can include extended family members (such as grandparents or cousins), relatives of a close friend, or teachers and ministers.[208] These people can foster trust and a sense of coherence, give "second chance" opportunities to acquire competence and confidence, and provide emotional support encouraging autonomy and initiative.[209] Involvement

203. Cf. Consortium 1994, 271.

204. Wills at al. (1996, 121) has found that without adult support youth may be more vulnerable to modeling effects of peer substance use.

205. Werner and Smith (1992, 68–69; and cf. 46) found that "while more of the resilient women (63.6%) were eager to help their friends who encountered problems, the majority of the resilient men (66.7%) tended to withdraw from others' troubles."

206. Cf. Clarke and Clarke 1992, 149; Lösel 1994, 9; Tousignant 1998, 67.

207. Cf. Vanistendael 1995[2]; Musick et al. 1987, 249.

208. Cf. Werner and Smith 1986, 97.

209. Cf. Werner and Smith 1992, 185–87, 192, 198–200; and 1986, 134–35.

with the wider community provides support in other forms, such as schools that value children and encourage them to learn; teachers who act as role models, assisting the youths with realistic educational and vocational plans; involvement in employment and local clubs and societies; and participation in a close-knit neighborhood.[210] On the contrary, risk variables include experiences of academic failure, low commitment to school, and low expectations from teachers; availability of abusable substances, extreme neighborhood deprivation, and disorganization;[211] and larger problems underlying particular cultures.[212]

We face another serious matter: play. As mentioned earlier, Eisen has found that play serves serious roles in the lives of children and adults.[213] Playful activities aid in processing information, solving problems, coping, learning survival techniques, and strengthening parent-child contact.[214] In extreme and normal situations, play serves in adaptation (for suffering loss-death) and promotion of survival.[215] Moreover, D. W. Winnicott posits that play positively correlates with a sense of self. He hypothesizes that the "relaxation in conditions of trust based on experience [gives way to] creative, physical and mental activity manifested in play [so that finally there is a] summation of these experiences forming the basis for a sense of self."[216] Numerous anecdotal indications suggest that play and contact with nature positively correlate to mental and physical health. They also serve as a psychological buffer and reestablish social stability and order in the face of crisis.[217]

210. Cf. Clarke and Clarke 1992, 153; Werner and Smith 1986, 97; Booth and Booth 1997, 113.

211. Cf. Consortium 1994, 271.

212. For example, Garmezy notes the prevalence of major problems found in the USA, such as depression as a widespread mental disorder, family breakup, racial disharmony, limitations in treating chronic childhood illnesses, effects on behavior of social class variations, school difficulties in ensuring children's later well-being through education and socialization (cf. Garmezy 1994, 6–7).

213. George Eisen (1988, 7) has studied children at play in the Shoah. He noted that a unique set of rules governed children's play. He observes that play displays a higher order than seriousness, since it can include the latter, but seriousness cannot include play.

214. In difficult situations, these activities can help us to understand the absurd, forget hunger, face fear, relieve stress, and find a person-environment balance (cf. Eisen 1988, 98).

215. Survival behavior learned through play can include resistance, protest, and defiance. Cf. Eisen 1988, 11 and 88f.

216. Winnicott 1971, 56; cf. Winnicott 1987. Alasdair MacIntyre (1999) argues that the unqualified trust of a caregiver can serve in releasing the creative physical and intellectual powers that we express in forms of play and result in a larger sense of self-sufficiency and independence in practical reasoning. In addition, he demonstrates that play permits us to explore reality. Play releases us from the pressures of felt need. It enables the pursuit of a range of activities that are worthwhile, pleasant. It allows the exercise and expansion of one's intellectual capacities.

217. Cf. G. Eisen 1988, 41. Eisen (1988, 60) tells of how children, deprived of contact with the city

Social Relationships and Religion

For a more direct treatment of the social dimension of spiritual and religious resilience, we shall take a closer look at the religious dimensions of community, peer, and family contexts.[218] Fundamental issues for social support and resources in resilience concern the principles and processes of social relationships that engender the religious community. According to Meyer and Lausell, a spiritual belief system provides a sense of community among believers, as well as principles that direct and govern not only personal behavior, but also relationships with others and joint efforts.[219] These principles sometimes conflict through diverse interpretations of religion's control and support functions.[220] As a control, religion offers direction for human action through divinely legislated law. As motivation, religion offers support, while leaving the interpretation to one's conscience. These foundational relationships and principles of action have special import when adolescents seek support from beyond the family.

The religious influence in society or culture has been found to (1) strengthen the "moral community"; (2) contribute to overall (average) mental health; and (3) deter delinquency and criminality. First, sociologists have found that religion significantly strengthens the moral community, in terms of both moral and social integration. It facilitates unity through shared be-

parks in the Warsaw Jewish ghetto, expressed a keen desire for contact with plants, flowers, and animals, even on their deathbeds. For a philosophical approach to drug-abuse rehabilitation using nature (through pilgrimage, mountain climbing, and desert survival) and ritual, see Albrecht and Zermatten 1994.

218. In various ways, resilience research has found that faith and spiritual resources are relational, social matters; this relational quality is perhaps clearer for "religion," which by definition includes relationships with other people and with God more often than does "spirituality." According to Gina O'Connell Higgins (1994, 175): "From its inception at a person's birth, when the most fundamental meanings about life are shaped within early care-taking relationships, convictional faith is forged with others." Fowler and Parks also interrelate faith and relationships. In the section on cognitive processes and meaning, we already outlined the roles of religious rituals and religious social support concerning positive coping outcomes, cf. Pargament et al. 1990, 814–16.

219. Notions such as "the Christian concept of brothers and sisters in Christ" or the Hindu ashram can build up that sense of community; while principles like the Ten Commandments of the Judeo-Christian tradition and the Four Noble Truths of Buddhism underlie religious agency. Meyer and Lausell (1996, 121) have investigated these issues regarding adolescent violence prevention and optimal development.

220. According to D'Antonio and Aldous (1983, 15–16), there is a struggle over the primacy and focus of the social control and social support functions of religion that manifests itself differently depending on particular cultures. According to D'Antonio and Cavanaugh (1983, 160), American Catholics have switched the emphasis for moral and religious guidance from dependence on legislation from above to dependence on the personal conscience.

liefs and social bonds.[221] Second, sociologists have identified a relationship between mental health and the strength of a community's cohesion. Naroll calls this the "moral net," which is mediated through social bonds, shared religious beliefs, and rituals.[222] Third, studies positively correlate moral-religious society to the deterrence of delinquency and criminality; they distinguish between the roles of religious belief and social bonds, as well as different types of criminality. Sociologists posit religion's social basis for deterrence in the social bonds of the community context (society and city, neighborhood and family). When a community is highly religious, certain crimes (assault, robbery, burglary, and larceny) are deterred, although no statistically significant deterrence correlates with others (murder and rape).[223] In "irreligious" cities (where there are low rates of church attendance) this deterrence functions to a lesser degree.[224]

Studies have found that in high-risk homes participation in a faith-community is a feature of success and resilience. According to Baldwin, Baldwin, and Cole's (1990) research on stress-resistant families and children, the successful families put particular importance on the religious community in their lives. In a psychosocial perspective, they conjecture that the church community contributes to the stress-resistance of children by reinforcing parental policy and providing peer influences consonant with parental values.[225] Anthony has furthermore found that intense religious affiliations can aid in overcoming disadvantage. This effect occurs most prevalently when the religious community wholeheartedly accepts individuals who are extremely vulnerable or alienated from society at large.[226] How-

221. Sociologists following Emile Durkheim (1988, 1995) have postulated that religion contributes significantly to the strength of moral community. Cf. Bainbridge 1992, 207.

222. Concerning religion's place in a society's moral net, according to Schumaker (1992, 66), "Naroll (1983) demonstrated that average mental health varies greatly from one society to another. He explained this in terms of his concept of the 'moral net,' and theorized that societies with intact moral nets should have better mental health, on average, than societies in which this net is weakened. According to Naroll, socially sanctioned religious beliefs and rituals are an important feature of the moral net. Consequently, erosion of conventional religious systems serves to unravel the moral net, one effect being lessened psychological health in all members of that society."

223. This latter observation is thought to hold since it is a crime of "passion." William S. Bainbridge (1992, 205–7) tries to distinguish hedonistic and larceny types of deviance.

224. Bainbridge (1992, 208) also found both that religious individuals in irreligious communities contribute to crime rates and, on the contrary, that individually irreligious people embedded in moral communities may be somewhat deterred by the religion of the people with whom they have social bonds.

225. Cf. Baldwin, Baldwin, and Cole 1990, 277–78.

226. Cf. Anthony and Cohler 1987, 38; Watt et al. 1990; Murphy and Moriarty 1976, 37–38.

ever, Meyer and Lausell have found negative effects of church involvement as well. For example, it leads to the avoidance of dialogue under certain conceptions of the separation of church and state.[227]

Other studies concentrate specifically on the religious and spiritual dimensions of friends and peers. As in the earlier observations, here both positive and negative correlations between friendship and religiosity are found. This ambivalence highlights the need for further nuances,[228] two of which concern the operative social process and the individual's interior affiliation with the religious beliefs. The first point stresses the influences of friends. According to Stark and Bainbridge, since religious beliefs are not automatically salient for human action (behavior), the influence of friends can reinforce or undermine the moral import of these beliefs.[229] The second point, however, is the crucial issue: whether religion becomes internalized. Indeed its impact on human agency occurs only when someone freely brings religious beliefs into their own motivations and decisions.

Transition: Resilience Insights for Philosophical Anthropology

As a transition to the upcoming dialogue with Aquinas' understanding of the emotions and virtues that arise in response to difficulty, we shall indicate key insights from this representative sampling of psychosocial theories on resilience research that can contribute to an enriched philosophical anthropology. First, temperament, as the product of both our genetic heritage and social interactions, contributes to our character, without being the last word. Empirical studies suggest that a person's individual situation alters resilience outcomes related to temperament. In the face of specific adversity, temperament traits that promote resilience in another situation can on the

227. Cf. Meyer and Lausell 1996, 129.

228. Darwin Thomas and Craig Carver's (1990) study positively correlates resilient behavior with religious peers and mentors, while Bahr, Hawks, and Wang (1993) found a negative correlation between religious friendship and deviant behavior. In particular, their study focused on substance abuse, the influence of friends, and the bonds of religion; it found no relationship between "religious conformity" and drug use. However, it has been considered inconclusive in that it did not adequately treat the influence of religion in regard to friends and peers. According to Meyer and Lausell (1996, 123), Bahr, Hawks, and Wang's conceptual error is twofold. First, they conceptualized religion only in terms of a code of behavior and as a sense of identification, without including the intrinsic value of spirituality as a personal experience concerning one's relationship with a "higher power." Second, they in effect also left out study of the motivational, support element in religion and the friendship relationships.

229. Cf. Stark and Bainbridge 1985, 325–45; and Bainbridge 1992.

contrary open us to new vulnerability. Difficulty does not affect each temperament type uniformly. Nonetheless, when the individual becomes more aware of his own temperament, particularly his own strengths and weaknesses, resources and limits, his behavior can become more personally responsible.

Second, psychosocial approaches evoke the significance of emotions for resilience. Emotions involve a type of judgment about meaning, insofar as they express emotional intelligence or contain cognitive content. They can either facilitate or hinder further perception and action. In a routine situation, they serve to appraise meaning. In a strenuous challenge, they can either help or hinder tripartite coping, self-protective and constructive responses. Studies demonstrate that social bonds (which are emotionally, as well as volitionally, based) reinforce behavioral modeling and emotional competency. For example, well-attached people exhibit greater confidence under certain kinds of stress. Moreover, studies suggest that the physiological reactions underlying emotions are more or less educable. Through rational behavior and social support, we can to some degree train our emotional reactions. However, differing anthropological perspectives on the value and management of emotions give diverging resilience and risk prognoses.

Third, cognitive processes underlie human resilience. They serve our search for meaning and purpose. In order to appraise ways to overcome risk or to solve problems, we rely heavily but not exclusively on cognition. Challenges of all kinds engage our comprehension of meaning. More serious ones even threaten our understanding of life goals and fulfillment. Cognitive skills involve conscious appreciation of our self-esteem and self-efficacy, the exercise of planfulness and problem-solving competencies, and the modification of risk. They often demand the aid of other social actors. We experience both stress and loss in a social context; we construct and adapt meaning with the help of family and friends. The cognitive capacities of our social environment help us to overcome adversity, understand a situation, and plan a solution. Likewise, religious and spiritual resources offer insights into ultimate meaning, purpose, and flourishing; they provide cognitive foundations and support to face difficult questions concerning evil and suffering.

Fourth, resilience outcomes draw tangibly from volitional processes, such as attention, motivation, and coping. Research indicates that the type of attention contributes to either resilience or vulnerability. Attention processes involve not only physiological influences (lowering physiological arousal in order to acquire a capacity for sustained concentration), but also positive and negative interactions with cognitive and emotional processes. Studies suggest that we can acquire attention-related stress regulation dispositions that help both promote homeostasis and serve higher goals. Furthermore, motivation and coping are other key volitional aspects of resilience or risk. For example, when it serves as part of coping processes, religion can play a resilience-promoting role. In turn, successful coping can strength religious engagement. Religion motivates human beings and communities, insofar as spiritual goals, meaning, and hope move them to act. Unfortunately, religious sentiments and associations can be manipulated as well. Other resilience insights involve how motivational competencies are not single deeds, but dispositional patterns acquired through past acts and ready for future use.

Fifth, family, religious, peer, and other interactions can have resilient or risk effects. Resilience researchers primarily focus on how the availability and quality of such external support systems encourage and reinforce our coping efforts and competency; open instead of close opportunities at life's turning points; communicate a sense of optimism and trust in interpersonal relationships; and provide a spiritual framework of meaning and motivational support. Researchers describe sources for social resilience as a stable emotional relationship; supportive relationships outside the home; and involvement in an external support system that rewards competence and provides a sense of coherence. On the other hand, they describe social risk in terms of family discord and conflict, a lack of emotional security, and a lack of strong affective ties, and of negative influences (e.g., criminal) from family, neighborhood, and environment, and socioeconomic status. The interrelated social systems and the physical environment give another dimension of meaning to the term "resilience." They suggest a sort of ecological theory composed of pertinent individual dispositions, social and religious support, and the physical, historical, and cultural environment.

Sixth, what does research say about promoting resilience? The two sides of the coin involve risk reduction and protection promotion. In the case of crisis or simple difficulty, when we restore balance or attain a goal, we establish an increased capacity for future adaptation and goal pursuit. We resiliently adapt to a situation by either decreasing our exposure to risk and stress or increasing personal and social protection. To reduce risk, we need to break the link between stressors and adverse outcomes. We can influence environmental, individual, and behavioral risk. To increase protection, we can promote rehabilitation and preventive policy and practices, at social and cultural levels. Prevention efforts cannot eliminate problematic outcomes or risk, however. Even if they could, it may not be wise to do so. Indeed, human development depends upon challenges. Nonetheless, by preparing to face challenges, we can reduce potentially destructive effects and facilitate the incidence of potential outcomes, such as personal, moral, and spiritual development. The promotion of protective factors and processes likewise cannot eradicate risk. It can nonetheless reduce its impact and related negative chain reaction, which contribute to human dysfunction. It can open up positive opportunities as well. Both risk reduction and protection concern personal and communal dimensions, as well as physical, psychosocial, and spiritual ones. These issues contribute to understanding the development of and education in virtue.

Lastly, a major question in resilience and vulnerability research concerns the staying power of these qualities. If either or both of them are acquirable, how do we account for subsequent change? If there is change, is any acquisition a stable life pattern? A common position in this research is that neither resiliency nor vulnerability is absolute. Both change, although we can expect some stability. Nonetheless, both change and stability in resiliency and vulnerability need explanation; and negative experiences do not inevitably precipitate negative outcomes. According to Rutter (1994b, 356; 1994a), negative life events have a tendency to accentuate rather than redirect human characteristics. Adaptive characteristics tend to persist, and maladaptive ones do as well. What resilience and vulnerability therefore do have in common is that we acquire them in the face of difficulty. Resilience entails that we acquire emotional, volitional, cognitive, and social competencies that are won in the midst of the challenge, threat, or loss. The contrary entails that we acquire a tendency to carry forward vulnerability to later stress and adversity.

Some vulnerabilities and resilience qualities persist for a short time; others are long-term. Most youth resolve their transitory problems without profound consequences for their lives. However, an individual's chronic stress and disorder or persistent resource deficits can contribute to a long-term burden of distress and dysfunction. Such susceptibilities correlate with the early inability to develop adequate protective resources. These factors enhance our exposure to stress and vulnerability to dysfunction, which we acquire through acts and events over time.

This chapter has offered a systematic, yet open-ended, psychosocial synthesis of resilience findings on human nature and society. It portrays empirical research that awaits correction, confirmation, and completion concerning the origins of human resources that aid our response to difficulty. The following chapter will address how these insights can contribute toward a renewed philosophical anthropology at the level of understanding the development of human hardiness under stress.

3

Renewing Moral Theology

Aquinas' Virtue Theory and Resilience Research

In order to contribute to the renewal of moral theology,[1] I shall critically assess, contrast, and integrate two levels of observation and reflection concerning human agency: a psychosocial resilience perspective, on the one hand, and St. Thomas Aquinas' virtue theory and theology of character, on the other. Previously, we saw that resilience research offers anthropological insights about extreme cases of adversity, as well as more typical challenges to growth. In this chapter, I widen the focus, by addressing how these studies relate to ethical principles and moral reflection. Aquinas' virtue anthropology and moral theology offer a qualitative vision of human agency's origin and finality, in a way that psychosocial resilience research cannot. At the

1. Without giving an overview of all the currents working toward the renewal of moral theology, I presently revisit Aquinas' sources and method to establish the import of a constructive virtue theory. In this regard, Servais-Théodore Pinckaers (1993, 439) suggests *first* reading the sources of Aquinas' thought, beginning with Scripture, while employing the historical method. This positive method consists "in interpreting his text, no longer by materials that came after him in time, but rather by what came before; not so much by consulting his commentators, in a chiefly speculative reflection, but rather by reading his sources, beginning with Scripture, thus using the historical method."

same time, his philosophical approach involves a philosophical psychology and social theory that can be used to integrate such contemporary reflections at the level of understanding growth in character and practical moral judgments.

Aquinas' Moral Theology and Resilience Research

The task here is not apologetic, but expository of the assumptions and principles that underlie a nonexclusive Thomistic model.[2] I shall interrogate Aquinas' texts and teachings in the light of contemporary critiques and resilience research. In order to do so, we need to recognize that both resilience research and virtue theory are mixed disciplines. They each contain scientific, ethical, and religious assumptions, concepts, and language. Nonetheless, they have their own specificities.[3] First, each approach has distinct primary research foci: either external or internal. Second, each generates either a-personal or personal knowledge.[4] Each human or behavioral science attains a particular dimension of human agency's complexity and depth. It is "limited" or "focused" inasmuch as its method inhibits it from adequately approaching human agency's moral, religious, and spiritual dimensions. However, it is "reductionistic" only when its assumptions deny the relevancy of the other dimensions.[5] I intend to approach progressively these deeper dimensions through resilience research, ethical theory, and moral theology. Aquinas beneficially provides a theoretical, ethical, and theological standpoint to integrate insights found in other human and psychosocial sciences. The wisdom of his approach involves integrating the truth and relevance of apparently divergent positions in nuanced ways.

2. Throughout this book, unless the context dictates otherwise, I use "Thomist" to refer to the person and work of St. Thomas Aquinas himself, not to a particular Thomist or Thomistic school.

3. See Browning 1987, 8.

4. See Pinckaers' 1993, 48–82, especially the section on "The Difference between Moral Theology and the Behavioral Sciences."

5. Lumsden and Wilson (1981, 381) define "reductionism" as an "oversimplification in the explanation of a complex system owing to the attempt to account for the system solely on the basis of the properties of its components. Usually ascribed by social scientists to biologists, by biologists to chemists, and by chemists to physicists." Steven Rose (1998, 273), besides demonstrating the inadequacy and seduction of reductionist explanations, critiques "reductionism as ideology," which is "the tendency, very marked in recent years, to insist on the primacy of reductionist over any other type of explanation, and to seek to account for very complex matters of animal—and above all human—behavior and social organization in terms of a reductionist precipice which begins with a social question and terminates with a molecule—often a gene." Cf. Cottier 1980, 164–65; E. O. Wilson 1998, 128; Rose 1998, 295.

The Specificity of Aquinas' Virtue-Based Ethical Theory

Identifying the specificity (nature, sources, and method) of Aquinas' virtue theory and moral theology will allow us to establish the basis for a multidisciplinary dialogue with the psychosocial resilience studies. Aquinas neither gave a definition of moral theology nor used the term "resilience." Theology was not yet so subdivided as to require such a definition, and the human reality of resilience was not yet conceptualized as such. Nonetheless, the *Secunda pars* of his *Summa theologiae* harbors the method and content of his moral theology. At the same time, it addresses the deeper issues of human resilience.

The structure of the *Secunda pars* expresses the order of discipline that Aquinas uses in morality, which we need to understand as a dynamic whole rather than as disjointed parts.[6] It is both faithful to the tradition and original in its approach to human agency.[7] It emphasizes movement: the human movement of being created in the image of God *(ad imaginem Dei)*.[8] Aquinas announces the depth and extent of this movement when he identifies the heart of his moral teaching, which treats "of the rational creature's advance towards God."[9]

Aquinas starts the *Prima Secundae* with a treatise on happiness or flourishing that we can understand only in the context of the evangelical beatitudes and the Sermon on the Mount (Mt 5–7).[10] His masterful analysis

6. The prologues in the *Prima secundae* introduce the structure and content of his moral study *(moralis): ST* I-II 1 prol., 6 prol., and so on. Aquinas also refers to *moralis* in other prologues of his *Summa theologiae: ST* I 22 prol. and *ST* I 84 prol. In addition to *scientia moralis,* he uses other phrases to denote moral science: e.g., *philosophia moralis, doctrina moralis, consideratio moralis, moralia* (cf. Jordan 1994, 82–83).

7. In the *Prima secundae,* Aquinas offers a fourfold innovation in textual arrangement and emphasis; he presents the soul's powers in a differentiated way; places beatitude up front; treats extensively the passions; and postpones the treatment of law and grace until the end (cf. Jordan 1994, 84–91). In the *Secunda secundae,* he innovates by applying a philosophical structure to a rather unruly theological tradition of *sententiae,* exhortations, *exempla,* and *pastoralia* (cf. Jordan 1994, 91–95).

8. For an intelligent creature, growing into this image involves free will and self-movement. The movement involved in being created *"ad imaginem Dei"* is not always evident in translations of and commentary on Aquinas' text (I-II prologue). In order to understand his teaching, we need to recognize that he distinguishes two types of image (I 35.2 ad 3): first, an image of the same specific nature, from second, an image of a different nature. While Christ alone is properly the Image of the Father (first sense), a human is an image of God only in an imperfect way (second sense). Although imperfect, this image present in a human person expresses a dynamic movement of its tendency toward its perfection, who is God.

9. *ST* I 2, Prologue.

10. Pinckaers (1997, 24–26) goes so far as to say that the *Secunda pars* as a whole is a theological commentary on the Sermon on the Mount. Cf. St. Augustine *De sermone Domini in monte; CCC* 1965–70.

of human acts and voluntariness, goodness and evil, and the emotions prepares the way for him to treat human *habitus,* virtues, and vices. More rationalist approaches have taken his treatment of law and natural law, which follows, as the heart of morality. But this sub-treatise and the whole treatment of morality are incomplete without their apex: the New, or evangelical, Law. The New Law is an interior law (the grace of the Holy Spirit) that serves as the unifying element in the *Summa.*[11]

In the *Secunda secundae* (the larger and more detailed of the two parts), he addresses the particular virtues. He gives preeminence to faith, hope, and charity as the roots of Christian moral action, and considers the other virtues in their theological dimension. While ethicists commonly recognize that Aquinas is a theologian, many do not comprehend the significance he grants to the gifts of the Holy Spirit and the beatitudes in moral theology. The way that he links them to each major virtue illustrates that, for Aquinas, Christian moral action involves a spiritual, even mystical, quality. Aquinas thus anchors Christian morality in grace, charity and justice.

As *sacra doctrina* or theology in general, morality has two dimensions: connaturality (habitual and practical knowledge and judgments) and science (separated, abstract knowledge of judgments and principles).[12] How are these two dimensions of morality sources of resilience? They offer us sources of resilience inasmuch as they involve our practical and speculative capacities and dispositions. First, through the gifts of the Holy Spirit, we connaturally judge about divine things through wisdom, counsel, piety, reverence, fortitude, and so on. Aquinas speaks of an *instinctus* of the Holy Spirit, which firmly and surely establishes our moral judgment. We employ this type of practical morality like an art *(ars)* that requires our intimate involvement. Although to act precisely depends on our participation and mastery, we can act accurately without manifesting technical cognitive precision *(scientia).* Second, through the study of the principles identified in revelation and nature, we gain knowledge of moral judgments. We discover a source that we need to apply in moral acts. We discern this second aspect of the twofold nature of moral knowledge and judgment through the study of morality (ethical theory), where we gain knowledge of right and good judgments and principles. We acquire the first aspect of moral knowledge,

11. Cf. *ST* I-II qq. 106–108; Pinckaers (1993, 434–45).
12. Cf. Titus 1990; Jordan 1994.

however, in the virtues, through which we have connatural knowledge and inclinations to judge well.[13]

In this line of thought,[14] S.-T. Pinckaers says that moral theology "is the branch of theology that studies human acts so as to direct them to a loving vision of God seen as our true, complete happiness and our final end. This vision is attained by means of grace, the virtues, and the gifts, in the light of revelation and reason."[15] Pinckaers highlights Aquinas' notion that theology is speculative or contemplative, not as opposed to being practical, but as the basis for the relationship with God that underlies the believer's practical life. To behold the face of God is the final end of the moral life. This communion is the reason and goal for human life. Inasmuch as we love, we act for someone and seek to be united to him or her. God's love empowers all other true loves.

Thomas's moral theology offers a model that draws upon a plethora of sources. They include scientific, philosophical, and properly religious sources. At different levels, each offers us information about human acts. Aquinas uses these sources to complete his ethical theory and moral theology, while trusting that faith and reason give harmonious witness to the unity of truth. The properly religious sources encompass Scripture and tradition. They include not only conciliar, magisterial, patristic, and explicitly theological tradition, but also less thematized personal and communal religious experience and *sensus fidelium*. Through these interior sources, Aquinas recognizes that morality is more than making judgments and applying external principles. It demands an internal knowledge, experience, and involvement. Aquinas' not-specifically-religious sources involve philosophical approaches to human nature and agency. In the spirit of his pursuit of truth, we furthermore can embrace contemporary disciplines such as psychosocial sciences, history, and literature, including resilience findings and narratives. In their own domains, each source has its own particular assumptions, principles, methodologies, and types of knowledge. These sources (scientific, phil-

13. Cf. *ST* I 1.5 ad 2.

14. *Veritatis Splendor* (1993, no. 29) says that: "'moral theology' [is] a science which accepts and examines Divine Revelation while at the same time responding to the demands of human reason. Moral theology is a reflection concerned with 'morality,' with the good and the evil of human acts and of the person who performs them; in this sense it is accessible to all people. But it is also 'theology,' inasmuch as it acknowledges that the origin and end of moral action are found in the One who 'alone is good' and who, by giving himself to man in Christ, offers him the flourishing of divine life."

15. Pinckaers 1995a, 8 (cf. 8–13, 44). He extensively explains this definition calling upon its scriptural foundations. For his more complete definition, see 1985, 55.

osophical, and theological; external and internal) account for human resilience in their own ways.

Treating the nature and method of Thomas's theology in general within a work of moral theology may surprise people. First, this method may seem curious in contrast to a current tendency in Christian ethics that restricts itself to normative issues: what is right and wrong; what is allowed and forbidden. Because of this tendency I need to confirm and explicate the theological nature of moral teaching in the Catholic tradition. Second, this approach may seem curious in contrast to much of the resilience research that is silent or minimalist in regard to spiritual resources for resilience. If there is a spiritual-religious component to human resilience, how can we investigate it? In order to explore spiritual-religious resilience, I propose to use Aquinas' approach to *sacra doctrina* (theology), in the context of his moral theology. He provides a model (albeit theological and moral) through which we can account for resilience experiences and reflect upon their spiritual dimension.

Resilience Research: Challenges for Moral Theology

The psychosocial sciences have brought important insights on human experience, concerning human resilience, for example. They have also brought challenges for theology, concerning their relevance and normativity in particular. In order to employ this research in moral theology, we should be aware of the psychosocial sciences' presuppositions and evolution, and distinguish their various methods. What presuppositions, promises, and limits of the psychosocial sciences concern moral theology?

Resilience approaches are riding the crest of an antireductionist wave. Nonetheless, a first challenge involves lingering positivist and materialist assumptions. This scientific renewal, in the best of cases, recognizes that scientific laws, theories, and hypotheses have limited depth and applicability. The various psychosocial methods cannot explore the whole of the human person and society, especially the very origin of human life and spirit. However, when psychosocial specialists presuppose that their findings alone are valid or objective, a triple misunderstanding occurs: they exaggerate these sciences' comprehensiveness (often due to a sort of determinism or materialism);[16] they overstate their scope (attempting to be a-subjective through

16. Cf. Rose 1998.

external observation and detached from presuppositions or the use of imagination); and they deny the reliability of interior, reflective, or moral and spiritual aspects of human life and society.[17]

A second challenge involves contrary presuppositions that claim objective knowledge is impossible. The very process of observation exerts an effect on the object. Physicists, following the Heisenberg indeterminacy principle, therefore commonly hold that on the subatomic level we can "accurately" study either velocity or position (of an electron, for example), but not both at once.[18] Critical and postmodern perspectives transfer this principle to philosophical and social sciences. They seek to bolster claims that human observers cannot be absolutely "objective." They can escape neither from their own ideas and emotions, nor from effects of the observation process on the observed person or community,[19] nor from the reductionism due to statistical analysis.

Certain psychosocial approaches attempt to compensate for these weaknesses and overcome lingering types of positivism, determinism, and relativism.[20] For example, narrative and evocative approaches to resilience in its various manifestations enrich social science statistical research and clinical observations.[21] We can therefore neither equate the resilience perspective with statistical psychosocial research on resilience nor all resilience findings with reductionistic or deterministic approaches. Complementary efforts in resilience research seek to remain more open to spiritual-religious experience, attempting to provide "thicker" accounts of human experience.[22] None-

17. Carolyn Osiek (1989, 275–77), for example, has reservations concerning the use of social analysis in Biblical hermeneutics. Social analysis in itself poses questions about (1) the historical distance between the present and the target group; (2) the uncertainty of the sampling; (3) the purpose of the Biblical texts (not sociological data, but faith documents); (4) the problematic of using modern categories in a comparative way; (5) reductionism and determinism; (6) problems of objectivity and subjectivity (text and interpreter).

18. This theory is known as the Heisenberg indeterminacy or uncertainty principle. In contrast to the confident worldview spawned by Newtonian physics, quantum mechanics introduced a degree of uncertainty into knowledge about the physical world (cf. Heisenberg's principle, and wave-particle dualism). Three interpretations of the nature of the uncertainty intrinsic to theories of physics involve the source of uncertainty, which is rooted in either (1) temporary human ignorance (Einstein, Bohm); (2) unavoidable experimental or conceptual limitations (Bohr); or (3) the uncertainty of nature itself (Heisenberg; cf. Mannoia 1980, 109–11; Polanyi 1958; Puddefort 1998, 1076–77).

19. See Karl Popper's *Objective Knowledge* (1972) for a realist, fallibilist theory of scientific knowledge, which grows through critical selection and seeks an objective theory of essentially conjectural knowledge.

20. Cf. Gould 1981/1996; Vanistendael and Lecomte 2000; Rose 1998.

21. Cf. Vanistendael and Lecomte 2000; Manciaux et al. 2001.

22. Clifford Geertz, for example, enriches the tradition of Weberian sociology. He reopens science

theless, the unobservable or unquantifiable aspects of spiritual-religious experience will continue to escape quantifiable measurement.

Resilience Research: Opportunities for Moral Theology

Moral theory seeks to explain rational human agency. Resilience research concurs, at least partially, by exploring the cognitive dimension of human coping, self-conservation, and positive construction in difficulty. Indeed, the fuller meaning that sacred doctrine draws from its first principles (God's action in creation and promises of happiness and redemption) counts primarily on faith and not on knowledge acquired through "scientific method."[23] Nonetheless, a reflexive approach to sacred doctrine and moral theology does not neglect scientific and philosophical domains.[24] A longstanding Catholic practice in moral theology ascribes an important place to philosophical sources, their reflections and findings.[25] However, while scientists employ reason to understand the human person and society, not every rational perspective on moral agency has the same compatibility with theology. We risk two extremes: (1) a suspicion that reason (and reasoned interpretations of human experience) cannot have any role in Christian faith,[26]

to semiotic/semantic, "thick descriptions" found in narrative, religion, literature, and art in order to understand better such cultural systems. He (1973, 30) says that "to look at the symbolic dimensions of social action—art, religion, ideology, science, law, morality, common sense—is not to turn away from the existential dilemmas of life for some empyrean realm of de-emotionalized forms; it is to plunge into the midst of them. The essential vocation of interpretative anthropology is not to answer our deepest questions, but to make available to us answers that others, guarding other sheep in other valleys, have given, and thus to include them in the consultable record of what man has said" (cf. Geertz 1973, 87–125). Geertz cites Gilbert Ryle as the source of "thick description," which is found in two of Ryle's essays: "Thinking and Reflecting" and "The Thinking of Thoughts" (reprinted in vol. 1 of his *Collected Papers*).

23. If one does not believe in their veracity (through theological faith), such principles hold no sway, and theology can only attempt to answer difficulties posed by the nonbeliever. But for those who believe, there are further "demonstrations," as when St. Paul argues for belief in the general resurrection from belief in Christ's resurrection. These demonstrations include indicating how revealed truths do not conflict with human reason and experience (cf. *ST* I 1.8; 1 Cor 15:12ff.).

24. Aquinas would underline the pride of place that divine reason and grace play in moral adjudication, without ignoring the importance of metaphysical and (philosophical) anthropological, epistemological, and psychological domains (cf. *ST* I-II 91.1, concerning divine reason—*divina ratio*). Not all of these domains are necessarily addressed in certain contemporary approaches (cf. Schweiker 1996, 77).

25. This tradition is traced to St. Paul, for example, who employs Epicurean and Stoic wisdom to attract the Athenians to believe in the Gospel of Jesus Christ; Acts 17:16–34. The encyclical *Fides et Ratio (FR)*, for its part, gives a history of the use of wisdom in seeking God, without directly addressing the place of reason in moral theology.

26. St. Paul expresses a suspicion concerning a type of Greek "wisdom" that judges the Christian message of the cross as "folly" (cf. 1 Cor 1:22ff.). This view of natural reason's limits and weakness finds its roots in the Fall, one of the consequences of which is ignorance (cf. Augustine, *De nat. et grat.* 21, 403). Protestant thought (e.g., Luther, Calvin, and their followers) generally has harbored a hostility to

and (2) an overzealous affirmation of reason's capabilities. While affirming the superiority of reason illuminated by faith, various magisterial teachings highlight the place of reason in seeking to understand faith and morals.[27] Thomas's approach to faith and reason provides us a middle ground and several bases for integrating resilience insights.

First, it advocates a unified theory of truth and wisdom (whose one source is God—divine *ratio*). Aquinas affirms that reason and faith have the common foundation of truth and that the Holy Spirit serves a unitive role as source of all truth.[28] One's perspective on truth is significant for the meaning dimension of resilience.

Second, Thomas views reason as "perfective" of faith. Reason helps faith uncover a further level of understanding, knowledge, or science, and in turn to expound a theological measure. *Sacra doctrina* benefits from the clarity brought by other sciences as handmaidens *(ancillae)*, in particular by philosophical reflection that is based on experience.[29]

Third, Aquinas' approach considers faith as "perfective" of reason. In their collaboration, *sacra doctrina* perfects philosophy (descriptive and normative sciences) as grace perfects nature.[30] Faith informs both fundamental presuppositions and rational investigations.

Lastly, Thomas explores a conception of reason that finds its prime analogate in divine reason. Through this metaphysical conception, he examines the meaning of ultimate happiness, moral finality, human agency, liberty, virtuous and vicious acts, nature and grace. According to Aquinas, reason more broadly conceived as including divine reason *(ratio)* and grace constitutes the criterion for adjudicating whether an action is good, done for a fitting purpose and in a suitable way. It exposes and establishes the meaning of the act. If the action diverges from right reason it is judged an evil act, even if it promotes short-term, "resilient" survival.[31]

---

natural theology, preferring a theology organized around revelation. There are notable exceptions, especially in more recent Protestant theology, which has shown an interest in fundamental theology (e.g., E. Brunner, W. Pannenberg, W. Joest). Cf. Lacoste 1998, 973–4.

27. The First Vatican Council affirms that "the one and true God, our Creator and Lord, can [. . .] be known certainly by the natural light of human reason" (*Denzinger* 3026). Various nineteenth- and twentieth-century Roman declarations affirm that natural reason can know, for example, the soul's existence, immortality, and freedom (*Denzinger* 2766, 2812) and the natural moral law (*Denzinger* 2866, 3875). More recently *VS* and *FR* have made important contributions.

28. Cf. *ST* I-II 109.1 ad 1; *In 1 Cor.* ch. 1, lect. III, no. 43; *ST* II-II 45.1 ad 2 and 45.2; *FR* 44; *GE* 10; *SC* 68.

29. Cf. *ST* I 1.5 ad 2; *ST* I 1.8 ad 2; Geenan 1952, 115; *SCG* I.8–9; *ST* II-II 1.5 ad 2; *ST* II-II 2.10 ad 2.

30. Cf. *ST* I 1.8 ad 2; cf. *In Boet. De Trin.* 2.3; *FR* 43.

31. Cf. *ST* I-II 4.4, and *ST* I-II qq. 18–20; Woods 1998, 315.

A dialogue with resilience insights offers hope to renew Aquinas' virtue-based ethical theory and moral theology at the level of philosophical reflection on the human experience of overcoming difficulty, not at the level of theological and moral first principles.

Employing Psychosocial Resilience Findings in Moral Theology

In order to understand how psychosocial resilience findings might enrich philosophical anthropology and moral theology, we must adjudicate the adequacy of various models of collaboration between descriptive, normative, and theological sciences. Our inquiry focuses on how to identify the limits of each method and how to integrate psychosocial science insights in theological reflection, without importing reductionistic effects or confusing claims to health, normalcy, or ethical normativity.[32] We shall first address what normative or ethical claims the psychosocial sciences in general, and resilience findings in particular, can make.

Resilience Findings and Normativity

In order to employ psychosocial sciences in a virtue ethics and moral theology, we need to face at least three problems: (1) how to determine the relevancy of the psychosocial data and concepts; (2) how to adjudicate their "scientific" authority; and (3) how to identify normative and value biases of particular studies.[33] A fuller treatment of these questions would demand that we address the place of finality and norms in moral theory, which I shall do later in this chapter. In this section, I shall illustrate briefly the debate on the normativity of psychosocial sciences. We shall start with some pertinent issues raised by the resilience perspective, and suggest that Aquinas' approach to prudence and ethical norms offers a philosophy of nature and normative framework to incorporate resilience findings.

Each resilience approach employs notions of normality (if not normativity per se) in order to establish whether an individual has exhibited resilience or not. When can we affirm that a person or group has coped well

32. For a treatment of how moral theology can collaborate in the social sciences, see Philibert 1980. For a general treatment of how the sciences interrelate and demand a philosophy of nature, see Wallace 1996, and Ashley 1985 and 1961.

33. James M. Gustafson (1971/1989, 437) identifies these three major problems involved in employing the empirical sciences in moral thought. First, ethicists have problems judging the relevancy of data and concepts. Second, questions arise concerning the principles of interpretation. Third, ethicists have difficulties identifying the normative or value biases in empirical studies.

in difficulty, resisted self-destruction in a fitting way, or constructed in an acceptable fashion? What are the standards or norms for survival or human flourishing? Without such notions, resilience would mean "survival at all costs." If norms were simply a function of convention, then the sole criteria for inclusion or exclusion would be ideological or pragmatic agreement. And if statistical analyses were to provide a normative understanding of human resilience, then the psychosocial sciences would establish norms directly from observation-based calculations.

In order to adjudicate whether or not these sciences can determine a normative framework, we shall outline the two main positions. On the one hand, E. O. Wilson claims that science, or sociobiology in particular, can identify the norms behind human behavior based on the explanatory power of causal chains.[34] Critics have found fault with Wilson's headlong fall into a "naturalistic fallacy." He claims in *Sociobiology* that social facts can establish social norms, and in *Consilience* that natural science methods can obtain unified knowledge.[35] Stephen J. Pope criticizes this type of sociobiology in general when it moves simplistically from factually describing behavior to a normative approval of it. This reductionistic tendency in some cases construes human behavior exclusively in organic, chemical, and genetic terms, and reduces culture to an expression of genetic influences.[36]

On the other end of the spectrum, the English social scientist Albert F. Osborn claims that resilience cannot be a good in itself: that is, simple coping, self-conserving, or constructing cannot be an uncontrolled norm. Otherwise one would have to praise and promote "resilient" survival by thievery, murder, or terrorism, as well. He says, on the contrary, "the means by which an individual avoids the potential consequences of adversity must be so-

34. Edward O. Wilson (1975/1978, 201) construes this causal basis of law (including normative laws) in terms of scientific materialism and evolutionary theory. Furthermore, as regards sociobiology and religion, Wilson holds that science and religion are of two different realms, each with its own values and purposes. Religion has motivational importance for human survival (even if there is no transcendental foundation for it). The roles of religion and science differ and converge in most areas of moral reasoning.

35. E. O. Wilson first expressed his unabashed advocacy of sociobiology's ability to provide norms for moral agency in *Sociobiology* (1975/1978). Afterward he retracted this position, and then reaffirmed it in a more glaring form in his *Consilience: The Unity of Knowledge* (1998). His theory of consilience is "an integration, literally a 'jumping together' of knowledge by the linking of facts and fact-based theory across disciplines to create a common groundwork of explanation" (1998, 8). According to J. Wentzel Van Huyssteen (1999, 25), this project exhibits Wilson's "massive and reductionist scientism."

36. According to Stephen J. Pope (1998a, 281), sociobiology attempts to observe the "options of good and evil" and falls into the naturalistic fallacy (neglecting the fact-value gap), while further applying itself to the domains of law, psychology, and sociology.

cially acceptable. [. . .] Survival itself is not sufficient. It must be socially approved survival."[37] What can the psychosocial sciences tell us of what is "socially acceptable"? Osborn claims that to determine social normativity is not the role of the social sciences, whose task stops at the level of formulating theories and describing events and tendencies.[38] As mentioned earlier, he is not alone.[39] Other specialists recognize that empirical observation cannot provide such standards. These researchers hold that empirical resilience studies, which employ notions of adjustment, survival, and fulfillment, need further justification, preliminary presuppositions, and foundational theories.[40]

To concede that the ethical framework must come from elsewhere than external observation denies the "naturalistic" solution. It does not, however, so simply solve the problem of naturalism in ethics and moral theology. The "naturalistic fallacy" or the "is/ought" controversy surfaces due to confusions between fact and value, between what *is* and what *ought* to be.[41] First, terminological and technical issues arise. On the one hand, specialists use the word "good" differently in "good economics" and "good ethics." On the other hand, within morality, terminological and metaphysical differences cause certain differences in adjudication between moral goods.[42] Second, problems arise in statistical methods, such as those that attempt to develop sci-

37. Osborn 1994, 13; cf. Consortium on the School-based Promotion of Social Competence 1994, 275.

38. As a social scientist, Osborn (1994, 13) has nonetheless recognized that religious faith *may* play a significant role in establishing what is socially acceptable. The French neurologist Bernard-François Michel (1998, 91–108), moreover, holds that it is for ethics, moral theology, and religion to provide the normative and spiritual framework for resilience. Geertz (1973, 30), furthermore, expresses a similar view.

39. For instance, according to the Swiss psychologists Meinrad Perrez and Michael Reicherts (1992b, 163–64), coping behavior is "adequate or appropriate if it corresponds to several criteria of rationality." They state that the means we use to cope and to reduce stress must be "ethically acceptable" and effective, and must positively correlate the cost with the benefit. Cf. Murphy 1987, 101.

40. Cf. Wolin and Wolin.

41. Concerning the debate about the "is-ought" question in moral philosophy, see D. Hume, *A Treatise of Human Nature*, 1888; G. E. Moore, *Principia Ethica* 1903; Hudson et al. 1969; Gustafson 1971/1989; Flew 1978; MacIntyre 1983; Robinson 2002. Concerning the naturalistic fallacy and theology, see Pope 1994, 1998a, 1998b; Arnould 1996 (esp. 230–32); Porter 1999.

42. For instance, some proportionalists (B. Schüller, F. Böckle, and others) differentiate the categories "morally right" from "morally good," and premoral, ontic, or physical good from moral good, they argue that these distinctions permit them to derive a moral claim by "weighing" the goods involved. This approach to distinguish goods seems to fall into a naturalistic or physicalistic error inasmuch as it claims that we can adjudicate moral rightness simply by optimizing premoral goods. This issue is beyond the scope of my treatise. I merely pose the question of whether foundational insufficiencies of such proportionalist systems lead to mistaken and overly technical notions of morality. The following critiques also attest to problems with these positions: *VS*, Pinckaers 1995b. According to Rhonheimer (2000, 365–400 and 582), the proportionalist systems of B. Schüller and F. Böckle fall into the "naturalistic fallacy"

entific notions of what is "statistically human."[43] What limits do they face in studying normality? Serious reasons inhibit us from simply elevating statistical averages of externally observed human behavior and social patterns to the level of moral and spiritual norms. The psychosocial sciences study people and societies in the past. They cannot say more than the research has already demonstrated. Epistemological (and metaphysical) problems arise concerning our relationship to the future though, especially inasmuch as life projects, goals, and finality can motivate moral acts. Much psychosocial research cannot appropriate the future-tending dynamic inherent to personal and communal action.

The resilience testimony expressed in narrative, however, highlights how humans build toward the future, in view of past experience and present convictions. According to child psychiatrist Stanislaw Tomkiewicz, scientists can never forget that they (as scientists using the model of positivist science) do not know the future.[44] Specialists sometimes do project statistical analyses into the future; they thus predict rates of suicide, mental health and illness, and so on. Yet on the individual level, we cannot predict a person's future. Even though a sociological survey might quantify personal opinions concerning good and evil, it neither establishes norms nor creates a normative framework. It can even tend to evaporate the richness of the notion of the human person; that is, unless the specialist compensates for methodological limitations and recognizes more comprehensive reflections, which are the proper domain of ethics and religion.

Even if we cannot derive moral norms from the psychosocial sciences, one can ask what types of input their concepts and findings contribute to understanding better the normative dimensions of human anthropology, goals, and society.

Types of Resilience Input from the Psychosocial Sciences

The diverse psychosocial sciences seek precise observations and statistical analysis of human behavior at a different level than moral theology's

---

when attempting to "optimize" premoral goods. They attempt nonetheless to establish a foundation in value (Böckle) or a love ethics (Schüller), which remain unsatisfactory frameworks inasmuch as they do not provide the way to hierarchize adequately actions and values, nor to correlate moral rectitude and goodness.

43. Gustafson (1971/1989, 433–35) identifies problems related to statistically developed notions of normality, especially when used as norms to employ life-taking measures (abortion, infanticide) or to stop life-prolonging treatments.

44. Cf. Tomkiewicz 2001.

observations and ethical reflections. The former seek factors that underlie resilience and vulnerability, health and illness, social support and isolation, and so forth. The latter refers above all to finality and flourishing, norms and virtues, nature and grace, which outstrip the competency of the psycho-social sciences.

Social or behavioral science (sociology) supplies concepts, data, and narratives about behavior and institutions, gender relationships and class structure. Sociological research offers particular resilience insights concerning the family: harmony, stress management, disruption and socio-economic status. It also investigates interactions outside the family: the quality of the larger environment, in particular relationships with friends and caregivers. The study of social support and resources tells us something about how we interact in social and religious relationships. The limitations to the studies involve a partial and external observation that quantifies facts without being able to address internal intentions and spiritual states. Notwithstanding their limitations, these types of insights concerning human society can enrich moral theology with thematized observations. They also offer social and historical contexts for understanding key texts of biblical revelation.[45] They offer insights into patterns of social interaction that "thicken" the social aspect of anthropology.[46]

Behavioral biology, evolutionary psychology, and sociobiology seek to answer questions about the evolved constitution of human emotions and human nature's biological ends.[47] Their limitations are evident when some researchers, such as E. O. Wilson, conflate sociobiology accounts and ethical normativity.[48] However, other specialists tend to differentiate between descriptive and normative domains. They distinguish the biological ends of human nature from its properly moral ends. Studies on the ordering of nature and the natural human constitution thus give us a partial view of human life.[49] This view, when taken as properly partial, serves further ethical

45. Cf. Osiek 1989, 278, and Gustafson 1971/1989, 122–37.

46. Cf. Cottier 1980; Pope 1994, 1996; Geertz 1973.

47. Cf. Arnould 1996, 223, and Pope 1996, 177.

48. Wilson's earlier work, entitled *Sociobiology: The New Synthesis* (1975/1978, 53), offers a biological theory of morality; he goes so far as to say that "genes hold culture on a leash"; in this work, he claims to establish a code of ethics that is "genetically accurate and hence completely fair" (Wilson 1975/1978, 575; cf. Rose 1998, 278).

49. According to Pope (1996, 177; cf. 179) while behavioral biologists and evolutionary psychologists need to distinguish the biological from moral ends of human nature, we can discern the properly moral ends of human nature only through moral and religious reflection. See Gustafson (1994, 104); Noonan (1998, 144).

and religious reflection. According to Alasdair MacIntyre, it is an error to suppose that an ethics independent of biology is possible. On the one hand, accounts of the good, rules, and virtues need to consider the way in which human beings are biologically constituted and progress. On the other hand, we can better understand human development in comparison with other intelligent animal species and, perhaps surprisingly, with humans who are vulnerable and disabled.[50]

Psychology and developmental theories address other issues related to mental health, behavior, and flourishing.[51] We cannot equate psychology, which generally employs rigorous observation, with narrower reductionistic approaches.[52] Psychologists, for the most part, do not claim to completely induce their knowledge of mental health and pathology from experimental or clinical observations;[53] those that still attempt this approach use more reductionistic methods.[54] The various types of psychology (modern experimental, clinical, and philosophical psychologies)[55] are mixed disciplines. They all contain more or less explicit instances of scientific, ethical, and religious languages and presuppositions. They resemble ethical theory and moral theology inasmuch as they provide concepts and techniques for ordering the interior life,[56] and in using hypotheses, imagination, and heuristic models in their research and explanations.[57] We can recognize the compatibility of psychotherapy and moral theories, when psychosocial health—or its reestablishment through some therapy—is a necessary, but not sufficient, condition for the capacity to chose good and to avoid evil,[58] and to develop moral virtue. Among the schools of moral growth rooted in

50. Cf. MacIntyre 1999, x.

51. Cf. Gustafson 1971/1989, 122–37.

52. Cf. Mannoia 1980, 5–29.

53. Cf. Goleman 1995, 40.

54. Although such psychologies may have some predictive value, they tend to have less therapeutic utility. In distinguishing scientific from nonscientific aspects of psychological theory, Paul C. Vitz (1997) identifies three different conceptual levels. At the first level, terms and categories are closely tied to observation, such as those of clinical psychology (e.g., extroversion/introversion, separation anxiety). At the second level, he distinguishes conceptual and theoretical concepts for the various theories (Oedipus complex, Jungian archetypes—persona, shadow, animus/anima). At the third level, general presuppositions, which are often religious, metaphysical, or ethical in nature, underlie the theory. Because of the importance of levels two and three for most psychological theories, they involve more an applied philosophy of life than the result of a scientific investigation. According to Vitz (1997, 20–21): "in general, there is little reliable scientific evidence for any Level Two concept." Furthermore, level three concepts are clearly assumptions, neither provable nor disprovable by empirical science.

55. Cf. Dent 1984.

56. Cf. Browning 1987, 3–8.

57. Cf. Watts and Williams 1988, 52.

58. Cf. Höffe 1983, 162.

psychology,[59] cognitive development models provide different types of input for resilience and virtue perspectives.

Cognitive theories of developmental psychology, based on the groundbreaking work of Jean Piaget, have influenced schools of moral and faith development.[60] They provide a basis for understanding the development of character and virtue. However, the various schools involve different philosophical and religious presuppositions about what constitutes psychological and ethical development. For example, Lawrence Kohlberg's structural-developmental approach proposes a six-stage theory of development, based on intuitions and empirical studies, as well as on particular philosophical approaches (Kant and Rawls). Kohlberg's highest stage concerns "universal, ethical principles," in particular justice understood as "equality and reciprocity,"[61] as respect for other persons as ends, not means. Notwithstanding its potential to help understand growth in virtue and resilience, Kohlberg's approach draws critiques concerning its presuppositions (bracketing-out of religious dimension, overreliance on Kantian deontology, and oversimplified focus on logic), its conceptions (invariant stage-sequences and gender- and culture-specific foci), and its assessments (inadequate treatment of human affective, behavioral, and symbolic capacities).[62]

Such critiques raise questions about the way in which developmental theories, and psychosocial science in general, can collaborate with moral theology.

Models of Collaboration and Scientific Pretensions

To formulate a model of collaboration between psychosocial and philosophico-theological disciplines, we need to establish the standards that accredit its scientific character. Previously, I mentioned that Aquinas' approach to moral theology calls upon the probable and external authority that philosophical reasoning brings through its use of experience and scientific observation according to the limited competencies of the different domains.[63] In this perspective, the psychosocial sciences' accounts of human nature, be-

59. Cf. Durkin 1995, 463–503.

60. Cf. Fowler 1974, 1981, 1982; and Crossin 1985, 94–100.

61. Kohlberg claims that "no principle other than justice has been shown to meet the formal conception of a universal, prescriptive principle." Kohlberg 1971, 221; cited in Crossin 1985, 86.

62. Cf. Crossin 1985, 87–91; Gilligan 1982 and 1992 (cf. Larrabee 1992); and Philibert 1975, 455–79, who compares and contrasts Kohlberg's approach to classical Aristotelian-Thomistic traditions of virtue ethics.

63. Philosophical-scientific sources are the third source for *sacra doctrina*. According Aquinas, there

havior, and society serve philosophical reflection as so many partial observations.[64] Nonetheless, we need to ask further questions. Inasmuch as grace perfects nature, how might moral theology employ the insights provided by these sciences?[65] Aquinas' thought sustains a natural law approach, which asserts a critical realism about knowledge of moral agency and affirms God's role in it.[66] Thomas conceives the natural law as the "rational creature's participation in the eternal law."[67] In following his method, we can turn to science for insights about human nature and behavior.[68] We need to examine how we can ground our ethical reflection in knowledge of basic human goods and in the proper ends of human life, intelligently grasped through human natural inclinations, intuition, and reason.[69] Toward this end, specialists have employed various consequentialist,[70] disclosure,[71] bricolage,[72] concordat,[73] and critical appropriation models. I will focus on the latter.

---

are: first, the authority of canonical Scripture as "proper and necessary" arguments *(proprie, ex necessitate argumentando)*; second, the authority of doctors of the Church "as proper, but probable" arguments *(quasi arguendo ex propriis, sed probabiliter)*; and third, the authority of philosophers as "extrinsic and probable" arguments *(quasi extraneis argumentis, et probabilibus)*. Cf. *ST* I 1.8 ad. 2; Geenan 1952, 128; Waldstein 1994, 81.

64. Gustafson suggests that empirical sciences assist moral understanding concerning the nature of persons as moral agents; the context in which decisions and actions occur; the potential consequences of action (and their predictability); and the identification of moral norms; cf. Gustafson 1971/1989, 122–37.

65. Cf. Van Huyssteen 1999 and 1998.

66. Cf. Hittinger 1999 and 2003, Porter 1999 and 2004, Cessario 2001, Pope 1998b.

67. *ST* I-II 91.2.

68. For example, Pope (1998b, 551) argues that evolutionary psychology (cf. Buss) can provide material for ethical reflection inasmuch as it assesses and orders (a healthy expression of) the full range of natural desires in the project of a good moral life. Pope says that "theologians might associate Buss's observations about the relatively indiscriminate nature of sexual desire in males, for example, with the sensitive account of 'concupiscence,' or disordered sexual desire, classically depicted in Saint Augustine's *Confessions* [1992, trans. Chadwick, Oxford, pp. 24–34]."

69. Pope (1996, 180) holds that through the exercise of the virtue of prudence *(phronesis)*, abstract knowledge of universal human goods is complemented in the concrete.

70. For example in Lisa Sowle Cahill's (1980/1989, 551–62) consequentialist model, the behavioral sciences (as well as personal narratives) contribute descriptive and normative accounts of human experience that, along with Scripture and tradition, compose the primary sources of moral theology. Cahill's interdisciplinary approach calls for correlating the interdependent reference points with the goal of attempting "an appropriate and critical hermeneutic of each in relation to all" (551); that is of Scripture, tradition, and descriptive and normative accounts. She generalizes the narrative contributions and behavioral studies and seeks a consensual adjudication of ethical issues (557).

71. Disclosure models relate scientific and religious knowledge as analogies pointing toward truth, giving "insights" about truth: (1) scientific insights entail discovery; (2) psychotherapeutic insights impact and transform the emotions and motivation (feeling and commitment); (3) religious insights illuminate truth, as well as arouse feeling and commitment (more often than science). Cf. Watts and Williams 1988, 151–52.

72. Cf. Stout 1988, 74–77; Lewis 1991, 6–9.

73. Stephan Jay Gould's principle of NOMA (Non-Overlapping Magisteria) advocates "a respectful, even loving, concordat between the magisteria of science and religion" (1999, 9).

Stephen J. Pope uses a model for the critical appropriation of current scientific insights in his dialogue with evolutionary theory and sociobiology concerning altruism and the ordering of love.[74] Relying on arguments from scientific authority, as a theologian and not as a scientist, he recognizes that his employment of provisional scientific findings gives only tentative "non-scientific conclusions," which are modest in scope and open to revision in light of new findings and theories. He attempts to differentiate speculative hypotheses from more definitive explanations, recognizing that sociobiology provides insights or hypotheses rather than axiomatic truths, due to its own methodological restrictions. Following James M. Gustafson, Pope holds that we can make a stronger or weaker claim. Either we claim to employ the "scientific" authority established by the source (such as Freud or Skinner), or we make a weaker claim, that the findings of science serve as sources of "insight" about human nature and behavior. In the second case, the authority depends on the moral theologian's use of the sources and the coherence of his own arguments' implicit empirical reference and anthropology.[75] Pope advocates the second model. He neither opposes nor identifies Christian ethics and the human sciences. Rather he considers these disciplines as mutually interdependent; his approach contrasts with others that reduce morality to a human adaptive capacity or that construe morality as independent of evolutionary developments.[76]

In order to integrate resilience findings into virtue theory and moral theology, I shall employ some of Pope's critical appropriation model. The tasks and visions of the empirical scientist and the moralist enrich each other; each needs the other to sharpen its specific method. They both contribute to a fuller understanding of the richness of human agency in a constructive effort that seeks to master both the wealth of observations and reflections and their limitations. We shall neglect neither the richness of observations about human action found through statistical analyses nor their limits. Likewise, we shall neglect neither the "thicker" narrative descriptions of internal aspects of human nature and moral agency nor their imprecision. Even if these scientific methods focus on different specific domains of human action, we need an overarching perspective that integrates and synthesizes the others. This method does not mean, however, that the overarching

74. Pope 1994 and 1996. Another who uses an appropriation model is Philibert 1980.

75. Cf. Gustafson 1971/1989 and 1981, and Pope 1994.

76. Cf. Pope 1998b, 545.

approach assumes the accumulated "scientific" prerogative of the others. Indeed, moral science attempts to examine human agency through these tools, while integrating a deeper reflection on the moral life. It relies on normative presuppositions and arguments that are the proper domain of philosophical reflection, divine revelation, and religious magisterium. Descriptive observations about human patterns of behavior will continually conflict with ethical norms (established through ethical reflection or religious sources). However, description does not outweigh prescription or normativity. One of the explanations of this descriptive-normative tension is the nature of human history and contingency, as well as social and personal sin.

In this model, how might these sciences offer insights for understanding an act, for example, a robbery? Psychosocial specialists can study the pick-pocketing of an unsuspecting pedestrian through theoretical observations and clinical analyses. Artists can re-represent the event in evocative ways. The agent (thief) himself can recount his choices, his motives, and the circumstances that led up to the robbery. They all bring their own observations and presuppositions. The moralist, for her part, attempts to draw together these accounts to understand the moral dimension of the act. If she wishes to do more that pass judgment that thievery is wrong, she needs them all, including the account of the thief and his underlying dispositions. Moreover, she must go further in analysis and deeper in supposition. As engaged observers, moralists (and other nonreductionistic thinkers) also reflect upon their own internal personal and communal experience, as well as deeper moral and religious principles. In addition to the specifically ethical realm, moral theologians recognize the negative influence of past sinful acts, as well as positive influences of communion and grace. They consider theological virtues and gifts, especially knowledge, understanding, and wisdom.

Within such a critical appropriation perspective, the next question involves how a theological approach elevates and completes psychosocial observations, information, and explanations.

Prudence, Norms, and Resilience

Aquinas helps us to understand the ways in which the practice of prudence and the knowledge of moral norms offer a moral framework for resilience research and motivate resilient lives. Aquinas' moral theory, however, philosophically investigates normativity through prudent adjudication, which at theoretical level offers the means to integrate resilience insights in ethics and moral theology, and at practical level in ethical and religious action.

Thomas argues that the norm of human action is prudence, through which we use practical reason in a free moral act to apply the goals of the virtues and precepts to personal action in concrete circumstances.[77] Prudence perfects practical reason through either acquired or infused means. He affirms that humans need to develop the virtue of prudence in order to face challenges with intellectual and moral fidelity and creativity. Prudence especially helps us to act resiliently when we meet acute complexity in evaluating the nature of the act's object and the applicability of moral principles.[78] Prudential judgment entails a global act that transforms the agent in his decision to act. It comprises intelligence, experience, effort, and vigilance, which involve human reason and will (including faith-informed reason).

While Aquinas recognizes intrinsic and extrinsic principles in prudential agency,[79] the key to human morality is that intelligent agents act for an end.[80] At both internal and external levels, Providence (and divine law) provides the ultimate source and goal of this intelligent ordering.[81] A commonly supposed dichotomy between practical reason and law (especially providential law) is resolved if we understand that humans choose freely to participate in divine Providence; this participation involves practical reason in the form of virtue. Through a virtuous disposition, as an interior principle of action, we develop natural inclinations and their related capacities, so as to act with more spontaneity, ease, and freedom. Law, for its part, serves two roles.[82] As an external principle of action, it leads us to attain goals and avoid extremes. The New Law, on the contrary, demands that we internalize the principle. Or rather, it is the presence and action of the Holy Spirit that transforms the believer's heart according to the principle.

77. As an intellectual virtue the seat of prudence is the practical intellect, in terms of "rectified judgment about things to be done" (I-II 56.4), while as a moral virtue its seat is "practical intellect charged with good will" (I-II 56.3). Cf. Westberg 1992, 290; Pinckaers 1997, 25–26.

78. Cf. *ST* I-II 94.4.

79. Cf. *ST* I-II 90.1; *ST* I-II 90.1 ad 1.

80. Cf. *ST* I-II 1.2. Alasdair MacIntyre (1999, 111–12) concurs that it is necessary to refer to flourishing as the human *telos* when involved in practical reasoning.

81. Cf. *ST* I 22.2 corpus and ad 4.

82. Aquinas' definition of law (*ST* I-II 90.4) is supple enough to apply to natural and eternal law, human and divine law, as well as the Old and New Law. It is only from within such a wide spectrum of law and moral norms that we can adequately formulate Aquinas' teaching on natural law (as well as the New Law). Nonetheless, such a simple distinction inadequately resolves disputes concerning natural law per se, and nature in general.

When law—especially the New Law—becomes an internal source of human agency, it promotes human freedom and spiritual resilience. Aquinas defines the New Law *(lex nova)* precisely as an interior law, which the Holy Spirit writes in the hearts of the faithful and works through love.[83] The full array of law crowned by the New Law moves us to participate in God's plan of wisdom.[84] Through these laws, God reproduces the image of his Son in human beings. Aquinas' view of the New Law neither exaggerates human autonomy nor overrides it. The eternal law is the source in which human beings freely participate through the use of reason. God is the author of this law, which sets the norms and goals for true freedom and resilience. The human mind goes on to make new rules (norms), because it is first ruled.

This participation in a higher norm is the standard human condition and the basis of a freedom for excellence. For Aquinas, human beings can direct themselves only because they are first directed.[85] In this context, we can construe (1) conscience more as a witness to natural law (as participating in the eternal law) than to human power, and (2) liberty more in terms of excellence than indifference. In a parallel way, a spiritual resilience will bear witness in action to natural law as participating in eternal law, and will have a qualitative dimension (excellence), rather than merely a quantitative one (survival).

In order to understand how the natural law's and the New Law's participation in the eternal law correlates with human virtue and resilience, we shall examine the normativity of law, precepts, and virtue—and whether they can serve as norms for spiritual resilience.

83. The New Law is the perfection of charity (cf. *ST* II-II 23.2 ad 1; *VS* 45). In the human active participation in the New Law, Thomas offers a coherent vision of how through the acquired and infused virtue of prudence we actualize natural and divine law. Aquinas' teaching on the New Law permits us to appreciate more completely how humans participate in, and God contributes to, morality (cf. Pinckaers 1989, 1978b). It highlights how nature correlates with grace, how we put natural and divine law into practice.

84. According to Aquinas, natural law participates in the eternal law, serves as a foundation for civil law, corresponds to the Decalogue (the epitome of the Old Law), and is fulfilled in the New Law of Christ taught in the Sermon on the Mount (cf. *ST* I-II qq. 106–108, esp. 108.3 *sed contra* and corpus; Mt 5:1–7:27; Lk 6:17–49; S.-Th. Pinckaers 2000b).

85. John Paul II speaks of this idea of natural law as "theonomy, or participated theonomy, since man's free obedience to God's law effectively implies that human reason and human will participate in God's wisdom and providence" (*VS* 41.2). His position recalls the Scholastic adage "the human reason is a measuring measure *(mensura mensurans)* only insofar as it is first a measured measure *(mensura mensurata)*," as relayed by Hittinger (1999, n. 48).

First, in Aquinas' view, morality is not simply a science of obligations, duties, or norms. Nonetheless, both rules and virtues are an integral part of morality.[86] Secondly, the need for prudent (wise) application of principles and norms causes us neither to discredit moral norms nor to deny intrinsically evil acts nor to promote moral relativism. Rather a rational study of the way in which the moral law unfolds through time explains how the underlying norms remain true in substance while needing to be specified in the light of historical circumstances.[87] Inasmuch as norms help us to build desirable self-attending and social behavior, they promote resilience. We shall explore this idea in the upcoming chapters.

According to Thomas, we make prudent judgments inspired by the primary precepts of natural law and the Decalogue,[88] the normativity of Gospel narrative and New Testament *paraclesis,* and the myriad variables in practical actions. These norms play a pedagogical role. They help us to actualize virtuous dispositions and acts. On the one hand, through prudence, we employ reason to unite the moral life under right judgment, employing operative principles (norms) of right practical reason such as do good and avoid evil. Infused prudence, on the other hand, offers a further rational measure that is informed by faith and its operative principles such as forgive others as you would have them forgive you; aid the poor; do not lead astray one of these little ones, and so on. Thomas's pedagogical approach seeks to identify, establish, and promote moral norms that are useful for mature Christian lives, for growth in character. If Scripture (as spiritual narrative and moral *paraclesis*) and the living tradition of the Church serve as a source of virtue narratives and moral-spiritual norms, then both the content and the motivation of moral theology will differ from moral philosophy—that is, if the latter excludes these theological sources. Likewise, the content and motivation for parallel sorts of resilience will differ inasmuch as these theological principles are not operative in psychosocial presuppositions and studies. Spiritual resilience, moreover, will differ from philosophical or psychosocial resilience, if the latter do not support a theological framework, content, and motivation.

86. According to MacIntyre (1999, 109–11), a community (network of givers and receivers) needs both virtues and rules. In particular virtues (e.g., truthfulness), no rule delivers an answer in particular situations; rule following is only a part of what we need for virtuous activity.

87. John Paul II takes such an approach to norms in *Veritatis Splendor* (no. 53).

88. Cf. *ST* I-II 97.4 ad 3, and 100.8.

In concluding this section, I recall that we have rejected a naturalistic approach that would directly draw a normative framework from the psychosocial sciences, from any aspect of the tripartite resilience findings: coping with difficulty, resisting destruction, or promoting construction. We cannot derive ethics (and core ethical principles) in a direct way from nature (from a scientific description of human behavior or natural ends). Rather we need a basis of philosophy of nature, philosophical anthropology, ethical theory, and prudent reflection in order for normative science to interpret and integrate descriptive observations. Aquinas' thought on prudence and law aids us in better understanding reason's role in both moral theory (and natural resilience) and moral theology (and spiritual resilience). Although resilience studies need such a larger normative framework, they offer poignant observations about human frailty and strength that can help us to understand moral behavior and judgments. In order to understand the way in which resilience and Aquinas' virtue approach can collaborate further toward an enriched moral anthropology, we shall next explore the role that flourishing plays in human action and resilience.

Flourishing in Aquinas' Moral Theory and Resilience Theory

Flourishing fascinates everyone. It interests psychosocial researchers, ethicists, and theologians alike. The human quest for happiness traverses resilience research and a virtue-approach to morality.

The Goal for Virtue Ethics: Flourishing

Although space limits prohibit us from revisiting Aquinas' moral anthropology systematically, we have good reason to give an overview of the place of flourishing or happiness, as a foundation and capstone, in his virtue-based moral theory. Aquinas starts his specifically moral treatise in the *Summa theologiae* (the *Secunda pars*) with a question neither about what is law, conscience, and freedom, nor about what is right or wrong. Rather, he first inquires about the finality of moral agency. He demonstrates that a person's ultimate goal is complete flourishing or happiness *(beatitudo)*. However, many candidates pretend to make us happy. Aquinas explores different variants on the ways through which humans seek fulfillment.

First, Thomas establishes that humans seek flourishing as the primary goal of their moral acts. Understandings of what makes us happy differ though. According to Aquinas, the ultimate goal that enlightens and motivates moral acts is the virtue of love (friendship-love with God) and the flourishing that it engenders and promises. The relationship of friendship-love and flourishing is based upon the human person being created in (toward) the image of God *(ad imaginem Dei)*.[89] Aquinas structures the discussion on human flourishing as follows (I-II qq. 1–5). Question one considers the human being's last end *(ultimus finis)*, which Aquinas identifies as happiness in God.[90] In Question two, he considers a rather exhaustive list of objects as candidates for human happiness. Does it consist in: wealth, honor, fame or glory, power, any bodily good, pleasure, any good of the soul, or any created good (aa. 1–8)? He finds that none of these goods can provide complete and lasting human flourishing. Question three treats of the nature of flourishing (from its subjective side). Thomas distinguishes the incomplete flourishing of this life from the complete flourishing that is possible only in the vision of God, with the company of the saints and angels in the coming new creation. Questions four and five successively treat what we require for complete flourishing and how we attain it. He says that the perfection of charity is essential to the happiness found in loving God; he describes this perfection of charity in Johannine terms, as friendship.[91]

Notwithstanding Aquinas' striking clarity, his exposition raises questions concerning the place of incomplete and complete *beatitudo* in moral theory and theology. What major transmutations has *beatitudo*'s etymology undergone?[92] First, when Thomas or the ancients speak of *beatitudo*,

89. Cf. *ST* II-II 23.1.

90. Aquinas structures his arguments around the insights of Aristotle, Augustine, and others. For example, Thomas (*ST* I-II 1.7 sc) cites Augustine's *De Trinitate* (xiii.3: *PL* 42, 1018) claim "that all men agree in desiring the last end, which is flourishing." While Augustine's global reflections bring a theological vision to philosophical treatments of happiness, Aquinas employs Aristotle to complete the Augustinian critique of the limits of earthly flourishing (cf. Sherwin 2005b).

91. Cf. *ST* I-II 4.8 ad 3; *ST* II-II 26.3; Jn 15:15.

92. According to the *OED* (1989, VI:1097), "happiness" or "the quality or condition of being happy" can mean: "1. Good fortune or luck in life or in a particular affair; success, prosperity. 2. The state of pleasurable content of mind, which results from success or the attainment of what is considered good. 3. Successful or felicitous aptitude, fitness, suitability, or appropriateness; felicity." This complex definition highlights happiness in terms of an external, objective, desirable situation (n. 1); its subjective appreciation (n. 2); as well as a quality that seems more active in promoting the good (n. 3). Happiness and happy have the Middle English root of "hap," meaning fortune, or "hap"-pening by chance. Nussbaum's (1994, 15 n. 5) reflection on Aristotelian "eudaimonia" is pertinent here: "*Eudaimonia* is often rendered happiness: but this is misleading, since it misses the emphasis on activity, and on completeness of life, there is (as Aristotle cogently argues) present in ordinary use of the Greek term, and wrongly suggests that what is at issue must be a state of feeling of satisfaction. (Pre-Utilitarian English-language uses of "happiness" had much of this breadth; but in our time the word is unavoidably colored by Utilitarian associations.)" Nussbaum thus translates *eudaimonia* as "human flourishing."

they mean flourishing as a reality of nature. Human beings naturally seek to flourish. The mature Aquinas used the word *beatitudo* to cover the notions of both complete and incomplete flourishing.[93] For him *beatitudo* can have objective and subjective as well as passive and active sides. I have resisted translating *beatitudo* as "happiness" when referring to the incomplete state and "flourishing" when referring to the complete one. By employing the term "flourishing" throughout, I hope to safeguard the unity and correlation between incomplete and complete states of *beatitudo* so important for Aquinas and for a fuller understanding of this reality.

A fuller notion of flourishing (in the sense of complete *beatitudo*) does not always hold a central place in moral theory. Since Aquinas' time, in different circles, "happiness" has undergone three substantial modifications. First, some thinkers no longer construe morality in terms of a natural tendency of the will toward flourishing. Second, others hold that flourishing is a matter of personal choice—one can choose to be, or not to be, happy. Third, writers have restricted flourishing to involve a subjective, egotistical motivator—the happiness of one person is thus pitted against that of others. Even though Kant's critique of eudemonism (moral theory based on flourishing) does not directly address the moral theory of Aquinas (or Aristotle and Plato), it has permeated moral discussions across the board. Since writers now often focus "happiness" on the subjective psychological aspect of ethics as well, we need to use the term "happiness" with care, and recall that Aquinas uses *beatitudo* more comprehensively.

Now let us discuss more in depth the challenges that changes in the meanings of flourishing pose to virtue theory and human resilience. While addressing particular aspects of Thomas's notion of the role of flourishing in moral theory, we need to ask whether his thought can escape not only the Kantian, but also the positivist and postmodern, critiques.

Aquinas builds his treatment of finality in human flourishing upon his understanding of human rationality, which is anything but premodern rationalism (although it is sometimes taken as such).[94] The notion of final-

93. While this usage holds true for the *ST*, it does not for the *SCG*, where Aquinas was seemingly searching for the appropriate vocabulary. In the *SCG*, he distinguishes between human incomplete flourishing *(felicitas)* and complete flourishing that originates in God *(beatitudo)*. However, in the treatise on *beatitudo* found in the *ST* (I-II qq. 1–5), he employs *"felicitas"* only in the quotes of Aristotle's Latin translation (I-II 2.2 obj. 1; 3.2 sc; 3.6 obj. 1; 4.1 obj. 3; 4.5 obj. 4) or in direct discussions of Aristotle (I-II 4.5; 4.5 ad 4; 4.7; 4.8; 5.4).

94. Aquinas acknowledges the limits of his own notion of finality: e.g., the analogous nature of

ity has suffered transformations since Aquinas. On the one hand, strains of premodern or Enlightenment rationalism have exaggerated the capacity of human rationality. On the other hand, positivist sciences have rejected finality, and certain postmodern critiques have radically questioned rationality itself. Forms of determinism and materialism have in certain cases replaced final causes.

In order to understand how Aquinas' moral theory fares in front of these critiques, a question needs to be asked: what does he mean by "finality" and "reason"? Thomas claims that we are able to act for an end (a goal) thanks to our capacity to reason. However, this finality is continuous. It is not simply the finality occasioned by a particular act. In contrast to positivist science's notion of finality (an occasional finality), Thomas holds that human beings can order even personal acts. We aim our desires and loves (through virtues of charity-friendship and prudence) at one single and ultimate end (a continuous finality). This movement grants an access to the end. Aquinas thus does not consider the end a disposable means or instrument. Rather, we participate in the end (God as source of ultimate flourishing) through knowing and loving.[95]

Aquinas' approach distinguishes, yet actively interrelates, two dimensions of flourishing: that in which human flourishing consists (from the human side), and that which makes us flourish (the external source).[96] This realist, metaphysical approach once again flies in the face of contemporary emphases on "subjective" flourishing, which often recognizes God's influence on humans only according to a person's subjective appreciation of it. With the advances of genetic sciences, some thinkers tend to identify hap-

---

knowledge concerning the last end (God); cf. *ST* I 1. He treats the issue of finality in human flourishing in *ST* I-II q. 1.

95. Aquinas' approach does more than distinguish between "secondary end and means." He does not use "means" without a specific relationship to the end. His expression *"ea quae sunt ad finem"* affirms a participation in the ultimate end, while distinguishing between (1) the acquisition *(adeptio)* of the end (what he sometimes refers to as "secondary ends")—these real ends pertain to the order of the love of friendship, for example; and (2) the use *(usus)* of the end (what he sometimes calls "means")—these instruments pertain to the realm of utility, although they involve a sort of acquisition *(ad consecutionem finis)*. Cf. *ST* I-II 1.8; Pinckaers 1998, 38.

96. Using Aristotle's principle, Aquinas introduces (I-II 1.8 corpus) a twofold distinction about the ends concerning flourishing: the end "for which" *(finis cuius)* humans seek flourishing and the end "by which" *(finis quo)* humans seek flourishing. On the one hand, human flourishing *finis cuius* is the end as the very source of flourishing *(loquamur de ultimo fine hominis quantum ad ipsam rem quae est finis)*. On the other hand, human flourishing *finis quo* is the way in which we participate in flourishing. By knowing and loving, human beings partake in the source of flourishing, who is God (cf. *ST* I-II 2.7 corpus and ad 3; *ST* III 2.10; and Sherwin 2005a).

piness-states with related genetic predispositions and hormone levels. This approach opens the way to attempts to chemically induce states of "happiness and well-being."

How can Aquinas' approach face such challenges? He defines *beatitudo* in a twofold way: "Flourishing, itself, since it is a perfection of the soul, is an inherent good of the soul; but that which constitutes flourishing, viz. which makes humans happy, is something outside one's soul."[97] The second, or ontological, dimension *(beatitudo ut res)*, involves goods, which merit and demand that we love them for themselves. When seeking these goods, we attempt to fulfill the basic human desire for flourishing.

After reviewing all the major candidates for human flourishing, Aquinas rejects all created things as inadequate for ultimate fulfillment—here we can add all parallel human processes, such as temperamental and emotional, genetic and hormonal, and chemically induced ones. He concludes: "God alone constitutes man's fulfillment."[98] From the standpoint of *beatitudo ut adeptio rei* (flourishing as the acquisition of something), he asks what human actions make a person happy; he recognizes that flourishing corresponds with the good *(bonum)*. Following Augustine, Thomas holds that the term *bonum* itself inseparably contains the ideas of good and flourishing. What is good will make one flourish; and what is evil makes one wretched.[99] Aquinas places a primacy on the role of the intellect, the speculative intellect (a. 5), and the vision of the Divine essence (a. 8) in ultimate flourishing. His emphasis on the beatific vision does not, however, distance the whole person from the search for and participation in that flourishing that already finds partial fulfillment in the present through love of the good, prayerful meditation, contemplation of beauty, and study of truth.

Fulfilled Human Flourishing and Graced Flourishing

Aquinas' notion of complete flourishing calls for an explanation of its relationship with the incomplete or partial components of human happiness.[100] What is the good (happiness-effect) found in the beauty and orderliness of created things, and the fulfillment of human faculties that do not

97. *ST* I-II 2.7 ad 3; cf. *ST* I-II 2.7; *ST* I-II 1.8.

98. *ST* I-II 2.8. In establishing this principle, Aquinas call upon Psalms 143:15 and 102:5, and Augustine *De Civ. Dei* XIX.2: 252, b, 26–27; cf. *ST* I 12.1; *SCG* IV.54.

99. Cf. Pinckaers 1998, 37.

100. Cf. *ST* I-II q. 4.

directly compose ultimate human happiness? Aquinas' moral theory, which concerns developing the full range of human powers,[101] employs analogous senses of flourishing. First, human flourishing takes shape in the excellence of the natural virtues. They specify fulfilled aspects of life at the natural level. Second, these natural (excellent though imperfect) types of flourishing have a certain order toward graced flourishing. We employ our body and the active life of moral virtue as a means of contemplation.[102] However, we need to ask, what roles do natural desire, will, and intellect play in the ordering between incomplete and complete flourishing?

Aquinas conceives of the ordering of love (natural desire and will) as an integral part of rational moral activity.[103] The foundational natural desire to see or know God as the Source of Truth[104] not only directs the intellect toward complete flourishing, but also inseparably motivates the will toward God as the Universal Good.[105] Throughout his moral theory, the desire for flourishing intertwines with (1) the knowledge of truth that moves the intellect and (2) the love of goodness that moves the will toward the action that is an integral part of coming to flourishing.[106] Aquinas puts these issues at the top of his treatment of morality (I-II 1–5) and of charity (II-II 23.1). Flourishing and friendship supply the backbone for his whole virtue theory.

A discussion of flourishing inevitably must respond to the Kantian critique of intuition, desire, and happiness. Kant claims that only a good will is a fitting foundational moral criterion. How can a Thomistic teleological approach, dominated by flourishing as its ultimate end, avoid the critique that it is hedonistic, egocentric, and utilitarian? Aquinas' response would recall that the root of the desire for flourishing and the heart of charity is friendship-love (love of friendship), which permits this type of morality to avoid getting bogged down in calculations of utility and pleasure, or duty and obligation.[107] For Aquinas, the love of friendship (with God essentially,

101. MacIntyre (1999, 64) reminds us that we need to understand "flourishing" in its analogous sense, in terms of developing "the distinctive powers that it possesses qua member of that species.

102. It is the fullest notion of flourishing that orders and serves as the major criterion in the development of virtue. Cf. *ST* I-II 1–5; Pinckaers 2001a.

103. Cf. Pope 1994.

104. An affirmation of this teaching on the natural desire to see God is found in the opening lines of the encyclical *Fides et ratio*.

105. Cf. *ST* I 2.8; *ST* I 2.7; *ST* I 5.1.

106. Cf. *ST* III 9.2 ad 3; Pinckaers 1976, 255–73; Bujo 1984.

107. The Kantian critique receives a threefold response. First, Aquinas construes the desire of flour-

and with neighbors concomitantly) is the most primal and final element in flourishing.[108] It serves as the true basis for the desire for flourishing, which beyond temptations and deviations is the desire to come to love God and neighbor in truth.[109] The desire for flourishing is an inchoate perception of the perfection of this love. This desire is not egocentric, but rather polycentric (including neighbors and other creatures). It is certainly theocentric.

As the last end and final cause, flourishing provides the higher criteria governing Aquinas' principal moral treatises. In the treatise on human acts, imperfect flourishing serves to direct human actions and passions through practical intellect.[110] Imperfect flourishing is inadequate or conflictive unless ordered to perfect and complete flourishing. For Aquinas, the virtuous dispositions (as efficient causes of good acts) direct humans to flourishing. Virtuous acts (and dispositions to act) in effect are the formal causes of flourishing. Through the moral, intellectual, and theological virtues, we flourish according to specific capacities and sources of strength and wisdom.[111] The type of flourishing (natural and graced) specifies a hierarchy among virtues according to their final cause.[112] Furthermore, Aquinas contrasts true flourishing with sin and its effects, chiefly mortal sin.[113] Flourishing is complete

---

ishing as spiritual in its central core. As part of our higher sensibility, it makes us react to and appreciate moral realities: good and evil, truth and deception (untruth), virtues and vices, joy and pain. Beyond the purely sensible appearances (phenomena), through this spiritual capacity we are attracted by goods and can perceive their deep nature. Secondly, this desire is open to others; it is not egocentric. The desire of flourishing, rooted in love of friendship, makes us search the good of the other, as our own good, as well as the common good. Thirdly, this desire goes beyond utilitarianism's focus on limited human capacities of pleasure, and the maximization of pleasure. The desire of flourishing, as grounded on the love of friendship, seeks the Good, which is desirable in itself as well as useful, but not useful in the same way as that which can be purchased with money; we can attain it only through sacrifice, as Pinckaers (1989, 185–89) reminds us.

108. In the complete flourishing of the Fatherland *(patria)*, the perfect love of God is essential, while the love of friendship (of neighbors) is concomitant. Cf. I-II 4.8 ad 3.

109. For Aquinas, friends are real ends (albeit secondary ones) in the order of the love of friendship. They are not "means" to final beatitude, as a disposable instrument pertaining to the realm of utility. Thinkers are sometimes confused when speaking of Aquinas' use of the expression *"ea quae sunt ad finem."* The *ea* share already in the nature of the end. They already begin to attain the end, of which they already express an imperfect fruition. Aquinas does not conceptually separate the *ea* and the *finis* in the ways that most contemporary ethical discussions separate "means" and "end." The good of the end is present in the *ea,* which we need to understand in a certain unity, since the *ea* participates in the *finis.* For these reasons, Thomas's term *ea* covers two separate English terms, "secondary ends" and "means."

110. Cf. *ST* I-II 3.5; *ST* I-II 6, prologue; *ST* I-II 69.3.

111. Concerning *moral virtues* see *ST* I-II 60.1 obj.3 and ad 3. Concerning *intellectual virtues* see *ST* I-II 57.1, where Aquinas cites Aristotle: "flourishing is the reward of virtue" *NE* i.9: 1099, b, 16–18; cf. *ST* I-II 3.7. Concerning *theological virtues* see *ST* I-II 62.1, where Aquinas cites 2 Peter 1:4, indicating that through Christ we are made "partakers of the Divine nature"; and *ST* I-II 62.2.

112. Cf. *ST* I-II 5.5 and 5.7.

113. Cf. *ST* I-II 72.5; *ST* I-II 85.6.

and sure only with the support of the grace of the Holy Spirit in the New Law. This law of love also perfects the acquired virtues. Through charity and prudence, we collaborate in truly human and Christlike acts.[114]

Health and Normality: Resilience Research Contributions to Aquinas on Flourishing

Psychosocial sciences have developed evaluative notions in order to promote "optimal development" and adjudicate between health and disease, and between normality and deviancy.[115] In this context, resilience theory and findings raise questions for Aquinas' virtue-approach to flourishing: How might psychosocial resilience research's underlying notions of flourishing, normality, and health enhance Aquinas' approach to complete and incomplete flourishing?

First, few people would equate physical health with human flourishing (even though we might on rare occasions, as when we are in severe pain or close to death). Nonetheless, physical well-being contributes to human flourishing. Notions of physical health are important because of the perspective that they assume and promote. On the one hand, the tendency to define health as an absence of physical disease involves a pathogenic perspective that concentrates on disease, illness, or abnormality.[116] On the other, the tendency to define health in terms of personal and social capacities to cope with and overcome physical challenges involves a resilience perspective that focuses first on healing and well-being. This second approach concentrates primarily on the resources for and dynamics of physical healing, and in a secondary sense on causes of disease.

Second, psychological health perspectives offer complementary consid-

114. Cf. *ST* I-II 107.1; 108.3; Pinckaers 1998, 35.

115. The World Health Organization defines health as "a state of complete physical, mental and social well-being and not merely the absence of disease or infirmity" (14 May 2002; www.who.int/about-who/en/definition.html). The *WEUD* (1989, 653) defines "health" first of all as "the general condition of the body or mind with reference to soundness and vigor"; and secondly as "soundness of body or mind; freedom from disease or ailment: *to have one's health; to lose one's health.*" The primary reference in both cases is soundness or wholeness, which is often taken as a static notion. The OED (1989, VII:53) defines health as follows: "soundness of body; that condition in which functions are duly and efficiently discharged."

Furthermore, the meaning of "disease" simply indicts the opposite of being whole. In regard to mental health, "sane" according to *WEUD* (1989, 1266) is defined as: "1. free from mental derangement; having a sound, healthy mind: *a sane person.* 2. having or showing reason, sound judgment or good sense: *sane advice.* 3. sound, healthy."

116. Cf. Moberg and Cohn 1991, 32; Schumaker 1992, 9.

erations for human flourishing. In particular, they consider subjective flourishing. Descriptions of psychological health include: "positive mental health" (Jahoda 1958); "self-actualization" (Rogers 1961; Maslow 1971); "optimal living" (Rosenhan and Seligman 1984); psychological well-being (Perrez and Reicherts 1992a; Chamberlain and Zika 1992); successful (physiological, psychological, and social) adaptation and survival (Brooks 1998, 229; Cicchetti 1990); overall functioning (Dubos 1959); or coping well with stress.[117] Of particular interest is a continuum model of health that identifies neither with any one definition nor with the popular notion of health as a static state. Instead it views health as a continuum or composite of sensation and perception, cognition and emotion, which forms an overall healthy pattern of experience and behavior.[118] This model might offer a way to appreciate competing aspects of human flourishing, such as intermediate human goals (some attained, some thwarted) and fluctuating experiences (joy and disappointment; pleasure and pain).

Thirdly, notions of social health address another dimension of human well-being and being human. On the one hand, some social science approaches employ reductionistic, empirical, and statistical methods to identify human, moral, and social normality or health as resilience phenomena. We need to resist facile attempts to equate statistical calculations of empirical normality with moral normativity, for example: (1) the range of efforts to bestow a moral status on the statistical analysis of the *homme moyen*,[119] (2) the "average type,"[120] and (3) the is/ought problematic in the more properly ethical realm. Furthermore, there are limitations imposed by realist and normative claims of the social facts identified by nomic methods,[121] evolutionary theories,[122] and more skeptical reductionistic approaches.[123]

In what way can Aquinas' approach to flourishing (virtue theory and moral theology) appropriate insights on physiological well-being? First, physical health concerns every human inasmuch as we are mortal and vulnerable to disease. Particular virtues are occasions of confronting barriers

117. Perrez and Reicherts (1992a, 137) note some of the researchers who make an explicit connection between mental health and coping behavior include: Platt and Spivack 1974, Ilfeld 1980, Becker 1984a, Fisher 1986, Schumaker 1992.

118. Cf. Radke-Yarrow and Sherman 1990; Schumaker 1992; Allport 1950/1967; Antonovsky 1998, 1987; Achenbach 1990; Rolf et alia 1990; Garmezy 1994.

119. Cf. Quetelet 1842, x; Turner 1986, 64–71.

120. Cf. Durkheim 1982.

121. Cf. Comte 1875; Mill 1861; Turner 1986.

122. Cf. Wilson 1975; Buss 1994.

123. Cf. Pearson 1911; Gould 1996.

that inhibit our health (prudence and courage), putting up with illness or suffering (patience), and participating actively in regaining health or preventing illness (initiative-talking). Furthermore, research on the neurochemical bases for human *habitus* helps us understand the corporal, and something of the emotional, and cognitive development of the moral virtues and vices. In turn, Thomas's anthropology offers an ethical and theological framework in which we can evaluate these insights. Through this larger perspective, we can better understand the role of physical health and resilience in moral development and spiritual flourishing. Research on human disease contributes to identifying physical obstacles to human flourishing, which can help us to differentiate them from moral and spiritual ones. We should not, for example, confuse biochemical malfunction with the effects of ignorance, social injustice, or sin, which in their own ways hinder flourishing.

Second, a moral anthropology needs to adjudicate the adequacy of pertinent insights from psychological descriptions of health. As mentioned earlier, we must evaluate such psychological insights in the context of their underlying anthropological theories. We can pose the following diagnostic questions: In what way does a particular psychological notion of health and flourishing appropriate sources beyond the human psyche? For example, does it restrict itself to simple peak experiences (e.g., Maslow)? Lisa S. Cahill, for her part, finds that "the underlying definition of human 'health'" employed by empirical science is inadequate for use as such in Christian moral theory, inasmuch as it does not include basic Christian norms ("suffering, self-sacrifice and self-denial for others"). Such norms depend neither on statistical frequency nor on psychological and physical standards alone.[124] Because of these sciences' self-imposed, methodological limits, we cannot expect results concerning phenomena outside of their competency, or a larger vision of meaning. Nonetheless, psychological theories and findings can help us to understand the development of character, especially at emotional and cognitive levels.

Third, how can social theories of health, normality, and resilience enhance Aquinas' view of flourishing? Social science approaches (e.g., cultural anthropology or ethnology) can apprehend or translate an extra dimension of the diversity in cultural and human experience. Nonetheless, we must interpret this data in terms of an anthropological and moral framework, in

124. Cf. Cahill 1980/1989, 557; *VS* no. 112.

order to discern its value for "thicker" notions of human flourishing. In the empirical approach, classical ethnology uses digital-descriptive analyses to report human, social, moral, and religious practices in an "objective" and abstracted way. Moreover, analogical-evocative methods try to provide "thick" reports of "mentalities" and cultures.[125] Through art, literature, and writing, this latter approach uses analogy and metaphor to recreate and communicate its object.[126] As an art form, narrative expressions can evoke social experiences and "mental behavior." They can thus provide Aquinas' moral anthropology with insights into the importance of cultural heritage for human behavior, moral agency, and religious practice. Nonetheless, we must evaluate the limits of statistical approaches to social analysis and public opinion, lest such accounts of normality take hostage morality and notions of flourishing. Otherwise, we risk taking the "normality" of social happenings (such as murder, rape, pederasty, or child abuse) as morally acceptable, or public opinion about them as normative. This risk is especially great when adjudicating statistical analyses of human satisfaction and flourishing.

Psychosocial science research, moreover, cannot directly access spiritual resilience and vulnerability, which we can more directly see only through reflection in a community that supports, affirms, and challenges the work of the person. Inasmuch as we can narratively report and statistically analyze personal experiences of meaning and purpose, these sciences can approach something more of the reality of spiritual resilience. However, we should expect that each of these disciplines offers only a partial view of human individuals, societies, and cultures.[127] Christian moral theology, while drawing on the insights of these disciplines, will need to employ them in the context of a philosophical anthropology[128] and moral theology framework that also draws its principles, content, and experiences from a scriptural, patristic, magisterial, and theological tradition. In this richer approach, Aquinas' moral theology purports to understand and promote better flourishing, as well as to support growth in prudence and to elaborate moral principles and norms.

In conclusion, Aquinas specifies human finality and flourishing as cen-

125. Cf. Geertz 1968, and 1973.

126. Cf. G. E. Marcus and M. Fischer 1986.

127. See Pope Paul VI, *Lettre au Cardinal Roy*, no. 40 and no. 30; cited in Jullien 1983, 481–97. On the nature of truth, see *ST* I-II 109.1 ad 1; *FR* 44; *GE*, 10.

128. Cf. Cottier 1980, 167.

tral elements of his moral theory and virtue approach. However, in the present intellectual arena, writers do not always appreciate this perspective. The problems are numerous. Happiness and flourishing are not univocal terms. Thomas supposes a different basis and finality when speaking of flourishing than do some contemporary psychosocial theorists and practitioners. We need to attend to the presuppositions imported in language, theories, and practices concerning flourishing in order to understand how research and theory might converge. The revival of Aquinas' virtue ethics demands exploring the place of incomplete and complete flourishing in both moral anthropology and theology. His approach inhabits a larger moral domain than that delimited by psychosocial approaches. It implies going beyond a duty-based framework (of what is right and wrong), simply identifying norms (and their exceptions), or promoting human physical, mental, or social health and well-being. Nonetheless, his approach inherently seeks empirical and theoretical input. It can take into account insights from resilience findings, which serve to enrich Aquinas' understanding of human flourishing and his contribution to spiritual resilience, especially developmental pathways and social interaction.

Aquinas on Emotions and Moral Development

We have set the stage with psychosocial resilience research and Aquinas' virtue theory on health and flourishing. We can now constructively revisit Aquinas' teaching on emotion and morality in order to understand related aspects of human agency and resiliency.

The Appreciation of Emotions in Moral Agency

Before we compare Aquinas' and other ethical approaches to human emotions, we shall situate his teaching on emotions in general. Aquinas follows the Aristotelian tradition in acknowledging that the human composite has five faculties or powers:[129] the intellective, the motive (volitional), the appetitive (emotional), the sensitive, and the vegetative.[130] He uses the word

129. Cf. *ST* I qq. 77–81; Aristotle, *De Anima* II.3 (414a29–32); Pinckaers 1990, 382, 384; Jordan 1986a, 87–96; King 1999, 101.

130. The vegetative part of the soul for a medieval thinker like Aquinas involves psychological experiences founded solely on physical reactivity: hunger, thirst, sexual urge, and so on. As more primitive motivational forces, both medieval thinkers and modern psychologists distinguish them from the passions of the soul, or emotions; the latter call vegetative movements "urges" or "drives." Cf. P. King 1999, 101.

passio or *passiones*[131] to refer to what contemporary psychology calls human emotions, feelings, affections, or sentiments.[132] While contemporary usage distinguishes emotions and passions,[133] often reserving the later for negative, vehement, or overpowering feelings (e.g., anger or love), I use the term "passions" in a larger sense, as synonymous with emotions and feelings.[134]

In his philosophical psychology, an emotion in general is (1) a movement of a passive power, as acted on by an agent; and more precisely, (2) a movement of an appetitive power; and more properly still, (3) a transmutation of an appetitive power having a bodily organ. The passions related to evil, such as fear and sorrow, specifically also involve (4) "some deterioration" *(aliquod nocumentum)* of the organ, inasmuch as an evil overcomes a particular good.[135] This last seemingly derogatory reference properly concerns how evil influences some emotions. It does not, however, eradicate the positive potential of the emotions, even of those related to evil, as we shall see later.

Thomas distinguishes the concupiscible and irascible appetites as two general emotive powers, which involve sub-layers of interrelated human capacities, or passions of the soul *(passiones animae).*[136] Both of these appetites appraise good and evil. The concupiscible appetite's object is sensible good or evil considered absolutely, while the object of the irascible emotions is sensible good or evil in hardship. Both of them are integral for human efforts of fortitude and resilience, since the difficult is rooted in what precedes it, and is drawn on by the good that finalizes it.

Aquinas outlines and describes the concupiscible appetite in a sixfold way, in two sets of three symmetrically opposing emotions: (1) *amor* (love), (2) *desiderium* or *concupiscentia* (desire), and (3) *delectatio* (pleasure) or *gaudium* (joy); and their contraries, (1) *odium* (hatred), (2) *fuga* (avoidance)

131. Aristotle uses the terms πάθη and πάθος. Other terms used by Aquinas' sources to translate the Greek include *motus animi* (St. Augustine, *De Civ. Dei* ix, 4), *perturbationes*, and *affectiones* (Cicero, *Tusc.* iv, 5). Cf. *ST* I-II 22.2 sc; Brachtendorf 1997, 290.

132. See chapter 1 for our more extensive discussion on the modern conception of emotions, their impact on perception, and the influence of attachment, solidarity, and emotional competency.

133. The *OED* (1989, IV:309–10) defines *passion* as "any kind of feeling by which the mind is powerfully affected or moved; a vehement commanding, or overpowering emotion; in psychology and art, any mode in which the mind is affected or acted upon (whether vehemently or not)." In a psychological sense, the *OED* (V:183) defines *emotion* as "a mental 'feeling' or 'affection' (e.g. of pleasure or pain, desire or aversion, surprise, hope or fear), as distinguished from cognitive or volitional states of consciousness. Also 'feeling' is distinguished from the other classes of mental phenomena."

134. See Leighton (1980, 203–37) article on Aristotle and the emotions.

135. Cf. *ST* I-II 41.1; *ST* I-II 22.

136. Cf. *ST* I-II 23.1 and 23.2.

or *abominatio* (dislike), and (3) *dolor* (pain) or *tristitia* (sorrow).[137] Once human beings know a good object, their first concupiscible movement is love (*amor*) for it. Thomas says that "a good produces in an appetitive faculty an inclination towards the good, a sense of affinity, a connaturality towards the good; this is the emotion called love."[138] His application of this conception of love surpasses pure sensuality; he raises it to include delight, charity, and friendship. In order to understand the depth of love, Aquinas distinguishes love as an emotion from love as an act of the will.[139] Next, through desire (*desiderium*) the appetite further inclines toward the good loved. It continues what love starts, moving toward union with the beloved.[140] Finally, delight or joy (*delectatio* or *gaudium*) involves that our appetite rest in the loved-good that we have reached, attained, or joined. Connatural union with the loved object brings pleasure and joy.[141]

In contrast, three concupiscible passions relate to evil: hatred (*odium*) disdains the evil; dislike (*abominatio*) or aversion (*fuga*) seeks to avoid and flee from it; while the presence of evil causes pain (*dolor*), sorrow, and depression (*tristitia*). Temperance and its related virtues govern this group of emotions, which we need to direct through the good of reason.

The object of the irascible appetite is sensible good or evil, but as difficult or arduous. Aquinas differentiates the irascible appetite in a fivefold way: *spes* (hope) and its contrary, *desparatio* (despair); *timor* (fear) and its contrary, *audacia* (daring); and *ira* (anger), which has no opposite.[142] Aquinas says that "the irascible passions are not all of one order, but are directed to different things: for daring and fear are about some great danger; hope and despair are about some difficult good; while anger seeks to overcome something contrary which has wrought harm."[143] He considers fortitude as the cardinal virtue for the irascible appetite. The root *ira* (anger) only lends its name to this particular human capacity. Anger is the greatest of the passions related to this power, in the sense that it manifests itself more vividly than the other emotions do.[144] Nonetheless, Aquinas does not construe it

137. See *ST* I-II 26–39, and especially questions 23.2; 25.2 ad 1; 35.2.
138. *ST* I-II 23.4; cf. *ST* I-II 26.1.
139. Cf. *ST* I-II 25 articles 3 and 4; *ST* II-II 23.1; Pinckaers 1990, 382.
140. Cf. *ST* I-II 62.3.
141. Cf. *ST* I-II 32.3 ad 3.
142. Cf. *ST* I-II 23.2; 23.3; 35.2. These emotions are treated in *ST* I-II 40–48.
143. *ST* I-II 60.4; cf. *ST* I-II 25.1; *ST* I-II 40–48.
144. Cf. *ST* I-II 25.3 ad 1 and 25.2 ad 1; *ST* I 59.1 ad 2; *ST* I-II 46.1 ad 1.

as the principal focus of the irascible appetite, since the fear of death is the strongest of its emotions.[145]

In order to illustrate Thomas's viewpoint on emotions, we shall ask: how does his ethical view of the passions correlate with other approaches to emotions and morality?[146] Identifying diverse schools of thought on emotions and moral agency will help us to situate Aquinas and lead into a dialogue with contemporary psychology. I divide the major positions on human emotions into three groups.[147] The first group views the emotions as irrational and evil (or at least always inclined to evil). For example, the Stoics teach that the passions are disturbances to reason that the sage suppresses through the practice of *apatheia*.[148] Post-Tridentine moral manuals construe emotions as enemies of voluntariness and obstacles to freedom.[149] The casuist approach, moreover, often focuses exclusively on the dangers of emotions for moral action. A second position holds that passions are suspicious or ambiguous in themselves; at best, emotions are morally relevant inasmuch as reason and will succeed in controlling them. The Platonic,[150] Kantian,[151] and sociobiology traditions in various ways fit here.[152] A third

145. Cf. *De virt. com.* 12, 26.

146. Aquinas' extensive treatment of the passions includes whether the passions are good or evil; how they are differentiated; the subject and object, cause and effect, of the eleven major passions, and so on (I-II qq. 22–48). For recent discussions of Aquinas on the passions in the context of habituation and virtue, see Jordan 1986a, 71–97; Pinckaers 1990, 379–91; Harak 1993, 71–98; Cates 1997, 16–30; King 1999, 101–32.

147. For a fourth group, the passions contain the highest good. The Epicureans, for example, pursue flourishing at the level of the passions, seeking to increase their pleasures and abstain from pain. Their goal of life is pleasure, conceived as a static freedom from distress. Cf. Sorabji 2002, 201ff.

148. A. A. Long and D. N. Sedley (1987) question whether Stoic *apatheia* maintained a limited place for emotions, which might not have been called passions once under the guidance of virtue (cf. Sorabji 2002). According to J. Brachtendorf (1997, 290), the Stoic view—also held by Cicero—was not a simplistic stimulus-response theory. Rather an intermediary evaluative intellectual activity (a practical syllogism) gives forth a reasonable movement of the soul when the objects are real goods (or real evils), whereas passions precipitate when the object only seems to be good or evil. Cf. M. Nussbaum (1994) who speaks of the Stoic "extirpation of passion."

149. Even within the Thomist tradition (a virtue tradition), some authors, such as D. M. Prümmer (1953), interpreted human emotions as obstacles to freedom.

150. Plato, for example, uses the image of two unruly horses representing the irascible and concupiscible passions. We can also mention here the cognitivist tradition of psychology, including Kohlberg 1980.

151. Kant distrusts emotions since they are neither always fitting and reliable, nor always a positive motivation for action. While emphasizing the authority of autonomous reason and good will in morality, nonetheless Kant insists that we must cultivate emotions in order to act from principle with right affective engagements (cf. *The Doctrine of Virtue* 386–87, 456; cited in Sherman 1997, 142–43, cf. 6, 141–58).

152. Sociobiology ascribes a "profound moral ambiguity" to "evolved natural emotional proclivities,"

position construes the passions as (neutral) energies that can become morally good or evil by participating in reason.[153] The distinction between this and the previous two positions is a fine one, and has important consequences for the way in which passions interact with reason in a moral act. To recognize passions as trainable neutral energies affirms both their positive potential in responsible action and also their capacity to render someone their prisoner.[154]

This third view is more properly Aquinas' position. Here emotions concern the whole range of emotive states that interrelate with the other human powers of sensation, volition, and intellection. They are more than felt reactions. They are both object-directed and pre-rational attractions or repulsions. On the one hand, as object-directed, they first arise from the appetitive rather than the apprehensive (cognitive) part of the human being (soul), since they relate and are ordered to things in themselves and not merely to human perceptions.[155] On the other hand, as pre-rational movements of soul, evaluative-thought-contents (cognitive, intellective, and even unconscious ones) constitute and interact with our emotions.[156] For example, perceiving a quickly moving dark object, we can experience fear. And the recognition of a person in need can stir mercy toward him.

The emotions, however, do not remain the initial affective-appraisal. Through our practical intellect, we rationally adjudicate the adequacy of the initial perception made through the senses; thus we further identify good and/or evil aspects of the object.

Aquinas' account of the emotions becomes clear in terms of his doctrine of habituation, virtue, and vice. Misconceptions of his position on how emotions increase or decrease the goodness or malice of an act often involve a simplified temporal reading of the "antecedent" and "consequent" distinction. Aquinas does not hold that every emotion that precedes intellectu-

---

which might no longer be adaptive and fitting. Emotions may motivate bad character and lead to wrong behavior; in any case they have their origin in natural selection rather than ethical principles or a larger view of an ordered creation (cf. E. O. Wilson 1975/1978; and critique by Pope 1998a, 288, and 1998b, 551).

153. Cf. *ST* I-II 24.1; *ST* I-II 18.5. The passions are neither morally good nor bad considered absolutely (*ST* I-II 24.1 ad 3). They are moral according to their usage. An expression of a passion is adjudicated according to the rationality of its moral object as the way it participates in reason, which serves as Aquinas' standard for moral agency.

154. Cf. *ST* I-II 24.3; *ST* I-II 10.3.

155. Cf. Aristotle, *Metaphysics* (vi.4, 1027b25–29); Aquinas (*ST* I-II 22.2).

156. Cf. *ST* I-II 17.7; Barad 1991, 397–403.

al adjudication of the situation decreases goodness and voluntariness, although some do. Particular emotions, which spring from virtuously shaped emotive capacities, first prepare and point us toward acting in a way that we have habitually done in the past. In a second intellectual step, we rationally evaluate the situation and the felt emotion. For example, our initial feeling of mercy does not deprive us from rationally and freely choosing an act of charity.[157] It serves rather both as a sign of the intensity of the will and as a chosen self-motivator to act; it renders us more attentive to the plight of our neighbor.[158] It needs further intellectual involvement. We need to evaluate rationally and choose freely to act. Thomas follows Aristotle in holding that virtue involves both actions and passions. If our passions come to participate in our reason, then we habituate them to become in some way even more fine-tuned, object-directed, and reasonable (without saying rational) movements of the soul. On the contrary, adverse and uncontrolled passions can attenuate an act's voluntariness and an agent's moral responsibility.[159] In either case, emotions are part and parcel of human agency.

Can Emotions Be Intelligent? Do We Need Emotions to Act Morally?

Recent neurological research has renewed the debate on how emotions support moral judgments. Neurological specialists have posed questions of vital interest for morality and the emotions. While juxtaposing rational intelligence with "emotional intelligence," neurological specialists hypothesize that emotions sometimes exhibit a cognitive content.[160] This "emotional intelligence" involves expressing a certain control over emotions. Daniel Goleman (1995, 34) says that emotional intelligence involves "abilities such as being able to motivate oneself and persist in the face of frustrations; to control impulse and delay gratification; to regulate one's moods and keep distress from swamping the ability to think; to empathize and to hope." This approach sets rational intelligence in parallel with "emotional intelligence," and

157. A locus of misinterpretation is Aquinas' article on "whether passion increases or decreases the goodness or malice of an act" (*ST* I-II 24.3). The prior two articles of the *Summa theologiae* affirm that passions can be good insofar as they participate in reason and will; this principle must serve in interpreting article three. The heart of the problem concerns (1) whether passions are good prior to, or only posterior to, a movement of the reason and will, and (2) whether the antecedent/consequent distinction is simply temporal, or also causal in nature. Cf. *ST* I-II 24.3 ad 1; *ST* I-II 77.6.

158. Cf. *ST* I-II 24.3 ad 1. On the contrary, Aquinas explains that it is less laudable to act simply from the passion of mercy without a judgment of reason.

159. Cf. *ST* I-II 6.6 and 6.7.

160. Cf. Goleman 1995, 42ff..

even speaks in terms of two minds—one rational and the other emotional. It recognizes the cognitive element of the emotions and their social dimension. In what way do these researchers construe emotions as intelligent? They observe that human emotions involve intuitive signals, gut feelings, and the emotional wisdom that we garner through experience.[161] Humans express emotional intelligence when we intelligently manage emotions, when we recognize their cognitive content and then use them for larger personal and social purposes. For these researchers, emotional intelligence means that we can employ our emotions in intelligent ways, but also that emotions affect the way in which we reason with our rational mind. Antonio Damasio's research (1994) goes so far as to suggest that without emotions we cannot act rationally (that is, we cannot act according to our rational principles and goals).

To acknowledge the potential intelligence of emotions leads us to ask how emotion and rationality correlate. Can we rationally manage our emotions? According to Goleman, the "emotional mind" exercises a range of control over emotions: "the more intense the feeling, the more dominant the emotional mind becomes—and the more ineffectual the rational."[162] In particular, certain emotions (such as anger and fear) are more than just initial reactions; they do more than give a first impression of the situation.[163] They also press the agent to act. A seemingly simple emotion-charged perception quickly puts the body into flight-or-fight postures. Nonetheless, except in extreme cases, emotions do not involve a fixed response.[164] The internal emotional manager (the prefrontal neocortex) regularly acts to control emotions.[165]

Lastly, emotional intelligence extends to the social domain in at least two regards, according to Goleman. On the one hand, to exhibit emotional intelligence, we must recognize emotions in others. Goleman conjectures a twofold social utility here: (1) empathizing with others enkindles altruism toward them. This empathy can start us on the way to an altruistic act. And

161. Cf. Bowlby 1969/1982; Ainsworth et al. 1978.

162. Cf. Goleman 1995, 8–9.

163. Cf. Goleman 1995, 17–21.

164. Cf. Goleman 1995.

165. When the emotional and rational minds interact well, according to Goleman (1995, 28–29), "emotional intelligence arises—as does intellectual ability. This turns the old understanding of the tension between reason and feeling on its head: it is not that we want to do away with emotion and put reason in its place, as Erasmus had it, but instead find the intelligent balance of the two. The old paradigm held an ideal of reason freed of the pull of emotion. The new paradigm urges us to harmonize head and heart."

(2) when we catch subtle social signals of the needs of others, we can more competently convey to them our own emotional signals and verbal communications.[166] On the other hand, we display emotional intelligence when we are capable of handling other people's emotions. This art of relationships involves not only recognizing their emotions, but also acquiring competence to help manage them.[167] Social emotional competence concerns more than just taking the emotional temperature of the social group. It involves how group members manage their emotional lives together. How they employ emotions in larger projects of meaning. How emotions motivate us to act in tune with an intelligent life. On the contrary, it describes also how emotions can lead us to act against our goals.

This notion of "emotional intelligence" offers us several insights on and challenges to understanding human resilience and Aquinas' anthropology. An emotional intelligence approach marks a positive turn in the recent history of how specialists correlate intelligence with emotion. To manage emotions intelligently in difficult situations involves a type of emotional resilience (resilience-producing use of emotional energy). In a group furthermore, it constitutes an element of social resilience. Indeed, social interactions aid us to manage our emotions, and an individual's emotional intelligence (intelligent use of emotions) influences human rationality and social agency.

Goleman describes the neural workings that underlie emotion, but his construal of an "emotional mind" causes us to think. Indeed, the functioning of the human brain and nervous system do not spell the whole of emotion for Aquinas, nor do they constitute a separate mind (in classical terms). For Thomas, the intellect (reason and will) operates through the senses and through emotion. However, reason and will are distinct from senses and emotion, as stated earlier. Aquinas addresses the interplay of emotion and intellect in his theory of moral habituation, as we shall see in the next section. Nevertheless, Goleman's work on "emotional intelligence" offers insights for Aquinas' approach to emotions and morality. He enhances Aquinas' view with parallel and complementary observations about intelligent personal and social uses of emotion. He presents ample reflections and examples of pedagogical implications of the intelligent management

166. Cf. Goleman 1995, 96–110.

167. See Goleman 1995, 111–26, for suggestions.

of emotions. Aquinas' position, however, outstrips Goleman's treatment of "emotional intelligence," especially concerning how the virtues instill intelligence in emotions so that we act with practical wisdom. Aquinas' teaching on finality and motivation provides a larger framework and depth of insight as well.

Thomas deems that emotions participate in reason by command and by habituation.[168] Reason and will, in his developmental-pedagogical sense, inform the emotive faculties and experience of emotion. In turn, emotions inform human reasoning about the situation on hand. First, as commanded by reason, human emotions participate in a political (non-despotic) type of rule.[169] Second, as participating in reason by habituation (i.e., through acquired virtue), human emotions become principles of well-ordered human action. Through virtuous habituation of human emotions, we confirm the emotion's "natural aptitude to obey reason,"[170] and correct emotional disordering.[171] Aquinas recognizes that we need well-formed emotions in order to act morally. Such emotions render our acts more praiseworthy and help us to complete good acts.[172]

Antonio Damasio poses a second, innovative question, on whether we need emotions to act morally. Often classic manuals of morality treat only the culpability of emotions; at most, they exonerate emotions from negative influence. Conversely, Damasio's neurological research construes emotions as vital for morality. His research makes the claim that emotions are indispensable for moral evaluation and behavior.[173] Through observing neurologically impaired subjects, Damasio has found that a person's higher-level intellectual abilities (such as attention, perception, memory, language, intelligence) can remain intact while their moral judgment and decision-making is impaired by the disturbance to lower-level emotion-related neurological activities. Damasio construes this connection of absent emotions and immoral behavior as meaning that (1) higher-level intellectual activities do not suffice for moral action, and (2) we need emotions to reason and act moral-

168. Aquinas' approach to the pedagogy of virtue can be found in *ST* I-II 56.4.

169. Cf. *ST* I-II 24.1 corpus and ad 3; 24.3 ad 1; and 56.4 ad 3; in this Aquinas follows Aristotle's *Pol.* i.3, 1254b4–5.

170. *ST* I-II 56.4.

171. Cf. *ST* I-II 56.4 ad 2; *ST* I-II 82.3; *ST* I-II 91.6; *ST* I-II 93.3 ad 1; *ST* III 15.2; and *ST* III 27.3.

172. Cf. *ST* I-II 17.7 ad 2; *ST* I-II 17.9 ad 3; *ST* I-II 22.2 ad 3; *ST* I-II 24.2 ad 2. On praiseworthiness and emotions, see *ST* I-II 24.3; *De verit.* 26.7; and McDermott 1999, 37.

173. Cf. Damasio 1994; Wallwork 1999.

ly.[174] This approach goes further than Aristotle and other thinkers who hold that through dispositions, our emotions can serve moral judgments. Damasio furthermore accounts for the personal historical component of habitual agency by what neurophysiology calls "somatic markers." He maintains that neurochemical profiles facilitate decisions, and extend past predispositions and choices.[175]

Although Damasio cannot demonstrate the way in which emotions and somatic markers directly contribute to reasoned decision-making, his research does convincingly show that disturbances to the emotional neurological circuitry precipitate problems in moral judgments. His research opens the way for further reflection on the importance, and even necessity, of emotions for moral life.

What do these observations, findings, and theories offer in rapport with Aquinas' anthropology and virtue theory? Damasio's neurological research demonstrates that emotions do not simply accompany, but rather are indispensable for, moral evaluation and behavior. His work goes further than Aquinas,[176] insofar as it involves a scientific discovery that damage to or lack of emotional neural-circuitry can impair moral agency. It provides a scientific neurological foundation for acknowledging that emotions constitute necessary, even positive, elements in moral agency. This insight, which correlates morality and emotion, nonetheless needs a larger theory of moral agency and finality, and in particular, of the development of moral *habitus* and virtue education.

According to Stocker and Hegeman (1996), moreover, an act done without emotion not only is less than perfect, but can be a sign of illness, either psychological or spiritual.[177] This position concurs with an aspect of Aquinas' position. Neurobiological and psychological studies on the necessity of emotions in moral reasoning and the development of emotional intelligence confirm the importance of emotions in morality, but also something of their function and trainability. Nonetheless, these sciences lack in themselves a larger view of human flourishing and normativity. The evolutionary researchers leave a vast field of meaning and purpose out of their investigation.

174. See Damasio 1994, 53.

175. Cf. Pope 1998b, 552; and Damasio 1994, 191.

176. Aquinas, nonetheless, already holds the principle that fully perfect human agency springs from well-formed will *and* passion (cf. *ST* I-II 24.3).

177. Cf. Stocker and Hegeman 1996, 1–2.

Moral Habituation and Natural Inclinations

In order to understand moral agency, we must also address moral habituation *(habitus)* and its relationship to natural inclinations. *Habitus* is the developmental backbone of Aquinas' moral thought.[178] It serves his virtue theory in three ways. First, a *habitus* integrates the moral building blocks: the goal of flourishing, basic inclinations, and emotions. We develop a *habitus* through goal-directed, rational interaction with our natural inclinations and emotions. Second, it permits continuity and creativity in moral acts. Third, a *habitus* serves as a psychological foundation for understanding virtue and vice, as well as sin, law, and grace.

Aquinas defines *habitus* as an acquired quality that we alter only with difficulty. It is a disposition to act that has become second nature *(connaturalis)*.[179] Aquinas uses *habitus* to cover the full range of mental, sensory, and organic states. He follows Aristotle in distinguishing a *habitus* of the body, or entitative *habitus*,[180] from a *habitus* of the mind, or operative *habitus*.[181] Operative *habitus* cover three closely related domains: (1) temperament or character traits, such as shyness and kindness; (2) acquired stable dispositions to act, that is, the virtues and vices; and (3) single acts. Operative *habitus* are hard-to-change qualities, connatural dispositions. They aid us to act with three key characteristics: ease, promptness, and joy.[182] Among operative *habitus*, Aquinas distinguishes cognitive or intellectual *habitus* (*ST* I-II 50, 3) from orectic or moral ones.

The contemporary use of the word "habit" is inadequate to render the richness of Aquinas' use of its cognate (especially in regard to moral and intellectual *habitus*).[183] The term *habitus* does not focus on external, non-

178. Aquinas' thought on *habitus* develops from a sketch in his *Commentary on the Sentences* of Peter Lombard to a full treatise in the *Summa theologiae*. After discussing the faculties as sources of action in the *Prima pars* of the *Summa theologiae* and the goal of flourishing and the passions early in the *Prima secundae*, he presents his treatise on *habitus* in questions 49–54 of the *Prima secundae*. He discusses *habitus* in terms first of acquired particular qualities relating to action (q. 49), then of how they differ when found in the body per se or also in the soul, intellect, and will (q. 50). Afterward he inquires whether *habitus* are innate, caused by one or several human actions, or infused into human beings by God (q. 51). Finally he treats the nature of *habitus*' growth and decay (qq. 52 and 53). Only after the building blocks of *habitus* are explored does Aquinas more fully address how moral *habitus* applies to virtue (I-II 55–67) and to vice in general (I-II 71–80), as well as to particular virtues and vices in the *Secunda secundae*.

179. Cf. *ST* II-II 156.3; *ST* I-II 49.1; *ST* I-II 78.2; *De verit.* 20.2.

180. Cf. *ST* I-II 50.1; *ST* I-II 49.2 ad 1; *ST* I-II 49.3 ad 3; and *ST* I-II 49.4.

181. Cf. *ST* I-II 50.1.

182. Cf. *De verit.* 20, 2; *SCG* 3, 150, nr 7.

183. *The Oxford English Dictionary* (*OED* 1993, V15), for example, says that a "habit" is "1. some outer

voluntary acts, for example, the habit of scratching one's nose. Furthermore, unlike a habit, a *habitus* is not an uncontrolled or involuntary motor reaction that impedes the freedom needed for moral action; for example, in the habit of smoking, an involuntary compulsion drives one to slavishly light up a cigarette.[184] Aquinas, however, views *habitus* as a disposition toward a chosen goal. They aid us to act knowingly, freely, and firmly.[185]

The place of volition in moral *habitus* is critical. For Aquinas, we choose to exercise our *habitus*.[186] A *habitus* pertains not only to the nature of the possessor, but also to the action that is either "the goal of the nature or something leading to the goal."[187] Therefore moral *habitus* do not become "almost or quite involuntary," but rather they allow us to act more voluntarily. They constitute an element of creative liberty, through which we fulfill our well-formed will. One who has the virtue of piano playing can creatively interpret a musical score, or write a new one. Inasmuch as a faculty or power's nature correlates with action, then the disposition will direct us to act in new ways. In this classical worldview, the *habitus* of the will thus affects our being and consequent operation, since our action follows our nature (being).[188]

The need to acquire moral *habitus* seems more obvious when we comprehend the diversity of uses to which humans can put rational faculties. We can approach our goals through different means, and we can more or less develop our moral skills. Aquinas says that "every faculty which can be exercised in more than one way needs a *habitus* to ensure that it is exercised in the right way."[189] *Habitus* help us know more clearly and act more surely. Aquinas for his part uses the notion of act and potency to analyze how we acquire *habitus*. We can habitually dispose a faculty only if it is not naturally determined, but rather open to further specification. Two critical open faculties are reason and will. In particular, to adapt a rational power accord-

nal deportment, constitution, appearance, [. . .] or behavior; [. . .] or 2. a settled disposition or tendency to act in a certain way, especially one acquired by frequent repetition of the same act until it becomes almost or quite involuntary. [. . .] 3. The way in which a person is mentally or morally constituted; the sum of the mental and moral qualities; mental constitution, disposition, character."

184. Cf. Pinckaers 1979, 144–47.

185. Cf. *ST* I-II 32.6.

186. In this regard, Aquinas draws support from his main patristic mentor Augustine, who says that "*habitus est quo aliquid agitur cum opus est.*" (*De bono coniungali* 21, 25; *PL* 40, 390; cited in *ST* I-II 49.3 sc.); and from Averroes, who indicates "*quod habitus est quo quis agit cum voluerit*" (*Commentary on III de Anima*, 18; cited in *ST* I-II 49.3 sc).

187. *ST I-II* 49.3.

188. This view is formulated as "*agere sequitur esse*" (cf. Cessario 2001, 23).

189. *ST* I-II 50.5.

ing to its nature, operation, or goal requires three conditions. First, the possessor of the power needs to have a potentiality. The related action must be neither impossible, nor in conflict with its nature, nor previously determined. Second, the rational agent must have alternatives to realize the potential. Third, the rational faculty seeks to analyze and synthesize complex elements.[190] In sum, in order for us to acquire a rational *habitus,* we must have as yet undetermined potential, different possibilities, and the ability for rational investigation.

According to Aquinas' anthropology,[191] human nature itself inclines a person toward good *habitus,* toward virtue.[192] We have what he calls the "seeds of virtue."[193] These natural or spiritual inclinations are preparatory principles or inclinations toward a proper object (e.g., the principles of natural right). Such inclinations belong to their respective powers, which serve as the basis for developing *habitus.* Casuist approaches have much misunderstood or neglected Thomas's position on the natural inclinations. They have seen in them simply the effects of original, if not also social, sin. Furthermore, contemporary psychological theorists have sometimes neglected the input of such inclinations (at least at nonrational levels, e.g., in cognitive theories). They have treated instincts in a descriptive or therapeutic, but nonmoral framework.

Aquinas' treatment of *habitus* and natural inclinations distinguishes between cognitive and appetitive faculties, as well as between their rudimentary states. First, rudimentary cognitive or intellectual *habitus* belong by nature to the soul itself;[194] for example, the principle of noncontradiction.[195] Second, the cognitive faculties possess natural inclinations that order humans to their connatural ends. Such an inclination, according to Aquinas, "starts from first universal principles known to us through the natural light of reason both in speculative and in practical matters."[196] These first principles tend reason toward conclusions, which aid us in forming intellectual

190. Cf. *ST* I-II 49.4.

191. Aquinas' optimism is of course tempered by the acknowledgement that this "connatural inclination" toward good is lessened through sin. Habitually disordered acts are not merely isolated incidences of sin, but stable patterns of vice (cf. *ST* I-II 85.1).

192. Cf. *ST* I-II 94.3; *ST* I-II 85.1.

193. *ST* I-II 51.1; cf. *ST* I-II 63.1; 3 *Sent.* d. 33, q. 1, a. 2, sol. 3, co.

194. Cf. *ST* I-II 51.1.

195. Cf. *ST* I-II 94.1 and 94.2.

196. *ST* I-II 62.3. Humans naturally know the first principles in practical matters through a *habitus* called *synderesis* (*ST* I 79.12).

habitus. Reason in turn moves the appetitive powers, which likewise can develop corresponding appetitive *habitus*, that is, concerning human passions and volition.[197] Third, the appetitive faculties have preparatory principles, certain inclinations, that direct the faculties toward their objects. As Aquinas says: "a thing's appetite naturally is moved and tends towards its connatural end."[198] The human rational appetitive faculty has a natural inclination, which orders us to our connatural ends, "from the rightness of will tending naturally to good according to reason."[199]

Aquinas says that such seeds of intellectual and moral virtues are naturally present in human reason, in that humans have a "natural desire for good in accordance with reason."[200] According to Thomas, the natural inclinations toward seeking the truth, pursuing the good, and living in community give direction to derivative moral action.[201] These inclinations are based on the first principle of practical reason: "that good is to be sought and done, evil to be avoided."[202] Aquinas analyzes human natural tendencies in three aspects of human nature: basic existence, animality, and rationality. First, in common with all substances, humans tend to the good of our nature. In particular, each human being has "an appetite to preserve its own natural being."[203] We maintain and defend the basic needs of human life, for example, when we eat healthily and protect ourselves from social and environmental threats. Secondly, the social aspect of human nature, which we have in common with other animals, instructs us concerning "the coupling of male and female, the bringing up of the young, and so forth."[204] Thirdly, humans have "an appetite for the good of our nature as rational," which inclines us to seek to know truths about God and to live well in society.[205] Given human spiritual nature, Thomas maintains that these inclinations are both natural and spiritual. This third level pertains to human nature as rational. Nonetheless, all three levels of natural inclinations underlie the orientations of our innate emotional reactions, and volitional and rational principles.

197. Cf. *ST* I-II 51.2.

198. *ST* I-II 62.4; cf. *De Car.* 1, 9; *ST* II-II 141.1 ad 1.

199. *ST* I-II 62.3.

200. *ST* I-II 63.1; cf. *ST* I-II 51.1.

201. Aquinas' account of these natural inclinations (*ST* I-II 94.2) is strikingly like that of Cicero (cf. *De off.* 1, 4), although his systematization and analysis is more complex than that of the Roman philosopher. However, it is uncertain that Aquinas directly saw Cicero's text, for even though Aquinas frequently refers to this work, he never cites this passage. Cf. Pinckaers 1995a.

202. *ST* I-II 94.2.

203. Ibid.

204. Ibid.

205. Ibid.

Even though they are underspecified and surrounded by the effects of original, personal, and social sin, these inclinations involve inchoate goals. They are a first step: to conserve our health and being, to commit ourselves to the marriage union and the educating of children, to live in society, as well as to know truth, and to love the good known. We must, however, rationally investigate these inclinations and goals. In order to pursue the underlying goals more thoroughly, Aquinas establishes his moral framework of flourishing and excellence. The inclinations demand further habituation. It is not enough to recognize intellectually a moral order. We need to construct *habitus* (virtues) that positively make these inclinations more than mere promptings.

Since native dispositions and social environments differ, however, humans do not all develop these inclinations in an identical way. For example, since natural individual intelligence differs according to the condition and use of sensory organs, we do not understand the first principles of understanding with the same clarity. Other dissimilarities spring from corporeal and appetitive differences.[206] According to Aquinas, some people's bodily constitution disposes them to chastity or mildness of temper, and so on.[207] Aquinas even astutely observes that being naturally disposed to one virtue, such as fortitude, might well render a person less disposed to a contrary virtue, such as meekness. Indeed, we employ conflicting tendencies when pursuing arduous goods (courage) and restraining irascible emotions (meekness).[208] However, he notes that reason inclines humans to all virtues, counterbalancing initial dissimilarities in natural dispositions. Although the inclinations as "seeds of virtue" direct us, we can develop them in multiple ways.[209]

Nature and Nurture: The Development of Habitus

Like Aristotle and other researchers involved in temperament, character, and virtue studies, Aquinas asks whether interior mental and moral qualities of *habitus* are innate or acquired. He queries about how much we can know and do by nature, and how much by experience. We shall now inquire

206. Cf. *ST* I-II 51.1.

207. Cf. *ST* II-II 47.15; *ST* II-II 141.1 ad 2; *ST* I-II 63.1.

208. Cf. *De virt. com.* 8 ad 10.

209. On how natural inclination is perfected in virtue: cf. *ST* I-II 51.1; *ST* II-II 108.2; and *ST* II-II 117.1, ad 1.

whether we can enrich Aquinas' approach with studies on genetic influences, neurochemical circuitry, and evolutionary reactions.

With the exception of extreme sociobiology theories (e.g., E. O. Wilson), contemporary researchers on genetic heritage admit that nurture or human experience and environment in some way influence our genetic emotional makeup. Sociobiology and evolutionary psychology suggest that the emotional "predispositions" selected by nature's evolutionary pressures do not overpower our thoughts and choices. They stand, nonetheless, in need of cultural instantiation, training, and habituation.[210] As these sciences indicate, and Aquinas concurs, the human emotions, as well as the natural inclinations, need shaping and do not start in a pure, passive state (a *tabula rasa*).

Neurobiological studies promise to reveal at least some of the mechanisms that underlie habitual dispositions and emotions. According to Damasio, cognitive processes and neurochemical substances stimulate each other. On the one hand, our repeated or habitual acts shape emotions and their neurochemical profiles (somatic markers). On the other hand, emotions and their neurochemical profiles form our dispositions to act.[211] Habitual dispositions to act have a historical, personal neurochemical profile that interacts with cognitive, volitional, and emotional processes.

Although they cannot approach the spiritual center of intelligent and volitional activity, human neurochemistry and evolutionary psychology offer insights concerning certain aspects of moral progress and growth in virtue. As Stephen J. Pope suggests, "moral conversion, moreover, might lead to not only a modification of thoughts, words, and deeds but also, by the repeated physiological effect of appropriate action (to some extent perhaps) even a reordering of this neurochemistry, particularly in the prefrontal cortices."[212] The question becomes: how can neurochemical profiles (personal historical component) for habitual action, which neurophysiology calls "somatic markers," facilitate our moral discernment and choices in complex social situations, or on the contrary, promote counter-moral decisions?[213]

In order to respond to this question and to evaluate this research and reflection further, let us differentiate the types of *habitus* and recall the larg-

210. Cf. Pope 1994, 154; de Waal 1997 and 1999.
211. Cf. Damasio 1994, 149–50.
212. Pope 1998b, 552; cf. Damasio 1994, 182–83.
213. Cf. Pope 1998b, 552; Damasio 1994, 191.

er context of virtue theory. According to Aquinas, human agents develop *habitus*, either vices or virtues, in active and receptive ways. We both cause these changes and are the subject of them.[214] In particular, we produce moral *habitus* in our own appetitive faculties (with their neurochemical circuitry) through the repeated use of reason. We produce intellectual *habitus* (scientific and practical knowledge) in the mind when we reflect on human experience and investigate primary propositions.[215] While entitative *habitus* and sensory faculties are primarily instinctual and only indirectly capable of rational influences,[216] the interior cognitive sense faculties of memory and imagination on the other hand have an innate basis that we rationally control and develop (at least to some extent). The *habitus* that inform these latter faculties bring rational (non-despotic) control to the nonrational parts of the soul: to the concupiscible and irascible parts through the virtues associated with temperance and courage respectively.[217]

For Aquinas, intellect itself, in our reasoning and willing capacities, is by nature both determined and malleable. Human reason is naturally adapted (determined) to truth in general as its object. Although we are receptive to the variety of things that we perceive (sense knowledge), we also actively think, critique, and recall knowledge. We acquire intellectual *habitus* through such rational activities.[218] Will, as an intellectual faculty, naturally inclines to the good in general. Nonetheless, its natural inclination for the good per se is underspecified for particular moral choices. We need additional volitional dispositions to ensure sure and prompt action toward particular goods.[219] We must have further *habitus* to direct us mediately toward our final goal and particular human goals, concerning which conflicting concrete goods often present themselves.

If any of these capacities are at first undetermined, or underdetermined, then we can actualize their potency through a *habitus*.[220] Aquinas explores the reasons for this habituation. In an acquired *habitus*, our faculty, such as the will, becomes connaturalized through a gradual transformation. An innate inclination to love the good, on the contrary, involves an immediate

214. Cf. *ST* I-II 51.2; *De virt. com.* 1, 9.

215. Cf. *ST* I-II 51.2.

216. Nonetheless, entitative habitus can be morally significant to the extent that the physical state and sensory faculties influence human mental activity; cf. *ST* I-II 50.2 and 50.3; Zagar 1984, 187.

217. Aristotle, *NE* iii.13, 1117 b 23–4; and Aquinas, *ST* I-II 50.3 sc.

218. Cf. *ST* I-II 50.4.

219. Cf. *ST* I-II 50.5 ad 3.

220. Cf. *De virt. com.* 1, 9.

union of the appetite with the good object. When we repeat acts, the *habitus'* potencies adapt to the object. Choices become easier through experience. This acquired connaturality functions differently than does an innate one. Through acquired connaturality, we can order ourselves to have right judgment.[221] In the case of good moral *habitus,* or virtue, we qualitatively alter a power or nature through repeated acts.[222] We do not, however, acquire *habitus* through simple repetition of external acts. Rather, we attend primarily to the interior quality of the acts, while not neglecting their external qualities. Instead of a life of unrelated singular acts, *habitus* supposes moral continuity as well as conversion in a moral history that becomes our character.[223]

Such *habitus* are principles for further action. As a result of *habitus,* we can use the connaturalized power at will.[224] Aquinas judges it necessary to acquire such *habitus* concerning the particular principles of actions and their ends. In prudence, for example, a human being "needs to be perfected by a certain *habitus,* through which it becomes, as it were connatural to him to judge rightly about an end."[225] Such a connaturalization or transformation demands an identity of end and person. Aquinas makes no qualms about following Aristotle's principle: "such as one is, such does the end seem to one."[226]

We should not undervalue the spiritual nature of human beings, as an impetus to act (from a deeper level). The human soul's power to influence human agency is more than a mere parallel to basic genetic and neurobiological wiring of natural inclinations. Nonetheless, human rational and volitional powers influence the whole person. We should not reduce these spiritual powers to evolutionary pressures on the species, nor the physical body with its myriad of interrelated sensate, biological, and neurological systems. This discussion of the spiritual soul raises further questions about the acquisition of intellectual and moral *habitus* (that can be considered to promote resilience and decrease vulnerability). Aquinas offers a nuanced and extensive response. *Habitus* in general have a multitude of sources. They can

221. Cf. *ST* II-II 45.2; *ST* I 1.6 ad 3; *ST* II-II 156.3.
222. Cf. *ST* I-II 56.5.
223. Cf. Zagar 1984, 183.
224. Cf. 3 *Sent.* d. 33, q. 1, a. 1, from a previously unedited text of St. Thomas (P.-M. Gils 1962, 618).
225. *ST* I-II 58.5.
226. Aristotle in the *NE* iii.5, 1114a32, as quoted by Aquinas in *ST* I-II 58.5.

originate either strictly from nature, or partly from nature and partly from the efforts of agents (and the influence of their environments). Concerning this second kind, we acquire some *habitus* through human effort, while God infuses others.[227]

In conclusion, to seek progress demands that we extend basic inclinations, the seeds of virtue, to more fully specified dispositions. As Aquinas says, "besides these natural principles, the *habitus* of virtue is required for the perfection of a human being according to the mode connatural to him."[228] It is in free and intelligent acts aimed toward temporal and eternal goals while employing instrumental goods that we actualize virtue in ourselves. A problem arises, however, when one thinks that an automation of morality is possible and even desirable. Moral acts involve principled and loving adaptation, rather than blind repetition. Another problem arises when we neglect human animality, or forget the indications about the resilience and risk effects of our acts, dispositions, and social relationships. It is important to recall the essential place of human animality (the body) in virtue, as has been remarkably done by Alasdair MacIntyre (1999) and the psychosocial sciences. Nonetheless, we need to supplement these sources with a doctrine of the natural inclinations that involves ontological, animal, and rational qualities (cf. *ST* I-II 94.2). Aquinas' teaching on natural-spiritual inclinations offers several pertinent correctives. It recognizes (1) that human action finds a vital principle in inclinations to preserve our existence, to develop life in family and society, and to seek actively truth and goodness; (2) that these inclinations are of a spiritual order (we cannot reduce them to evolutionary pressures on the human species); and (3) that we should not too sharply separate them from each other, when we seek to understand how virtues develop and correlate.

Aquinas on Virtue, Education, and Resilience

To make moral progress, we train our emotional and intellectual capacities. We promote moral behavior as well as avoid conditions that tend to activate "undesirable aspects of our evolved 'incentive systems.'"[229] We can

227. A more detailed treatment of infused virtue is found in chapter 7, in regard to the infused virtue of fortitude, its associated virtues, and their correlation with the gift the Holy Spirit.

228. *De virt. com.* 1, 10.

229. Pope 1998b, 552. This moral behavior is called "social ecology" by Bellah et al. (1986, 284).

develop both rational and emotional intelligence, as Goleman has put it. Aquinas, for his part, describes the way we instill intelligibility in virtuous *habitus* of emotions, will, and reason. His brand of emotional intelligence does not confuse or collapse the *habitus* of the emotions with simple intelligence, reason, or will. As intelligent, appropriate, and virtuous as an initial emotional judgment might be, we must rationally adjudicate the situation in order to act morally. We shall now investigate Aquinas' approach to virtue education in dialogue with the psychosocial approach to resilience.

Virtue Education

The relationship between human agency, reason, and resilience raises difficult questions, when we consider the moral complexity and immoral compromises often expressed in everyday action. Even in the post-lapsus human condition—with all the disordered effects on human individuals and society—Aquinas claims that "the seeds of virtue, which are in us, are an ordering of the will and reason to the good connatural to us."[230] This innate starting point not only directs our will and reason to the good (moral and spiritual goods), but also directs them away from evil.[231] Nonetheless these seeds are inadequate in themselves for responsible moral action or for understanding growth in resilience and virtue.

"Virtue" has many meanings in contemporary language.[232] Different cultures and times have established diverse lists of virtues.[233] We can understand Aquinas' technical use of the term "virtue" only in the context of his typology (study of the types) of *habitus*. Virtue and its contrary, vice, are operative *habitus;* they differ according to their rapport with reason. Thomas

230. Cf. *ST* I-II 51.1; *ST* I-II 63.1; *ST* I-II 27.3; 3 *Sent.* d. 33, q. 1, a. 2, sol. 3, co.

231. Cf. 4 *Sent.* d. 49, q. 5, a. 5, sol. 3, ex.

232. "Virtue" has numerous contemporary meanings that we should not confuse when approaching Aquinas' treatment of *virtus.* First, the *OED* recognizes that the Latin word *virtus* has the following senses: "valour, worth, merit, moral perfection"; and that its root, *vir,* means "man." Furthermore, the *OED* defines "virtue": "I. As a quality of persons. 1. The power or operative influence inherent in a supernatural or divine being. [. . .] 2. Conformity of life and conduct with the principles of morality; [. . .] 3. With a and pl. A particular moral excellence; a special manifestation of the influence of moral principles in life or conduct ME." Furthermore the *WEUD* lists the following senses of "virtue": "1. moral excellence; goodness; righteousness. 2. conformity of one's life and conduct to moral and ethical principles; uprightness; rectitude. 3. chastity, esp. in a girl or a woman [. . .] 4. a particular moral excellence. 5. a good or admirable quality." The list goes on.

233. The following recent studies illustrate the variety of virtue approaches: cf. MacIntyre 1981/1985; 1988; Pinckaers 1985, 1995a; Crossin 1985; Porter 1990; Comte-Sponville 1995. In these studies, the divergences in the lists of virtues are rooted in differing beliefs concerning human nature and its potential. The list we gave earlier can complete these.

says: "virtuous deeds are connatural to reason, but vicious acts are contrary to it."[234]

Aquinas' treatment of virtues is one of the masterpieces of medieval Scholastic moral theology. It was the fullest study of human agency to date and established several novelties as it developed.[235] The richness of Aquinas' virtue doctrine demands that he establish several definitions of virtue. In the *Summa theologiae,* the most basic philosophical definition asserts that "virtue denotes a determinate perfection of a power."[236] This perfection involves the way in which the power correlates to its end or proper act. In this section, we focus on the type of virtue produced in rational powers, without neglecting emotional ones. Human rational powers are not determined to one act. Such specifically human virtue entails a good operative *habitus,* which, as a perfection of a natural human power, is good by definition.[237] This good not only correlates to the basic ordering of nature, but it is also directed by the order of human reason.[238]

Concerning the potency and internal causes of virtue that exist in the moral agent, Aquinas does not stop with the standard definition of virtue, but rather argues that all acquired virtues (intellectual and moral) "arise from certain natural principles pre-existing in us."[239] The early or preliminary stages of virtue are natural to human beings in two ways: according to our specific nature and according to one's individual nature. First, virtue is natural inchoatively, since through experience nature instills in human rea-

234. *ST* I-II 70.4 ad 1.

235. As in the case of *habitus,* Aquinas' thought on virtue changes in its organization and deepens in its content between his *Commentary on the Sentences* and his *Summa theologiae.* In the earlier work he follows Peter Lombard's approach of addressing virtues in terms of whether Christ had them, while developing major reflections on virtue that go beyond the Lombard's structure and content. For example, to the Lombard's framework of whether Christ had the theological virtues of faith, hope, and charity, Aquinas adds a treatise on virtue in general (3 *Sent.* d. 23, q. 1); and after the Lombard's short treatise on the four principle virtues, Aquinas adds an extensive treatment of the common moral virtues, the cardinal virtues, and the parts of the moral virtues (3 *Sent.* d. 33, q. 1–3). In his *Summa theologiae,* Aquinas develops the topic further while employing a novel structural organization. He lays the foundation for understanding virtue by explicating the goal of flourishing, the nature of human acts, the principles of morality, the passions and *habitus* (*ST* I-II 1–54). This preparation then leads to his progressive elaboration of the virtues, which addresses the nature and seat of virtue, the intellectual virtues and their difference with the moral virtues, the cardinal and the theological virtues, the cause and mean of virtue, the reciprocity among virtues, and their comparison and duration (*ST* I-II 55–67).

236. *ST* I-II 56.1; *ST* I-II 55.4

237. Cf. *ST* I-II 55.3.

238. Aquinas draws from both scriptural and Ciceronian authority in this regard. See *ST* II-II 58.3; *ST* II-II 58.12 sc; 3 *Sent.* d. 33, q. 1, a. 2, sed c. 2.

239. *ST* I-II 63.3; cf. *ST* I-II 51.1; *ST* I-II 63.1; *ST* I-II 63.2.

son naturally known principles of knowledge and action. Along with the will's natural appetite for good in accordance with reason, these principles serve as seeds for intellectual and moral virtue.[240] Nonetheless, we must actively develop these principles.

Secondly, our individual bodily dispositions affect the way in which we are disposed to virtue. The dispositions of bodily sensory powers and emotions consequently aid or hinder the rational powers that they serve,[241] as we already saw in our study of emotions and temperaments. At this level, humans have unequal natural aptitudes: either for science, or for fortitude, or for temperance, and so on. As previously discussed, for Aquinas, the virtues build upon two natural bases. On the one hand, we extend the basic human inclinations to know truth, to love the good known, to conserve oneself in health and being, to commit oneself to the marriage union and the educating of children, and to live in society.[242] On the other hand, we use and amend the natural dispositions (such as kindness, friendliness, courageousness, and so on). We develop these initial aptitudes for virtue into virtue through virtuous acts. To acquire virtues, we need to actualize what we have as potencies.

Virtues have different natural and supernatural causes. The efficient causes of the virtues involve human intelligent and divine sources. At the natural level, reason and will produce virtuous acts and the formation of the underlying dispositions. For Aquinas, inasmuch as any natural good action correlates with the Source of goodness, God is also the efficacious cause through a help *(auxilio Dei)* that is typical of the goodness endemic to nature. At the supernatural level, God efficaciously produces the infused virtues, but not without human graced collaboration. Aquinas moreover holds that God is the first cause of the virtues, since in Him exist the exemplar virtues.[243] The final cause of the virtues, moreover, directs and motivates human beings. The perfect virtues of Christ and the saints in glory spell out the content of promised complete happiness, and thus serve to direct and motivate human efforts.[244] Lastly, the formal causes of the virtues constitute the reasons that make the act and disposition virtuous. In this regard, human social nature informs natural virtue according to our emotional, ratio-

240. Cf. *ST* I-II 63.1.

241. Ibid.

242. Cf. *ST* I-II 94.2.

243. Cf. *ST* I-II 61.5.

244. Cf. *ST* I-II 1–5; *ST* I-II 61.5.

nal, and volitional capacities, while the grace of the Holy Spirit and graced charity molds all Christian virtue.[245]

The process of acquiring virtue is based in human potencies and demands time. According to Aquinas, it traverses steps as well. He distinguishes three stages, although he does not construct a strict developmental stage theory. He describes three degrees of charity, which might serve as a model for the development of the other virtues (cf. II-II 24.9). The first stage involves beginners, the second progressives, and the third the mature. Aquinas does not order them according to chronological age, but to maturity in experienced, knowledgeable, and discerning judgment. They advance toward firm and constant dispositions. First, these three steps of virtue parallel three stages in human development. They illustrate how we progress from childhood to adolescence and finally to adulthood. Second, they resemble three qualities of moral development. To begin with, we need discipline in order to act morally. Then we make progress in virtues. And finally we become capable of mature action in freedom. Third, they correlate with three sources of morality in Scripture: the precepts of the Decalogue, the encouragement of the beatitudes, and the inspiration of the New Law. Fourth, these stages of growth in virtue involve three aspects of the mystics' spiritual progress. They advance from the purgative stage to the illuminative and finally to the unitive stage.[246]

Although in this section I cannot address other pedagogical ramifications of this model of virtue development, we should highlight its perspective on charity and on the roles of the teacher and of law therein. Although the theological nature of the experience of charity is not exactly parallel to moral virtues, it nonetheless manifests other similarities, especially in developmental trajectory. First, charity illustrates how virtue develops as a process of connaturalization with the end, the good that attracts us. Charity is more than the natural inclination or feeling of attraction for a good. For Aquinas, in charity we acquire a sort of connatural knowledge through an

245. Cf. *ST* II-II 23.8; *ST* I-II 61.5. See also Aquinas' discussion of the "perfecting virtues" (cf. *ST* I-II 61.5).

246. These stages can be put into diagram form (cf. *ST* II-II 24.9; Pinckaers 1995a, 354–78):

Stages	*human development*	*moral qualities*	*Scripture*	*mystics*
Beginners	childhood	discipline	Decalogue	purgative
Progressives	adolescence	progress in virtues	beatitudes	illuminative
Mature	adulthood	maturity in freedom	New Law	unitive

experience of the Good (ultimately God, who is the source of all good). The experiential basis for acquired knowledge of the Good serves in turn as the basis for contemplation and for action. Since charity plays the primary role in this perspective, the connatural knowledge affected by experiential charity enlivens the whole range of our action. It serves as the foundational source for the other virtues. It is expansive, rather than restricted by norms. The highest form of mature charity involves spontaneity and exceeds the normative and conventional demands.[247] In the upcoming chapters, these three degrees of virtue serve as a point of convergence with the behavioral sciences and a contrast with Kohlberg's developmental model.[248]

Secondly, the roles of the teacher and of the law are to aid the student in such self-actualization and maturity. Aquinas emphasizes that a natural aptitude for virtue is inadequate. Humans must acquire virtue by means of some kind of training.[249] We must apply ourselves. Yet a human being cannot train himself alone. We need training from another, in order to attain to the perfection of virtue in both disposition and act. In every case, we need paternal/maternal training. But when we are prone to vice and unamenable to instruction, it is useful that law restrain us from evil by force and fear.

Human law disciplines us. Through fear of punishment, it causes us to do what virtue would freely dictate, at least minimally. Aquinas follows Aristotle in this understanding of our capacity for the heights of virtue and the depths of human depravity.[250] Human law's purpose is to establish peace and harmony. It aims to create a culture for advancing not only virtuous acts, but even virtuous dispositions. Aquinas' Christian understanding of the Decalogue, the beatitudes, and the New Law of the Holy Spirit goes further than the natural level. Yet in order to understand it, we need to distinguish further the internal and external sources of growth in virtue and spiritual resilience.

Internal and External Sources of Learning and Instruction

What internal and external sources underlie human moral agency, virtue, and resiliency? How do the active correlation of learning and instruction underlie moral and spiritual agency? In order to exemplify virtue education, Aquinas correlates the way we acquire virtue and knowledge. He

247. Cf. Pinckaers 1995a, 365.

248. Cf. Philibert 1975, 1980.

249. Cf. *ST* I-II 95.1.

250. Ibid.

uses two principal images—the student and teacher, and the arts, especially the art of building—in order to demonstrate the act of teaching *(docere)* and learning.[251] Aquinas borrows insights from the Greek philosophical tradition of *paideia* (*παιδεία*). He renews them though his Christian treatment of the relationship between master and disciple.[252]

Aquinas constructs his approach to teaching and learning neither on Averroes' theory of the direct transfer of phantasms nor on Plato's theory of reminiscence.[253] Rather, led by Aristotle's mediate position, Thomas argues that we learn through interior and external causes[254] that advance us from potency to act. What are these internal and external sources?

The internal sources occupy a primary place in both moral agency and theory. They involve the emotional, intellectual, and spiritual sources that constitute natural and supernatural feelings, knowledge, and love. They entail personal and communal experience. Aquinas does not confuse moral virtue and moral knowledge. Nonetheless, in order to study moral science, we need moral experience. In his general discussion of science, Aquinas notes that, in order to elaborate a science (including *sacra doctrina*, or theology and moral theology), we need related personal experience.[255] On the one hand, mathematics and physics require that we abstract principles and knowledge from sensible things. Counting apples aids us to understand addition. Moral wisdom, on the other hand, requires moral practice and experience. Aquinas says that its "natural principles, which are not abstracted from sensible things, are known through experience, for which a long time is required."[256] We understand principles of practical prudence better because of experiences of others' and our own prudent acts.

Aquinas emphasizes, however, that an ethicist is not made by raw experience alone. Experience is insufficient, unless we acquire freedom from slavery to the emotions. Moral character helps us study morality.[257] Aqui-

251. Cf. Pinckaers 1995a, 359–74; Verbeke 1994.

252. For Aquinas, the Master or Teacher par excellence is Christ (cf. *ST* III 7.7), who is followed in this role by the Apostles, bishops, and the masters of theology who teach and comment on sacred Scripture. In this perspective, Aquinas regroups the gifts of the Holy Spirit (cf. 1 Cor 12) around the teacher, since through instruction one human can act upon another on the spiritual level (cf. *ST* I-II 111.4).

253. Aquinas critiques these two theories in *ST* I 117.1 and *De verit.* 11.1.

254. His scriptural commentaries add further reflections on the acquisition of virtue as well (cf. *Commentary on Philippians*, Sct 4–1; on verse 4:8.

255. See Aquinas, *in Meta*, A 981a14–15; *In lib. causis* (lect. 1); and Aristotle *NE* (i.3, 1095a2–11) and *Metaphysics* (A 981a14–15).

256. *In Eth.* 6, 7, 1209; cf. *NE* i.3, 1095a2–11; and *In Eth.* 1, 3, 38–40.

257. Cf. *In Eth.* 6, 7, 1211; *In Eth.* 1, 3, 40; cf. *NE* i.3, 1095a2–11.

nas insists that the virtues correlate with each other. Moral virtue (temperance, courage, justice, and prudence) assists intellectual virtue (understanding, science, and wisdom; and prudence and art); and vice versa. In ethics, we speculatively examine practical moral experience, our own and that of others. In moral theology, we examine the experiences communicated in Scripture, tradition, and the faith-community (liturgical and non-liturgical prayer), as well.[258]

A study of moral and spiritual resilience includes how these sources address human suffering and failure, aspirations and efforts. Theological reflection involves a regular movement back and forth between experience and speculation in order that the one aids in interpreting, guiding, and rectifying the other. We construct a personal synthesis born of reexamining the text (e.g., Scripture) and significant events (such as personal experience of good and evil, as well as other events open through to history and faith, such as the exodus, Christ's Passion, Auschwitz, Hiroshima). We revisit these texts and events neither qua historical text nor qua historical event. Rather we examine them to better understand their import for contemporary audiences and ourselves. They help us to meet the challenges that we face concerning meaning and commitment, coping and constancy, and constructing something good out of human suffering and failure.

Indispensably, external sources for moral agency, theory, and theologizing involve those events and persons that help us to better understand the pleasures and pains of the human journey toward happiness. Aquinas' analysis of teaching and learning emphasizes both internal and external sources.[259] He explains how we learn from our joy-filled, painful, and innocuous experiences through the master-and-disciple archetype. We use the light of the intellect (personal reason and will) and various sources of light (both outside teachers and God).[260] The master (exterior principle) leads the disciple (interior principle) to acquire personal knowledge. Aquinas emphasizes that an external teacher does not directly cause us to learn. Yet we depend upon a teacher's aid in order to appropriate human experience personally. External masters can involve nonformal interactions with unlikely teachers:

258. Cf. Pinckaers 1993, 439–41.

259. Cf. *ST* I 117.1, *ST* II-II 181.3 corpus and ad 2, and parallel places: *II Sent.* dist. 9.2 ad 4; dist. 28.5 ad 3; *SCG* II.75; *De verit.* 11.1; Opusc. XVI, *De unit. intell.*, 5.

260. For Aquinas, the Holy Spirit accomplishes the goal of Scripture, which is human instruction and learning *(eruditio)*, through the saints' scriptural commentaries (cf. *QDL* 12.17 sc).

the poor and weak, young and old alike. They lead us from things unknown by us to those known by them, in a twofold way. First, the master provides instructive aids *(auxilia vel instrumenta)* in order that our intellects can acquire knowledge *(scientia)*. Secondly, the master strengthens our intellects by proposing the order of proceeding from principles to conclusions. We need such demonstrations until we can continue on our own.[261]

St. Thomas highlights a correlated and nonconflicting interior principle. We might call it an external-internal principle—an external principle that becomes internal. In addition to the interior light of the intellect, which is a principal cause of knowledge and virtue, God is also a principal cause of light, knowledge, and virtue.[262] Thomas identifies the second interior source not only as an interior source of light (the Word through faith) but also as an interior inclination to act (grace of the Holy Spirit through hope and charity).[263] He recognizes it as the evangelical or New Law that the grace of the Holy Spirit inscribes in the believer's heart. The Spirit, as a unique external-interior source and Master, actively provides the understanding of Scriptures and knowledge of Providence. He is more fully associated with the gifts of the Holy Spirit that accompany the virtues, as we shall discuss later. The Spirit endows us with strength for action.[264] Christian moral theology thus takes as its basis the experience of the new resilient life in the Spirit.[265] The twofold light of truth (human and divine reason) shines through the summit of the human mind to the depth of his heart. It permeates our judgments about the true goodness and good truth that we discern in the thoughts and action of other people and ourselves.[266] The Teacher empowers us. He instructs us in this fuller path, and enables us to attain our goals through the presence and gift of the Holy Spirit. The pedagogical insight here involves the internalizing effect of law, especially the New Law. The goal is full maturity in the virtues of faith, hope, and charity, which constitute freedom for a life of excellence.

261. Cf. *ST* I 117.1.

262. In this regard, Aquinas quotes the Psalms (93.10 and 4.7) in *ST* I 117.1 ad 1. See also *SCG* (II.75 ad 3) and *ST* I II 9.6, where Aquinas draws from Phil 2:13.

263. Cf. *ST* I 1.10; *Ad Gal.* ch. 5, lect. 7; *QDL* 7.6 art. 15; de Lubac 1964, 2:272ff.; Pinckaers 2002, 11.

264. Cf. *ST* I-II 106.1 ad 2.

265. St. Paul describes this type of resilient life of the Spirit in his letter to the Romans (Rm 7:21–8:11). This new life entails living (and longing to live) by the Spirit, instead of the flesh.

266. Cf. Pinckaers 2002, 10.

Moral Experience and Knowledge as Sources of Resilience

Practical reflections on both ethical theory and resilience have a common starting point: resilient moral experience and virtue. Aquinas' approach to personal, social, and divine sources would inseparably intertwine morality and resilience. He would not make resilience a standard for human agency, unless it was integrated with morality and religion. In following Aquinas, we avoid two extremes when correlating moral experience, knowledge, and virtue to resilience.[267] One side of the dichotomy favors a rational study of moral norms, while neglecting experiences of responsibility, virtue, and excellence. Moral norms, as a priori principles, would simply need application, a rational step; knowing would produce doing, for example, Socrates. Likewise, resilience would simply mean learning to apply resilience rules. The other extreme overshadows moral norms in favor of personal experience, which then would serve as the only criteria in the moral domain. Unfortunately, this extreme could involve abuses to liberty.[268] Resilience would then be experience per se, even normless experience.

Aquinas forges a middle ground between extremes. His approach accords a basic priority to the moral experience (virtuous character) that grows through virtuous acts, enlivened by moral, social, and spiritual support. Herein of course, he reserves an important, but subservient, place for establishing norms and prudent decision making. A parallel type of resilience would draw upon experience, norms, and virtuous dispositions. It would demand a complete type of action.

Aquinas understands experience in a moral and theological framework. "Experience" etymologically finds its roots in the practical knowledge, skill, or competence *(peritia)* that we draw from a trial or danger *(periculum)* once overcome.[269] However, not all experience exhibits overcoming difficulty in the same way. What are the different sorts of experience? Even though a basic unity underlies being human, we have emotional and psychological experiences; sensual and intellectual ones; and moral and spiritual ones. We need to reflect upon experience in order to gain moral science, virtue, and resilience. However, not all experiences will serve as a basis for moral or resilient knowledge, judgment, and action in the same way.[270]

267. Cf. Pinckaers 1995a, 91.

268. St. Paul warns of such abuses of liberty in Romans ch. 8.

269. Cf. Bruguès 1995, 33; *WEUD* 1989, 501.

270. For there are specifically shallow, immoral experiences; cf. Pinckaers 1995a, 91–94.

Interior experience is particular. We amass it developmentally in at least two ways.[271] First, each of the two interior dimensions (human and divine) of Christian experience is progressive. We acquire both only with time and in function of our own particular genetic heritage and personal history, gender and relationships, culture and society, and so on. *Gratia praesupponit naturam.*[272] Second, when we develop moral theology and virtue, the utility of our personal and social context manifests itself in dialogue between our personal experiences and those of others: not only other theologians or ethicists from similar backgrounds, but also those who are young or inexperienced, weak or sick, dependent or crippled, who all have their lessons to offer.[273] Beyond its particularity, each person's experience has a certain universality, and for the better part, resilience.

The dialogue between our own experience and that of others is made possible through (1) being in relationship with others; (2) understanding the other person as another self; (3) having confidence that other human beings' experiences are real and can be critically integrated to serve as a source for one's own moral judgments; and (4) believing that we share a common humanity between people of all genders, cultures, and times. Thus we can learn from another person's and other people's experience, and we can learn how theorized sciences (including both the theological and psychosocial sciences) can gain insights into human resilient experience through that of particular individuals and communities.[274]

What type of moral knowledge can we attain through these different sources? In the light of Aquinas' example, ethical theory and moral theology involve the rational elaboration of moral experience and sources: we reflect upon human experiences of successful and failed resilience; and we call upon different sciences—literary and human sciences, philosophical, and theological ones. Moving from outside appearances to inner sources, to levels that we cannot measure,[275] moral theology takes the point of view of the responsible faith-filled person and his origin of knowledge and volition, af-

271. Cf. Philibert 1975.

272. Concerning the like parallel between faith and natural knowledge, with explicit reference to grace and nature, see *ST* I 2.2 ad 1; *ST* I 1.8 ad 2; *De verit.* 14.10 ad 9.

273. Cf. MacIntyre 1999, 6–7; Pinckaers 2000a.

274. The moral theorization of experience considers both insights from one's personal experience and those gleaned through the observations of the social sciences (cf. *VS*, n. 111 and 112; Bruguès, 1995, 32–36), which analyze aspects of the diversity and richness of human experience and narrative in order to refine a moral anthropology in terms of spiritual-religious experience and philosophical, sociological, psychological, neurophysiological, and biological data.

275. Cf. *VS* 54–64; *GS* 16; Pinckaers 1995a.

fect and action. According to Pinckaers, it involves four types of knowledge: basic, intuitive, reflective, and systematic. These types of knowledge incorporate the resources available through our own person and gifts, friends and family, music and art, nature and environment, in differing ways.[276] This involves a progressive appropriation of particular sources of resilience in virtuous dispositions.

First, through our basic (fontal or causal) knowledge, although hazily, we grasp a whole action. The origin of knowledge—our basic self-awareness—grows out of the experience.[277] We encounter a deep unity of intellect and sensation, acts and goals, intentions and circumstances. This deepest level of knowledge is direct, dynamic, and creative, an encounter of human inclinations and motives with grace and the Holy Spirit. It is inexhaustible. We cannot adequately express it in words. It precedes both ideas and words. *For example, it is the foundational, existential aspect of an encounter with a caregiving friend or a peaceful sonata that as a basic experience nourishes human resilience and serves as the origin for reflection.* This origin of knowledge underlies later more developed types of knowledge.

Second, when we develop moral reflection and seek self-understanding, we acquire a reflex or intuitive knowledge. Here we observe experience and ourselves. Rather than an action itself, this type of knowledge involves speculative self-vision. Such intuitive knowledge entails a reflection of human action and basic knowledge in our conscience. Language can articulate some of this event. It cannot, however, entirely express the basic knowledge, just as words can only partially express the movements of the heart. *This reflex knowledge involves, for example, an intuitive glimpse of the cognitive and affective resilience-significance related to having contact with the friend or listening to the sonata.*

Third, when we ask the questions "why" and "how," we attain more specified, reflective knowledge. We produce a practically oriented knowledge, which starts to establish a process of generalization, but not yet systematization. Through this reflection, we seek the goals, motives, circumstances, and consequences of the act.[278] We express reflective knowledge in narra-

276. Cf. Pinckaers 1995a, 49–55.

277. This origin of knowledge (and experience) is described in different ways (which are not all equivalent): as the heart (biblical conception, cf. 1 Cor 2:11; Rom 8:16); as subconscious (Freud); as premoral good and evil (Curran, McCormick, Cahill); as superconscience, "fontal," or causal knowledge (Pinckaers); and so on.

278. It attempts to "explain, justify, critique, or improve it" as well as to "draw lessons, resolutions,

tive, instructive, and wisdom literature, as well as in precepts and laws. *For example, it describes and recounts the resilience wisdom and guidance, or support and love that we gain through the friend; it communicates the comfort and sense of order that we receive when listening to the music.*[279]

Fourth, in theoretic or systematic knowledge, we attempt scientific discourse. We employ reason and logic to transform, generalize, and universalize reflective, reflex, and basic knowledge. We even attempt to predict and verify the relevance of the way in which we theorize this knowledge. Parts of the New Testament exhibit this process of theoretical organization and systematization. More developed expressions include scholastic and contemporary theology. *Thus we provide theories in order to explicate the resilience and existential significance of friendship and beauty.*

Language in some way always remains inadequate to explain moral experience and resilience, while at the same time being a key to significant aspects of them. Nonetheless, actually resilient lives and virtuous individuals provide a rich source for reflection on resilience and morality. In order to appropriate deeper dimensions of spiritual experience and resilience, we shall resist the secularization of knowledge and reductionistic methods. In this spirit of renewal, Aquinas' moral anthropology proves to be a resilient model. We have confirmed and adapted his virtue theory and moral theology. They constitute a framework and provide insights into how moral experience helps aids us acquire and understand resilience. This chapter's dialogue has served as a methodological, theoretical, and anthropological introduction to the following chapters on fortitude and its related virtues.

---

practical advice, and directives for living," employing memories of past experiences (cf. Pinckaers 1995a, 53).

279. We find examples in the sapiential and moral teaching of Scripture and of spiritual works, inasmuch as they are written in concrete and ordinary language.

PART TWO

APPLICATIONS

4

Resilience and Aquinas' Virtue of Fortitude

If any of our communities, families, or selves were invulnerable, we would need neither emotions such as fear, hope, and daring, nor virtues such as fortitude. Even in the most protected environments, we rightly experience fear when faced with real and potential deformation, destruction, or loss. Fear is based on human vulnerabilities that extend from physical to psychological, from economic to social, and from moral to spiritual levels. Can we prevent fear from causing deeper anxiety? Can we prepare ourselves in order to better control fearful situations? Can we resist fear without forgoing what is good, right, and true? Courage and its related virtues offer practical responses to these questions. As the British analytic philosopher P. T. Geach says: "Courage is what we all need in the end; we all have to die, and for none of us can the possibility be excluded of dying nastily: in great pain, or after a long disabling illness."[1] The ultimate vulnerability of mortality produces manifold expressions of strong emotionally charged fear. However, human beings also need courage to rebuild after less serious losses, and for more common danger and toil. Fortitude entails that we avoid going to

1. Geach 1977/1979, 150.

extremes when faced with extreme or threatening situations. Its associated virtues—which Aquinas calls magnanimity, magnificence, patience, and perseverance—bring balance and focus to our actions in the difficult situations of ordering everyday life that concern initiative taking and resisting.

Aquinas on the Virtue of Fortitude

Without giving a history of fortitude[2] or Aquinas' contribution thereof, in this section, we establish an anthropological context for our in-depth treatment of fortitude. We concentrate on Aquinas' philosophical anthropology and his insights on how fortitude helps us to manage fear and daring. Furthermore, we highlight the way that resilience input enriches our understanding of this virtue.

Types of Fortitude

Aquinas makes an extensive study of the types (typology) of fortitude and its related virtues.[3] He establishes that fortitude can be a general or a specific virtue. Thomas's typology of fortitude helps us to discuss fortitude philosophically and to avoid confusing its various senses. It also allows us to see how resilience resembles this virtue in certain ways.

2. We can nevertheless recall a number of historical points in order to understand Aquinas' synthetic account of fortitude. The ancients (taken cumulatively) hold to the following. Characteristically courage (1) is undeniably tied to the good, which distinguishes "true fortitude" from semblances thereof; (2) has a constitutive social dimension; (3) manages fear and affronts the greatest dangers of life; (4) demands patient suffering and firm resistance in the face of adversity; and (5) employs daring to confront danger in order either to overcome it or to manifest truth and defend justice, even in the face of an inevitable defeat. Modern and postmodern discussions have introduced new questions, tendencies, and distinctions, which have had a decisive and altering impact on contemporary conceptions of courage. Some thinkers challenge the basic characteristics that typify the ancient worldview and Aquinas' Christian synthesis. Modern philosophical approaches more often than not sever or weaken the bond between fortitude and the good. They sometimes maintain that courage is not a virtue (because we can abuse or wrongly use it), or is outdated and misplaced (because we no longer need the courage of epic heroes). In its place, they claim that other more pertinent virtues need cultivating, such as imaginative compromise, ironical detachment, and political adeptness (to avoid situations that would otherwise need courage). Furthermore, they replace magnanimity and magnificence with generosity. Other transformations include (1) a shift away from courage as the mastery of fear to focus on daring or despair as the motor for courage; and (2) a denial or skepticism of the need for or possibility of heroic courage. This brief overview of diverse views on and critiques of courage sets the philosophical stage for a constructive treatment of courage in the light of Aquinas. Nonetheless, it does not pretend to be complete. Several recent works ably recount the history of fortitude: Gauthier 1951; Canto-Sperber 1996b. Attempts at addressing Aquinas' treatment of fortitude in historical context include Lottin 1942–60; Gauthier 1951; Congar 1974.

3. St. Thomas (1992) uses *fortitudo* frequently—2,228 times in his collected works—and in different ways.

In addressing Aquinas' reflections on *fortitudo*, authors translate the word as either "fortitude" or "courage."[4] Contemporary philosophers who discuss this cardinal virtue tend to employ more readily the term "courage," which etymologically finds its origin in Latin *cor* and old French *cuer* (heart). Nonetheless, other philosophers and theologians employ "fortitude," which finds its roots in the Latin *fortis* (strong or vigorous). In this work, I shall primarily use "fortitude" in translating Aquinas' *fortitudo*; yet I shall also use "courage" as its synonym.

Fortitude is not a question of simple physical strength or brash daring, for Aquinas. As a moral virtue, it is manifest by truly courageous and good acts and dispositions that are in accord with reason. The rational faculty serves as a primary reference in managing efficaciously all aspects of life including our emotions, as discussed in chapter 2. Emotions are a significant aspect of the virtue of fortitude. Difficult obstacles can disincline the will to follow reason. Hardship often excites an emotion such as fear, daring, hope, or sorrow. "In order to remove this obstacle fortitude of the mind is requisite, whereby to resist the aforesaid difficulty even as a man, by fortitude of body, overcomes and removes bodily obstacles,"[5] as Aquinas says.

In order to study the treatise on fortitude (*Summa theologiae* II-II 123–140),[6] St. Thomas's analysis distinguishes (1) fortitude as a specific virtue (and its integral related virtues), when it specifically faces the fear of death,[7] and (2) fortitude as signifying secondary and connected virtues (potential parts of fortitude), as when the matter is some lesser difficulty[8] or as when it is a condition for all virtues (fortitude as a general virtue).[9] Fortitude as a specific virtue has no subjective parts (different types of fortitude),[10] since we cannot differentiate it further according to another object, or break it

4. In the compilation of English translations of Aquinas' works found in the *Past Masters*, "fortitude" is found 653 times, while "courage" is used 93 times, and only for other Latin expressions (i.e., not for *fortitudo*). English-speaking contemporary philosophers and theologians split on the use of "fortitude" and "courage." The following authors use "fortitude": R. Cessario (1991), J. Porter (1990, 1995), and the *Summa Theologiae* (*ST*) translation by the Fathers of the English Dominican Province (1947 and 1981). Others use "courage," such as D. N. Walton (1986), Y.-M. Congar (1974), A. Ross and P. G. Walsh (1966, Blackfriars translation of *ST*).

5. *ST* II-II, 123.1.

6. The treatise on fortitude was most likely composed in 1272 in Paris; the commentary on the *NE* was done in 1271–72 (cf. Torrell 1996, 146–47, 227–28, 333; Congar 1974, 333). In distinguishing the parts of the virtue of fortitude in the *Summa theologiae* (II-II 128), Aquinas uses Cicero, Aristotle, Macrobius, and Andronicus as his principal philosophical sources.

7. Cf. *ST* II-II 123.2.

8. Cf. *De virt. com.* 12, 27.

9. Cf. *ST* II-II 128.1 ad 5.

10. Cf. *ST* II-II 143.1.

*The Virtue of Fortitude and Its Principal Parts**

Virtue	*Object*	*Proximate Matter*	*Remote Matter*	*Opposing Vice*
Fortitude	persisting in the good of reason	fear and daring	dangers of death	Cowardice Fearlessness
(Virtues of initiative taking)				
Magnanimity	attaining greatness in good	hope	being worthy of great honors	Presumption (works) Ambition (honors) Vainglory (praise) Pusillanimity
Magnificence	attaining greatness in deeds	hope	great spending	Profusion Meanness
(Virtues of resisting)				
Patience	remaining in the good	sorrow	afflicting evil	Unresponsiveness Weakness / Cowardice
Longanimity	knowing how to wait	hope	delays, length of time from the goal	Lack of enthusiasm / Inconsistency Discouragement
Perseverance	persisting in the effort	fear	duration of time needed, delay	Hard-headedness Weakness, Softness
Constancy	continuing the effort	sorrow	toil / renewed obstacles	Stubbornness Inconstancy

*Chart adapted from Labourdette (1961–2, 47).

down into distinct species. Aquinas thus construes fortitude to have such a unity that it has no higher universal concept that could collect distinct types of fortitude.[11]

Aquinas divides fortitude into four (quasi-) integral parts: magnanimity, magnificence, patience and perseverance.[12] He recognizes two acts of

11. We might ask why fortitude has no subjective parts. Has Aquinas so precisely conceived of fortitude's object that he limits different types of fortitude: domestic, economic, political, military, and so on (cf. *NE* iii.11, 1116a16–1117a28)? Aquinas responds by saying that we might best construe these divisions as modes of fortitude rather than parts, since they lack the true notion of virtue (*ST* II-II 128.1 ad 5). Aquinas divided the virtues according to the faculties, as a perfection or *habitus* of a power (*potentiae perfectionem*).

12. Cicero divides fortitude into four (quasi-) integral parts according to its four inclinations (*appetitiones* and *contemptiones*). Cicero considers these inclinations to involve passions, feelings, or emotions, rather than being abstracted or separated as merely intellectual components. Aquinas, however, prefers magnanimity, rather than Cicero's "confidence" (cf. *ST* II-II 128.1; Cicero *Rhet.* II, 54). Aquinas was not

fortitude: initiative taking *(aggredi)* and endurance *(sustinere)*.[13] The act of initiative taking (aggressiveness) underlies the virtues of magnanimity and magnificence that either combat or undertake some enterprise; these virtues employ and moderate aggressiveness.[14] The act of endurance lies beneath the virtues of patience and perseverance that resist death and destruction; these virtues master endurance. Aquinas argues that patience and perseverance are more uniquely characteristic of fortitude. These four virtuous acts or dispositions are quasi-integral parts of fortitude when they apply to the proper matter of fortitude, namely the fear of death. They are potential parts, or secondary virtues related to, yet distinct from, fortitude, when we apply them to another kind of hardship. Aquinas identifies longanimity and constancy as two other potential parts of fortitude.

A diagram of the way Aquinas subdivides the virtues and passions related to fortitude demonstrates the structure through which he articulates his philosophical psychology. This diagram displays how Aquinas relates fortitude and its associated virtues to their objects, emotions (proximate matter), remote matters, and opposing vices.

This sketch of Aquinas' typology of fortitude gives us a context to discuss how particular types of fortitude serve as functional equivalents to resilience and how resilience insights enrich our understanding of the virtues related to difficulty.

The General Virtue of Fortitude and Resilience

Aquinas depicts how truly courageous actions accord with reason and resist difficulty in two ways, with two virtue-types of fortitude. First, as strength of mind, affection, and action, fortitude is a general virtue. It is a quality necessary for all the virtues. In this regard, we can construe fortitude as a type of, or at least a source for, moral resilience. Second, fortitude is

---

alone in following Cicero's quadruple division of fortitude. Others who did the same include Abelard in his *Ysagoge* (c. 1150); William (Guillaume) of Auxerre in his *Summa Aurea* (c. 1220); John de la Rochelle in his *De virtutibus;* Albert the Great in his *Com. super sententiis* (cf. Lottin 1960, III:187–94). Nevertheless, we should note that Aquinas distinctly assigns Aristotle a central role in structuring this treatise. Aquinas is also original in his synthesis of Aristotelian and prevailing Abelardian conceptions of courage and associated virtues.

13. Aquinas draws from the Stoic division of courage, but not from its content. He follows Philip the Chancellor in holding that the parts of courage are integral parts, but he uses a different conception than Philip, who thought that courage has one act with six parts. Aquinas holds that it has two acts: *aggredi* and *sustenire*. Cf. Gauthier 1951, 360–63

14. Cf. *ST* II-II 123.3 and 123.6; *ST* II-II 128.1.

the special capacity to control fear and daring when resisting or overcoming some life-threatening danger.

In claiming that fortitude is a *virtus generalis,* Aquinas affirms that the virtues interrelate. As a general virtue, fortitude qualifies the other virtues, which, inasmuch as they are specific virtues, have their own proper object. In other words, the general virtue of fortitude involves the strength or resilience that is one of the universal qualities of every virtue. The exercise of the other virtues involves consistency, truth, and stability, which are necessary conditions for every virtue or act of virtue.[15] Otherwise, a virtue would be transient or simply a singular act. Indeed, each excellence must stand firm in its own matter.

According to Aquinas, this first sense of fortitude, which applies in general to all virtues, involves "the power of resisting corruptions,"[16] "all constancy of soul,"[17] "the principle of action [as] a *habitus* whereby someone acts well,"[18] the "firmness of mind in face of assaults of all kinds,"[19] "a disposition whereby the soul is strengthened for that which is in accord with reason, against any assaults of the emotions, or the toil involved by any operations,"[20] the common formal principle, which "strengthens the mind,"[21] or the firmness of mind "required both in doing good and in enduring evil, especially with regard to goods or evils that are difficult."[22] The general sense of fortitude makes fortitude a constitutive element of each virtue. It is the cement that, when added to other ingredients (a specific matter, action, or faculty), becomes a solid foundation for the life of excellence.

Evoking the description of general resilience in chapter 1, I would like to suggest that general fortitude (the general virtue of fortitude) is a functional equivalent to the resilience quality identified as general strength in difficulty. It manifests coping, resisting, and constructive supports. I also recall that studies on "emotional intelligence" provide parallel insights into what Aquinas would call moral virtue in general and the general virtue of fortitude.[23] Fortitude as a general virtue recalls the steeling aspect of resilience. Seen as

15. Cf. *Qu. disp. de virtutibus* 1, 12, 23; 5, 1, 1.
16. *ST* II-II 123.2 ad 1.
17. *In Eth.* 2, 8, 337; cf. *ST* II-II 123.2; *In Eth.* 2, 4, 283. *ST* I-II 61, art. 3 and 4.
18. *ST* II-II 123.2 ad 1, which he takes from Aristotle's *Rhet.* i.9, 1366a36–b1.
19. *ST* II-II 123.2 ad 2; *ST* I-II 65.1, *In Eth.* 2, 8, 336–37.
20. *ST* I-II 61.4; cf. *ST* I-II 61.4 ad 3.
21. *ST* I-II 61.3.
22. *ST* II-II 139.1; *ST* II-II 123.3.
23. Cf. Goleman 1998 and 1995.

a quality of all virtues, it also resembles an analogue for acquired and in-grained qualities that underlie more than singular instances of resilience.

The Special Virtue of Fortitude and Moral Resilience

When Aquinas further specifies the virtue according to its matter, his notion of courage offers added interest to the resilience dialogue. In addition to concerning the good of reason (like the other virtues), fortitude concerns danger and labor. As a specific or special virtue, "fortitude may be taken to denote firmness only in bearing and withstanding those things wherein it is most difficult to be firm, namely in certain grave dangers."[24] Aquinas does not stop at this general definition though. His philosophical project proceeds by progressive nuances, which examine specific phenomena of fortitude.

Aquinas demonstrates that, even as a specific virtue, fortitude procures a general strength in resisting destruction to our dispositions and our person.[25] Aquinas holds that a natural power involves both a capacity to resist degradation and a principle to act. As the extreme activity of a power, he identifies the second (a principle to act) as the more common determination of virtue in general. But the first (being a power to resist corruptions) indicates an indispensable quality of virtue and a particular quality of the specific virtue of fortitude. Aquinas says, "even as a special virtue with a determinate matter, it helps to resist the assaults of all vices. For he that can stand firm in things that are most difficult to bear is prepared, in consequence, to resist those which are less difficult."[26]

Fortitude helps us to resist in accordance with how we have become ordered to our ultimate goal, flourishing. Aquinas does not construe goods to be all of the same level or importance. Rather, he argues that human beings will more fully attain flourishing by seeking it through a definitely ordered hierarchy of goods. For example, holding firmly to the good of reason (*bonum rationis*) is more important than either avoiding bodily evils or seeking bodily goods, which by themselves are patent sources of attraction or repulsion. If the will's courageous disposition to the good of reason holds

24. *ST* II-II 123.2. To add support to this affirmation, he quotes Cicero, St. Gregory the Great, and Aristotle. Cicero's *Rhet.* II.54.

25. Thomas's argument (*ST* II-II 123.2 ad 1) builds upon, yet outstrips, two Aristotelian principles (cf. *De Caelo* i.116; and *Metaphysics* v.12).

26. *ST* II-II 123.2 ad 2; cf. ad 1.

in the most fearful situations, it should do so in less fearful ones. This rationale gives Aquinas the basis for identifying the specific nature of the virtue of fortitude. He claims that "fortitude of soul must be that which binds the will firmly to the good of reason in face of the greatest evil."[27] Thomas's hierarchy specifies not only the types of fear, but also the types of rational truths and volitional goods.

Aquinas' argument deepens. He contends that fortitude is more precisely about fear and daring (*ST* II-II 123.3), the fear of death (*ST* II-II 123.4), and most specially death in battle (*ST* II-II 123.5). While building upon the basis of a natural virtue, he widens the cultural context and extent of its application. Thomas pushes beyond the notions of courage's fulfillment as identified by Aristotle and Cicero. According to Aquinas, the highest form of fortitude is more than death in battle to defend the polis (Aristotle) or in a political effort for the common good (Cicero), as we shall see in a later section.

Fortitude's place in the hierarchy of virtues further illuminates Aquinas' conception of this specific virtue. Even though fortitude concerns difficulty, Aquinas emphasizes the ordering due to excellence and the good, rather than difficulty per se. He says "simply speaking, that virtue is more excellent, which has the more excellent object,"[28] and "virtue essentially regards the good rather than the difficult."[29] Thus, intellectual virtues are more excellent than moral virtues (I-II 63.3); and among moral virtues, prudence and justice are more so than the other cardinal virtues, because they concern the perfection of reason itself and establishing this good of reason in human affairs.[30] This hierarchy of virtues by no means belittles the place and utility of the moral virtues though.

Evidently, other factors differentiate the four cardinal virtues and their associated virtues, including their necessity for flourishing.[31] One of the virtues without the others leads to situations that can no longer be considered virtuous. Fortitude in particular needs the virtue of justice, lest we put it to bad use. Aquinas integrates the notion of justice in true courage. Aquinas thus cites Ambrose, who says: "fortitude without justice is an occasion of injustice; since the stronger a man is the more ready is he to oppress the

27. *ST* II-II 123.4.
28. *ST* I-II 66.3.
29. *ST* II-II 123.12 ad 1.
30. Cf. *ST* II-II 123.12; *ST* I-II 61.2; *ST* I-II 61.3 and 61.4.
31. See Aristotle's *Politics* 1323b20–1323b35.

weaker."[32] In the fuller sense, specific fortitude has a general utility in safeguarding justice, temperance, and the other virtues.[33] As a specific virtue, fortitude involves the capacity to cope with difficulties and resist the destruction of our dispositions. This moral resilience especially helps us to act according to our reasoned commitments and long-term projects when facing the danger of death.

We can find analogues of fortitude in related domains such as altruism, generosity, and self-sacrifice, which contrast self-preservation and egotism. Individuals and groups confront and overcome threats to life, truth, and goodness with natural and acquired reactions, dispositions, and strategies. For example, seeking to protect other individuals and social groups or ourselves involves an intellectual, volitional, and emotional tenor in order not to be distracted from these goals and to overcome the challenge actively. On the contrary, the inclinations to self-preservation when controlled by selfish tendencies can undercut generous and altruistic acts.

Even though the language of "courage" or "fortitude" per se is not particularly central to the social sciences, researchers employ related terms when treating the management of emotions, especially fear and daring.[34] Synonyms of fortitude or related concepts that lend themselves to this investigation include hardiness, dauntlessness, intrepidity, pluck, spirit, heroism, daring, gallantry, bravery, valor, bravado, security, self-confidence, and self-efficacy. Contrasts to fortitude aid the illustration of its content and dynamics as well. Psychosocial researchers demonstrate the disruptive nature of extreme emotions, which would oppose this virtue: (1) fear, anxiety, fright, terror, cowardice, timidity, and the pathologies of hypochondria, panic, and phobia; and (2) fearlessness, aggression, audacity, rashness, recklessness, and indifference.[35]

Fortitude and its related virtues are most evident when we need to cope with stress-filled, difficult, or dangerous situations. This virtue group parallels major aspects of resilience. For example, the situation-behavior (psy-

32. *ST* II-II 123.12 ad 3 cites Ambrose's *De offic.* (I.35.176: *PL* 16.75A). In this regard Aquinas and Ambrose follow Cicero, who holds a reserve concerning those who exhibit fortitude without yet having proved their general moral equilibrium. The Roman statesman and philosopher warns that "a courageous spirit in a human who has not attained perfection and ideal wisdom is generally too impetuous" (*De off.* I.46; cf. I.7, 62–63, 66; II.33–34, 38).

33. *ST* II-II 123.12 corpus and ad 5; *ST* II-II 142.3 ad 1; *De verit.* 1, 12, 23; and 5, 1, 1.

34. Cf. Lazarus and Lazarus 1994.

35. Cf. Goleman 1995, 289–90.

chology) approach has investigated the dynamic of coping, as an aspect of resilience.[36] It theorizes that courageous, resisting, and initiative-taking acts are types of coping responses to different kinds of stress. Building upon a detailed taxonomy of coping,[37] Perrez and Reicherts[38] hypothesize that one type of stress-producing situation (type I) promotes more passive (hesitate and wait) and evasive (escape and avoid) reactions.[39] Another (type II) tends to promote more active and instrumental reactions and interventions.[40] They conjecture that these situations promote different emotions. Type I situations engender more depressive emotions and ones that aid in disengaging the agent from the danger or difficulty.[41] Type II situations involve more positive emotions that favor active engagement in the environment and direct confrontation with the stressor. Perrez and Reicherts suggest that this second type of stressful events, which humans interpret as controllable and not likely to reoccur, activates the agent positively to influence the stressor. I suggest that the first type of situation-oriented coping response can enrich our understanding of the virtues of resistance (patience and perseverance, and courage as a specific virtue), while the second can do so with the virtues of courage (as a general virtue) and initiative taking (magnanimity and magnificence).

36. According to Perrez and Reicherts (1992a, 5), the situation-behavior approach to coping, which is "transactional, contextual and process-centered, began to appear in the late 1970's stimulated by cognitive-relational theories of stress and emotion, which were a part of the broad cognitive movement in psychology." This work is contrasted with an earlier "psychoanalytical ego-psychology outlook in which the emphasis was placed on coping as a personality style," e.g., defensive strategies (repression-sensitization).

37. Meinrad Perrez (1992, 5–8) develops an extended coping taxonomy, which involves the following classifications: (1) coping with a situation can demand instrumental, passive or evasive action; (2) the agent can cognitively relate to (represent) the situation in either seeking or suppressing information; and (3) the agent can opt to either chose to reevaluate the situation or change his goals. Insights into these "coping responses" involve the way in which they distinguish between objective parameters and subjective perceptions.

38. We should associate Perrez and Reicherts' (1992a, 29) "situation-oriented" approach with two other types of coping operation: (1) the representation-oriented type of coping that searches for or suppresses information; as well as (2) evaluation-oriented coping, which changes intentions and goals, or reevaluates the situation.

39. The Type I coping situation is characterized as follows: "If a stressful event is perceived as of low controllability and with high expected probability for reappearance, subjects react with rather negative emotions and with stronger evasion, passivity and disengagement" (Perrez 1992, 13). This type of stress situation can have a tendency to promote a depressive emotional pattern.

40. Cf. Perrez 1992, 6 and 13; Lazarus and Folkman 1984.

41. Cf. Perrez 1992, 6; Klinger 1977; Lazarus, Kanner and Kolkman 1980; Fridja 1987, 295, 298.

Managing Human Fear

Neurophysiological Science on Fear and Timidity

In order to understand fear-related moral phenomena and dispositions, we need to observe how humans experience fear. The contemporary neurological and physiological sciences offer detailed analyses of fear and timidity, as well as daring and boldness To chart the phenomena of human fear at neurological and physiological levels offers us a further tool to know and manage fear. For example, we can log the trajectory of a fear-evoking sound. What spontaneous neurological and physiological reactions does a fear-inspiring noise precipitate in us? Through our ear, brainstem, and thalamus, we first sort out the physical sound wave. With the amygdala and hippocampus, we compare it with other sounds. Finally with the auditory cortex, we analyze it in order to determine its origin. This process startles us into alertness.

If we cannot pinpoint the source and meaning of the sound, then we start a more in-depth analysis; we use the amygdala, hippocampus and prefrontal cortex, which at the same time heighten our uncertainty and fix our attention on the sound's potential sources. If this process fails to resolve the query about the noise's origin, the amygdala sounds an alarm that activates the hypothalamus, brainstem and autonomic nervous system. We then experience apprehension, subliminal anxiety, and edginess. The body prepares itself for movement as the autonomic nervous system (through the emergency-response hormone—corticotrophin) charges the cardiovascular system, muscles, and gut to act. The muscles of the vocal cords tighten, giving a higher-pitched voice. Norepinephrine (noradrenaline) heightens the sensory circuit's receptivity. At this point, unconscious anxiety pierces consciousness, and we start to feel fear.

We experience other related fear-reactions, such as a blanched face and fearful facial expression; tensed muscles; an increased heart rate and heightened blood pressure; slower breathing; focused attention on the source of fear; and a racing of the mind that seeks to resolve the fear-dilemma or to respond to the related danger.[42] This neurophysiological description is not the whole story of human management of fear.

At a second level, temperament traits involve fearfulness and timidity.

42. Cf. Goleman 1995, 6; 297–300 and Kagan 1994.

Jerome Kagan (1994) identifies timidity and its contrary, boldness, as two of the four major temperament types.[43] As mentioned in chapter 2, according to Allport and a wide consensus of psychologists, temperament is a dynamic of behavioral, emotional, and cognitive patterns.[44] Temperament is a collection of types of personality differences, which we can detect at an early age. It influences how we develop our characters, involve ourselves socially, and manage fearful situations. Its impact is due to underlying physiology and neurochemical levels of reactivity, which we can educate to a certain extent.

Having an easily aroused neurochemistry (and neural circuitry), timid personalities tend to avoid the unfamiliar, shy away from the uncertain, talk less to strangers, and more easily suffer anxiety. Timid children have higher levels of reactivity across the range of sympathetic nervous system indices (resting blood pressure, pupil dilatation, norepinephrine markers). From birth, their hearts beat faster than other infants' when faced with novel or strange situations. This easy arousal seems to underlie their timid temperament, which means they are more likely to react to new people or situations as if they were threats.[45]

These indicators suggest why we should consider an individual's acquired vulnerability and resilience in the context of temperament and character developments. Not that our temperament is our destiny, but temperament types can heighten risk or protection for an individual in a particular situation. An individual's neurological reactivity, with which he is born, serves as the basis for learning to cope in social interactions or to build on the temperament as a strength.[46] This second factor helps us to further understand fear and timidity. As for the neurological effects of fear, considerations of an individual's temperament are necessary but insufficient to explain the moral quality of human agency and character.

43. Kagan (a University of Harvard researcher) posits at least four temperamental types: timid, bold, upbeat, and melancholy. Each type involves a particular pattern of brain activity. These types nonetheless are involved in further innumerable differences in temperamental endowment. On the dimension of temperament that ranges from boldness to timidity, cf. Kagan 1994, esp. 155–57.

44. Cf. Allport 1937/1961; Durkin 1995, 71.

45. Furthermore, Goleman (1995, 216–18; 221–23) notes that they have been found to be at higher risk for developing anxiety disorders, such as panic attacks.

46. As in chapter 3, a timid temperament has been shown to be a protective dynamic in situations demanding violence avoidance and intellectual/academic achievement; cf. Consortium 1994, 275.

Psychosocial Sciences on Fear and Attachment

The emotion of fear is more than its neurochemistry and neurophysiology or its relation to temperament traits. Other important domains involve its relationship to attachment, its utility, its purpose, and its evolutionary origin.

Sociobiologists and psychologists deem fear a survival-promoting tendency;[47] it responds in the face of certain "natural clues to an increased risk of danger."[48] Without having to learn how to formally assess the particular risks involved, an individual has survival advantages based in his ingrained capacities to respond appropriately with avoidance, flight, resistance, or the like.[49] John Bowlby identifies some natural clues of danger for humans: strangeness (unfamiliarity), sudden change of stimulation, rapid approach, height, and being alone.[50] He correlates fear and attachment, which are not simply opposites. When we feel secure (well attached), we are not fearful. Inversely, when we feel afraid, we are not secure. The same circumstances often activate fear and attachment behavior together. When feeling afraid, people not only exhibit fear behavior, but also attachment behavior. For example, infants cling to their mother or father; children run for peer or adult protection; adults find shelter in the tried and true sources of support, such as spouses and friends. Likewise, when people feel secure they are more apt to explore potentially fearful new situations. Infants momentarily distance themselves from a parental source of attachment and security while probing a new surrounding.[51]

What implications for resilience and courage arise from this correlation

47. By natural tendency, they mean a disposition that (1) promotes the survival advantage for the individual, his/her genes, or related gene pool (species) and (2) has been acquired through natural selection and is passed on through genes or conditioning. Cf. E. O. Wilson 1975/1978; Pope 1994.

48. Bowlby's attachment theory (1969/1982) is embedded in a general theory of behavior employing several trends from biology and social sciences: psychoanalytic orientation; the biological discipline of ethology, which views behavior in an evolutionary context; psychobiology; control-systems theory; Piaget's structural approach. Cf. Ainsworth et al. 1978, 3–4, 20.

49. Daniel Goleman (1995, 297) efficaciously summarizes contemporary psychosocial theory (in an evolutionary perspective) on the utility of fear: "'The emotional mind is our radar for danger: if we (or our forefathers in evolution) waited for the rational mind to make some of these judgments, we might not only be wrong—we might be dead. The drawback is that these impressions and intuitive judgments, because they are made in the snap of a finger, may be mistaken or misguided. [. . .] Fear, in evolution, has a special prominence: perhaps more than any other emotion it is crucial for survival. Of course in modern times misplaced fears are the bane of daily life, leaving us suffering from frets, angst, and garden variety worries—or at pathological extreme, from panic attacks, phobias, or obsessive-compulsive disorder."

50. Bowlby also notes the tendency to respond more strongly when two or more natural clues are simultaneously present (cf. Ainsworth et al. 1978, 20).

51. Cf. Ainsworth 1978, 22.

between fear and attachment? And how might courage be rooted in attachment not only to an affective source, but also to rational meaning? First, the "survival advantage" (evolutionary resilience) and disadvantage (vulnerability) of fear reactions depend upon the situation and individual. For example, the short-term advantages of being reactive to real danger can become a lasting problem when the brain resets its reactivity according to an experience of trauma. In this case, the brain's predispositions react "like a car stuck in perpetual high gear";[52] we then need to reestablish emotional calm.[53]

When inadequately attached, moreover, we can exhibit an increased flight tendency. Bowlby's research suggests that when humans have no personal attachment, we more readily exhibit a flight, rather than a fight, movement. To flee a dangerous situation is necessarily neither inappropriate nor uncourageous. However, we need to counter such a tendency when the situation involves a cause worth defending. Likewise, the lack of attachment security in the face of fear can disrupt our attention,[54] self-confidence, and self-efficacy.[55] This situation can incapacitate the rational analysis we need to adequately assess what is appropriate, what is courageous.

Second, in terms of resilience, security-producing attachments can contribute to the strength we need to assess the situation calmly and rationally, in order either to flee or to fight in a free and fitting way. We might also extend these reflections on attachment-based security to the emotional and affective (and not simply intellectual) attachment to sources of meaning and truth. If feeling attached includes a secure sense of meaning and finality, then attachment involves a source of strength to control fear and to more readily confront its source.[56] In summary, fear and attachment correlate in both uncourageous vulnerability and courageous resilience. Ill-adapted fear

52. Goleman (1995, 206) notes that there can be excessive fear or hypersensitivity to it, when the amygdala and its connected regions fix a new setpoint during the moment of trauma.

53. In emotional relearning, as when overcoming the learned fear of a post-traumatic stress disorder (PTSD), the neocortex is critical in redressing the amygdala in having an appropriate, milder reaction to objects related to the trauma. Natural relearning occurs when we encounter the feared object without truly scary consequences. However, in a PTSD, this spontaneous relearning fails to occur. According to Goleman (1995, 207–8), "but given the right experiences, even PTSD can lift; strong emotional memories, and the patterns of thought and reaction that they trigger, can change with time. This relearning, Charney proposes, is cortical."

54. As was illustrated earlier (Wilson and Gottman 1996, 201), the high levels of arousal, such as when we are deeply under the influence of fear, can have detrimental effects on attentional process and in turn on our resiliency.

55. Cf. Bandura 1986; Rutter 1990.

56. Cf. Ainsworth et al. 1978, 20–22; Bowlby 1969/1982.

reactions and inadequate attachment can accentuate vulnerability.[57] On the contrary, emotional, willed, and intellectual attachment to sources of meaning and truth and to stable and solid relationships can serve resilience.

Enhancing Aquinas' Analysis of Fear and Timidity

In spite of his archaic theory of the movement of body heat and vital spirits, Aquinas makes pertinent phenomenological observations about the physiological and psychological effects of fear.[58] For example, we experience a chilling and a loss of spirit, speechlessness and trembling, blushing (from shame as a type of fear) or turning pale (when facing the fear of death), as well as attack-wariness and heightened flight-readiness, to name but a few.[59] While retaining some relevance, these insights are incomplete, and his physiology is outdated. We can renew Aquinas' anthropology through integrating neurobiological and physiological observations on the effects of fear and daring and contemporary temperament theory on timidity. In their well-defined domains, these contemporary sciences help us to understand fear and timidity more fully. Yet, we need a moral context, which Aquinas can provide, in order to understand better how fear and timidity influence our moral acts and dispositions.

57. Certain existential and psychoanalytical insights further illustrate the dynamics of fear and anxiety. In particular these approaches widen the domain of fear beyond considerations of death and physical danger. According to Paul Tillich's existentialist approach (1952/2000), fear and anxiety have three objects: first, physical dangers and death; second, doubt and meaninglessness; and third, guilt and condemnation. Tillich illustrates the need for courage to assume the existential (irresolvable) anxiety that constitutes the way that human beings must face not only death and physical dangers, but also threats to meaning and social participation (including salvation). This insight has value and application beyond the limitations of his existential project. It suggests distinguishing two basic types of fear: (1) an everyday fear whose concrete object threatens physical life and meaning, and (2) an ultimate fear whose object concerns at least a moral order. This ultimate fear also refers to a revealed moral order and our relationship with God. This discussion will continue later in the context of Aquinas treatment of acquired and infused virtues of fortitude, in chapter 7.

Erik H. Erikson, furthermore, in his psychoanalytical approach, construes anxiety to influence the three human processes: the somatic processes inherent to the organism, the ego processes that organize experience, and the social processes that involve interpersonal roles and activities. At the somatic or biological level, we experience pain and tension. At the psychological level, ego undergoes a type of anxiety that puts pressures on self-individuation. Finally, at the social science level, we face the panic emanating from a group. Cf. Erikson 1950/1985, 34–37. According to Erikson (1950/1985, 24–25), the psychotherapist "deals above all with human anxiety," which is based in conflicts that are present already in young children. This emphasis on conflict finds its origin in Freud's first focusing on mental disturbance.

58. We should further specify Aquinas' physiology of emotions: e.g., fear involves the sensitive appetite, accompanied by a transmutation; Aquinas in this regard takes his leads from Aristotle and from Damascene, the latter of whom uses the image of contraction (*sustolen*) to speak of fear (*De fide orth.* III.23; cf. *ST* I-II 41.1 sc and obj.1).

59. Cf. *ST* I-II 44.2 obj/ad 1; 44.2 obj/ad 2; 44.3; 44.2 obj/ad. 3; *ST* II-II 125.

Aquinas' interest in how human animality interrelates with moral and spiritual life leads him to pay searching attention to how human emotional capacities relate to moral acts and dispositions. In chapter 3, we treated Aquinas' theory of emotions and virtue. Here we need to specify the roles that fear and daring play in his approach to the virtue of fortitude.

While aiming to integrate pertinent neurophysiological observations on fear phenomena, we need to look beyond these phenomena for a rational and moral domain. For Aquinas, fear is an emotion of the soul *(passio animae)*.[60] Through it, we relate to an evil that seeks to overcome a particular good.[61] Through the virtue of fortitude, we master such fear, as a special emotion whose object is "a future evil, difficult and [almost] unavoidable."[62] Fear and daring, although of key importance for us to understand resilience, are only a part of the emotional picture. In general, the irascible or contending emotions help us to manage sensible good and evil that are arduous to attain or avoid.[63] Fear and daring face some great danger. However, these emotions are supported by the other irascible emotions: hope and anger.[64]

We cannot understand human fear however without reference to love of particular goods. Love underlies all human agency. Likewise, resilience studies cannot simply focus on the emotions directly rooted in difficulty. Our emotions and efforts in hardship find their sources in the love and desires that motivate and sustain us.[65] Aquinas recognizes that our two major emotional capacities—the concupiscible and irascible appetites—collaborate in morality. The concupiscible appetite aims at sensible good or evil per se. The irascible, on the contrary, perceives the good or evil in hardship. Aquinas says that the passions of the irascible faculty relate primarily, if not

60. Aquinas treats fear as a passion (cf. *ST* I-II 23.4; *ST* I-II 41–44) and as a gift of the Holy Spirit (cf. *ST* II-II 19.1–12).

61. Cf. *ST* I-II 41.1 co.

62. *ST* I-II 41.2; cf. *ST* I-II 42.1. Aquinas sometimes speaks of the evil as being irresistible or unavoidable (cf. *ST* I-II 41.2; 41.4; and so on) and at other moments as being *almost* unavoidable (cf. *ST* I-II 41.2 ad 3; 42.3; 42.4; 43.1). The second seems to be the general meaning since he explains that when the evil is *absolutely* unavoidable even fear is lost in despair; for fear requires hope of escaping the future evil. Cf. *ST* I-II 42.2; and *Rhet.* ii.5, where Aristotle claims that those who are on the scaffold, facing immanent death, are not afraid.

63. Cf. *ST* I-II 60.4; cf. *ST* I-II 25.1; *ST* I-II 40–48.

64. Cf. *ST* I-II 23.2; 23.3; 35.2; *ST* I-II 40–48.

65. We need to recall also that Aquinas distinguishes love as emotion from love as an act of the will. His understanding of love outstrips sensuality, since we find fulfillment in the joy of charity, the highest form of friendship. Cf. *ST* II-II 23.1; *ST* I-II 25.3 and 25.4; *ST* I-II 28.

exclusively, to the two movements of *aggredi* (initiative and attack) and *sustinere* (resistance and endurance).[66]

He does maintain that neither anger nor hope[67] (nor their related virtues—meekness and magnanimity or humility) are the cardinal points of the irascible power, since, as he observes, "anger and hope do not move men as does fear of death."[68] The irascible appetite concerns an ordered configuration of the passions of fear and daring, hope and despair, and anger, which respectively relate to the virtues of fortitude, magnanimity, and meekness, in addition to the other virtues related to fortitude.

The clarity of Aquinas' philosophical psychology is admirable, but how useful is it for moral theory confronted with contemporary psychology and neurophysiology? We find its pertinence in his theory of moral habituation and virtue, where (as suggested in chapter 3) Aquinas' views cast needed light on the way in which we can employ human emotions to confront and overcome human difficulties. However, Aquinas considers the natural temperaments or psychosomatic forces toward being courageous,[69] without the neurological and biochemical nuance possible through contemporary research and theories. Nonetheless, his moral teaching provides relevant lessons and a larger moral framework. In particular, his moral theory resists confusing natural character traits (or neurological reactions) with the virtue (acquired disposition) of fortitude. It also offers a basis to counter reductionistic tendencies, which assert that natural temperaments render this virtue redundant or disprove its existence. For Aquinas, character traits (temperaments) are in some way natural, although given in unequal measures—one person has more or less than another. Even though the powers in which these traits are found correlate with the virtue of fortitude (forming its material basis), we acquire this virtue through courageous acts, and we diminish it through contrary ones. Although a natural temperament to-

66. *ST* I-II 25.1; 25.3.

67. In one sense, we can hold that hope (the human passion) is the greatest of human passions since through it we attain all of our human projects. Hope is an effect of the arduous desired good on the human person. Human action is a result of working toward the hoped-for future good. Unless one is plagued by constant fear or anger, hope is the motor for the majority of human action (cf. *ST* I-II 25.3).

68. *De virt. com.* 12, 26.

69. See *ST* II-II 123.1 ad 3; *ST* I-II 63.1. In this regard, Aristotle distinguishes natural virtue from virtue in the strict sense; cf. *NE* vi.13 1144b3, 1144b34–1145a1. Aquinas discusses natural or innate: *dispositio* (*ST* II-II 141.1 ad 2; *ST* I-II 63.1), *inclinatio* (I-II 6.5 ad 2), *habitus* (I-II 51.1), *potentia* (*ST* II-II 4.1; *ST* I-II 10.2).

ward courageousness may make the further acquisition of that virtue easier, fortitude in act or disposition is not assured.

The natural inclinations, which are on a different level than temperament, serve as a basis for Aquinas' virtue theory. They establish a dynamic foundation for the virtue of fortitude and for understanding emotional phenomena of fear and temperamental timidity.[70] We can find reasons to be courageous and to master fear, at different levels, in the inclinations toward self-preservation, family and social life, goodness and truth, and flourishing.[71] These inclinations provide a formal cause for fortitude. They indicate a larger framework for managing emotions, that of natural law.

The natural desire to know truth, for example, leads us to seek not only to extend our knowledge, but also to communicate and even courageously defend it when fear affects us. Truth's effusive effect aids us in overcoming timidity and fear through particular acts of fortitude. When a friend is slandered, our inclination to truth predisposes us to defend the truth that we have come to know (and love). Our fear of others or of their malicious slander and our natural timidity might hinder our efforts. Yet the thirst and quest for truth serves as an efficient cause of the courageous defense of particular truths. An inclination is already a movement toward action. However, we each need to expound reasoned responses and strategies in order to overcome fear and to prevent similar situations in the future. Admittedly, in the case of calumny against a friend, we rely on more than an inclination to truth. In this example, our will is engaged because of our friendship and our inclination to the good of social life, which provide further efficacious causes for action.

Although aspects of Aquinas' discussion of the physiological transmutations related to fear are outdated, his understanding of the formal element, the movement of the appetitive power of the soul, remains pertinent,[72] though misunderstood. While needing further defense, Aquinas' hylomorphic principle provides a deeper philosophical basis on which to graft contemporary insights of neurobiology and temperament theory. The human soul, as principle for human agency, interacts with our emotions. As we have argued in chapter 3, Thomas's explanation of emotion and bodily

70. Aquinas does not neatly distinguish natural from rational inclinations. An excessively definite split results from later philosophical and theological developments. Cf. Kent 1995.

71. Cf. *ST* I-II 94.2.

72. Cf. *ST* I-II 44.1; and *ST* I-II 28.5.

changes, at least at one level, sounds contemporary. However, we cannot understand Aquinas' insights unless we take them in the context of the existence of a human soul and its rational capacities for moral judgment; that is, we must employ a realist metaphysical framework. He uses the notion of the human soul to explain the rational movement involved in moral agency and emotions. This conception of the soul, which needs further explication, can assure a unity and depth to morality that is not evident in neurological and physiological theories when specified as exclusive (reductionist) approaches. Aquinas' framework for and understanding of the deeper rational (cognitive and volitional) roots of fear-provoking phenomena thus provides additional explanatory power concerning human responsibility for actions done in or from fear. In effect, his anthropology and moral theory allow us to analyze another level involved in managing hardship, a moral resilience.

Aquinas' Typology and Moral Evaluation of Fear

Neurophysiological, psychological, and social insights on fear, timidity, and anxiety contribute a better understanding of different types of fear and resilience. Thomas distinguishes fear according to its objects, causes, and effects, which are in turn relevant for adjudicating the morality of acts done in or from fear. Aquinas bases his moral evaluation upon the act's rationality, voluntariness, and goodness.[73] He notes that fear can influence voluntariness for the better and for the worst.

Aquinas distinguishes natural from nonnatural emotions and fears by the diversity of their objects.[74] He calls a movement in general and a passion in particular "natural" when nature inclines us thereto, either with or without the apprehensive faculty. In the case of the natural emotions of love, desire and hope, natural inclinations lead us to pursue what is good and to avoid what is evil. Thus, we naturally fear death, as a *malum naturae*.[75] We naturally shun and fear a life-threatening evil, because we naturally desire to exist.[76] On the other hand, we exhibit a material and nonnatural fear of painful evil when we shrink from fighting evil, simply because of the pain

73. Aquinas requires that the intention and the object be good and the circumstances be favorable (cf. *ST* I-II 6–21).

74. Cf. *ST* I-II 41.3.

75. Cf. *ST* I-II 42.2. In other passions however, the natural inclination is not sufficient, for we need perception or knowledge for pleasure and sorrow; cf. *ST* I-II 31.1, 31.3; 35.1.

76. Aquinas (I-II 41.3) follows Aristotle (*Rhet.* ii 5 1382a22) in distinguishing painful and corruptive evil, the latter of which involves death.

involved.[77] These intuitive and nonintuitive insights underlie his more developed theory and typology of the emotions.

Thomas defends a typology of fear, which has enduring features and resembles cognitive theory. He argues that humans exhibit six types of fear: "laziness, shamefacedness, shame, amazement, stupor, and anxiety."[78] Aquinas explains that we experience them according to the diversity of the objects of fear and certain special reasons. Fear can have either an internal or an external object: the evil in our own action or in some external thing. On the internal level, humans beings fear the toils that burden our capacities. Thus laziness *(segnities)* arises when we back away from an effort for fear of the labor involved. We also fear disgrace in the sight of others, which involves disgrace from future (shamefacedness—*erubescentia*) or past deeds (shame—*verecundia*). On the external level, evil overcomes the human rational capacity of resistance. Dumfounded amazement *(admiratio)* arises when the magnitude of the evil surpasses our ability to rationally master it. Unusual and rare evil stupefies us *(stupor)*. Lastly, anxiety *(agonia)* concerns an unforeseen or unforeseeable evil, which surpasses our capacity to resist it, for example, when unpredictable misfortunes cause us anxiety.

Significantly, love is the primary cause of fear, as already mentioned. Aquinas confirms that love serves as the basis of human emotions and moral agency. It causes fear either as an efficient cause or as a material disposition.[79] Cognitive, volitional, and affective objects inform fear, which as a passion of the soul takes its species from both natural and artificial objects. The efficient cause of the object of fear inflicts the feared evil (on the part of the person feared). While our material disposition to be fearfully affected by such an object causes fear inasmuch as it disposes the thing to be an evil for us. Therefore, love causes fear, both since the evil of losing or not attaining the loved-good is fear's object and since loving that good is the basis for our fear of being deprived of it.

According to Aquinas, human beings do not fear what we can control

77. Since this fear of pain opposes the natural inclination for self-preservation, Aquinas deems it nonnatural. The fact that we experience pain in attempting to prevent our own death is not a natural deterrent, when we understand the severity of the threat. Shunning pain demands an inclination toward, knowledge of, and commitment to a higher goal; cf. *ST* I-II 41.3.

78. He follows St. John Damascene: *ST* I-II 41.4 (cf. obj./ad 1 and sc); *De fide orth.* ii.15: PG 94.932C. Here Aquinas delicately declines from following Aristotle, who divides the species of fear according to four species of sorrow (cf. *Rhet.* II.5 1382a22).

79. In order to illustrate the role of love in fear, Aquinas (*ST* I-II 43.1 sc) cites St Augustine: *OQ.* 83, qu. 33; *PL* 40.23. BA 10.97.

(what is within our power and will). He applies this principle to whether a human can fear sin or even can fear fear itself. Since a human being can normally control his own will,[80] we do not, properly speaking, fear the evil of sin. Sin involves a voluntary act, and at a natural level we abhor evil; the basic inclination of the will moves toward good rather than evil. In a secondary sense, however, we fear sin insofar as an external cause can attract our volition toward sin.[81] Furthermore, we fear fear itself through a natural reaction, which we can nonetheless overcome by intelligent choice.[82]

These ontological and psychological types of fear prepare for further moral ones. Aquinas distinguishes praiseworthy and blameworthy fear. As a general avoidance tendency *(universaliter fugam)*, however, it contains the notion *(ratio)* neither of moral good nor of moral evil.[83] It is natural.[84] For Aquinas, we adjudicate fear as praiseworthy (good) or blameworthy (evil) only when it concerns ordinate or inordinate reason and behavior. The good of human agency consists in its being duly ordered; evil acts consist in the opposite. Accordingly, we need to duly dispose the emotions (and will) through the rule both of human reason and of eternal law or God's reason.[85] Human reason acts as the proximate and homogeneous cause of the action, while divine reason acts as the primary cause of rectitude. This due ordering demands that we subject the emotion to reason's rule (a loving rule), indicating that we should shun *(fugienda)* some things and pursue *(prosequenda)* others. Thus, inordinate fear involves shunning what reason adjudicates that we need to endure. Ordinate fear, on the contrary, involves shunning what reason requires us to shun.[86] We morally evaluate detrimen-

80. Weakness of will and the acquired internal dispositions to vice are not the free voluntary acts that Aquinas refers to here. See his reflections on vice: *ST* I-II 71–89.

81. Aquinas holds that external causes (such as association with wicked people) can incline the will to sin; cf. *ST* I-II 42.3. Furthermore, we should fear the evil of sin as regarding the effect of sin (such as separation from God, cf. *ST* I-II 42.3 ad 1).

82. An emotion first arises from an external cause (an imminent evil) that incites our imagination. In this sense, we fear the necessity of fearing the threat of such a great evil. However, as subject to the will, the lower appetite obeys reason in driving away inordinate fear. Indeed, we do not normally will to fear "fear itself" Cf. *ST* I-II 42.4. This insight recalls the modern expression of F. D. Roosevelt, "The only thing we have to fear is fear itself" (*First Inaugural Address*, 4 March 1933).

83. Cf. *ST* II-II 125.1 ad 1; *ST* I-II 24.1 and 24.3. Aquinas follows Aristotle in this regard (cf. *NE* ii.4, 1105b31–1106a2).

84. This aspect of the emotion of fear is natural according to Thomas and Aristotle (cf. *NE* iii.10 1115b26–8; cited in *ST* II-II 125.1 obj. 3). As natural, fear cannot be the matter of sin according to St. John Damascene (cf. *De fide orth.* II.4 and II.30: PG 94.876A and 976A; cited in *ST* II-II 125.1 obj. 3).

85. Cf. *ST* I-II 71.6; *ST* II-II 109.2.

86. Cf. *ST* II-II 125.1.

tal or constructive effects of fear in terms of how fear correlates with reason, volition, and action; we can furthermore rationally weigh even fear that surfaces from preconscious or unconscious levels.

Aquinas reports a number of ways in which fear can hinder action. It can disturb reason, upset the imagination (promote failure in concentration-demanding tasks), and deflate motivation (inhibit action through fear of toil).[87] Since bodily members instrumentally cause external actions, fear can perturb an act by hindering the bodily members through disturbances to human reason, imagination, or motivation.[88] The correlation of fear and counsel illustrates this point. Aquinas says: "when a human is affected [. . .] by a passion, things seem to him greater or smaller than they really are: thus [. . .] to him that fears, what he fears seems more dreadful. Consequently when wanting of right judgment, every passion, considered in itself, hinders the faculty of giving good counsel."[89] He affirms that a certain type of fear unravels reason, insofar as it "drives away all thought and dislocates the mind." In particular, the stronger the passion the more detrimentally it sways us. In extreme cases of fear, even though we seek counsel, we are unable to use it appropriately.

Aquinas resists, however, the opinion that every type of passion or fear "disturbs repose" and hinders reason.[90] Fear does not hinder human agency always or in every way. Thomas affirms that we need fear "so as to shun what reason requires to be shunned."[91] Such positive types of fear move us to take counsel and to pay greater attention (work with solicitude). According to Aquinas, fear can be conducive to action "insofar as it inclines the will to do that whereby a man escapes from what he fears."[92] Especially in the face of a great, proximate, or difficult-to-overcome evil, moderate fear that does not disrupt reason can incite us not only to work well and to employ our own rational guidance, but also to seek counsel.[93] Aquinas highlights how this moderate fear can help us to apply ourselves with greater attention

87. Cf. *ST* I-II 44.4.

88. Aquinas' principle is sound, although he explains its function in an outmoded physiology; for example, he says that the bodily members are unable to act appropriately since fear deprives them of their "heat" (cf. *ST* I-II 44.4).

89. *ST* I-II 44.2 corpus (and ad 2). Aquinas draws support from Cicero (cf. *De quaest. Tuscul.* IV.8.).

90. Cf. *ST* I-II 44.2 obj. 1 and corpus.

91. *ST* I-II 125.1.

92. *ST* I-II 44.4 ad 3.

93. Cf. *ST* I-II 44.4. *ST* I-II 44.2 ad 3; and *Rhet* II.5, cited *ST* I-II 44.2 sc.

and carefulness.[94] For example, an ordinate fear can help servants to not neglect their service and to work more carefully.[95] This insight parallels those on positive types of anxiety that promote focused attention, as found in resilience research, which aids in accomplishing tasks and overcoming fear.[96]

In conclusion, Aquinas recognizes four characteristics of positive fear: (1) we realistically fear what is fearful; (2) it motivates us to seek counsel and social support; (3) it does not gravely disturb our reasoning; but rather (4) it even heightens our attention, reflection, and carefulness. Intense fear, on the other hand, blocks adequate reflection and leads to compromised choices. For example, when fear limits our considerations to what can go wrong, it robs our confidence to do what is good and right;[97] furthermore, when it focuses our attention on a real but lower-level evil, it hinders us from freely pursuing larger considerations and more important projects. Fear promotes or hinders not only human survival (resilience and vulnerability), but also moral agency and flourishing (moral resilience). In Aquinas' perspective, survival-promoting tendencies must be weighed in the context of other natural tendencies that give us the fuller context—in particular, the tendencies to family and social life, goodness and truth, flourishing and ultimate goals. Reflections on resilience and human attention furnish phenomenological and neurological descriptions of the anatomy of fear. Aquinas furnishes a moral theory that enlarges these observations and reflections to include considerations of normative agency and human flourishing. The above-mentioned distinction between praiseworthy and blameworthy fear in action, furthermore, ultimately evolves around not only the nature of related acts, but also the degree to which we do an action voluntarily or not, which leads us to a more direct treatment of the virtue of fortitude.

Fortitude: Characteristics and Context of Moral Resilience

The previous discussion on the emotion of fear serves as a prelude to a dialogue on the virtue of fortitude: its definition, characteristics, and context. Indeed, we have not yet fully addressed Aquinas' definition of forti-

94. Cf. *ST* I-II 44.2 ad 2; Bowlin 1996.

95. We need not restrict St. Paul's insight about service to mundane matters; see Eph 6:5, which Aquinas cites (*ST* II-II 125.1 obj./ad 2). Cf. *ST* I-II 44.2 ad 2 and ad 3.

96. See chapter 2's study on "Volitional Processes: Attention and Competency." Cf. Wilson and Gottman 1996.

97. Cf. DeMarco 1996, 45.

tude. In order to do so, we need to examine the inclination and emotion of daring, as well as further moral and social issues concerning fear.

Resilience as Courageous Coping with Fear and Daring

The various types, means, and social dimensions of fear raise questions about how human beings can best manage fear phenomena. Triggered by impending pain, danger, evil, illness, and separation, a simple fear reaction can lead to bouts of worrying or inactivity. In extreme situations, such fear can become chronic or pathological.[98] Without blurring the spectrum of fear phenomena, I shall examine resilient coping with fear and daring. However, before addressing strategies and perspectives on managing fear and daring, I shall reiterate neurobiology's findings on positive and negative types of fear. Neurobiology situates fear's survival advantage in a tendency to be alert to dangers. As a vigilance response, it can serve as a type of buffer against difficulty. Fear triggers the emotional brain to focus its attention on the source of worry, ignoring any other concerns for a time, until a viable solution surfaces.[99] When having trouble finding straightforward solutions to the source of fear, we find a further survival advantage in a constructive reflex to mull over a problem at hand; this mulling is called worry. Furthermore, fear or anxiety can serve in protecting us against an experience. According to Freud, a non-neurotic type of anxiety can signal in advance a disturbing encounter, and thus protect a person, as would a shield.[100] Researchers have shown that worry can protect the subject from certain effects of anxiety.[101] To keep in mind fear's positive basis and effects is important in order to understand the negative side to fear and its management as well.

The danger of fear, from the resilience perspective, is that it can lead into a vicious circle, where worry, anxiety, and fretting distract and debilitate us. Vulnerabilities increase when failure leads to fears of failure, which in turn lead to beliefs that we shall continue to fail.[102] Michael Rutter's research

98. Pathologies related to fear include phobias, obsessions and compulsions, panic attacks, obsessive-compulsive disorder, generalized anxiety disorder, fright neurosis, and so on. Cf. Freud 1922/1955, 27; Anthony and Cohler 1987, 13; Goleman 1995, 65–69.

99. Cf. Goleman 1995.

100. It can protect one from the stimuli, which could otherwise be damaging. This insight follows Freud's theory that protection from stimuli is almost more important that the reception of stimuli. Cf. Freud 1922/1955, 27; and Anthony and Cohler 1987, 13.

101. Cf. Roemer and Borkovec 1993; Goleman 1995, 68.

102. There are other risks involved with disordered fear and anxiety. According to Murphy and Moriarty (1976, 202–3), "Increases in vulnerability are seen when the interaction between the child and

(1990) suggests that resilience processes reduce fear-failure chain reactions. But how can we stop vicious circles of anxiety-producing interchanges? Indeed, researchers have suggested that self-soothing, game playing, and self-confidence can help us manage fear and control anxiety.

Emotion researchers demonstrate that self-soothing is one of the basic life skills in question. According to psychoanalytic thinkers, such as John Bowlby and D. W. Winnicott, the art of soothing oneself in the face of fear is a fundamental skill. They even hold that it is one of the most important psychic tools, whose strength comes from our primary attachments; these attachments serve as the basis for handling fear, as well as daring.[103] Lizabeth Roemer and Thomas Borkovec (1993), psychologists from Pennsylvania State University, have studied fears and phobias in order to identify strategies for calming vehement emotions. They have found that insomnia patients' anxiety surfaces in cognitive and somatic forms. The cognitive form (worrisome thoughts) disrupts sleep more than somatic arousal (sweating, a racing heart, and muscle tension). One solution involves shifting attention away from the worries in order to break the cycle of fear or to uproot its persuasive power. Roemer and Borkovec offer a twofold analysis of this solution. On the one hand, we must become mindful of the fear and evaluate its causes. Through self-awareness, we attempt to recognize as early as possible the start of a worry episode. Then we can actively challenge the worrisome thoughts through self-talk and investigation: Are they well founded? Are there other possible outcomes than the one we fear? What constructive steps can we take? And so on. This activity can decrease the neural activation (limbic drive) underlying low-grade anxiety. On the other hand, inducing a relaxed state can counter our anxiety signals. Once aware of anxiety, we can exercise relaxation efforts to calm the body so that we can better handle sources of stress.[104]

Researchers have found that children's play serves as a coping tool.

---

the environment results in new limitations or difficulties, new threats to homeostasis and to integration, new obstacles to learning, increased difficulties in mastering anxiety, or negative expectancies." According to Norman Garmezy (1990, 530), the compounding of anxieties might constitute a component of low social class status that relates to the actualization of risk and inhibits escape from it.

103. Cf. Bowlby 1969/1982, 1973; Winnicott 1971, 1987. Goleman (1995, 57) explains: "The theory holds that emotionally sound infants learn to soothe themselves by treating themselves as their caretakers have treated them, leaving them less vulnerable to the upheavals of the emotional brain."

104. In more extreme cases, phobia, obsessive-compulsive disorder, or panic disorder, Goleman (1995, 69) suggests that medication might be used to interrupt the anxiety cycle, while a therapy is still needed to lessen its recurrence.

George Eisen (1988) has studied play as a strategy for managing fear. His interdisciplinary study has demonstrated how children's play helps them to understand and manage otherwise unbearable situations. Indeed, children's play can promote information processing (even in the face of the absurd), problem solving (proximate and long-term solutions) and coping (facing fear and finding balance "in both spiritual and physical realms" in the midst of threats and hardships). It can even function as a survival technique in extreme cases. Play can make such contributions at both conscious and unconscious levels. At a conscious level, the skills that we acquire through complex problem-solving games, in playing chess or other strategic games, for example, can aid us in resolving, or at least not being overwhelmed when we have to face, complex situations, unexpected events, or even chaos. At the unconscious level, through play, the mind can find a balance. For example, when faced with trauma, play facilitated distraction can allow the mind time to decipher the situation and to settle itself.[105] These insights on children's play give hints for similar benefits that certain types of games (and recreation) might have for people of all ages.

Psychosocial researchers have shown that hope, self-confidence, self-assertiveness, and initiative taking help us to confront, to counter, and to correct difficulties. They can help us manage the obstructive and debilitating nature of fear. Belief in our own self-efficacy, according to Stanford psychologist Albert Bandura, underlies our sense of optimism or hope, and how we use our capacities. Those who do not believe in their own self-efficacy have a greater fear of failure and fear of seeming inept.[106] Lazarus maintains that hope is an expression of intellectual intelligence, which resists anxiety and depression.[107] Timid and pessimistic temperament traits, however, need not impede positive emotions and dispositions. According to Kagan, natural timidity, for example, does not obstruct humans from becoming self-

105. Eisen (1988, 98) says: "Looking beyond the external, we must also consider a subconscious drive, a constant striving on the part of the human organism to reestablish an equilibrium in an utterly irrational and unpredictable universe. Techniques of opposition, coping, and survival were reflected in children's play—not unexpectedly—for play practices and behavior became compensatory agents in relieving stress and providing a process for accommodating the painful and traumatic existence of that time."

106. Cf. Bandura 1986. According to Rutter (1990, 206–7, 197), evidence suggests that the establishment or maintenance of self-esteem, self-confidence, and self-efficacy through supportive personal relationships or successful task accomplishment serves as a protective process when facing difficulty (cf. Bowlby 1969/1982 and 1973; Wilson and Gottman 1996, 190–220; Yule 1992, 191; Maughan 1988, 214; Consortium 1994, 276).

107. Cf. Goleman 1995, 87; Lazarus and Lazarus 1994, 74.

confident, hopeful, and even bold in practice.[108] Assertiveness training for passive or impulsive individuals can promote balanced responses, rather than passive or aggressive ones.[109]

Seeking a Mean between Fear and Daring

Aquinas utilizes the philosophical tradition of Aristotle to establish that fortitude is a mean between fear and daring.[110] Fortitude is a mean, a middle ground where reason manages the proper use of fear and of daring—each with its own benefits, drawbacks, opportunities, and threats.[111] We search for a mean between fear and daring for various reasons: situations differ; not everyone acts (perceives, feels, thinks, and chooses) the same way when faced with the same dangers and labor; we neither realize the gravity of the situation nor feel fear or daring in equal measure.[112]

Aquinas argues that this just mean has a particular tenor. Fortitude primarily concerns fear and flight from the impending evil, and only secondarily concerns daring and fighting the difficulty, "for it is more difficult to allay fear than to moderate daring, since the danger which is the object of daring and fear, tends by its very nature to check daring, but to increase fear,"[113] as Thomas says. In between fear and fearlessness, we experience security, in which we hold firm in the face of fear. Fortitude calls immediately upon security in order to overcome fear or at least hold it at bay.[114] Through this virtue, we establish security, based on confidence, hope, and the other pertinent virtues.

Although fortitude directly regards fear and security, it indirectly regards hope and confidence, inasmuch as fortitude makes use of daring. This collaboration of fear (or security) and daring (or confidence) highlights two

108. Cf. Kagan 1994; Goleman 1998, 68–72.

109. Cf. Bloom 1996, 99–100.

110. The Philosopher discusses fortitude as a type of mean or just measure in regard to both fear and daring or confidence (as Barnes translates it). It is a just means between the extremes (*mesotes*) of fearlessness or rashness and cowardliness. Thanks to well-established dispositions and well-engaged rational, volitional, and affective management, the courageous person experiences fear and confidence when he should, how he should, and where he should (cf. *NE* iii.6, 1115a12–13). Aquinas refers to chapters 2 and 3 of Aristotle's *NE*, in which the Philosopher gives a rich explanation of fortitude. Aquinas' own commentary on the *NE* on these chapters is also very illuminating (*In Eth.* 2, 8, 341; 3, 14, 529 and 3, 18, 583).

111. Cf. *ST* II-II 123.3.

112. Cf. Aquinas' *Commentary on the NE*, and Aristotle's *NE* iii.8, 1116 a 16.

113. *ST* II-II 123.6. Cf. Aquinas' *Commentary on the NE: In Eth.* 3, 18, 583.

114. Cf. *ST* II-II 129.7; and *ST* I-II 45.2.

aspects of fortitude. In addition to managing emotions (an internal dimension), the virtue of fortitude draws upon skills and dispositions needed in posing related external acts. Thus, we employ a social dimension that goes beyond the acts themselves.

Personal skills and our sense of self-efficacy are not insignificant, when we face danger, as Stanford psychologist Albert Bandura's research demonstrates.[115] Indeed, the internal dimension of fortitude is necessary, but not always sufficient, to resolve the situation. Fortitude (as managing emotions of fear and daring, of flight and fight tendencies, of security and confidence) will not of itself overcome the difficulty and danger. Nor does it necessarily accompany prudence, or skilled navigating, or temperance, which are all needed in situations such as storms at sea. Bravery is only part of the picture; other skills in the end will save the day (and the ship). Likewise, other virtues will complete fortitude. To overcome fear, courage employs audacity or confidence, which has its source in hope, inasmuch as it is the mother of daring.[116] Hope and confidence always have important roles to play in courage and its related virtues. Later we shall examine how fortitude moderates fear of failure and how initiative-taking virtues bolster hope and confidence.

Why does fortitude need to correct fear more than daring? Fear inclines us to withdraw from a menacing evil. If we calm fear, then our volition will not be disinclined from following reason; we can apply reason to resolve the situation on hand; in turn, we can more clearly adjudicate the type of initiative to employ in order to overcome the difficulty.

Aquinas argues that fear in a certain way is more primary to the virtue than daring or confidence because of the centrality and universality of the fear of death.[117] Like the other virtues, fortitude is built upon natural human inclinations. It is natural to love one's own life, and to fear and resist the loss of it.[118] In the hierarchy of goods, nonetheless, the goods of family and society are even more important than one's own life. The undeniable so-

115. According to Bandura, who pioneered studies in self-efficacy (1986), self-confidence positively correlates with self-efficacy, the belief we have about our own capacity to perform. Skill alone is not enough though, we have to believe in our skills and the way that they can develop. Especially in resolution of a difficult task, those who doubt themselves perform less efficaciously than do those who believe in their abilities (their self-efficacy).

116. Cf. Labourdette 1961–62, 23–40.

117. *ST* II-II 141.3; *ST* II-II 123.3; *ST* I-II 45.1 corpus and ad 2.

118. Cf. *ST* II-II 123.4 ad 2.

cial dimension of these natural inclinations inhibits an egotistical reading of fortitude. Fortitude of soul assures that no fear of the loss of a bodily good or the facing of a bodily evil—the loss of one's own life being the greatest—will deter us from following the greater goods of reason.[119] This vision of fortitude has several practical ramifications.

First of all, Aquinas argues that if we stand firm in the most fearful of situations (the danger of death) then we should be able to stand firm in the lesser ones.[120] However, the opposite is not necessarily the case. Aquinas is not simply identifying the logical divisions of a virtue and its determinate matter here. Rather, there are pedagogical implications concerning how we develop our own self-image and attachments; how we judge what holds the greatest value in life; and how we foresee our own death.

Secondly, although the virtue pertains to an extreme, we should not confuse fortitude with the lesser instances where humans also need to manage fear bravely.[121] Other virtues also deal with the fear of failing or losing different lovable things, such as money (generosity, magnificence), pleasure (temperance), and the like. The specific virtue of fortitude more properly concerns the danger of death, which is the most fearful and most inevitable extreme. Fear, rather than daring, has a certain priority in fortitude,[122] because human beings are mortal, and must pass through the experience of death. Ultimately neither daring nor skills, neither medical treatment nor wisdom and the like can liberate us from the inevitability of death. Because it is more difficult to allay fear when faced with danger than to move to attack, endurance is the chief act of fortitude,[123] as we shall discuss more in the context of the endurance found in patience and perseverance and the capacity for attacking or enterprise found in magnanimity and magnificence (in the next two chapters).

Aquinas argues that properly speaking, fortitude concerns the fear of the fatal danger, rather than every kind of constancy, when facing difficulty.[124] Fortitude as a special or specific virtue, "strengthens against dangers of death,"[125] moderates "fear and daring in connection with dangers of

119. In this context, Aquinas once again quotes Augustine to ensure that the discussion remains on a spiritual level: *De morib. eccl.* (i, 15; *PL* 32, 1322), cited in *ST* II-II 123.4 obj. 1.

120. Cf. *ST* II-II 123.4.

121. Cf. *ST* II-II 123.4 ad 1.

122. Cf. *ST* II-II 123.3.

123. Cf. *ST* II-II 123.6.

124. See Aquinas' *Commentary on the NE: In Eth.* 2, 8, 339; and *ST* I-II 61.4.

125. *ST* I-II 61.3.

death,"[126] and endures "not any kind of hardship, but only those connected with the danger of death."[127] This further specification of the special virtue of fortitude does not diminish Aquinas' or our interest in a whole range of levels and types of fear and daring. It rather focuses on intense passions that concern unavoidable situations.

We shall finish this section with the question of false fortitude, which raises important issues for resilience in general, and moral resilience in particular. The tradition of distinguishing true fortitude from its semblances predates Aquinas. Although his full definition of fortitude admits a larger range of acts, it denies the status of "true fortitude" to acts that merely resemble it.[128] Semblances of courage are inadequate in several ways. Two people might perform the same external act, without having an adequate goal, motive, understanding, or intention. The moral quality of their acts can also differ because of significant circumstances. Aquinas enumerates five semblances of fortitude; they are acts that we do (1) since we have miscalculated the danger involved because of our ignorance; (2) since we have already escaped from similar situations; (3) since we count on own capacities or skills; (4) since emotions have moved us, such as sadness or anger; and (5) since we seek egotistical self-interest, personal honor, pleasure, or profit.[129] For Aquinas' perspective, fortitude is more than standing steadfast in the face of danger. This insight offers correctives for reductionist approaches to resilience theory and ethics.

Social Dimension: Human Struggles and the Common Good

Aquinas addresses the social dimension of true fortitude more clearly in the context and finality of courageous acts and dispositions. Fortitude per se is neither instinctive optimism nor firm confidence in our natural or acquired abilities. It is more than fighting fitness, or brute resilience.[130] It demands an ordered social resolve.

Not every fear-producing object is of equal value. Since some are more

126. *ST* II-II 137.1.

127. *ST* II-II 147.2 ad 3.

128. Aquinas associates true virtue and true fortitude, which he distinguishes from counterfeit fortitude (cf. *ST* II-II 123.10 ad 3; *ST* II-II 123.1 ad 2; *ST* II-II 128 ad 7; *ST* II-II 64.5 ad 5; *ST* II-II 23.7 sc and corpus; *ST* II-II 61.4 obj; *ST* I-II 65.1).

129. Aquinas comments directly upon Aristotle's analysis (*NE* iii.2: 1116a16–1117a27); cf. *ST* II-II 123.1 ad 2; *In Eth.* 3, 16, 557–60; and 3, 17, 571–82; *De virt. com.* 6 ad 4; *De virt. card.* a. 2; *ST* I-II 58.4 ad 3.

130. Cf. Pieper 1949–59/1966, 117–21 and 126–27.

worthwhile, useful, and socially fitting, Aquinas seeks the most worthy object for true fortitude. Thus, he explores the social dimension of fear and this virtue. St. Thomas affirms (to a certain extent) Aristotle's position that courage in battle is more honorable than courage at sea. To allay the fear born of human vulnerability in battle-ready fortitude is more honorable because of its social import. But how do morality and the social value of our acts correlate? Aquinas employs Aristotle's definition that "fortitude is chiefly about death in battle"[131] in order to explore the social hierarchy of fortitude. The notion of battle, for both these thinkers, is not primarily synonymous with alleviating fear, but rather with protecting and promoting the common good.

While employing Aristotelian social thought on fortitude, Aquinas goes beyond it in the ways in which he construes both battle and the common good. Thomas, on the one hand, enlarges Aristotle's notion of battle. Aristotle argues that not just any risky business deserves the highest and most proper name of fortitude, but only that concerning military warfare.[132] Although Aquinas follows Aristotle in his *Commentary on the Nicomachean Ethics*,[133] he nuances and expands his own position later in the *Summa theologiae* to include the danger of death in different types of struggle and effort.

Aquinas widens the notion of what type of action we fittingly call fortitude, from the narrow category of military battles to a broader category including private (nonmilitary) struggles that aim at a higher good. Aquinas affirms not only that fortitude involves voluntarily putting ourselves in danger of death, but also that it results from having directly chosen some higher good. Thomas also specifies that true fortitude involves only the dangers that ensue "directly on account of some good," as when defending "the common good by a just fight."[134] We can draw at least two conclusions: true fortitude for Aquinas is found (1) neither in unjust battles (2) nor in just battles in which we have engaged for reasons other than the common good.

131. *NE*, iii.9, 1115a34–35, cited in *ST* II-II 123.5; cf. *In Eth*. 3, 14, 537 and 540.

132. The dangers of death due to sickness, storms, journeys, and the like do not concern fortitude strictly speaking for the Greek philosopher. For Aristotle the truly brave person is the citizen-solder, not the professional soldier. The former is brave not because of compulsion, nor profit, nor thinking his side is stronger, but rather because it is noble, virtuous to be so. Such a citizen-soldier does not flee from the post in the face of danger, but prefers death to disgrace. Cf. *NE* 1116a15–1116b2 and 15–22.

133. *In Eth*. 3, 14, 542; cf. *ST* II-II 123.5.

134. *ST* II-II 123.5.

Contemporary writers have taken up these issues, while often denying that they need to tie fortitude to the common good, or good per se.[135]

For Aquinas, defending the common good through a just battle or struggle can take military or nonmilitary forms. The judge or private person who does not waver from a just judgment because of death threats illustrates this latter case. Aquinas construes such situations to include personal assaults, struggles, or battles.[136] He can thus, unlike Aristotle, affirm that humans express true fortitude when we attend to a sick friend while fearing a deadly infection, or when we labor to support a family or accomplish a pious action that involves facing the danger of death during a journey, for example, on business trips or on pilgrimages, which were particularly tiring and perilous in Aquinas' time.[137]

On the other hand, Aquinas widens Aristotle's notion of the common good as well. He holds that fortitude is concerned not only with the greatest dangers (i.e., threats to life) but also with the noblest of dangers, defending the common good with one's own life.[138] Although they agree here, and Aristotle's notions of fortitude *(ἀνδρεία)*, honor *(καλός)*, virtue *(ἀρετή)*, flourishing *(εὐδαιμονία)*, and common good[139] are parallel in key ways to Aquinas', Thomas outstrips Aristotle's notions, especially that of the common good. In particular, Aristotle's notion of the common good does not extend to all mankind, and it seems to be culturally and historically bound.[140]

Aquinas uses both Cicero and the Christian tradition to expand this notion of common good. First, Cicero extends the notions of common good and fortitude beyond that of a state at war.[141] This movement is developed in the Ciceronian and Stoic consideration that fortitude deals with all virtuous matters *(honestas)* when we face fear and daring.[142] They also maintain that we must use this virtue in service of the common good *(salute commu-*

135. Cf. Porter 1998b; Canto-Sperber 1996b; Cunningham 1985; Dent 1981; and von Wright 1963.

136. Cf. *ST* II-II 123.5.

137. Cf. *ST* II-II 123.5; Congar 1974, 338.

138. Cf. *In Eth.* 3, 14, 537–38.

139. Cf. *NE* ix.1169a10–11.

140. Aristotle's use of the notion of the common good has been critiqued because of its limitations to the particular realm of family, friends, and the *polis* in which one lives. Some critiques admonish Aristotle for his limiting the application of virtue, in particular justice. Although he had rather extensive knowledge of other states—he studied some 159 different constitutions in his *Politics*—he remained provincial in his view of justice and the common good, according to MacIntyre 1988 and 1966/1999, and Randall 1960.

141. Aquinas quotes Cicero's *Off.* (I.22) in his *ST* II-II 123.5 obj. 2.

142. Cf. *Rhet. ad Her.* III, iv, 9.

ni) and not only for one's self.[143] Stoics were the first in the Greco-Roman world to hold systematically that justice concerned humanity as such, irrespective of the *polis*.[144] The basis for this widening of justice and the common good was the Stoic vision of the universality of the supreme law, which binds all rational creatures to obey it, and human nature, through which we recognize the humanity of others.[145]

Aquinas takes inspiration from these philosophers to establish an ordering of types of fear and responsibility in fortitude. However, he nuances such movements (acts and dispositions) with a notion of the ordering of love that finds its inspiration and definition in the Christian tradition. Indeed, the philosophical fortitude that Aquinas promotes involves moral standards that offer the foundation for moral resilience.

Progress and Failure in Fortitude

A series of diagnostic questions on the resilience of fortitude-building and fear-management strategies will guide our dialogue with Aquinas on the development of fortitude. What can failed fortitude teach us about moral vulnerability? How can the resilience perspective aid us in understanding developmental matters and educative strategies related to fear and difficulty?

Failed Fortitude, Failed Resilience

According to Aquinas, we learn fortitude not only through positive experiences of managing fear and daring, but also through experiences of failed fortitude. His treatment of failed fortitude is found in the context of his moral evaluation of fear in fortitude and his understanding of the vic-

143. Cicero affirms, "the Stoics correctly define courage *(fortitudo)* as 'that virtue which champions the cause of right.'" *Off.* I.62. It is not enough to avoid doing injury to others, but the courageous person must prevent injury (*Off.* I.65). One strives to be virtuous in deed and not simply to be thought virtuous.

144. However, the Stoic account of justice and law did not prevail against the dominant practices of Greek and Roman polities (cf. MacIntyre 1988, 147–52).

145. Nonetheless, their hierarchy of responsibilities involves family, city, and then universe; notably, foreigners fall in this latter category. Cicero explains that we owe foreigners a very limited fare: water, fire, and honest counsel—whatever is common property. Private property is not owed to others; since "the resources of individuals are limited and the number of needy is infinite, this spirit of universal liberality must be regulated [. . .] in order that we may continue to have the means for being generous to our friends." *Off.* I.52.

es opposing fortitude: timidity and cowardliness, rashness and recklessness. Through cowardliness or rashness (in act or *habitus*), we at least temporarily override or dismiss a higher good for the sake of a disordered attachment to a lower one. We do not, however, always face two viable and equal options. When we do not abide in the good prescribed by reason (a reasonable good) because of excesses of fear or aggressivity, we miss the mark of courage. We do not persevere in the goals and intermediate ends (means) that we have conceived as good and fitting. We might cede to the threat of losing external goods: prestige, reputation, honor, power, wealth, bodily integrity, and even physical life. We can fail to courageously manage our emotions when faced with dreadful bodily ills, especially death.[146] We can even fail because of more mundane dangers, toil, or assaults.

We can unsuccessfully express fortitude either in a single act (of weakness, for example), in an underdeveloped disposition, or in an ingrained vice (*vitium*). Aquinas distinguishes vicious dispositions from virtuous ones according to their rapport with reason.[147] Both are operative *habitus;* yet both do not have the same relation to cognition and volition. In failed fortitude, we redirect a primary inclination in a way contrary to the common good, our flourishing, and ultimate goals. We acquire a bad *habitus* when we have connaturalized ourselves to an activity that contradicts reason, human nature, and the virtue.[148] For Aquinas, fortitude entails that we manage, in a just mean, the two emotions of fear and daring.[149] We seek a just measure involved in situations that inspire confidence and fright.[150]

146. Cf. *ST* II-II 123.4.

147. Cf. *ST* I-II 70.4 ad 1.

148. Therefore, a bad *habitus* is not a *habitus* in the same way as a good *habitus*, since a good *habitus* is a connaturalization according to nature, according to human reason—while a bad one is a deformation, or a connaturalization against the ends proper to human nature. A bad habit can be further differentiated from an evil *habitus*, the former of which lacks freedom and could be caused by bad environment, culture, family upbringing, and so on, while the later of which involves voluntary choice for evil. Vices have three characteristics. They involve acting (1) wrongly, badly, or evilly, (2) connaturally, with the pleasure of habitualization, and (3) without resistance of reason (I-II 78.3 ad 1).

149. Aquinas follows Aristotle, for whom courage is an intermediary disposition between the vices of cowardliness and rashness. Aristotle says: "With regard to feelings of fear and confidence courage is the mean; of the people who exceed, he who exceeds in fearlessness has no name (many of the states have no name), while the man who exceeds in confidence is rash, and he who exceeds in fear and falls short in confidence is a coward." (Ross and Urmson trans. of *NE* ii.7, 1107a33–1107b3. Cf. *NE* iii.6, 1115a6; *EE* 1228a38; *EE* 1228b4.

150. Cf. *NE* iii.7, 1116a10; iii.6, 1115a27–28; iii.8, 1117a30. The moral virtue of courage for Aristotle involves disposing the irrational part of the soul to participate in the principle of reason in order to develop further our virtuous dispositions and to act concretely in situations that inspire confidence and fear.

Properly speaking, timidity or fearfulness *(timiditas)* is the opposite of fortitude. The danger of death[151] and, in a secondary way, other difficulties causes us to act without due confidence or without proper estimation of the stakes at hand. Aquinas chiefly adjudicates human acts according to their end,[152] which allows him to hold that bravery is not found in dying (or killing oneself) in order to avoid disagreeable situations such as poverty, lust, or slavery.[153] Inasmuch as fortitude involves daring or audacity that draws upon hope, inordinate fear of death (or other objects) tends toward despair and undercuts the movement of this disposition.[154] His conception of fortitude is not physical resilience at any cost. The moral dimension leads human agency toward a particular type of resilience that involves normative standards.

The distinction between praiseworthy and blameworthy fear in action hinges on how voluntarily we act.[155] A person can be responsible for an act done when experiencing fear, if he doesn't let the emotive reaction control his reasoning (that is, if he contains fear at the level of sensate appetite, protecting his reason and rational appetite). In most cases, we can and must intentionally rectify our relationship with the person or thing that produces fear in us. Otherwise, we conform ourselves to the fear; we accept or even will the effect of fear (which opposes our rational good). That we will the effect of fear (e.g., being immobilized by a fearful situation) does not simply concern that we experience a real cause for fear. Rather, it specifically involves that we handle the cause of fear in an unreasonable way. According to Aquinas, fear's inordinateness is due to the will inasmuch as we "deliberately shun something against the dictate of reason."[156] In order to override the inhibitive effect of fear we need to act with reasoned daring or patient perseverance.

The question remains: when does fear excuse us from sin and willed moral vulnerability?[157] For Aquinas, acting from fear involves an admixture

151. Cf. *ST* II-II 125.2.

152. Cf. *ST* I-II 1.3, *ST* I-II 18.6.

153. Cf. *ST* II-II 125.2 ad 2. Here he once again follows Aristotle.

154. Cf. *ST* II-II 125.2 ad 3; *ST* I-II 45.2. The sin of fear (the act of inordinate fear) is the beginning of despair: cf. *ST* I-II 40.4; *ST* I-II 45.2; and *ST* II-II 20.1–4. We shall discuss the relationship of hope and daring further in chapter 5.

155. Aquinas also uses a number of scriptural quotes in bolstering his arguments on sin and fear in *ST* II-II 125 (in order of citation): Ps 18:8; Eph 6:5; Mt 10:28; Ez 2:6; Ps 127:1; Mt 27:44; Jgs 7:3; Dt 20:8; Rv 21:8; Ps 18:8. Aquinas (cf. *ST* II-II 125.3) even asks: when is fear a mortal sin?

156. *ST* II-II 125.3.

157. Cf. *ST* II-II 125.4.

of voluntariness and involuntariness.[158] Fear-precipitated acts extenuate our responsibility to the degree that we are under the necessity of an imminent fear. Nonetheless, Aquinas also distinguishes between levels of voluntariness and responsibility. He says that "the evils of the soul are more to be feared than the evils of the body; and evils of the body more than evils of external things."[159] These three levels prioritize fearful objects. We rightfully fear most the evils of the soul that underlie moral vulnerability (the contrary of good and virtuous acts that underlie moral resilience). We should not fear such evils any less than the others, since love presses us to cling to good. Even though the second and third types of object are truly fearful, they should not cause us to renounce the good of virtue.[160] Whenever we adjudicate the dangers and evils of the body or external things as more fearful than the losing of the goods of the soul, we improperly order our loves and fears. Although fears may weaken our voluntary capacities, the virtue of fortitude constitutes the way to remain firm in the more fundamental goods and truths, even in the face of really dreadful evils.

How do misdirected passions and acts create *habitus* (vices) of timidity and cowardliness, fearlessness, and recklessness? Let us recall that through fortitude, we cope well with the emotions of fear, daring,[161] and pain when facing threats, especially to our own life; we discern, choose, and act in ordered, intelligent, and loving ways. We fail in fortitude, on the contrary, when we voluntarily let disordered passions of fear and daring affect our thought, will, and action. We can understand this latter case more fully in dialogue with the psychosocial sciences on issues such as learned helplessness and aggressiveness. Voluntary accord with disordered passions leads to acquired dispositions (at psychological and neurobiological levels) that prolong their effect of vulnerability. We thus acquire a moral weakness. We accept distraction (even relishing it) instead of concentrating our energies on more important goods, even those that we have identified as priorities for ourselves. We ingrain in ourselves patterns of fearful reserve and overbearing aggressivity.

When asking whether blameworthy fear opposes fortitude, Aquinas recalls that all fear arises out of love.[162] While we find the general source

158. Cf. *ST* II-II 125.4, where Aquinas cites Aristotle's *NE* (iii.1, 1110a4–19).

159. *ST* II-II 125.4.

160. Augustine, the Peripatetics, and Aquinas concur on this (cf. *ST* II-II 125.4 ad 3).

161. Cf. *ST* II-II 129.1 ad 2; *ST* II-II 123, articles 4 and 5.

162. Cf. *ST* II-II 125.2. Aquinas finds a source for this principle in St. Augustine (*Octoginta trium Quest.* q. 33: *PL* 40, 22), whom he quotes in *ST* II-II 19.3 and *ST* I-II 43.1.

of every virtue in ordinate love, every sin (disordered act) likewise finds its general source in inordinate fear—our inordinate fear of losing money (covetousness), pleasure (intemperance), and so forth.[163] In this extreme and exaggerated sense we even fear fear itself.

Fearlessness is another way in which we fail in fortitude. We can bring disaster, in seemingly heroic acts, through shortsighted audacity. We do not reasonably estimate the danger present to self or the community. We manifest fearlessness in unreflected recklessness from three sources.[164] According to Thomas, we can act fearlessly when we do not love self, others, or God in due measure.[165] We can also, through pride, err by favoring ourselves, while despising others. Lastly, we can act without due fear through a defect in reason. Through fearlessness, we fear neither what we ought to fear nor as we ought to fear it.[166]

Neurological, physiological, and psychological descriptions of these disordered dispositions add further nuance to the underlying biological and psychic interactions. They enrich our understanding of human anthropology. Nonetheless, they are not enough to comprehend the entirety of the moral act, neither as a disordered moral *habitus*, nor as failure in moral resilience. From Aquinas' moral analysis, fortitude fails when we act without a fitting and possible response, albeit at intellectual (reason and will) or emotional levels. Such failure can be a single happening. However, we form a moral *habitus* or vice in proportion as we repeat disordered acts. In turn, such an acquired vice disposes us to act more readily in similar ways. It makes us more vulnerable to the risks that fearful situations involve.

Aquinas' Developmental Perspective on Fortitude

What does Aquinas' developmental approach offer in the light of psychosocial reflections and research on managing fear and daring? In this section, I shall analyze Thomas's developmental insights and perspective

163. Cf. *ST* II-II 125.2 corpus and ad 1.

164. Cf. *ST* II-II 126.1.

165. Thomas recalls this fearlessness in regard to the unjust judge who feared neither God nor other people. Cf. Lk 18:2; *ST* II-II 126.1 sc. In the corpus of the response, Aquinas also quotes St. Paul's letter to the Ephesians (5:29). For Aquinas, although the vice of fearlessness mitigates our natural inclinations to love self, others, and God, it can never erase these natural inclinations, even in the case of suicide, through which someone seeks liberation from present stress, pain, and suffering, rather that being cutting off from these sources of love.

166. Cf. *ST* II-II 126.2.

in terms of the causes that ward off fear and the place that the natural inclinations and emotions have in the development of fortitude. His perspective illustrates a type of connaturalization that occurs through experiences of fear and difficulties, in the context of our quests for flourishing. Before attempting a response to our opening question, I would like to note that some thinkers have criticized Thomas's approach for its psychological shortcomings regarding human and social development. According to Jean Porter, although his account of the virtues remains fundamentally sound and normative, it needs reformulation since, as she says, he "has no sense of the dynamic development of the psyche, and, perhaps more importantly, he also has very little sense of the significance of social forces in shaping individual identity."[167] This critique, while expressing a valid concern to advance Aquinas and the tradition's reflections on virtue, seems overstated. There is no reason to defend Thomas for not having foreseen contemporary debates (and advances) concerning human individuation and socialization. However, we need to look deeper in order to examine the developmental insights that Aquinas expresses through his moral anthropology.

Aquinas cites Aristotle in identifying a number of causes (some of which are social) that drive fear away. The Philosopher says: "wealth, strength, a multitude of friends, and power drive fear away."[168] From this quote, Thomas draws on two psychological insights for warding off fear. First, concerning the material disposition to fear, he says: "some defect is, of itself, the cause of fear: for it is owing to some lack of power that one is unable easily to repulse a threatening evil." For example, we lack confidence of victory, when we fear not to have ample personal strength. Second, concerning the efficient cause of fear (of the person feared), he says, "it is owing to the fact

167. Porter 1995, 167. Porter (1995, 168) "reformulates" an education perspective on virtue, based on "how the prudent and virtuous person [. . .] is capable of rational self-criticism and transformation of her individual and cultural ideals for virtue, precisely in and through her continued reflective practice of the virtues." In particular, she (1995, 169) identifies "that the formation of a sense of individual identity, and the awareness of oneself as one human being among others, are both dependent on a capacity for empathetic identification with others. This capacity for identification begins to emerge as the child is taught to observe the norms of her society, to participate in its rituals, and, not least, to talk, and it continues as she tries on the roles and the recurrent narratives of her community through role-playing." A practical commitment to life and to being good (in whatever language it might take) is a basic condition for virtue education (including self-education). Porter expounds a framework (and ordering of the questions of morality) that emphasizes the interaction between individual persons and their wider communities. Concerning "the difficulties" in Aquinas' account of human faculties, she refers us to Anthony Kenny (1993, 145–160).

168. *Rhet.* ii.5, 1383b1–3; cited in *ST* I-II 43.2 sc.

that the cause apprehended as harmful is powerful, that its effect cannot be repulsed." For example, when the opponent is strong, or when we face an evil beyond the measure of fear (when in the throes of being executed, for example).[169] In this context, the place and utility of hope stand out; they become even more apparent when understood in the context of how we acquire virtue. In both extremely fearful things and more mundane ones, fear diminishes inasmuch as hope increases. According to Aquinas, whatever increases a person's power *(potestas)*, such as experience *(experientia)*, fosters a person's agency; it thereby strengthens our hope and weakens our fear.[170] These causes provide insights into personal development within a social context (friends, battles, society).

The natural inclinations, which serve as the formal basis to establish virtue, serve fortitude in a particular fashion. For Aquinas, the expression and development of the virtue of fortitude involves the interaction of several natural inclinations: the natural inclination to preserve one's own life; as well as the natural inclinations to pursue what is good and true, family life, and social interaction. We need to prudently seek a just mean;[171] in the case of danger and toil, especially concerning life-threatening situations (death in battle or for the common good), we need to develop proper relationships between these inclinations and more explicit personal and social goals.

In particular, the danger of death for a just cause demands that we adjudicate between the natural inclination to preserve one's own life (and perhaps to support our family) and the natural inclinations toward the good, the true. and the common good (and the ultimate good). Does such a situation involve a conflict between inclinations? In discussing fearlessness, Aquinas clearly speaks of this potential ambiguity of the natural inclination to self-love and protection: "And every man has it instilled in him by nature to love his own life and whatever is directed thereto; and to do so in due measure, that is, to love these things not as placing his end therein, but as things to be used for the sake of his last end."[172] His placement of the doctrine of human inclination in a larger framework of finality demands further pedagogical efforts. It demands that we nurture and educate such loves and inclinations in order to arrive at a "due measure." As we shall ex-

169. Cf. *ST* I-II 43.2.
170. Cf. *ST* I-II 42.5 corpus and ad 1; *ST* I-II 40.5.
171. Cf. *ST* II-II 123.3.
172. *ST* II-II 126.1.

plore later, Aquinas modifies the Aristotelian doctrine of the mean with Ciceronian teaching on natural inclinations, but also with Christian teaching on the place of community and the ordered relationship of human ends and flourishing.

While clinging to and pursuing good and resisting or avoiding evil are difficult, we develop fortitude through understanding, feeling, and acting well for difficult good ends, by employing good intermediate ends. We make such efforts only within the larger perspective of the other virtues and the whole gambit of human social potential. Aquinas uses the concept of connaturality to explain how the acquired virtue of fortitude entails a certain mental and emotional firmness, which does not lack a sense of development and finality. A human being "can achieve this steadfastness in a way which is connatural and peculiar to him, so that he does not abandon the good because of the difficulty of either fulfilling some strenuous task or enduring some oppressive ill."[173] This mental and emotional steadfastness entails a connaturalization of the emotions so that we use reason to guide our actions even in the face of oppressive difficulties. Aquinas holds that the actions that virtue produces resemble the actions that produce virtue (as a disposition). He says, "We become brave by accustoming ourselves to despise and endure terrors, and having become brave we are very capable of enduring terrors."[174] As discussed earlier, Thomas promotes the role of parents, teachers, and the law in the growth of virtue;[175] his conception of good dynamically leads from self-love to common good to ultimate good.

Pleasure and pain play a special role in fortitude and in its associated virtues.[176] Love and the natural inclination to preserve one's own life serve human motivation and action. Fortitude concerns loving some present or future good that an impending danger and difficulty threatens. However, it is not about pleasure and pain as its proper matter, which is rather fear and daring. Nor is it about a false bravery, through which we do what appears to be brave, when really seeking some temporal good—pleasure, honor, gain—

173. *ST* II-II 139.1.

174. *In Eth.* 2, 2, 264 (cf. *NE* 1104b1–3).

175. Cf. *ST* I-II 95.1; *ST* I-II 63.1; *ST* I-II 94.3.

176. As was demonstrated earlier, Aquinas' position on education in virtue in general and fortitude in particular is marked by Aristotle, who promotes a right education (*παιδεία*) of moral excellence that trains human pleasures and pains in order to "to delight in and to be pained by the things that we ought" (*NE* Book II.3 1104b7–8). Aristotle's three definitions of courage as an acquired disposition help to illuminate education in courage. Cf. Smoes 1995, 210–12.

or avoiding some disadvantage—pain, blame, loss.[177] In moral virtues, pleasure and pain serve as intermediate ends, through which we acquire a good end or avoid an evil one. Fortitude, however, is more complicated than some incidences of moral virtue, whereby pleasure accompanies but also characterizes the virtuous activity.[178] It involves difficulty and therefore a mixture of pleasure and pain.[179]

Thomas's focus on the philosophical physiognomy of fortitude does not spell forgetfulness about finality and flourishing. Flourishing is the continual motive and dynamic end that animates human life, especially when we face fear.[180] It involves a cognitive, motivational, and emotional coping tool. A contemporary question is whether we necessarily need to tie fortitude with flourishing (and goodness). Aquinas affirms that brave persons do what is fitting to the virtue of fortitude, while they seek, at the same time, eternal and human flourishing and goodness.[181] Fortitude itself is good. Yet it loses its fullest meaning and power to move us when we abstract it from our love, desire, and pursuit of complete flourishing (including its social dimension, the common good, and ultimate good).

In order to complete Aquinas' position on fortitude and to identify its relevance for moral resilience, we need to at least mention the architectonic position that anger (and the other passions) plays in the operation of this virtue, especially regarding daring, enterprise, and aggression. In the practice of virtue, moderate anger is instrumentally useful to reason. Particularly in regard to fortitude, inasmuch as anger cooperates with reason, it renders action more prompt and more resistant.[182] These considerations of the development or employment of fortitude lead to others on education in this virtue.

Education in Fortitude

Thomas's developmental perspective becomes clearer through an investigation of his counsel concerning how we prepare ourselves for fearful situ-

177. *ST* II-II 123.1 ad 2; *In Eth.* 3, 18, 583 and 587; see also Aristotle, *NE* 1116a15–1117a28.

178. Cf. *ST* II-II 58.9 ad 1, citing Aristotle (*NE* i.8, 1099a18–22).

179. Cf. *ST* II-II 123.8; see also *ST* I-II 31.3–5.

180. In his discussion on whether brave people act for the good of this *habitus*, Aquinas gives a striking example of how flourishing serves as a motivation (cf. *ST* II-II 123.7).

181. On the goodness of fortitude, Aquinas cites Aristotle (*NE* iii.10, 1115b21–24). On the relationship between fortitude and flourishing, Aquinas (*ST* II-II 123.7 obj. 3) quotes St. Augustine (*De Trin.* xiii.8: *PL* 42, 1022–23, and *De morib. eccl.* xv. i, 15: *PL* 32, 1322).

182. Cf. *ST* II-II 123.10; see William C. Mattison's (2001) treatment of Aquinas on virtuous anger.

ations. It suggests a narrative method that employs imaginative foresight and self-calming efforts. In Aquinas' virtue theory, the courageous disposition is informed by reason and rendered more obedient and docile to reason through our successive experiences of mastering fear. We can draw from previously ingrained dispositions, which we have acquired through formally similar experiences and actions.[183]

To prepare oneself for the unforeseen is an integral, yet progressively acquired, characteristic of the virtue of fortitude.[184] Aquinas explains that courage involves both what is foreseen and what is unforeseen. Although fortitude concerns action in the face of sudden occurrences and unexpected dangers, it nonetheless involves the requirement that we prepare ourselves through imaginative and narrative efforts. For example, in choosing to ponder courageous people and stories, we progressively prepare ourselves for unpredicted events. Aquinas draws upon Saint Gregory the Great in this regard, when he says:

> the brave man chooses to think beforehand of the dangers that may arise, in order to be able to withstand them, or to bear them more easily: since according to Gregory, "the blow that is foreseen strikes with less force, and we are able more easily to bear earthly wrongs, if we are forearmed with the shield of foreknowledge."[185]

We should choose to prepare ourselves for a good number of dangerous and toilsome things and in so doing become at least remotely prepared for them. Such mental planning and narrative imagination is important: we can forecast some dangers and toil in life's great projects (involving family and education, business and politics, personal and ecclesial life); all people can expect to die, and we cannot exclude beforehand a painful or violent death.[186] The need for preparation has significant pedagogical implications, even concerning sudden events or surprises.

183. Aquinas draws heavily from Aristotle's insight on the acquisition of courage. In particular, Aristotle says that "by doing the acts that we do in the presence of danger, and being habituated to feel fear or confidence, we become brave or cowardly" (*NE* ii.1, 1103b17–18). Just as humans are usually strengthened through eating and physical exertion, so likewise in the case of fortitude; Aristotle argues that by "being habituated to despise things that are terrible and to stand our ground against them we become brave, and it is when we have become so that we shall be most able to stand our ground against them" (*NE* ii.3, 1104a28–1104b3).

184. Cf. *ST* II-II 123.9, where Aquinas once again cites Aristotle's *NE* (iii.9, 1115a32–35).

185. Hom. xxv *In Evang.* I: *PL* 76, 1259 c; cited in *ST* II-II 123.9.

186. Cf. *ST* II-II 123.11 ad 3.

Fortitude as a *habitus* is "made manifest chiefly in sudden dangers,"[187] according to Aquinas. To bravely confront unpredicted dangers (including dangers of death) without weakening or disorientation demonstrates that we have become disposed for courageous acts. Being prepared to be surprised is part and parcel of this virtue. Indeed, surprise exacerbates efforts to repulse evil in two ways. First, fear can overcome our capacities, when the magnitude of the evil startles us. Aquinas affirms that we can diminish such fear by premeditation. We train ourselves by thinking about possible situations of evil, even sudden, great, or long-lasting ones. Preparation helps us to correct emotion's tendency to exaggerate threat.[188] Secondly, a fearful surprise can further weaken us, when for lack of time it deprives us of the remedies and strategies that we might have mustered otherwise. In both these cases, suddenness can aggravate our vulnerability to fearfulness, while premeditative preparation for sudden fearful difficulty can aid us in mastering it rationally with emotional composure and a firm will.

The fact that we cannot know exactly when or how we shall die raises an epistemological-moral question: how can we be sure to exercise real bravery, that is, fortitude, in the fullest sense? It is only when we are actually faced with the danger of death that we shall know whether we shall be truly courageous or not. A similar query concerns whether we are really and fully resilient, before the final test. Aquinas uses a principle that is reasonable, yet difficult to verify. It concerns facing real and not imagined near-death situations. He claims that if we are able to do what is more difficult, then we shall be capable of what is less so.[189] A well-disposed capacity, though, does not guarantee we shall use it well; extreme situations have their ways of uprooting our best-laid plans. Not everyone, furthermore, has faced a real, sudden, or immanent danger of death, nor should we purposely put someone into such a situation. Imaginative proximity is another story. Those who have bravely faced a sudden danger of death, on the contrary, cannot count on their laurels. Nonetheless, given the nature of *habitus* and remote preparation, we can face real and imagined situations of death with relative confidence, according to Aquinas.

187. *NE* iii.11, 1117a17–22, cited *ST* II-II 123.9.
188. Cf. *ST* I-II 42.5 corpus and ad 3; *ST* I-II 42.6.
189. Cf. *ST* II-II 123.4.

Concluding Remarks on Fortitude and Resilience

St. Thomas develops a philosophical notion of moral fortitude that contains the following characteristics. Due to the virtue of fortitude, we firmly, rationally, and deliberately face dangers and bear toil. We find a mean between the extremes of fear (principally) and daring (secondarily). We confront death in the context of a just war or political engagement for the common good. His comprehension of fortitude and its contribution to moral resilience is richer than it might seem from this slim characterization. From Aquinas' moral, developmental, and relational approach to fortitude, we can extrapolate a moral resilience and a resilient fortitude.

Some other characteristics of fortitude underscore the contributions offered by resilience research. Resilience research has well illustrated that resilient individuals should not rest on their laurels or social supports. They need to apply themselves diligently in each situation that tests their acquired strengths. The virtue of fortitude, as an acquired strength, involves a dynamic interaction between perception, emotion, reason, and will. Neither do humans resiliently strengthen a virtuous disposition, like fortitude, by blindly copying a previous external act. Nor do we do so in isolation from other dispositions. Courage demands that we act creatively in a new situation that endangers us and causes fear. Courageous coping with conflict draws upon the expertise of virtues such as prudence, justice, and temperance. How can we courageously stand firm, if we misconstrue the adversity, or sacrifice the rights of others in our place, or cede instead to a desire for comfort? According to Aquinas, the principal virtues support each other. We can understand reasons for fortitude only in the context of our deeper goals, loves, and moral norms. Our courageous character shapes our irascible capacity, which serves not only our loves, but also the whole range of inclinations and emotions, cognitions, and volitions. Aquinas' doctrine of the connection of the virtues does not involve static perfection. It suggests a type of pedagogy toward growth and completion, which draws on internal and external collaboration and support. Psychosocial resilience research has highlighted the sociobiological and physiological working of fear and aggression, attention, and concentration.

This study has highlighted fortitude-related resilience-promoting strategies: self-soothing techniques, self-efficacy, and confidence, and so forth. A Thomistic anthropology can integrate these elements while offering a larger framework and guidance. Indeed, Aquinas provides a basis to promote a moral type of resilience. Not that the other bases are immoral. Yet the sciences, according to their own methods, either admittedly depend on fitting moral assumptions, make fallacious moral inductions, or ignore the issue. Admittedly, this Thomistic moral appreciation of resilience is neither modern nor postmodern in the limited sense of both terms. Rather, it represents a tradition that resists rationalistic and voluntaristic movements. In particular, it makes its own contribution to a moral type of resilience through its insights on ultimate finality, cognitive orientation and normativeness, affective motivation, and emotional and intellectual dispositions.

St. Thomas contributes his own insights regarding educational strategies as well. Courageous response demands self-knowledge and information about the origin of fear. It draws from our intended goals and commitments to norms, in addition to cognitive, motivational, and emotional dispositions to act courageously. We increase courageous outcomes when we imaginatively foresee events, such as physical and social difficulties, as well as moral and spiritual challenges. This type of virtue encourages self-preparation, vigilance, and practiced emotional control. It suggests the educational significance of literature and the arts that project difficult experiences that humans encounter. Our efforts at a controlled practice of emotions concerning hardships and trials demand that we do more than passively observe the situation. Rather, with active discernment, we select the objects of our attention and evaluate their effect on our society and selves.

In addition to the foreseeable events for which we can and should prepare ourselves, Aquinas recalls that sudden occurrences can surprise us. In the latter, we must mobilize our moral and intellectual virtues and other resources in creative ways. In order to continue on a virtuous developmental trajectory, such as a resilient type of fortitude, we prepare for the foreseeably unforeseeable future. The unexpected event calls us to apply our intellectual, moral, and emotional skills to new terrain; we need our wits to do so. We can learn from our successes and failures, from our good decisions and mistakes. We need to be vigilant in order to continue to do the truth in love.

As rich as this philosophical study of Aquinas and resilience research on the dispositional and emotional range of courage might be, it is incomplete. It needs to treat the philosophical dimension of the virtues of initiative and resisting in the next chapter, and the theological dimension of these virtues and related emotions in the last ones.

5

Constructive Resilience and Aquinas' Virtues of Initiative

The resilient child is oriented toward the future, is living ahead, with hope.

MURPHY 1987, 101.

Hope and foresight are vital for constructive resilience. Through individual and communal resilience resources, we muster hope, confidence, and generosity toward initiatives that have a twofold effect. Not only do they promote personal flourishing, they also promote community. Constructive resilience entails rebuilding in the wake of disasters. It empowers us to face the challenges present in worthwhile but difficult projects, enabling us to build something positive out of destructive events. The concept of constructive resilience can help to deepen our understanding of Aquinas' treatment of initiative. For Aquinas, besides what is specific to the virtues of courage and patience, there are the initiative-taking virtues of magnanimity (*magnanimitas*) and magnificence (*magnificentia*). Magnanimity, as a natural virtue of hope, regulates our emotional attachment to attaining possible goods, while it also strengthens us through the hardships involved in pursuing them. We can attain such goods only by investing ourselves in life's projects and by drawing upon the resources of others. The dynamics of human hope in initiative serves in the coping, resisting, and transformative effects active in the other virtues as well.

Arduous Activity: Confronting Difficulty with the Energy of the Passions of Hope and Daring

An analysis of Aquinas' notion of *magnanimitas* and *magnificentia* can help us to understand the dynamics of facing difficulty, of rebuilding life in the aftermath of destruction, and of performing generous acts that require confident risk taking to accomplish an important good. For Aquinas, these virtues are the key movements in the act of initiative taking or enterprise.[1] They pertain to self-preparation for and execution of excellent deeds. Through *magnanimitas,* we mentally and emotionally prepare ourselves for an arduous undertaking. For Thomas, the mind and will need to be assured and hopeful in great and honorable efforts.[2] We prepare our mind and whole person by measuring and imagining the opportunities and risks involved. *Magnificentia* involves not only the start, but also the development and the completion, of the act. It engenders external, generous acts of making or doing. We imagine magnificence's stages in the first moments of magnanimity (seen as a more general virtue), but need actually to execute the act without wavering from our initial confidence and purpose.[3]

Aquinas on Arduum: The Difficult Good

The difficulty involved in human initiative, especially magnanimous efforts, invites an initial study of what Aquinas calls *bonum arduum* (the difficult good).[4] In fact, his complex notion of magnanimity seems to concern all the difficulties included in seeking flourishing, which he and classical thinkers purport to be life's major project. Thomas associates *magnanimi-*

1. We already discussed Aquinas' notion of the irascible faculty in chapter 4.

2. In *ST* II-II 128.1 Aquinas borrows this key notion of magnanimity from Cicero's (*Rhet.* ii: 10–12) understanding of "confidence."

3. Cf. *ST* II-II 128.1; Cicero *Rhet.* ii: 7–10.

4. Cf. *ST* I-II 60.4; *ST* I-II 67.4 ad 3; *ST* I-II 40.1 ad 1; *ST* I-II 30.2 ad 3; *ST* II-II 161.1.

tas or *fidentia* with the disposition that prepares our minds for action in the face of the dangers of death (as a quasi-integral part of fortitude) or in any lesser hardship (as a secondary virtue related to fortitude).[5] Indeed the virtue of magnanimity includes the range of difficulties involved in the passion of hope (defined in terms of a difficult good)[6] and in the notions of greatness and excellence, as well as in honor itself.

Thomas construes virtue in general to concern the difficult and the good (*difficile et bonum*).[7] Indeed, we face continual challenges and opportunities in establishing the rational mean of the intellectual virtues and justice.[8] Because of the specific adversity in managing the passions in a rational way, we need the other moral virtues.[9] Even at the level of the sensitive appetite, which as a natural inclination is naturally subject to reason, both the passions themselves and their objects (when they are complex) resist reason. Rational failures are even more widespread when we aspire to an object that contains an aspect of greatness. Magnanimity involves a rational way of hoping for something great. Aquinas addresses the correlation of reason and great efforts time and again. Magnanimity saves the good of reason in managing our hope of greatness (I-II 60.4) or our desire for greatness (*De malo* 8, 2); putting a just measure in our aspiration for it (*In II sent.*, 42, 2, 4); and imposing a rational mode in these aspirations (*ST* II-II 129.3–4).

As mentioned earlier in regard to fortitude in general, the irascible faculty is in charge of managing difficulties, even though its passion of hope is entrenched in the concupiscible faculty. That is, hope concerns something we love that is difficult to attain.[10] This insight opens the door for reappropriating Aquinas' understanding of *arduum*, in which the object of hope involves not only difficulty, but above all an attractive good, a good capable of drawing us toward itself. Often writers take the Latin terms *arduum* and *difficile* as synonymous.[11] According to René-Antoine Gauthier, we should, however, translate *arduum* as "great" (*grand* in French),[12] rather than "diffi-

5. Cf. *ST* II-II 128.1; 123.4–5; 129.1 ad 2.

6. Cf. *ST* II-II 129.1; *ST* II-II 129.8; *ST* II-II 131.2 ad 1; *ST* II-II 17.5 ad 4; Gauthier 1951, 316–7; Labourdette 1961–62, 28–29.

7. Cf. *ST* I-II 60.5; *In Eth.* 2, 3, 278. In this regard, he follows Aristotle: cf. *NE* iii.2, 1105a9–13.

8. Cf. *ST* II-II 129.2.

9. Aquinas (*ST* II-II 129.2), drawing from Dionysius (*Div. nom.* iv, 4), holds that the passions can resist reason. Sometimes passions even resist reason in a way that requires two moral virtues: one for the extreme object, the other for the common case.

10. Cf. *ST* I-II 40.1; *ST* I-II 23.1; *ST* I-II 25.1; Gauthier 1951, 331–32.

11. Cf. Deferrari 1983.

12. Gauthier thinks that the term *arduum* is foreign to Greek philosophy and that it was introduced

cult." This distinction helps us to understand Aquinas' psychology of the irascible appetite, which while linked to the notion of *difficile, arduum* is not always simply synonymous with it. Rather, as was the case for his contemporaries, *arduum* refers first of all to greatness and excellence.[13] Thomas uses the following terms to express the meaning of *arduum: magnum, altum, elevatum, excellens, meloiora;* it is the opposite of *parvum.*[14] When thus associating the great and the difficult, *arduum* becomes what is great in two senses: objectively great, and great relative to our faculties. *Arduum* does not necessarily surpass our capacities, but it surpasses their easy exercise, their normal use. It demands a concerted effort. The greatness of hope is thereby not simply external to our greatness, for it entails personal involvement and personal difficulty. Inversely, what is difficult for our faculties implies that it is great, at least for us.

In Thomas's understanding of *arduum,* hope is based on an instinct, appetite, or power *(potentia)* of initiative, enterprise, and conquering aimed at the difficult good. It entails a twofold movement. On the one hand, the concupiscible appetite—as the instinct of possession, pleasure, and joy—finds difficulty repulsive. On the other hand, the irascible appetite[15] involves the instinct of assertiveness, combat, conquest, and domination to overcome the difficultly involved in seeking the good (or avoiding evil). For the instinct of assertiveness, nothing is more moving than something great and difficult. But it does not focus on the difficultly in itself or as a source of suffering, but rather on the great in its aspect of being difficult to attain. This *arduum* is greatness not as source of difficulty, but as source of dominating the difficulty.[16] Thomas thus considers the irascible under the aspects of both struggling and fighting, as well as victory and domination,[17] which seem to be elements in resilience efforts. His thought on hope and greatness in achieving the difficult good needs further exploration.

---

by twelfth-century masters, the *quidam* or *aliqui* as Aquinas refers to them (cf. *In de anima,* bk. III, lec. 14; Gauthier 1951, 321, nn. 1 and 2). He notes that there were diverging conceptions of *arduitas,* e.g., the Salamancan Carmelites; Duns Scotus for his part struck *arduitas* from his theology of hope.

13. Aquinas' contemporaries use *arduum* in the following ways. Alexander of Hales: *arduum* is above one's powers to undertake; St. Albert: *arduum* is that which is high and elevated; St. Bonaventure: *arduum* equals *magnum,* great, *excellens,* eminent, superior, and so on. Cf. Gauthier 1951, 322–23 and 325–27.

14. See *In III Sent.,* d. 26, qu. 1, obj. 1; *ST* II-II 136.5; Gauthier 1951, 323, n. 3; 324–25. In *ST* II-II 129.2 (on whether magnanimity concerns great honors), Aquinas says that *difficile* and *magnum* pertain to the same thing.

15. Cf. *ST* I-II 23.1 ad 3.

16. Cf. Gauthier 1951, 329; and 329–30, nn. 1 and 2.

17. Cf. *ST* I-II 32.6 ad 3.

Great Attention and Firmness of Mind

Human efforts of struggle, accomplishment, enterprise, and conquest demand concentration. Aquinas highlights the importance of great attention *(magna attentio)* and firmness of mind *(firmitas animi)* in magnanimously managing difficulty. Before exploring Thomas's ideas in this regard, we shall turn to resilience (and neurobiology) research on attentional processes that serve in overcoming adversity and hardship. As extensively discussed in chapter 2, the human capacity to manage attention is basic to a number of risk and resilience factors.[18] Important, complex, or urgent human initiatives can tax our basic skills; they demand maximal use of our personal and social resources. In order to organize these resources, we need to control our capacities, direct our mind to the goal, and remain conscious of pertinent surrounding issues.

Our attention shuttles between perceptions, emotions, and cognitions in order to manage resiliently our responses to the situation, our moods and feelings, and our social relationships. An abundance of stimuli can distract us. We must focus our attention and calm ourselves in order not to be captured by the latest stimulus. In this regard, Beverly J. Wilson and John M. Gottman distinguish two types of arousal and performance. On the one hand, high levels of "incentive arousal" as an active coping response aid in motivating and focusing attention on a primary task, while keeping contact with secondary ones, and even lowering levels of effort and energy dispensed. On the other hand, high levels of "anxiety arousal" tend to affect performance detrimentally because of anxiety's negative cognitions, such as self-doubt and fear of failure.[19] Wilson and Gottman furthermore claim that attentional styles and processes are influenced by (1) personality type and past personal experiences, (2) past and present physiological arousals, our capacities and emotional states, surroundings, and relationships, and (3) present goals for the future. In turn, effective attention management underlies resiliency strategies.

The parallels between this research and virtue theory raise a question and invite a dialogue with Aquinas' thought on the great attention and firmness of mind needed in magnanimity. How do these attentional styles

18. Cf. Wilson and Gottman 1996; Wallwork 1999; Eysenck 1982.
19. Cf. Wilson and Gottman 1996, 194–95.

enhance Thomas's approach to great objects of hope, which involve difficulty and stress in attaining them? First, Aquinas for his part draws from insights retrieved in Aristotle, whose version of this quality of strong attention might well be found in the magnanimous person's lack of interest in anything that is not great, and conversely his piercing interest in what is noteworthy. According to Aristotle, the magnanimous man's "gait is slow, his voice deep, and his utterance calm."[20] This description might at first glance seem irrelevant or even an inside joke. Critiques of Aristotle's thought have attacked his magnanimous man's aloofness and self-absorption, and have found his characteristics no more than humorous.[21]

Aquinas nonetheless finds meaning in the phenomenon of focused attention, which he cites twice in treating magnanimity, as well as elsewhere regarding learning.[22] He says that "the magnanimous person is intent only on great things; these are few and require great attention *(magna attentione)*, wherefore they call for slow movement."[23] Such great attention and firmness of mind is necessary in every virtue, but especially magnanimity and fortitude, both of which employ this mental attitude or psychological stance aimed at formidable deeds and overcoming hardship.[24] Thus, magnanimous people stretch forth their minds to great things, exemplified basically in accomplishing great and difficult acts.[25]

Aquinas' complementary insights on solicitude, moral responsibility, and human social nature help him to avoid the critiques leveled at Aristotle's no-

20. *NE* iv.3. In the *Physiognomics* (809b15–36 p. 1244), which Barnes (1984) judges as spurious, Pseudo-Aristotle's conception of the lion "moves slowly with a large stride, rolling his shoulders as he goes. Such is his bodily appearance, and in soul he is generous and liberal, proud and ambitious, yet gentle and just and affectionate to his comrades."

21. According to W. F. R. Hardie (1978), Aristotle's *μεγαλοψυχος* "does not command our modern sympathy" (Stewart 1892), is "unpleasing" and "offensive" (Ross 1964), or is a "product of his time" which modern readers find repulsive; B. Russell (1946) goes so far as to say that Aristotle's whole system is "unduly smug and comfortable." Alasdair MacIntyre (1966/1999[2], 79) says in insult that the *μεγαλοψυχος* "is very nearly an English gentleman." According to Martha Nussbaum (1988), furthermore *μεγαλοψυχία* is the "relativists'" favorite target.

22. Aquinas (I-II 37.1) draws upon the insights of St. Augustine (*Soliloq.* I.12.21; *PL* 32.880) and Proverbs (2:4–5) when discussing the need for attention in learning. A focused attention is necessary and depends on the quality of our love. Pain can distract us even from what we have previously learned. Nonetheless, love makes the difference. Aquinas observes that the stronger our love, the more it retains the attention of our mind and overcomes the distractions of pain.

23. *ST* II-II 129.3 ad 3. Aquinas discusses the more culturally dependent properties in *ST* II-II 129.3 ad 5.

24. The virtue of fortitude, however, demands more firmness of mind than magnanimity, since its object is more difficult. Cf. *ST* II-II 129.5; *ST* II-II 139; *ST* II-II 123.2; *ST* I-II 61.3.

25. Cf. *ST* II-II 129.1–2; Horner 1998, 428.

tion of magnanimity. First, Thomas highlights the importance of the magnanimous person's solicitude, which is neither slowness nor disinterest per se. Rather, through solicitude we focus on the things that truly need counsel and watchfulness, while trusting in regard to other secondary things, when it is fitting to do so.[26] Second, according to Aquinas, free and moral agency demands control of our attentional focus, which is so important for proper knowledge, intelligent willing and loving. Although the type of desire that follows reason and will *(passio consequens)* increases moral responsibility, a second type of desire that inhibits knowledge and voluntariness by limiting attention can distract us and diminish our moral responsibility.[27] Thus, for Aquinas, human agents must master their attentional focus on fitting objects, while resisting distraction in order to exercise their full moral responsibility. Third, Thomas's notion of magnanimity involves giving one's whole attention *(tota ejus intentio)* to the good of others.[28] This type of attention is a long way from the purported self-absorption charged of Aristotle's version, and demonstrates that in important regards, Aquinas' notion of greatness has less to do with Aristotle's than is commonly thought.

With these three aspects of attention and strength of mind, Aquinas illustrates a type of effort that constructively elicits movement toward a goal. Rather than a demobilizing fear and anxiety, it involves an active attraction toward some good. Indeed, at the very center of this virtue of great deeds and his virtue theory in general, Aquinas specifies an attentional style that is of the incentive rather than anxiety type, according to neurobiological typology. This aspect of virtue underlines another noteworthy characteristic of constructive resilience.

Daring, Aggressiveness, and Initiative: Temperament and Emotion

The arduous good interacts with our emotions and temperaments; it captures the human intellect. The temperaments and emotions related to daring and aggressiveness can serve or hinder our initiatives to attain the difficult good. According to Thomas, we use raw aggressiveness or asser-

26. Cf. *ST* II-II 47.9 ad 3.

27. The reason and will manage to resist excessive diminishing of attention when they resist the belittling effect of sensual desire. Thomas discusses these types of distraction in his article on moral responsibility and the sensitive appetite (I-II 77; see especially articles 1, 2, 6 and 7). For Aquinas, we are responsible for our desires and their objects, with two exceptions: (1) antecedent passion that diminishes attention, knowledge, and voluntariness; and (2) the desire that renders someone crazy *(in amentibus)*.

28. *In Eth.* 4, 10, 779. Aquinas widens the import of the Philosopher's thought.

tiveness *(aggredi)* for building up or tearing down. Hope gives rise to daring, which as an emotion or temperament trait we further use for good or evil. For Aquinas, the rational mastery of personal temperament and the passions of hope and fear are at the heart of turning simple assertiveness into well-reasoned initiative.[29]

Before going further, I should clarify the terminology of daring and aggressiveness. For Thomas, *audacia* (daring) refers to three things: a basic passion, an underlying natural temperament, and an acquired disposition.[30] We employ *audacia* both when we make a quick response *(operatio festina)* that we moderate with reason *(moderata ratione)*, and when we quickly act without adequate reflection and counsel.[31] This second aspect can involve a culpable act. Contemporary English discussions likewise attribute positive and negative senses to human daring. As an emotion and an act, the terms daring, assertiveness, boldness, and audacity have positive or neutral connotations, while aggression, rashness, recklessness, fearlessness, and indifference connote a negative extreme. For example, the term "aggression" is commonly used only in reference to violent and unreasonable emotion or action. Although daring, assertiveness, boldness, and audacity can also indicate a negative extreme, I have chosen to use them in the positive sense, akin to fortitude and courageousness, unless otherwise indicated by the context.[32]

Contemporary sciences track the physiological and neurochemical bases of daring and aggressive phenomena involved in the cognitive and emotive appreciation of a threat as something to be overcome through confrontation and in the motivation to do so. This tendency is the fight aspect of the basic human flight-or-fight reaction. The apprehended threat precipitates a physiological arousal, hormonal secretion, and neurological activity. The limbic system (the amygdala and septum lobes) activates these emotions, while the neocortex can intervene in managing them according to higher goals. Primordial, evolutionary responses to the situation are not the last

29. Cf. Congar 1974.

30. I need also to note another sense, which is more the lack of this quality. Aquinas uses the term *pusillanimitas* to indicate the absence of due daring. Later we shall discuss this inordinate act. Cf. *ST* II-II 133.1–2.

31. Cf. *ST* II-II 127.1 corpus and ad 2. Aquinas affirms the value of daring, calling on the authority of St. Gregory the Great (*Moral.* XXXI.24 al. 11, in vet. 19, n. 43; *PL* 76.597B) and Aristotle (*NE* vi.10, 1142b4–5). He calls upon Ecclesiasticus (8:18) to denote the sin of audacity.

32. For example, the *WEUD* (1989) defines "daring": "*n.* (1) adventurous courage; boldness.—*adj.* (2) bold; intrepid; adventurous." Its synonyms count: (1) audacity, bravery. (2) dauntless, undaunted, venturesome, audacious, brave, courageous.

word; humans dialogue with them through acquired temperament, emotion, volition, and cognition as well as memory and imagination. A person, moreover, consciously and unconsciously employs a web of family, socioeconomic, and religious dispositions and resources in eventually producing an act of daring.[33]

Fearful and timid temperament types (as discussed in chapter 3) react quite differently than bold and daring ones, which again differ from aggressive ones. A bold temperament can be characterized as involving a nervous system that is calibrated for a higher threshold of amygdala arousal. This type of personality results in the individual's being not only less easily frightened, but also more naturally outgoing. It can mean that the individual will more easily explore new places and meet new people. It offers some obvious resilience advantages.[34]

Aggressive personality types, on the contrary, entail an extreme form of reactivity, in which learned experience is an important determinant, according to Daniel Goleman. They involve a perceptual flaw, which assumes that the other human or animal or the situation is hostile. Aggressiveness is more than a normal cautionary limbic reaction when faced with a potential threat. It goes to an extreme in nurturing and acquiring a mental appreciation that presumes others are malevolent rather than innocent. Furthermore, aggressiveness is clear in another reactional flaw, where the individual tends to "aggress" automatically on the other, instead of exercising self-control and employing communication, negotiation, or compromise to clarify and adjudicate the situation. The aggressive reaction can take the form of accusations and personal insults, as well as other learned behaviors involving the use of weapons and physical force.[35]

Recalling again the psychosocial discussion on resilience and tempera-

33. As Craig L. Nessan (1998, 50) observes, the complexity of human daring and aggression is such that "a complete taxonomy of human aggression and violence would require examination of physiological, evolutionary, developmental (family and socialization), emotional, cognitive, cultural, socio-economic, and religious factors."

34. Cf. Goleman 1995, 196–97, 234–39.

35. The related problems are numerous: impulse control and coercive style, learning disorders, hyperactivity and academic failures, as well as more gender-specific violence in adolescent boys and unplanned pregnancies in adolescent girls. In general, aggressiveness can be the result of emotionally inept parenting, and can be modeled through violent behavior among friends and in gangs. Nonetheless, it can in some cases be tamed through mentoring situations. Emotionally inept parenting is arbitrary and harshly punitive. The parents of aggressive children typically alternate neglect with extreme and capricious punishments, resulting in making the children somewhat paranoid and combative. Cf. Goleman 1995, 196–97, 234–9; Wilson 1975.

ment in chapter 3, different styles of aggressiveness can expose an individual to risks or can promote resilience. In contrast to a bold temperament, it would seem that in most cases, an aggressive temperament lends itself to further risk and vulnerability, for both the individual and the social group. According to Michael Rutter's findings, antisocial aggressive behavior can in turn elicit aggressive and negative responses from other people. A chain of such behavior and responses can create a vicious cycle of negative experiences.[36] Nonetheless, in extreme situations such as famine or emergencies, one's aggressiveness turns into a resilience factor, when because of a more demanding attitude, someone prevails in acquiring limited resources, such as food or medical aid.[37] Furthermore, in everyday life, one can accomplish more typical situations and ordinary goals aided by a daring temperament or the reasonable management of our emotional drives.

In order to put these insights into dialogue with Aquinas' on daring, we must first, include his understanding of natural inclinations and physiological reactions; second, consider the relationship of the emotion of daring with fear and hope; and finally, study the related virtues, especially magnanimity.

Thomas recognizes that the movement of daring involves our taking the offensive against what opposes us. We are inclined by nature to attack the source of opposition, insofar as we are free from fear and mobilized by a hope of overcoming the threat.[38] The lack of reasonable aggression or daring is timidity or cowardliness; the excess of reasonable aggression is audacity and fearlessness.

Aquinas draws his sources' insights on aggressiveness or assertiveness into his architectonic structure of the irascible emotions, which are charged with energy for action when faced with the difficult good that appears possible to overcome.[39] While Aquinas' notion of hope, strictly speaking, in-

36. Cf. Rutter 1994a, 371–72.

37. Cf. the De Vries study on child survivors of the Zimbabwe famine (cited by Rutter 1998, 48).

38. Cf. *ST* II-II 127.2 ad 3.

39. St. Thomas's synthesis of ideas concerning magnanimity does not shy away from Stoic and medieval contemporary (his references to *quidam* and *aliqui*) insights on hope, daring, aggressiveness, and initiative. In particular, both Cicero's and Peter Abelard's thoughts are important for Aquinas' understanding of hope in daring action, as well as of confidence and security in magnanimous initiatives. In interpreting Cicero's fourfold division of the virtue of fortitude, Aquinas inserts "magnanimity" in the place of Cicero's "confidence," while appropriating confidence as an aspect of the virtue of magnanimity. Peter Abelard (1079–1142) and this current maintain that the first degree of courage is initiating difficult projects in a spontaneous and reasonable way. This virtue undertakes an initiative in a way capable of

volves the difficult good *(bonum arduum)*, his notion of daring concerns the overcoming of some great danger through the virtue of fortitude, which manages fear and daring.[40]

Daring and hope creatively and positively interact. Firstly, daring can support hope. It is the emotional power in magnanimity to overcome the difficulty involved to attain the *bonum arduum* as well as to avoid the *malum arduum*.[41] Both hope and daring involve movement toward *(accessus)* the object,[42] hope to embrace the good aspect, and daring in order to overcome an evil aspect (through the virtue of fortitude) as well as to obtain the difficult good (through magnanimity).[43] The irascible appetite is the gateway for the passions of motion and the foundation for human initiative.[44] This enterprising side of magnanimity is a companion and corrective for the movements related to patience, which can tend toward passivity and play into helplessness. Magnanimity mobilizes our resources, calms the fear of failure, and converts us in natural hope.

The presence of hope and the lack of fear in the face of difficulty, secondly, produce daring action.[45] Aquinas explains that daring ensues from the emotion of hope, "since it is in the hope of overcoming the threatening object of fear, that one attacks it boldly."[46] Hope puts aside fear and incites us to daring acts, but only when hope is strong enough.[47] Thomas analyses the working of fear, daring, and hope in terms of the corporeal effects of the passions (bodily transmutations and appetitive movements) that can participate in virtue.[48] He does not balk at the physical aspect of the energy of daring that arises when an object grounds hope or banishes fear.[49] Such

---

completing it. Abelard's thought was passed on through the *Moralia dogma* and Philip the Chancellor, as mentioned earlier. It is important to note here that St. Albert did not integrate these insights in the same way as Aquinas, since he was even more set on finding inspiration in Aristotle (cf. Dixsaut 1996).

40. Cf. *ST* I-II 45.1–4; *ST* I-II 40–44; *ST* I-II 23.2–3; *ST* I-II 35.2; *ST* I-II 59.4 ad 3.

41. *ST* I-II 23.2; cf. *ST* I-II 23.1 and *ST* I-II 23.4.

42. Cf. *ST* I-II 45.1 ad 2; *ST* I-II 23.2; *ST* I-II 40.4.

43. Cf. 129.6 ad 2.

44. Cf. *ST* I-II 25.1.

45. See *ST* I-II 45.3 and chapter 4 on how banishing fear gives rise to daring.

46. *ST* I-II 45.2; cf. *ST* II-II 123.3 ad 3.

47. Cf. *ST* I-II 45.2 ad 2; *ST* II-II 125.2 ad 3.

48. Thomas quotes Aristotle as an authority on how hope causes daring, and how daring ensues from hope. The Philosopher notes that "those [who] are hopeful are full of daring" (*NE* iii.8) and that daring "is caused by the presence in the imagination of the hope that the means of safety are nearby, and that the things to be feared are either non-existent or far off" (*Rhet.* ii.5, 1383a17–18; cited in *ST* I-II 45.3; "daring" is also translated as "confidence" by Richard McKeon (in Aristotle 1941). Aquinas, however, goes further than Aristotle in recognizing the very corporeal effects of the passions in works of virtue.

49. Cf. *ST* I-II 45.3.

an understanding of readiness to act encompasses all aspects of the human person.[50] Daring is not concerned only with the emotions of hope and fear, but also with the content of one's virtue and character.[51]

Thomas's view of the larger teleological purpose of the emotion and acts of daring contrasts certain views from evolutionary psychology. In an extreme form of sociobiology, Richard Dawkins measures animal behavior (including that of humans) according to what most efficiently propagates the individual's genes. In particular the human "survival machine" employs the aggressive drives and instincts for self-preserving purposes.[52] These insights, while explaining an aspect of animal instinct, do not, however, adequately integrate the whole of human moral agency and purpose. Nessan corroborates this critique. He argues that the human being is not only capable of "bottom-up" behavior based on drives and instincts. It also employs "top-down" behavior based on conscious intention and decision. Observations of human agents demonstrate that they can override certain basic instincts for a consciously chosen end.

What does a virtue-based moral approach contribute to this debate? According to Nessan, the human brain's capacity for reflective self-consciousness integrates self-awareness, awareness of other human selves, symbolic language, culture, religion, art, music, and so forth.[53] We need to consider the proclivity for aggression, as an adaptive behavior, in liaison

50. As Josef Pieper (1949–59/1966, 129–30) says in regard to the bravery and confident hope in aggressive human acts. "The brave man not only knows how to bear inevitable evil with equanimity; he will also not hesitate to 'pounce upon' evil and to bar its way, if this can reasonably be done." This attitude requires readiness to attack, courage, self-confidence, and hope of success; "the trust that is a part of fortitude signifies the hope which a man puts in himself: naturally in subordination to God." This aspect of virtue is sometimes quite foreign to contemporary Christian views of ethics, which is partly due, according to Pieper, to an evident mistrust of passions in ethics. There is an intellectual Stoicism that is actually more Kantian, in associating ethics with duty, rather with such brazen acts of courage and magnanimity.

51. Cf. *ST* I 95.3 ad 2.

52. Self-preservation is so central for Dawkins (1976, 2 and 71ff.) that his reasoning verges on either reducing all other inclinations to self-preservation or making it the key inclination that orders all others. Dawkins's mind experiments attempt to demonstrate cost benefit calculations of fighting and aggressiveness; their statistical basis, however, does not permit a non-reductionistic inclusion of deeper aspects of empathy, altruism, and benevolence.

53. Religions can use symbols, myths, and rituals for either partisan support or elimination of violence. The human capacity of knowing how our actions affect others establishes the moral dimension to human activity that is not immediately incumbent on animal instincts (cf. Nessan 1998, 445–46, 451). Darwin L. Thomas and Craig Carver's (1990, 195) findings suggest that religion can significantly reduce negative social types of aggression. We need to contrast this position, though, with a fundamentalist promotion of aggression, for example, in the form of planned terrorism.

with human "reflective self-consciousness," which humans can put to rational use either for violence or for "empathy and altruism." Human beings can employ their intellectual capacity to plan ever more sophisticated forms of violence, such as verbal and physical abuse, spouse and child abuse, rape and torture, slavery and capital punishment, murder and war. They even make weapons for non-ritualized violence and routinely regard watching violence as recreation.[54] On the contrary, human beings can employ reflective self-consciousness in developing empathetic and altruistic alternatives to primordial violence.

One of the greatest human struggles, according to Nessan, is to master violence, using models for resolving conflict and building human community without violence. Thus we employ our energy to promote positive interactions and constructions.[55] Ambiguities will remain, however, since local cultures can also promote the survival function of certain undesirable behaviors.[56] A Thomistic virtue perspective furthermore takes these insights to a deeper personal and communal level, to involve human dispositions and history in order to focus human energies toward creative and peaceful activities. While we recognize aggression or assertiveness as a necessary survival instinct, human beings can couple aggressiveness with intellectual capacities to create or to avoid violence, to dissimilate, or to promote peace. In addition to extreme cases, humans muster assertiveness and daring in mundane initiatives. Aquinas' position is consistent with Nessan's corrective critique of a raw evolutionary perspective. Thomas, though, insists that we need to train temperaments through well-disposed virtues in order to harness daring and aggressiveness for the common good. Aquinas takes this discussion further when addressing the place of daring in confident action.

54. Nessan (1998, 451) notes that as the inflicted psychological or physical harm that imposes an individual's or group's will on others through nonverbal, verbal, or physical means, violence is a uniquely human potential.

55. Human beings can use their intellectual functioning in relation to their sociobiological phenomena (sex, aggression, pain) to "either direct humans toward ever more destructive ways of perpetuating the self or redirect them toward the betterment of human community. [. . .] Human beings demonstrate their fallen condition insofar as they fail to realize their capacity to *redirect* sociobiological inclinations for the sake of their neighbor." Nessan 1998, 453; cf. 450–51; Rose 1998, 277; 290–91nn20, 21.

56. According to research (Consortium 1994, 275), "in certain cultures, neighborhoods and situations, so-called undesirable behaviors (e.g. aggressiveness, selfish, or passive behaviors) may be required if one is to be perceived as 'well adjusted' or to avoid being subject to harm."

The Harnessing of Daring: Aquinas on Confident Action

Aquinas distinguishes the person who has acquired the virtuous dispositions of fortitude and magnanimity from the one moved by the emotion of daring alone. Those moved by these virtues face danger according to the judgment of reason, with due deliberation and foresight, and "on account of the good of virtue which is the abiding object of their will. Whereas men of daring [*audaces*] face the danger on account of a mere thought giving rise to hope and banishing fear";[57] or according to an evolutionary perspective, on account of an aggressive instinct based on a genetic drive to reproduce or protect one's gene pool (as Dawkins would say). Through a stable intention, disposition, and rational adjudication courageous and magnanimous people master both fear and daring. They are misdirected by neither one nor the other emotion. Aquinas sets demanding standards. A merely daring person aims at an object that calls forth hope and banishes fear, and may even accomplish a good effort. His act is nevertheless shortsighted, insofar as it lacks some measure of correct rational judgment, due to deliberation and foresight.[58]

A discussion of daring raises questions about the Gospel dictum to turn the other cheek. Are Christians who follow such messages more vulnerable to aggression than others? Indeed, Aquinas and the Christian tradition's attempts to temper aggressive behavior toward strangers and to instill benevolence toward hostile enemies have attracted extensive critiques.[59] Aquinas' position on just wrath, however, provides a partial rebuttal to the claim that Christians are underprotected from natural hostility. Indeed, by positive use of assertiveness just wrath serves to overcome the injustices that waylay our personal and social projects. Anger is especially helpful in attack and in establishing justice, when it pounces upon evil and acts to right a wrong. Aquinas' vision of the positive potential of anger is strikingly different from that of the Stoics, and it offers an at least partial response to contemporary critiques.[60]

57. *ST* I-II 45.4. Aristotle views hope and optimism as negative elements; he notes that the mercenary, the optimist, and the rash person resemble each other in having too much confidence. Cf. *NE* iii.7, 1116a7–9; Smoes 1995, 227–34.

58. On daring and attack arising from hope see *ST* I-II 45.2; *ST* II-II 123.3 ad 3; and *NE* 1116b 23. On the precepts relating to hope and fear see *ST* II-II 22.

59. We shall address the critiques of F. Nietzsche and S. Freud in the following theological section.

60. On how fortitude and wrath work directly upon each other, see *ST* I-II qq. 46–48; Pieper 1949–59/1966, 130; Mattison 2001.

Further questions arise though. Can we harness aggressive instincts for positive endeavors? And can we turn "negative" aggression toward positive efforts? We find Aquinas' response to these questions in the way in which he construes that basic human inclinations motivate self-confidence, self-efficacy, and so on. Thomas associates confidence *(fiducia)* with the virtue of fortitude and identifies it with magnanimity.[61] Confidence qualifies the strength of hope that serves "magnanimity [which] is chiefly about the hope of something difficult,"[62] according to Thomas. As an integral part of fortitude, confidence is not a separate virtue. But when identified with magnanimity, as fortified hope,[63] it strengthens us to obtain a difficult good.

When hope causes a daring confrontation of difficulty and evil, confidence contributes both to magnanimity's overcoming despair and to fortitude's harnessing daring and banishing fear.[64] Confidence relates not only to hope but also to faith *(fides)*, from which it takes its name; and as such, it believes something or believes in someone. Insofar as human beings are not self-sufficient, we need the assistance of others, in whom we must put our trust.

According to Thomas, internal and external sources can rouse us to confidence and hope for victory: to recognize our own strengths and resources and to observe friends' capacities and other sources of help.[65] First, we find confidence in our own abilities and correct appreciation of them. We can also undermine it by our lack of a proper sense of self-efficacy, which we learn through observing our own accomplishments. We establish self-assurance by recognizing how we are successful agents with (some degree of) control over the positive outcomes we have experienced, as resilience research has affirmed. Observing our past achievements can give us a self-confidence that nonetheless depends upon self-correction.

Second, we find confidence when we observe the availability of resources of friends and relatives. We need to recall past occasions of their aid and when we have aided them; such cases give us reason to believe that reciproc-

61. Aquinas follows Cicero's quadruple division of fortitude with this exception. Thomas replaces *magnanimitas* with Cicero's *fiducia* (*Rhet.* II, 54), while guarding the content of the latter's teaching. Cf. *ST* II-II 128.1; 129.6 ad 3; Horner 1998, 428.

62. Aquinas moreover claims that we can be confident when hope is strengthened by a strong opinion. Cf. *ST* II-II 129.6; *ST* II-II 129.6–7; *ST* II-II 129.1 ad 2.

63. Cf. *ST* II-II 129.6 ad 3; *ST* 128.

64. Cf. *ST* II-II 129.6 ad 2; *ST* II-II 129.7; *ST* I-II 45.2.

65. Cf. *ST* I-II 45.3; *ST* II-II 129.6 ad 1.

ity will continue. Furthermore, it is advantageous (even a point of excellence for Aquinas) to have people willing and able to render us service (not only friends and relatives, but colleagues, employees, and servants). Even with this experience though, we still must "believe" or "have faith" that they will help us again when we are in need. Likewise, we may reasonably assume that public resources will be attributed to us in strict distributive justice, although it does not always happen. History illustrates the "unexpected" in economic and civil crises, wars, and disasters. Therefore, we need here also to have careful confidence, lest we be debilitated by mundane worries. For Aquinas, a person must trust not only in himself, but also in other human beings and in society.

Security collaborates indirectly with magnanimity in calming fear, despair, and anything that perturbs the mind.[66] Not only can fear cause despair, but it destabilizes hope. Security, on the contrary, "denotes a perfect freedom of the mind from fear,"[67] as well as the process of attaining it. Such security involves neither oblivion to fear nor its denial. Rather, it results from a person taking counsel and acting in order to find a way to avoid, remove, or overcome the cause of fear. In the fears that arise from human resistance, intrigue, and bad fortune *(perturbationi fortunae)*,[68] magnanimity brings about security by overcoming fear and banishing despair, through its efforts that establish a confident hope of attaining the difficult-to-attain good. Each virtue in its excellence, as a difficult-to-obtain good, must overcome the resistance of human intrigue and bad fortune. The firmness and certitude of hope depends on the removal of such fear, which acts as an obstacle to hope and action.[69]

In conclusion, when one is faced with trying circumstances, natural inclinations can produce an initial assertiveness, which can form the first step toward acting to protect the well-being of one's society, family, or self; defending a child in need of protection; speaking out for justice in a community, and so forth. When the virtuous person can do something to overcome the danger or achieve the difficult good, he does not simply endure the difficulty and wait. Rather the person of virtue attempts to surmount the barriers and to combat the danger, employing energy drawn from the emotion of daring. Since not every attack or effort is appropriate, the person of virtue

66. Cf. *ST* II-II 129.7.

67. *ST* II-II 129.7.

68. Aquinas cites Cicero *Off.* I.20 as the authority in *ST* II-II 129.7 sc.

69. Cf. *ST* II-II 128.1 ad 6; *ST* I-II 40.4 ad 1.

must also reason and deliberate. Consequently, beyond our natural inclinations, we seek to acquire dispositions to aid us in moving quickly once we have taken counsel. Like fear and anxiety, daring and audacity can be well-founded and appropriate emotions; yet they can also be disproportionate reactions to the situation at hand. We need to make a distinction. Through audacity, we deviate from the aim and measure of fortitude. The audacious person mistakenly adjudicates his own capacities and the difficulties entailed in the effort. He presumptuously errs about himself and the nature of the enterprise. On the contrary, through assertiveness, the positive sense of *aggredi,* we employ careful strength and healthy disdain for obstacles in a worthy initiative.

Magnificentia *as the Virtue of Making and Generosity?*

Magnanimity and magnificence are intertwined. They both depend on related notions not only of greatness, but also of nobility and morality. *Magnificentia* has undergone many mutations, which we could chart from the conceptions of Greek and Roman nobility to medieval codes of chivalry, Aquinas' philosophical-theological synthesis, the Cartesian reaction against the concept of nobility of his time, and Kant's exclusive turn to the universality of the good will. In modern conceptions, magnificence has been narrowed to the concept of "generosity." Nietzsche furthermore reduces this generosity, as well as greatness, to an illusion (or at least reverses the values of generosity and greatness, giving them an extra-moral sense), and thus plays a decisive role in undermining modern notions of heroic morality and virtue ethics.[70] Nonetheless, after recent critiques of modernity and the resurgence of philosophical virtue theory, contemporary scholars have initiated a wider treatment of magnificence that reappropriates the richer tradition. What is the interest of Aquinas and resilience research in this regard?

Aquinas on Projects of Quantity, Value, and Dignity

For Aquinas, *magnificentia* concerns making or doing something great, realizing projects of "quantity, value or dignity."[71] It involves a sort of self-efficacy and excellence in agency. It includes but is distinct from the excel-

70. On the history of the concept of *magnanimitas,* see Dixsaut 1996, 596 and 598–9; Gauthier 1951. It is telling to observe how Dixsaut amalgamates magnificence and magnanimity in her conception of generosity.

71. *ST* II-II 134.2.

lence and greatness in acts that belong to the very notion of virtue.[72] More specifically, *magnificentia* concerns excellence in bringing about great external acts,[73] which secondarily involve great expense. While it is not an art itself, it is nonetheless a virtue of art.[74] Given Thomas's social context and personal experience, as well as the diversity of his sources, we must ask to whom does his notion of magnificence refer. Is it for monastic procurators, medieval cathedral builders, and aristocratic philanthropists? Does it apply to the business community and venture capitalists? Does it have anything to say to those who altruistically give themselves and their possessions toward any worthwhile project?

The etymology of magnificence (*magna facere:* to make great things) directs Aquinas in developing a comprehensive definition, involving both strict and broader senses. In a broader sense, *magnificentia* concerns the *habitus* or disposition behind the deed. We can be magnificent without actually accomplishing great projects, if we do not have the financial means or a fitting opportunity. Someone who has even the most meager of means can nurture the disposition of *magnificentia;* even the poor person can be magnificent, for Aquinas. In this sense, he says that the virtue of *magnificentia* is at the heart of the generous person *(liberalitas)* either through a proximate disposition or through the interconnection of the virtues.[75] Thomas's conception integrates a Stoic notion of the self-sufficiency of virtue.[76] He even says that the poor person who is magnificent can accomplish an act that is proportionately great, "although little in itself."[77] Thus, we can count the widow's mite as great, in terms of merit and efficacy.[78] Magnificent people have a virtuous inclination of the irascible appetite to make good use of the

72. Cf. *ST* II-II 134.1.

73. Both Cicero and Albert consider magnanimity as a part of the virtue of magnificence. Albert defended Cicero's classification of the four parts of fortitude found in his *De inventione rhetorica* (II, 54): magnificence, confidence, patience, and perseverance. Furthermore, for Albert (as for Cicero) magnanimity is a potential part of magnificence, which has two parts: (1) to confront difficulty with greatness of soul *(magnanimitas)*, and (2) to bring these sentiments into act, i.e., to do great things. Thus, magnificence concerns both achievement of great works and also initiative-taking (enterprise). (Cf. Gauthier 1951, 306–7)

74. Cf. *ST* II-II 134.1 ad 4.

75. Cf. *ST* II-II 134.1 ad 1; *ST* I-II 65.1 ad 1; *ST* II-II 129.3 ad 2. Diane Fritz Cates' (1997, 229) insights on compassion are pertinent here, since it serves as cognitive, volitional, affective, and pedagogical bases for liberality.

76. In *ST* II-II 134.3 obj. 4, Aquinas takes his cue from Seneca's *De ira* (ch. 9) and *De vita beata* (16.28–9).

77. Since the chief act of virtue is the inward choice, even the poor person can be magnificent. Cf. *ST* II-II 134.3 ad 4.

78. Aquinas esteems the widow's act of giving her two copper coins (cf. Mk 12:43; Lk 21:3) to be

rule of art in regard to things to be made, especially in situations that press their resources to the limit.[79] On the contrary, obstacles that inhibit us from engaging our resources in a "great work" (projects, gifts, and expenditures) involve inordinate attachment to our money and other resources.[80]

In a strict sense, *magnificentia* concerns actually great deeds and the disposition that underlies them.[81] This virtue, as a disposition or habitus, entails a mean in the order of reason concerning a certain extreme quantity of an external work.[82] As a virtue of making, we acquire it through art and external deeds. Thomas considers a work of art magnificent inasmuch as the work produced is something great in goodness in terms of "quantity, value, or dignity."[83] He claims that the strict sense of magnificence concerns both inward intending and outward accomplishment of "great and lofty undertakings."[84]

While magnanimity concerns greatness in every matter, magnificence concerns more specifically external works. *Magnanimitas*'s primary focus is on the sole aspect of greatness, whereas *magnificentia* is a special virtue of doing and tending to do great things.[85] Magnificence prolongs magnanimity in material realizations, in artistic and technical orders, in all that is done (*faire*).[86] But this extension does not stop at the quantity of the material project; rather it reaches beyond to the project's purpose and effect, in terms of self-flourishing and social benefit.

Self-esteem and Resilience in Taking Initiatives

The present focus on great projects does not sidetrack us from considering the place of self-knowledge and self-worth in accomplishing initiatives.

---

proportionately great; this greatness relates to the merit due (good deeds, cf. *ST* I 95.4) and the spiritual efficacy (almsgiving, cf. *ST* II-II 32.4 corpus and ad 3).

79. Cf. *ST* II-II 134.1 ad 4; and *ST* II-II 134.3 ad 4.

80. Cf. *ST* II-II 134.3 ad 2. An ordinate affection is necessary lest one err through prodigality or covetousness.

81. Aquinas contrasts the strict with a broader sense of making or doing (*facere*) something great, which applies to any action, both external action as well as activities that remain in the agent, on the level of intellect and will (cf. 134.2). Thus, there is a type of greatness (excellence) in each virtue, in which there is the excellence due to its genus. Each virtue's primary focus is on its principal object. For example, an excellence in the virtue of temperance manages the concupiscible appetite according to right reason (cf. *ST* II-II 141). In this broader sense, he escapes a narrower reading of Aristotle's virtue of magnificence.

82. *ST* II-II 134.1 ad 2.

83. *ST* II-II 134.2.

84. See *ST* II-II 134.2 ad 2, where he cites Cicero (*Rhet.* ii.54); *ST* II-II 128.1.

85. Cf. *ST* II-II 134.2 ad 2.

86. Cf. Labourdette 1961–62, 26.

In particular, recent studies focusing on the place of self-esteem in resilient actions present both promises and problems that we face in creative projects. Resilience research highlights the importance of self-esteem as a motivating factor in human action. As the ongoing debate demonstrates, however, we can make further nuances. As mentioned in chapter 2, researchers have contrasting views of self-esteem: some conceptualize it as a means to an end, others as an end in itself. Some researchers correlate self-esteem with how someone is doing in life. It is a simple indicator. Other researchers construe self-esteem as of primary importance for one's self-realization and resilience.[87] In the present section, we shall introduce the typology of self-esteem and distinguish the import of diverse self-valuation styles on social interaction and moral agency.

Pro-social self-esteem as a temperament trait, according to numerous researchers, tends to elicit a positive response from family and community.[88] As a feeling, furthermore, self-esteem has resilience value when it aids motivation and action that resist external and internal negative pressures.[89] However, other researchers have discovered that unwarranted self-esteem can lead to problems and vulnerability. Important questions arise: what are the bases of cognitions and feelings of self-worth? And in turn, what are the effects of different types of self-esteem?

According to Martin E. P. Seligman, the basis for our self-esteem influences the way that we react in strenuous efforts. He posits two types of foundation for self-worth: one is unfounded in a realist evaluation of one's capacities and acts, and the other is based on an overly positive evaluation. He speculates that teaching unwarrantedly high self-esteem to children can lead to problems such as violence and depression, which tend to surface when a person's unrealistic self-esteem conflicts with strenuous challenges and personal failures.[90] On the contrary, research suggests that realistic evaluations of personal accomplishments increase feelings and cognitions of self-efficacy[91] that serves as a basis for coping. Rutter conjectures that the

87. Cf. Seligman 1991/1998, vi–vii; Baumeister, Smart, and Boden 1996.

88. Cf. Rutter 1990, 182; Garmezy 1985.

89. Emotional processes underlying self-esteem seem to spring from both emotional predispositions (temperament) and acquired dispositions (both conscious and unconscious ones). Cf. Rutter 1990, 197–207; Yule 1992, 191.

90. Cf. Seligman 1991/1998, vii; Lösel 1994, 9.

91. Cf. Werner and Smith 1992, 185–86, and 207; Maughan 1988, 214; Werner and Smith 1986; Seligman 1991/1998, vi–vii; Baumeister, Smart, and Boden 1996.

cognitive dimension of self-esteem functions through the carry forward of cognitive sets concerning positive events and their relation to self-esteem and self-efficacy.[92] Personal attentional capacities, which help us to manage emotional and social experiences, also seem to contribute in forming feelings and cognitions of self-esteem and self-efficacy. Negative or low self-images, however, increase vulnerability and inactivity. These sources are multiple and difficult to analyze: having a history of personal failures, being crushed by external events, being abandoned in front of overwhelming tasks, and so on. The repetition of such events can lower our self-image, leading us to depression, underachievement, and a sense of incompetence.

Since the notion of self-esteem is not independent from social interaction, another important question arises. What kind of resilience impact on agency results from social relationships? In addition to the social influence on self-evaluation, a person's self-efficacy is shaped through feelings and relationships of social solidarity.[93] A social network can supply affectional, intellectual, and practical support that models not only external behavior but also internal emotional competency.[94] Family influences the types of self-esteem that we practice. Some families model constructive self-esteem through fitting emotional support and effective communication.[95] Family disruption and marital conflict can conversely produce cognitive sets of helplessness and low self-esteem, leading to psychiatric vulnerability.[96] In certain cases, nonetheless, we can compensate for inadequate family support by relevant experiences in another domain (e.g., other relationships, schools, communities, and society).[97]

This typology suggests that interrelations between self-esteem and resilient self-efficacy are complex. We need to affectively apply ourselves in order to perform well. We draw upon cognitive, affective, and social elements in planning and executing acts. As was argued earlier, Aquinas' virtue theory favors considering the affective, cognitive, and volitional aspects of human agency with reference to larger purposes. He would deem that proper self-evaluation needs realistic external references, without neglecting the

92. Cf. Rutter 1994a, 373–74.

93. Cf. J. Bowlby 1969/1982, and 1973; Ainsworth et al. 1978.

94. Cf. Clarke and Clarke 1992, 153; Rutter 1990, 203–10; Maughan 1988, 214; Werner and Smith 1992, 5.

95. Cf. Wills 1996, 115; Wilson and Gottman 1996, 220.

96. Cf. Watt et al. 1990, 300; Rutter 1990, 200; Tousignant 1998, 64.

97. Cf. Rutter 1990, 197.

internal ones. Aquinas' notion of the virtues of magnificence and generosity, especially when understood in relation to other pertinent virtues such as prudence, temperance, hope, and love, enriches these considerations of agency, resilience, and vulnerability.

Conspicuous Consumption or Generosity at the Service of Survival and Flourishing

A cultural anthropology perspective investigates how types of generous and status-building initiatives measure up as survival tendencies. The research of James L. Boone (1998), for example, investigates the evolution of generosity and magnificence.[98] He advances a Darwinian explanation of conspicuous consumption (wasting time and energy on risky or decorative ventures) as a form of adaptive energy expenditure that reinforces social status and in turn brings fitness benefits. Boone uses a form of "optimization theory" from human behavioral ecology to explain the interaction of variations in fitness affecting behaviors (such as foraging or conspicuous consumption) with environmental conditions. He relates human subsistence and reproductive strategies in function of the time or energy expended (cost) and the energy or fitness acquired (benefit). Then, he predicts the optimal behavior that maximizes the net fitness gain (energy, surviving offspring, and so on).

Boone's evolutionary theory observes that conspicuous consumption is omnipresent in rich and poor alike, in the forms of nonessential or elaborate decorations, clothing, housing, and recreation. What benefit does wasting time, energy, and resources on such things bring? He hypothesizes that conspicuous consumption is advertising; it is a costly signaling of an unobservable phenotypic quality in the sender.[99] The quality that one advertises is social status.[100] But what are the short- and long-term reproductive ben-

98. His article is entitled "The Evolution of Magnanimity" (in *Human Nature* 9 [1998]: 1–21). We should note that the article title takes "magnanimity" in a contemporary sense to mean magnificence or generosity, as a "costly helping behavior," in contrast to "non-altruistic costly displays" (15). This use of "magnificence" means "conspicuous consumption" rather than a Classic notion of great-souledness. Boone is a cultural anthropologist (University of New Mexico) who does research on behavioral ecology and the archaeology of complex societies.

99. Boone (1998, 9; cf. 2–5) says, "The key idea in strategic handicap theory is that a signal is effective and reliable because it lowers one component of a signaler's fitness while raising another through the production of the display. I have argued above that social power is an underlying, usually unobservable quality that must be signaled or advertised in order to be effective."

100. Cf. ibid., 5–9.

efits of reinforcing social status? He identifies fitness benefits; conspicuous consumption increases the "probability of survival through relatively infrequent, but recurrent, demographic bottlenecks by determining individual or familial priority of access to resources accumulated, produced, or defended by the social group during infrequent but serious shortages."[101] But why and under what evolutionary ecological circumstances does status competition take altruistic rather than violent forms? He argues that competitive altruism prevails over violence and against rivals in social groups for two reasons. First, aggression and violence are more costly and less successful. Second, costly helping behavior is more likely to attract collaboration (supporters, mates, and so forth), thus allowing dominants to stay so, and demonstrating a capacity to rally defense against outsiders.[102]

One of the major problems in this type of analysis is uncertainty (not only for the scientist, but for the individual) in tracking the long- and short-term effects on survival and fitness needs of altruistic conspicuous consumption.[103] In the long term, humans need to be ready for infrequent, unpredictable demographic bottlenecks (such as famine, economic crisis, or war) that put personal and lineage survival in jeopardy. He argues that social status has the primary evolutionary raison d'être of promoting survival in such risky situations. Nonetheless, shorter-term needs related to fitness also expend time and energy: nutrient acquisition, avoidance of environmental hazards and pathogens, parental investment, mating efforts and so forth.[104] He concludes that social status reinforcement is an adaptive, state-dependent strategy that involves short- and long-term costs and benefits.[105]

101. Boone (ibid., 10) analyses strategies that favor fewer offspring and more offspring in the short term. He compares survival during two nineteenth-century famines (in India and Ireland) over the long term. He (11–12) observes a higher population (higher survival rates, i.e., less deaths in famine crises) in the first instance. It seems to me that he uses two extreme cases, which seem to prove his point; but which in a larger analysis might not.

102. Boone (ibid., 15–16) argues furthermore that altruistic generous displays "as distinctive, emergent, group-level characteristics" are complex because (1) they involve economic transactions—problems of interpreting history or effect; and (2) a transfer of good or service reduces the fitness differential (at least in the short term).

103. Another problem would be if political propaganda or social studies would promote the contrary—for example, that aggression and violence are less costly and more successful for survival. Thus, we need moral norms.

104. Boone (1998, 18) assumes, contrary to popular opinion, that socioeconomic status and fitness is not isomorphic, that it is not definable simply in terms of total annual income or some measure of total accumulated wealth.

105. Boone (1998, 18) says, "It seems at least possible that a group of individuals or families that have identical annual incomes or accumulated wealth might expend widely variable proportions of income

These theories provide theoretical and observation-based support promoting generous altruism rather than egotistical miserliness as a survival strategy. They offer constructive insights concerning the utility of altruistic generosity for oneself and one's offspring as well as for the social whole.[106] This evolutionary approach comes to some conclusions similar to Aquinas', but for different reasons and with different import.

Aquinas holds that the virtues of magnificence and generosity have personal and social import. Magnificence is primarily about accomplishing great ventures, but secondarily about the expenditures needed to complete these works.[107] It concerns the emotions involved in such feats. First, the context of the virtues of magnificence and generosity is explicitly moral and social; we must explicitly intend and plan to bring benefit to others through our ventures and expenditures. They both involve a larger social impact. Neither generous nor magnificent people are egocentric, but rather they recognize that "one's person is little in comparison with [. . .] the affairs of the community at large."[108] Aquinas affirms that excess of riches is meant to be generously distributed, without impoverishing the giver.[109] This view gives us indications of the larger social context and the related virtues, such as justice and prudence.

Secondly, Aquinas attends to how our emotions and intellects interact in these virtues. He identifies great expenditure and the love of money as the critical points of magnificence. He compares and contrasts this virtue with generosity. Generosity or liberality extends to all riches, money and possessions. It immediately concerns the concupiscible passions of loving, desiring, pleasure, and sorrow, which we experience when we liberate things from our ownership. Generosity in effect demonstrates that our mind is free from attachment to these things.[110] It moderates our love of money.

---

on (a) conspicuous consumption and other status reinforcement displays, (b) the production and rearing of offspring (Kaplan 1996), and (c) conservation of resources that can be passed on to offspring in the form of bequests (Rogers 1990)." He leaves for future research more detailed hypotheses about the relationship between socioeconomic conditions, wealth allocation, and other components of long- and short-term fitness.

106. However, he makes what I judge to be an inconclusive argument about the tradeoff between social status and fertility. Cf. Boone and Kessler 1999.

107. Cf. *ST* II-II 135.1.

108. *ST* II-II 134.1 ad 3.

109. Cf. *ST* II-II 117.1 ad 1, citing Ambrose (Serm. 81 *de temp.*: *PL* 17.593–4) and Basil's (Hom. 6 in Luc xxi.18: PG 31.264C, 276 C) commentaries on the Gospel of Luke (12:18) in order to define the context and purpose for excess riches. In addition to the function of distributing wealth, Aquinas speaks in terms of the merit due the person that gives to those in need.

110. Cf. *ST* II-II 117.2.

Magnificence, in contrast, addresses these same two objects at different levels.[111] First, it relates to the difficulty concerning monetary transactions and possessions that are properly proportioned to great works. A magnificent person directs his efforts, using reason to find a proportion of expenditure fitting for the great works at hand. Second, humans must efficaciously manage the related passions—the love and desire for these great means—amidst the project's difficulty. The passions are more strongly influenced since these great goods and works confront risks; we may incur great loss.[112] For these reasons, the irascible passions are more central than the concupiscible. We need to hope that we can complete the project and not be dispossessed of our property in the process.[113] Although the proportions differ, both generous and magnificent people spend their money and give their possessions readily and with pleasure.[114]

The outlay needed for a great project is a secondary aspect of the virtue of magnificence. It concerns both intellectual planning and emotional engagement. Only once we have adjudicated that a venture is a fitting end can we set about to find appropriate means to accomplish it. We must calculate the details in terms of their suitability and cost. Through magnificence, we seek to maximize the quality of the work for the expense.[115] Through waste or meanness, however, we can derail this effort.

Meanness or stinginess involves several problematics. First, on the level of the passions, it entails an inordinate attachment to our own goods. The possibility of failure related to great projects produces greater fear of being dispossessed and thus exasperates tightfistedness. Second, in the measure of the end, the miserly person intends something little, where it is fitting to aim higher, and where magnanimous people intend something great. The latter tend to great projects, because of the good involved; then they calculate and accept the expense in turn. While the stingy person first measures the expense, looking to minimize his outlay; then he intends to do a small work.[116] He fails by aiming below the mark, by not even considering other goods, except in the optic of their material expense. Inhibited by love of

111. Cf. *ST* II-II 134.3.

112. Cf. *ST* II-II 134.4 ad 3.

113. Cf. *ST* II-II 134.4 ad 1.

114. Cf. *ST* II-II 135.1 ad 3.

115. See *ST* II-II 134.3 and *ST* II-II 135.1, where Aquinas quotes Aristotle (*NE* iv.4, 1122b13–18; *In Eth.* 4, 6, 718). This idea concerns the proportion—a more adequate relationship between cost and the quality of the project. It involves reason applied in art—the virtue of art in relation to the cost of the work.

116. Cf. *ST* II-II 135.1.

possessions, he will not spend for a project of philanthropic or entrepreneurial value. Third, he "does not regulate his affections according to reason, but, on the contrary, makes use of his reason in pursuance of his inordinate affections."[117] Such greedy and ungenerous people spend only with sadness and delay.[118]

Conversely, when one is wasteful, one spends more than is reasonable for a project. One overestimates the value of the venture. Thomas recognizes that a particular work calls for a proportioned expenditure.[119] Thomas uses the Latin term *consumptio*, since this type of spending acts like a fire that consumes all for no good purpose.[120]

How does the evolutionary approach on altruistic conspicuous consumption and survival compare with Aquinas' virtue approach to magnificence and generosity? Both approaches promote an altruistic type of generosity. We find a major difference though in the moral and social dimension. Inasmuch as cultural anthropology involves an abstraction from moral adjudication and does not attend to important aspects of an act's intentionality, it seems to neglect a deeper analysis of personal involvement in promoting not only the physical survival but also the moral flourishing of one's self, family, and society. We need to incorporate fuller notions of justice and common good, unless we accept leaving the quality of survival to the invisible hand of altruistic conspicuous consumption to distribute basic goods to those in need. Aquinas' fundamental definitions of magnificence and generosity, on the contrary, cannot be separated from their larger context, which specifies a moral and just type of survival and resilience. In this case, we must correlate the difficulty of using money and possessions with the other virtues that direct them to the common good, the good of others, and one's own excellence. In particular, the virtues of justice, prudence, fortitude, and temperance necessarily underlie works of magnificence and generosity, and weigh them with a different measure than pure physical survival.[121] In the end, they involve the physical and moral flourishing of individuals and society. Magnificence and generosity interrelate with the natural virtues of magnanimity and hope, which we shall now address more fully.

117. *ST* II-II 135.1 ad 2.
118. Cf. *ST* II-II 135.1 ad 3.
119. Cf. *ST* II-II 135.2.
120. Cf. *ST* II-II 135.2. Such waste can be caused by another vice, such as the pursuit of vainglory (cf. *ST* II-II 135.2 ad 3). Moreover, in regard to the virtue of generosity or liberality (*ST* II-II 117), Thomas treats the related vices of covetousness (*ST* II-II 118) and prodigality (*ST* II-II 119).
121. Cf. *ST* II-II 117.6.

Magnanimitas *as the Natural Virtue of Hope*

We can now return to examine the way that humans confront adversity with the energy of the emotions through the disposition that Aquinas calls *magnanimitas*. By following Thomas, we can avoid a narrow concept of the emotion, disposition, and act of hope. He associates magnanimity with the management of honor, great deeds, and excellence. Here resilience is of particular benefit again; it analyzes the roles that human hope and optimism play in temperament, attitudes, and behavior.

The internal complexity of Thomas's notion of *magnanimitas* and the emotions it manages are entrenched in an obscure historical evolution and etymology. How might one best translate his notion of *magnanimitas* today? Is "greatness of soul" or "great-souledness" more illustrative than "magnanimity"? The problems of *magnanimitas* is well exemplified through the history of its Greek forbearer *μεγαμλοψυχία*, which is etymologically concerned with greatness of soul, and by definition it concerns great things (*περί μεγάλα*).[122] Seeking to avoid coloring the interpretation of this virtue with any one of its numerous facets (and thereby either infelicitously limiting it or unjustly overcharging the definition), some English translators of Aquinas have translated *magnanimitas* literally, as "magnanimity."[123] I shall follow this practice, while trying both to highlight the abundant richness of the concept and not to stray too far afield from its associations with resilience.

Other etymological problems arise concerning hope. We need to distinguish the emotion of hope and optimistic temperament from the vir-

122. Cf. *NE* 1123a34. Before Aristotle, *μεγαλοψυχία* was a part of common language that signified successively clemency, magnificence, heroic courage, grandiose ambition, pride, and finally impassivity when faced with bad fortune. Aristotle's specifically ethical treatment attempts to reconcile the vestigial Homeric values of greatness and grandeur with the newer values of moderation and the mean. For example, a heated debate among Aristotle's commentators exists about the meaning and relevancy of his definition and description of *μεγαλοψυχία*. Its meaning has perhaps elicited more divergent interpretation in recent scholarship than any other of his virtues. Some people reject it as culturally irrelevant, and others hold it as Aristotle's highest, synthetic virtue. Some of the difficulty is expressed in the way in which different thinkers translate *μεγαλοψυχία* (cf. Curzer 1990, 532 and 518; Gauthier 1951, 37–41, 52, 55–118, 273; Smoes 1995; Somme 1999).

123. Besides its literal renderings of magnanimity (Horner 1998; Rackham 1983; Curzer 1990 and 1991; Gauthier 1951; Tricot 1959; Gauthier and Jolif 1970; Somme 1999), and great-souledness or greatness of soul (Thomson 1953; MacIntyre 1966/1999; Dalimier 1992; Smoes 1995, 267), other translations include: pride or proper pride (Ross 1923/1959, McKeon 1941), high-mindedness (Greaves 1964), superiority (Thomson 1953), and dignity (Joachim 1951).

tues that bear the same name. Etymologically, the English language is poor in this regard. We use "hope" both for the theologal virtue and for everyday wishes, desires, and expectations, such as an optimistic attitude or our hopes at work, in child raising, and so forth.[124] Although lacking a clear terminological distinction in English, I shall contrast everyday hopes (in the plural), rooted in the natural passion of hope, from the fundamental theological hope (singular), which also involves grace and divine initiative. Aquinas identifies magnanimity as the virtue that manages the passions of hope and despair. Yet he also discusses it in terms of managing honor and excellence.

Optimism and Resilience: Attitudes, Emotions, and the Virtue of Hope

From a virtue perspective, individuals' natural dispositions differ. As for timidity and boldness, some humans are more hopeful, others more pessimistic. But such differences are not static. Through our actions, we modify not only our way of experiencing such emotions, but also our temperaments and dispositions.

The psychosocial sciences widely consider optimism or hopefulness as a temperament trait that tends toward acting with the expectation of attaining a good result.[125] For example, Lois Barclay Murphy conceives of optimism as "a bias evoking resilience";[126] C. R. Snyder defines it "as a generalized expectancy that good things will happen";[127] and Richard S. Lazarus and Bernice N. Lazarus describe it as "a positive expectation about what will happen."[128] Such a temperament quality elicits positive social responses

124. English, like Latin *(spes)*, German *(hoffnung)*, and Italian *(speranza)*, has only one noun for hope. French on the contrary has the advantage of possessing two separate words *(espoir* and *espérance)* that are sometimes used in order to distinguish a natural virtue, with its everyday hopes *(espoirs)*, from a fundamental or theological virtue *(espérance)*. For other reflections on this distinction between everyday or ordinary hopes and fundamental hope, see B. Schumacher (2000, 116ff.), who distinguishes *"espoir"* or *"espoirs ordinaires"* from *"l'espérance fondamentale"*; J. Pieper, who differentiates *die "Alltags-hoffnungen"* from *die "fundamentale" Hoffnung* (1967/1994, 24–28); or J. B. Brantschen, who distinguishes *die vielen "vorletzten Hoffnungen"* from *die "letzte Hoffnung"* (1992, 24–33).

125. Cf. Wills et al. 1996, 128; Murphy 1987; Rutter 1990, 182; Garmezy 1985; Seligman 1991/1998; Goleman 1995.

126. Murphy 1987, 104.

127. Snyder et al. (1991a, 571) also cite Scheier and Carver (1985), who "argue that optimists maintain positive expectations that are not limited to a specific domain or class of settings."

128. Lazarus and Lazarus (1994, 73) say: "Optimism is having a positive expectation about what will happen. In optimism one is primed for a good outcome. This is sometimes imprudent because one

from the human environment. While involving human genes, these sciences recognize that humans can develop a temperament disposition such as hopefulness in diverse fashions through interaction with their surroundings throughout life. In both individual and social domains, they construe optimism as one of the basic attitudinal dimensions of coping.

Cognitive psychologists construe hope as an emotional or sentimental reaction to a situation that one senses as beneficial, yet associated with something unfavorable. Lazarus and Lazarus (1994) deem hope an emotion with coping value, since it seldom involves a cool detachment, but rather brings emotion to action.[129] They say that:

> People generate the feeling of hope as a way of *coping* with the trouble because it is better than giving into despair. The personal meaning is that there is some chance, either by virtue of what one does or merely as a result of good luck, that the outcome we dread—and hope against—will not be as bad as was feared, or that despite what we dread, everything will ultimately turn out okay.[130]

The feeling of hope forcefully sustains us in the midst of difficult conditions. They emphasize moreover that hope is not simply a positive state of mind. Rather, as rooted in some difficulty, it is "essentially an antidote to despair." Since hope precedes a positive outcome, we need to anticipate it, without falling into "false hope."[131] They emphasize though that even vain hope gives people a footing against despair. The danger of this kind of hope, however, according to Lazarus and Lazarus, "is that the person will continue to seek what is denied and, therefore, fail to redirect his or her thoughts and energies toward a more realistic outcome."[132]

This discussion of the attitude of optimism and the emotion of hope leads to further queries about learned optimism and resilience, that is, about an acquired virtue of hope. Today's difficult encounter might render a

---

may have risked too much, and, when things go sour, it is all the more dismaying, costly, and even disillusioning. Mostly, one hopes a bad situation will improve."

129. Lazarus and Lazarus (1994, 73) describe the emotion of hope as: "a wish for better conditions of life in an ambiguous but difficult situation. Other words, such as faith, trust, security, conviction, confidence, all seem too positive and secure to carry the more tentative meaning of hope." They maintain that promise, expectation, and anticipation are synonyms for hope (72).

130. Ibid., 74.

131. Lazarus and Lazarus 1994, 72. Furthermore they say: "To the extent that hoping sustains our ability to cope actively with the way things are and to maintain a positive outlook on life, any claim about its falseness seems to lack wisdom" (71).

132. Ibid., 74.

different emotional result than yesterday's. Beyond emotive reactions, hope serves as a basis for further action. When it involves an operative disposition, a virtue for creative action, hope entails more than its associated acts, according to Aquinas. In order to understand hope-filled human agency, we need to examine emotional reactions and attitudes in the context of a person's experiences, acts, and dispositions (at social, intellectual, volitional, emotional, genetic levels), as well as the present situation.[133]

As an acquired tendency for creative action, hope is more than a temperament trait or an emotional experience or even a judgment. According to both Thomas and resilience researchers, temperament and emotional styles form a natural basis for acquired qualities that we can more fully understand only in terms of cognitive and volitional input, in a more global perspective on the human person. Having or not having an optimistic temperament is not the last word. If we can learn hopefulness, then we can extend or correct to some extent genetic patrimony and personal history.[134] A person can learn to knowingly and willingly act in the expectation of attaining a goal, and can thus ingrain such an optimistic tendency in emotion, imagination, thought, and will;[135] or correct contrary tendencies as a sort of recovery, therapy, or conversion.[136] Learned helplessness, in contrast, as a "failure to escape traumatic shock" can reinforce early pessimistic attitudes or reorient a hopeful temperament.

133. In certain cases, researchers call hope an emotion, even though they conceive it in a very complete way, even including intellectual perception and complex judgments about possible future solutions, and volition involvement in goal acquisition. For example, Janice Post-White (1998, 281) says: "Hope is an emotion in human experience that entails finding meaning in a situation, perceiving a possible solution, envisioning a future goal, and participating to achieve that goal (Lynch 1965; Stotland 1969). Hope is a situational, learned response that motivates the individual to achieve realistic, important goals (Mowrer 1969)."

134. For example, Murphy (1987, 104) describes the basic roots and early development of acquired optimism; she says: "I have shown here that the roots of early coping skills lie in the baby's active protests and selectivity, and the young child's capacity to accept substitutes and restructure experiences of gratification of needs, of being able to count on life feeling good. The optimism and hope that come from the earliest satisfying, restorative experiences are reinforced in the next few years when separations are followed by reunions, frustrations bring support in coping, pain is followed by comfort, initiatives are backed, and the child develops confidence that he and the environment will be able to manage any problem. There are ups and downs, downs and ups, and the growing child begins to feel that he can get out of the downs and help to make his life good. As Helen said at the age of 10, 'Bad things can turn into good things.'"

135. See Damasio (1999a and 1999b) on the relationship between human consciousness, emotions, and genes.

136. For example, Murphy (1987: 101) construes "learned hopefulness" in the perspective of resilience, as recovery involving aspects of the whole person.

Seligman takes a cognitive and attribution approach to understanding optimism, pessimism, and their related effects on human capacities to confront difficulty.[137] He defines optimism as a habit of the mind that enables those who face misfortune to think of it as temporally limited, as having an external cause and as being restricted in its import.[138] Confronted with setbacks and frustrations, optimism means expecting that, in general, things will turn out well. Attitudes and cognitive narrative styles are of utmost importance for optimism, which is not a static attitude. Rather Seligman conceives of it as a flexible quality that aims to increase our control over the way we think about adversity.[139] He theorizes that optimistic explanatory styles not only decrease the down time after a defeat, but also promote renewed activity.[140]

Besides his empirical approach to studying optimism, Seligman draws from several theoretical and experimental sources, namely control theory and attribution theory. The first theory identifies control as the psychological process of harnessing events and circumstances. We strive to appreciate the world's causal texture in function of our own self-efficacy: which events we can master, and which ones we cannot. To be able to meaningfully harness ongoing events and direct our activity lends itself to optimism for the present and future. However, Seligman highlights risks from two extremes: an unresponsive world and expectation of too much control. If our situation is truly unresponsive, perceived control could be counterproductive. It can lead not only to depression, but also to alternative strategies such as an energy saving, coping strategy of limited "helplessness."[141] On the contrary, expecting exaggerated responsiveness and "personal control" in internal and external forums can make us more vulnerable to crushing defeats.[142] Since

137. In addition to his notable work on optimism, Seligman is perhaps best known for his research and theories on helplessness; cf. Seligman 1975; Garber and Seligman 1980; Peterson, Maier, and Seligman 1993.

138. Seligman (1991/1998, 4–5) says that optimists and pessimists think about their hard knocks in opposite ways. The optimists "tend to believe defeat is just a temporary setback, that its causes are confined to this one case. The optimists believe defeat is not their fault: Circumstances, bad luck, or other people brought it about. Such people are unfazed by defeat. Confronted by a bad situation, they perceive it as a challenge and try harder."

139. Cf. Seligman 1991/1998, 208, and 281ff.; Goleman 1995, 88.

140. Cf. Seligman 1991/1998 and 1995.

141. Peterson, Maier, and Seligman (1993, 306; cf. 305) say that, in this case: "helplessness may be less a deficit than an alternative way of operating, a way of laying low and keeping one's eyes open when the world becomes unresponsive." Cf. Seligman 1975; Garber and Seligman 1980.

142. According to Peterson, Maier, and Seligman (1993, 307–9), the "era of personal control" can

our beliefs about our own capacities affect how those capacities are used, our performances can vary according to our sense of self-efficacy in bouncing back after failure and managing the situation positively instead of seeing defeat before starting.[143]

The second and perhaps most important theoretical aspect of Seligman's theory of learned optimism involves attribution theory. He describes it as the "explanatory style," which individuals use in attributing causality to their actions, successes, and failures.[144] Seligman's theory involves styles of explanation, instead of single narratives for single failures.[145] He proposes three dimensions of explanation (permanence, pervasiveness, and personalization), which vary according to optimistic or pessimistic narrative styles. First, optimists view good events as having permanent causes, negative events as having temporary ones. He warns that "permanent explanations for bad events produce long-lasting helplessness and temporary explanations produce resilience."[146] Second, pervasiveness contrasts universal versus specific explanations. He says: "The optimist believes that the bad events have specific causes, while good events will enhance everything he does; the pessimist believes that bad events have universal causes and that good events are caused by specific factors."[147] Thirdly, personalization identifies the target of blame for the difficulty. Optimists externalize the cause, blaming other people and circumstances; pessimists internalize the blame on themselves.

While Seligman's paradigm is in many ways convincing, it raises several

---

promote various problems: depression in young adults (a disorder of personal control); the seduction of technology (preferring the immediate but shallow responsiveness of technology, instead of person-to-person interaction); the rejection of the social world; and the promotion of egotism and special-interest mentalities (a lack of interdependence and common-good orientations in society).

143. Cf. Goleman 1995, 89; Bandura 1977.

144. Seligman takes his inspiration from Bernard Weiner, a social psychologist, who at UCLA in the late 1960s developed attribution theory. Weiner sought the factors to which people attribute their successes and failures—why some are high achievers and others not. Attribution theory runs against the Skinnerian theory about achievement, demonstrated (in the 1930s) by the partial reinforcement extinction effect (PREE). Attribution theory postulates that human behavior is controlled not only by an external environment-based "schedule of reinforcement," but also by an internal mental state, which is seen through the explanations that people make for why the environment has scheduled their reinforcements in this particular way (cf. Seligman 1991/1998, 40–41).

145. In this regard, Seligman's theory differs from Weiner's. Other differences include: a third category of explanation (pervasiveness), not included by Weiner; and a focus on achievement, while Weiner studied mental illness and therapy (cf. Seligman 1991/1998, 43–44).

146. Seligman 1991/1998, 47.

147. For Seligman (ibid., 47–8), hope depends on both the pervasiveness and permanence dimensions of explanatory style: "Finding temporary and specific causes for misfortune is the art of hope."

questions. First, is his vision of optimism based in reality? Does it rest on an explanatory theory that promotes self-delusion instead of truthfulness? We can establish one rebuttal to this charge in his approach to self-esteem. He opposes the promotion of groundless self-valuation and provides striking counter-indications of educational practices that attempt to promote self-esteem without any basis in personal worth. Unmerited self-esteem correlates with violence, aggression, and depression when the individual confronts a harsh experience.[148] Seligman does not promote empty self-esteem, but rather concentrates on skill acquisition in overcoming defeat and misfortune. Self-esteem follows then as a natural consequence.[149]

The second question is: In promoting external blaming-strategy (blaming other people and circumstances, rather than our own shortcomings), does Seligman at the same time encourage an egotistical orientation and an antisocial mentality? Elsewhere, he attempts to provide a social context for his theory of optimism promoting narrative style. For example, he claims that "becoming an optimist consists not of learning to be more selfish and self-assertive, and to present yourself to others in overbearing ways, but simply of learning a set of skills about how to talk to yourself when you suffer a personal defeat [. . .] from a more encouraging viewpoint."[150] Seligman's approach to learned optimism offers merit and illustrates facets of acquired resilience. Its close proximity to a virtue approach on hope invites a more in-depth investigation.

The Virtue of Hope: Goals, Agency, and Developmental Pathways

Psychosocial studies on goal-directed behavior aid us in further differentiating hope from optimism. They have distinguished goal perception from goal attainment and desire for an outcome from efficacious behavior.[151]

148. Baumeister, Smart, and Boden (1996) indicate that self-esteem can be a factor that causes violence in criminals. Seligman's conclusion is that "if you teach unwarrantedly high self-esteem to children, problems will ensue," such as violence and depression (Seligman 1991/1998, vii). On the importance of self-esteem for resilience, see Lösel 1994, 9.

149. Seligman recognizes that achievement is a function of talent, as well as the capacities of explanatory style that withstand defeat. Cf. Peterson, Maier, and Seligman 1993, 310; and Goleman 1995, 89.

150. Seligman 1991/1998, 207.

151. Researchers often contrast hope with optimism. According to Snyder et al. (1991a, 571), "Hope is similar to optimism in that it is conceptualized as a stable cognitive set reflecting general rather than specific outcome expectancies. Hope and optimism differ, however, in the hypothesized relationship between outcome and efficacy expectancies and the role that this relationship plays in the prediction of goal-directed behavior."

These studies have made advancements. Previously, a predominant view associated greater hope (as a goal orientation) with positive outcomes and exceptionally low expectancies for goal attainment with somatic disturbance and psychopathology.[152] More recent research, however, attempts to identify the means through which hope renders human acts adaptive; it draws on goal concepts to elucidate hope's cognitive sets.[153] Within this goal-setting framework, Snyder proposes two intertwining elements of hope: agency (efficacy expectancies) and pathways (outcome expectancies). This perspective invites a dialogue with Aquinas' virtue theory of hope.

Snyder defines hope "as a cognitive set that is based on a reciprocally derived sense of successful (a) agency (goal-directed determination) and (b) pathways (planning of ways to meet goals)."[154] First, our sense of "agency," including our will to accomplish our goals, increases hope. We gain a sense of positive agency through individual participation in goal attainment. We successfully motivate ourselves and gain a feeling of resourcefulness in front of the challenge. Second, the perceived availability of successful "pathways" to a goal bolsters hope. We seek to generate successful projects, to break down formidable tasks into manageable pieces, and to modify plans when the goals are unattainable. We employ cognitive capacities related to problem solving, but also to resisting anxiety, defeatist attitudes, or depression when faced with setbacks. Both agency and pathways involve more than single acts. They constitute "an enduring disposition" of hope, which we subjectively construct as we set goals for ourselves and attempt to attain them.[155]

Snyder's theory expects that a person's levels of facility and motivation in dealing with goals correlate with the person's behavior and achievements.

152. Cf. Post-White 1998; Erickson, Post, and Paige 1975; Stotland 1969; Frankl 1963/1984.

153. Cf. Snyder et al. 1991a; Pervin 1989; Lee, Locke, and Latham 1989.

154. Snyder et al. (1991a, 570–71). C. R. Snyder is a University of Kansas psychologist, who furthermore posits that "the two components of hope [agency and pathways] are reciprocal, additive, and positively related, although they are not synonymous" (571). Snyder et al. integrate two dominant theories (that of Bandura and that of Scheier and Carver), while disagreeing with both Bandura's emphasis on efficacy expectancies and Scheier and Carver's reliance on outcome expectancies. Snyder et al. argue (571) that "if self-related cognitions pertaining to goal-directed behavior are the sum of the reciprocal action of efficacy expectancies and outcome expectancies, as we have posited in the present hope model, then focusing on either type of expectancy alone will not completely tap the cognitive set."

155. Snyder et al. (1991a, 571) distinguish the emotion of hope from this disposition of hope. They say that "the cognitive emphasis of the present model does not imply that emotions are irrelevant, but rather that emotions are the sequelae of cognitive appraisals of goal-related activities. The quality of emotion for a particular goal-related setting depends on the person's perceived hope in that setting." Cf. Goleman 1995, 87.

His study confirms that people with a higher level of hope not only undertook a larger number of goals than people with a lower level, but also set more difficult goals.[156] Nonetheless, while the higher-hope people were "more certain" to attain their goals, the lower-hope people were found to be equally likely to attain their own goals, although these were objectively less challenging and fewer in number.[157] Snyder's health-as-an-adaptive-human-behavior perspective construes hope as relevant insofar as "health-related matters are easily conceptualized in terms of people's goals."[158] His extrapolations on this study suggest a positive correlation between hope and health levels.

What can Snyder's research and theory on hope in agency and pathways offer to enhance Aquinas' approach to the passion and virtues of hope? For Aquinas, the natural passion of hope is rooted in human love *(amor)* and desire *(passio)* and is manifest in the longing for flourishing *(beatitudo)* and the natural inclinations of the will toward the good and communion, of the intelligence toward the true and the beautiful, of the whole person toward love, family, and life in society. Thomas's perspective attends to both human origins and finality. Goals and their attachment are of ultimate and intermediate importance. In his philosophical psychology and philosophical anthropology, a person loves and desires some good thing because of the nature of the good object to attract us. In this natural dimension, we move from loving a certain good to desiring it (if we have not attained it) to hoping for it (if it is difficult but possible to achieve) and finally to experiencing joy (when we are united with it).[159] Although the underlying passion of hope relates most

156. Snyder et al. (1991a, 581–82) were surprised to find no gender differences in the level of reported hope. They speculate, however, "that gender differences in hope may emerge when different goals are explored in subsequent research."

157. Cf. Snyder et al. 1991a, 582.

158. Snyder et al. 1991a, 583; Snyder et al. 1991b. Another suggestive study on the relationship of hope and health is that of Janice Post-White (1998), which indicates a probable correlation between hopefulness, quality of life, and a strong SOC (sense of coherence). The SOC (discussed in chapter 2) is seen as reducing tension and improving health by modulating the psychological, neurological, hormonal, and immune systems. Positive effects in terms of immune function, cancer outcome, and quality of life—cognitive, psychological, and social levels—are expected, based on the three coping-related effects of stress on the immune function: 1. Poor coping skills decrease natural killer (NK) cell activity, while good coping skills and a positive attitude increase NK and neutrophil function. 2. Social support buffers stress and contributes to increased NK function. 3. "Negative emotional states that result from the psychological response to stressors may explain how psychosocial events produce immuno-suppression (Kiecolt-Glaser and Glaser 1991) and contribute to the increased incidence of infections, autoimmune disease, and cancer." (Post-White 1998, 280)

159. Cf. *De verit.*, 28, 4; *ST* I.5 ad 1; *ST* I-II 40.8; *NE* i.1, 1094a3; Pinckaers 1976, 266–71; Pieper 1967/1994, 20–24.

directly to everyday hopes, it also relates to fundamental human hope and longings. What can Snyder's approach to agency and pathways tell us about the natural level—the emotion and the virtue of everyday hopes?

Hope, as the central passion for the virtue of *magnanimitas*, tends to expect great goods, according to Thomas.[160] This hope in the midst of action, moving toward an end, is intrinsically teleological. It is not simply an optimistic attitude or temperament. Thus initiative taking, in the larger sense of *aggredi*, mobilizes human activity, including our own and other resources toward a difficult goal. In order to complete acts of maximal intensity, we muster a battery of personal energy and social resources. For Aquinas, magnanimous people have the power to focus their emotional and intellectual energies on life's important tasks.[161] This attentional and effective capacity involves natural and acquired emotional and bodily dispositions and moral and intellectual character.

Through magnanimity, we employ the stimulus of hope as well as daring, in addition to justified fear of failure and related passions. What is great and difficult can elicit hope, just as it can elicit despair. It can mobilize action, just as it can freeze human initiative.[162] The difference between hope and despair is found in the possibility of attaining the object. More than a logical possibility, the agent must possess the needed physical power, psychological energy, intellectual plan, and needed external assistance.[163] Desire confronted with difficulty is transformed into hope only when we judge that we can attain the desired object.[164] Snyder's typology of high and low levels of hope usefully illustrates the power of great goals to attract us and the immobility that comes when we do not have the agency or pathways for attaining the goal. His speculation about the connection of hope and health is suggestive not only for everyday hopes but also for our fundamen-

160. Cf. *ST* II-II 129.5 obj.3 and ad 3.

161. Cf. *ST* II-II 129.3 ad 4.

162. According to Aquinas, the difficulty and greatness at which hope aims precipitate repulsion and frightened retreat. Cf. *ST* I-II 23.2; *ST* I-II 25.3, ad 2; *ST* II-II 161.1.

163. Cf. *ST* I-II 40.3 ad 2; Gauthier 1951, 327–28.

164. Cf. *ST* I-II 40.1. We recall also Breznitz's interesting insight into a psychology of hope, despair, and hopelessness. He describes despair as having nothing left to lose (but something to gain through the involved risk). The risks involved in an act of desperation are extreme because of the extreme situation. According to Breznitz (1986, 303), the "opposite of hope is not despair, but the absence of hope. Whereas, in despair there is nothing to lose; in the absence of hope, there is nothing to gain. Despair may yet act as a motivating force for acts of despair, whereas, in the absence of hope, there is no energy left." One can reasonably ask whether such acts have only tragic results (e.g., suicide terrorism) or also surprisingly good ones (altruistic death-defying acts).

tal hope. Nonetheless, Thomas offers a deeper philosophical anthropology concerning the natural movement of hope in terms of finality and the development of magnanimity as an operative disposition. In order to demonstrate this point more fully, we shall now examine how personal and social resources motivate hope.

Hope and Resources: Oneself and Others

The emotion and the natural virtue of hope do not simply aim at goals that are within the reach of a person's attainment. Hoping can pertain to oneself and to others. Its pathways are not only personal, but also social and theological. Thomas makes an important distinction between hoping in our own personal capacities (*sperare tantum*) and hoping in the assistance of another (*exspectare* or *expectare*). Medieval thinkers understood *exspectare* (to look at, to consider) and *exspectatio* (consideration) as the cognitive act preceding the movement of the passion of hope. This cognitive process considers both a hoped-for great good and another person, through whom we obtain it. Through this kind of hope, we keep our eyes not only on the sought-after good and our personal capacities, but also on the other (*ex alio spectare*). Thomas considers *sperare tantum* (hoping in one's own capacities) as pure human hope, and *exspectare* as hope linked to the expectation of needing the help of others.

On the one hand, the object of a human hope is a difficult and great good we can attain by ourselves, through our own means and strength, our own planning and execution. This hope is the primal form (archetype) of the passion of hope as *sperare tantum*, which, according to Aquinas, the virtue of magnanimity manages.[165] Resilience research has demonstrated that competency can breed hope inasmuch as our experiences of overcoming difficulty give rise to hope for future successes. When we cope with hardship, for example, we build up a type of immunity, which involves a situational mastery and learned hopefulness. This immunity counteracts learned helplessness and past experiences of failure.[166]

Human expectation on the other hand is involved in a second kind of hope. We derive it from the first type, which always serves as the basis of pure impetus—the simple movement of the appetite, since it has but one

165. Cf. *ST* I-II 40.2 ad 1; cf. Gauthier 1951, 341 n. 3.

166. Cf. Werner and Smith 1986, 157; Werner and Smith 1992, 209; Meyer and Lausell 1996, 125.

object. When in certain cases we need the help of others in order to attain the sought-after goal, we feel hope in our own capacities as well as a confident expectation in the help of another. The other (person or group) supplies a second object to hope.[167] This type of *exspectare* does not mean delay, immobility, or simple possibility, however. It implies neither pure receptivity of hoped-for goods nor a lack of an effort to reach for them. Rather here, we consider the good in terms of the means of attaining it, which establishes confidence in oneself and the other.[168] Aquinas employs one underlying psychological structure for both types of hope (*sperare* and *exspectare*): a good object (which is future, great, and difficult) and the accompanying confidence (in another and in oneself).

Aquinas identifies three characteristics of the virtue of *magnanimitas* that illustrate how it is a type of constructive resilience. First, magnanimity concerns the passions of hope and despair concerning doing great things.[169] It manages extremes in both directions concerning future goods that are difficult but possible for us to obtain. Second, it has two sources of efficacy. It tends to something that is within one's own power properly, and secondary only with someone's assistance.[170] Third, the object desired is a good. This emotional aspect demonstrates why magnanimity is the virtue of hope (as a natural passion) for Aquinas.[171] His notion of magnanimity, however, is not so simple; this virtue also manages honor and excellence in human agency.

Sidetracked by False Hopes, Presumption, and Despair

Because of false hopes, presumption, despair, and faintheartedness, we fail to accomplish fitting ventures. These unresilient dispositions represent a vulnerability to fail in constructive initiatives. But before treating St. Thomas's approach to these psychological and moral weaknesses, we shall examine psychosocial insights on the functional advantages or pseudo-resilience of non-hope phenomena, such as despair, denial, and depression.

Empirical research on hardship has observed not only the efficacy of

167. Cf. *ST* I-II 40.2 ad 1; *ST* I-II 40.7; *ST* I-II 42.1; *ST* I-II 43.1 ad 1 and ad 2; *ST* I-II 62.4; cf. Gauthier 1951, 342 n. 2.

168. Concerning *fiducia*, see *ST* II-II 129.6; Gauthier 1951, 344.

169. Cf. *ST* I-II 60.3; *ST* I-II 60.4.

170. Cf. *ST* II-II 17.5 ad 4; *ST* II-II 17.1.

171. The following scholars also hold that Aquinas' notion of magnanimity is the natural virtue managing the passion of hope: Gauthier 1951; Horner 1998, 430; B. N. Schumacher 2000.

hope, but also the utility of denial and despair in certain situations. Breznitz says: "even an ineffective coping mode is better than none at all" and denial and despair can be psychological "vital signs" in an individual's struggle to cope.[172] He argues that the opposite of hope is not despair, but rather the absence of hope. He continues: "whereas in despair there is nothing to lose; in the absence of hope, there is nothing to gain. Despair may yet act as a motivating force for acts of despair, whereas, in the absence of hope, there is no energy left." The energy that drives acts of despair may well exist, but the moral and resilience question involves where we direct such deeds. Breznitz's understanding of despair moreover guards an element of hope and thus differs from Aquinas'.

Researchers likewise argue that depression can have positive consequences. Pelham's survey of psychosocial studies suggests "that depressed people react to their acute distress by engaging in self-serving biases and striving to develop positive self-views."[173] He argues that the use of compensatory self-enhancement can offset losses in one dimension of the self-concept by boosting self-perceptions in another.[174] Once again moral and resilience questions arise. What is the reality behind our self-concepts, especially when we "enhance" them? And how long can we consciously deceive ourselves with false hope? If artificially enhanced self-concepts serve as short-term tools to overcome depression, we can include them in a larger context of health, realism, and finality. Aquinas' notions of presumption and other failures in constructive resilience illustrate this broader vision, but should integrate (in a developmental perspective) the manner that self-serving bias (enhaced self-concepts) may aid a long-term goal.

Presumption as an excess of hope implies an immoderate expectation of what we can accomplish through our own powers. According to Aquinas, we cannot attain all arduous goods through human power. Moreover, not all humans can equally do what others can. Exceptionally gifted people tend to make others marvel by their great deeds. But each human is unique in background, training, native gifts, social network, and so forth. And while we need each other's strengths to attain our goals, it is presumptuous to

172. Breznitz 1986, 303.

173. Pelham 1991, 670–71.

174. Pelham (1991, 670) furthermore points out that most depressed people manage to escape by themselves (with their own personal and local resources) from their depression without psycho-medical interventions.

think that each human can do the same job as well as another. However, presumption is not simply the sin of the weak, of those who are incapable of great things.[175] We can presume too much of our capacities for several reasons. We mislead ourselves by a false appreciation of our capacities (lack of self-knowledge or confusion of riches with ability or self-worth). A type of false bravery also comes through overestimating the skills acquired through experience. Such false hopes spring from the anger that blinds us to the larger context and to what we really need in order to resolve the situation. They also hope that we shall triumph merely because we have succeeded before, not because of any personal skill acquired through experience.[176] A desire for inordinate honor, glory, money, or success can mislead us.[177] When we press such ventures beyond due measure, we doom them to failure.[178]

In addition to false hopes and presumption, Thomas considers the ways that despair, insecurity, and faintheartedness sidetrack hope and initiative. Fear produces despair and causes one to conclude that the future arduous good is impossible to attain.[179] Such fear overrides hope, which is also weakened by laziness, impurity, and depressive sadness, according to Aquinas.[180]

In hoping to accomplish great deeds, we can also err through insecurity. When insecure we lack due confidence in our own excellence and abilities. We misapprehend our external resources and ourselves. Through lack of proper self-esteem, we overly criticize and thereby undercut our own efficacy. In addition to having a relationship with our genetic constitution, environmental support, and interpersonal attachments, sustainable self-esteem is rooted in skill acquisition rather than empty ego inflation. The negative side of flattery-based self-esteem mirrors the positive traits of authentic competency-based self-esteem. The former favor violence and aggression, while the latter bolster pro-social motivation. Security, according to Aquinas, counts on an intertwined web of personal and social resources. Errors in self-inspection and evaluation of past deeds can make us fearful, even to the point of despair. Insecurity can immobilize us or, less severely, simply

175. Cf. Gauthier 1951, 354–55.

176. See Aquinas' *Commentary on the NE* (*In Ethics*, 1, 3, 17, 577).

177. Cf. *ST* II-II 130.2 ad 3.

178. In the context of theological hope, Aquinas distinguishes two types of presumption, one of which concerns the virtue of magnanimity, when we immoderately hope in our own capacity to attain an arduous good (cf. *ST* II-II 21.1).

179. Cf. *ST* I-II 40.4; *ST* I-II 45.2; and *ST* II-II 20.1–4.

180. Cf. *ST* II-II 20.4.

present undue barriers to action: for example, as when we do not even hope for the things that are within our reach. When insecure, we do not strive for the great deeds of which we are capable; we are overcome by fear of failure or immobilized in despair.[181] This point recalls the insights of John Bowlby and attachment theory concerning the importance of bonding relationships, as well as Aquinas' account of security and confident action that build upon an intertwined web of personal and social resources.

In the face of impressive difficulty and opportunities for excellence, we can show ourselves to be great or timid, even in minor things. Aquinas calls the latter littleness of soul or faintheartedness, by which we deem ourselves unworthy of things within our grasp.[182] In this vice of unused strength, we are discouraged by pride, fear, or a lack of self-confidence. Through pride, we can cling too resolutely to a false opinion about our incompetency.[183] We can desist from fittingly taking on a great project, because of either fear or ignorance.[184] Fear of failing in matters that we falsely judge beyond ourselves can cause us to shrink from the great things of which we are worthy and capable. Ignorance of our true capacities can be caused by laziness when we neither consider our own ability nor accomplish what is within our power.[185]

Aquinas holds that we have a natural inclination to act commensurately with our capacities. While presumption exceeds what is proportionate with our capacities, faintheartedness falls short of this measure. We are timid inasmuch as we have abilities, natural disposition, knowledge, and external fortune, but fail to use them for excellence.[186] He illustrates this extreme through the parable of the slothful servant who out of fear faintheartedly buries instead of trades with the money left in his charge.[187] In timid acts, we err not only by leaving our potential undeveloped, but also by not doing what benefits others.[188]

A natural moral virtue of hope (as magnanimity), according to Aqui-

181. Cf. *ST* II-II 129.7.

182. *ST* II-II 133.2; cf. *NE* iv.7, 1123b9–13; *In Eth.* 4, 8, 740; cited in *ST* II-II 133.1 obj. 2 and obj. 4. Faintheartedness takes various forms, which oppose the exaggerated greatness found in presumption, ambition, or vainglory.

183. Cf. *ST* II-II 133.1.

184. Cf. *ST* II-II 133.2.

185. Cf. *ST* II-II 133.2 ad 1; cf. *NE* iv.9, 1125a23–24: *In Eth.* 4, 11, 786. This sloth is opposed to solicitude (cf. *ST* II-II 47.9).

186. Cf. *ST* II-II 133.1 ad 2.

187. Aquinas refers to Mt 25:14–30 and Lk 19:11–27 in *ST* II-II 133.1.

188. In *ST* II-II 133.1 ad 1, Aquinas calls upon both Aristotle *NE* iv.9; 1125a18–19; *In Eth.* 4, 11, 784; and St. Gregory *Pastorali* I, 5: *PL* 77, 19 C.

nas, specifically assures a rational mean in hoping for a future good. It seeks avoiding the extremes of false hope, presumption, despair, and weakness.[189] Its finality involves truth and realism, although we may make slow progress in approaching them through well-developed virtue. Indeed the intermediate steps involved in attaining everyday hopes are necessarily complex. For example, an object of hope might motivate an action that has become possible to hope for only because competing objects have been wrongly abandoned through despairing their possibility or through indiscriminate choice. Natural hope-phenomena, as illustrated by Breznitz's example, are not always normative; they can prove to be maladapted. We must rectify human hopes in terms of our intermediate and ultimate goals. Aquinas offers a metaphysical, moral, and psychological foundation for a further analysis of such phenomena of failed and resilient hopes.

Accenting Honors or Excellence?

Hope, optimism, and their contraries do not explain the whole of initiative. At least Aquinas' notion of *magnanimitas* recognizes that honors and excellence play constitutive roles in human agency as well. Two practical questions, though, concern the accent he accords honor and excellence in hope-filled action, and what difference it makes for constructive resilience.

Aquinas on Virtue Guiding Honor

St. Thomas emphasizes magnanimity's rational management of natural hope. Why then should he concern himself with saving a place for honor in his treatment of this virtue? This question might not trouble one, since modern and postmodern disregards for honor minimalize this concept.[190] Honor is nonetheless one of the gateways to exploring the magnanimous person's sociability for Aquinas. Any but the most individualistic evaluations of human efforts raise questions about honor. What place of honor does Thomas accord to human efforts? Can an honor-seeking motivation be unambiguous? We miss the full depth of these questions and Aquinas' perspective if we construe honor as self-centered reference to a non-social ideal of the human being.

189. On the need for a mean in moral virtue, see *ST* I-II 60.4.

190. Peter Berger (1983, 172–81) outlines the violent abuses that people have perpetrated in the name of honor.

Studies in cultural anthropology remind us that conceptions of honor define the value that we have in our own eyes, but also in those of others. In regard to the ancient, medieval, and modern Mediterranean worlds, cultural anthropologists have found that honor is a "pivotal value" expressed in a general honor code as well as local ones.[191] They suggest that social forms of honor have varied according to cultural influences, in particular according to a given culture's dominant values, such as veracity, self-renunciation, loyalty, or military courage.

Ancient and medieval worldviews are intent on archetypal and hierarchically ordered social roles, practices, and institutions in which honor has a particular regulatory function. Both modern and postmodern conceptions of the self, on the contrary, define self-worth in terms of human dignity instead of public recognition and honor. Thus, Martha Nussbaum can reappropriate magnanimity by simply grounding its "attitudes and actions with respect to one's own worth" without acknowledging the place that a hierarchical system of goods play in self-valuation.[192] Nonetheless, the social aspects of honor, as being integral to related notions such as self-worth, are essential for understanding Aquinas' magnanimous person.

Thomas's notion of *magnanimitas* synthesizes the rich doctrines of Aristotle, Cicero, and Scripture on the finality and function of honor in human agency, especially in great and difficult deeds, but also in more ordinary experience. Following Aristotle, Aquinas identifies two virtues concerned with honors. The first involved with ordinary honors is nameless, while its extremes are called *philotimia,* love of honor, and *aphilotimia,* lacking love of honor. The second is *magnanimitas,* which like other moral virtues manages that which is great in a passion, in this case great honors.[193] It is curious that a whole philosophical tradition lacks a name for the virtue that manages the ordinary honors. Does this absence mean that every honor is conceptualized in relationship to great honors, that even the unsung glory of a normal life finds motivation in great ideals?

191. According to Jerome Neyrey (1998, 5–8), honor and shame are the key concepts for understanding sacred Scripture. In a historical-critical perspective, he contends that we correctly understand Scripture only by taking into consideration the local culture. In particular, we understand the culture of honor and shame through a study using the models and efforts of modern cultural anthropology in dialogue with ancient rhetorical theory (i.e., Aristotle, Cicero, Quintilian), which in practice influenced the elite and the non-elite, the rural and urban populations, males and females, although in different ways.

192. Daniel McInerny (1997, 78–79) makes this charge concerning Nussbaum's "Non-Relative Virtues: An Aristotelian Approach" (1988, 32–53).

193. Cf. *ST* II-II 129.2.

This perspective on honor is that of the ancient world and Aquinas, who target nothing less than flourishing through human acts. In particular for Aquinas, the search for flourishing not only is great in itself, but also informs the relatively great difficulties in virtuously managing more mundane honors and shame. Thomas claims that the mode of reason observed in virtuously employing and seeking great honors is much more difficult than for normal honors.[194] What is great serves as a training ground for lesser trials of honor and shame. People who make good use of great honors are more able to make good use of lesser honors, as well as being well-ordered in regard to dishonor or shame. We must resist the ways honor can mislead us, and avoid extreme relationships with honor.

Aquinas holds that honor has several purposes. In general, it serves as a source of motivation (as a final cause), for in order to attain honor and avoid shame, people set aside all other things.[195] It aids in focusing one's attention, efforts, and even affections. Furthermore, it has a social function (an efficacious causality), for he considers that excellent qualities should be praised in order to benefit others.[196] We should use honor to benefit others. For example, one can translate the honors that come with a position of dignity into assistance for others. Although human honor is not the ultimate source of good, it is a useful good.[197]

Even though an ordinate desire of honor can hearten people to do good and to avoid evil, humans can abuse honor.[198] Aquinas follows Cicero in holding that the inordinate desire for honor tends to lead us to unjustly dominate others.[199] Such tests of the social dimension of magnanimity contrast with Aristotle's self-absorbed magnanimous person. Aquinas' sense of overall goodness does not focus exclusively on interior or personal goods or autonomy.[200] Rather this conception of the virtue of magnanimity involves an other-regarding tension. As the crown of the virtues, it is the fulfillment of the other virtues. For Aquinas as for Aristotle, contrary to the position of Nietzsche, a person cannot be both wicked and magnanimous.[201] Rather, magnanimous people focus their attention totally on the goods of com-

194. Cf. *ST* II-II 129.2 ad 1.
195. Cf. *ST* II-II 129.1.
196. Cf. *ST* II-II 131.1.
197. Cf. *ST* II-II 131.1 ad 3.
198. Cf. *ST* II-II 131.1 ad 1.
199. Cf. *ST* II-II 131.2 sc.
200. Nonetheless, Aquinas does consider magnanimity as overall goodness, with a certain priority on the interior life, since the magnanimous person is fully concerned with the internal goods, which are truly great. See *In Eth.* 4, 10, 777.
201. Cf. Horner 1998, 431.

munity and God in actions that are "beneficent, generous, and grateful."[202]

According to Thomas, while we should not care disproportionately for honors, we should not care too little for them either. Reason should regulate such desires for good.[203] A deficiency in appreciation for honor can lead a person to asocial habits: not avoiding what is contrary to honor, not seeking to be worthy of honor, not honoring the good that others do—that is, a slothful inertia. A deficient sense of honor can lead us to inappropriate levels of shame as well. In general, shame functions to dissuade us from doing what is base.[204] Not only honor, but also shame, depends upon social networks. According to Thomas, anonymity can weaken a sense of shame, while proper levels and types of shame, on the contrary, encourage us to act aright when peers support us.[205] According to Aquinas, the perfectly virtuous person does not experience shame, since he does not even imagine doing what is evil. In the meantime, for those developing in virtue, it serves a pedagogical function.

How do these indications on the finality and function of honor and shame relate to those previously mentioned concerning hope, despair, and resilience? When Aquinas says that magnanimity is primarily about the emotions of hope and despair (rather than the emotions of honor and shame),[206] he does not discredit honor. While he defines magnanimity as immediately concerning the passion of hope (as its proximate matter), honor on the other hand is placed as the intermediate object of magnanimity.[207] Even though Aquinas provides us with a key to understand how hope and honor correlate, we need to ask how he saves a place for honor.

First, although Aquinas places such importance on honor, it is a secondary object for the virtue of magnanimity. As the greatest external object of the passion of hope, honor "tends to the difficult good."[208] Even though it is not the greatest difficulty, which involves the danger of death and concerns directly the virtue of fortitude,[209] magnanimity strengthens the mind in

202. *In Eth.* 4, 10, 779; cf. *ST* II-II 129, 4, ad 2.

203. Aquinas (*ST* II-II 131.1 ad 1) demonstrates similarities to Stoic teaching in this regard.

204. Cf. *ST* II-II 144 articles 1–4. Aquinas cites St. John Damascene (*De fide orth.* ii, 15) and Nemesius (*De nat. hom.* xx) in *ST* II-II 144.2 sc. He cites Aristotle throughout his discussion, see especially *NE.* iv, 9 (cited in *ST* II-II 144.4 sc). Cf. *ST* II-II 72 on reviling; and *ST* II-II 74 on derision.

205. Aquinas finds support for this insight from Aristotle; cf. *Rhet.* II.6, cited in *ST* II-II 144.3.

206. Cf. *ST* I-II 60.4.

207. Cf. *ST* I-II 129.1 ad 2; *ST* I-II 60.5. Aquinas' original insight is an innovation in regard to Aristotle's position, which despises hope inasmuch as it implies weakness.

208. *ST* II-II 129.1 ad 2; cf. *ST* I-II 40.1; *ST* I-II 45.1; *ST* I-II 60.5.

209. Cf. *ST* II-II 129.5.

hope against challenges of being worthy of honor. He says: "magnanimity by its very name denotes stretching forth of the mind to great things."[210] This stretching forth of the mind, soul, or spirit can relate to many objects and acts, including the best use of the greatest goods; it concerns both all virtues and being honored for virtue. Honor is the greatest of external things, that is, honor as an attestation of virtue, in particular concerning great and difficult matters.[211] Honor is positive contact with a social realm, inasmuch as the latter can appreciate the level of honor due. Second, Thomas's correlation of hope and honor becomes clearer when we look more deeply at how they interact in his treatment of excellence in great and difficult action.

Magnanimitas *as a Life of Excellence?*

To seek to be worthy of honor leads one to pursue excellence. The ordering of honor toward excellence, however, is not always so evident. Different schools of thought have tried to work excellence into the notion of magnanimity. Although Aristotle defined magnanimity solely in terms of a person's being worthy of honor (because of their excellence), one can legitimately ask whether honor provides sufficient matter for a virtue. Indeed, scholars have debated this issue for centuries. Abelard, for example, defined magnanimity in terms of initiative taking and great action. Although St. Albert follows closely Aristotle's emphasis on honors, St. Thomas seems more conscious of the limitations inherent in this view. He attempts a synthesis between Aristotle and Abelard.[212]

Aquinas' *Commentary on Aristotle's NE* emphasizes initiative taking concerning great actions and enterprising aspirations,[213] offering a triple correction of Aristotle. First, while Aristotle says that magnanimity implies that we desire great things, Aquinas adds a gloss to the effect that the magnanimous soul *(animus)* focuses on *accomplishing* a great action.[214] Second-

210. *ST* II-II 129.1.

211. Cf. ibid.; *ST* II-II 103.1 ad 2; *ST* II-II 129.4 ad 1. We should not forget that for Aquinas honors are also important because they are given to God and to the best. This view of honor rectifies a disregard of virtue.

212. This synthesis can be said to find its formula in Aristotle, and its "soul" in the Abelardian current (via Philip the Chancellor and the *Moralium dogma*); cf. Gauthier 1951, 282 and 310. According to Horner (1998, 433), "Aquinas, filling out Aristotle's account, manages to preserve both the minimal requirements of ordinary virtue and the maximal requirements of extraordinary virtue. The maximal is rooted in the minimal; in going beyond it does not replace, subvert, or compete with it."

213. Gauthier (1951, 315) thinks that Aquinas takes this tack only after a few hesitations about the importance to give to honors in magnanimity.

214. Cf. *ST* II-II 129.1; *NE* 1123a 34–5.

ly, while Aristotle's magnanimous people judge themselves to be worthy of great things, Aquinas' gloss describes a type of self-esteem that comes from being worthy of *doing* great things.[215] Thirdly, Aristotelian magnanimous people seek what is great in each virtue, which Thomas explains as magnanimity inclining us to *do* what is great in each virtue.[216] Aquinas emphasizes a type of agency, greatness in action.

We need to ask whether Aquinas is treating only extraordinary excellence in the context of magnanimity. Some scholars affirm this interpretation for both Aquinas' and Aristotle's conceptions of magnanimity.[217] Aquinas, however, explains that "an act may be called great in two ways: in one way proportionately, in another absolutely. An act may be called great proportionately, even if it consists in the use of some small or ordinary thing, if, for instance, one makes a very good use of it: but an act is simply and absolutely great when it consists in the best use of the greatest thing."[218] Concerning external things, honor is simply the greatest, since it is most akin to virtue. Although it is integrally related, it is nevertheless secondary to human flourishing.

This response leaves the question of how becoming worthy of honor depends on having requisite means at our disposal and on human action. We need to have a certain security of means in order to attain great honor or accomplish something great. Aquinas describes such means as the good not only of fortune, riches, or power, but also friends.[219] As in the case of virtue in general, which involves a level of self-sufficiency,[220] magnanimity employs external means and engages human relationships in order to act more expeditiously,[221] remaining nonetheless detached from these external goods. The magnanimous person does not waver in their presence or absence, neither rejoicing at obtaining them nor grieving at losing them, except in the case of friendship. He esteems them as useful for accomplishing virtuous deeds and living a virtuous life.[222]

215. Cf. *In Eth.* 4, 8, 736.

216. Cf. *NE* 1123b30; *ST* I-II 66.4 obj. 3; *ST* II-II 129.4 ad 1; *ST* II-II 134.2 ad 2; *De virt. card.* 1, obj. 15; *In Boet. De Trin.* qu. 3, ad 2; cited in Gauthier 1951, 315 n. 4, which includes references to the *In sententiarum*.

217. Cf. Horner 1998, 436–37.

218. *ST* II-II 129.1.

219. *ST* II-II 129.8; cf. Aristotle, *NE* i.9, 1099a32–b7; *In Eth.* 1, 13, 163; *ST* I-II 4.7–8.

220. Aquinas' source here is Seneca, *De ira* i: *De vita beata* xvi.

221. Cf. *ST* II-II 129.8 ad 1.

222. Cf. *ST* II-II 129.8, ad 2 and ad 3.

The magnanimous person tends toward doing great deeds in regard to any virtue,[223] in seeking all human goods;[224] thereby he tends to what is worthy of great honors. For Aquinas, since honors are due to every virtue, magnanimity concerns all the virtues.[225] He in effect holds that a magnanimous person tends toward what is excellent and shuns what is defective. One does acts of beneficence, generosity, and gratefulness because they are excellent things to do; one disdains the contrary because they are not fitting to true excellence and greatness.[226]

Aquinas also distinguishes magnanimity, as a general virtue,[227] which has a certain priority in a sphere of human agency. The cardinal virtues have neither an absolute priority nor primacy in all regards. Rather, repeatedly Thomas introduces the case of magnanimity in order to show that other virtues can be greater in different ways.[228] Being a general virtue is one such distinction of greatness that he gives to magnanimity. It might well entail an aspect of constructive resilience. When discussing general virtues, Aquinas differentiates between three types of generality: genre, cause, and effect.[229] He specifies that magnanimity is a general virtue as a universal cause of other virtues. It is like the sun, which is the general cause of all that grows. Such a general virtue extends its influence over the whole moral life. This extension is possible for the virtues whose ends are high enough to embrace the ends of other virtues. They thereby command the other virtues to serve this higher end.[230] Beyond this ordinary sense of magnanimity, Aquinas remarks that magnanimity has a universal effect, inasmuch as it needs many other virtues to operate in fulfilling its condition. As a universal effect, it adds an extra allure to the beauty of all the virtues. The virtue of magna-

223. *ST* II-II 129.4 ad 1. As such, it is a special virtue as establishing the mode of reason in a determinate matter of honors.

224. Cf. *De malo* 8, 2; *ST* I-II 84.2; *ST* II-II 162.2. ad 4.

225. Cf. *ST* II-II 129.4; *ST* II-II 103.1 ad 2.

226. Cf. *ST* II-II 129.4 ad 2; Horner 1998, 433.

227. There are three general virtues of the moral life that serve the highest goals of the natural order: the greatness of man (magnanimity), the good of the community (justice), and the honor of God (religion). Each embraces harmoniously all the other virtues and directs them to its end, in the order of acquired virtue. At the level of grace, the infused virtue of magnanimity is completed by theological hope and charity. Charity is the general virtue par excellence for the Christian. It orders the whole life to its goal of God as Father and as Friend, and leads infused magnanimity to seek greatness by friendship with God. Cf. Gauthier 1951, 370–71.

228. Cf. *ST* I-II 61.3; see list Gauthier 1951, 364 nn. 1 and 2.

229. Cf. *ST* I-II 46.1.

230. This general virtue must then be a special (or proper) virtue with its specific end, to which it then orders a large number of other virtues (cf. *ST* II-II 58.6; cf. *In III S.*, d. 9, qu. 1, a. 1 qle 2).

nimity confirms the mind in "hoping for or obtaining the greatest goods."[231] Such firmness of mind is a quality present in every virtue, but chiefly in virtues tending to a difficult good. This firmness concerns both magnanimity and fortitude, the latter of which serves as a virtue-type for the former.[232] These qualities entail general aspects that also constitute a person's moral resilience.

Misplaced Excellence: Vainglory and Ambition

Misplaced excellence is a danger endemic to worthy projects. The emotional and intellectual energy that drives us to excellence can lead us to impasses, excesses, and vulnerability. Such failed resilience is as much a social issue as it is an individual and moral one. Thomas identifies the classic pitfalls to initiative taking as the vices of vainglory, ambition, and false humility. Concerning possible failings in human initiative, resilience research also offers insights on individual and social planes.

Competency and excellence ordinarily call forth praise. We receive rightful praise as a result of individual or joint efforts: in completing a worthwhile project (achieving peace in the midst of conflict), in overcoming major difficulty (rebuilding after disaster), or in attaining noteworthy qualities (breakthroughs in science and medicine). Glory itself is an effect of honor and praise, which make known the excellence of a person, according to St. Thomas.[233] Being glorified means being brought into the light,[234] which makes known one's qualities either to the multitude, to a few, or to oneself. It involves social recognition as well as self-knowledge. Aquinas both illustrates the positive side to glory and investigates the means by which we should seek it.

First for Aquinas, glory is basically good, true, and useful. Glory's utility does not degrade its true value or goodness. It should be sought for the good of others. Indeed, glory can edify others, who see the effect of the excellent things done by the person who receives it. Second, glory serves to motive one's own actions to better oneself and to strive one's utmost.[235] Al-

231. *ST* II-II 129.5.

232. Cf. *ST* II-II 129.5; and *ST* II-II 129.6 ad 3.

233. Cf. *ST* II-II 132.1–2; *ST* II-II 103.1 ad 3. In *ST* II-II 132.4 ad 2, he says that honor and praise cause glory (as their end) as a renown in the knowledge of others.

234. Aquinas (cf. *ST* II-II 132.1) quotes Augustine's Commentary *Super Joan.* tracts: 82, 1 (re: 15:8); 100, 1 (re: 16:13); 104, 3 (re: 17:1) *PL* 35, 1842–43, 1891, 1903.

235. Here, Aquinas (*ST* II-II 132.1 obj. 2) cites Cicero (*De Tusc. quest.* I, 2).

though both true glory and vainglory can motivate good works, Thomas nonetheless considers the works of vainglory not to be truly virtuous. The aim of the latter is vacuous self-pleasure.[236] All told, Aquinas affirms that we should not primarily seek human praise and glory in themselves nor strive for the pleasure that they bring; they nonetheless aid us to persevere in goodness, seek to better ourselves, and edify our neighbor.[237]

According to Aquinas, seeking praise and glory for our own excellence can go astray in two extremes that he calls vainglory or ambition and false humility, the latter of which was discussed earlier. In vainglory, we err in manifesting excellence[238] and precipitate instead related vices. Aquinas outlines three types of desire for vainglory: one concerns unworthy things (when we overestimate the value of something frail and perishable), another comes from uncertain sources (when we overrate judgments from fallible human sources), and the third lacks a due end (when it does not also reflect its ultimate source and contribute to the common good).[239]

Secondary (but important) risks accompany a desire for glory. First, a disordered passion for vainglory might enslave our minds.[240] We can ask, what is the long-term resilience of the human glory acquired through non-truth and injustice? As when politicians fall because of wrongdoing, through which they acquired popularity at the polls, we see that misdeeds, once revealed, bring dishonor and vulnerability at individual and social levels. Second, we run the risk of developing a disposition toward other vices, especially pride, self-complacency, presumption, and over-self-confidence.[241] In this tradition, pride denotes an "inordinate desire of excellence"[242] and is considered an utmost danger. Aquinas enumerates vainglory as one of the seven capital vices (or as the queen of all the vices) and identifies seven other vices relating to it: boasting, love for novelties, hypocrisy, obstinacy, discord, contention, and disobedience.[243] These dangers pertain to every effort, which we can do well and which can occasion public recognition.

Aquinas distinguishes vainglory from ambition. The ambitious person

236. Thomas follows Augustine (cf. *De Civ. Dei* 5, 12, 4: *PL* 41, 156), whom he cited in *ST* II-II 132.1 ad 2 and ad 3; cf. *ST* II-II 103.1 ad 3 on the distinction between honor, praise, and glory.

237. Cf. *ST* II-II 132.1 ad 3.

238. Cf. *ST* II-II 132.5; *ST* II-II 132.1; and *ST* II-II 132.4.

239. Cf. *ST* II-II 132.1.

240. Aquinas quotes Cicero *Off.* I.20 in *ST* II-II 132.2 sc.

241. Cf. *ST* II-II 132.1 ad 1; *ST* II-II 132.4; *ST* II-II 132.3 ad 3.

242. ST II-II 132.4; cf. *ST* II-II 162.1–2.

243. *ST* II-II 132.5. Thomas finds support here from St. Gregory the Great, as he does in regard to

seeks honors for excellent qualities that he does not possess or deeds that he did not do. We might seek recognition for superior knowledge through plagiarizing an essay or cheating on an exam. We might seek honor from inappropriate sources or for compromising reasons. Aquinas is however quite aware that honor and glory motivate people both in doing good and in avoiding evil. In this regard, he quotes Cicero, who says that "honor fosters the arts."[244] We can nevertheless rightfully wonder about the disproportionate (blind or shallow) honor that society and the media sometimes give to entertainers, sports stars, and politicians, who indeed have certain excellent qualities and can symbolize the hopes and dreams of youth and nations. Aquinas would consider that the honor attributed because of artistic, technical, popular, or financial success is unworthy of being desired, unless it is rooted in virtue and used toward higher goals.[245]

In order to avoid such pitfalls and acquired vulnerabilities, magnanimous people glory neither in little things (as true as they may be) nor in human opinion (truth is of the utmost importance) nor in an excess of glory in rapport with their deserts, and certainly not in contending for vainglory.[246] Rather the magnanimous are solidly rooted in honesty and flee self-complacency. For this reason, they shun not only false humility (which concerns the intellect) and vainglory (concerning social recognition), but also isolationism and individualism. According to Aquinas, we should use glory in moderation and only for good ends. Indeed, through being acknowledged by others, one "acquires clarity,"[247] which one must in turn reflect on its sources. This social dimension of resilience and vulnerability is more profound and extensive than at first sight. It entails a social dimension of virtue, which consists of the person's proper relationship to reality and social networks, as well as the way that the social entourage gives recognition to its members in order to motive their growth in excellence.

---

the analysis of other failures in virtue. Aquinas cites Gregory's *Moralia in Job* (ch. 31: *PL* 76, 621 A) in *ST* II-II 132.4 sc and corpus, and *ST* II-II 132.5 sc.

244. *De Tusc. quest.* 1; cited in *ST* II-II 131.1 obj. 3. He also quotes Aristotle and Sallust in this regard.

245. Cf. *ST* II-II 131.1 ad 3.

246. Cf. *ST* II-II 132.2 ad 1, ad 2 and ad 3.

247. *ST* II-II 132.2.

Conclusion: Constructive Resilience and Virtues of Initiative

Courage and resilience entail more than the management of fear in the face of danger. They empower us to overcome the obstacles involved in constructive human acts with concentration and hope, as well as a drive for flourishing. By doing something rather than nothing, we expose ourselves to the risks of failure. Likewise, when pursuing excellence in great and small projects, we multiply the need for resilience in the face of opposition. We demonstrate another facet of fortitude and another facet of resilience: constructive resilience and virtues of initiative.

Considerations of constructive resilience have enriched our study of Aquinas' approach to the initiative-taking virtues of magnificence and magnanimity. Placed in dialogue, resilience research and his virtue theory aid us to understand how humans not only can build life in the face of difficulty, but also can face the difficulty of building. In order to accomplish endeavors, we employ our emotional and intellectual dispositions. We engage our emotions of hope and assertiveness. We manage our desires for excellence, honor, confidence, and security. At the same time, we overcome the counterforces found in insecurity, presumption, timidity, meanness, vainglory, and ambition.

Resilience research enhances Aquinas' conception of magnanimity through its insights on optimism and hope. Through initiative-taking virtues, we mobilize hope and daring in an active and constructive resilience. These virtues are more than simple coping responses to different kinds of stress, challenge, or loss. We can differentiate them according to their sources of motivation: the quality and finality of goals, competencies, and dispositions. Social support from family, friends, and society can also make us optimistic and trusting in people's assistance. Hope and motivation underlie human agency. Our motivation increases with hopefulness, and more hopeful people are motivated to attain more challenging and more numerous goals. On the contrary, when friends and family fail us, we can acquire a sense of pessimism and distrust. Social and personal insecurity also hinder our endeavors.

The efficacy, purpose, and resilience of another type of initiative revolve around generosity and magnanimity in Aquinas' language. Evolutionary psychology offers insights on the impact that resource management styles—such as generosity, sharing, and status promotion—can have on human development and survival. They offer benefits such as returned energy, acquired fitness, and offspring survival. Aquinas, in contrast, situates generosity and magnanimity in the larger framework of truth, goodness, honor, and excellence. He measures the use of resources in terms of their contribution to the common good, personal flourishing, and a veritable search for honor that depends on the verity of the excellence sought. This perspective might or might not serve the survival advantage of individuals (and their gene pools) in a particular historical-cultural crisis. It demonstrates that virtue theory and resilience theory do not always have the same norms. Indeed, the measure of success determines outcome appraisals.

Aquinas offers insights into the misplaced searches for excellence, such as vainglory, ambitiousness, and false humility, that would counteract constructive resilience. He promotes a type of initiative that finds its roots in a truth-seeking estimate of our own resources and need for assistance. This type of initiative promotes resilience in several ways. It avoids the vulnerability endemic in false self-esteem, timidity, and other-blaming. It involves a social relationality that seeks human flourishing while building up the common good. It discerns our own capacities and limits, as well as the assistance offered through social circles. A magnanimous disposition courageously stretches us from strength to strength, while it resists overstepping rational limits. It maximizes the investment of time and energy in great and seemingly little things. It focuses collaborative human agency on necessary goals, while recognizing that lesser goals might not be achieved. Such great initiatives are synonymous with a lifestyle that seeks moral excellence and employs constructive resilience.

6

Resistant Resilience and Aquinas' Virtues of Endurance

Fortitude fails if we only intermittently stand firm to fearful things and take initiatives to accomplish our goals. In order to resist the destructive effects of adversity, rather, we need to endure with consistency and master the emotions and dispositions that give us staying power. We must endure the difficulty, hold firm in the good, resist self-destruction, and persist until we accomplish our goal. Thomas identifies two movements and distinct virtues here: patience and perseverance.[1] These virtues are key elements in his virtue theory and in understanding moral and spiritual resiliency and vulnerability.

Emotions Related to Sorrow, Suffering, and Waiting

Resilience and Social Sciences on Pain, Suffering, and Loss

Resilience research and the psychosocial sciences—such as psychoanalytical theory and neurochemical and developmental sciences—treat the

1. Cf. *ST* II-II 128; *III sent.* 33, 3, 3.

destructive and steeling effects of pain, suffering, waiting, and loss. E. J. Anthony has documented this phenomenon in regard to children who seem to have become capable of mastering life and its obstacles in the midst of painful episodes.[2] Differentiating the sources of human pain, suffering, and loss gives us a nuanced way to approach the matter of how they can be sources of risk or opportunity for resilience.

The psychoanalyst Erik Erikson's typology of human suffering proposes three levels: physical pain, psychological anxiety, and social panic.[3] On the organismic plane, experiences of physical suffering can lead to heightened thresholds of pain. This adaptation can have several effects. It can halp us to not be distracted from more important goals by physical pain and discomfort. It nonetheless can open us to vulnerability when pushed too far. This capacity is detrimental when, for example, a premature baby's ability to support pain leads him to unresilient behavior, including not avoiding excessive amounts of physical pain and the bodily damage and danger that accompanies it.[4]

The types of psychological suffering are numerous: anxiety, phobias, loneliness, loss, and so on. Resilience research has found that certain personality types and developed emotional styles present themselves as added risks or protection for certain kinds of suffering. First, timidity, for example, involves added risk of suffering anxiety due to having an easily aroused neurochemical circuitry, to avoiding unfamiliar situations, and to shying away from uncertainty. However, timidity can be a source of resilience when shy behavior protects someone from the marked dangers of a violent neighborhood or from contact with dangerous strangers. It can aid someone in focusing to accomplish tasks that are more amenable to their personality strengths. In a pacific ambiance, on the contrary, it can spell isolationism and missed opportunities.[5] According to Daniel Goleman, timid children are at higher risk for developing anxiety disorders, such as panic attacks.[6]

Second, the emotion of fear can have positive and negative effects on human psychological well-being. Fear is crucial for survival, aiding our per-

2. Cf. E. J. Anthony 1987, 180; Wills et al. 1996, 108; Lösel 1994, 9.

3. Cf. E. Erikson 1950/1985, 36. This psychoanalytical perspective is based on his conception of a human being in terms of three continuously interrelating processes of organization: as a physical organism, as a psychological ego, and as a member of society. We discussed this more extensively in chapter 3.

4. Cf. Petit, et al. 1998, 3045–46.

5. Cf. Cowan, Cowan, and Schulz 1996, 10; Consortium 1994, 275.

6. Cf. Goleman 1995, 218.

ceiving dangers, as well as avoiding and even overcoming them. Misplaced fears, on the contrary, are counter-resilient. According to Goleman, they involve the more ordinary suffering of daily frets, angst, and worries, as well as pathological extremes of phobias, obsessive-compulsive disorders, and the like.[7] Lastly, types of psychological suffering come from a heightened threshold of psychological discomfort. They can open us to vulnerabilities, as when codependent persons unnecessarily abide excessive psychological suffering.[8] However, resistance to psychological suffering also gives us endurance in pursuing a difficult good.

We also confront social sources of suffering, such as parental favoritism, family violence, discrimination, social injustice, and so forth. According to Norman Watt, children of divorced parents suffer from immediate disruptions and parental hostility (violence), and further progressive costs from latent psychological insults, such as loss, estrangement or tarnishing of primary identification figures, disintegration of family structure, sentiments of social stigma and isolation, and excessive challenges such as prematurely imposed self-reliance.[9] Social injustices produce suffering and vulnerability at family and extra-familial level, as when parents display favoritism among children or when children suffer prejudices in school. Michel Tousignant estimates that such phenomena are cumulative factors for already vulnerable children's becoming even more so.[10] An added risk arises from excessively supporting pain through social passivity.

The capacity to persist in difficulty can be risky in extremis; it can also promote resilience when rationally measured for a good end. In the second regard, we can avail ourselves of numerous fitting pathways to a goal. Yet it might be more resilient to take another tack or even to stop for some time before taking up a difficult pursuit. Researchers demonstrate that strategies of rest, humor, and play facilitate long-term effects of coping with a difficult situation, task, or goal. These strategies actually contribute to solving problems that cannot be resolved in more conventional ways.[11] Furthermore, at-

7. Cf. ibid., 297.

8. This vulnerability is only one aspect of dependent and codependent people's suffering. Cf. Beattie 1987; Albrecht and Zermatten 1994.

9. According to Watt et al. (1990, 300), divorce spells the opportunity for both acquired vulnerability and resilience.

10. Cf. Tousignant 1998, 64. According to Erikson (1950/1985, 36), as members of society, humans are susceptible to the group's panic.

11. Cf. Eisen 1988.

tachment researchers have positively correlated attachment and confidence in challenges. Lutkenhaus's experiment on the tower-building performance of three-year-olds who were securely or insecurely attached found that securely attached children tended to speed up under pressure, whereas insecurely attached children tended to slow down.[12] According to Michael Rutter, this tendency implies that "secure attachments led to a sense of confidence in their ability to meet challenges, whereas insecurity was followed by a tendency to give up under pressure." These findings suggest that the quality of our perseverance finds roots in our strategies, not only conventional cognitive goals and volitional approaches, but also those underestimated resources found in rest and humor, play and interpersonal attachments. Once again these strategies and resources show themselves to be important for the quality of life and efficacious goal achievement.

Aquinas' Typology of Sorrow and Suffering

What are Aquinas' framework, conception, and typology of sorrow and suffering? In order to understand Aquinas' conception, we shall distinguish *tristitia* (sorrow) from *dolor* (pain). In a general sense, we might translate his term *tristitia* as both sorrow (or sadness) and pain (or suffering). Thomas identifies sorrow or *tristitia* as one of four principal passions, inasmuch as it arises from all the other passions when an evil is present or a good is absent.[13]

In his more frequent and technical use however, he defines *tristitia* as a species of *dolor*.[14] Nonetheless, he then differentiates *dolor* as bodily pain from *tristitia* as the internal suffering of the soul.[15] Pain and sorrow are the counterparts of pleasure and joy respectively.[16] Two things are requisite for the experience of pain in general: the encountering of some evil and the perception of this event. Sorrow, on the contrary, is the pain that is caused

12. Rutter (1990, 200) cites the research of Lutkenhaus et al. 1985.

13. The other principal passions are joy *(gaudium)*, hope *(spes)* and fear *(timor)*. In his question on whether there are four principal passions (I-II 25.4), Aquinas supports this division of the passions with the authority of Boethius' *De consolation* (I, 7, *PL* 63, 657A–658A). Augustine's list of the four principal passions contains *tristitia*, but replaces *spes* with *cupiditas* (*De Civ. Dei* xiv.3.2 and 3.7; *PL* 41.406 and 410; which Thomas cites in *ST* I-II 25.4 obj. 1). Comparable divisions can be found in Cicero *Fin.* III, x, 35; and St. Jerome *In Ezechiel* I, i, 7, *PL* 25, 23 BC.

14. *ST* I-II 35.2.

15. Thomas (I-II 35.2) cites Augustine's *De Civ. Dei* (xiv.7; *PL* 41.411) and Aristotle's *NE* iii.13, 1118a16–23. Cf. *In Eth.* 3, 19, 610–11, and 3, 20, 613–14.

16. Cf. *ST* I-II 35.3; Deferrari 1986, 1051–52.

by an interior apprehension of the intellect or imagination. This inward pain—sorrow, sadness, and grief—is both greater and more universal than the exterior or bodily pain.[17]

We cannot understand sorrow and suffering in Aquinas' conception unless we relate them to the good and study them in the context of the other concupiscible emotions. Indeed, while a type of sorrow is managed by patience in the irascible faculty, sorrow and suffering in general arise from the concupiscible emotions: from loving something that is good, through desiring it, to the pleasure of being in union with the good *(delectatio* or *gaudium).*[18] This series in turn has its contraries: hatred of an evil object or the rejection of a good, the avoidance or dislike of it, and finally pain or sorrow when a good is not attained or an evil is present.[19]

Sorrow on the occasion of contact with evil is both an evil, inasmuch as one experiences something that is evil (even if only imaginary), and a good, since being pained or saddened at the presence of evil is a sign of the goodness rooted in the ordering of the faculty.[20] Aquinas affirms that sorrow can be good and righteous, when it involves a proper disposition to evil. The right relationship with evil depends on the proper use of reason and will, and takes emotional form in righteous expressions of sorrow and anger and virtuous form in patience and perseverance principally.

Sorrow is caused most properly by the presence of an evil,[21] which does not involve just the simple absence of good. Indeed, the apprehension of evil focuses on the undue and undesired absence of a particular good.[22] Aquinas claims that the proper cause of sorrow is the personal experience of evil, which triggers a certain repulsion of the appetite.[23] Aquinas identifies four different types of sorrow: pity, envy, anxiety, and apathy.[24] Each of these types of sorrow involves applying the notion of sorrow to its cause (object) or effect. This simple causal typology should not be read outside of

17. Aquinas (*ST* I-II 35.7) supports this insight with one authority, that of Ecclesiasticus 25:17.

18. Cf. *ST* I-II 23.1–3; and *ST* I-II 35–39.

19. Cf. *ST* I-II 23.2, and *ST* I-II 35.2. Thomas extensively treats the concupiscible virtues in *ST* I-II 26–39, drawing from Aristotle and other philosophers, St. Augustine, and patristic sources, as well as scriptural texts.

20. Cf. *ST* I-II 39.2.

21. Cf. *ST* I-II 36.1 sc, citing John Damascene (*De fide orth.* ii, 12).

22. Cf. *ST* I-II 36.1; *ST* II-II 136.3.

23. Cf. *ST* II-II 34.6; *ST* II-II 136.3.

24. Cf. *ST* I-II 35.8 corpus and obj 3, where Aquinas refers to the division of sorrow presented by Nemesius (mistakenly attributed to Gregory of Nyssa), *Nemesius* 1; PG 40, 688A.

Aquinas' realism, which includes not only physical, psychological, and social realms but also the underlying moral, metaphysical, and spiritual ones.

Through pity or mercy, we consider the evil experienced by another as our own. In the archetype of mercy, friendship-love impels us to act on behalf of the other as another self.[25] In a second type of pity, we feel sorrow for the other person, because we might fall into the same predicament.[26] Such empathetic expressions are deeply social in nature.

Through envy, we consider the good experienced by another as our own evil. Strictly speaking, envy contradicts charity, which should rejoice at our neighbor's good. This vice engenders risks to the social order when we seek to denigrate the good of the other or to emulate evildoers who unjustly cumulate material wealth.[27]

Through anxiety, distress, or perplexity, we have a certain burden on the mind, making escape from the evil seem impossible,[28] for example, when future unforeseen fears surpass our capacity to resist them.[29] The larger the source of fear and its social consequence, the more troubling the anxiety will be.

Through torpor, apathy, or depression, we are so weighed down by the evil as to be rendered motionless, speechless, and closed in on ourselves. Inasmuch as it hinders the will from enjoying some good, the presence of evil is repugnant to our movement and thus depresses or burdens the soul. The hindrance to the soul can even express itself through bodily paralysis. The strength of the sorrow depends on whether and to what degree we continue to hope to evade the evil, as will be clarified in the upcoming section on patience and hope. Aquinas adds that, in general, pain and sorrow hinder action that they produce; nonetheless, pain and sorrow serve as a type of cause when we attempt to overcome them.[30]

How can psychosocial research and Aquinas' typology of sorrow enhance each other? Resilience research observes the emotional phenomena and their developmental trajectory, especially how they lead to a positive self-organization and self-construction. Erikson's tripartite division of

25. Aquinas supports his arguments with insights drawn from St. Augustine (*De Civ. Dei*, ix.5; *PL* 41.261), St. Paul (Rm 12:15) and Aristotle (*NE* ix.4, 1166a7–10).

26. Cf. *ST* II-II 30.1 and *ST* II-II 30.2.

27. On envy, see *ST* II-II 36.1–2.

28. On anxiety or perplexity, see *ST* I-II 37.2.

29. Cf. *ST* I-II 41.4; *ST* I-II 35.2 obj 2; *ST* I-II 67.1.

30. Cf. *ST* I-II 37.3, and *ST* I-II 37.2.

sources of pain, anxiety, and panic from the physical, psychological, and social spheres benefits from a further metaphysical and moral analysis of the structure of fear and evil. Although the immediate ramifications for Thomas's analysis of these emotions are psychological, they extend to deeper moral issues. His virtue theory is more than a phenomenology of emotional states; nevertheless it benefits from a realist, metaphysically based phenomenology, especially one focused on the resources that we need to overcome and to resist adversity. Aquinas' approach to virtues leads us to inquiry into the way that humans can develop dispositions to act more responsibly. If we wish to more fully understand human agency, psychosocial insights about how humans can be resistant to acquiring vulnerability and to external destructive pressures must be read in a normative project: the goal of human growth in excellence its contribution to a more just society. These reflections serve as a propaedeutic for discussing the resilience of the virtues of patience and perseverance and the vulnerability of their contraries.

The Virtues of Patience and Perseverance in a Resilience Perspective

Aquinas on the Virtue and Act of Patience

In establishing patience as one of the four parts of fortitude (*ST* II-II 128), Aquinas analyzes how it principally involves enduring hardship or suffering in order that good be achieved or evil avoided. He employs the definition of patience that Cicero gives in his *Rhetorica:* "patience is the voluntary and prolonged endurance of arduous and difficult things for the sake of virtue or benefit."[31] To this moral definition of patience, Aquinas adds the notion of managing sorrow. For Thomas, patience (and perseverance) relates to fortitude either as one of its potential parts, when we deal with any minor adversity, or as an integral part of fortitude, when we deal virtuously with the greatest danger, specifically death for the common good.[32]

Aquinas furthermore establishes that patience concerns the mind remaining strong when faced with the sorrow and suffering that comes from withstanding evil. Aquinas extensively treats suffering and pain in his moral theory.[33] We can best understand this emphasis on suffering in the context

31. *Rhet.* II.54; cited in the *ST* II-II 128.1, and *III Sent.* 33, 3, 3, co.

32. Cf. *ST* II-II 128, ad 4, and *ST* II-II 136.4; see also chapter 3.

33. Thomas devotes twenty-five articles to sorrow and pain (cf. *ST* I-II 35–39), as well as the questions on courage, patience, perseverance, and the gift of fortitude (cf. *ST* II-II 123–140).

of the importance his virtue theory places on flourishing. He says that the role of the virtue of patience is to assure that "the mind be not broken by sorrow, and fall away from its greatness, by reason of the stress of threatening evil."[34] The object and act of patience entail safeguarding the good of reason from the sorrowful impulse of the passions, which arises from bearing evil. Aquinas goes so far as to claim that we can develop sorrow as a virtuous good.[35] Indeed, we have to wait for the possession and enjoyment of longed-for goods (especially the ultimate good). One can understand patience's object and act only in relation to the difficulty of the good and the passion of sorrow.

The philosophical framework and foundation for Thomas's explication of patience involves a natural virtue that raises many theological questions in the next chapter. However, for the time being, in order to dialogue with resilience insights better, I shall focus on its philosophical and psychological dimensions. Thomas's analysis of how patience resists the disturbance of sorrow is unique and important enough that he modifies (see italics) the classic definition from Augustine's *De Patientia:* "human patience is whereby we bear evil with an equal mind, *i.e. without being disturbed by sorrow,* lest we abandon with an unequal mind the goods whereby we may advance to better things."[36] Evil and difficulty firstly produce sorrow, then anger, hatred, and unjust injury; we employ other virtues to manage the latter three directly.[37] However, since sorrow itself has different sources, patience thus demands the aid of different virtues: temperance to manage the pain (as opposite of physical pleasure) that comes from alimentary and conjugal abstinence and fortitude to manage the sorrows (evil, suffering, and pain) that are inflicted by other people through deeds or words.[38] Even so, patience has a certain perfection or excellence; thus, Aquinas interprets the letter of James (1:4) "Patience hath a perfect work,"[39] as illustrating how patience bears hardships and plucks up any related inordinate sorrow.[40]

34. *ST* II-II 128.

35. Cf. *ST* I-II 39.2 corpus and sc.

36. *ST* II-II 136.1; citing Augustine, *De patientia* ii; *PL* 40.611.

37. While the virtue of patience manages and moderates feelings of sorrow, meekness does so for anger, charity, for hatred and justice, for unjust injury (cf. *ST* II-II 136.2 ad 1).

38. Cf. *ST* II-II 136.4 ad 2; *ST* II-II 72.3.

39. *ST* I-II 66.4 ad 2, *ST* II-II 136.2 obj. 1 and ad 1, et al.

40. Indeed, sorrow causes emotions such as hatred and anger (cf. *ST* I-II 66.4 ad 2; *ST* II-II 136, 2 ad 1). Patience also has a certain perfection in being an effect of the abundance of charity, through which

The act of patience involves not only bearing evil and not giving into sorrow, but also holding fast with a calm spirit. Patience serves all the virtues (as a general virtue) through its calming effect on the soul.[41] It indirectly serves as a foundation and protection for the virtues inasmuch as it manages the passions that are precipitated by adversity and disturb the soul.[42] Patience allows us a certain undisturbed self-domination, control, or ownership. Lastly, patience produces pleasure as a fruit that helps in overcoming sorrow and calming the soul.[43]

While patience concerns not being broken by the sorrow of the difficult effort at hand, longanimity, or long-suffering, describes the dimension of waiting, how we must remain and endure.[44] Longanimity relates to waiting in a way different than does hope. The expectation implied in hope does not emphasize the delay of what we hope for, as does long-suffering.[45] Indeed, longanimity describes how we tend to something a long way off. In facing difficulty, it participates in the dynamic of hope as a passion (instead of the passions of sorrow, daring, or fear per se). In this way it is like magnanimity, which participates in the passion of hope while daringly confronting adversity.

Longanimity relates to patience insofar as waiting causes difficulty, suffering, and sorrow. It describes how we need strength to endure over time some difficulty for the sake of good. As it is less difficult to endure the same trial for a shorter time, so we need more strength, longanimity, or long-suffering, if the trial lasts a longer time. Delay itself causes sorrow. Indeed, a delay in overcoming evil or in waiting for the good entails a certain suffering.[46] Longanimity bears the sorrow of not only facing and resisting evil but also the delay needed before enjoying the good.

In the context of his analysis of patience, Aquinas distinguishes longanimity from constancy: longanimity concerns the waiting or delay in the patient effort, and constancy concerns the involved toil. Constancy precisely

---

one bears hardships patiently (cf. *ST* II-II 184.1 ad 3). It is in this context that Aquinas quotes Romans 8:35: "Who shall separate us from the love of Christ? Shall tribulation? or distress?"

41. In this regard, Aquinas (*ST* II-II 136.2 obj 3) quotes St. Gregory the Great (*Hom. xxxv in Ev.* n. 41 *PL* 76, 1261 D) on Luke 21:19.

42. Cf. *ST* II-II 136.2 ad 2, *ST* II-II 136.2 ad 3; *III Sent.* 33, 3, 3 ad 1.

43. Cf. *ST* II-II 136.1 ad 3.

44. Cf. *III Sent.* 26, 2, 2, ad 3.

45. Cf. *ST* II-II 17.5 ad 3.

46. In this regard, Aquinas (*ST* II-II 136.5) quotes Proverbs 13:12: "Hope deferred makes the heart sick."

refers to the toil needed in persistently confronting some evil for the sake of good, or in accomplishing some good while resisting evil.

Perseverance, the Virtue of Active Waiting

Aquinas' treatment of perseverance is akin to patience, in philosophical and psychological framework. He explores perseverance as the virtue that aids us to not weary, for we need to stay attached to the future good and to resist evil when difficulty persists.[47] Aquinas reasons that a virtue may concern difficulty or goodness, either by its object or by a special difficulty. He deems the length of time, that is, persisting for a long while, a special difficulty that demands a specific virtue: perseverance.[48] He stresses the attainment of the goal, for we must "persist in good for a long time until the end."[49] He distinguishes this perseverance from the general quality of every virtue to persevere inasmuch as it is a quality difficult to change.[50]

Following Cicero (*Rhet.* II, 54), Aquinas annexes perseverance to fortitude as a secondary virtue, as they both do for patience.[51] Thomas construes fortitude, as a specific virtue, to outstrip perseverance in the order of difficulty and the way of handling it. He subordinates perseverance, as the "endurance of difficulty arising from delay in accomplishing a good work,"[52] to the difficulty addressed in fortitude, concerning the fear of fatal danger. These virtues interrelate since both perseverance and fortitude are in the irascible appetite. In particular, perseverance moderates the passion of fear as related to weariness or failure because of the length of delay entailed.

Aquinas' own definition adds, or puts an emphasis on, the duration of time in a way different from classical philosophers.[53] He says: "perseverance is a special virtue, since it consists in enduring delays in the above [temperance and fortitude] or other virtuous deeds, so far as necessity requires."[54] He notes that we shall have more occasions to persist for a certain time concerning matters of moderating pleasures (of touch) rather than the fear of death. Indeed, most often the fear of the danger of death is not endured for a long time.

47. Cf. *ST* II-II 128.1.

48. Cf. *ST* II-II 137.1.

49. *ST* II-II 137.1 ad 3.

50. Cf. *ST* II-II 137.1 ad 3; Aristotle, *NE* ii.4 1105a 32 b 5.

51. Aquinas (*ST* II-II 137.1) borrows from, yet enriches, classical definitions of perseverance found in Cicero, Andronicus (Chrysippus), and Augustine.

52. *ST* II-II 137.2.

53. Cf. *ST* II-II 137.1 sc.

54. *ST* II-II 137.1.

Aquinas remarks that a virtue sometimes also has the same name as its act, which is the case for perseverance.[55] Thomas's distinction between the habit and the act of perseverance is a useful heuristic tool. As a *habitus*, perseverance refers to the human tendency to complete a task, to achieve a goal or to persist in it. But we fulfill, or do not, a *habitus* in a particular act. As an act, Aquinas specifies two types of perseverance, according to two different types of ends: a work and a life. Some acts cannot find completion until the end of life. This distinction allows Aquinas to explain Augustine's dictum that "no one can be said to have perseverance while living, unless he persevere until death."[56] Thomas does not construe perseverance as merely a human natural virtue related to completing acts important for this life, such as building, planting, and maintaining familial and friendship relationships.

Aquinas says that constancy relates in a special way to perseverance, since both refer to the same end, persisting firmly in some good (*ST* II-II 137.3). But they differ in regard to what makes it difficult to persist in this way. Perseverance specifically pertains to the delay itself, while constancy pertains to other difficulties that come from external hindrances. According to Aquinas, the delay itself is more intrinsic to virtue than the external matters considered in constancy. As mentioned before in relation to longanimity, constancy is also a matter of moderating sorrow, since it handles difficulties. In this regard, it is also associated with patience. In concerning delays and duration, both longanimity and constancy resemble perseverance, which adds the notion of completing the act, of arriving at the end.

Not much commentary on resilience is perhaps necessary here. Perseverance serves as a synonym for resilience efforts that demand completion over time: coping, conserving, and constructing. Can everything that is said about perseverance be said about persisting resilience? Once again, context and finality are important to fix comparative standards. Aquinas discusses perseverance in a moral context, which serves to expand reductionistic notions of resilience.

The Vices in Opposition to Perseverance

In order to expand Aquinas' treatment of perseverance and to enhance resilience research, we shall examine counterexamples of failed persever-

55. Cf. *ST* II-II 137.1 ad 2.

56. *De persever.* i; quoted in *ST* II-II 137.1 obj. 2; see also chapter 9.

ance. Aquinas recognizes two vices that oppose perseverance, as extremes to a rational mean: softness or moral weakness *(mollities)* and pertinacity. He uses a tactile image to illustrate moral weakness. Thomas deems as *mollities* a person who is "ready to forsake a good on account of difficulties which he cannot endure. This is what we understand by *softness*, because a thing is said to be 'soft' if it readily yields to the touch."[57] This softness or weakness does not find its corrective virtue in indestructibility. The resilience research has demonstrated the dangers of such an exaggerated extreme.

Indeed even a strong wall will fall to the battering ram, as Thomas says. Rather, this type of weakness refers to the person who does not resist or struggle in order to stand firm.[58] Thomas claims that in this soft condition a lack of pleasure causes sorrow, when one tends to withdraw from the difficult pursuit of some good, in order to pursue a bodily pleasure. Both the intended good and the specified pleasure vie for our limited time, memory, attention, and so on. According to Aquinas, a higher good or more complete goal requires a well-ordered mind, heart, and affections. Pleasure, although good in itself, is sometimes desired inordinately or from unfitting sources, which would mean desiring and pursuing a lower pleasure instead of accomplishing a more important good with its accompanying, but delayed, joy.

Aquinas says that softness or moral weakness can be caused by natural disposition or custom, by nature, or by nurture. First, he remarks how temperamental frailties can make the mind less persevering.[59] We have examined such genetic or natural weaknesses, for example, in terms of attention deficit disorder. Aquinas, following Aristotle and the anthropology of their times, judges that women are more delicate and weaker than men and therefore demonstrate a natural frailty, making them less fit for toil and less persevering.[60] Aristotle and Aquinas must be corrected in this regard, for while males may in general have more brute physical force, women demon-

57. I offer "softness" as a modified translation, since the English edition renders *mollitiei* as "effeminacy," which is rightly to be avoided. I prefer "moral weakness" in general, and "softness" here because of the literal context. Cf. *ST* II-II 137.1. Aquinas cites Aristotle's analysis of pain in terms of softness and perseverance: *NE* vii.7, 1150a24ff.

58. See *ST* II-II 138.1, which quotes Aristotle (*NE* vii.7, 1150b6–16).

59. Cf. *ST* II-II 138.1 ad 1.

60. Cf. ibid.; *NE* 1150b15. Aristotle curiously claims that these traits of weakness are hereditary with the kings of the Scythians. Aquinas additionally quotes Deuteronomy 28:56 in a similar regard (cf. *ST* II-II 138.1 ad 2).

strate physical stamina, as well as perseverance, not only in their efforts of child-bearing and -rearing, but also in efforts at justice, compassion, and so forth.[61]

Second, we become accustomed to enjoy pleasures to the extent that it becomes difficult to stand lacking them.[62] Our imagination and memory are permeated with the attraction to pleasure in such a way that a greater good is either disregarded or considered out of its full context. We may still recognize the greater good as more important than the particular pleasure, but the distraction unsettles our concentration. Aquinas notes that indulgence in such pleasure diminishes the actual participation in the good. Moreover, he illustrates several types and causes of moral weakness. Some people are delicate and cannot support toil, since it diminishes pleasure. Others inordinately seek play, relaxation, or rest, and are thus unable to endure toil.[63]

The opposite extreme of softness is called pertinacity, in which we inordinately hold on to the good in the face of sorrow.[64] This inordinate perseverance entails a disordered consideration for the importance of oneself or one's opinion. In holding on to some good in order to seek our own glory (vainglory), pertinacious people disorder their pursuit of good.[65] In exaggerating the significance of their own views or opinions, the pertinacious err. Lastly, in persisting in something against difficulties, they inordinately desire the consequent pleasure and shun the opposing pain.[66]

The Development of Patience, Perseverance, and Resistant Resilience

Resilience Findings on Suffering and Resilient Patience

Resilience approaches suggest patience-like attitudes, activities, and character traits for overcoming pain, suffering, and loss. The term "patience," though, is infrequently found in resilience findings. More often, however, we do find patience-like phenomena in discussions on managing pain, suf-

61. Cf. M. Schumacher (2003).

62. Cf. *ST* II-II 138.1 ad 1.

63. Cf. *ST* II-II 138.1 ad 2 and ad 3.

64. See *ST* II-II 138.2, where he quotes Isidore (*Etymol.* x, ad litt. P, nn 213, 211: *PL* 82, 390 A, 389 C).

65. St. Gregory says that pertinacity arises from vainglory; Thomas (*ST* II-II 138.2 obj. 1) quotes his *Moral.* xxxi.45 al. 17, in vet. 31.88: *PL* 76.621A. Gregory is especially important support for Aquinas in regard to the theological dimension of virtues in contrast to their vices.

66. Cf. *ST* II-II 138.2 ad 2.

fering, loss, distress, and so forth. Indeed, a focus on patience-like phenomena needs to search transversally across the three resilience aspects of coping, resisting, and constructing, through different schools of psychology. I shall simply focus on cognitive and evolutionary psychology.

Cognitive psychologists, such as Richard Lazarus, Meinrad Perrez and Michael Reicherts, identify a type of coping reaction that I construe as paralleling the notion of patience. They establish a phenomenological taxonomy that systematizes coping in regard to the function and temporality of the stressor (past, present, and future). The coping response functions to alleviate our discomfort by reestablishing homeostasis. This process may involve choosing high levels of discomfort in order to obtain long-term goals.[67] As discussed earlier, cognitivists identify a situation-oriented (type I) coping operation in which coping reactions involve either active influence on the situation or passive (understood as a standing firm or waiting reaction) and evasive strategies.[68] I suggest that the coping activities of evasion or withdrawal and passivity parallel patience in noncomprehensive ways. In this schema, these activities are served by representation-oriented (type II) and evaluation-oriented (type III) coping operations, as prudence, knowledge, and wisdom serve patience in virtue theory. These researchers confirm that coping sometimes needs to involve what they call passive or evasive activities. This first observation starts to assemble elements for patience strategies.

In addition to evasive and passive coping operations, patience functions in cognitive appreciations to aid us to bear or to overcome suffering. In the midst of physical and psychological pain, we find that a sense of solidarity and justice (moral order) serves as anchoring experiences, which give us strength to weather the difficulty. According to Tousignant's findings,[69] children who have faced the injustices of parental favoritism find it easier to cope when their siblings show compassion or suffer with them. Understanding that suffering is not limited to themselves, that it is pervasive in the world, permits an opening to understand that others suffer as well. This experience establishes a basis for understanding morality. Tousignant thus suggests that resilience is born out of perceptions of solidarity and a larger moral order in hardship. Rutter likewise finds that bad experiences as well

67. Cf. Perrez and Reicherts 1992a, 28.

68. Cf. ibid., 28–9.

69. Cf. Tousignant 1998, 64.

as good ones can serve in promoting adaptive behavior and coherent self-concepts.[70]

Efforts to establish appropriate types of patient relationships to pain and to our neighbor demand that we manage sociobiological inclinations. As mentioned earlier, we need to develop sociobiological inclinations involving conjugal love, aggression, and pain. From the evolutionary perspective, the biochemical alarms (the pain caused by particular objects) provide incentive to an organism with self-awareness to correct the painful relationship with an object, as well as to plan to avoid it in the future. According to Antonio R. Damasio, self-awareness of these alarms and avoidance of painful objects rewards us with survival advantage.[71] Craig L. Nessan, however, goes further. He argues that humans can employ their intellectual functioning in order to direct sociobiological phenomena either toward destructive expressions of self or toward the bettering of human society.[72] He holds that humans demonstrate their fallen condition or moral weakness when they fail to redirect sociobiological inclinations for the sake of neighbor and instead have unreflective and simply self-serving reactions to pain. More needs to be said on this topic, especially on human efforts at putting a reasoned order between pain and altruistic projects.[73]

Resilience researchers suggest that optimism and hope also help us to cope with pain and to build something positive out of hardship. They have identified some processes used by optimists to overcome suffering. First, optimism is conducive to flexibility, intentional adaptation, and hope for restoration of normalcy. It involves the acquired capacities to accept substitutes, to restructure our expectations of need gratification, and to count on comfort following pain. According to Lois Barclay Murphy, these roots of optimism support not only coping skills, but also the capacity to transform bad situations into good ones, to build something positive out of what is negative.[74] Secondly, according to the research of Martin E. P. Seligman, a key skill of optimists is the active and acquired capacity of talking to themselves when suffering personal challenges.[75] They encourage themselves in

70. Cf. Rutter 1990, 206.

71. Cf. Damasio 1999b, 79.

72. Cf. Nessan 1998, 451–53.

73. Stephen J. Pope (1994) examines the complexity of this task, which must consider community and neighbor, family and self, in an ordered ethical way. He discusses the differentiated way that humans express an *ordo amoris* (an ordering in their loves) and an *ordo caritatis*.

74. Cf. Murphy 1987, 104.

75. Cf. Seligman 1991/1998, 207.

the midst of pain and suffering; they project new goals and imagine other desirable outcomes when temporarily defeated. Optimistic strategies spell active ways to face suffering and hardship; they involve a sort of confidence that eventually we shall manage the problem at hand. This confidence in the midst of challenge, threat, or loss can be rooted in different sources such as secure attachment,[76] compensatory self-enhancement,[77] or existential hope.

Optimist or not, one of the major sources of suffering is bereavement. According to C. Clark David, protective factors related to facing death include anticipation of death, a clear concept of death, and previous experience of a loved one's death.[78] These factors can help us to mourn and to recover from the feelings of grief. According to Eisen's findings, play activities help us to adapt after suffering the death of someone as well. They promote survival by including resistance, protest, and defiance behaviors.[79] These insights might well enlighten experiences such as disability, loss of friendship or employment, and so on.

Research and experience differentiate, yet interrelate, developmental tutors of patience and resilience tutors of patience.[80] First, developmental tutors of patience or perseverance involve the telltale ways in which we acquire patterns of resisting and persisting attitudes, behaviors, and characters through everyday situations. This process includes facing the suffering and pain, distress and waiting, that come in birth, growth, and death: for example, the unavoidable difficulty involved in individuating, separating, seeking justice, and moving residences. From early on, temperament traits, like robustness in the face of suffering and pain, can elicit positive social responses. Such temperamental bases help us to face adversity and to establish strong attachment relationships that in turn serve as a social safety net.[81] However, even without optimal temperament traits, social interaction and support from social groups can promote self-worth and strengthen personal resistance to exter-

76. Cf. Rutter 1990, 200; Bjorck and Klewicki 1997.

77. Cf. Pelham 1991, 671. He has found that we can compensate for losses in one dimension of our self-concept by enhancing another area.

78. Cf. David 1994, 101 and 133. Early parental loss, however, has been found to create vulnerability to psychiatric disorders, especially when associated with risk variables such as cognitive sets of helplessness and low self-esteem (cf. Rutter 1990, 200).

79. Cf. Eisen 1988, 11 and 88f.

80. B. Cyrulnik during a lecture in Geneva (HUG, 9/2001) discussed tutors of resilience, which involved mostly extreme cases—he defined resilience in terms of extreme loss, difficulty, or suffering. In turn, I extend the idea of tutors to include to a type of everyday growth as well.

81. Cf. Werner and Smith 1992, 192.

nal and internal negative pressures and suffering.[82] These are just examples of more ordinary developmental pathways toward patterns of resilience and resisting in the face of suffering and waiting.

Second, resilience tutors of patience and perseverance involve the more extreme situations in which we have to prove ourselves resilient through suffering and pain, separation and threats of death. "Extreme" might be "everyday" for the street child or the refugee family. In any case, it pushes human capacities to their limits. In most every case, one already has some basic strength that he has won through everyday life to date. However, by definition, the extreme situation puts human dispositions to the test. Will the person prove resilient or vulnerable in this situation? Unsurprisingly, normal adaptation often proves solid and resilient under trial. On the contrary, surprisingly, certain qualities that are maladaptive for normal situations seem instrumental for overcoming extreme situations. For example, the DeVries Zimbabwe famine study found that a demanding temperament and low tolerance for pain, hunger, and suffering, while sources of distancing a child from caregivers in normal situations, served the survival needs of children in famine.[83] While educational projects revolve around everyday situations, the extreme situation is the locus of undesirable testing that can, nonetheless, provide a resilience tutor for patience and perseverance.

Although a good number of individuals resiliently overcome extreme situations, having coped with pain, resisted self-destruction, and even built something positive out of a negative situation, others need therapeutic intervention. In both cases, the complexity of development and trauma makes resilience theories an evolving commodity. In both everyday and extreme cases, resilience involves exploiting the numerous ways in which we find personal and social resources to affront and overcome the adversity or loss. It is difficult to distinguish these two categories too neatly, since we acquire the disposition for resilient patience and perseverance both through ordinary developmental pathways and through more extreme hardships.

I suggest that patience-phenomena spring from the three aspects of resilience: we creatively cope with sorrow-producing situations; we actively

82. The social development model suggests that motivation serves to protect an individual through social bonding with family and other social units. This attachment can regulate behavior according to the group's standards (cf. Consortium 1994, 300).

83. Cf. De Vries study (cited in M. Rutter 1998); Anne M. Clarke and Alan D. B. Clarke 1992 hypothesize that temperamental irritability can become a resilience mechanism in extreme situations.

resist suffering, deformation, and loss; and we constantly build out of the painful situation. Without having depleted the resilience research, we shall now use it to enhance our understanding of patience in managing suffering and adversity, and perseverance in the face of waiting for and attaining a far-off goal.

Strategies for Managing Sorrow and Pain and Virtuous Sorrow

Although Aquinas did not devote a systematic treatise to education, he has pertinent insights on the development of patience, in terms of strategies for managing sorrow and pain.[84] Thomas, in his *Summa theologiae*, explains five such strategies that involve the employment of pleasure, emotional venting, receiving of sympathy, contemplation of truth, and refreshment through sleep and baths.[85] He first describes how pleasure can drive away sorrow. Not only the pleasures directly contrary to the given pains or sorrows, but any pleasure in some way pacifies them. Indeed, according to Aquinas' anthropology and psychology, as sorrow wearies the appetite, so pleasure refreshes it.[86] He observes that when seeking pleasure to overcome sorrow, more people seek bodily pleasures because sensible goods are more widely known than spiritual goods and pleasures.[87]

Aquinas holds, secondly, that "tears and groans, naturally assuage sorrow."[88] Hurtful things pain us more when we are intent upon them and when they are kept inside. Inward sorrow is lessened when sorrow manifests itself in tears, groans, and words. Such action befits the sorrowful condition, accords a certain pleasure, and lightens sorrow further. As true as this may be, exceptions exist, and we need to avoid extreme types of emotional venting. The excessive venting of emotions such as sorrow has drawbacks, especially when we cannot break the grip of the disordered emotion (e.g., being inconsolable). An expressive, yet self-soothing and corrective, manifestation of sorrow can put the cause of sorrowing into a larger perspective.

The sympathy of friends, thirdly, brings consolation to the sorrowing in two ways. The heavy, depressing effect is lightened through other peo-

84. Various questions in the *ST* relate more or less directly to patience (including the questions on sorrow that we address below), and others relate more or less directly to education (including most pertinently *De verit.* 11, 1, and *ST* I 117.1, as we discussed earlier).

85. Cf. *ST* I-II 38.1–5.

86. Cf. *ST* I-II 38.1. Here Aquinas draws upon Aristotle, *NE* VII.15, 1154b13–15.

87. Cf. *ST* I-II 31.5 ad 1. We shall discuss spiritual good and pleasures in chapter 7.

88. *ST* I-II 38.2; cf. Augustine *Conf.* iv.7.

ple's helping to bear the burden. Furthermore, the love expressed through a friend's sympathetic sorrowing serves as a source of pleasure, which sedates the sorrow. In both these regards, Aquinas acknowledges the importance of social bonding, the highest and most pervasive form being friendship-love.[89]

Fourth, Aquinas holds that the contemplation of truth, which is the greatest of all pleasures, calms pain and sorrow.[90] Contemplation of truth calms us; the higher powers of the soul influence the lower ones. Once again this action gives a form of pleasure (joy, in this case) overcoming pain, for a truth-inspired-joy lightens both physical pain and psychological sorrow. Although contemplation itself is a good (based on the natural and spiritual inclination to truth) and naturally pleasant, Thomas claims that the more a person is a lover of wisdom, the more the contemplation of truth can assuage suffering and even sensual pain.

Lastly, he notes the remedial effects of sleep and baths, which "bring nature back to its normal state."[91] By restoring the bodily nature to its due condition of vitality and giving a certain pleasure, sleep and baths lighten both pain and sorrow. Aquinas demonstrates a well-balanced understanding of human corporality, and the effect of the body on the soul. The body serves the soul. Bodily pleasures and even simple caring for the body can help to overcome pains that are on the same level, as well as sorrows that are on another.[92] Here the reprieve that refreshment and sleep offer may be short-lived, if resolution of the problem is elsewhere. Nonetheless, it may grant us physical energy to address the more profound issue.

If we were to stop the study here, Aquinas' strategies for managing pain and suffering might seem lacking on both psychological and philosophical levels. His five strategies for managing sorrow and pain might seem unexpectedly venial. But his understanding of human nature and of metaphysics gives these strategies further relevance. Indeed, his strategies for managing pain and sorrow are varied elements for developing the virtues of patience

89. Aquinas (*ST* I-II 38.3) here draws from the insights concerning love and friendship from St. Augustine's *Confessions* (cf. *Conf* iv.9, *PL* 32.699) and concerning sympathy and friends from Aristotle's *NE* (ix.11, 1171a29–30). See also the ultimate context for friendship-love as the highest form of charity in *ST* II-II 23.1.

90. *ST* I-II 38.4.

91. *ST* I-II 38.5.

92. The classic tradition supports Aquinas' claim. See Augustine, *Conf.* ix, 12, 32: *PL* 32, 777; and Ambrose, *Deus Creator omnium: PL* 16, 1410; both quoted in *ST* I-II 38.5 sc.

and perseverance. Employing these strategies in a way that orders them toward the goals that give life meaning requires prudence. Aquinas astutely uses these strategies—to which we should join the other resilience strategies earlier discussed—in order to develop his idea of virtuous sorrow. Patience and perseverance strategies are ways to develop the ability to sorrow virtuously.

Virtuous sorrow, for Aquinas, involves a disposition to resolve situations of sorrow in the larger moral (and resilience) framework.[93] Indeed, the framework sets the standard for the type of virtue and resilience that we exercise through patience and perseverance. If patience strategies are not in rational relationship with some good, then the implied endurance of pain and sorrow will be more a hardness of heart than the virtue of patience.[94] Aquinas argues that virtuous sorrow is expressed in relation to a virtuous good. It is an interior sorrow that follows a right measure and rectitude of reason and will.[95] The virtue of patience thus is not simply a matter of managing pain, suffering, and sorrow; it entails virtuous sorrow. Thomas identifies virtuous sorrow as one that entails the perception and rejection of evil, either through shunning bodily pain or through making a right rational judgment of the evil situation, which should then lead us to act appropriately.[96]

Virtuous sorrow is useful when it moves us to expel the saddening evil, the source of the suffering. It adds another motive for avoiding evil as well. It does so in two ways. It entails avoiding things that are evil in themselves or that are occasions of evil. It also rectifies disordered sorrows, as when we rejoice at evil or when we are saddened by good. For Aquinas, we need to refine all the soul's passions by the rule of reason.[97] In excessive sorrow, our passions are not properly under reason. It is patience's role to manage sorrow in general and especially when it moves us toward excess. This virtue involves rejecting the temptation to revel in sorrow. Inordinate sorrow is an

93. We have taken this notion of "virtuous sorrow," from Aquinas' discussion of "Whether sorrow can be a virtuous good" (*ST* I-II 39.2). Since Aquinas affirmatively responds, it would seem that we can speak of a "virtuous sorrow" as we explain here following. He also describes how sorrow is useful or beneficial in *ST* I-II 39.3. Furthermore, even though Aquinas does not mention "patience" in this discussion of virtuous sorrow, patience serves as the conceptual context, as the virtue implied in managing sorrowful situations well and not going to extremes for the sake of charity (in the fullest sense).

94. Cf. *ST* II-II 136.1 ad 2 from a quotation of St. Augustine, *De pat.* ii.

95. Aquinas identifies the rational and volitional dimensions of virtuous sorrow in *ST* I-II 39.2.

96. Cf. *ST* I-II 39.2. He also describes how sorrow is compatible with moral virtue: cf. *ST* I-II 59.3.

97. Cf. *ST* I-II 39. 2 ad 1; cf. *ST* I-II 24.1.

obstacle to flourishing. However, cultivating virtuous sorrow does not mean that one chooses to be sorrowful per se, as if sorrow were a good in itself and certainly not as an end in itself. Although we can nurture the character from which emanates particular emotions, we do not choose to be sorrowful inasmuch as we do not choose the evil that is the source of the sorrow. Rather, we patiently choose and perseveringly long for the good end and the intermediate good in the face of suffering and sorrow.

Some Conclusions on Patience, Perseverance, and Resistant Resilience

When something impedes the enjoyment of a desired good, we have at least two options. First, we can labor to overcome the obstacle, seeking to solve the problem in order to attain the desired good. The virtues of initiative primarily manage the acts of daring and hope required by this option. Second, if the desired good is unattainable, we can respond by patiently keeping our wits in the midst of the inevitable sorrow. We perseveringly hold on to our goal by waiting and wisely working on practical remedies to alleviate or mitigate the sorrow. It is through the virtues of patience and perseverance that we withstand suffering, sorrowing, and waiting needed in route to our intermediate and ultimate goals.

For Aquinas, the virtue of patience safeguards the good of reason. It strengthens the mind in the face of sorrow and suffering that inevitably arise from bearing evil. We need to recall two elements of Aquinas' anthropology here. First, we withstand difficulty only for the sake of some good. Second, the nature of sorrow, suffering, and delay enter into direct conflict with our fundamental search for flourishing. We can understand how patience bears with the evil, does not give into sorrow, and holds fast with a calm spirit, only in the overall quest for goodness, truth, and happiness. It produces undisturbed self-domination and control, as well as a joy in the process. The virtue of long-suffering specifically relates to the dimension of waiting and enduring in the midst of the delay in attaining what is hoped for, especially when it is a long way off. Constancy specifically manages the toil required in persistently confronting some evil for the sake of good, or conversely in accomplishing good while resisting evil. Lastly, perseverance pertains to the specific difficulties involved in persisting for a long time until the good is accomplished and the goal attained. It moderates fear of failure or weariness due to the length of delay in our efforts. Thomas's insights on virtues of enduring provide a developmental framework that has psychological, philosophical, and metaphysical tenor, while not offering the last word on the study of resisting persisting phenomena or on the promotion of developmental strategies.

Resilience findings aid in enhancing virtue theory concerning how humans endure difficulty or suffering, hold firm in a painful struggle, resist self-destructive pressures, wait for the attainment of good, persist until the accomplishment of some goal, and even express sorrow as a virtuous good. The social and developmental lines of insight are especially strong in cognitive, evolutionary, and social developmental sciences. Their insights into the three aspects of resilience that involve coping, resisting, and constructing suggest a nuanced grid through which to cull insights for the virtues of enduring. In general, the resilience perspective affirms that pain, suffering, and loss can have detrimental as well as steeling effects on humans at physical, psychological, and social levels. In particular, the concept of coping as formulated by cognitive psychology parallels the notions of patience and perseverance. We can use "coping" to understand how humans develop active, passive, and evasive strategies to reestablish homeostasis in the face of suffering, or even choose high levels of discomfort in order to achieve a goal. Representation-oriented and evaluation-oriented coping operations parallel the role of prudence, knowledge, and wisdom in virtue theory. Some resilience research even speculates that cognitive appreciations of a moral order (e.g., sense of solidarity and justice) can aid us in bearing suffering and managing sociobiological inclinations concerning pain in altruistic perspectives. As in the case of the virtues of initiative, resilience research has found that optimism or hope positively correlates with both coping with pain or suffering and building something positive out of the painful hardship.

Researchers have sometimes confused enduring, resisting, and passivity. Distinguishing between levels of action, intention, and finality, however, helps to resolve this confusion. Moreover, we need to differentiate the battle from the war. Overall success may demand that we endure a certain kind of defeat or firmly hold far-off goals in the midst of the proximate struggle. What appears to be a passive defeat, a waste of time, or the result of weakness may be a vital stepping-stone in a larger event. To understand this type of activity, we must admit a difference of perspective. Aquinas recognizes that in the midst of a difficult struggle for the good we cannot always engage in an initiative that will immediately right the wrong or resolve the difficulty. Sometimes we need to stand firm in the midst of an onslaught that will spell a loss on one level, in order to achieve a gain on another: losing a contract because we will make only an honest bid, losing a job in order to retain moral principle, suffering for defying an unjust law, and so on. This is more than a trade-off. Patience resists the vulnerability of passivity. It manages sorrow and resists evil, while remaining resolutely attached to a moral good. Perseverance resists significant compromise and the vulnerability of misplaced suffering, persisting for as long as it takes to procure the ultimate victory.

PART THREE

FORTITUDE *and* RESILIENCE TRANSCENDED

I have delayed treating explicitly the theological aspect of fortitude until now in order to allow clear terrain for dialogue between resilience research and Aquinas' virtue anthropology. The previous chapters serve as a foundation concerning his vision of human agency in adversity and the way in which resilience research offer psychosocial insights on human development and resilience in difficulty. By treating the theological aspects of virtue and resilience apart from the philosophical and psychosocial aspects, I do not mean to imply that the subject (person or community) examined philosophically and scientifically differs from the subject examined spiritually and theologically. Rather the approach (principles, sources, and method) differs. I seek to model this work on that of Aquinas' moral theology, which is pervasively theology in dialogue with philosophical and scientific sources. Our object thus becomes more explicitly theological: God as source and goal for human agency, and human beings as cooperators therein. In this theological dialogue between resilience and Aquinas, I shall continue to explain his thought, while offering complementary resilience insights. In doing so, however, I cannot draw upon specific resilience research as directly as before; no resilience studies pursue properly theological questions. Nevertheless, inasmuch as grace builds up nature, the resilience perspective and a resilience-enriched anthropology offer bases for further theological reflections on the human person and community. Our definition of spiritual resilience now serves as a means to deepen our theological understanding of the virtues in question. Spiritual resilience involves the ethical, religious, and theological processes (personal qualities, communal resources, and efficacious goals) that render human persons and communities able (1) to cope actively with difficulty, (2) to resist disintegration of actual competencies, and (3) to construct positively out of adverse situations.

7

Aquinas' Theological Transformation of Fortitude and Resilience

The Lord is my strength and my song.
(PSALM 118:4)

In order to investigate the infused virtue of fortitude and its relationship with spiritual resilience, next we shall examine Aquinas' teaching on martyrdom and the centrality of the gifts, beatitudes, and fruits of the Holy Spirit in Christian fortitude. We thus build upon the reflections on resilience and the virtue of fortitude found in chapter 4.

The Infused Virtue of Fortitude

Distinguishing Acquired and Infused Virtues

Before entering into the content of the infused virtue of fortitude, I shall address how Aquinas distinguishes acquired and infused virtue.[1] In gener-

1. On Aquinas' teaching concerning the acquired and infused virtues and the gifts of the Holy Spirit, see Sherwin 2005a; Cessario 2001; Porter 1992.

al, Aquinas distinguishes virtue as either acquired or infused in order to account for the interplay of divine grace in human agency. Even with his large definition of virtue, he has proper notions of how complete virtue accomplishes actions that are purely good.[2] Rather than employing Aristotle's definition of virtue, Aquinas uses a customary definition of infused virtue (attributed to Augustine) in order to discuss the perfection of virtue: "virtue is a good quality of the mind, by which we live righteously, of which no one can make bad use, which God works in us, without us."[3] Thomas thus identifies three characteristics of infused virtue: its object is God; only God can infuse it; and its object depends on divine revelation.[4] He also differentiates acquired and infused virtues according to their final, formal, and efficient causes.

A specific distinction between these types of virtue arises from what they subserve, their finality or goal: either the sociopolitical or divine order. The goal or final cause of the acquired and infused virtues directs and motivates human beings. The acquired virtues aim at the good of the earthly city, whereas the infused virtues aim at acting well as members of the household of God. As Aquinas says, citing St. Paul's letter to the Ephesians, in acquired moral virtue "people behave well in relation to human affairs," while in infused moral virtue "people behave well as *fellow-citizens with the saints, and of the household of God*."[5] The acquired and the infused virtues differ according to their relation to these ends. The perfect virtues of Christ and the saints in glory spell out the content of promised complete flourishing, and thus serve to direct and motivate human efforts that are transformed by infused virtue.[6]

Aquinas specifies that the acquired and infused virtues also differ according to their formal cause, which constitutes the reasons that make acts and dispositions virtuous. Acquired virtues use the measure fixed by human reason, establishing the mean according to a virtue's matter. Human social nature informs acquired virtue toward human flourishing in accord with the common good.[7] Infused virtues use the measure of divine rule (ul-

2. Cf. *ST* I-II 65.1.

3. *De libero arbitrio*, II.19: *PL* 32.1268, which Aquinas quotes in *ST* I-II 55.4; cf. *ST* I-II 65.1. According to Odon Lottin (1942, 371), although this definition is customarily attributed to St. Augustine, it is probably from Peter of Poiters in his commentary on the Sentences (III, I. *PL* 211, 1041). Cf. Porter 1998a, 1219.

4. Cf. *ST* I-II 62.1; *ST* I-II 63.3.

5. *ST* I-II 63.4.

6. Cf. *ST* I-II 1–5; *ST* I-II 61.5.

7. Cf. *ST* II-II 23.8; *ST* I-II 61.5; *ST* I-II 63.4.

timately) and reason informed by faith (mediately).[8] They operate through faith and charity, which grant a higher principle and surer will.[9] For Thomas, human beings can rationally participate in divine reason, as created in the image of God and guided by God's Spirit. The Holy Spirit and graced charity thus form all Christian virtue.

Ultimately, our good is eternal flourishing, being face to face with God and experiencing the beatific vision. However, natural, spiritual inclinations toward acquiring virtue and human rational and volitional powers cannot efficiently cause the virtues needed to obtain this supernatural good. While the natural principles and seeds of virtue are ordered to eternal glory, they cannot cause the virtues proportioned to this end.[10] Rather here we need God's grace and the theological virtues of faith, hope, and charity, as well as the infused moral virtues.[11] The Holy Spirit, through the grace received in the infused virtues, perfects our natural powers so that we attain the theological object of divine flourishing and act more faithfully toward every good.

Aquinas' teaching on the efficacy of grace follows at least three basic principles: (1) that which is received into one is received according to one's nature: "even though the divine power is infinite in its cause, and so acts without limits, the effect of this power depends upon the capacity of the recipient and upon God's own plan";[12] (2) that our operations are perfected, not destroyed, by grace; and (3) that we are *capax Dei*—able to enjoy communion with God—although unable to achieve this union on our own, that is, without grace.

The last qualification of Augustine's definition of perfect virtue—"which God works in us, without us"—refers specifically to God as the efficient cause of infused virtues. Thomas identifies how human intelligent and divine sources cause virtues. At the natural level, reason and will produce virtuous acts and the formation of the underlying dispositions, as we discussed extensively in chapters 3 through 6.[13] At the supernatural level, God effica-

8. Cf. *ST* I-II 63.4. I have already correlated natural and infused prudence with moral and theological norms in chapter 3.

9. Cf. *ST* I-II 91.4 ad 1; *ST* II-II 23.1.

10. Cf. *ST* II-II 24.3 ad 2; *ST* I-II 4.3; *ST* I-II 111.3.

11. Cf. *ST* I-II 63.2; 3 *Sent*. d. 33, q. 1, a. 2.

12. *ST* III 57.3 ad 3. Also see *ST* I 75.5; *ST* I 79.6; *ST* I 89.4; *ST* III 54.2 ad 1, and *SCG* 3, 150, ad 7.

13. However, insofar as any natural good action correlates with the Source of goodness, God is also its first and efficacious cause through a help that is typical of the goodness endemic to nature, which Aquinas calls *auxilio divino* or *auxilio Dei* (*ST* I-II 109 articles 1 and 3; *ST* I-II 61.5).

ciously produces the infused virtues, but not without human graced collaboration. Infused virtue enables an excellence of performance that we could not assure otherwise.[14] This flourishing is not a purely human progressive self-elevation toward God. Rather, it entails a twofold action: a gift from God and a response of the believer. First, God's gift involves calling us into union with Himself. This union is primarily His movement toward and presence in us, rather than our moving ourselves.[15] His grace is the common root for two distinct but simultaneous effects: "the enlightenment of the mind and the enkindling of the affections."[16] This "God-like form" given to the believer through grace is not something other than the perfecting of what God started in creating us.[17] Humans are created toward God's image in that we have an intelligent nature, comprising both reason and will. We imitate God most completely when we emulate "God's understanding and loving of himself."[18]

A second aspect of transformation in the image of God entails our being capable of receiving grace *(capax Dei)*,[19] as well as our active cooperation in using the grace granted through applying our intelligence, through freedom in judgment, and through progression in self-mastery.[20] The divine indwelling, as well as created grace and virtue, direct and attract us in our freedom to fully return to God.[21] We, however, are not slavishly driven to believe, to hope, or to love. Rather, we remain free. Insofar as it fulfills our human nature, Aquinas deems that we are freest when we choose to be in union with the one who fulfils us. The gifts of grace given to us—in which God becomes present to us in a new way—do not destroy our human nature.[22] On the contrary, they enable us to do things that we otherwise would not (because of the deforming effects of sin) and to know and to believe things we otherwise would not (because of our intellectual limitations, ignorance, and pride).

On the natural level, our intellect starts with the first universal principles of truth (such as the principle of noncontradiction), and our will be-

14. Cf. *De verit.* 14.10.
15. Cf. Eph 1:5f; *ST* I 20.2 ad 3, and *ST* I-II 110.1; 1 *Sent.* d. 14, q. 2, a. 1, s. 1; cf. *ST* I 43.5.
16. *ST* I 43.5 ad 3.
17. Cf. Gn 1:26–27; 1 Cor 11:7; Eph 4:24; Col 3:10.
18. *ST* I 93.4.
19. Cf. *ST* I 12.1; *ST* I 12.4 ad 3; *ST* I-II 3.8; *ST* II-II 2.3.
20. *Prima secundae*, Prologue.
21. Cf. 1 *Sent.* d. 14, q. 2, a. 2.
22. Cf. *ST* I 43.3.

gins with a natural tendency toward the good of reason. On the supernatural level, the Holy Spirit directs us into divine flourishing here and now insofar as our intellects are transformed and our wills rectified.[23] Thus, the Spirit shapes us according to the beatitudes and the commandment of love, which encompasses all the others. In the infused virtues, God's grace is the transforming agent and the fuller foundation through which reason works and the virtues are built.

Acquired and Infused Moral Virtues: The Case of Fortitude

As an infused virtue, fortitude, according to Thomas, involves a graced strength in difficulty to face fear and anxiety, especially in terms of death and destruction. Aquinas construes this virtue in the context of the theological virtues (especially friendship-love of God and neighbor), but also the life projects that concern created things and that have personal and social extension. A series of questions arises about the correlative exercise of acquired and moral infused virtues, especially in the face of the lingering effects of vicious dispositions or undeveloped acquired virtues. For Aquinas, charity is the heart of the solution to these questions. God infuses all the moral virtues into the believer, contemporaneously with faith, hope, and charity.[24] Through grace a person can exercise perfect virtue, not only infused charity, but also infused fortitude and temperance. However, a person might at the same time have great difficulty and no pleasure in infused moral virtue.

Through well-developed acquired virtues, we normally act with ease, promptness, and joy (or pleasure).[25] These properties also underlie well-established resilience qualities. Nevertheless, Aquinas recognizes that they are not always evident when someone is fatigued or ill. Furthermore, although charity itself brings joy, one can find it difficult and pleasureless to do works of infused moral virtue for their own sake. As Thomas explains, "certain contrary dispositions remaining from previous acts" can inhibit someone from facility in moral matters.[26] Indeed, we obtain and use infused

23. Cf. *ST* I-II 62.3.

24. Cf. *ST* I-II 65.3 and 65.4.

25. Cf. *De verit.* 20, 2; *SCG* 3, 150, n. 7. According to Romanus Cessario, "The grace of the infused moral virtues shapes and energizes our human operative capacities, intellect, will, and sense appetites, so that a human person can act promptly, joyfully, and easily in those areas of human conduct that are governed by the Gospel precepts." Cessario 1996, 5; cf. Cessario 2001, 200–205.

26. *ST* I-II 65.3 ad 2.

and acquired virtues in different ways. Since we receive infused virtues without necessarily having yet developed the underlying moral faculties rightly, we have to overcome past negative dispositions before we can gain the connatural ease, promptness, and pleasure that come with perfect virtue. Nevertheless, God in his divine pedagogy does extraordinarily grant pleasure in order to encourage one soul, or withdraw it in order to strengthen another. In resilience terms, this insight explains how infused virtues can concomitantly exist with an acquired moral vulnerability or without ease in action. Yet for Aquinas, the infused virtues involve a source of strength that can consistently overcome moral weakness (even though the individual might suffer an internal struggle in the process).

In the case of fortitude, Aquinas claims that "sometimes it does not lie within human power to attain the end of one's work, or to escape evils or dangers, since these sometimes press in upon us to the point of death."[27] In a state of intact nature (pre-lapsus state of original justice), we could achieve such a natural good, as well as the supreme good, by well-proportioned acts. In both cases now we need the help of grace in the infused virtues.[28] For Aquinas, God's help (*auxilio Dei* for natural virtue and grace proper for infused ones) underlies any goodness present in human acts, any goodness in the distinct types of fortitude.

How does Aquinas understand the specifically theological dimension of infused fortitude? The virtues of faith, hope, and charity establish this infused virtue's context and finality. God directs us to our supernatural end through divinely bestowed theological virtues. Because of charity's place therein, infused fortitude goes beyond the range of its acquired counterpart, in which human beings in our capacity as citizens order our actions to the common good. Charity commands infused fortitude (and martyrdom), ordering it to the ultimate end, the vision of God. Infused fortitude's very acts are formally acts of charity, since it takes its species formally from charity. However, it is not due only to infused fortitude being formally an act of charity that infused and acquired fortitude differ. Rather, they specifically differ because infused fortitude's acts establish a mean ordered to the ultimate end, that is, the object of charity, while acquired fortitude is ordered to the common good.[29] Furthermore, the rational means established by ac-

27. *ST* II-II 139.1.

28. Cf. *SCG* 3, 150, ad 7.

29. Cf. *De virt. com.* 10 ad 10.

quired and infused fortitude can vary. In the *Sentences* Aquinas specifies that "what is excessive according to the norms of civic virtue may be truly moderate, according to infused virtue; for example, that a man fast or offer himself voluntarily to die in defense of the faith."[30]

Aquinas argues that the theological virtues of faith, hope, and charity parallel the natural principles of acquired virtue, in that they have infused *habitus* that are correspondingly proportioned to the acquired moral and intellectual virtues. Nonetheless, the acquired moral and intellectual virtues do not themselves exactly match (or make superfluous) the theological virtues.[31] Although we need faith, hope, and charity to shape us according to our supernatural end, to God, we also need the other "infused virtues in regard to created things, though as subordinate to God."[32] According to Aquinas, fortitude and the other infused moral virtues of the emotions involve that through grace we progressively transform the dispositions related to the emotions of fear and daring in the face of danger and difficulty.[33] Although reason and will participate, Aquinas holds that further dispositions proper to our emotions take new shape in infused moral virtue. The time needed to reorder our emotional dispositions involves added difficulty in the process. In the *Summa theologiae,* Aquinas inscribes his discussion of the virtue of fortitude in the context of the human need for grace.

Fear and Trials: Theologically Transforming Fortitude and Resilience

Although Aquinas' technical virtue-terminology is philosophical in origin, it is pervasively theological in content when he applies it to the infused virtue of fortitude, which he transforms theologically using the Christian tradition. He transposes Aristotle's virtue theory and the definition of courage to involve not only management of fear and daring through our natural means, but also the theological dimensions of the virtue. He likewise employs Cicero's insights on the structure, ordering, and political end of cour-

30. *III Sent.* 33, q. 1, a. 2 Sol. 4. ad 2. He also affirms the specificity of infused virtues in the *ST*: cf. *ST* I-II 63.4 corpus, ad 1 and ad 2.

31. Cf. *ST* I-II 63.3 ad 1.

32. *ST* I-II 63.3 ad 2.

33. For Aquinas both the acquired and the infused virtues bring right ordering to the emotions. Thomas says that these virtues impress reason on these appetites (cf. *ST* I-II 60.1). Another part of the tradition focuses on the will in the infused moral virtues. For example, St. Bonaventure construes the infused moral virtues as a matter of will without any lasting effect on the development of our emotional dispositions (cf. Cessario 2002, 203; Kent 1995).

age in order to establish its fulfillment in the act of martyrdom rather than in the act of facing death either in the political arena (Cicero) or on the battlefield (Aristotle). Because of this extension, beyond strictly politico-philosophical bounds, we cannot completely understand the depth of Aquinas' general definition of fortitude without treating its principal act, martyrdom, as well as its relationship to related emotions, virtues, and gifts of the Holy Spirit.

Rich and varied reflections on the relationship of fear and religion are found throughout the history of thought. Certain thinkers posit that fear and other emotions have engendered religion and quests for God (or gods).[34] On a more pragmatic level, some thinkers observe that religion produces and controls fear.[35] William James, for his part, catalogues the variety of emotions involved in religious intention: "religious fear, religious love, religious awe, religious joy, and so forth."[36] However, negative interpretations of religion's role in fear management include Freud's reductionistic thesis, which considers religion as an immature response to coping with fear and helplessness.[37] Other critiques claim that some types of religion are potentially detrimental to mental health, for example, by "creating anxiety and fear by beliefs in punishment (e.g., hell) for our evil ways."[38] Positive interpretations, however, are not wanting. Pargament speculates that religious faith reduces fear of death and aids in managing fear in general.[39] Certain studies even suggest that potential health benefits ensue when religion (1) reduces existential anxiety through cognitive explanations of the chaotic; (2) offers a sense of hope, meaning, and purpose, as well as a resulting sense of emotional well-being; or (3) solves, at least partially, the problem of mortality.[40] Taking the negative interpretations as a partial warning about the potential shortcomings of religion, and the positive as leads to develop, this study turns to back Aquinas.

34. Lucretius held that "Fear begets Gods"; Hume thought that the first ideas of religion originate in concerns for life and human fear; Feuerbach construed "primitive" religion as exclusively focusing on frightful aspects of nature; some recent empirical approaches pose similar foundations (cf. Hood et al. 1996, 18–20 and 9–13; Allport 1950/1967, 161).

35. Cf. Thomas and Carver 1990, 195.

36. Allport 1950/1967, 10–11.

37. The illusion of God, as an ideal father figure who protects and controls (Oedipal phase) is created in order to cope with the unpleasant details of reality and to reduce fears of helplessness (cf. Watts and Williams 1988, 27).

38. Schumaker 1992, 3–4.

39. Cf. Pargament et al., 1990, 797–98.

40. John F. Schumaker (1992, 3) furthermore offers a list of other potential health benefits from religion.

Aquinas' focus on the philosophical physiognomy of fortitude and its management of fear does not imply forgetfulness about theological finality and flourishing. Rather, theological flourishing is the continual motive and end animating human life[41] and involves cognitive, motivational, and emotional coping toward this end. A contemporary question is whether fortitude needs to be linked with flourishing (and goodness). Aquinas affirms that a brave person does what is fittingly brave, while seeking eternal flourishing at the same time. Fortitude itself is good, but this virtue taken out of the context of our loving flourishing loses its fullest power to courageously face fearful obstacles and move us to act. For Aquinas, God remains the first mover, the efficacious center, and the final end of fortitude.[42]

Fortitude's foundations are weakened, however, when fear of violent death dissuades us, when we deem physical life the highest value, or when avoidance of confrontation at all costs rules our attitudes.[43] A myth of terrestrial satisfaction, in terms of wealth, goodness, or flourishing can offset the resilient endurance we need throughout life's journey. It involves a forgetfulness of ultimate sources of flourishing and fear. On the contrary, when flourishing that is rooted in divine beatitude serves as a goal and motivation, fortitude counteracts the temptation to shortchange theologal flourishing for an apparently easier life. This type of courage connotes spiritual resilience, which does not construe human existence merely in physical terms.

For a faith perspective, Aquinas recalls the scriptural precepts concerning "fearing the Lord" (with filial rather than servile fear).[44] He contrasts this type of fear with the scriptural precept not to fear what is naturally fearful. We are not to excessively fear bodily death, the enemy, and so on, in order to remain duly attached to the goods of faith, hope, and charity.[45] These instances demonstrate how the soul through ordinate relationships to fearful objects can manage fear, how it respects natural objects of fear, and how it can supersede them for a reason.

When Aquinas describes how fortitude concerns fear and daring, once

41. Cf. *ST* II-II 123.7.

42. Aquinas (*ST* II-II 123.7) cites Aristotle (*NE* iii.10, 1115b21–24) on the goodness of fortitude and Augustine (*De Trin.* xiii.8: *PL* 42, 1022–1023; *De morib. eccl.* xv, i, 15: *PL* 32, 1322) on the relationship between theological fortitude and flourishing.

43. Cf. Forschner 1983, 33–34.

44. Cf. Psalm 127:1 cited in *ST* II-II 125.2 obj. 1. On Aquinas' typology of fear and the Gift of fear, see *ST* II-II 19.1–12.

45. Cf. Mt 10:28; Ez 2:6; cited in *ST* II-II 125.1 sc.

again he does not hide the theological dimension of fortitude. In quoting St. Gregory he reaffirms that as a special virtue fortitude consists in "loving the trials of this life for the sake of an eternal reward."[46] This insight introduces the importance of testing, trials, and tribulation that we overlook too quickly when examining fortitude only in terms of fear and daring. These realities illustrate a basic aspect of resilience and courage. In the midst of testing, we need to cope with adversity and to retain our own integrity. Testing not only proves the strength and genuineness of the protagonist, it also is a means to establish further strength, faith, and goodness. The way in which Scripture handles strength in weakness, and testing can serve as analogues (functional equivalents) for Aquinas' treatment of fortitude as a general virtue.[47] Aquinas mines Scripture but is necessarily selective. A wider look at Scripture identifies pertinent teaching concerning strength (as an analogue for both fortitude in general and resilience) and strength in weakness (as a functional equivalent for moral virtue and moral resilience), as well as testing, trials, and tribulation (which are especially akin to resilience). Indeed, a primary aspect of human experience is the testing that not only can reveal human vulnerability, but whose primary function (according to Aquinas) is both to show a person's integrity and to serve in expanding spiritual capacities. Thus physical, psychosocial, and spiritual types of resilience are uncovered through testing, trials, and tribulations. Hardships can either test, prove, and build up those involved, or tempt, distract, and weaken them.[48] Overcoming our fears in the midst of courageous action involves a strange strengthening of human weakness through trials.

46. *ST* II-II 123.3 ad 1.

47. The resilience and faithfulness of God's chosen ones are tested time and again in the Old Testament: Adam and Eve (Gn 2:17), Abraham (Gn 22:1), the Exodus (Ex 15:25). They are proven, purified, or strengthened by the ordeal. New Testament accounts of resilience in trial and testing include the archetypal resilience in trial of Jesus Christ through his passion and death (Jn 12:27f; 3:14f.); his paradigmatic resilience is a spiritual resilience that includes ontic, moral, and salvific dimensions, and is manifest only in the resurrection. In turn the trials of the Church and of Christians correlate with those of Jesus Christ. In one way or another, everyone must pass through trials. Jesus Christ announces that those who follow him will face their own ordeals (cf. Mk 10:38f, Heb 10:32–9). The intended purpose and effect of testing is multiple: investigating the qualities and endurance of God's servants; causing their improvement and development; and offering them a reward.

48. Etymologically, "experience" finds its roots in the practical knowledge, skill or competence *(peritia)* drawn from trial or danger *(periculum)* once surmounted; cf. *WEUD* 1989, 501; *OED* 1998.

Strength in Weakness: A Test for Infused Fortitude and Spiritual Resilience

Christian notions of strength in weakness and humility challenge a virtue approach to fortitude. Thomas takes this challenge as the place to examine how human and divine competences interact.[49] Aquinas and the Christian tradition's conceptions of strength fly in the face of certain cultural standards. The very notion of God is put to the test in the humble Jesus Christ, who dies on a cross. Furthermore, Christian doctrines and practices relating to suffering and death have spawned numerous sometimes conflicting notions and practices that range from the glorification of suffering per se (dolorism) to the denial of any benefit from human effort. Critiques arise from certain philosophers (Nietzsche and Marx) and resilience researchers (Cyrulnik) who slight some manifestations of Christianity for promoting weakness and glorifying suffering.

Aquinas' treatment of the problematic Pauline adage "strength in weakness" helps to illustrate Christian fortitude, as well as spiritual resilience. The rather problematic scriptural formula "strength in weakness" tests infused fortitude's resilience. First, the enigma of strength in weakness is pertinent for Christian fortitude and education. This problem is poignantly posed through St. Paul's Second Letter to the Corinthians (12:9) concerning "virtue being perfected in infirmity."[50] The Pauline text is so significant that Aquinas uses it as the first potential objection concerning whether fortitude can be a Christian virtue.

Before addressing Aquinas' interpretation, I would like to note several pertinent points of exegesis. First, according to Jerome Murphy-O'Connor, Paul's text refers to human weakness as the means whereby we acquire the power of God, rather than the virtue of fortitude per se.[51] Secondly, considering the cultural milieu, according to Timothy Savage, Paul's weakness refers to being conformed to the poor and vulnerable Christ, rather than to the self-exalting tendencies of the Corinthians.[52] This type

49. See also Gauthier (1951, 475ff.) and Yearly (1971, 557–80) on the thirteenth-century debate about the importance of humility.

50. This translation of the Vulgate differs from the *RSV*: "my power is made perfect in weakness."

51. According to Murphy-O'Connor (1990, 828), this weakness can involve not only the general weakness of the human condition, but also that of individuals put in particular situations. In this context, Paul refers to the power that God accords him for his ministry, as well as the weaknesses that are obstacles to it (cf. 2 Cor 3:5–6).

52. The Corinthians find fault with Paul in four areas: boasting (Paul refused to follow the cultural

of weakness does not mean that Paul was weak in practice, but rather that he understood that a minister of Christ will resist certain cultural pressures.[53] Thirdly, Paul's so-called weakness refers to his aptitude for apostolic adaptation and for glorifying the "power of God for salvation for everyone who has faith."[54] Paul does not exalt the divine power over the nothingness of mortals, but rather, he opposes the strength that human beings find in God versus the impotence found in being without God.[55] Paul testifies to the strength that Christ's Spirit works in the believer who is brought into God's own fullness.[56] Such strength unfolds in the midst of weakness and often does so through testing, the proving grounds for spiritual resilience.

Aquinas, for his part, employs Paul's text to affirm that Christian fortitude has human and graced dimensions. In the midst of the human capacity of fortitude, humans are weak and need continuing help from God. Aquinas interprets St. Paul as distinguishing weaknesses regarding the flesh from weaknesses of the mind. Aquinas' spiritual interpretation goes beyond the literal text. The weaknesses of the flesh concern emotional and dispositional frailty; they are not physical debility per se. He does not want Paul read as encouraging spiritual weakness. Rather fortitude entails strength of spirit in handling weaknesses of the flesh. The strengths (virtues) of the

practice of boasting); physical presence (Paul's physical demeanor was unimpressive); speech (unskilled, in an arena that prized powerful and polished rhetoric); support (Paul would not accept monetary support; he lived a simple life and thus deprived the community of a reason to be proud of their generosity). Cf. Savage 1996, 54–99.

53. In this case, the Corinthian culture had exaggerated practices of boasting about one's own importance, making displays of physical presence, delivering grandiose and abusive oratory, and displaying ostentatious wealth. This context sheds light upon the antithesis of strength in weakness as in the rest of the series of dyads (antitheses) that Paul employs in 2 Corinthians: comfort experienced through suffering (ch. 1); glory manifested through shame (ch. 3); life working in death (ch. 4); riches won through poverty (ch. 6); and finally power expressed through weakness (chs. 12 and 13). Cf. Savage 1996, 1, and 164–92.

54. Romans 1:16. According to Paul, although faith is a gift (1 Cor 12:9), its strength varies: (a) Abraham "grew strong with respect of faith" (Rom 4:20); (b) certain gifts are to be employed in proportion to faith (Rom 12:3); (c) faith is individuated (Rom 14:22; cf. Sampley 1995).

55. Being without God is folly, while even the simple means that God employs is wisdom. As Paul says: "For the foolishness of God is wiser than men, and the weakness of God is stronger than men" (1 Cor 1:25). God's method is clear: "God chose what is foolish in the world to shame the wise, God chose what is weak in the world to shame the strong, God chose what is low and despised in the world, even things that are not, to bring to nothing things that are, so that no human being might boast in the presence of God" (1 Cor 1:27–29; cf. Jo 23:10; Lv 26:8; Phil 4:13).

56. Paul's teaching on the Spirit is clear in his letters to the Philippians and Ephesians, especially Phil 3:10f; Eph 3:14–19, and Eph 6:10–20. In order to fulfill his ministry in Christ, Paul has inner strength (2 Cor 4:6), the power of Christ dwelling in him (2 Cor 12:9), the resilience of Christ.

soul that are thusly developed are patience or fortitude (in regard to bearing the infirmities of the body bravely) and humility (in courageously recognizing our own weaknesses and our need for social and graced support).[57] In recognizing our weaknesses and need for grace in order to do good with consistency, we can be stronger in practicing the virtues, especially when the object of the virtue is supernatural. This type of graced-virtue in the midst of human weakness does not simply limit, but rather puts further demands on, human efforts.

In the debate on weakness, strength, and humility some scholars have feared that Aquinas has completely missed St. Paul's meaning of "flesh," and has actually contradicted the sense of the Second Letter to the Corinthians (12:9);[58] other Scripture scholars point to different meanings.[59] The Pauline notion of strength in weakness is certainly at odds with a Pelagian understanding of Aristotelian virtue theory, especially of fortitude. The juxtaposition of these two notions in Aquinas' dialogue does not yield a hybrid Pauline Aristotelianism or an Aristotelian St. Paul. Aquinas figures that he is respecting both Aristotle and Paul, and that the truth of each is both preserved and advanced. How does he do so?

First, the Creator has endowed humans with natural capacities for good action and excellence, including the natural, acquired virtue of fortitude. Thomas nonetheless takes into consideration the disordering effects of original, personal, and social (structural) sin. Second, God's wisdom and strength is far beyond human strength, which depends on divine help to assure natural fortitude and on divine grace to receive infused fortitude and the gift of courage. Aquinas presumes that grace builds up and brings completion to nature in infused virtues. On the one hand, the natural, acquired virtue of fortitude demands reason, while also being demanded by reason (it requires the prudent exercise of reason, while also protecting our reason from the sway of excess emotion). On the other hand, acquired fortitude underlies the psychological experience (pleasure), moral ease, and promptness that accompany infused fortitude. Nonetheless, according to Aquinas, acts of infused fortitude per se do not create a perfect acquired virtue of

57. Cf. *ST* II-II 129.3 ad 4 on the utility of recognizing one's own faults.

58. Cf. Congar (1974, 342) and Pinckaers (1996).

59. *The Jerusalem Bible* and the *Jerome Biblical Commentary* (O'Rourke 1968, 52:42) suggest that it refers either to a disease (with severe attacks, an "angel of Satan") or persecution (from Israelites, his brothers "according to the flesh"). See also Savage's (1996) interpretation presented above.

fortitude.[60] When we have developed moral courage, infused acts of fortitude contemporaneously strengthen it. But when we do not have an underlying moral virtue, we experience the difficulty and a lack of promptness and pleasure in acts of infused fortitude.[61] In a more direct response to this objection, Aquinas recognizes that the human person cannot be both weak and strong in the same way, at the same time. Therefore through fortitude (acquired and infused) the mind manages our own emotional weakness with the help of God, and through humility we recognize our limitations and need for God's continued grace and, secondarily, for the assistance of others.

Infused fortitude concerns fearful things that have a theological tenor, or the natural ones that attempt to cut us off from our theological goals. It sharpens our acquired capacities to act calmly in danger. However, an acquired virtue must provide a foundation with which the infused virtues confer a further measure to reason and an added surety to acts. Infused fortitude does not make the acquired virtue redundant; nor does acquired fortitude make infused fortitude superfluous. Infused fortitude neither replaces human efforts to master fearfulness nor creates a full-blown acquired virtue of fortitude, without cooperation in human habituation. Progress in the acquired virtue of fortitude, nonetheless, can find further support in the infused virtues of faith, hope, and charity. Scriptural and other narratives, liturgy and hagiography, as well as contemporary struggles for peace and justice provide training grounds for learning to conquer fearful situations and to acquire fortitude.[62]

Resilience in Martyrdom?

If resisting human mortality is *the* criterion for resilience, then martyrdom will be nonsensical vulnerability. The pride of place that the NT and the Christian tradition give to martyrdom can be disturbing, especially in

60. Cf. *ST* I-II 51.4 ad 3; *De virt. com.* 10 ad 19.

61. This distinction of natural and supernatural fortitude is not a simple one, for "the idea of grace perfecting nature coupled with the notion of the continuing presence of the supernatural end forces the recognition that no clear, simple, and neat distinction can be made between natural and supernatural activity." Yearley 1971, 578; see also M. Labourdette 1961–62, 15.

62. Indeed, both life and fiction instruct us in managing emotions in accord with virtuous goals. Children, youth, and adults learn fortitude from the experiences of mothers and fathers, friends, and the community at large. Aquinas did not develop a theory of narrative. For more developed theories of narrative and its relationship with virtue see MacIntyre 1981/1985; Hauerwas 1981; Hall 1994, and so on.

view of the way in which Christ's passion and death (martyrdom) is the archetype for charity.[63] The key text for Aquinas in this regard is Jesus' farewell discourse in the Gospel of John: "Greater love has no man than this, that a man lay down his life for his friends."[64] The martyr fulfills the vocation of every Christian to holiness[65] and is motivated by faith and truth, and by hope in promised life eternal. Thomas crowns fortitude by the discussion of martyrdom (*ST* II-II 124) that directly follows his initial question about the virtue.

Martyrdom and the Virtue of Faith

In demonstrating the pertinence of martyrdom for natural and theological fortitude, Aquinas draws upon the etymology of *martus*, which means witness *(testis)*. He calls upon both scriptural and patristic sources to explain that martyrdom involves a witness to one's faith in Christ,[66] which finds its principal motivation in charity. Since the second half of the second century for Christians,[67] the "martyr" has referred to those who have witnessed with their lives (that is, at the cost of their physical lives) to the truth of the Gospel of Jesus Christ and the coming Kingdom of God.[68] The NT has several senses of the word "*μάρτυς*," three of which are more central to Aquinas' focus:[69] (1) the active proclamation of personal experience, (2) the witness of one's acts, including (3) the witness in giving one's life. First of all, biblical martyrs are more than simple eyewitnesses; they actively proclaim

63. In treating martyrdom, Thomas principally utilizes sacred Scripture and patristic sources to illustrate his uniquely Christian notion. He employs a plethora of Scripture citations on martyrdom in question 124 of the *Secunda secundae*, in which he cites the following (in order): Mt 5:10 (2x); Acts 1:8; Jn 15:13 (2x); 1 Cor 13:3; Rom 3:22; Rom 10:10; 1 Jn 3:16; Col 3:14; Phil 2:8; Heb 10:34; Heb ch. 11; Jb 2:4; 1 Pt 4:15–16; Jas 2:18; Ti 1:6; Rom 8:9; Gal 5:24. Although martyrdom has held an important place in the tradition from the beginning, Aquinas has a novel way of recognizing that the act of martyrdom is the supreme act of courage (cf. Congar 1974). Stanley Hauerwas (1993) poignantly highlights the significance of the differences between the traditions of Aristotle and Aquinas on fortitude (and martyrdom).

64. John 15:13, which Aquinas cites on numerous occasions in this regard: cf. *ST* II-II 122.1 ad 1; *ST* II-II 124.3 (2x); *ST* II-II 140.1 ad 3.

65. Cf. Rom 1:17, 1 Cor 1:2; 1 Pt 2:9; Ws 2:12; Is 5:20; *VS* no. 93.

66. Aquinas (in *ST* II-II 124.2 obj. 1) cites both Scripture (Acts 1:8) and a notable patristic source (St. Maximus the Confessor, *De natali S.S. Mart.* 3, al. Serm. 88; *PL* 57, 708B).

67. The technical distinction between "martyr" and "confessor" (one who suffered for Christ without dying from it) was not made until the second half of the second century with the *Martyrdom of Polycarp* (cf. Louth 1998, 711).

68. The NT martyrs witness to the world to come, to the Kingdom of God: e.g., the eighth beatitude (Mt 5:10), Jesus' promise of paradise to the good thief (cf. Lk 23:43), and both Steven (Acts 7:56) and John's visions of heaven (Rv 1:9). Cf. Heb 10:34; Louth 1998, 711.

69. Furthermore, *μάρτυς*, can have the sense of the juridical testimony of a person who has been present to a material fact, or a conclusion of a juridical operation. Cf. Spicq 1991, 969–74.

what they have seen and what they know. For example, the mission of the twelve apostles is to bear witness to the resurrection of Jesus Christ.[70] Second, examples of the witness of one's actions are found in Jesus Christ's acts of healing, which testify to the veracity of his message as well as to his origin and his mission.[71] Third, the ultimate test of martyrdom is the witness of one's own life. Christ is thus the archetype for all Christian martyrs;[72] he expresses what for Aquinas is the highest form of friendship-love, which lays down one's own life for one's friends.[73]

Martyrdom shares the general characteristics of virtue (voluntariness and protecting the good of reason), as well as those of fortitude.[74] Faith assures the content of a martyr's witness and the vision of his goal. As Aquinas says, citing Hebrews 11, "a martyr is so called as being a witness to the Christian faith, which teaches us to despise things visible for the sake of things invisible."[75] Although human beings naturally prefer to lose possessions and suffer pain rather than die, a martyr bears witness to the faith in the radical way that he subjugates visible goods to invisible ones. Thomas affirms that the perfect notion of martyrdom requires that a man suffer in body unto death and that he does so for Christ's sake,[76] instead of any mere reason or truth. Witnessing to Christ can be done in word or any virtuous deed (including the avoiding of sin) provided that it refers to God or divine truth, which renders a virtuous deed a profession of faith.[77] Aquinas draws upon scriptural authority to establish this necessary interrelation between word and deed.[78] The key is that the martyr be Christ's through doing virtuous deeds that are activated by the Spirit of Christ (cf. Rom 8:9). Thus

70. Cf. Lk 24:48; Jn 19:35; 1 Cor. 15:15; Mk 13:11; Acts 1:8.

71. Cf. Jn 5:36; Jn 10:25, 37–38.

72. Cf. Lk 13:33; 9:51; Jn 18:37; 1 Tim 6:13; Rv 1:5; 3:14; Phil 2:8; Is 53:11; Mt 20:28; Heb 9:12, 22; as well as Augrain 1995, 723–24; Louth 1998, 712.

73. Cf. Jn 15:13; *ST* II-II 124.

74. Cf. *ST* II-II 124.2; where cites St. Paul (Rom 3:22); and draws from the authority of: St. Maximus the Confessor (*De natali S.S. Mart.* 3, al. Serm. 88; *PL* 57, 708B) and St. Cyprian (whom St. Augustine cites in *Serm.* 311, al. De Div. 115.1: *PL* 38.1414).

75. *ST* II-II 124.4; cf. Heb 11:1–40 and 2 Cor 4:17–18.

76. Cf. *ST* II-II 124.4.

77. Cf. *ST* II-II 124.5; 124.5 ad 1. Aquinas employs the tradition's identification of the eighth beatitude with martyrdom as the basis of justifying that in addition to faith, other virtues pertain to martyrdom (cf. *ST* II-II 124.5 sc).

78. In this regard, Thomas (in *ST* II-II 124) employs not only the letter of James (2:18) but even St. Paul's letter to the Romans (8:9 and 10:10). Aquinas finds no necessary animosity between faith and deeds. He can employ the Romans text without divorcing its teaching on justification by faith from its moral demands and exhortations.

he imitates Christ in avoiding sin (cf. Gal 5:24), in confessing faith, and in doing good. Because of this wider understanding of witnessing to faith, Aquinas deems John the Baptist a martyr even though he suffered death for reproving adultery instead of defending an article of faith per se. This understanding of the interrelationship of faith and morals is crucial for the type of resilience expressed therein.

In looking at the fortitude engendered in Christian faith, we need to be careful not to construct a false dichotomy between reason and faith, by opposing a rational fortitude to either a courageous faith or a faith-inspired courage.[79] In Aquinas' perspective, though, faith does not abandon reason but only the pretensions of unaided erroneous reason; and reason does not denigrate faith, but only realizes a relationship that does not do violence to human reason. Both reason and faith offer a corrective according to each one's proper pretensions. Such remedies are especially pertinent concerning the rational and faith issues operative in an act of martyrdom, especially concerning the role of charity in fortitude, martyrdom, and, we can add, spiritual resilience as well.

Charity as Its Unifier, Motivator, and Greatest Expression

As a pinnacle among the expressions of Christian virtue, martyrdom demands and expresses the unity of the virtues. The fortitude involved in martyrdom faces the danger of death for the sake of the good, the common good, and the greatest good (God and our friendship with God), in a spiritual combat. It demands infused virtue, which can be supported (or not) by the person's natural, moral virtue of fortitude. Aquinas construes charity and the infused virtue of martyrdom in terms of the threefold character and reception of infused virtue: its object is God; only God can infuse it; and its object depends on divine revelation.[80]

Charity's two dimensions, friendship-love with God and neighbor,[81] or-

79. This dichotomy opposes two vertiginous extremes regarding faith. A fear of faith's risks and unknowns accepts only experimental certitude and positive reason. On the contrary, an overreaching confidence in the content of faith shuns any dialogue or relationship with the sciences (cf. P. Secretan 1993, 311).

80. Cf. *ST* I-II 62.1; *ST* I-II 63.3; *ST* I-II 65.3.

81. See *ST* II-II 27, 8, where Aquinas uses 1 John 4:21 to emphasize the interrelation of these two aspects of love: a love of neighbor, which includes that love of God as well as a love of God which includes love of neighbor. There is nonetheless an ordering in finality: that God be loved with one's whole being—principally since God is the source of love—and one's neighbor be loved as oneself—secondarily, but with the important measure of one's natural inclinations to self-regard and -protection (cf. *ST* II-II

der the act and virtue of martyrdom. The preeminence of love for God and neighbor specifies that the ultimate (self-fulfilling) purpose of one's life is self-giving. This counterintuitive and seemingly counter-resilient teaching is at the very center of Christ's Gospel. One can understand it only in the context of faith in His life, death, and resurrection; of hope in His promises of resurrection and eternal life; and of charity. These theological virtues serve as the necessary basis for acts of infused fortitude and martyrdom.[82]

The relationship of charity to martyrdom occasions various confusions. First, how can an act that disregards natural love of one's body be resilient? Will not such a basic conflict inhibit even the loftiest motivation, and render senseless all natural optimism and strength?[83] Besides the natural inclination to preserve oneself, which would tend to offer resistance to putting one's physical life in jeopardy, two motivators support the virtue of martyrdom. Charity is its chief and principal motivation, while fortitude is its proper motivation.[84] These two virtues collaborate in a determinate fashion: charity commands martyrdom, fortitude elicits it. As in the case of all Christian virtue, without charity one has neither merit nor complete virtue, as St. Paul says: "If I should deliver my body to be burned, and have not charity, it profits me nothing."[85] For Aquinas, martyrdom is not fully courageous in simply enduring forced death *per se*, for it must express the charity, which is the driving force and reason to endure such a hateful act. It is the greatest love (Jn 15:13), the love of Christ that is victorious in the martyr, according to Aquinas.[86] This charity puts the love of one's life in a larger context. The natural inclination to preserve one's physical life is drawn up within the spiritual inclination to preserve one's life with God. Although natural abhorrence to death remains, faith, hope, and charity provide the renewed object and motivation to pursue our ultimate flourishing.

Martyrdom as the greatest expression of love poses a second resilience problem. Is it not counterintuitive and even counter-resilient to claim that martyrdom expresses greatness or perfection? Is it not the ultimate folly

184.3 and his sources Dt 6:5, Lev 19:18, and Mt 22:40, and also *ST* II-II 26.3 and *Ad Joan*. ch. 4, lect. 4, with reference to Origen).

82. Cf. *ST* II-II 4.3; *De carit*. 3 ad 13.

83. Pieper (1949–59/1966: 127) also asks such questions.

84. Cf. *ST* II-II 124.2 ad 2.

85. Cor 13:3; cf. *ST* II-II 124.2 obj.2.

86. In this regard, Aquinas (*ST* II-II 124.2 obj.2; *ST* II-II 124.5) cites St. Maximus, *Sermon* 16; *PL* 57.708B.

neither to fight nor flee if faced with a way out of death? In a seeming paradox, Aquinas directly acknowledges that life is the good of this present world that humans treasure most, and that death, especially a painful one, is most naturally shunned.[87] In blatant opposition to one's natural inclinations to preserve one's own physical life and to hate pain and death, Aquinas claims that one still rationally reckons martyrdom the most perfect completion to human life. The suffering of death itself is the greatest perfection (although the species of the act is not praiseworthy itself) inasmuch as death is directed to something else by its principal object and motivation, it takes on a deeper meaning. If human life is more than its physical manifestation, then there can be something greater than preserving one's body.

Aquinas argues that not only does the love of charity, as the principal motivation of martyrdom, bring perfection to the act of martyrdom,[88] but that the act of martyrdom demonstrates the greatest proof of charity. Since death is so naturally despicable and life so naturally embraced, martyrdom can be the most perfect of human acts, as the sign of the greatest charity.[89] If the primacy of charity is not recognized however, Christianity and the pride of place it apportions to martyrdom will appear glaringly anti-resilient, as sources of ultimate and fatal vulnerability.

Martyrdom Defending the Good of Reason: Truth, Justice, and Prudence

We can ask whether Aquinas' conception of martyrdom conforms to the criteria of moral resilience: does it defend the good of reason and is it voluntary? Martyrdom safeguards the good of reason in several ways, including justice as its proper effect. Aquinas argues that "martyrdom essentially consists in standing firmly to truth and justice against the assaults of persecution."[90] His source for this insight is the eighth beatitude (Mt 5:10): "Blessed are they that suffer persecution for justice's sake, for theirs is the kingdom

87. Cf. *ST* II-II 124.3; and *ST* II-II 124.4, where he also quotes Job 2.4.

88. Aquinas (*ST* II-II 124.3) cites St. Paul (Col 3.14): "charity . . . is the bond of perfection." In the *sed contra*, Aquinas furthermore draws upon St. Augustine's (*De Sancta Virgin* 46.47: *PL* 40.424) authority to affirm that martyrdom is even more perfect than virginity.

89. Here Aquinas once again draws upon the teaching of Christ found in the Gospel of John 15:13 (cf. *ST* II-II 124.3). Furthermore, martyrdom is also a sign of the greatest possible obedience, since through it one follows Christ who became "obedient unto death" (Phil 2:8; cited by Aquinas in *ST* II-II 124.3 ad 2).

90. *ST* II-II 124.1. On truth and justice, see *ST* II-II 109.1–3.

of heaven."[91] This beatitude serves not only to establish that martyrdom is a virtue, but also to identify certain of its principal qualities. Martyrdom demands that we remain firm in justice, as the habit of establishing the order of reason in human affairs.[92] It involves the right endurance of suffering related to not committing injustice and to resisting injustice actively,[93] which excludes acts of suicide or terrorism being considered as Christian martyrdom. This good of reason that we achieve through acts of justice not only is that of practical reason (prudence), but also includes that of infused speculative reason (faith).

Aquinas also attests to the importance of patience drawing out other important moral, pedagogical, and psychological features of martyrdom.[94] He acknowledges that the chief act of fortitude found in martyrdom is endurance rather than initiative or aggressiveness. St. Thomas defends martyrdom against possible misconceptions and objections about its being involuntary, illicit, or presumptuous.[95] First, martyrdom must be voluntary in order to be a moral act.[96] Second, it is not suicide.[97] Third, it demands some mental and emotional preparation. Such preparation may seem rash, even presumptuous. Aquinas, however, argues that it is virtuous to prepare oneself for martyrdom. The precepts of the Divine Law thus aid one in preparing one's mind and heart to suffer martyrdom, when it is expedient.[98] Preparation is especially helpful, since it is so difficult to "rightly endure sufferings that are unjustly inflicted," as Aquinas says.[99] We do not, however, find the most powerful source for martyrdom, the Spirit of Christ, in hu-

91. Aquinas (*ST* II-II 124.5 sc) calls upon tradition (a gloss) and St. Jerome's commentary in linking the eighth beatitude to the act and virtue of martyrdom.

92. Cf. *ST* II-II 123.12.

93. Cf. *ST* II-II 124.1 ad 3; *ST* II-II 124.5 ad 1.

94. On martyrdom and patience, Aquinas (*ST* II-II 123.6) cites St. Augustine's sermon on St. Cyprian in *Serm.* 311, al. De Div. 115.1: *PL* 38.1414.

95. Cf. *ST* II-II 124.1 obj. 1–3.

96. The voluntary nature of martyrdom is problematic when considering the Holy Innocents as martyrs for Christ's sake. Even though St. Hilary attributes the glory of martyrdom to children of such a young age, Aquinas, following Augustine, recognizes that they merit this glory not for the voluntary aspect of their death, but rather due to their suffering in the place of Christ. It is by God's grace that they attain what others do through collaboration with their own wills. Cf. *ST* II-II 124.1 obj/ad 1; and *ST* II-II 124.4 ad 4.

97. Augustine attests that certain women martyrs during persecution seemed to have illicitly killed themselves. Aquinas resists any association of martyrdom with suicide, yet claims that these women are fittingly honored. Cf. *ST* II-II 124.1 ad 2; *ST* II-II 64.5; *ST* II-II 64.1 ad 2.

98. The theme of preparing the soul for martyrdom in several places: *ST* II-II 124.1 ad 3; *ST* II-II 124.3 ad 1.

99. *ST* II-II 124.1 ad 3.

man training.[100] Human self-preparation is necessary but not sufficient for martyrdom.

In addition to defending the good of reason by standing firm in truth through the virtues of justice and patience, infused fortitude and martyrdom also indispensably draw upon prudence. Common language, however, often opposes fortitude and prudence: martyrdom or fortitude is seen as an audacious recklessness or imprudent boldness, and prudence is often conceived of as a spineless caution or self-serving protectionism. However, far from being contrary virtues, fortitude and prudence positively correlate in a way particular to their objects, effects, and causes. Aquinas expresses the interrelation of fortitude and prudence as perfect virtues in two ways.[101] First, as general properties, they need each other in order to habitually do the good well. Aquinas describes prudence's qualities overflowing into other virtues, inasmuch as prudence directs and guides them.[102]

Thomas differentiates prudence and fortitude according to their determinate matters.[103] Prudence pertains to the proper functioning of reason, and fortitude to that of the irascible faculty.[104] Nonetheless, in martyrdom they interact since their determinate matters depend on each other for perfect virtue. In particular, prudence, being in the cognitive power, informs fortitude.[105] Prudence overcomes the illusions that threaten courage. If one takes his courage to be all the strength needed to overcome the adversary, he can be heartily wrong. The courageous stature of a person or a whole community might be necessary but not sufficient. We can render a desperate situation all the more disastrous by the illusion that alone we shall save the world. In order to bring a framework to courage, prudence must measure well the objective danger and the resources on hand. It quantifies the fra-

100. Cf. Acts 1:8; Gal 5:24; which are cited respectively in *ST* II-II 124.2 obj.1 and *ST* II-II 124.5 ad 1. Furthermore, Aquinas mentions another source of strength for the martyr. In *De verit.* 13.3 ad 9, he draws from Augustine's insights to explain that a "sprinkling" of divine glory (i.e., a non-beatific vision of God's essence) enables the martyrs to live temperately, justly, bravely, and prudently when faced with temptations. Cf. St. Augustine, *De genesi ad litteram*, XII, 26 (*PL* 34:476).

101. Cf. *ST* I-II 65.1.

102. See *ST* I-II 61.4 ad 1, which responds to Gregory (*Moral.* xxii, 1). Furthermore, the human being who seeks perfection, by rectitude of will directs every virtue in its appropriate matter; cf. *De virt. com.* 5, 23.

103. In this regard, Aquinas (*ST* I-II 61.3–4; *ST* I-II 65.1; *ST* II-II 47.4 sc; *De virt. com.* 5, 23) employs: Aristotle (*NE* ii.7, 1107a33ff or vi.13, 1144b36ff); the Book of Wisdom (8:7); St. Gregory the Great (*Moralia in Job*, xxii.1; and ii.49); and Augustine (*De morib. eccl.*, xi and *De Trin.*, VI.4).

104. Cf. *ST* I-II 61.2; *ST* I-II 66.1; *ST* I-II 85.3; *De malo* 4 ad 4; *De virt. gen.* 12.25; *In Meta.* lect. 20.1064.

105. Cf. *De carit.* 3.13; *ST* I-II 61.4; *ST* I-II 66.1; *In Eth.* bk. 10, lect. 12.

gility and strength found in those around us and in ourselves. It calculates what we shall gain or lose in acting and not acting in a particular way.[106]

Aquinas' moral analysis of infused fortitude and martyrdom not only respects moral resilience, but also pushes it to its logical limit. A perfect moral expression of our intellectual powers of reason and will demands other criteria than the good of reason and a good will. We can absolutely trust neither our brave reactions nor isolated acts of fortitude. Only the prudent person can be brave on a consistent basis. Human fragility and vulnerability demand infused fortitude and prudence in order to adjudicate the fitting type of witness and acts that might lead to martyrdom. The question of martyrdom's criteria leads Aquinas to turn to Christ as the archetype for managing fear and death.

Fear in Christ as the Archetypal Model of Martyrdom

A study of St. Thomas's treatment of Christ's agony, passion, and death specifies the place of fear in Christ and in Christian martyrdom.[107] Of more than passing interest, the experience of fear in Christ has ontological, moral, Christological, and soteriological ramifications. Although Aquinas' analysis of fear in Christ relies extensively on his treatment of the passion of fear,[108] Thomas's basis for discussion is positive—the Gospel of Mark's account of Christ's suffering in the garden of Gethsemane, which testifies that "Jesus began to fear and to be greatly troubled."[109] This quote is the only record of Christ's fear in the Gospels. Its straightforward simplicity has nonetheless spawned opposing interpretations that Aquinas aims to integrate by adding a further nuance concerning Christ's fear: in short, he affirms that Christ

106. See *ST* II-II 50.4 ad 3 and, on the counterexample of fearlessness, *ST* II-II 126.2 ad 2.

107. In *ST* III 15.7, Thomas asks "Whether Christ experienced fear." As important as the management of fear is for fortitude, it is curious to find that Aquinas does not directly discuss fear in his treatise on martyrdom (*ST* II-II 124). This absence does not mean that the martyr does not face fear. Rather it is typical of Aquinas' dialectical method and intent to minimize repetition. The context is clear. His treatment of martyrdom is situated in the larger context of the treatise of fortitude, which extensively addresses fear, and of the earlier treatise on the passion of fear (ST I-II 41–44). Aquinas treats fear and daring in *ST* II-II 123 (on fortitude), *ST* II-II 125 (on fear), *ST* II-II 126 (on fearlessness), *ST* II-II 127 (on daring), and extensively through other parts of the whole treatise on fortitude (*ST* II-II 123–140).

108. His sources are scriptural (Mk 14:33; Prv 28:1), patristic (St. Hilary's *De Trin.* X.10; Damascene *De fide orthod.* III.23; Jerome, *Com. in Matt.* IV.26 and 27); and philosophical (Aristotle *Rhet.* II.5).

109. Aquinas (*ST* III 15.7 sc) cites the Vulgate (Mk 14:33). Paul Gondreau (2002) laments a "regrettable omission" in Aquinas' not making more explicit reference to this text in his argumentation. Gondreau rightfully remarks that further use of the only extant record of Christ's fear amplifies the argument with more existential vigor.

experienced fear, but not in a way that would deprive him of his rational use of his faculty of reason. This simple nuance, which applies to moral resilience, needs further explanation in order to appropriate insights for fully Christian resilience.

Jesus Christ in his human nature experienced fear, as the body "naturally retreats" from a perceived future evil. Moreover, during the agony in the garden, Jesus experienced in effect two other types of fear. Fear proper moved him inasmuch as he still had a glimmer of hope that he might not have to suffer death. Furthermore, he experienced sorrow when realizing that it was inevitable.[110] His fear was precipitated and exacerbated by the proximity of the evil, being deserted by his friends (cf. Mk 14:37), and his foreknowledge of the physical torment that lay ahead.[111]

According to Thomas, however, Jesus did not experience fear due to ignorance concerning the source, timing, or certainty of the death that he was facing. Jesus Christ did not confront his terror as one would a strange sound in the night. Aquinas is keen to deny that there was any ignorance in Christ,[112] or any need for learning from experience. The claim of perfect knowledge and perfection in general demonstrates Aquinas' tendency to attribute glorified and exalted status to Christ's psychology, rather than an itinerant one with the developmental need of acquiring human knowledge through experience.[113]

Aquinas affirms that Christ experienced fear not just as a natural repulsion to death, but also within his choice to not evade his foreseeable death, to accept the "cup" that is offered, to do the Father's will. In responding to the objection found in Proverbs (18:1), "the just, bold as a lion, shall be without dread," Aquinas explains that Christ's fear did not compromise his rational judgment. In this regard, Aquinas introduces St. Jerome's distinction

110. Cf. *ST* III 15.7; Mk 14:35.

111. Cf. Lk 22:43–44. To illustrate Christ's natural or spontaneous fear of and aversion to death, Aquinas distinguishes between desiring by natural instinct and desiring as modified by reason. In this regard, see Gondreau's (2002, 375ff.) excellent discussion on Aquinas' use of Damascene in relation with Maximus Confessor, Peter Lombard, Hugh of St. Victor, Alexander of Hales, and Bonaventure.

112. Aquinas affirms that Christ had full knowledge even of future events (cf. *ST* III 15.7; where he cites Damascene *De fide orth.* III.23), because Christ was not subject to the *fomes* of sin (which include ignorance) and because of his human nature's union with the Divine hypostasis (cf. *ST* III 15.3 corpus and ad 2, where he cites Jn 1:14).

113. Such development is reflected in Hebrews 5:8: "Although he was Son, he learned obedience through what he suffered" (cf. Phil 2:7). Concerning the debate on Aquinas and the knowledge of Christ see the bibliography found in Torrell 1994, 394–409, and 1999, 1:135–49; and Gondreau 2002.

between a pure passion and a propassion.[114] While a pure passion has the post-lapsus tendency to derange reason, a propassion involves an emotional and a rational apprehension of the source of evil without the blurring of reason or the inhibiting of the will. Christ is able to will freely to follow the Father's plan that he continue his mission, while fully realizing the fearfulness of the death to be imposed upon him by those who oppose him. He does so with an unmitigated command of reason and will. The realism of Christ's psychosomatic experience of fear meets the criteria of Aquinas' Christology and soteriology, which demands that Christ be fully human and fully divine.[115]

Aquinas does not contradict himself when he transforms Greco-Roman notions of fortitude into Christian martyrdom. This transformation simply demonstrates how human wisdom is extended through a fuller wisdom, which is based on divine revelation, informed by a life of grace, and expressed through faith, hope, and charity. It also demonstrates a larger sense of resilience. On an initial reading of Aquinas' account of fortitude, the evolution of the arguments might seem anything but theological. Fortitude, as the virtue that most properly deals with the fear of death in battle for the common good, seems restricted to the military arena. Nonetheless, the basic definition of fortitude, when seen in the context of the whole treatise involving the ultimate fortitude needed for martyrdom, provides a wider basis to understand theological fortitude. Aquinas uses warfare in a wider sense to include the situation not only of private persons in everyday struggles, but also of the martyrs, who "have been made valiant in battle."[116] Christ thus serves as an example for martyrs, who meet similar ontological and moral situations of fear. Is he also thereby a model for resilience? Aquinas' claim that Christ is the exemplar for all virtue suggests that he is the model for resilience as well.[117] But what type of resilience? Notwithstanding

114. See *ST* III 15.7 ad 1, which draws on Jerome's *Com in Matt.* IV.26:37 (on Mk 14:33).

115. This admission of Christ's vulnerability to pain, suffering, and fear, also avoids any doubt of Docetism in Aquinas' position. Cf. *ST* III 15.7 ad 2 and ad 3; Gondreau 2002.

116. Aquinas (*ST* II-II 123.5 ad 1 and *ST* II-II 124.2) quotes from Hebrews 11:34, which was in Aquinas' time the Epistle for the Mass of the martyrs SS. Fabian and Sebastian.

117. According to L.-B. Gillon (1959), the theme of *Imitatio Christi* is neither very present nor explicit, although not absent, in Aquinas' works (cf. Congar 1974: 344). Aquinas' approach in the *Summa* differs from other approaches, such as Thomas à Kempis's *Imitatio Christi* and the spirituality of the *devotio modera*. Inasmuch as its style is more analytical, it demands a resynthesis in order to more fully draw out such a theme.

the martyrs in ancient Israel,[118] martyrdom takes on a new meaning rooted in the experience of Jesus Christ. When we open the resilience concept to this faith perspective, we must root Christian resilience not only in Christ's passion and death, but also in hope in his resurrection. The Christian martyr imitates Christ and participates in his salvific work.[119] Jesus foretells that, like himself, his followers will be persecuted and put to death.[120] This type of resilience requires that we face fear and remain strong in our faith in God; we hope in the eventual fruitfulness of the evident loss; and we be drawn on by charity even for those who persecute us.

The Gift of Fortitude and the Beatitude of the Just

In martyrdom, the spiritual dimension of Christian fortitude and resilience reaches a peak, but is not exhausted. Aquinas surpasses his treatment of fortitude as a natural virtue or an infused virtue (in the case of martyrdom) in his teaching on fortitude as a gift of the Holy Spirit, in relation to the beatitude of those who hunger and thirst for justice, and in the precept of fortitude. Thomas is consistent here with his vision of the possibility for human participation in the divine life through knowledge and affection of the Word of Christ and through the Holy Spirit's prompting, sanctification, and strengthening.[121] In different ways, all the virtues and gifts of the Holy Spirit are useful; not one of them is redundant. However, the diversity of their origin and exercise raises a host of challenges for more restricted notions of resilience.

The Gift of Fortitude

The sevenfold gift of the Holy Spirit is not a secondary element in Aquinas' moral theology, nor is it unimportant for human and spiritual resilience. Nonetheless, it raises difficulties concerning its relationship to moral agency and to virtues in general. First, for Aquinas this sevenfold gift concerns how the Holy Spirit moves our minds and hearts. Through these gifts the

118. For example, Eleazar, the seven brothers, and their mother martyred under Antiochus (2 Mac 6–7).

119. Cf. *ST* II-II 124.5 ad 1; Gal 5:24.

120. Cf. Jn 15:20 and 12:24.

121. It is difficult to overestimate the importance that Aquinas places on the Holy Spirit's role in Christian life (cf. *ST* I-II 106.1; 108.1–2).

Holy Spirit prompts the human person, who is disposed to be so perfected.[122] Such a conception of the gifts, though, raises a difficulty for conceptions of voluntariness and responsibility that permit no external influences. Aquinas' larger sense of voluntariness, however, specifies that an external influence does not necessarily diminish human autonomy. This insight recalls Aquinas' teaching on the dual principle of human movement: internal (reason and will) and external (God and human teachers).[123] In particular, when the external source is reliable and contributes to the goals of true freedom (freedom for excellence), then it even assists and completes human agency in its moral quest for flourishing, truth, and goodness. As contributing to human perfection, a prompting of the Holy Spirit leads human moral agency without diminishing it.

Secondly, a gift of the Holy Spirit does not oppose a human virtue, nor does a human virtue oppose a gift, for Aquinas. A human virtue perfects a human capacity in doing something well, while a gift refers to a cause of the action.[124] Virtues are interior principles that lead people toward happiness. The gifts bring greater perfection to the virtues. They add a further docility to the movements of the Spirit. It is thus that morality can become the life according to the Spirit. The domain of human virtue is that which is natural for us to do through reason. The domain of the gifts is a spiritual sensibility, an instinct of the Holy Spirit in both the reason and will that adds further perfection through being more certain (since the act is informed by a "principle higher than human reason") and more sure (since one is disposed to follow the inner promptings of divine instinct).[125] Aquinas' original contribution to the theology of the gifts is twofold. First, they are superhuman dispositions *(habitus)* of human agency, proportionate to our supernatural calling. Second, in the *Prima secundae,* Aquinas explains this mode in terms of the prompting of the Holy Spirit.[126] The gifts are thus dispositions to

122. Cf. *ST* II-II 139.1; and *ST* I-II 68.1–3.

123. See *ST* I-II 9.4 and 9.6, as well as our chapter 3. Aquinas follows a work attributed to Aristotle called the *De bona fortuna.* Concerning the many problems with this text see Deman 1928, 38–58; O'Connor 1974, 142–47.

124. Cf. *ST* I-II 68.1; *ST* I-II 63.3.

125. Aquinas innovates while drawing heavily from the tradition. His primary sources include Isaiah (11:2–3), St. Gregory the Great, St. Augustine, and Aristotle. In an extraordinarily long corpus concerning the gifts of the Holy Spirit (*ST* I-II 68), St. Thomas addresses diverse erroneous positions. On the debates that Aquinas' teaching has precipitated, see Pinckaers 1995a, 26; O'Connor 1974; Labourdette 1957.

126. Aquinas' teaching has become the most common Catholic position on the gifts of the Holy

be open to the Holy Spirit, as well as promptings of the Spirit; nonetheless they interrelate with the virtues (as *habitus*) in the search for goodness, truth, and flourishing. If one admits the moral dimension of the gifts of the Holy Spirit (which some philosophers and psychologists find difficult), then one can welcome a further source of resilience. What does this insight mean in the case of fortitude?

The gift of fortitude addresses human suffering. It supports humans in managing to keep our eternal perspective and grounds us in God (as first cause and last end), while facing suffering, as either a present evil or the toil needed to accomplish some good. We can examine this instinct, as a graced disposition to follow the lead of the Spirit, in two types of situation. First, it can elevate human fortitude; however, this construction does not involve putting one block on top of another. Rather it entails an extension, a transformative completion, the coming to blossom of the image of God at the very core of our humanity when facing fearful situations. Second, it can even function without the naturally developed disposition or *habitus* needed for a mature moral virtue of fortitude. This idea can cause some psychologists or scientists to raise their eyebrows, and ask what could be the source of such an act. However, would they discredit all outside influences and relationships that help a person to act responsibly? Through instruction, discipline, and suggestion, our instructors, family, and friends can encourage particular acts and the development of dispositions. The gift (as the influence of God's relationship with us) goes beyond the present limits of our personal natural *habitus*, as does the impact of a friend who influences us to be courageous when we otherwise might well let fear control our activities. The gift per se does not create a natural disposition, although it strengthens already existing ones. A good act facilitated by the gift serves as a further basis to develop human fortitude and undo opposing cowardliness.

The firmness of mind denoted by the virtue of fortitude, as either a general virtue or a special one (when concerning difficulties in facing death), involves a mode that is proper and connatural to human beings in accomplishing arduous efforts and in enduring grievous evil.[127] Through the gift of fortitude, however, the Holy Spirit prompts the human mind to per-

Spirit. See Pope Leo XIII, *Divinum illud munus* (9 May 1897); CCC (1266, and 1830–31); O'Connor 1974.

127. Cf. *ST* II-II 139.1; *ST* II-II 123.2; *ST* I-II 61.3.

sist in order to attain the sought-for end and to avoid threatening perils.[128] Such persistent strength is not always naturally possible, nor do we necessarily experience it psychologically in the same way as an acquired virtue, especially when faced with the fear of death. In particular the Holy Spirit strengthens the mind (1) by infusing confidence about God's bringing us to everlasting life—the end of all good deeds—and about God's releasing us from all perils, and (2) by expelling any fear to the contrary.[129] Even though God (through the Holy Spirit) is present in every moment of goodness, including all courageous acts, the gift of fortitude comes as a completion, not a destruction, of human nature and efforts. The Holy Spirit moves us further in the general strength of each virtue, as well as in specific acts of fortitude and the martyr's witness.[130] God thus promotes a spontaneous living of Christian resilience, the life of the Spirit.

This spontaneity nonetheless does not exclude an intense struggle at the level of human *habitus*, because of vice, the lack of virtue, and the effort needed in developing virtue. The work of the Spirit, through a person's willing cooperation with the grace of God, can assure action that is fitting for salvation, even though everyone does not have the same natural ease, promptness, and joy (moral maturity) in their use of intellect, will, and emotion. The tricky issue of the coexistence of acquired vice or underdeveloped virtue with infused virtues and supernatural gifts is critical for spiritual resilience. Aquinas' moral theology gives some key insights into understanding how the theological resilience of infused virtues and the sevenfold gift of the Holy Spirit can assure salvation, even in the face of the need to overcome the effects of a human vice, the lack of natural capacities, or struggles in maturation. Acts of theological resilience at the same time strengthen preexisting natural dispositions, which involve separate efforts to develop through the steps of debutant, progress, and self-mastery or maturity.[131]

Fortitude and the Beatitude of the Just

The beatitudes also play an integral role in moral theology and in fortitude. Aquinas construes the beatitudes as fruits or perfect acts of both the virtues and the gifts, and as such they cap Christian resilience. In the

128. Cf. *ST* II-II 139.1 ad 3; *ST* I-II 68.2; *ST* I-II 68.4 ad 3; Bowlin 1996, 414.

129. Cf. *ST* II-II 139.1.

130. Cf. *Ad Eph.* ch. 3, lec. 4, p 140.

131. Cf. *ST* I-II 51.4; *ST* I-II 63.3; *ST* I-II 63.4; *III Sent.* 33, q. 1, a. 2; and q. 1a. 3.

accomplishment of the beatitudes, we move (1) from what virtue inclines us toward according to the measure of reason, (2) to what the gifts inspire according to the higher measure of the Holy Spirit. In this regard, Aquinas follows Augustine's principal ordering of the virtues, the gifts, and the beatitudes,[132] even though their approaches differ.[133] Aquinas explores the nature of how the beatitudes, gifts, and virtues interrelate, and draws upon a host of sources in a classic patristic moral interpretation of the beatitudes as tracing a series of virtues leading to the Kingdom: poverty and humility, docility (or meekness), justice, mercy, purity, and peace.[134]

The spiritual progression among the beatitudes leads to purity of heart, the will for peace, and even the witness of martyrdom as their summit. Aquinas ties this movement to the search for flourishing; he views the beatitudes as Christ's response to the question of human flourishing. Although St. Thomas introduces many insights and nuances on flourishing throughout the first five questions of the *Prima secundae*, that so-called treatise on beatitude seems curiously incomplete. Servais-Théodore Pinckaers has argued that the treatise does not end there (*ST* I-II 1–5), but rather culminates with the question on the beatitudes (*ST* I-II 69), as well as the questions concerning the New Law (*ST* I-II 106–8).[135] This spiritual progression illustrates Christian resilience; it becomes evident in the way in which Aquinas treats how the beatitudes correlate with the virtues and the gifts.

How does Aquinas relate fortitude (as acquired and infused virtues and

132. In his influential commentary on the Sermon on the Mount (*De sermone Domini in monte: PL* 34), Augustine is the first to correlate the beatitudes, the gifts, and the petitions of the *Pater*. In doing so, he reworks their division and order. This innovation is motivated by the patristic tradition's affinity for finding seven a symbol of plenitude. Prior to Augustine, writers customarily recognized only six petitions in the *Pater*. Augustine identifies the petition on temptations as distinct from that on evil. Likewise, he finds seven beatitudes in Matthew's Sermon on the Mount (unlike St. Ambrose, who finds an eightfold division in Matthew, and unlike the Gospel of Luke's fivefold division). Cf. Pinckaers 1995a, 145–46; 1998, 46–48; O'Connor 1974, 90–2.

133. Augustine's perspective relies extensively on his own experience, quest for flourishing, and desire for God. Aquinas seeks these realities' source and their interconnection in action; cf. *ST* II-II 121.2.

134. Aquinas especially draws on the following sources in his treatment of the evangelical beatitudes (in the *ST* I-II 69.1–4): the Gospels of Matthew and Luke, St. Augustine and St. Ambrose, Isaiah (ch. 11), and St. Paul, as well as the philosophical categories of Aristotle (cf. Pinckaers 1998, 44–45). Pinckaers (1997, 25–26) deems the *Secunda pars* a type of commentary on the beatitudes and the Sermon on the Mount.

135. Cf. Pinckaers (1998, 42–43). A complete treatment of flourishing should even include Aquinas' discussion of grace (*ST* I-II 109–113). Furthermore, the concrete realization of post-lapserian human participation in beatitude needs to consider not only the most pertinent virtues (esp. charity, cf. *ST* II-II 23–46), but also Aquinas' treatment of redemption and the sacraments in the *Tertia pars*.

as a gift) to the beatitude of the just: "Happy those that hunger and thirst for what is right: they shall be satisfied"?[136] Although the ordering is Augustine's, the approach is Aquinas'. Augustine, in his *Commentary on the Sermon on the Mount,* explains that fortitude is becoming of those who hunger and thirst for justice, since it involves toil in order to enjoy true goods and to avoid being trapped in our love of material things. Aquinas confirms this interrelation while arguing that this match is fitting since fortitude is about difficult things and this beatitude is about very difficult things involved not only in works of justice (virtuous deeds), but in doing them with an insatiable desire designated by the beatitude's phrase, "hunger and thirst for justice/what is right."[137] Aquinas interprets "justice" as the universal justice involved in all virtuous deeds[138] and "desire" as including the charity at the root of each virtue and gift.[139] Furthermore, he signals that patience (in enduring evils) and longanimity (regarding long delays and accomplishing good actions) are the related fruits.[140] Thomas explains that the beatitudes in general are not only acts, but also rewards,[141] which fulfill the desires that underlie them on a higher plane. Thus, the beatitude of those that hunger and thirst for justice involves already a certain fulfillment in terms of patient persisting in the face of difficult labor, persevering to the end, resisting invading evil, and accomplishing the difficult good. Aquinas thus demonstrates an expression of fortitude (that I deem typical of Christian resilience), which finds deeper foundations and fuller expressions in the sevenfold gift of the Holy Spirit and the beatitudes.

Precepts of Fortitude and Its Development

Given that law and precepts are principles external to moral action, it might seem extraordinary to address the place and resilience-effect of the precepts concerning fortitude (and its annex virtues) after the related gift

136. Mt 5:6 *(JB)*. The *RSV* reads: "Blessed are those who hunger and thirst for righteousness, for they shall be satisfied." Cf. *ST* II-II 139.2.

137. When discussing whether the beatitudes are suitably enumerated, Aquinas—following Augustine—also makes this match based on the motive *(motiva)* that it is principally fortitude of soul that moves one to hunger for the works of justice (I-II 69.3 ad 3). Nonetheless, Aquinas draws other relationships between the gifts, virtues, and beatitudes. For example, following St. Ambrose's commentary on the St. Luke's list of beatitudes (*Super Lucam,* 6:22), he matches them according to the likeness of matter, which he divides according to human faculties.

138. Aquinas (*ST* II-II 139.2 ad 1) follows St. John Chrysostom (*Super Matth.* Hom. 15.4: *PL* 57.227) and Aristotle (*NE* III, 1129b14–19).

139. Cf. *ST* II-II 139.2 ad 2; *ST* II-II 23.8 ad 3; *ST* I-II 68.4 ad 3.

140. Cf. *ST* II-II 139.2 ad 3; *ST* I-II 70.3.

141. Cf. *ST* I-II 69.3.

and beatitude. Nonetheless, the topic and this ordering are that of Aquinas, and for good reason. The New Law, as consisting chiefly in the grace of the Holy Spirit,[142] has not only an external, but also an internal, character. First, temporally it is an external principle of human agency that becomes internal inasmuch as through the infused virtues and gifts of the Holy Spirit it yields a spiritual spontaneity. Spiritual spontaneity, expressed in the practice of virtues and gifts, comes from the interior. It grows out of the natural inclinations, is further moved by the presence of the Holy Spirit (through created grace), and is confirmed by reason and will.[143] Created in the image of God, human beings have this internal principle of motion, within which the Holy Spirit works without destroying human autonomy. In particular, the spontaneity of the New Law inscribed in our hearts serves the human development of virtue and attainment of flourishing, through the inspiration of the Holy Spirit, who acts as master for the attentive disciple.[144] It serves acquired virtue inasmuch as we act freely and knowingly (even through understanding only after the fact that we have acted in accord with an inspiration). Such reflective and free acts are bases for further actions and for the development of *habitus*.

Secondly, even though one can distinguish the precepts of the Old and New Law, they both lead to flourishing and serve growth in virtue, insofar as they assist the process whereby the prescribed good becomes second nature.[145] Precepts are about acts of virtue, as Aquinas repeatedly says (*ST* II-II 124.1 ad 3). Thus he can say that external law is a first step in forming the debutante in the combat against sin and in reforming vices, as discussed in regard to education in fortitude. The precepts of the New Law, which are efficacious through the gifts of the Holy Spirit and grace, aid in assuring good and prompt action. These good acts lead to growth in virtues and have friendship-love with God and with neighbor as their ultimate end.

St. Thomas frames the different precepts of fortitude according to their source, for example according to human laws or to Divine Law. He draws chiefly from scriptural sources in addressing the precepts of fortitude.[146] As

142. Cf. *ST* I-II 106.1–2, *ST* I-II 108.1. The grace of the Holy Spirit received by the Christian in the New Law works through the form of faith, hope, and charity, with the tools of Scripture and the sacraments.

143. Cf. *ST* I-II 106.1, employing Augustine's *De Spiritu et lettera*, C. 21: *PL* 44.222.

144. Cf. Pinckaers 1995a, 17ff. and 400ff., and Pinckaers 1999.

145. Cf. *ST* I-II 99.2; *ST* I-II 107.1; *ST* I-II 108–109; Pinckaers 1989.

146. Cf. *ST* II-II 140.1–2, in which Aquinas quotes the following scriptural passages: Dt 20:3–4,

is the case for all precepts, scriptural precepts direct people to the end established by the lawgiver. The end to which the Divine Law directs human beings is to adhere to God (through friendship-love with God and with neighbor). Thus, precepts of fortitude direct the mind and heart to God and neighbor. Aquinas cites Deuteronomy 20:3–4 to illustrate how a divine precept of fortitude works. Even in the midst of fearful situations, God's word and presence can give one strength, confidence, and ease when realizing that God is near. The archetypical NT precept is that of Christ: "Fear not; it is I."[147] These words are more than moral exhortation, when they are freely accepted in grace and thereby become morally efficacious.

The promises of both the Old and New Testaments serve in understanding the motivation of fortitude. Aquinas follows Augustine in adjudicating that the OT involves temporal promises, while the NT entails spiritual ones.[148] Likewise the battles are of different sorts. The OT teaches how to fight a bodily contest, while the NT instructs us how to fight spiritually in order to possess eternal life.

We can ask whether focusing on the spiritual battle is less resilient than focusing on the bodily one. Aquinas recognizes the centrality and primacy of the spiritual aspect of doing battle and living aright.[149] Nonetheless he confirms that we also have to prepare ourselves to confront the fear involved in bodily death.[150] The general message of these precepts is threefold: to fear not (neither spiritual nor physical dangers), to resist evil (from the devil, others, and self) and to hold firm in faith. Once again, Aquinas' approach is an ordered one; the precepts lead from what is more manifest to what is less so. The intention of the law and the lawgiver aims at making humans virtuous. In this vein, the precepts of fortitude are less direct than the precepts of the Decalogue, while leading to rich, yet less obvious, aspects of Christ's teaching: (1) that even the dangers of bodily death are not to be excessively feared; and (2) that the highest form of virtue is the friendship-love that lays down one's life for one's friend.[151]

Mt 11:12; 1 Pt 5:8–9; Jas 4:7; Mt 10:28. Furthermore, he draws from St. Augustine and St. Gregory the Great.

147. Cf. Mt 28:10 and Mt 14:27.

148. In ST II-II 140.1, Aquinas cites *Contra Faust* book iv, c. 2; ML 42.217–218.

149. Thomas (*ST* II-II 140.1 ad 1) cites three scriptural passages to bolster his case: Mt 11:12; 1 Pt 5:8–9; Jas 4:7.

150. In this regard, he cites Mt 10:28; cf. *ST* II-II 140.1 ad 1.

151. Cf. *ST* II-II 140.1 ad 3; *ST* II-II 122.1 ad 1; Jn 15:13.

Aquinas faces a problematic distinction attributed to sacred Scripture in regard to the virtues associated with fortitude, some of which are promoted by precepts and others by counsels.[152] First, there are precepts for the virtues of patience and perseverance. Precepts are fitting in regard to what is more difficult, for it is easier to know what to do in general concerning lesser hardships and toils.[153] Second, there are counsels for magnanimity and magnificence, since they belong to the genus of fortitude only because of the greatness in their respective matters.[154] Furthermore, Aquinas distinguishes between affirmative and negative precepts. The precepts of patience and perseverance are affirmative, while those of fortitude are (primarily) negative.[155] Aquinas clarifies that "although affirmative precepts are always binding, they are not binding for always, but according to place and time."[156] As in the case of the precept for martyrdom, this type of affirmative precept involves a preparedness of mind to act when it is appropriate.[157] Negative ones can be more concrete, while the affirmative ones must remain more general.

Aquinas fittingly finishes his reflection on the precepts of fortitude and the whole treatise on fortitude by affirming that because of the greatness of danger associated with fortitude, we must proceed with caution without fixing particular determinate responses ahead of time about what we should do.[158] He intends that these precepts should not infringe upon the creativity and spontaneity of the virtues at the practical level; rather they aid us in acquiring stable virtuous dispositions and performing good acts. This insight verifies the flexibility promoted in his conception of resilient fortitude.

152. Cf. *ST* II-II 140.2 sc.

153. Cf. *ST* II-II 140.2 ad 2 and ad 3.

154. Cf. *ST* II-II 140.2 ad 1.

155. Cf. *ST* II-II 140.1 ad 2.

156. *ST* II-II 140.2 ad 2.

157. Cf. *ST* II-II 140.2 ad 2. Aquinas interprets the martyrdom precepts in the NT, which literally applies in certain cases, to pertain in general to a preparation of the mind and heart for martyrdom. Aquinas cites Rom 10.10 and 1 John 3:16 as examples of precepts concerning martyrdom in *ST* II-II 124.3 ad 1; cf. 124.1 ad 3; I-II 108.1 ad 4.

158. Cf. *ST* II-II 140.2 ad 3; Congar 1974, 339.

8

A Theological Dimension of Resilient Initiative-Taking?

Our theological reflections on human initiatives and divine purpose lead us to wonder about the variety of goals that humans pursue and the strength needed to accomplish them. What is the potential theological extension of the virtues and emotions of initiative in relation to constructive resilience, as examined in chapter 5?

Infused Greatness and Initiative: Theological Dimensions of Magnificentia *and* Magnanimitas

This juncture of the study raises several problems of vocabulary and definition. On the one hand, terms borrowed from non-Christian cultures need interpretation. For example, Aristotle or Cicero's language and vision of the virtuous human can seem so tightly bound with Greek and Roman cultures that we find it difficult to imagine it pertaining to the humble Christ or to large segments of the Christian tradition, in particular the monastic perspective of fleeing the snares of the world (*fuga mundi*). On the other hand, we have the problem of applying resilience to a theological domain—in particular, the psychosocial sciences' use the concepts of hope, hopelessness, optimism, and pessimism with great fluidity. Their meanings can imply more or less strictly philosophical or psychological foundations, and are neither always inclusive nor always exclusive of religious senses. Furthermore, resilience research does not necessarily attain the deepest levels of spiritual causality. We must make any appropriations in this theological study with due respect for the research.

Humility and Greatness in Human Agency

Many writers have queried about the Christian character of magnanimity and magnificence. Aquinas' treatment of these virtues has seemed difficult to stomach for some people, especially when read with an indebtedness to Aristotle in mind. It can invoke a sense of "greatness of spirit" and "grandeur of project" with which few contemporary people feel at ease. At first glance, these virtues might evoke the prejudices of an epoch that is neither Christian nor postmodern, let alone that of a twenty-first-century entrepreneur or refugee child. Such notions of aristocratic greatness seem more akin to the imagined greatness of a Greek hero, a Roman senator, or a Renaissance architect. We can even imagine it being personified in a Nietzschean *übermensche*[1] or an English gentleman of yesteryear.

These misgivings denote the lines of debate on magnanimity and humility in Christian agency. With these suspicions on the table, I should recall that before Aquinas and his master, St. Albert the Great,[2] there was a propensity among theologians to make a mystical transposition whereby they identified magnanimity with either theological hope or humility.[3] This position results in identifying the magnanimity of the philosophers with

1. Nietzsche expresses alarm at the way in which greatness had disappeared in the nineteenth century, when he says that "people [. . .] are becoming smaller and smaller" (*Thus Spoke Zarathustra* 1954, 169; cited in Curzer 1991, 150; cf. Congar 1974, 339–40).

2. Albert integrated the Aristotelian notion of magnanimity into Christian theology. Nonetheless, Albert's solution (at least as he formulated it in his *Summa de bono*, written between 1244–48; Albert changed his position during a course on the *NE* between 1268–70) is different from that of Aristotle and Aquinas. In his early position, Albert affirms with Aristotle that magnanimity is a virtue, distinct from *fortitudo*, and concerns having a soul big enough to undertake the conquest of a great object, such as honor. Albert, however, reverses Aristotle's ordering of virtues concerning honor, by according great honors to Aristotle's unnamed virtue (Albert's *mavortia*, which concerns great honors due to those in charge of public affairs), and according little honors to magnanimity. Thus we have an etymological contradiction, which eliminates the idea of greatness from magnanimity (cf. Gauthier 1951, 307–9, and 492).

3. St. Bernard and St. Bonaventure, for example, supported a certain mystical transposition of magnanimity, as theologians suspicious of Abelardian and Aristotelian humanism (cf. Gauthier 1951, 282–92, 317–18).

Christian humility and the magnanimity of the politicians with Christian hope. However, both cases empty the Christian ideal of *human* greatness, at least according to René-Antoine Gauthier.[4] Aquinas avoids such pitfalls, for Yves-Marie Congar, when trying to give full recognition to human nature and collaboration, without depreciating divine initiative and efficacious grace.[5] By so doing, Aquinas emphasizes the grandeur of human hope and enterprise in efforts at innovation. He admires those who realize projects that fully employ human energies and capacities.

But does St. Thomas succeed in capturing the spirit of the Christian tradition, or does he lead it astray? Gauthier has said that Aquinas' doctrine on *magnanimitas* reconciles the "diviniste" spirituality of the Fathers with a humanist spirituality; that it produces a spirituality, which is typically for the lay person who is engaged in the world, searching God mediately through human beings and creation.[6] Congar for his part suggests that magnanimity has the first place of the virtues and commands all the others on the level of personal life, as social justice does for community life,[7] without deprecating the primacy of theological love and Christian humility. Such suggestions do not offer final conclusions, but rather directions for further debate on the relationship of Aquinas' notion of magnanimity and initiative with humility and resilience research.[8]

We find that Aquinas widens his notion not only in social, but also theological, directions. For Aquinas, *magnanimitas* involves giving one's whole attention to the good of others and God.[9] This socio-theological vision is a long stride from the purported self-absorption charged to Aristotle's version; it also demonstrates that in important regards, Aquinas' notion of greatness has less to do with Aristotle's than is commonly thought. At the very center of his virtue of great deeds and virtue theory in general,

4. Cf. Gauthier 1951, 295.
5. Cf. Congar 1974, 340.
6. Cf. Gauthier 1951, 496.
7. Cf. Congar 1974, 341.
8. Indeed, in addition to employing Cicero and Aristotle, Aquinas proposes a synthesis of sources whose diversity of insight on *magnanimitas* makes it even more difficult to identify a contemporary name for this virtue (or group of virtues). Diverse notions of greatness, for example, modify the import of magnanimous acts. Thus for Cicero, it is a greatness in self-confidence and being worthy of honor by acting for the public good; for the Fathers of the Church, its source and end is divine greatness; for St. Albert, it entails the great scope of theological hope; for St. Bonaventure, it involves a greatness in being humble; for the voluntarist, it is a greatness in doing the will of God; for Descartes, a greatness in generosity; for Nietzsche, a greatness in striving for excellence above and beyond the crowd, even above and beyond morality. Cf. M. Dixsaut 1996, 596.
9. Aquinas' *In Eth.* 4, 10, 779.

Aquinas intends an attentional style that is akin to the incentive rather than the anxiety type, as mentioned earlier in the psychosocial research.[10] Indeed for Aquinas, the focusing of one's whole attention on common and divine goods is not a source of anxiety, but rather the result of a liberating movement that draws forth excellence. To maintain that this insight involves an incentive attentional style suggests another potential characteristic of spiritual resilience: that social and divine goals serve as incentives to focus and accomplish our tasks.

Magnanimity mobilizes our resources, calms the fear of failure, and converts us in natural hope. Regarding the theological virtue of hope on the contrary, magnanimity is a result of being converted in hope. Christian daring and confidence harness a restrained aggressiveness, a specifically Christian reasoned standard of action. Aquinas not only specifies that magnanimity involves the correct judgment of reason, due deliberation, and foresight in general,[11] he follows the exacting requirements of the Christian tradition, which demands one to overcome aggressive behavior toward strangers and to love hostile enemies. This teaching seems repugnant to the human evolutionary tendency to protect oneself and one's gene pool.

Christian teachings on pardon, nonaggressiveness, and love of enemies have made Christians appear soft in the view of certain critiques. A case in point is Freud, whose critique of Christianity's stance on aggression rings loud. He takes aim at a Christian preoccupation with self-sacrifice in the form of love for neighbors, strangers, and enemies. His criticisms attack what he believes is the Christian underestimation of aggressive human nature. Unconstrained by natural affections, humans tend to be hostile to strangers. The Christian is overly exposed to the aggression of others. Without using the term "resilience," Freud basically judges Christianity to be unresilient to human hostility and aggression.[12]

Aquinas' teachings on the virtues of magnanimity, hope, courage, and martyrdom bring a response to this critique and a corrective to this view of Christian passivity. The Christian is called to lay down one's life for one's friend, because it is in doing so that we can not only defend the weak and promote social justice (rather than simple self-interest), but also participate

10. Cf. Wilson and Gottman 1996, 194–95.
11. Cf. *ST* I-II 45.2; *ST* II-II 123.3 ad 3; and *NE* 1116b23.
12. Cf. Freud 1961, 57; Browning 1999, 134.

in Christ's salvific work of building up the Kingdom of God. Aquinas promotes a profound notion of human social nature. He does not deny the inclination for self-protection, but recognizes that it interacts in the larger context of other inclinations toward family life, society, and Church, as well as seeking truth, goodness, and flourishing. Are not these tendencies even more powerful in the long run? A further rebuttal of Freud's claim that Christians are underprotected from natural hostility is Aquinas' position on just wrath.[13] Rather than being absolute, the counsel to turn the other cheek to insult has its limits. Action, empowered by just wrath, must correct certain types of wrong.

Humility is endemic to Aquinas' approach to Christian greatness and initiative. Insofar as human beings are neither their own creator nor completely self-sufficient, they need the assistance of others (human and divine) and must put trust in them. The resources for this confident hope that we can triumph involve (1) recognizing the real dimension of our own strengths and resources, (2) observing friends' capacity to aid us and other sources of help, and (3) believing in promises of divine assistance.[14] This third area, divine help, is the heart of Aquinas' teaching on humility, even though it applies to the other two areas as well. Indeed even when we have self-confidence, Aquinas reminds us that "a person hopes in himself, yet under God withal,"[15] and that our natural hope is also a "confidence in God."[16] Consequently, a person must have confidence not only in himself, in other human beings, and in society, but above all in the assistance and promises of God.[17] It is fitting to recall the importance of the interaction of the virtues and the gift that render us docile to the guidance of the Holy Spirit. Confidence derives its strength of hope from these sources, in which one must believe while lacking personal control of them. This point demonstrates the non-Pelagian nature of Aquinas' position, and invites a further examination of the related virtues.

13. On anger and Christian action, see *ST* II-II 123.10; *ST* I-II 46.5; *ST* II-II 136.2 ad 1; *ST* II-II 157 (meekness and anger); *ST* II-II 158 (the vice of anger).

14. Cf. *ST* I-II 45.3; *ST* II-II 129.6 ad 1.

15. *ST* II-II 17.5; and *ST* I-II 62.3; cf. *ST* II-II 128.1 ad 2.

16. *De virt. com.* 1, 12.

17. *ST* II-II 129.6 ad 1.

The Theological Measure of Magnificentia *and Generosity*

Anthropological studies suggest that conspicuous consumption and altruistic giving can promote the survival advantage of an individual and his gene pool. I have argued that Aquinas' views on generosity and magnificence offer a larger moral and metaphysical framework to adjudicate efforts at self-giving and wealth sharing. Now I shall situate these comments in his theological view on magnificence and generosity.

Aquinas' treatment of *magnificentia* avoids the risk of a narrow anthropocentric self-sufficiency by considering human virtue as a participation in divine power and purpose.[18] He construes the fullness of magnificence according to its theological and social content. The magnificent person is not egocentric, but rather recognizes that "one's person is little in comparison with that which regards Divine things, or even the affairs of the community at large."[19] Once again, humility marks Thomas's notion of greatness and society.

Human works are ordered to an end, the greatest of which is the honor of God, wherefore we enact magnificence's greatest work with reference to divine honor and glory. Aquinas denotes a unity to great works that are intended not only to glorify God, but also to sanctify human beings.[20] He recognizes that we must measure the greatness of human action in the world in regard to its effects on human holiness and religion.[21] Aquinas aligns his notion of magnificence to the measure of holiness whose chief effect is directed to religion, the worship of God, and the sanctification of the human community for God's glory.[22]

These theological considerations about religious practice raise a question about how religion and spirituality might enhance or degrade both self-

18. Cf. *ST* II-II 134.1 sc; where he quotes Ps 67:35 [68:34] and thus marks the theological dimension of a discussion that we might otherwise take as merely philosophical.

19. *ST* II-II 134.1 ad 3.

20. Aquinas takes his cues on the relationship between magnificence, glory, and sanctification from Scripture. From St. Jerome's Vulgate, he quotes the Book of Exodus (15:11), "*Magnificus in sanctitate,*" as well as the Psalm (95:6), "*Sanctitas et magnificentia in sanctificatione eius*" (cf. *ST* II II 134.2 obj. 3). Thomas's insight stands, even though contemporary Scripture scholarship offers us translations without the term "*magnificentia.*" He even employs Aristotle, who likewise considers the chief object of magnificence to concern God, namely expenditure for divine sacrifices; cf. *NE* ii.5, 1122b19–23; 33–35, which he cites in *ST* II-II 134.1 ad 3.

21. Cf. *ST* II-II 81.8.

22. Cf. *ST* II-II 134.2 ad 3.

esteem and self-efficacy. Resilience studies suggest that enhancement of self-esteem and social competence comes from an internalized religion, whose role in self-valuation and agency involves providing meaning, purpose, identity, self-realization, and motivation. When we are faced with denigration or great efforts, religion can thus affirm us in our (faith-established) origin and purpose, as well as offer resources to overcome difficulty in both internal and external forums.[23] Negative experiences of religion, on the contrary, can have adverse emotional and antisocial effects, and an extreme emphasis on human decrepitude can negatively impact self-esteem and efficacy.[24]

Aquinas' teaching on the centrality of the virtue of religion and its place in magnificence affirms the basis for an internal type of religious practice. According to resilience research, such an internal type of religion correlates with increased self-esteem and self-efficacy. We cannot take these qualities as synonymous with sanctification. Yet they might involve a significant resilience effect of the meaning and purpose that an active religious relationship with God and neighbor confirms.

Aquinas' view of magnificence, though, is not simply a question of religious worship and its internal resilience effects on its practitioners. It concerns a social agenda tied to the betterment of our neighbor's situation. In this regard, although Aquinas takes many cues from Cicero, the range of the virtues of magnificence and generosity is vastly different for the Roman philosopher. Cicero does consider that human nature has a universal scope. Nonetheless, his conception of the commonweal involves a different hierarchical ordering of responsibilities and reciprocities: family, city-state, and then universe, foreigners falling in this latter category. Moral obligation first demands to render practical services to our country and then to our parents and friends.[25] Private property is not owed to others, according to Cicero,[26] for "the resources of individuals are limited and the number of needy is infinite, this spirit of universal liberality must be regulated [. . .] in order that we may continue to have the means for being generous to our friends."[27] For

23. Cf. Lösel 1994, 8–12; Meyer and Lausell 1996, 129; Chamberlain and Zika 1992, 139; Pargament et al. 1990, 793, and 814–16; Thomas and Carver 1990, 195ff.

24. Cf. Meyer and Lausell 1996, 129.

25. These objections are surpassed only by the "first duty to the immortal gods" (cf. *Off.* I.160; *Off.* I.53–59; McNamee 1960, 45–46; Griffin 1991, xxiii).

26. Here we see Cicero's social conservatism. He even identifies one of justice's two principal functions as promoting the proper use of private and common property (the other being to prevent *iniuria*, or unprovoked aggression; cf. *Off.* I.20).

27. See *Off.* I.20; *Off.* I.52. Even though being far from the Christian vision of charity, this stoic

Cicero, generosity as an aspect of justice is very tightly bound by the limits of his political program.

Aquinas' Christian conception of neighbor, generosity, and magnificence prophetically calls us to reconsider the relationship that we have with our own resources and our relationships with others. This reconsideration includes a special respect and love not only for the least among us, but also for our enemies.[28] Aquinas construes an *ordo caritatis*, an ordering of love.[29] Nevertheless, this *ordo* calls for a sense of responsibility that involves that we cannot rest while others are still in need. Indeed, our lives flourish when we give glory to God, sanctify ourselves, while generously doing good to our neighbors who are in need. In generosity and magnificence, we intellectually adjudicate (prudence) that so much is inadequate (stinginess), more is appropriate (generosity), and beyond is extravagant (largesse). However, for Aquinas greatness goes hand in hand with humility, which invites us to learn from Christ's magnificence and generosity, while being meek and humble in action.

In sum, we cannot separate Aquinas' fundamental definitions of magnificence and generosity from their larger context, which indicates a moral and spiritual type of survival that is akin to spiritual resilience. In this case, one must construe the use of money and possessions in relation to the other virtues that direct them to the divine good (God's glory), the good of others (the common good and justice), and one's own excellence (sanctification and justice). In particular, the virtues of religion, justice, fortitude, temperance, and prudence necessarily support works of magnificence and generosity, and weigh them in a different measure than pure physical survival.[30] Ultimately, Aquinas identifies a spiritual basis for these virtues, which yield a spiritual wealth, survival, and resilience.[31]

Infused Magnanimity

First, we need to ask whether Aquinas' doctrine of magnanimity has a theological dimension. Numerous authors have disputed whether Aquinas' moral theory is theology, philosophy, or both. In passing, I have already dis-

vision is employed by St. Augustine and other Christian thinkers to illustrate that the eternal law is known to all, that is, to illustrate Romans 2:14–15. For a further discussion see MacIntyre 1988, 152–53; Long 1995, 240.

28. Cf. *ST* II-II 129.4 ad 2; Aristotle *Rhet.* 1366b17; Horner 1998, 433.

29. Cf. Pope 1994.

30. Cf. *ST* II-II 117.6.

31. Cf. *ST* II-II 117.1 ad 1; Lk ch. 12.

tinguished between the virtue of magnanimity's focus on the passions of hope and despair and the theological virtue of hope. This distinction does not, however, necessarily negate the possibility of two types of magnanimity, one philosophical and another theological. In establishing the latter in the writings of Aquinas, I intend to illustrate another aspect of spiritual resilience in initiative taking, the way in which the theological builds up the philosophical through unexpected turns. Aquinas' conception of magnanimity would thus differ from Aristotle's in other significant ways. We have already seen how Thomas extends the Philosopher's notion of greatness by affirming in his *Commentary on the NE* that the magnanimous person's "entire attention is concerned with the goods of the community and God."[32] But Aquinas' position goes further.

Inasmuch as magnanimity concerns managing hope, despair, and daring in life's foremost projects, we employ this virtue to seek human flourishing, which for Aquinas ultimately aims at a theological reality. As an acquired virtue, magnanimity develops as we train our passions of hope and daring that we experience in relation to important goals. Acquired magnanimity achieves that which is great in every virtue; it moves toward a harmonious development that is not only physical and psychological, but also spiritual. Although morality involves living according to right reason as expressed in natural moral virtues, faith informs right reason with a further participation in divine reason and Providence as expressed in the Christian virtues.

Infused magnanimity therefore comprises reason informed by faith,[33] grace infused by God.[34] In establishing the shape and texture of magnanimity, the theological virtues aid us in identifying another rational mean that appropriates our theological end. Through the grace received at baptism, the Christian possesses the infused virtue of magnanimity, by an infused proximate disposition. Thereby we are disposed to practice the act of magnanimity, "if it were competent to him according to his state."[35] If we have a great opportunity, grace can dispose us to great acts that even exceed our past experiences. Nonetheless, infused magnanimity invites spiritual training.

In addition to being concerned for physical development, the Christian knows through grace that the body requires the special training of spiritual

32. *In Eth.* 4, 10, 779.

33. See *De malo*, 8, 2.

34. Cf. *ST* I-II 63.4.

35. *ST* II-II 129.3 ad 2.

discipline (penance and mortification). This need for development applies to all domains. All our faculties have been wounded by sin and need to be healed from the tendency to evil. The Christian magnanimous person does not simply strive for fulfillment of his personality within the limits of his post-lapsus condition, but rather he seeks the graced-filled restoration of his wounded personality, and more. He discerns true greatness, which for the Christian is found in following Christ.[36] The infused virtues make for a greatness that God can work in us. This greatness can even be in disproportion to our strength.[37] With the infused virtue of magnanimity, we measure our own capacities (strengths), and having found them to be adequate, in the context of grace, undertake great and difficult theological works; such is the case with the acquired virtue on the natural level. They both suppose the strengths that the subject possesses in our human, connatural way.

The theological form of magnanimity, however, according to Aquinas, "makes a man deem himself worthy of great things in consideration of the gifts he holds from God: thus if his soul is endowed with great virtue, magnanimity makes him tend to perfect works of virtue; and the same is to be said of the use of any other good, such as science or external fortune."[38] We strive to deserve honor, even though we do not "think much of the honor accorded by man."[39] This attitude helps us not to fall away from God's gifts, nor to do wrong on account of seeking human honors. Such magnanimity completes humility, which "makes us honor others and esteem them better than ourselves, insofar as we see some of God's gifts in them."[40] We need a great soul in order to follow the resilient Christ through conversion, attempting to live the beatitudes, being docile to the Spirit, remaining faithful to our baptism, and proclaiming ourselves disciples of God. Greatness's principal purpose is theologal hope: the wait and expectation for entry into divine beatitude, which shakes up our lives, by conferring an unexpected perspective.[41] Magnanimity mobilizes all the resources of hope in the greatest enterprises. It involves a spiritual resilience that strengthens us to affront the inevitable risks and perils and even awakens in us distaste for failure.

36. Cf. Gauthier 1951, 348–49.

37. Cf. *In III S.*, 34, 1, 2; Gauthier 1951, 354).

38. *ST* II-II 129.3 ad 4.

39. *ST* II-II 129.1 ad 3.

40. *ST* II-II 129.3 ad. 4. Instead of Aristotle, Aquinas draws here upon Psalm 14:4 concerning the just man who "honors them that fear the Lord." This theological perspective demonstrates the reverential bearing of both *magnanimitas* and humility for Aquinas. See also *ST* II-II 161.1 ad 3.

41. Cf. Brugués 1991, 252.

The Theologal Virtue of Hope

The energy of the passions of hope and daring empowers the virtues of initiative. Although the underlying passion of hope is related most directly to everyday hopes, is it not also related to the most fundamental human hope, the theological level? Aquinas treats two virtues of hope that are in some way both grounded in the passion of hope and that are both active elements in spiritual resilience.

Without presenting a complete treatise on theologal hope, I shall trace its principal elements in order to complete our study of initiative and resilience in Aquinas' Christian perspective. As already mentioned, Thomas specifies that hope's object is a good that lies in the future and that it is difficult but possible to attain. This view of hope seems almost synonymous with a resilience trajectory, one that seeks the agency and pathways to attain the future goal. The virtue of hope as a natural virtue (magnanimity) is rooted in human desire, and manifest in the longing for flourishing. For Aquinas, however, it is impossible with one's own natural capacities to attain the vision of God, or even to hope in Him. The human person is not self-sufficient, and human natural inclinations point beyond themselves for their fulfillment.[42] The dialectic of hope, which is rooted in natural desire, passes through trials before finding the fulfillment of all its fundamental longings in God. God makes known His promises to bring us at the end of time *(eschaton)* to complete beatitude; it is only through the means of grace in the present that we can truly begin to hope theologically.[43] God alone can make us fully happy.[44]

Hope as a supernatural virtue "makes one sphere of human activity to be good and to reach one of the rules it is supposed to reach."[45] This hope is not an emotion, but a *habitus* of the spirit; that is, its subject is not the sense appetite, but the intellective appetite, the will.[46] Hope finds its roots in the human person being created in the image of God.[47] Although it is expressed in a primitive form through the natural desire for communion with God and the rest of creation, and through the other spiritual inclinations,

42. Cf. *De spe* 1, ad 6.

43. Cf. Pinckaers 1995a, 313–17; and 1978a, 165–77; *LG* no. 48d.

44. Cf. *ST* I-II 5.5; *ST* II-II 17.4.

45. *ST* II-II 17.1; cf. *ST* I-II 40.1.

46. Cf. *ST* II-II 17.1 ad 1; *ST* II-II 18.1.

47. Cf. Gn 1:26–27; 1 Cor 11:7; Eph 4:24; Col 3:10; *ST* I 93.4; *ST* I 12.1; *ST* I 12.4 ad 3; *ST* I-II 3.8; *ST* II-II 2.3; *GS* 12.

hope is properly a virtue of the will, which is situated in a spiritual disposition of hope (the rational appetite beyond the sense appetite or the emotion of hope).[48]

Hope is a theological virtue when its principal object is God and the eternal flourishing that he offers us, according to Aquinas.[49] The secondary object of theological hope is divine assistance, which is necessary to attain eternal flourishing.[50] The arduous nature of the object of hope has several implications though.[51] God as the object of hope makes theological hope a theological magnanimity, as seeking to attain the greatest (and most difficult) good, which is God. Divine assistance as an object of hope, moreover, makes it a theological humility, as recognizing our absolute dependence on God's help. Although divine assistance figures as the secondary object of hope, it is principal as its first efficient cause.[52] In liaison with the virtues of charity and faith, hope furthermore offers a unitive link with God, bringing about a personal relationship with God as source of absolute goodness and help toward blessed flourishing.[53]

Faith precedes hope, since the hoped-for good must be made known and appear possible, and since faith manifests the hoped-for good of eternal life, parousia, and resurrection, as well as the means that makes them possible for us, divine help.[54] Belief in God's existence, power, and promise to save must come before we start to hope in partaking in these goods. Although of a volitional and affective nature, hope's certainty is derived "from faith's certitude found in the cognitive power."[55] This certitude entails a certain moderation or measure, not as if one could have too much hope; rather, we must avoid presumption and despair.[56]

Aquinas views charity's relationship to hope in two different ways. First, hope is prior to charity. For, "hope can initiate one into charity to the extent, namely, that one hoping to be rewarded by God becomes inspired to love him and observe his precepts."[57] Such hope is a type of imperfect love of another, since it loves "something not for its own sake, but as it brings some

48. See *ST* II-II 22.1 ad 1; *ST* I-II 56.6; *De virt. com.* 5; *ST* I-II 62.3 ad 2; Gauthier 1951, 320.

49. Cf. *ST* II-II 17.6; *ST* II-II 17.2.

50. Cf. *ST* II-II 17.5 ad 3.

51. Cf. *ST* I 59.4 ad 3.

52. Cf. *ST* II-II 17.4; *ST* I-II 40.7; Pinckaers 1978a, 226–30.

53. Cf. *ST* II-II 17.6.

54. See *ST* II-II 17.7, where Aquinas cites Hebrews (11:6) as an authority.

55. *ST* II-II 18.4.

56. Cf. *ST* II-II 17.5 ad 2; *ST* II-II 20–21.

57. *ST* II-II 17.8. On the precepts relating to hope and fear see *ST* II-II 22.

good."[58] Hope precedes charity, as the imperfect anticipates the perfect. Secondly, hope follows charity in a sequence of excellence. Indeed, "with the advent of charity hope is rendered more perfect, since we are most of all inclined to be hopeful when we have friends to rely upon."[59] Here the perfection of charity's form purifies hope, which is imperfect in comparison to charity.

Another corrective and guide for hope in initiative taking comes from the gift of the fear of the Lord; this gift is commensurate with the theological virtue of hope and comes to the aid of the infused virtue of magnanimity. Aquinas distinguishes two types of fear concerning our relationship with God: servile fear and filial or chaste fear. Servile fear incites us to convert to God and remain close to him through fear of punishment. Filial fear involves our fearing to offend God and indicates a filial relationship.[60] To illustrate how filial or chaste fear is rooted in affection and love, Thomas employs St. Paul's image of adoptive sonship through which we call out, "Abba, Father," and a spousal image of chaste union.[61] Aquinas emphasizes that this second type of fear regards God as a source neither of punishment nor "of moral fault, but as a goal from which separation as a consequence of fault is to be avoided."[62] The fear of the Lord supports hope. This gift is rooted not in self-love, but rather in charity. It does not fear the loss of what we hope to obtain by divine help, but rather our own disregard of God's help.

Filial fear and hope interrelate and perfect each other,[63] becoming more intense with the increase of charity.[64] They are accompanied by an increase in confidence in God's grace, which draws us ever closer to God through our theological projects. This process explains how fear is rooted in love (emotion), how the gift of fear is rooted in charity (virtue), and how in fortitude and magnanimity we are driven by neither fear or fearlessness per se. A courageous and great-spirited person resists excessive fear of evil, which can move us into that evil and separate us from God. Moreover, quoting Ecclesiasticus, "he that feareth the Lord shall tremble at nothing,"[65] Aquinas

58. *ST* II-II 17.8.

59. Ibid.

60. Cf. *ST* II-II 19.2 and 19.6.

61. See Rom 8:15 and 2 Cor 11:2, cited in ST II-II 19.2 ad 3.

62. *ST* II-II 19.5 ad 2.

63. Cf. *ST* II-II 19.9 ad 1.

64. Cf. *ST* II-II 19.10.

65. Aquinas cites Ecclesiasticus 34:17 (34:14, *RSV*) in *ST* II-II 126.1 and *In symb. apost* art. 5; cf. Pieper, 1949–59/1966, 126–27.

explains that the love of God also involves the reverse side, a type of fear of the ultimately dreadful thing, the loss of that love.

Even if Christian hope chiefly concerns eternal flourishing as the good we seek and the divine assistance needed in attaining it, this virtue also concerns other objects of our prayers and the lesser subordinate ends of everyday actions.[66] These ordinary hopes, the natural dimension of family, friends, and society, concern the good human ends of life and mobilize a large part of our day. Work, family, and community involve plans that elicit hopes for their accomplishments. Resilience research has demonstrated the utility of hope, for example, for the displaced refugee. It is important for the refugee to have hope in some possible future and way to achieve it: reunion with family, return to homeland, establishment in a new community, health, and social security, and so on. But often they need to establish a new source of hope. At the natural level, this type of hope is common sense. One seeks the agency and pathways to attain a goal. On the spiritual level, ultimately (for the Christian) this search for hope must turn inside and look beyond, for a new interior and fundamental source of hope that grounds everyday ones. Indeed, ordinary hopes find their fuller meaning when rooted firmly in fundamental hope, for hoping in God renders hope active by confident prayer in God and by transformed action.

According to Thomas, we can achieve the act of hope, which reaches God, neither through personal effort nor through the help of other creatures, but only through God's infinite power. Nonetheless, we continue to seek secondarily the help of other human beings, the saints, and angels, as instrumental sources or subordinate agents of assistance, regarding both our fundamental hope and our everyday ones.[67] This theological perspective illustrates the interplay between theological hope and infused magnanimity, as well as the natural virtue of hope and the emotion of the same name. In resilience terms, theological hope secondarily serves to bolster natural efforts. Inasmuch as it also strengthens hope as an emotion and magnanimity as the natural virtue of hope, it is instrumental in all spiritual resilience that reaches natural levels of human agency.[68]

66. See Aquinas' Commentary on St. Paul's letter to the Philippians (4:5–6; *Ad Phil.* lect. 4.1), where he cites Mt 6:25; 1 Pt 5:7; and Rom 12:8.

67. Cf. *ST* II-II 17. 2, ad 2; and *ST* II-II 17.4.

68. See Brugués 1984, 47–58.

Theological Honor and Excellence

Spiritual resilience and vulnerability revolve around initiatives that seek greatness and humility, honor, and excellence and that can go awry in several ways. Aquinas' synthesis of related virtues walks a steady mean between excesses. His structuring of the virtues nonetheless raises further questions about the Christian character of his moral theory, inasmuch as it apparently (at least structurally) gives magnanimity and magnificence a place superior to humility. In particular, does Aquinas' attempt to save a place for honor and excellence weaken Christian humility?[69]

Fallen Greatness: False Hopes and Misplaced Excellence

Aquinas' virtue approach identifies dispositional vulnerabilities that we acquire when seeking great and small initiatives. False hopes, presumption, and despair sidetrack us from our goals. Misplaced honors, glory, and excellence lead us astray. Such failures promote vulnerability and underlie risks at natural and spiritual levels. Outlining the risks of vainglory or misplaced excellence in initiative demonstrates Aquinas' Christian measure. The theological dimension of initiative taking, magnanimity, and hope is clarified further in his treatment of other excesses that undermine it: namely false hopes, presumption, despair, and timidity.

Glory and honor motivate human actions. Aquinas is aware not only of the positive side of honor, but also of how vainglory can make us vulnerable and weak. We sidetrack ourselves from important and ultimate goals by desiring things unworthy of us, by overestimating their value. Although

69. Indeed Aquinas' solution to the issue of initiative taking attempts to integrate Aristotle's and Cicero's insights on magnanimity with the Christian tradition's notion of glory and honor. He addresses the polemic raised by Aristotle's two readings of magnanimity. The first gives primacy to the idea of greatness; here magnanimous people would consider themselves as worthy of great things, through greatness in each virtue, only doing what is great. The second gives primacy to the idea of honor; here magnanimous people act properly concerning the object of honor. According to Gauthier (1951, 302–4), a Christian focus limited to the first reading risks aspiring to greatness, not in order to assure that mankind dominate the world per se, but in order to restore lost human greatness with the intention of returning it to God. Taking the Aristotelian texts in this way adds to the Abelardian influence to make magnanimity the virtue that presides over our seeking to participate in our own perfection. A Christian focus limited to the second reading risks seeing magnanimity as a casuistry of glory and honors that one need flee from inasmuch as they take us from God and that one need search for inasmuch as they serve to give God glory. Instead of assuring human domination over the world, this perspective assures the human itinerary toward God. Taking the Aristotelian texts in this way can destroy the Abelardian influence in Aquinas' synthesis, reducing magnanimity to a precise question of casuistry.

we might not consciously place a temporal good over an eternal one, the neglect of ultimate goods can effectively exaggerate our attachment to worldly ones. Furthermore, when seeking human glory, as if it had eternal consequence, we desire honor from unreliable sources. These sources can redirect our time and energy in wasteful ways. Moreover, for Aquinas, glory has a purpose. When we do not use it for the common good or do not acknowledge its ultimate source, we employ glory without proper respect for its due end. Aquinas deems that we should use glory to honor God and to aid our neighbor spiritually.[70]

Aquinas distinguishes spiritual risks when humans misuse honor from spiritual benefits when we use it well. Vainglory especially opposes charity concerning either the matter in which we glorify ourselves (personal wisdom, strength, and riches) or the intended use of glory.[71] Nonetheless, Thomas affirms the importance of recognizing "the things that are given us from God" and the utility of letting them be known to others.[72] Even God seeks to be glorified for our sake, since we need to know God's glory and to glorify God in order to attain flourishing.[73] Likewise, human beings should seek honor for the good of other people and in order to glorify God aright.[74] True glory is promised from God for good works, and in turn serves to encourage them.[75] Aquinas thus specifies that human praise and glory are not to be desired in themselves, but can be useful in four ways:[76] to glorify God, to edify our neighbor, to persevere in goodness, and to better ourselves. This spiritual utility is also based upon humanity's social nature: the goods of our relationships with God and others.

Presumption also causes dispositional risks revolving around the use and abuse of our capacities. According to Aquinas, presumption strictly concerns striving for great deeds that are not proportioned to our abilities.[77] Since divine reason orders nature, human reason and action ought to imi-

70. Cf. *ST* II-II 132.1.

71. Cf. *ST* II-II 132.3.

72. In *ST* II-II 132.1; Thomas quotes Augustine in warning about the danger of loving praise; nonetheless, Aquinas finds that Scripture (notably 1 Cor 2:12, Mt 5:16, and Ps 4:3) recognizes glory's positive purpose.

73. Aquinas (*ST* II-II 132.1 ad 1) quotes Augustine's Commentary *Super Joan.* tract 58. 3 (re: Jn 13:13); *PL* 35, 1793.

74. In this regard, Aquinas (*ST* II-II 132.1 ad 1) quotes Mt 5:16.

75. Aquinas (*ST* II-II 132.1 ad 2) supports this teaching by citing Rom 2:7 and 2 Cor 10:17–18.

76. Cf. *ST* II-II 132.1 ad 3.

77. See *ST* II-II 130.1; *ST* II-II 130.2.

tate creatively the order that God has established in nature. Through prudence and wisdom, we scrutinize the commensurability of planned action and the agent's power to accomplish it.[78] Each person being endowed and educated differently face actions more or less adapted to them, at different moments in their natural and spiritual developments. Through difficult activities that push us beyond the limits of previous experience, we can become capable of more or we can fail. The muscle stretched to, but not beyond, its limit becomes even stronger, all things being equal. The human intellect is likewise sharpened through its exercise in particularly difficult domains. Even a non-devastating failure can be a source of further growth and resilience.

According to Aquinas, we have a natural inclination to strive for more, as well as to remain within the limits of our capacities. When presumptuous, we overstep our boundaries. Aquinas gives several examples. First, it is presumptuous to endeavor to advance toward perfect virtue only when one does not possess the means. In theological matters, we need not only personal ability, but also God's assistance. Thus St. Paul, while not considering himself to be already perfect, "strains forward" to the things that were before him, because Christ has strengthened him to do so.[79] According to Thomas, it is fitting to think and do good and to accomplish virtuous deeds with confidence in God's assistance.[80] Second, it is presumptuous to do what it becomes God to do, to have inordinate confidence in divine mercy, or to seek glory without merit.[81] Nonetheless it is not presumptuous, but rather timid and unresilient, not to strive to be united to God in reason and will. Likewise, we fall into vulnerable timidity if we neither trust in divine forgiveness for those who seek pardon[82] nor attempt the great things that are within our reach. On the contrary, through pride, we cling too resolutely to a false opinion about our incompetency, even refusing to obey divine commands[83] or accept the worthiness granted by a divine grace.[84]

Despair, furthermore, destroys initiatives. As hope is driven by love, so despair is produced through fear, which causes one to conclude that the fu-

78. Cf. *ST* II-II 130.1.

79. Phil 3:12–14, cited in *ST* II-II 130.1 ad 1.

80. Cf. *ST* II-II 130.1 ad 3.

81. Cf. *ST* II-II 21.1.

82. Cf. *ST* II-II 130.1 ad 2; *ST* II-II 130.2 ad 1.

83. *ST* II-II 133.1 ad 3. Following Gregory (*Pastor.* I, 7: *PL* 77, 20 D), Aquinas cites the example of Moses, who avoids the double temptation of pride by undertaking a great task only with fitting trepidation and by not refusing to do the difficult task commanded by his Creator.

84. Cf. *ST* II-II 133.1 ad 4.

ture arduous good is impossible to attain.[85] Such fear overrides hope at natural and spiritual levels. Aquinas says that in order to exclude despair, we need to properly adjudicate our goal of flourishing as an arduous good (a spiritual good) that is possible. To overcome despair demands both that we nurture our desire and our hope for the spiritual good of flourishing and that we exclude sources of despair: impurity, laziness, and depressive sadness. These sources of despair all hinder in some way the perception and attainment of flourishing.[86]

Insofar as fortitude and magnanimity (as the acquired virtue of hope) are natural virtues, their impulses spring from the hopes born of the irascible part of the soul. However, insofar as hope is a theological virtue, it does not primarily concern the emotions, but the will; and its object is God and divine assistance. The promises and the difficulty that ground theological hope serve growth, moral agency and development of this virtue: hopes, human and divine. What is the distinguishing factor that enables such spiritual progress? For Aquinas, this spiritual resilience and growth demands the interaction of both God's grace and human conscious action that Aquinas differentiates in terms of virtues, gifts, and beatitudes. Hope plays vital roles in this spiritual resilience. Highlighting the developmental aspect of hope and the place that God's promises play therein, Origen says:

> That it may do this, that is, that the soul may become capable, the Lord our God as it were holds His promises out of our reach; He does not withdraw them. He so withholds them that we may stretch ourselves toward them. We strain, and therefore we grow. And so we grow, that we may reach what He promised us.[87]

This citation, collected by Aquinas, emphasizes the divine pedagogy that is active in Thomas's virtue theory and serves as a transition to the investigation of the place of honor, great deeds, and excellence in initiative taking and spiritual resilience.

Theological Virtue Guiding Honor

Aquinas' treatment of *magnanimitas* attempts to overcome an apparent conflict concerning the use of honor and excellence as criteria for action. The question in the theological realm becomes whether Aquinas' anthropol-

85. Cf. *ST* I-II 40.4; *ST* I-II 45.2; and *ST* II-II 20.1–4.
86. Cf. *ST* II-II 20.4.
87. Aquinas' *Catena aurea*, 17th Sunday after Pentecost, vol. 4.2, Origen 6.1.

ogy breaks down in front of particularly Christian virtues such as humility. Can we use acquired magnanimity, conceived in terms of honor and excellence, as a basis for infused magnanimity without deforming the Christian tradition in the process? Will it render the tradition vulnerable to itself?

For Aquinas, theological magnanimity parallels martyrdom, which is the apotheosis of courage. Fortitude's correlation with martyrdom does not degrade it, but puts it in the perspective of the highest possible form that we can understand only theologically. Natural magnanimity similarly tends toward theological fulfillment, although it is marked by a double absence. "Ordinary magnanimity" (concerning ordinary honors) remains nameless. Likewise, theological magnanimity (concerning great acts that merit honor from God) has no name.[88] Through the natural virtue, we have the disposition toward managing our emotions of daring and our acts in the face of greatness well. It involves a life of excellence, according to our opportunities and capacities. In order to understand how such excellence relates to Christian resilience, we need to explore Aquinas' theological perspective on honors and human agency.

Aquinas finds several reasons why the virtue of *magnanimitas* is absolutely about the proper use of a particular type of honor, "the best use of the greatest thing," as he says.[89] However, we must understand even this natural virtue in terms of his overall theological project. In particular, he analyzes three aspects of magnanimity's relationship with honors: (1) the reasons for honor and its source, (2) the people who are honored and the hierarchy of honors, as well as (3) the social purpose of honor.

Honors for Thomas are due attestation of a person's virtue.[90] As individualistic as Aquinas' definition of honor might seem to some interpreters, honor is a social and theological reality. Honor is the reward that others give for being virtuous; it is public recognition for goodness.[91] As attestations of virtue, honors are the best of external things. His conception follows, yet substantially contrasts, Aristotle's conception of magnanimity.[92]

88. Cf. *ST* II-II 129.3 ad 2.

89. *ST* II-II 129.1.

90. Cf. *ST* II-II 103.1 and 103.2.

91. Cf. *ST* II-II 131.1; *ST* II-II 103.1 and 103.2.

92. In particular, Aquinas reforms Aristotle's magnanimous man by turning five objectionable qualities of Aristotle's magnanimity toward more positive qualities (cf. *ST* II-II 129.3 obj 5). Moreover, he addresses the problem of self-absorption by focusing on the magnanimous man's great actions, in terms of a theologically grounded humility and a general respect for other humans as created in the image of God

For Aquinas and the Christian tradition, honor as an objective recognition of one's excellence does not primarily come from society, but rather it is ultimately from God. Indeed, God alone attests truly and completely to the worth and honor of our dispositions and acts. Such impartial and just recognition credits the virtuous person, whom society unjustly condemns, but also goes hand in hand with Christian humility. Although honor is good, the only adequate reward for being virtuous is flourishing rather than honor per se.[93]

Aquinas has a twofold typology of honor. Honor is offered either to God *(latria)* or to the best people *(dulia)*. The ancient and medieval worlds acknowledged an ordering of goods. Aquinas' hierarchy of goodness ultimately focuses the magnanimous person's interest on the life of grace.[94] We need to return all true human honors *(dulia)* in the form of praise, veneration, and adoration *(latria)* to God, who is present even in human virtues. Indeed, God is the principal source of human excellence, which Aquinas deems something divine in human garb.[95] On the contrary, ambition neither recognizes proximate and ultimate sources of one's excellence nor returns this honor to its due sources, especially the divine one.

Aquinas describes honor's purposes. Honor motivates our acts, as a final cause. We do or avoid things in order to attain honor or to shun shame.[96] Honor can thus aid in controlling our concentration, efforts, and emotions. Moreover, it has a social function, as an efficacious cause of action. Aquinas remarks that we should use God-given qualities of excellence to benefit others in two ways: we can aid them directly with outstanding acts, and we can use the recognition for such acts to further benefit others.[97] Although such human honor is clearly not an ultimate source of good or flourishing, it is nonetheless a real good.[98]

Although honor is important, it is only a secondary object of magnanimity for Thomas. Honor involves positive exchange with a social sphere.

(cf. *ST* II-II 129.3 ad 4; Horner 1998, 435). Furthermore, Aristotle stresses the importance of external goods (including being honored at social level) more than either the Stoics or Aquinas (cf. Horner 1998, 421 and nn. 34 and 35).

93. Cf. *ST* II-II 131.1 ad 2.
94. Cf. *ST* II-II 129.1 and 129.2; *ST* II-II 103.3.
95. Cf. *ST* II-II 131.1.
96. Cf. *ST* II-II 129.1.
97. Cf. *ST* II-II 131.1.
98. Cf. *ST* II-II 131.1 ad 3.

In the Christian context, magnanimity ultimately manages personal and social honor in order to glorify God and to advance the salvation of the world (sanctify human beings). His Christian conception of flourishing demands not only that we attain friendship with God, but also that we glorify God. The search for eternal flourishing is not only great in itself, but also informs the typically great difficulties in virtuously managing more mundane honors and shame. This virtue makes every virtue even greater, since it engages them in the perspective of seeking to be worthy of honor from God, and in returning any honor to God. It even makes the acts that Aquinas construes as great correlate with loving God and one's neighbor.[99] This work of Christian virtue constitutes a primary source and finality for Christian resilient action. Christian resilience then is especially apparent in the great and excellent action involved in the seemingly contradictory Christian excellence of meek magnanimity and magnanimous humility, which we shall now treat more extensively.

Christian Excellence: Meek and Humble Magnanimity

These insights on doing great deeds and using honor well do not exhaust the spiritual dimension of seeking excellence in Aquinas' perspective. Rather, he completes the doctrine on excellence with the Christian virtues of humility and meekness, as well as the beatitude of the meek. This excellence in the form of a meek and humble magnanimity refocuses the question of whether Christianity promotes a type of vulnerability. Aquinas integrally correlates magnanimity (and fortitude) with three aspects of meekness: (1) as an evangelical beatitude: "Blessed are the meek, for they shall inherit the earth" (Mt 5:5), (2) as a fruit of the Holy Spirit (Gal 5:23), and (3) as a virtue.[100] Thomas's virtue theory relates such beatitudes to virtues, as complete acts relate to dispositions to act; they both relate to fruits, which involve delight in the graced act. As a moral virtue, meekness develops a disposition of subjecting the emotion of anger to reason.[101] As a beatitude, meekness is a graced act of the virtue bearing the same name. As a fruit of the Holy Spirit, it involves delight taken in such a meek act.

Thomas highlights the necessity of meekness for magnanimity through

99. Cf. *ST* II-II 129.4 ad 2; Aristotle *Rhet.* 1366b17; Horner 1998, 433 and n. 106.

100. Cf. *ST* II-II 157.2 ad 3.

101. Thomas calls upon the authority of Seneca (*De clementia* II.5) and Aristotle (*NE* iv.5) in regard to mercy and meekness often throughout *ST* II-II 157.

the passion of anger, which we might otherwise overlook. Through magnanimity, we deal with arduous goods that can engender vengeance or anger and blind us to our rational project, even our ultimate goal. A particular challenge arises from the nature of anger. Anger can aid proper and prompt action.[102] Anger also needs to be carefully controlled. Meekness restrains the onslaught of anger and vengeance by mitigating this passion.[103] The impetuosity of anger comes from its clouding our free judgment of truth, according to Aquinas. The virtue of meekness involves an excellence, albeit a restricted one, among the virtues that resist evil inclinations, since it guards our self-possession. Highlighting meekness's theological import, Thomas emphasizes how it directs our minds to the knowledge of God, self-possessed mitigation of anger, and consistency with truth.[104] Meekness especially establishes a new balance and focus for aggressive or attack movements of the emotions, of which anger is one of the most powerful. In particular, meekness harnesses anger for a Christian response to overcoming injustices and other hardships. It describes an aspect of resilience that is both human and led by the example of Christ.

Aquinas also includes the Christian notion of humility in initiative and magnanimity.[105] Humility and magnanimity are a sort of dual virtue (*duplex virtus*) that address arduous goods.[106] This twofold virtue is a type of gen-

102. Cf. *ST* II-II 123.10; *ST* I-II 46.5; and *NE* iv.11 1126a30–31.

103. Cf. *ST* II-II 157.1 and 157.3.

104. Aquinas expresses the theological framework for understanding the proper use of anger employing Augustine (*De Civ. Dei.*, XIV, 9, 1: *PL* 41, 413; quoted in *ST* I-II 24.2 sc, and cited at the beginning of *ST* II-II 123.10).

105. Aquinas compares and interrelates magnanimity and humility in the following places: *ST* II-II 123.1 ad 1; *ST* II-II 129.3 ad 4; *ST* II-II 161.1 ad 3; *Ad Mat.* 5:16; *De vert. com.* 12, 26.

106. Cf. *ST* II-II 161.1. Before going further though, a historical note is in order. Thomas participates in the thirteenth-century controversy over the relation of *magnanimitas* and *humilitas* (cf. Pinckaers 1995a, 228, and 2002, 8; Congar 1974, 345–46; Kent 1995, 51–52, 72–74). His position differs both from the radical Aristotelians of the Faculty of Arts at the University of Paris and from eminent theologians such as St. Bonaventure. Part of the reason for this dissimilarity is the different use and appreciation of sources. Drawing on scriptural and patristic writers as their primary sources, both Aquinas and Bonaventure share the essentials and figure as part of the Catholic theological tradition, unlike the radical Aristotelians. Nonetheless, the two theologians illustrate two subtraditions, shaped not only by how they structure their theological sources, but also by the philosophical sources they employ. In particular they differ in the ways they interpret Aristotle's thought (cf. Gauthier 1951, 295–371; Torrell 1996; Pinckaers 2002; Kent 1995).

Both Thomas and Bonaventue oppose certain doctrines of the radical Aristotelians. And they both critique and integrate the Philosopher's thought in their own theology. Bonaventure considers these virtues to belong essentially to the rational part of the soul. On the contrary, Aquinas, while acknowledging the role of reason and will in these virtues, recognizes more fully the emotional bases involved. St.

eral virtue as well. An oft-overlooked hermeneutical principle for Thomas's treatise on the virtue of humility can be found in the *sed contra* of its first article, "whether humility is a virtue."[107] He starts the treatment of humility with a scriptural and patristic reference to Jesus Christ's admonition: "Learn from me, because I am meek, and humble of heart."[108] The position of such a quote in Thomas's scholastic approach, as well as its content, is highly significant. It serves as a narrative background and provides content for reading the whole treatise. This admonition is not simply an extrinsic rhetorical nicety, but rather a metaphysical and moral basis for Christian agency. It demands that one reread even the philosophical references to Aristotle (or Cicero) in the light of the Gospel narrative.[109] Such a theological appraisal is not always made.[110]

Aquinas' response to the question about the way humility and magnanimity interrelate (in the *Summa theologiae*) has sometimes been interpreted as abstract philosophy that has the following content. In controlling the impulses that arduous goods provoke, we would need a twofold virtue: first, humility, which restrains the mind from immoderately tending to things that are too high, and second, magnanimity, which strengthens the mind against despair and urges it to pursue what reason rightly dictates is truly good.[111] The rest of Aquinas' treatise would seem more philosophical than

---

Bonaventure's (1221–74) and Aquinas' differences can be illustrated in terms of the way in which these two great contemporaries developed their *Commentaries on the Sentences of Peter Lombard*. St. Bonaventure does not build a theology of virtue; he is less virtue-centric than Aquinas (whose *Commentary on the Sentences* is already based on the virtues, although only a sketch of his later works). In Bonaventure's conception, virtues such as fortitude reside in the part of the soul that is controlled by the rational (cf. *Com. on the Sent.* III, 33, 3). They are virtues of the will. For Aquinas, a moral virtue such as fortitude resides in the sensible appetite, and needs to be considered in the context of the gift of fortitude. For a sympathetic and nuanced reading of Bonaventure and his development, see Kent 1995.

107. Cf. *ST* II-II 161.1 sc. Likewise, at the very beginning of his treatment of the virtue of fortitude, Thomas acknowledges the importance of the virtue of humility in responding to St. Paul's understanding of virtue as being perfected in infirmity (2 Cor 12:9). Humility assures that we acknowledge our weaknesses and infirmities of body, in order that fortitude's strength of mind bear them bravely. We need to understand this reference to humility in its theological context (cf. *ST* II-II 123.1 obj 1 and ad 1).

108. Aquinas (*ST* II-II 161.1 sc) quotes the Gospel of Matthew (11:29) and makes reference to the Magnificat (Lk 1:48), through the commentary of Origen (Hom 8 in Luc.: PG 13.1821A; *PL* 26.236C).

109. Thomas's close association with Aristotle and a philosophical structuring of the virtues in general has attracted several critiques of Aquinas' teaching, and limited such a wider interpretation. Attacks target the distance between Aristotle's conception of magnanimity and Christian humility. They critique his associating humility with the virtue of temperance, which limits humility's focus, its pride of place among the virtues and its integration of scriptural teaching (cf. Pinckaers 1993, 442; 1995a, 228; Torrell 1996, 41; and discussions with M.-L. Ardoin).

110. See Nussbaum 1988, 38; and MacIntyre 1999, xi.

111. Cf. *ST* II-II 161.1; I-II 23.2; *ST* I-II 61.2.

theological, and would be summarized as such: (art. 2) humility is essentially in the appetite itself, as suppressing excessive hope, (art. 3) it does not demand us to necessarily subject ourselves to other people, and (art. 4) it is chiefly about restraining the passion of hope and is associated with the moral virtue of temperance. This philosophical dimension is Thomas's, but it is not the entirety of his teaching.

When we look deeper, in the light of the Matthean passage and the other biblical citations, another interpretation of Aquinas' teaching on humility comes alive. His articulation of humility depends on more than its philosophical citations and arguments. It necessitates a theological content and prime referent. Humility's tempering of presumptuous hope and immoderate self-confidence denotes our subjection to God, even as the Son is subjected to the Father in an ordered love. As Thomas says, it chiefly involves "divine reverence, which shows that man ought not to ascribe to himself more than is competent to him according to the position in which God has placed him."[112] This type of humility involves adoptive filiation, which has searching social features.

The theological content and pedagogy of Aquinas' approach to humility need to be more explicitly distinguished from that of Aristotle. That is not the major point however. The deeper emphasis is that humility adds a corrective to great and self-confident efforts; it serves in the dual virtue: meek and humble excellence and excellent humility. It recognizes the ordering of creation, redemption, human initiatives, and social goods. The resilience of humility in particular involves a perspective on divine help and ultimate goals. This vision of Christian humility is not the weak sort critiqued by Nietzsche, but rather an exuberant one that follows Christ, who dares to walk where even the strong would not tarry. This humility is a self-referential and other-respecting movement. To humble oneself, according to Aquinas, involves acknowledging our weaknesses and social needs, acclaiming God's greatness, and calling upon God as the source of grace and hope

112. Cf. *ST* II-II 161.2 ad 3. Thomas follows Augustine, who understands humility as poverty of spirit, while ascribing it to the gift of filial fear, whereby we revere God (he cites Augustine's *De serm. Dom. in monte* I.4,11: *PL* 34,1234). Also see the earlier treatment of this gift and its relationship with the theological virtue of hope (cf. *ST* II-II 19.1–12). Lastly, humble people, as the Letter of James (4:6) illustrates, obtain grace from God, who conversely resists the proud (cf. *ST* II-II 161.5 ad 2). If more space permitted, this analysis could treat Thomas's other theological, biblical, and patristic arguments and references, and in particular his objections to St. Benedict's division of humility into twelve degrees (cf. *ST* II-II 161.6).

for all that is great and perfect.[113] This Christian excellence in meek and humble form involves a type of resilience that we acknowledge as a gift from God, which at the same time is at risk due to personal infirmity and social injustice.[114] This meek excellence motivates a typically Christian constructive resilience that finds its standard for excellent initiative in Christ as the rule for thought, sentiment, and deed.

113. Cf. *ST* II-II 161.1 ad 4; cf. *SCG* III.97.
114. Cf. *ST* II-II 129.3 ad 4; McInerny 1997, 80.

9

Theological Dimension of the Virtues of Enduring

Through patience we have peace both in prosperous and adverse times.

AQUINAS, *IN ORAT. DOM.* PET. VII.

Is there a specifically Christian response to pain, suffering, and sorrow? For Aquinas, the infused virtues of patience and perseverance distinctly offer Christian criteria and models. They involve necessary dispositions for Christian maturity in the face of adversity. These infused virtues should not be confused with the acquired virtues of the same names or resistant resilience (chapter 6), even though they can strengthen already existing acquired virtues. Furthermore, the theological virtue of hope, the gift of knowledge, the fruit of patience, and the beatitude of mourners all constitute a Christian type of patience and perseverance. They are completed by Aquinas' understanding of virtuous sorrow and moral and spiritual progress.

Infused Patience, Perseverance, and Resilience

Aquinas on Patience, Grace, and Human Nature

Thomas masterfully addresses the dynamics of acquired and infused patience in the *Summa theologiae,* using both philosophical and theological sources.[1] He starts his treatment of patience by affirming that patience is a gift of God and a quality attributed to God.[2] This scripturally based insight serves to furnish the theological inspiration without which we cannot understand Aquinas' treatise.

When Aquinas asks, "whether it is possible to have patience without grace," he poses a question he does not directly ask of any other virtue associated with a cardinal virtue, except for perseverance.[3] He straightforwardly answers that we are not able to have "true patience" without the help of God. Many writers have heatedly debated the meaning of true patience and the implications of his text.[4] Some authors hold that Aquinas does not think that (true) patience exists without the help of grace.[5] Others hold that he thinks humans exercise a natural virtue of patience through their own nature and effort; this patience would be a moral, non-infused virtue.[6] The discussion revolves around not only the notion, object, and act of patience per se, but also those of the type of grace involved.

These questions of grace, virtue, and the quality of agency are not indifferent for resilience. In the Christian perspective, grace establishes the basis

1. Although the principal sources—not only in quantity—are Scripture and St. Augustine, the philosophical foundation is significant. Aquinas uses the following sources for *ST* II-II 136 (in order of frequency): Scripture (subtotal: 14): Is 49:10; Rv 7:16; Eccl 5:16; Gal 5:22; 2 Cor 7:10; Eccl 30:25; Jas 1:4; Lk 21:19; Ps 61:6; 1 Cor 13:4; Rom 5:5; Eccl 5:4; Rom 2:4; Prv 13:12; St. Augustine (subt. 9): *De Trin.* 14, 9; *De pat.* ch. i (twice) and ii and iii and iv (twice) and v; *De Civ. Dei* 14; *De morib. eccl.* xv; Ep. cxxxviii *(ad Marcellius)*; St. Gregory the Great (subt: 3): Hom. 35 *in Ev.* (twice); *Moral.* 22; Aristotle (subt: 2): *NE* i, 8; ii, 6; Cicero (subt: 2): *Rhet.* II.54 (twice); *Opus imperfectum* on Mt 4:40 (falsely ascribed to Chrysostom): *On Matt* 4,10; Origen (or gloss of P. Lombard): *Ad Rom* 2:4; Prosper: *Sent.* 811. Usage rather than frequency determines the importance of these citations. Not all citations are on the same footing. For example, quotes used in the *sed contra* have a certain priority; Aquinas uses them as superior authorities serving to enlighten the arguments (cf. Pinckaers 2002).

2. In the first *sed contra* (*ST* II-II 136.1 sc), Aquinas quotes Augustine's *De pat.* (I; *PL* 40.611).

3. *ST* II-II 136.3; and *ST* II-II 137.4. See also Thomas's treatise on the necessity of grace (I-II 109.1–10). Cf. Gilson 1946, 93.

4. For the history see Lottin 1942–60, III:186; on the related question of true happiness and true virtue see Sherwin 2005b, 325–28.

5. Cf. Labourdette 1961–62, 44; Gilson 1946, 93–104; Spanneut 1984b, 452.

6. Cf. Delhaye 1984, 247; Noble 1932, 296; van der Meersch 1925, VI.2:1578; Vansteenberghe 1932, XI.2:2248–49.

for spiritual resilience that cannot be measured or quantified, as can external acts. We necessarily presuppose a conception of human nature in any treatment of grace. The correlation of grace and nature is vital to understand how persons and communities rely on God's help consciously and unconsciously for ordinary development and patience, as well as for extraordinary resilience and perseverance.

Aquinas explores the necessity of grace and what it would mean to have natural patience by asking: "Is it possible to have patience without grace?"[7] An important reference point in reading this question is the authoritative wisdom that he quotes in the *sed contra*, which runs: "It is written (Ps. 61:6): *From Him*, i.e., from God, *is my patience*."[8] It is easy to understate the importance of this passage and its placement. For Aquinas however, the *sed contra* generally serves as a source of light, which refracts in different variants and intensities throughout the rest of the article and question. In this regard, the richness of the quote's larger context needs to be recalled. *Psalm* 61 (62) is one of the psalmist's most powerful expressions of trust in God. Not only does the psalmist express his trust in God in the face of harassment by enemies, vv. 2–5 (1–4), but he also invites the community to follow his example of trusting God, rather than human vanity, wealth, and power, vv. 6–10 (5–10). The full message of the quotation announces the tone of the response that Aquinas intends.

Aquinas dialectically presents objections to a Christian understanding of grace, nature, and patience. He poses a Pelagian objection, which claims that in following their rational natures and without grace, those who are evil can patiently suffer for the sake of an evil purpose.[9] Those who seek a good goal, thanks to their rational nature, should be all the more able to suffer patiently without grace. Aquinas responds, saying that even though it is reasonable to suffer evil for some good, there are two drawbacks to doing so. First, the inclination of reason toward the goal constantly prevails only in integral human nature, but not in our present, weakened (lapsarian) state of nature. Second, in this condition the concupiscible inclination makes hu-

7. *ST* II II 136.3.

8. *ST* II-II 136.3. This version of the Vulgate Psalm 61:6 (62:5 *JB*) is translated in different ways: "Rest in God alone, my soul! He is the source of my hope" (*JB*); "For God alone my soul waits in silence, for my hope if from him" (*RSV*); *verumtamen Deo retice anima mea ab ipso enim praestolatio mea* (*BS*, iuxta Hebr.).

9. Cf. *ST* II-II 136.3 obj1 and ad1.

man beings more prone to follow its desires than reason, in bearing evils for the sake of present pleasures rather than for future goods. "True patience" on the contrary endures evils for the sake of future goods that we desire in accordance with reason.[10]

Even though Aquinas' argument seems to mean that we might be truly patient in a particular situation, it also indicates that we are not able to assure our own consistent true patience. He says: "man is more prone to bear evils for the sake of goods in which the concupiscence delights here and now, than to endure evils for the sake of goods to come, which are desired in accordance with reason: and yet it is this that pertains to true patience."[11] While recalling the limitations of the present human condition, what he clarifies in this text is simply three criteria for the virtue of true patience: (1) endurance of evil (object), (2) for the sake of future goods (final end), and (3) desired in accordance with reason (intermediate end—*circa ea quae sunt ad finem*). We must see these issues in the fuller context of divine grace's interaction with human nature and of the particular "goods to come."

He addresses another objection concerning the criteria for true patience. It claims that nonbelievers have true patience, since while not in the state of grace they abhor sinful evils more than bodily ones, and in some cases have patiently endured many hardships rather than betray their country.[12] Aquinas answers that such social virtues—human beings acting well in human affairs—are commensurate with human nature and concern natural goods only.[13] Social virtues, whereby someone behaves well in human affairs, spring from human nature, which is social.[14] They are acquired in civil life and have the civil good as their end, that is, acquired moral virtues. They are possible without sanctifying grace (*gratia gratum faciens*), but not without the help of God (*auxilio Dei*).[15] This latter type of gift (*auxilium Dei*) assures the real-

10. Aquinas uses the terminology *vera patientia* or *est vere patientiam* only in *ST* II-II 136.3, where he carefully addresses Augustine's *De patientia*, which uses these terms throughout. Aquinas moreover is aware that these adages exist in a sermon of St. Cyprian, which is quoted in the *Catena aurea* (vol 2.1, part 2, 346; *On the Advantages of Patience*: *PL* 4.621).

11. *ST* II-II 136.3 ad 1. Gilson (1946, 100) argues in this regard that both Aquinas and Augustine deny that there can be a natural patience, i.e., patience without grace.

12. Cf. *ST* II-II 136.3 obj.2/ad2.

13. Cf. *ST* I-II 61.5; Pinckaers 1976, 255–73.

14. Aquinas speaks of these social or human virtues earlier in his *Summa theologiae*, where following Macrobius, he distinguishes them from two other types of human virtue: purgative and perfect virtues (cf. *ST* I-II 61.5). In these discussions, a fourth type of virtue (exemplar virtues) concerns God.

15. Cf. *ST* I-II 109.2.

ization of the good commensurate to human nature, and even though such divine help is from God, the human effect can nonetheless be called human natural virtue, since it is within human nature to commit such acts.

Types of Patience

Aquinas argues that human beings need God's gifts at two levels: (1) for doing natural good (acting well) and (2) for the healing of broken human nature (justification) and supernatural acts of virtue (such as the infused virtue of patience).[16] First, Thomas's theocentric anthropology posits that human beings are marked by the image of the divine Creator, who is the source of their being and co-origin of their perfections.[17] He says: "human nature needs the help of God as First Mover, to do or wish any good whatsoever."[18] All good, even natural good, comes from, is possible through, and returns to God. Aquinas affirms the continuing goodness of creation and the efficacy of divine exemplar virtues.[19] No natural good can be separated from God, who is the source and final goal for creation.

Second, in the present human state, grace is needed to heal deformed human nature, which is now more prone to follow proximate concupiscible desires rather than the future, promised goods. Human beings cannot fulfill all that is possible through human nature, although they are able by their natural endowments to act responsibly or to attain some particular, natural goods, such as building homes, planting vineyards, and having friends, as Aquinas specifies. "Yet [human nature] cannot do all the good connatural *(connaturale)* to it, so as to fall short in nothing; just as a sick man can of himself make some movements, yet he cannot be perfectly moved with the movements of one in health, unless by the help of medicine he be cured."[20] Thus in addition to needing divine help *(auxilio divino)* for the capacity to perform well any good action, one needs grace *(gratia gratum faciens)* in the

16. Aquinas distinguishes five effects of grace in supernatural acts (cf. *ST* I-II, 111.3).

17. Cf. *ST* I 93.1–9; *ST* I-II 110.2 ad 3.

18. *ST* I-II 109.2. Aquinas calls upon the authority of St. Paul (*Rom* 9:16) and Augustine (*De corrept.* ch. 2; *PL* 44, 917) in illustrating how God's grace is that source of every good thought, wish, love, or act. Furthermore in *ST* I-II 109.1 sc, Aquinas calls upon Augustine (in one of his later works, *Retract.* I, 4, 2; *PL* 32, 589) to affirm that sinners also can know many truths.

19. Through these preexisting *virtutes exemplares,* God "directs us to himself" (*ST* I-II 62.1 ad 2; cf. *ST* I-II 61.5; *SCG* I.54, I.92, and *ST* I.93; *III Sent.*, 33, 1, 4). Aquinas employs both Macrobius (1991, 1, referring to Plotinus and Plato) and St. Augustine (*De morib. eccl.* 6, n. 9–10; *PL* 32, 1314–1315) as sources for this position on exemplar virtues.

20. Cf. *ST* I-II 109.2; *ST* I-II 109.5.

form of infused moral virtues to heal human inconsistency and thus, even in the realm of social virtues, approach true, consistent, and complete natural patience.

In its integral state, human nature needed the assistance of sanctifying grace in order to be conformed most completely to the image of the Creator. All the more so now, true patience as an infused virtue counts on God's completing and purifying grace. This need for grace is also true for the theological virtues of faith, hope, love, and the other infused virtues. The question remains whether there is an acquired true patience without grace.

Aquinas' treatment of patience makes two original points:[21] that natural virtue needs God's help (in order to act well); and that it also requires sanctifying grace in order to heal the deformities in human nature and for acts of theological and infused virtue. Laboring to demonstrate the harmonious relationship of human and revealed wisdom, Aquinas acknowledges two types of patience, one a natural acquired moral virtue and the other an infused moral virtue. The question remains whether they both merit the Augustinian appellation of true patience.

In order to understand the two types of patience more fully, it is perhaps useful to compare how they parallel two types of flourishing. First, limited flourishing is possible in the present life. Second, complete flourishing is beyond our experiences at present, and further dependent on God for its realization.[22] Moreover, in the present life, there are two additional types of flourishing: (1) there is the incomplete flourishing achieved through various natural human activities;[23] (2) there is an imperfect participation in happiness, which is possible through the theologal life of the infused virtues.[24] At present, both natural patience and infused patience are incomplete (from the human side), and they participate differently in sources of strength and vision as well: one that is in the measure of this world, the other that participates in the security and completeness of the next.

21. While remaining faithful to Augustine's central insights, Aquinas' treatment of patience goes beyond them. A difference springs from these two theologians' approaches to doing theology and perspectives on society in general. Augustine emphasizes how true virtue opposes the pride endemic in the Roman pagan society of his time, especially the philosophical circles that he had frequented, where pagan pride manifests itself in the rejection of Scripture (he is also battling Pelagian errors). Aquinas on the contrary lives in another epoch and approaches pagan sources in a more conciliatory way, without the same bellicose rhetoric.

22. Cf. *ST* I-II 69.2; Pinckaers 1984, 80–94.

23. Cf. *ST* I-II 2.1–8; 5.1–8.

24. Cf. *ST* I-II 69.2 corpus and ad 3; Pinckaers 1995a; Cessario 1996, 2–5.

In parallel with this typology of patience, there are two types of resilience. Resilience as a natural good is empowered by God through natural means (as *auxilio Dei*). As a supernatural good, spiritual resilience can be likened to infused virtue insofar as the object of its act, its finality or future good, and its rational means (informed by faith) are theological in tenor.

Patience, Its Purpose and Motivation

Aquinas clarifies his position on patience's purpose by raising another objection to the need for grace in patience. It claims that often people without grace go through much pain and trouble in order to regain their own bodily health.[25] If the good of the soul is even more important, why cannot someone without grace endure many difficulties and much suffering in order to regain one's health and well-being? This position seems common sense, in the abstract.

Aquinas responds to this Pelagian argument by affirming that to seek the soul's supernatural good is itself on a different level than seeking bodily health. Salvation requires supernatural love, while health requires natural love. Sanctifying grace is already operative in our concern for salvation. Aquinas clarifies this point further in his treatment of prevenient grace, which describes how we desire the good of salvation before it is possessed.[26] Moreover, it is interesting to note how Aquinas here distinguishes the acts of natural and supernatural patience. He applies the word "patience" only to the realm of salvation, but uses *tolerantia malorum* (the tolerance of ills and evils) instead when referring to the endurance of difficulties to regain bodily health. This distinction seems to illustrate: (1) that the object of "true patience" is the eternal flourishing and the fulfillment of the Gospel promises needing the help of God that comes in sanctifying grace; and (2) that natural patience is the *tolerantia malorum*, which we sustain by natural love, although neither consistently nor completely.[27]

Aquinas argues that this virtue becomes intelligible when we realize that someone will patiently suffer through an ill only for the sake of some good goal.[28] Indeed, we will not patiently bear difficulties for the sake of

25. Cf. *ST* II-II 136.3 obj. 3.

26. Prevenient grace neither prevents nor forces but rather enables someone to take a free decision for faith. Cf. *ST* I-II 111.3; *SCG*, III.160; *Ad Joan.* 1.10, 206 and 1.4, 644; *Ad Eph.* 5.5; Augustine's *De natura et gratia* xxxi; Rom 11:6 and 6:23.

27. Noble 1932, 296.

28. Cf. *ST* II-II 136.3; and Augustine's argument about only suffering for some pleasure in *De pat.* iv.

something that we perceive as evil itself. Aquinas understands that those who do evil, who act for a bad end, misrepresent that end as a good. More than a simple epistemological mistake, it can result from a gradual accumulation of moral errors. In the hierarchy of goods, we will suffer evil for some greater goods, and we will do without some lesser goods even when their lack causes sorrow and demands patient endurance. The first type of good is more powerful since it enables us to bear some evil. It has a certain absolute character. For Aquinas, the good of grace (and the desire not to lose it) exemplifies this first type of good, which allows us to both suffer evil and endure patiently the sorrow of doing without other secondary goods.

Aquinas argues that if we prefer the good of grace to other lesser, natural goods it is because of charity. He thus recognizes that the infused virtue of patience has God as its source (in sanctifying grace—*gratia gratum faciens*) and as its final cause. In this fundamentally theological perspective, Aquinas deems that inasmuch as patience, at least indirectly, has as its end the future glory and flourishing that God alone grants, such patience depends upon sanctifying grace,[29] and insofar as it concerns not wanting to lose the good of grace, it depends on the grace of charity, through which we love God above all things.[30] Indeed, acts of patience, as well as of fortitude and all other virtues, are meritorious only if they are done out of charity.[31] Another effect of charity in the act of patience is excellence in bearing hardships.[32]

Although Aquinas clearly holds that it is impossible to have the patience based on charity without the help of actual grace,[33] he also affirms that even when sanctifying grace and the theological virtue of charity are absent, every good human act in the realm of social virtues entails another gift from God *(auxilio Dei)*. The natural political or social virtues involved in building homes, farming fields, and having friends must then involve a natural patience supported by the help of God *(auxilio Dei)* appropriate for natural goods. However, does Aquinas construe it as a "true" natural patience?[34] The

29. Cf. *SCG* III.151.

30. *ST* II-II 136.3; 1 Cor 13:4; *ST* II-II 23.4 ad 2; *ST* II-II 186.7 ad 1; *ST* I-II 65.3 ad 1.

31. Cf. *ST* I-II 114.4 ad 3.

32. See *ST* II-II 184.1 ad 3, which quotes Rom 8:35 and Jas 1:4.

33. Cf. *ST* II-II 136.3 and Rom 5:5.

34. In my reading, Aquinas does not clearly resolve this problem in question *ST* II-II 136, because he has already done so in *ST* II-II 23.7. According to Gilson (1946, 104), however, there is a "natural virtue of patience without grace," but no true natural patience. Gilson (104) would have us think that

question seems clarified by the principle that a natural virtue can be true, even though it is incomplete.[35] Calling lesser, natural human goods "true patience" need neither diminish the primacy put on charity-based patience, which finds its ultimate source and final cause in God's patience, nor disregard charity as the foundation of infused social virtue.

This typology of patience suggests a parallel for resilience: we acquire a resilience that is in the measure of our natural capacities (though not possible with consistency and completeness unless we are healed and strengthened by sanctifying grace); we receive a spiritual type of resilience that outstrips our natural capacities and needs the grace of the theological virtues in order to know, to motivate, and to hope to attain its theological object(s).

The Patience of God Expressed through Jesus Christ

This discussion demands a fuller examination of Aquinas' approach to the theological sources and manifestations of patience, in order to explain how the patience of God as expressed in Christ serves as the source and model of patience for others. Aquinas' scriptural commentaries[36] illustrate, in a manner less systematic than the *Summa theologiae*, how the blessing of God's patience expresses divine mercy and charity, which serve as a final cause for human action. God's patience is made known so that sinners may turn to God, believe in Christ, and come to eternal life.[37] God patiently (yet actively) waits[38] in the face of the evil that we suffer and that we do, of the good that we do not accomplish, and in anticipation of our participat-

---

Aquinas strictly follows Augustine, who is not unaccustomed to say that true patience pertains only to that which is inspired and sustained by charity. Gilson interprets Thomas as affirming that true patience is supernatural patience alone.

In adjudicating this issue, we need to ask what Aquinas intends by "future goods." Do they refer to the goods of social virtues as well, or only to strictly supernatural goods and ends? Aquinas' use of "future goods" needs to be considered in the larger context of his *ST* and the whole of his thought. In the *ST,* we find several examples where he makes a comparison between temporal and future goods (*ST* II-II 36.2; *ST* II-II 124.4; *Exp. Job,* ch. 2, p. 95 and ch. 27, p. 325).

35. Cf. *ST* II-II 23.7; *ST* II-II 136.3 ad 1.

36. Beyond the question devoted to patience (*ST* II-II 136), Aquinas treats this virtue in a less methodical way in his commentaries and *reportationes* on Scripture, on the Pater, and on the *Credo,* as well as in other loci of his *ST.*

37. Cf. *Ad Eph.* cap. 2, lect. 2 (Eph 2:4–7), where Aquinas cites 1 Tm 1:15; cf. cap. 3 lect. 2. Also see: *Ad Rom.* cap. 2, lect. 1 and 2 (Rom 2:4 and 7), where Aquinas illustrates this point further with reference to Ps 7:11–12; 2 Pt 3:9 and 3:15.

38. Aquinas attributes "patience" and "waiting" metaphorically to God, only inasmuch as we can intelligibly predicate these time-bound images to God's simplicity and eternity. See: *ST* II-II 136.1 and *ST* II-II 136.5, where he quotes Augustine *De pat.* 1, Cf. *Ad Mat.* cap. 17, no. 2; and *I Sent.* 30, 1, 2, ad 2.

ing more fully in God's own good. In particular, God's merciful patience is the means that God offers human beings to participate in the redemption wrought by Jesus Christ.[39]

Jesus' patience offers us a model of well-ordered suffering and sorrow. Aquinas establishes three criteria in order that Christ's passion and death serve as an efficacious exemplar: the reality of his suffering, its voluntariness, and its conformity to reason.[40]

Aquinas holds that Jesus Christ really suffered and experienced sorrow,[41] with moral and soteriological ramifications. Neither Jesus Christ's union with the Father and the joy of His divine contemplation, nor His perfect virtue kept Him from feeling human sadness.[42] Aquinas illustrates this by quoting Matthew (26:38): "My soul is sorrowful even unto death."[43] Jesus Christ was capable of joy and sorrow, since the divine Word, the second person of the Holy Trinity, assumed human nature.

Aquinas distinguishes between a passion and propassion,[44] in order to explain that Jesus had a true experience of sadness, which was rightly affected by the object, without unreasonable resultant action.[45] Jesus Christ's experience of sorrow and suffering was a propassion and not a disordered passion.[46] This difference does not make His sorrow radically different (human experiences of sorrow do not necessarily hinder reasonable action) nor does it diminish what He suffered (for He suffered immensely).[47] The difference concerns consistency, not type. His were moral acts. Aquinas dis-

39. Thomas explains the soteriological fruit of divine patience in his commentary on Romans 2:4 (*Ad Rom.* cap. 2, lect. 2). Cf. *ST* II-II 136.5 and *III Sent.* 19, 1, 5, ad 3.

40. Cf. *ST* III 46.6 ad 2.

41. Cf. *ST* III 18.2; *SCG* IV.8, IV.32, and IV.35.

42. Cf. *ST* I-II 59.3; and *ST* III 15.6.

43. Aquinas quotes this passage as the authority (of the *sed contra*) quoted in his article on "whether there was sorrow in Christ" (*ST* III 15.6 sc; cf. *ST* I-II 59.3 sc). In the *Comp. theo.* (ch. 232ff.), Aquinas asks what suffered in Christ? He responds that the Word of God, Christ, suffered in His soul, not only in His lower reason, imagination, and body. Gondreau (2002) skillfully addresses Aquinas' position on Christ's sorrow in the *Tertia pars* (*ST* III 15.6).

44. In general, for Aquinas, passion can have as its object what is unlawful to do, or it can forestall the judgment of reason. A propassion, however, does not hold sway over the soul and its functions. Cf. *ST* III 15.4; cf. *ST* III 15.6 ad 2. Also see Sorabji (2002, 344ff.) on Stoic and Christian discussions of propassions.

45. Cf. *ST* III 46.5–8; and *III Sent.* 2, 3, co.

46. See *III Sent* 15, 2, 2, co. Furthermore, in the *ST* (III 15.6 ad 1 and ad 2), Aquinas explicitly responds to the Stoics. He distinguishes well-ordered and inordinate management and experiences of passion, which are explained by the Stoics in terms of proper sorrowing, which pertains to the apprehending, through the sensitive appetite, of bodily or exterior evils without disturbing reason.

47. Cf. *ST* III 51.2 ad 1.

tinguishes Jesus' suffering as a "propassion" since in experiencing His own passion and death, and in sorrowing for the plight of others,[48] He was not deflected from His mission, which involved knowledge, freedom, and surety, that is, a moral act.

In facing great suffering and trials, even his own death, with tranquility of mind, Jesus Christ has become an example of patience, manifesting the patience of God the Father. The example of Christ is especially efficacious since He knew He would suffer death and torture, as a result of proclaiming the Gospel of salvation for all humankind, in accord with the plan and will of the Father. Christ did not voluntarily will His death and passion per se; however, He did chose them as ordained to the end, the redemption of humankind.[49] Jesus suffered for a purpose. He did not search for human glory. Rather, He knew His destiny, His glory to be revealed in the future, and knew that the path to the redemptive manifestation of this glory was His passion and humiliation.[50] Moreover, Aquinas specifies that when needing patience when faced with persecution, we in a more general sense also follow Jesus Christ's example through gentleness.[51] Patience demands such gentleness in order to not perturb right judgment and to withstand persecution.

St. Thomas employs Romans 15:5 in order to explain that the mercy and consolation of God is made manifest in the suffering of Jesus Christ, who serves as an example for us when we must face some suffering or evil.[52] Thomas explains that Jesus Christ gave an example of patience, a virtue that prevents sorrow from overwhelming humans in time of adversity; the greater the trials, the more splendidly does the virtue of patience shine forth in them. An example of perfect patience is afforded in the greatest of physical evils—death—if it is borne without distress of mind.[53]

This model is especially clear in His enduring passion on the cross. Aquinas says: "If you seek an example of patience, you will find it in its highest degree upon the Cross."[54]

48. Cf. *ST* III 15.6; and *ST* III 46.6. 49. Cf. *ST* III 15.6 ad 4.

50. See: *Ad Joh.* cap. 7, lect. 1 no. 1019, where Aquinas reinforces his commentary referring to Luke 24:26 and Romans 8:18; and *ST* III 15.6 sc, where he quotes Ambrose, *De Trin.* ii, Al., *De fide ad gratiam*, ii, 7.

51. Cf. *II ad Timoth.*, cap. 2, lect. 4 (2 Tim 2:24–25).

52. Cf. *Ad Rom.* cap. 15, lect. 1; Lk 22:42; Ps 93:19; 1 Pt 1:11; Jb 13:15; 2 Cor 1:3.

53. Cf. *Comp. theo.* 1, 2, 227; *ST* I-II 68.1; *III Sent* 34, 1, 1 co.

54. *In symb. apost.* art. 4. See also *ST* III 15.6 ad 4.

Aquinas sees the passion and cross of Jesus Christ as the exemplar not only of the virtue of patience, but of all virtues.[55] Illustrating that patience is not a static virtue, but mobile, dynamic, and fruitful, his commentary on the Apostle's Creed quotes the letter to the Hebrews (12:1–2): "Let us run by patience to the fight proposed to us; looking on Jesus, the author and finisher of faith, who, having joy set before Him endured the cross, despising the shame."[56] Christ for His part shows that being set on the reward of joy and future glory with the Father enabled Him to endure the cross. It is the promised joy of eternal life and glory with God the Father (as final cause) that makes the passion and death of Jesus Christ comprehensible, and in turn makes possible following His example in offering one's life for others, in martyrdom, and in other self-giving acts.[57] The "cloud of witnesses," mentioned in the Letter to the Hebrews (12:1), serves participatively as an active example of sharing spiritual consolation and showing how they were able to run the race more freely and surely by having laid down the weight (burden) of sin and earthly desires. Thomas also affirms that Paul and the "cloud of witnesses" serve as models of following Christ's suffering.[58]

By patiently enduring the dangers of death and other types of suffering, we enter into the life of glory. It is thus that Aquinas interprets what it means to "always carry in the body the death of Jesus" (2 Cor 4:10), to always be in His patience.[59] Aquinas recognizes that such fullness of patience as found in Christ must be rooted in charity; that is, the fullness of patience entails how we support evil and suffer difficulties following His example of self-giving love for God the Father, for humanity (our neighbors), and for all creation.[60]

Persisting to the End in Christ: The Virtue of Perseverance

Aquinas' treatment of the infused virtue of perseverance is akin to that of patience, and his sources are philosophical, patristic, and scriptur-

55. Cf. *ST* III 46.4; *In symb. apost.*, art. 4.

56. *In symb. apost.*, art. 4. Aquinas also quotes Heb 12:1–2 in his commentaries *Ad Phil.* cap. 2, lect. 1; and *Ad Thes.* cap. 1, lect. 1.

57. Cf. *Ad Heb.* cap. 12, lect. 1. Thomas mentions the patience of martyrs in numerous places, including *ST* II-II 124.2 ad 3; I 19.9 ad 1; I 22.2 ad 1; *ST* I-II 102.4 ad 8; *ST* I-II 114.4 obj. 3.

58. Cf. *I ad Thess* cap. 1, lect. 1 (1 Thess 1:6); *Ad Heb.* cap. 12, lect. 1 (Heb 12:1); Cf. *I ad Thess.* cap. 2, lect. 2 (1 Thes 2:6–10); and *II ad Thess.* cap. 3, lect. 1 (2 Thes 3:5); *Ad Rom.*, prologus.

59. *II ad Cor.* cap. 4, lect. 3.

60. In his commentary on 2 Thessalonians 3:5, Aquinas calls on a large number of scriptural sources to support this insight (*II ad Thess.* cap. 3, lect. 1): 1 Tm 1:5; Lk 21:19; Mt 5:11; 1 Pt 2:21.

al.[61] Aquinas does not construe perseverance as merely a human natural virtue through which we complete acts important for this life, such as building and planting, or familial and friendship relationships. We express two types of perseverant act according to two types of ends: a specific work and one's whole life. Some acts cannot find completion until the end of life. For example, the dispositions of faith, hope, and charity concern the fulfillment of our entire life, so that we persevere until the end. This distinction between perseverance as a *habitus* and as two types of act allows Aquinas to explain Augustine's dictum that "no one can be said to have perseverance while living, unless he persevere until death."[62]

Thomas explores the specifically Christian dimension of perseverance by asking whether it needs the help of grace. As with the virtue of patience, Augustine is the authority on the necessity of grace. He quotes Augustine as saying: "We hold that perseverance is a gift of God, whereby we persevere unto the end, in Christ."[63] Aquinas agrees, explaining two ways that someone needs grace in persevering. First, he considers the *habitus* of perseverance as an infused virtue, and therefore as needing the gift of habitual grace (*dono habitualis gratiae*). Second, he considers the act of perseverance as enduring in the good until the end of life, which needs not only the gift of habitual grace, but also another gratuitous gift of God.[64] Aquinas explains that the habitual grace of the infused virtue of perseverance does not take away the human capacity to choose otherwise than what is good. Even when the free will is repaired (healed), it is still malleable. While our free will is capable of persevering, it so happens that it is not in our power to accomplish alone our plan or choice to persevere. As Aquinas says: "for it is often in our power to choose, but not to accomplish."[65]

In his discussion on the necessity of grace, Thomas discusses three ways that we need grace to persevere in good. First, as a *habitus* of the mind, through perseverance we are disposed to resist the pressures of sadness and sorrow that sidetrack us from the good we intend to accomplish. Secondly,

61. Aquinas dialogues with the following sources on the virtue of perseverance (*ST* II-II 137) and on the vices opposed to perseverance (*ST* II-II 138), listed in order of frequency: Aristotle (subt: 15). *NE* 11.3; 11.4; vi.8; vii.7 (eight times); vii.8; vii.9 (three times); Augustine (subt. 7): *De persever.* I.1; I.6 (twice); *De lib. arbit.* ii.19; *Tract. in Joan.* lxxix.14; *De corrept.* xi.11; xi.12; Scripture (subtotal: 5): Dt 28:56; Ws 5:7; Mt 24:13; Rom 5:15; 1 Cor 6:9–10; Cicero (subt: 5): *Off.* I.20; *Rhet* ii.53; ii.54 (three times); Andronicus (Chrysippus) (subt. 2): *Definit.* III.578 (twice); St. Gregory the Great (subt: 1): *Moral.* 31.45; Isadore (subt: 1): *Etym.* X.213–214; Macrobius (subt. 1): *In somn. scip.* i.8.

62. *De persev.* I; quoted in *ST* II-II 137.1 obj. 2.

63. *De persev.* I; quoted in *ST* II-II 137.4 sc.

64. Cf. *ST* I-II 109.10.

65. *ST* II-II 137.4.

we need a particular intention to remain attached to the good until the end. Both these types of perseverance are infused in us along with grace. Aquinas remarks that we need this type of habitual grace for the other virtues,[66] and to heal wounded human nature. Although through justifying grace God redeems us and heals our minds, we need habitual grace that assists in the progressive recovery of the integrality of human nature that informs our intellects that are burdened by ignorance.[67] Thirdly, through perseverance, we abide in the good until the end of life. The grace of justification is not adequate. We need God's continuing assistance in habitual grace in order to resist evil and persist in the good; as Thomas observes, we also need "divine assistance guiding and guarding us against attacks of the passions."[68]

Aquinas addresses a false and static notion of perfection and passivity. He recognizes the humble nature of virtue, which, as a *habitus* inclining us to specific acts of excellence, must always be confirmed by the will. Therefore, even if we can consider that someone has the virtue of perseverance, as Aquinas does, "it does not follow that a person who has the *habitus* of virtue uses it unchangeably until death."[69] We are vulnerable because of our own status as voyagers. Complete and stable resilience is not assured by a singular resilient act; it needs to be progressively won. We need the special help of God's gratuitous grace, through which we actively persevere in faith and hope, which are the guides for spiritual resilience.[70]

Aquinas' approach to the Scripture-based precept of fortitude illustrates further that his notion of perseverance is not simply philosophical. This precept plays a pedagogical role in developing the disposition and preparing for acts of perseverance.[71] Following Augustine,[72] the precept is understood as a means for us to learn to persevere in order to gain eternal life. Indeed, the promise of the eternal flourishing serves a key role in understanding and

66. Cf. *ST* I-II 109.10.

67. Cf. *ST* I-II 109.9.

68. *ST* I-II 109.10; see also *ST* I-II 109.9 and *ST* II-II 137.4.

69. *ST* II-II 137.4 ad 1; cf. *ST* I-II 49.3 sc; *ST* I-II 50.1 ad 1; *ST* I-II 50.5.

70. Cf. *ST* II-II 137.4 ad 2 and ad 3; where Aquinas quotes Augustine *De corrept.* 12, 34–35 (*PL* 44.937).

71. St. Thomas (*ST* II-II 140.2 obj. 1) construes the following Scripture passages to involve precepts of perseverance: "He who endures to the end will be saved" (Mt 10:22); "Therefore, my brethren, be steadfast, immovable, always abounding in the work of the Lord, knowing that in the Lord your labor is not in vain" (1 Cor 15:58); "It is for discipline that you have to endure" (Heb 12:7).

72. Thomas (*ST* II-II 140.1 ad 1) cites Augustine's anti-Manichean *Contra Faust.* IV.2; *PL* 42.217–18.

motivating final perseverance. Thomas distinguishes the promises and effects of both the Old and New Testament teaching. When confronted with physical and especially mortal danger, Aquinas affirms that the NT teaches us to do spiritual battle, not only physical battle, as in the OT. In effect he interprets the violence mentioned in Matthew 11:12 to mean a spiritual struggle: "In the New Testament, men were to be taught how to come to the possession of eternal life by fighting spiritually."[73] In such spiritual battle we need to overcome the fear of death and to persevere until the end.[74]

Another aspect of this spiritual battle is the resisting and enduring that pertains more specifically to perseverance. In various epistles, Aquinas finds precepts of resistance, which are most connected with resisting evil and the devil.[75] Such resisting, at first glance, might seem negative. Practically speaking however, it is quite positive. It entails holding firm to something or someone. According to 1 Peter 5:9,[76] resisting the devil involves standing firm in faith and keeping friendship with God. Perseverance is to "stand fast in the Lord" (1 Thes 3:8); this virtue also serves as a source of fortitude and perseverance for others.[77]

This positive resisting recalls Augustine's insight that Aquinas makes his own. Patience, which is first the patience of God expressed in Christ, is the gift of active waiting. We sometimes push the human side of waiting and resisting to extremes, and enact unnecessary damage. Is such patience and perseverance a type of unresilient vulnerability? In Aquinas' theological perspective, what can seem to be folly (e.g., martyrdom, generosity, or social justice) can involve following the model of Christ and participating in his salvific act through patience and perseverance. Once again the difference between virtue and true folly is its rational measure. Acts of patience and perseverance are neither unpurposeful nor unreasonable acts of suffering. The reason informed by faith that guides our acts of patience and perseverance proves to be Aquinas' criterion for spiritual resilience.

Aquinas' treatise on the cardinal virtue of fortitude treats patience and perseverance last, in less space and with fewer articles.[78] Do these two vir-

73. *ST* II-II 140.1 ad 1.

74. Aquinas (*ST* II-II 140.1 ad 1) quotes Matthew 10:28, "Fear ye not them that kill the body."

75. In this regard, Aquinas (*ST* II-II 140.1 ad 1) quotes 1 Peter 5: 8–9 and James 4:7.

76. Aquinas quotes 1 Peter 5:9 in *ST* II-II 140.1 ad 1.

77. Cf. *I ad Thess.* lect. 3.1.

78. He writes a total of 3 questions and 11 articles on patience and perseverance, versus 7 questions

tues, which have such significance for spiritual resilience, get short shrift? Being last is not in this case a depreciating quality but rather a teleological one. Patience and perseverance are more central to the highest form of fortitude, which is martyrdom.[79] They involve resisting sorrow and remaining strong in the pursuit of good, in Christ, until the end of our lives, especially when it means following him through a martyr's death or being ready to do so. This ultimate dimension of the Christian life, persisting unto the end in Christ, spells the parameter of Christian resilience.

Theological Supports for Patience

In continuing to enhance our notion of spiritual resilience through Thomas's works on patience, we need to keep in mind the importance accorded to the patience of God the Father, the example of Jesus Christ, and patience's related gifts, beatitudes, and fruits of the Holy Spirit. All these elements contribute to a progressive fullness of patience for Aquinas. Beyond the two types of patience already explored (natural and infused patience), Aquinas articulates the way that patience progresses as a disposition and is enacted through these further theological sources. As with the virtue of fortitude, Thomas's analysis of patience involves a similar progression and transformation of a conception of virtue that we can no longer simply deem Stoic.

Hope as a Source of Patience

Aquinas says that the "hope set on the living God, who is Savior of all, especially of those who believe," gives the reason motivating all of life, especially in the midst of sorrow and toil.[80] For Aquinas, the promise of the life to come, as the final cause, inspires hope that underlies our patience in labor; likewise, this patience serves to fuel Christian hope. Patience is per-

---

and 25 articles for magnanimity and magnificence, and 5 questions and 25 articles for the virtue of fortitude itself and its principal act, martyrdom.

79. Although Aquinas does not go so far as to say that martyrdom is an act of patience rather than fortitude, he does deem that martyrdom is chiefly about fortitude's movement of endurance, which is expressed in patience and perseverance (cf. *ST* II-II 124.2 obj and ad 3; *ST* II-II 123.6). On patience, Aquinas quotes St. Cyprian and St. Augustine in *ST* II-II 124.2 in order to appreciate the way in which we can praise the martyr's patience (and faith).

80. Tm 4:10. Cf. *I ad Timoth.* cap. 4, lect. 2. 1 Tm 4:7–8 (in regard to training in piety or godliness) and also 2 Tm 2:6 (concerning hard work and rewards), and *Ad Eph.* cap. 2, lect. 2 (concerning final cause).

tinent not only in the waiting for the accomplishments of the hoped-for promises, but in actively doing what is fitting in the mean time. As the letter to the Hebrews says: "For you have need of endurance [ὑπομονή, patience], so that you may do the will of God and receive what is promised."[81] This promise is eternal life and a sharing in the true glory of God.[82] Aquinas explains that confidence in these rewards inclines us to handle sadness patiently, without exceeding what is reasonable, in regard to both suffering evil and waiting for the loved goods.[83]

In his Second Letter to the Corinthians, Paul illustrates the interrelationship between patience, hope, and consolation: "If we are afflicted, it is for your comfort and salvation; and if we are comforted, it is for your comfort, which you experience when you patiently endure the same sufferings that we suffer. Our hope for you is unshaken; for we know that as you share in our sufferings, you will also share in our comfort."[84] Aquinas says that this consolation, granted to Paul, is effective for others not only in being a means of consolation and salvation, but also in expressing the ordering of this consolation toward salvation. In patiently enduring as Paul did, we demonstrate patience in adversity as well as the fruit, which comes from this patience. This fruit is hope in eternal life. As Aquinas says in his commentary on 2 Corinthians: "From the suffering which the saints of God sustain for Christ springs forth their hope for eternal life: and the cause of this hope is the knowledge that *as you have shared in our suffering, so you shall share in our consolation;* that is eternal life."[85] The fullness of the graced virtue of hope is completed when it becomes embodied in the believer's experience of patience and perseverance in the face of the inevitable and unavoidable suffering and waiting that one must face while being true to Jesus Christ, in word and deed.

Hope is a key in Paul's understanding of how God strengthens the local churches against tribulation.[86] Aquinas interprets Paul's teaching on hope to be eschatological and Trinitarian. This hope allows us to patiently sup-

81. Heb 10:36 (*RSV*). *Ad Heb.* cap 10, lect. 4. Cf. *Ad Eph.* cap. 4, lect. 1 (Eph 4:2), where the quote illustrates why we rightly avoid impatience.

82. Cf. *ST* II-II 132, 1 ad 2; Rom 2:7; 2 Cor 10:17–18.

83. Cf. *Ad Heb.* cap. 10, lect. 4 (Heb 10:35–36).

84. Cor 1:6–7 (*RSV*).

85. *II ad Cor.* cap 1, lect. 3 (2 Cor 1:6–8). In this regard, he also quotes: Rom 5:3; 2 Tm 2:11; 1 Pt 4:14; and St. Gregory the Great. Cf. *Ad Eph.* cap. 4, lect. 1 (Eph 4:1–4).

86. Cf. 1 Thes 1:1–8; 2 Cor 1–11.

port adversity, with the joy inspired by the Holy Spirit;[87] it is based on the promises made known through Christ and his resurrection, which all lead us to God the Father.[88] The hope that we have, in the midst of trial, tribulation, and suffering, has to be based both in faith, which gives meaning to tribulations and expresses itself in good works,[89] and in charity, which endures and through which good works abound.[90] Observance of the law or human works alone separated from hope (as well as faith and charity) are inadequate for recognizing the sources and ends that inform, motivate, and empower patience.

We shall now recall the resilience research on hope and optimism, outlined in chapter 4, particularly the significance of having plans for the future and of hope's cognitive and social dimensions. The passion and virtues of hope express modalities of resistance that further specify Aquinas' typology of patience and perseverance. Hope and despair can involve either active or passive resistance to suffering. Thomas's typology and language of patience provide a counter-narrative to a misconstrued notion of patience that would promote a blind passivity and receptivity that effectively means violence and oppression to minorities, women, and children.[91] In the latter case, passive resisting spells defeat. It involves an inactive submission to oppression, abuse, and the like. This passivity can arise if we construe the evil or difficulty to be so powerful and permanent that it excludes any hope for evading or repulsing it; then we become depressed, immobilized, and even stupefied by it.[92] This type of defeated patience, where we simply suffer the present hardship as inevitable, lacks all redeeming qualities. It involves a vulnerable passivity.

On the contrary, according to Aquinas, if the evil that we are suffering is not strong enough so as to deprive us of all hope of release or of conquering it, then the depression of body and mind is relative. It might in-

87. In *I ad Thess.* cap. 1, lect. 1 (1 Thes 1:3–6), Aquinas refers to the plenitude of the Holy Spirit's works among Christ's followers who suffer: Acts 2:4; Acts 5:41; Acts 10:44; Heb 2:4; Mt 10:20; Jas 1:2.

88. Cf. *I ad Thess.* cap. 1, lect. 1 (1 Thes 1:3); where Aquinas argues in the light of the following Scripture passages: 1 Thes 4:9; Rom 12:12; Jas 5:2; 1 Pt 1:3; Mt 6:1; Heb 6:19.

89. Cf. *Ad Gal.* cap. 3, lect. 2 (Gal 3:4); where he cites Jas 2:26 and Rom 5:3.

90. Cf. *I ad Thess.* cap. 1, lect. 1 (1 Thes 1:3); 1 Cor 13:15; 1 Thes 4:9.

91. The Christian virtue tradition, which Aquinas represents so well, does not promote misogyny or child abuse by neglect. It furnishes ample conceptual, motivational, and communal means to resist abuse and rape, battery and oppression, in terms of virtues that must accompany patience: fortitude and initiative-taking virtues, chastity and martyrdom, prudence and justice, and so on. Cf. Whitmore 1999.

92. Cf. *ST* I-II 37.2.

volve a systemic (genetic and connatural) effort at group-preservation and self-conservation, which is a type of active passivity that waits for the prudent moment to repulse the evil. At the theological level, faith informs us that the final victory is God's; hope motivates us through his promises. At the natural level, prudent hope needs to render patience creative and ready for timely action. Without a plan and desire for resolving the problems on hand, we would have to simmer (stew) in our suffering or simply bend to oppression. Prudent hope provides a basis for patience and resilience at two levels: first, a cognitive re-appreciation of hardship and potential release or resolution (meaning), and second, a volitional resolve to wait for and persist in the promised good (motivation). It also assures that Christian patience does not passively give into neglect, oppression, or violence.

Patience in Gift, Beatitude, and Petition

Aquinas associates patience with the gifts, beatitudes, and fruits of the Holy Spirit as well as the petitions of the *Pater Noster* (the Lord's Prayer). He treats patience as both a specific virtue and a transversal quality (or a general virtue of Christian life) because of the way that patience and human sorrow interrelate and help us to understand the theological dimension of patience. Thomas's reflections invite two diagnostic questions.[93] Does a theological type of patience simply add a further motivation to philosophical patience (Stoic *apatheia*)? Or does it further specify the virtue, adding a Christological or theological measure?

Thomas attributes patience to the third Beatitude: "Blessed are they that mourn; for they shall be comforted." The relationship between mourning, comfort and patience is neither a free association nor a phenomenological progression nor a developmental stage analysis. Aquinas has a profound theological and metaphysical understanding of this interrelationship. It is too simple to observe (even by definition) that comfort can only follow suffering or sorrow. In more than an observation about temporal progression, Aquinas explains that the promised comfort is not received without having to go through internal suffering or sorrow.[94] The Beatitude of mourners is

93. Aquinas (*ST* II-II 83.9 ad 3) once again uses Augustine's insightful correlation of the gifts, beatitudes, and petitions of the *Pater Noster*, found in the latter's Commentary on the Sermon on the Mount (*De sermone* ii, 11, 38, *PL* 34, 1286), which correlates knowledge, mourning, and the third petition ("Thy will be done").

94. Cf. Mt 5:5; *ST* I-II 69.4; Pinckaers 1995a, 141–63.

grounded in charity and reflects the sorrow that is due to being in the body and absent from the Lord, as Paul indicates.[95]

In his commentary on this beatitude, Aquinas distinguishes three types of mourning that parallel three types of consolation.[96] First, we sorrow because of sin, both our own and others'; "for if we mourn those who have died physically, we should all the more mourn those who have died spiritually."[97] Second, we mourn because of having to live actually in a distressing condition, as well as in longing for our heavenly homeland. Third, we mourn worldly pleasures inasmuch as they distract us from coming to and remaining in Christ.[98] Aquinas offers St. Paul as a model of resisting worldly distractions that would distance us from Christ. He quotes the letter to the Galatians (6:14) in order to demonstrate how Paul does not seek the approval of others, nor worldly pleasures, but rather the glory of the cross of Jesus Christ, through which, as he says, "the world has been crucified to me, and I to the world." This patient resisting transforms mourning into comfort through a union with Christ's suffering and glory.

Aquinas identifies three types of consolation that parallel each group of mourners. First, those who mourn sin will receive the remission of sin as the effect of contrition and faith. Next, those who mourn the delay of heaven and the presence of misery receive consolation through the hope of eternal life. Thirdly, those who mourn worldly pleasures while the world rejoices receive consolation through divine charity. For when someone mourns the lack of a desirable thing, being given something greater more than suffices. Thus it is the gift of the Holy Spirit, divine charity, that brings joy to our hearts.[99] Mourning is transformed into comfort and eventually into joy, through the working of the theological virtues that underlie the life described in the beatitude of the mourners.

Aquinas goes so far as to claim that this beatitude of mourning inclines us to develop virtuous moderation in regard to being sorrowed, or even de-

95. Cf. 2 Cor 5:8; *ST* II-II 28.1 obj. 2 and ad 2.

96. Cf. *Ad Mat.* cap. 5-2. Aquinas' *Lectura* on the Gospel of Saint Matthew seems to have been written in 1269–70. Even though the passage that concerns us here (Mt 5:5) is authentic, a good deal of the rest of the commentary of the Sermon on the Mount in the currently circulated printed texts is instead by Peter of Scala (cf. Torrell 1996, 339).

97. *Ad Mat.* cap. 5-2. He holds that once someone had committed sin, refraining from further sin is not sufficient or satisfactory in itself.

98. Cf. *Ad Mat.* cap. 5-2.

99. See also *Ad Joan.* cap. 2, 1–9, where he quotes John 6:20 and Romans 8:18.

liberately choosing sorrow in order to promote some good thing. This inclination can happen in two ways. First, through a virtuous disposition, we gain a certain control and consistent right ordering of the concupiscible passions. Through experience and education we acquire the capacity to comprehend their functioning and to use (enjoy and suffer) them moderately.[100]

Second, through the gift of knowledge, we can achieve a heightened type of sorrow, for we come to know more fully the effect of our actions and the magnitude of the social situation, and also the way to participate in Christ's salvific works. In regard to the gift of knowledge, Augustine says: "Knowledge befits the mourner, who has discovered that he has been mastered by the evil which he coveted as though it were good."[101] Aquinas explains how right judgment about creatures entails the knowledge that we can be led astray from God, when creatures are mistakenly judged to be the last end and true good for humankind.[102] The gift of knowledge assures, in turn, an appropriate sorrowing for past errors, as well as the related consolation promised in the flourishing, "which begins in this life, and is perfected in the life to come."[103] It is thus that the gift of knowledge has a practical effect in the active life, by directing the operative act of the beatitude of mourning.[104] The knowledge of a sinful condition even serves as the principal motive for the beatitude of mourners: "whereby man knows his failings and those of worldly things, according to Eccles. 1:18: 'He that addeth knowledge, addeth also sorrow.'"[105] But this sorrow leads to joy in that, through faith, it merits eternal consolation. As Aquinas says: "the sorrows of the present life lead us to the comfort of the future life. Because by the mere fact that humans mourn for their sins, or for the delay of glory, they merit the consolation of eternity."[106] Contrition for sin and hopeful anticipation of God's promises result from this gift, and in turn are the formal reason for its merit.

In his homily on the *Pater Noster*,[107] Aquinas recognizes how the third

100. Cf. *ST* I-II 69.3.

101. *De sermone* i, 4; *PL* 34, 1234; quoted in *ST* II-II 9.4 sc.

102. Aquinas also notes how the third beatitude's right judgment and sorrow about evil committed relates to both the beatitude of poverty and the gift of fear of the Lord (*ST* I-II 69.3 ad 3). These gifts dispose the human faculties to be more readily obedient to the Spirit's promptings (cf. *ST* I-II 68.1).

103. Cf. *ST* II-II 9.4 ad 1; *ST* I-II 69.3 ad 4.

104. Cf. *ST* I-II 69.3 ad 2, and *Ad Mat.* cap. 5.2.

105. *ST* I-II 69.3 ad 3; cf. *ST* II-II 19.12; and *ST* I-II 69.3 ad 2.

106. *ST* I-II 35.3 ad 1; where Aquinas also relates humility with the third beatitude. Cf. *ST* II-II 161.5 ad 3; Mt 5:5 and Mt 6:19–20.

107. *In orat. dom.*, art. 3. The *collatio in orationem dominicam* is a homily or catechetical instruction

petition—"Let thy will be done on earth as it is in heaven"—helps to explain the third beatitude's relation to patience in a threefold manner. First, the beatitude of mourning manifests the desire for eternal life (cf. Ps 120:5). This sorrow is especially present among the saints, whose mourning becomes accidentally a longing for death (2 Cor 5:8), which would naturally be avoided. Second, those who will to keep the commandments are in sorrow, because of the difficulty for the body of the implied discipline (cf. Ps 126:6). Third, we sorrow because of the sins of the body; such sorrow has an expiating effect (cf. Ps 6:6). In this commentary on the *Pater*, moreover, he associates the beatitude of peacemakers and the gift of wisdom with patience. Through the Holy Spirit, believers are incited to pray and thereby obtain a certain blessedness of peace and trust even in the midst of difficulty and tribulation. For it is through patience that we are able to be at peace in prosperity and in adversity.[108]

Patience as a Fruit of the Holy Spirit

Aquinas' analysis of patience-related moral agency and grace does not stop with his correlation of the virtues, gifts, beatitudes, and petitions. He completes the Augustinian schema by explicating the nature and typology of the fruits of the Holy Spirit. Various scholastic attempts at including the fruits within this theological framework were already afoot preceding Aquinas.[109] Instead of a historical investigation, though, I shall examine his notion of the fruits of the Holy Spirit in view of identifying insights into resilience outcomes that they might offer.

The gifts, beatitudes, petitions of the *Pater*, and fruits of the Holy Spirit (*Gal* 5:22–3) are not neat, non-overlapping theological concepts, for St. Thomas. He distinguishes the fruits according to formal, yet flexible, rationale; they are types of goods enjoyed,[110] which complete and signify the flourishing of the spiritual life, as it is possible on earth.[111] He includes the

---

on the *Pater Noster*. It is thought to date from the last period of his life (1272–73); cf. Torrell 1996, 266, 358.

108. Cf. *In orat. dom.* art. 7; cf. art. 6. In articles 6 and 7, Aquinas addresses respectively the petitions of the *Pater Noster* on temptation and evil, and how patience is crucial for them both.

109. The fruits of the Holy Spirit had been included in the works of St. Bonaventure (*In III Sent.* 34.1.1.1), and St. Albert the Great, who makes them a higher perfection (*In III Sent.* 34.1), transforming the ascending order proposed by Philip the Chancellor (virtues, gifts and fruits together, beatitudes). Cf. *Summa de bono;* cited in Lottin 1942–60, III.363; cf. O'Connor 1974, 103.

110. Cf. *ST* I-II 70.3 ad 4.

111. Cf. *ST* I-II 70.3; *ST* II-II 139.2 ad 3.

fruits of the Holy Spirit in his moral theology, employing the images of seeds, trees, flowers, and fruit from a number of scriptural metaphors to suggest the nature, growth, and goal of these acts.[112]

Aquinas identifies the different senses of "fruit," the meaning of which he transfers from material to spiritual realities. Even though we either produce or gather fruit, not all that is produced or gathered is fruit. Virtuous human operations proceed from reason and will; such is the case for both acquired and infused virtues, the latter of which involve the fruit of reason and will informed by faith, hope, and charity. The spiritual sense of fruit connotes that which is last and gives pleasure. As Thomas argues: "man's fruit is his last end which is intended for his enjoyment."[113] The fruits involve the effect of the Holy Spirit on the human organism.[114] Both the infused virtues and the gifts of the Holy Spirit participate in producing fruitful acts. In particular, fruits spring forth through the virtues as sweetness and delight and through the gifts as being their "last and congruous products."[115]

Aquinas classes both the beatitudes and the fruits of the Holy Spirit as acts of the infused virtues and the gifts. While the beatitudes and the fruits resemble each other in being something ultimate and delightful, the beatitudes alone connote something perfect and excellent.[116] Aquinas follows the scriptural tradition of his time in enumerating twelve fruits of the Holy Spirit,[117] in contrast to the nine fruits named in critical editions of Paul's

112. Aquinas takes these images for his treatment of the fruits in the *ST* (I-II 70) from the following sources: Gal 5:22–3; Mt 12:33; Ws 3:15; Jn 4:36; 1 Jn 3:9; Eccl 24:23; Rom 6:22; Is 27:9; Mt 13:23; Rv 22:2.

113. *ST* I-II 70.1.

114. Cf. *ST* I-II 70.1, where Aquinas draws his insight from 1 John 3:9.

115. *Ad Gal.* cap. 5, lect. 6. In the *ST* (I-II 70.1 ad 2), Aquinas emphasizes that this type of pleasure in an ultimate thing formally concerns virtuous deeds. We rejoice in them because of their goodness, which is formally good although not the ultimate goodness. We do not rejoice in them as if they were a final cause of delight. God alone merits being delighted in for His own sake. Aquinas quotes St. Ambrose (*De Parad.* 13.6; *PL* 14.308B) in affirming that virtuous deeds are refreshing fruits.

116. Because of the beatitudes' central and final perspective in the moral and spiritual life, Aquinas construes the fruits of the Holy Spirit as subordinated to the beatitudes (cf. *ST* I-II 70.2 corpus and ad 2; *ST* I-II 69.1 ad 1).

117. Thomas employs the *Glossa ordinaria*, which contained the following twelve fruits: *caritas* (charity), *gaudium* (joy), *pax* (peace), *patientia* (patience), *longanimitas* (long-suffering), *bonitas* (goodness), *benignitas* (kindness), *mansuetudo* (mildness), *fides* (faithfulness), *modestia* (modesty), *continentia* (self-control), and *castitas* (chastity). This twelvefold tradition was the only one that Thomas knew; with further modifications it has persisted in theology and catechesis. The *Catechism of the Catholic Church* (CCC 1832) list twelve fruits with slight variation in order and content. Aquinas attributes twelve fruits to Paul's text in Galatians 5:22 (cf. *ST* I-II 70.3, and *Ad Gal.* cap. 5, lect. 6). He nonetheless quotes (in *ST* I-II 70.4) Augustine's commentary on Galatians 5:22–23 (n. 51; *PL* 35.2141–2142), in which the latter does not articulate twelve fruits; in particular Augustine refers to *longanimitas* and not *patientia*.

Letter to the Galatians (5:22).[118] The gift and presence of the Holy Spirit is source of this and all the fruits, which according to Aquinas incline us to remain in God. Aquinas argues furthermore that the Holy Spirit is the first gift, from which the particular gifts and fruits are portioned out.[119]

St. Thomas explains that patience is fittingly called a fruit of the Spirit even though it entails the contact with a painful object. Indeed "the fact of not being disturbed by painful things is something to delight in."[120] The operation of not being overcome by sorrow and difficulty is not the fruit of patience itself; rather this fruit is a result that follows upon such a virtuous operation.[121] Aquinas closely associates the fruits of patience and long-suffering,[122] and describes how they correlate with the fruits of charity, joy, and peace. These five are inward perfections, with social rather than individualistic overtones. Charity, joy, and peace more directly concern good,[123] whereas patience and longanimity face evil directly. In particular, the Holy Spirit leads a person to firmly face the evil that disrupts peace, by giving patient endurance in adversity. Concerning the evils that disturb joy, the Holy Spirit grants long-suffering; thus we can resist being broken by the delay in obtaining the loved object.[124] References to the fruit of patience and long-suffering should not be taken as a passive and self-destructive tendency; their association with the virtue of fortitude and its aspect of initiative taking entail that this patience is not an end in itself, but serves a larger purpose.[125]

118. Various discrepancies in the recensions of the fruits are due to the various Latin translations of Scripture, errors in recopying biblical manuscripts, and perhaps even efforts to reinforce other references to the Spirit. These additions might be due to the custom of glossing a text by adding synonyms between the lines. A scribe might have mistaken the interlinear gloss for the original text (cf. O'Connor 1974, 148). According to Charles-A. Bernard (1964, 1571–72), another theory speculates that the additions were made in function of the mystical connotations of the number twelve and the important reference in the book of *Revelation* (22:2), to "the tree of life with its twelve kinds of fruit."

The Greek NT text (Aland, 1976) and standard critical translations such as the *RSV*, as well as the Vulgate, name nine fruits of the Holy Spirit in Galatians 5:22. The *Glossa ordinaria* (used by Aquinas) contains *patientia* in addition to *longanimitas (μακροθυμία), mansuetudo* in addition to *fides (πίστις)* and *castitas* in addition to *continentia (ἐγκράτεια)*. Cf. O'Connor 1974, 148–49.

119. In *ST* I-II 70.3, Aquinas draws this insight from Romans 5:5, 1 John 4:16. It is well developed in *Prima pars* (*ST* I 38.2), where Aquinas draws further from Augustine's *De Trin.* (iv.20 and xv.24) as well as Aristotle's *Top.* (iv.4).

120. *ST* I-II 70.3 ad 3; cf. *ST* II-II 136.1 ad 3.

121. Cf. *De car.* art 2, 12.

122. Unlike Aquinas' Latin translation of Galatians 5:22, which lists two separate fruits, *patientia* and *longanimitas*, the *Vulgata* (1975) gives only *longanimitas*, and the original Greek only *μακροθυμία*, which is variously translated in this context as: "patience" *(RSV* and *JB)* or "patient endurance" *(NAB)*.

123. Cf. *ST* I-II 70.3 (citing Rom 5:5); *ST* I 37.1; and *Ad Gal.* cap 5, lect. 6.

124. Cf. *ST* I-II 70.3; *ST* II-II 136.5; *ST* II-II 139.2 ad 3; *Ad Gal.* cap. 5, lect 6.

125. Cf. *III Sent.* 34, 1, 5, co.

For Aquinas, to know the fruit involves that we know the tree, its needs, and its potential. Aquinas correlates the fruit with the nature of the tree. If the tree produces something against its nature, it is an oddity instead of a fruit. Likewise, the works of vice are against nature (as a deformation of nature), while the works of virtue are connatural to the human tree.[126] How might this metaphor of fruit serve to enhance the resilience perspective, and be enhanced in the process? In order to identify and promote resilience we have to understand the nature, needs, potential, and goals of the rational agent and community. In the case of a good that we cannot yet attain or can attain only with difficulty, patience phenomena involve acquired and infused supports that help us to cope with the hardship, to conserve ourselves under destructive pressures, and to persist toward the goal amidst delays. Aquinas helps us to understand how theological patience is a fruit of the human person and community, through the working of the Holy Spirit. Theological supports to patience result from revelation and grace: hope, the beatitudes, the gifts, and the fruits of the Holy Spirit. They are thus not observable in the same way as nonspiritual resilience phenomena. Nonetheless, Aquinas' theological anthropology illustrates the human and spiritual nature, needs, and finality that produce resisting and persisting resilience. His view of theological patience and perseverance demonstrate a rich (though empirically nonverifiable) way to depict spiritual resilience.

Development of Patience and Spiritual Resilience

Christian conceptions of patience and suffering must face challenges that arise from certain resilience and psychosocial research, for example, challenges that involve whether Christian patience creates vulnerable individuals and passive communities, who are willing to suffer wrong rather than correct it. Such questions lead us to explore Thomas's conception of virtuous sorrow, patience, and moral progress in dialogue with resilience insights.

Virtuous Sorrow

Aquinas' typology of patience and fortitude recalls his previously mentioned typology of sorrow. Since pleasure and pain can be of a bodily or

126. Cf. *ST* I-II 70.4 ad 1.

spiritual nature—the latter relating more primarily to the effect on the soul[127]—the brave and patient person can experience both spiritual joy and spiritual sorrow or pain at the same time.[128] On the one hand, one experiences spiritual sorrow at the thought of physical death or pain, as well as at the knowledge of spiritual death or evil. The nature of bodily pain on the other hand has a great number of sources, and is capable of making us insensible to other realities, such as the spiritual joy given through a virtuous act. On the physical level, pain is stronger than pleasure, and pain that leads to death causes the greatest distress to the mind, the greatest fears.[129] On the spiritual level, however, the virtue of fortitude and patience itself work to prevent bodily pain from completely overcoming reason. Indeed one experiences spiritual joy when achieving virtue or attaining the end at which virtue aims.[130] This end implies the love of God, love of neighbor, and complete flourishing. God grants spiritual joy by raising the soul above the blinding effect of spiritual sorrow and bodily pain, to the divine things that give delight.[131]

The framework of the virtues offers various strategies for overcoming sorrow or pain. First, in order that endurance entail virtuous patience rather than hardness of heart, one must aim at some good, rather than rejoice in the suffering itself.[132] The spiritual sorrow that expresses a virtuous good involves a sorrowing according to a right measure of reason and will.[133] Such virtuous sorrow is compatible with the joy of charity, "insofar as a man grieves for that which hinders the participation of the Divine good, either in us or in our neighbor, whom we love as ourselves."[134] More than being sim-

127. Cf. *ST* I-II 23.4; *ST* I-II 31.1; *ST* I-II 35.1.

128. Cf. *ST* II-II 123.8; see also *ST* I-II 31.3–5.

129. Cf. *ST* II-II 123.11.

130. Cf. *ST* II-II 123.8.

131. This type of joy is manifest in Aquinas' reference (*ST* II-II 123.8) to the Maccabean martyr Eleazar (2 Mc 6:30). When asking whether the brave person delights in his act, Aquinas explains that one can be supported by spiritual joy in the act and end of virtue, as well as experience spiritual sorrow because of the thought of losing his life and the pain involved.

132. Cf. *ST* II-II 136.1 ad 2 from a quotation of St. Augustine, *De pat.* ii.

133. One finds this notion of "virtuous sorrow" in *ST* I-II 39.2. The Sermon on the Mount, in particular the beatitude of mourners, which serves as the *sed contra* to the question, informs his notion of virtuous sorrow. Cf. *ST* I-II 39.3; and *ST* I-II 59.3.

134. *ST* II-II 28.2. In asking the question as to whether one can have both the joy of charity and sorrow, he distinguishes two types of joy. One type, which is more excellent, involves rejoicing in the divine good considered in itself (*ST* II-II 28.2). Since such joy's object is perfect, so is the resulting joy; neither this object (God) nor the resulting joy permits an admixture of sorrow (Cf. Phil 4:4). The other type is the joy of charity as our participation in the divine good. Such a participative joy can be hindered

ply compatible with it, virtuous sorrow both is informed by charity, which directs our perception of evil, and strengthens our resolve to reject evil. Furthermore, virtuous sorrow emanates from charity, inasmuch as living charity does not just react to such emotion, but is constitutive of the virtuous character that further orders the appetites toward the true good of the Gospel, so that we sorrow differently with charity than without it.

Both St. Paul and the book of Ecclesiasticus (Sirach) serve Thomas's illustration of sorrow's power to debilitate the human spirit and even to kill it.[135] In his Second Letter to the Corinthians, Paul distinguishes two types of sorrow that can be likened to two types of patience. God uses the first type of grief, sadness, or sorrow to bring someone to repentance, to return to God.[136] This type of virtuous sorrow produces spiritual benefits in two ways. Through it, we shun things that are in themselves evil, for example, sin, past, present, and future. Paul describes how the grief (or virtuous sorrow) that he provoked in the members of the community in Corinth served in their repenting and restoring good relations with him.[137] Such sorrow is useful not only in avoiding the evil of future sin, but also in repenting for sins already committed. Moreover, through virtuous sorrow, we spurn occasions of evil, for example, particular disordered relations with temporal goods.[138] Indeed, we can become too attached to temporal goods, loving them inordinately and thereby being distracted from our ultimate goal.

A second type of sadness, a worldly grief, brings destruction and death, since it depresses the soul through a present, experienced evil.[139] The virtue of patience resists this type of sorrow and embraces the first, inasmuch as graced sorrow is a catalyst for repentance, conversion, and returning to God. Aquinas furthermore distinguishes two sorts of graced sorrow that correspond to natural and infused patience.

The virtuous good of sorrow rectifies other disordered relations to sorrow, since inordinate sorrow is an obstacle to flourishing. Aquinas argues that "although in this unhappy abode we participate, after a fashion, in the

by anything contrary to the divine good (anything in us or in our neighbor), and therefore can be experienced at the same time as sorrow.

135. In *ST* II-II 136.1, Aquinas illustrates this point using 2 Corinthians 7:10 and Ecclesiasticus 30:25.

136. Cf. *ST* II II 136.5; *ST* I-II 37.2 ad 1; *ST* I-II 39.3; 2 Cor 7:10–11.

137. Cf. 2 Cor 7:9, quoted in *ST* I-II 39.3.

138. Cf. *ST* I-II 39.3.

139. See *ST* II-II 136.1, which quotes 2 Cor 7:10, and *ST* I-II 37.4 sc, which refers to Prv 17:22; Prv 25:20; Eccl (Sir) 30, 19.

Divine good, by knowledge and love, yet the unhappiness of this life is an obstacle to a perfect participation in the Divine good: hence this very sorrow, whereby a man grieves for the delay of glory, is connected with the hindrance to a participation of the Divine good."[140] Sorrow is chosen neither as a good in itself nor as an end in itself. Indeed, we do not choose evil as the source of sorrow. Nonetheless, we desire the good end and good object, rather than any associated evil. "And thus Christ's death and passion were of themselves involuntary, and caused sorrow, although they were voluntary as ordained to the end, which is the redemption of the human race."[141] As is evident in the beatitude concerning those who mourn, there can be a salutary connection between present sorrowing and flourishing, the fullness of which God alone offers in the world to come.[142]

Aquinas discusses how devotion to Christ (the practices of meditation and prayer) has the effect of both joy and sorrow and thus contributes to establishing virtuous sorrow. He says that it is "evident that the first and direct effect of devotion is joy, while the secondary and accidental effect is that 'sorrow which is according to God.'"[143] In meditation one comes to recognize that "in the consideration of Christ's Passion there is something that causes sorrow, namely, the human defect, the removal of which made it necessary for Christ to suffer; and there is something that causes joy, namely, God's loving-kindness to us in giving us such a deliverance."[144] The sorrow and joy related with the suffering and salvation wrought through Christ's passion, death, and resurrection offer a school of virtuous, Christ-like sorrow and joy. Jesus Christ's passion and the sorrow that he felt in his life and especially during his agony serve as an example of education in patience. Knowing the suffering that he would confront, Jesus prepared himself. Thomas suggests that we do the same through a virtuous sorrow that prepares the mind and is part of a larger spiritual and moral progress, and we might add, spiritual resilience.

Development of Patience and Spiritual Resilience

The resilience research identifies a typology of suffering that is often built on nonnormative and nonempirical foundations, which underlie psy-

140. *ST* II-II 28.2 ad 3.
141. *ST* III 15.6 ad 4.
142. Cf. Mt 5:5; *ST* I-II 39.2 sc; as discussed earlier.
143. *ST* II-II 82.4, quoting 2 Cor. 7:10.
144. *ST* II-II 82.4 ad 1; Lk 24:25.

chosocial theories about developmental pathways for the management of suffering. For example, Freud, in general, critiques the forces of civilization and religion that socialize, redirect, and sublimate human instinct. He speculates that while the instincts of life (*eros*) and death (*thanatos*) need to be controlled and ordered, a repressive society's overcontrol produces neurosis and needless suffering. In regard to Christianity, he finds that the principle "love your neighbor as yourself" is not only overcontrolling, but also psychologically impossible and thus not ethically binding.[145] This negative assessment touches the Christian conception of patience at its heart.

Freud's position is not self-evident, nor substantiated by empirical findings; although its influence is on the wane, it figures largely in contemporary psychosocial theories. Don S. Browning assesses Freud's position as simplistic and unscientific, while he offers at the same time a self-critique of Christianity, seeking to correct the oppression and exploitation experienced by such groups as women and minorities in the name of self-sacrifice and patience. Browning's criteria identify notions of self-esteem that specify more resistant manifestations of self-giving and that indicate pathways for developing patience. He distinguishes self-abnegation from truly appropriate forms of self-giving in the name of our neighbor.[146] Browning thus takes one step toward enhancing the idea that undifferentiated physical pain or psychological suffering is an inevitable aspect of individual triumph over hardship[147] and of Christian self-understanding. Although challenging goals demand effort and often pain to achieve them, not all suffering is necessary or appropriate. Christian self-esteem and self-awareness are not simply equated with undifferentiated pain and self-giving; rather it is necessary to include notions of both appropriate pain avoidance and self-giving, and to distinguish social and theological goals.

Such insights might well be carefully transferred not only to experiences such as disability, loss of friendship, or employment, but also to more specifically spiritual and religious domains. However, more specialized resilience research further clarifies the relationship between patient suffering and spirituality or religion. According to Garbarino and Bedard, the key to addressing problems of trauma, suffering, and evil is found in recognizing the multidimensional nature of the human person. In particular, they

145. Cf. Freud 1961; Browning 1987, 46ff.
146. Cf. Browning 1987, 160.
147. Cf. Radke-Yarrow and Sherman 1990, 114.

speculate that spirituality aids in overcoming such adversity because of its awareness that humans are more than physical beings, and that their spiritual existence has a certain primacy.[148] As mentioned in chapter 2, studies have indicated that religion can (1) work as a coping mechanism, with reports of "lower levels of reported pain and greater happiness,"[149] and (2) be beneficial to health by providing "a reassuring fatalism," enabling humans to better withstand suffering and pain.[150] It can also provide protection through the development of faith and religious practice, inasmuch as they offer a means of finding goals, purpose, and meaning in life, especially in the face of suffering and death, but also when confronted with the degradation of notions of self-esteem and self-efficacy.[151] The religious community can also provide support, as can the clergy, who have traditionally served a caring function.[152] This input concerning the interaction between spirituality and patient management of suffering, pain, and adversity can now be put in dialogue with Aquinas' formulation of these issues.

Aquinas bases his notion of how patience develops upon the dynamic interrelation between human inclinations, emotions, and virtues, on the one hand, and grace and the sevenfold gift of the Holy Spirit, on the other. For Thomas, the development of patience is a question of training, discipline, encouragement, character, and progress. One of the keys to growth in the fullness of Christian patience is personal training in God's ways, a being trained by God and others. In this regard, both docility (as discussed earlier) and piety are important. It is interesting to see how Aquinas handles the words of Paul: "Train yourself in godliness; for while bodily training is of some value, godliness is of value in every way, as it holds promise for the present life and also for the life to come."[153] Aquinas underlines the importance of the training of the affections and senses through practices such as abstinence, fasting, and almsgiving, which can serve as efficacious remedies. But he makes it clear that such training has eternal value only if it is rooted in charity. When informed by charity, godliness is useful in every way. It abolishes sin, promotes good, and receives God's special mercy.[154]

Patience develops through discipline, and conversely is a necessary

148. Cf. Garbarino and Bedard 1996, 470.

149. Cf. Pargament et al. 1990, 797–98.

150. Cf. Schumaker 1992, 3.

151. Cf. Lösel 1994, 8–12; Meyer and Lausell 1996, 120.

152. Cf. D'Antonio and Aldous 1983, 15–16, 106.

153. Tm 4:7–8 (*RSV*).

154. Cf. *I ad Timoth.* cap. 4, lect. 2.

means to receive discipline. Thomas recognizes the place of human and divine discipline, both of which are rooted in charity, for we do not discipline children unless we love them.[155] However, divine discipline is more complete in its duration (eternal life) and end (sanctification). Aquinas puts divine filiation and discipline in the context of the Church as the mother, whose spouse is God.[156] Recognizing that human senses and thoughts can be prone to evil, Aquinas underlines the necessity of discipline to correct such tendencies. The discipline administered to children medicinally directs them toward good and away from disordered tendencies. As medicine can be bitter and painful in facilitating the desired healing, so discipline can require traversing sorrow or pain before arriving at its fruit, which is peace and joy.[157]

Patience, for St. Thomas, also has a social function tied to aiding others in spiritual and moral growth. Indeed education takes patience and perseverance, which for Aquinas not only avoids doing evil ourselves, but also reprimands patiently a neighbor who has done evil. Our concern and caring for a neighbor include a learned and holy rebuking or admonition. In this regard, Aquinas quotes Paul: "Reprove, entreat, rebuke in all patience and doctrine."[158] We need not only patience in education, but also a sense of timeliness, which considers how the suggested correction will affect the person: whether it will be counterproductive; whether another time would better serve the effort; and how other people involved might be influenced.[159] Lastly, we should conjugate patience with sweetness and initiative-taking virtues in order to correct the dangers associated with patience, which are hardness of heart and passivity.[160]

Chapter 6 introduced other strategies for managing sorrow and pain, whose theological dimension we can now examine. For example, Aquinas construes the sympathy that consoles the sorrowing neighbor in terms of charity or friendship-love.[161] Concerning the pleasure of the contemplation

155. Cf. *Ad Heb.* cap. 12, lect. 2 (Heb 12:7).

156. Cf. *Ad Heb.* cap. 12, lect 2 (Heb 12:8).

157. He emphasizes that the Letter to the Hebrews admonishes us neither to neglect the discipline of the Lord nor to grow impatient of it, but rather to persevere in it so as to attain the promised fruit. Cf. *Ad Heb.* cap. 12, lect. 2 (Heb 12:5, 7, and 11).

158. Tm 4:2; quoted in *Ad Eph* cap. 5, lect. 4; where he also cites Eccl (Sir) 17:12.

159. In this regard, Aquinas quotes Augustine insights found in *De Civ. Dei,* I, 9 (*PL* 41, 22).

160. Cf. Bruguès 1984, 47–58.

161. Although Aquinas (*ST* I-II 38.3 corpus and ad 2) draws here from Aristotle's insights on the role friends play in comforting the sorrowing (*NE* ix.11, 1171a 29–30), he integrates theological insights

of truth that calms pain and sorrow, Aquinas says: "In the midst of tribulations men rejoice in the contemplation of Divine things and of future beatitude."[162] Truth-inspired joy lightens physical pain and psychological sorrow inasmuch as it puts us in touch with divine sources of strength, comfort, and flourishing.[163]

In this regard, Aquinas attends to the pedagogical functions and evangelical bases that the precepts of patience and perseverance have in handling pain and suffering and in developing these virtues. Being prepared for suffering, difficulty, and adversity is key to the virtue of patience. The precepts of patience[164] assist the proper formation and execution of this virtue. These precepts of the divine law have the purpose of directing the mind to God. Aquinas argues that it is fitting to have precepts of obligation concerning both patience and perseverance,[165] which involve the preparedness of mind. Aquinas says that this preparedness for patience concerns being ready to withstand things that are both done and said against us.[166] Although we ought to be prepared to turn the other cheek if necessary, Aquinas explains that we are not always bound to do so, and furthermore that we should be prepared also to be impatient in certain cases.

When being physically attacked or verbally reviled, it may not be expedient to remain patient, according to Thomas. He gives two reasons why we should not always withstand either being attacked or reviled (as Jesus did not in John 18:23). First, we must respect the good of the attacker or reviler, since correction may serve the good purpose of assisting that person out of error.[167] Second, we must consider the good of other people, who might be not any less concerned: indeed when the common good is endangered,

---

from the experiences of St. Augustine (*Confessions* viii.4 and iv.9), St. Paul, and the suffering Job, which are confirmed in Aquinas' commentaries: *In Eth.* lect 13; *Ad Eph.* 4. lect 1; *In Job* 2, 2, 16, lect. i; *Ad Rom.* 12, lect. 3.

162. *ST* I-II 38.4.

163. In *ST* I-II 38.4, Aquinas draws upon St. Augustine (*Soliloq.* 1, 12), upon the Letter of James, (1:2) and upon the martyr Tiburtius (Dominican breviary, 11 August) in order to bring Christian tradition and experience to support this phenomenon.

164. Thomas (*ST* II-II 140.1) identifies the following scriptural bases for precepts of patience: "Accept whatever is brought upon you, and in changes that humble you be patient" (Eccl [Sir] 2:4, *RSV*); "By your endurance you will gain your lives" (Lk 21:19, *RSV*); "rejoice in your hope, be patient in tribulation, be constant in prayer" (Rom 12:12, *RSV*). He finds precepts of perseverance in Mt 10:22; 1 Cor 15:58; Heb 12:7.

165. Cf. *ST* II-II 140.2 ad 1.

166. See *ST* II-II 72.3 and II-II 140.2, which draw on Augustine (*De sermone*, i.19); Scripture (Mt 5:39 and Lk 6:29); and St. Gregory the Great (*In Ev.*, hom. XXXV, 1; *PL* 76, 1259 BC).

167. Cf. *ST* II-II 72.3; where Thomas cites Jn 18:23; Prv 26:5; cf. St. Augustine, *De corrept.*

a country fights against its enemies;[168] or when a wrong reflects on God or on the Church, one should right the wrong in order to avoid undue scandal;[169] or when remaining silent to slander against public figures will hinder the moral and spiritual progress of others, we should correct detractors.[170] Aquinas does not hold that the virtue of patience entails always being "patient," in the sense of being passive in front of every adversity or evil. The virtue of patience also involves being prepared to be impatient; in that case, we call upon the virtues of fortitude and initiative empowered by righteous anger and prudent judgment.

Freud's critique of a certain notion of Christianity falls short of Thomas. Indeed, Aquinas' strategies for managing pain and sorrow and his interpretation of the precepts of patience and perseverance underlie a fuller conception of what it means to manage pain and sorrow. They demand an action readiness and hardiness that Freud did not grasp as Christian.

Patience in Moral and Spiritual Progress

Experiences of suffering and patience are testing grounds for spiritual progress and for spiritual resilience. However, psychosocial methods inhibit research from addressing theological treatments of suffering and patience as properly theological. For this reason, Thomas's observations on theological patience serve to complete at this level the dearth of input from the psychosocial sciences. In particular, Aquinas' scriptural commentaries provide us with narrative images from the tradition as well as philosophical and theological concepts to explicate pathways toward growth in spiritual patience.

Aquinas interprets spiritually the wines served at the wedding feast in Cana, in his *Commentary on the Gospel of John*. He illustrates how the bitter feeling of sorrow, and the need to manage it patiently, must be kept in the perspective of moral and spiritual progress, and the sweetness of salvation. He notes that sorrow is a characteristic of the first stages of this progress, while sweetness comes with the delights, joy, and glory to come. Christ does not serve the tastiest wine first, but rather proposes a way that is bitter and hard. It is only when we make progress in faith and teaching that we be-

168. Cf. *ST* II-II 136.4 ad 3, quoting Augustine's letter to *Marcellinus* (Ep. cxxxviii).

169. Cf. *ST* II-II 108, 1 ad 4; *ST* II-II 72.3; *ST* II-II 140.2 ad 2.

170. Cf. *ST* II-II 72.3, where Aquinas quotes St. Gregory's *Hom. super Ezech* (IX bk I, hom. 9, n. 18: *PL* 76.877D.

come more aware of the sweetness.[171] This spiritual progress involves the patient management of the sorrow and tribulations, measured against the joys that come through following Christ and being supported by the Holy Spirit.[172]

Aquinas notes that sorrow results when due progress is not achieved in ourselves and in others. Such is the sorrow that Paul feels because of the actions of the Ephesians (Gal 4:20). Paul is sorrowed and ashamed since they have turned from good to evil, according to Aquinas, who says: "For since a son is a thing of the father, and a disciple as such is a thing of his master, a master rejoices in the good he sees reflected in him and glories in it as though it were his own. Conversely, he is pained at evil and is ashamed."[173] This same concern of a father or a mother for the child and a master for the disciple is found in the discipline exacted by God, who intends that believers grow in their stature as God's children. Aquinas thus speaks of needing patience in correction, quoting Proverbs (3:11): "My son, do not despise the Lord's discipline or be weary of his reproof, for the Lord reproves him whom he loves, as a father the son in whom he delights."[174]

Thomas highlights the significance, place, and utility of affliction and temptation in regard to growing in patience. First, the human person is directed toward patience through adversity. He reasons that God made all creation good, according to nature. But if we suffer evil and adversity or confront some punishment, we should believe that the difficulty or punishment is from God; however, not as if God willed the blameworthy evil deed. "Because no evil is from God, except that which is ordained to good; and therefore if every punishment that humans suffer is from God, it should be endured patiently. For punishments purge sins, humble the guilty, and lead the good to love God."[175] Thus through patient endurance of evils and affliction, we can recognize that even such difficulties can be a way to know and love God more fully. We must recall, though, the need to prudently discern punishment from oppression and violence.

171. Cf. *Ad Joan*, ch. 2, lect. 1–9 (Jn 16:20), which also quotes Rom 8:18.

172. Aquinas discusses three degrees of spiritual progress in charity in *ST* II-II. 24.9. Cf. Pinckaers 1995a, 359–74.

173. *Ad Gal.* cap. 4, lect. 6; in this regard, Aquinas refers to Eccl (Sir) 22: 3.

174. *In orat. dom.* intro. In regard to correction and admonition, Aquinas also relies on St. Augustine' *Admonition and Grace (De correptine et gratia)*, quoted in the *ST* (I-II 109.2; II-II 72.3; II-II 137.4), *De verit.* (6.3), and *De car.* (art. 12).

175. Thus, Aquinas (*In symb. apost.* art. 1) considers punishment a type of evil and explains Job's (Jb 11:10) otherwise puzzling affirmations.

St. Paul's letter to the Romans (5:1–5) contains one of the most important texts describing the relationship of suffering and patience to faith, hope, and charity. Aquinas uses this text on numerous occasions in order to illustrate the relationship of trials to patience.[176] One of the reasons for the consequence of this text is the context of grace, which serves as a foundation for understanding patience and hope. Through grace, we have peace with God the Father, faith in Jesus Christ and hope of sharing future glory, the glory of God, in which we already participate through such hope. Aquinas notes that it is the strength of this hope that permits someone to endure difficulty and even bitter medicine for the sake of the hoped-for glory or healing.[177] Thus we can rejoice not only in the hope of future glory, but also in present trials, which open the way to this glory.[178]

This perspective on suffering is possible because of the faith, which enables us to know "that suffering produces endurance [*ὑπομονή*], and endurance produces character [*δοκιμὴ*], and character produces hope" (Rom 5:3–4, *RSV*). The suffering is not the efficient cause of the patience, but is the matter and occasion for exercising patience.[179] Aquinas explains that patience and character[180] both precede and result from suffering. They are both the condition for enduring it and the effect of the trial endured. The result is a hope that has been tried, is firm, and will not disappoint. The source of this confident hope is God's love, which God the Father manifests through the death and resurrection of Jesus Christ, and through the gift of the Holy Spirit. Aquinas notes that it is an expression of love when we suffer in the service of God.[181]

In the context of affirming how Jesus Christ's passion has freed us from the power of the devil, Aquinas observes that we can be bothered by temptation either as merited from our own guilt (a result of our own evil ac-

176. In addition to the commentary *Ad Rom.* cap. 5, lect. 1, Aquinas also quotes Rom 5:3 in *II ad Cor.* cap. 1, lect. 3; *Ad Gal.* cap. 3, lect. 2; *I ad Timoth.* cap. 4. lect. 2; *Ad Rom.* cap. 12, lect. 2; *De verit.* 2, 28, 8 sc 2; *IV Sent.* 15, 1, art. 4; *In Isaiam* 11; *In orat. dom.* art. 7; *In Psalmos* 9 [illegible].

177. Cf. *Ad Rom.* cap. 5, lect. 1 (Rom 5:3).

178. Aquinas (*Ad Rom.* cap. 5, lect 1) refers here to Acts 14:22 and Jas 1:2.

179. Cf. *Ad Rom.* cap. 5, lect. 2 (Rom 12,12); and *Ad Eph.* cap. 4, lect. 1.

180. In the Latin translation of St. Paul's Letter to the Romans used by Aquinas, *probatio* is used to translate *δοκιμή*. *Δοκιμὴ* literally means „the quality of being approved" through a test, trial. or ordeal, and hence it is also translated as „character" (*RSV*) or "perseverance" (*JB*). Aquinas' commentary on *probatio* (*Ad Rom.* cap. 5, lect. 2) employs James 1:3 in developing the notion of how the testing of one's faith produces patience.

181. Cf. *Ad Rom.* cap. 12, lect. 2.

tions) or in order to test us and to put patience into practice.[182] In this second regard, both Abraham and Job are examples of those who have suffered temptation in order to show others their patience in resisting evil and doing good.[183] In his commentary on the book of Job, Aquinas uses the image of gold being tested and made manifest by fire, in order to illustrate why Job's patience and virtue in general is put to the test in order to be a source of witness for others. In commenting on Job (23:10), "He will prove me like gold which passes through fire," Aquinas says: "just as gold does not become true gold but its genuineness is manifested to men as a result of the fire, so Job has been proved through adversity not so that his virtue might appear before God but so that it might be manifested to men."[184]

Aquinas correlates the development of patience with Paul's teaching on corporal mortification (Col 3:5–17).[185] Aquinas interprets Paul's directional metaphor, to seek what is above, as meaning focusing on Christ, the Kingdom of God, a restored life of justice, a justified relation with God (Mt 6:33); these are the greatest goods and give order to all earthly goods. In order to integrate this finality, that "our desire must be on him,"[186] we must put to death earthly ways, the old nature, and its practices. We must die to evil ways and mortify our carnal desires. Aquinas highlights that this is a life-giving rather than a morbid perspective. Taking off the old demands putting on the new way of life and being "renewed in knowledge after the image of its creator" (Col 3:10). Patience, forbearing others, and forgiveness are all tools specifically fit for facing adversity, when we need to remain rooted in the love of God and the rectitude of justice (patience), to endure others' weaknesses (forbearance), and to pardon their offenses (forgiveness).[187] Such virtues are the result of charity at work in the mortification of sinful, and enlivening of good, activities.

Aquinas' commentary on the Lord's Prayer explicitly notes the import of patience for transforming tribulations into something good. Aquinas recognizes that all who want to live in Christ will suffer tribulation or temptation (2 Tm 3, 12) and that the Lord's Prayer teaches us to pray more specifically *not to be led* into temptation. Aquinas emphasizes that this petition does not request a life without temptation, but rather that we do not con-

182. Cf. *III Sent.* 19, 1, 2, ad 2.

183. Cf. *In orat. dom.* pet. 6.

184. Cf. *In Job,* cap. 23, ln. 160–72.

185. Cf. *Ad Col.* cap. 3, lect. 1 and 2.

186. *Ad Col.* cap. 3, lect. 1; with references to Mt 24:28 and Mt 6:21.

187. Cf. *Ad Col.* cap. 3, lect. 3 (Col 3:16–17).

sent to the inevitable temptations experienced. For temptation gives the opportunity of receiving the crown of eternal life (Jas 1:12; Rom 5:3), of finding the liberty of the children of God (*In ora. dom.* pet. vi.), and of itself being transformed into untold good (*In ora. dom.* pet. vii). Aquinas says that it is God who frees us from temptation and evil, works consolation, and converts situations of temptation and tribulation into something good.

We shall note one last cognitive, or rather sapiential, point. Aquinas argues that God demonstrates his wisdom by freeing us from evil and by converting tribulations into something good: "This is a sign of the greatest wisdom, because wisdom orders evil toward the good through patience, which is realized through tribulations."[188] In particular, the Holy Spirit, working through the gift of wisdom, makes us ask to participate in the transformation of tribulation. Thus, we cooperate in acquiring the patience needed to become mature children of God. This type of intelligent patience is an all-weather virtue; as Aquinas says: "through patience, one has peace both in prosperity and adversity."[189]

188. *In orat. dom.* pet. vii.
189. Ibid.

10

Conclusions

Resilience Research and the Renewal of Moral Theology

> *You understand that your faith is only put to the test to make you patient, but patience too is to have its practical results so that you will become fully developed, complete, with nothing missing.*
>
> JAMES 1:3–4 (JB)*

The existential bridge that allows us to relate the psychosocial sciences and St. Thomas's virtue theory is not only the reality of difficulty, but also the resourcefulness needed to overcome it, that is, the individual and social capacities to cope with difficulty, to resist destruction under hardship, and to construct something positive out of an otherwise negative situation. Both the virtue of fortitude (with its associated virtues of initiative and endurance) and resilience (as concept, phenomenon, and practice) relate to

* The letter of James 1:4 is often used by Aquinas, in many of his Scripture commentaries (11 different ones) and in his *ST* in the following places: I-II 61.3 obj. 3; I-II 66.4 obj 2 and ad 2; II-II 136.2 obj. 1 and ad 1; II-II 184.1 obj. 3 and ad 3, as well as in *De virt. com.* 5, 1 obj. 14 and 5, 4 obj. 12

difficulty. Both fortitude and resilience contribute to a fundamentally positive perspective that counters an excessive focus on brokenness, vice, and the effects of sin and psychopathology.

The resilience metaphor has been applied to physical, psychosocial, and spiritual domains. In the latter, on philosophical and theological levels, resilience involves the ethical, spiritual, and religious processes that render humans capable to cope actively with difficulty, resist deformation of competencies, and construct from the unfavorable situation using spiritual resources. Through a meta-analysis of resilience findings on temperament, emotions, cognition, and volition, I have inductively identified resources and strategies that support resilience outcomes. In turn, I have brought these insights into a critical and constructive dialogue with Aquinas' understanding of philosophical anthropology, virtue theory, and Christian virtues in order to participate in renewing moral theology.

Methodology is the bane of any interdisciplinary research, perhaps especially for a moral theology that seeks to remain theological while integrating other sciences (Part One). Moral theology, when following Aquinas' example, brings the theological tradition of the Church into dialogue with the sciences on human nature and moral agency. I have made the case that we can employ resilience research to contribute to a more robust philosophy of nature and philosophical anthropology, to clarify moral analysis, and to continue a renewal in moral theology. The various domains of resilience research—psychology, developmental theories, social sciences, and evolutionary theory—offer insights into human nature and moral agency (the natural virtues, especially those that concern the management of adversity). But they do not offer, in and of themselves, a complete framework or analysis. As empirical and descriptive sciences or clinical theories, the psychosocial sciences need completion at the level of philosophical, metaphysical, and ethical bases and analyses. Philosophy and theology have contributions to make at these levels.

While moral theology draws resources from descriptive, normative, and theological sciences, the appropriation of these sciences does not involve an indiscriminate ordering. We do not pretend that moral theology simply acquires the accumulated "scientific" status of the study with which it dialogues. That is, we avoid a naturalistic approach that directly draws ethics from psychosocial sciences. We affirm a nonmechanistic view of nature that resists reductionism and materialism, while being open to experiential, realist reflections. We have thus followed the method of Aquinas, while employing insights from Stephen J. Pope's "critical appropriation model." In particular, Aquinas accords a tertiary, but important, place to philosophical and other scientific arguments and observations in doing moral theology. These sciences are not on the same level as Scripture and tradition, but they provide "extrinsic and probable" arguments for understanding human agency. This ordered approach does not denigrate the input that empirical and descriptive sciences bring at the level of human agency, but it puts them in a larger normative and theological context. In short, resilience insights coming from descriptive sciences can thus enrich Aquinas' virtue-based ethical theory and moral theology at the level of its philosophy of nature and philosophical anthropology, by offering bases to further explain and understand its notions of finality and flourishing, emotions in moral development, and virtue education.

On the level of acquired natural virtue (Part Two), reflections on fortitude are the most obvious dialogue partners for psychosocial resilience research—both concentrate on the human response to adversity and the place that fear and daring play therein. Psychosocial research, for its part, highlights fear's utility and purpose in resilience, as well as that of temperament (e.g., timidity and audacity). Research describes the neurological, physiological, and psychological interactions that underlie fear-related emotional, cognitive, and motivational dispositions. This research enriches Aquinas' analysis of fear. In particular, his model of thought can incorporate the physiological and neurological considerations of cognition, motivation, and emotion without reducing the human experience to the biophysical level. His experiential and realist metaphysical teaching on the natural virtue of fortitude constructively adds to our understanding of human agency in difficulty and of its interrelated causes, from the more proximate to the more profound. This approach provides a wider philosophical and psychological foundation to appreciate moral agency in the midst of fear. For Aquinas, we master or succumb to fear in the practice of fortitude, which demands foreseeing threats and hardships and learning from failures. He contributes a richer type of moral resilience to the debate. In particular, he treats fortitude developmentally and expounds a philosophical psychology of fear and daring with a social analysis of struggle, death, and the common good. On a normative level, this typology of fortitude helps us to comprehend human responsibility and moral resilience.

Aquinas' notions of the virtues of initiative (including *magnanimitas* and *magnificentia*) recognize the specific place of enterprise and resourcefulness in the face of difficulty. Sometimes we must attack or confront the source of adversity in order to overcome or change it. Resilience research, for its part, highlights the role of optimism and generosity in human initiatives. These qualities are important since we confront arduous projects through the energy of the emotions, especially hope and daring. Resilience research in particular shows how we harness daring in confident acts through our capacities to concentrate. Aquinas construes initiative taking in terms of a series of virtues that aim to master the use of the emotions of hope and daring. His approach to initiative focuses on the natural virtue of hope. This virtue of initiative taking manages temperament traits, emotions, and motivations in order to overcome hardship in attaining important and difficult goods. In hope-filled agency, Aquinas affirms that (a desire for and understanding of) excellence leads us to act for more worthwhile ends than does a motivation based on honors alone. Nonetheless, he accents the place of both honors and excellence in providing a further normative framework, while avoiding vainglory and ambition. Resilience research and Aquinas' reflections enrich each other to offer a nuanced typology of the natural virtue of hope. In this view, to overcome the difficulty involved in practical human acts, we need not only concentration and hope, but also a drive for flourishing and excellence. This type of natural hope and daring risk taking underlies constructive resilience.

In order to resist more consistently the destructive effects of adversity, we need to master the emotions and dispositions that underlie endurance as well. For Aquinas, we endure loss, suffering, and pain through the virtues of patience and perseverance. The resilience perspective on endurance responses to adversity helps us to appreciate and supplement Aquinas' typology of these virtues, as well as the related vices. In particular, research on the management of sorrow and waiting adds insights to Aquinas' moral theory. For example, it aids us in understanding moral progress and the role that patience and perseverance play in managing sorrow, pain, and suffering. In dialogue, Aquinas and the resilience research collaborate in offering a richer notion of the virtuous endurance that we might call resistant resilience.

Grace transforms the virtue of fortitude for Aquinas (Part Three). His theological vision of the transformation of natural fortitude has radical implications for the way in which spiritual resilience completes moral and psychosocial resilience. The theological tenor of fortitude (as an infused virtue, an act of martyrdom, the beatitude of the just, and the sevenfold gift of the Holy Spirit) specifies a type of markedly Christian resilience. Aquinas—following St. Augustine—recognizes that the Christian tradition emphasizes the gift of the Holy Spirit, the beatitudes (and the rest of the Sermon on the Mount), and the precepts of the Lord's Prayer in spiritual agency. Through fortitude, human beings participate in divine hardiness by (1) their openness to the gift of fortitude, (2) their acts aimed at the beatitude of those who hunger and thirst for justice, and (3) their following the inspiration of the precept of fortitude. As an infused virtue, fortitude illustrates a type of resilient agency that participates in divine strength, in the midst of human fear, trials, and weakness. Furthermore, Aquinas' conception of Christian martyrdom offers an archetype for spiritual resilience, based upon friendship-love and justice. It resists critiques that claim that Christianity nurtures vulnerability.

Aquinas' conception of grace that operates through the virtues of initiative taking opens the way for understanding a theological dimension in resilient initiative. Indeed, the theological extension of constructive resilience and of initiative-taking virtues illustrates the roles that being honorable and seeking excellence (involved in human initiatives and divine purpose) play in spiritual resilience. The infused greatness and initiative specified in constructive projects and generosity (that include acts of adoration and religion) and in great intentions and plans (that find their inspiration in the Gospel) display a particularly Christian type of resilience, as do theological honor and excellence that serve to plan, motivate, and complete projects whose source and finality is in God. This type of initiative involves interdependence, meekness, and humility, while seeking to honor God and serve others.

Aquinas gracefully articulates the theological difference involved in infused patience and perseverance, which illustrate the stamina of spiritual resilience. This theological extension of resistant resilience, modeled on the virtues of endurance, illustrates further ways to manage pain, suffering, and loss. Theological patience, perseverance, long-suffering, and constancy find their source in God's patience, as expressed through Jesus Christ, who serves as the archetype for a Christian response to pain and suffering, including the ultimate and extreme instances that we all need to face, especially near death. Aquinas identifies other theological developments that support patience. Grace completes and elevates emotions, reason, and will through resisting and overcoming the difficulties that punctuate our way to our ultimate good. This grace involves a theologically informed hope that permeates daily work as well. It enables our reception of the gift of knowledge and makes possible acts inspired by the beatitude of mourners and the fruit of patience. These theological movements extend patience and perseverance and illustrate a way to resist suffering and evil. On the developmental level, Aquinas' theological approach to enduring hardship and waiting for the attainment of good can transform psychosocial resilience insights on pain, suffering, and resisting. As an indispensable element, we have to integrate our own experience, which is based on our experience of God through the theological virtues of faith, hope, and love. At the same time, the experience of others—especially those who have resiliently overcome difficulty—offers us food for thought and a model for resilient behavior. Nonetheless, the level of supernatural or graced virtue cannot find empirical or statistical corroboration based on external observations alone. Aquinas' theological reflections on the life of grace involve the non–empirically verifiable, lived experience of the Christian tradition (scriptural, patristic, mystic, and liturgical sources) that finds able witnesses among the resilient followers of Christ.

Much remains to be done in the dialogue between the psychosocial sciences at the levels of anthropology, ethics, and moral theology. There is promise in the renewal of Christian anthropology based upon a dialogue with resilience research and positive psychologies, rather than on psychopathology alone (that is, rather than a focus on abnormal psychology or even sin per se). More extensive research on the application of Christian virtue theory in clinical settings and through empirical studies might help us to better articulate the deeper teachings of the tradition on human nature and agency, especially concerning human flourishing, freedom, and responsibility in pursuit of the good. It might help us to integrate better the biophysical, psychosocial, ethical, and spiritual dimensions of the human person and society into efforts at promoting health and overcoming illness, developing virtuously and overcoming vicious tendencies, and living in community toward a hope that is eschatological.

This method—and that of Aquinas—holds that truth is one. The truths about human resilience can help us better understand human virtues that face hardships. Nonetheless, resilience findings are shaped by the researcher's worldview and anthropology. Resilience itself—as if it were a pure phenomenon of survival, taken outside of a larger philosophy of nature and ethical context—might dangerously promote survival at any cost. The type of surviving and thriving that we promote is the issue. We can avoid reductionist tendencies if we understand that resilience is more than material survival of the fittest. In this book, I have therefore confidently sought to avoid the shortfalls of interdisciplinary methods that simplistically revamp major elements in philosophical or theological ethics based on the psychosocial sciences' tentative theories and empirical findings. Rather than simply providing conceptual clarifications or interpretations of empirical research, I have sought to employ them both in a larger and deeper understanding of the human person concerning human nature and agency in the midst of difficulty. Thereby, I do not intend to limit moral theology by any reductionist research method, but rather to suggest that an ordered interdisciplinary dialogue will help to renew moral theology and ethics, while being able to contribute to a heartier anthropology as well.

Our contemporary understanding of Aquinas and of Catholic moral theology is in a process of renewal. We are struggling to escape dualistic, underspecified, or misdirected ideas of human nature that reduce humans to our biophysical-neurological bases, to psychological tendencies, or to social interactions. We furthermore seek to overcome (1) exaggerated notions of rules and duty that eclipse the primacy and influence of faith, hope, and charity, as well as (2) narrowed notions of virtue that recognize neither the wounds of sin nor the transforming effects of grace. In turn, following the leads of Aquinas' virtue-based anthropology provides us a larger ethical and theological context than is possible in reductionist or nonintegrated psychosocial sciences alone. In this regard, Aquinas' natural-law approach to moral norms and pedagogy offers guidelines and a framework for human resilience; moreover, his approach to the New Law of grace and the infused virtues offers a fuller understanding of spiritual resilience. Aquinas offers us a vibrant realist, metaphysical model of moral theology. He offers more as well. His reflections on natural and graced life faced with adversity contain invaluable insights, but they cannot be understood without some interpretive effort. They serve as a valid basis for conversation with contemporary experience and research that aid the ongoing renewal in moral theology that is dear to us all.

Abbreviations

Theological Tradition: Revelation, Magisterium, and Patristic Sources

Aquinas, St. Thomas

Ad Col. *Super ad Coloss.*
Ad Eph. *Super ad Ephesios*
Ad Gal. *Super ad Galatas*
Ad Heb. *Super ad Hebr.*
Ad Phil. *Super ad Philippenses*
Ad Joan. *Super evangelium Joannis*
Ad Mat. *Com. ad evangelium Matthaei*
Ad Rom. *Com. in epistolam ad Romanos*
Catena aurea *Glossa continua super Evangelia*
Comp. theo. *Compendium theologiae*
De car. *Quaestiones disputatae de caritate*
De malo *Quaest. disputatae de malo*
De Trin. *In Librum Boethii de Trinitate*
De verit. *Quaest. disputatae de veritate*
De virt. card. *Quaest. disputatae de virtutibus cardinalibus*
De virt. com. *Quaest. disputatae de virtutibus in communi*
I ad Thess. *Super I ad Thess*
I ad Timoth. *Super I ad Timoth.*
II ad Cor. *Super II ad Corinthinios*

II ad Thess. *Super II ad Thess.*

II ad Timoth. *Super II ad Timoth.*

In De anima *Sententia libri De anima*

In Eth. *In decem libros Ethicorum Aristotelis ad Nic. expositio*

In Job *Expositio super Job*

In Lib. causis *In Librum de Causis*

In Meta. *In duodecim libros Meta-physicorum Aristotelis*

In orat. dom. *Collatio in orationem dominicam*

In Psalmos *Postilla super Psalmos*

In sal. ang. *In salutationem angelicam*

In symb. apost. *Collatio in Symbolum Apostolorum*

Rigans montes *Rigans montes de superioribus*

SCG *Summa contra Gentiles*

Sent. *Scriptum super liberos Sententiarum*

ST *Summa theologiae*

QDL *Quaestiones quodlibetales*

Bible (texts and translations)

Greek NT *The Greek New Testament*

LXX *Septuagint*

Vulgata *Biblia Sacra iuxta versionem*

RSV *Revised Standard Version*

JB *Jerusalem Bible*

NAB *New American Bible*

Magisterial Documents

CCC *Catechism of the Catholic Church*

FR *Fides et ratio*

GE *Gravissimum educationis*

GS *Gaudium et spes*

LG *Lumen gentium*

PDG *Pascendi Dominici gregis*

SC *Sapientia Christiana*

VS *Veritatis splendor*

Patristic and Ancient Sources

De fide orthod. St. John Damascene, *De fide orthodoxa*

De div. nom. Dionysius (pseudo-Areopagite), *De divinis nominibus*

De parad. St. Ambrose, *De paradiso*

De offic. St. Ambrose, *De officibus*
Definit. Chrysippus, *Dialectical Definitions*
Etym. St. Isadore of Seville, *Etymologies*
Hom. super Ezech. St. Gregory the Great, *Homiliae in Hiezechielem prophetam*
In Ev. St. Gregory the Great, *In Evangelia homiliae*
Moral. St. Gregory the Great, *Moralia in Job*

Augustine

Conf. *Confessiones*
Contra Faust. *Contra Faustum Manicheum*
De Civ. Dei *De Civitate Dei*
De corrept. *De correptione et gratia*
De lib. arbit. *De libero arbitrio*
De morib. eccl. *De moribus ecclesiae catholicae*
De nat. et grat. *De natura et gratia*
De pat. *De patientia*
De persev. *De perseverentia*
De sermone *De sermone Domini in monte*
De Trin. *De Trinitatis*
OQ *Octoginta trium quest.*
Retract. *Retractiones*
Soliloq. *Soliloquia*

Philosophical Sources

Aristotle

EE *Eudamean Ethics*
Metaph. *Metaphysics*
NE *Nicomachean Ethics*
Pol. *Politics*
Rhet. *Rhetoric*
Top. *Topica*

Cicero, Marcus Tullius

Fin. *De finibus bonorum et malorum*
Off. *De officiis*
Rhet. *De inventione rhetorica*
Rhet. ad Her. *Rhetorica ad Herennium*
Tusc. *Tusculanae disputationes*

Collective References

Journals, Dictionaries, Encyclopedias

AFP *Archivum Fratrum Praedicatorum*
Con *Concilium*
DCT *Dictionnaire critique de théologie*
Denzinger Denzinger and Schönmetzer, *Enchiridion Symbolorum*
DEPM *Dictionnaire d'éthique et de philosophie morale*
DdP *Dictionnaire de philosophie*
DOTTE *The New International Dictionary of Old Testament Theology and Exegesis*
DMC *Dictionnaire de moral catholique*
DS *Dictionnaire de la spiritualité*
DTC *Dictionnaire de théologie catholique*
ERE *Encyclopedia of Religion and Ethics*
EThL *Ephemerides theologicae. Lovanienses*
FZPT *Freiburger Zeitschrift für Philosophie und Theologie*
GELNT *Greek-English Lexicon of the New Testament and Other Early Christian Literature*
JSSR *Journal for the Scientific Study of Religion*
JRel *Journal of Religion*
JRE *Journal of Religious Ethics*
NCE *New Catholic Encyclopedia*
NDTh *New Dictionary of Theology*
NJBC *New Jerome Biblical Commentary*
NRT *Nouvelle revue théologique*
NV *Nova et vetera*
PG *Patrologia graeca, ed. J. P. Mignes*
PL *Patrologia latina, ed. J. P. Mignes*
RETM *Revue d'éthique et de théologie morale*
RT *Revue Thomiste*
RSPT *Revue des sciences philosophique et théologique*
RevScRel *Revue des sciences réligieuses*
RTAM *Recherches de théologie ancienne et médiévale*
RTL *Rivista teologica di Lugano*
TDNT *Theological Dictionary of the New Testament (Kittel)*
TS *Theological Studies*
VTB *Vocabulaire de théologie Biblique*
WEUD *Webster's Encyclopedia Unabridged Dictionary*
Zygon *Zygon: Journal of Religion and Science*

Bibliography

Primary Sources (in Theology and Philosophy)

Thomas Aquinas

Thomas Aquinas. *Thomae Aquinatis opera omnia:* cum hypertextibus CD-ROM. Edited by Roberto Busa. Milano: Ed. Elettronica Editel, 1992.

_______. *Summa theologiae,* Cura et studio Petri Caramello, cum textu ex recensione Leonina. Taurini, Romae: Marietti, 1952.

In consultation with these translations of Aquinas' works

_______. *Aristotle's De Anima with the Commentary of St. Thomas Aquinas.* Translated by K. Foster and S. Humphries. New Haven: Yale University Press, 1951.

_______. *Commentary on the Metaphysics of Aristotle.* Translated by J. P. Rowan. Chicago: Regnery, 1964.

_______. *Commentary on the Nichomachean Ethics.* Translated by C. I. Litzinger. Chicago: Regnery, 1964.

_______. *Commentary on St. John.* Translated by James A. Weisheipl with F. R. Larcher. Vol. 1. Albany, NY: Magi Books: 1980.

_______. *Commentary on St. Paul's Epistle to the Ephesians.* Translated by M. L. Lamb. Albany, NY: Magi Books, 1966.

_______. *Commentary on St. Paul's Epistle to the Galatians.* Translated by F. R. Larcher. Albany, NY: Magi Books, 1966.

_______. *Commentary on St. Paul's Epistle to the Philippians.* Translated by F. R. Larcher. Albany, NY: Magi Books, 1968.

_______. *Commentary on St. Paul's Epistle to the Thessalonians.* Translated by Michael Duffy. Albany, NY: Magi Books, 1968.

_______. *Compendium of Theology.* Translated by Cyril Vollert. Herder: St. Louis, 1947.

______. *The Division and Methods of the Sciences. Questions V and VI of his Commentary on the* De Trinitate *of Boethius.* Translated, intro., and notes by Armand Maurer. 4th ed. Toronto: Pontifical Institute of Mediaeval Studies, 1986.

______. *De Caelo,* by Aristotle. Translated by J. L. Stocks. In *The Works of Aristotle,* vol. 2, edited by W. D. Ross. Oxford: Clarendon Press, 1930.

______. *In Decem Libros Ethicorum Aristotelis ad Nicomachum,* cura ac studio Angeli M. Pirotta. Taurini: Marietti, 1934.

______. *The Disputed Questions on Truth.* Vol. 1, Translated by Robert William Mulligan, S.J. Chicago: Henry Regnery Co., 1952. Vol. 2, translated by James V. McGlynn, S.J. Chicago: Henry Regnery Co., 1953. Vol. 3, translated by Robert W. Schmidt, S.J. Chicago: Henry Regnery Co., 1954.

______. *On Evil.* Translated by Jean Oesterle. Notre Dame: University of Notre Dame Press, forthcoming.

______. *Faith, Reason, and Theology,* Questions I–IV of the Commentary on Boethius' De Trinitate. Translated by Armand Maurer. Toronto: Pontifical Institute of Mediaeval Studies, 1986.

______. *The Literal Exposition of Job: A Scriptural Commentary concerning Providence.* Translated by Anthony Damico. Atlanta: Scholars Press, 1989.

______. *On Charity.* Translated by L. H. Kendzierski. Milwaukee: Marquette University Press, 1960.

______. *On the Power of God.* Translated by English Dominican Fathers. London: Burns, Oates, and Washbourne, 1932–34.

______. *On the Virtues in General.* Translated by J. P. Reid. Providence, RI: Providence College Press, 1951.

______. *Questions on the Soul.* Translated by James H. Robb. Milwaukee: Marquette University Press, 1984.

______. *Quodlibetal Questions I and II.* Translated with an intro. and notes by Sandra Edwards. Toronto: Pontifical Institute of Mediaeval Studies, 1983.

______. *Somme théologique.* Translated by Aimon-Marie Roguet. Edited by Albert Raulin. Paris: Ed. du Cerf, 1990.

______. *Summa theologiae.* Translated by English Dominicans. London: Burns, Oates, and Washbourne, 1912–36. Repr. New York: Benzinger 1947–48; repr. New York: Christian Classics, 1981.

______. *Summa theologicae: Courage.* Vol. 42. Edited and translated by Anthony Ross and P. G. Walsh. London: Eyre and Spottiswoode, 1966.

______. *Summa Contra Gentiles.* Translated by English Dominicans. London: Burns, Oates, and Washbourne, 1934.

The Bible

Biblia Sacra. Iuxta Vulgatam Versionem (1975). 2nd corrected ed. 2 vols. Stuttgart: Württembergische Bibelanstalt.

The Greek New Testament (1976). Ed. Kurt Aland et al.. 3rd corrected ed. Stuttgart: United Bible Societies.

The Jerusalem Bible (1966). London: Darton, Longman and Todd.

New American Bible (1991). Translated by Catholic Biblical Association of America. New York: Catholic Book Publishing Co. Electronic version Liguori.

The New Jerusalem Bible (1985). Garden City, NY: Doubleday.

The New Oxford Annotated Bible with the Apocrypha, Revised Standard Version (1976). New York: Oxford University Press.

The Revised Standard Version of the Bible (1971). Division of Christian Education of the National Council of the Churches of Christ. Electronic version Liguori, 1995.

Aristotle

Aristotle. *The Complete Works of Aristotle.* Revised Oxford translation, edited by Jonathan Barnes. Princeton: Princeton University Press, 1984 (used for quotes in the text).

______. *The Basic Works of Aristotle.* Edited and introduction by Richard McKeon. New York: Random House, 1941.

______. *L'Ethique à Nicomaque.* Intro., translation, and commentary by R.-A. Gauthier and J.-Y. Jolif, ... vol. 2nd ed. Louvain: Publications Universitaires, 1970.

______. *Ethique de Nicomaque.* Nouvelle trad. avec introduction, note et index par J. Tricot. Paris: J. Vrin, 1959.

______. *Les Grands Livres d'Ethiques (La Grande Morale).* Translated by Catherine Dalimier, presentation and notes by Pierre Pellegrin. Paris: Arléa, 1992.

______. *The Nicomachean Ethics.* Translated by W. D. Ross. Revised by J. O. Urmson. In *The Complete Works of Aristotle,* ed. J. Barnes. Princeton: Princeton University Press, 1984.

______. *The Nicomachean Ethics.* With an English translation by H. Rackham. Cambridge, MA: Loeb Library, 1982.

______. *Nikomachische Ethik.* Translated by Franz Dirlmeier. Berlin: Akademie-Verlag, 1956.

______. *Opera Omnia, Greace et latine cum indice nominum et rerum.* Vol. 2. Edited by Cats Bussemaker. Hildesheim/New York: Georg Olms, 1973.

Augustine

Augustine. *St. Augustine Select Letters.* Translated by J. H. Baxter. London: W. Heinemann, 1965.

______. *De patientia, PL* 40, 611–26. *Patience.* Translated by L. Meagher. In *Treatises on Various Subjects.* Vol. 16. New York: Fathers of the Church, 1952.

______. *De sermone Domini in monte, PL* 34, col. 1229–1308. *Explication du sermon sur la montagne.* Presentation and translation by A. G. Hamman. Paris: Desclée de Brouwer, 1978.

______. *Oeuvres de Saint Augustin. II. Problèmes moraux.* Translated and notes by Gustave Combes. Paris: Desclée de Brouwer, 1937.

Cicero

Cicero, Marcus Tullius. *De finibus bonorum et malorum.* With English translation by H. Rackham. Cambridge, MA: Harvard University Press, 1994.

______. *De natura deorum.* With English translation by H. Rackham. Cambridge, MA: Harvard University Press, 1994.

______. *De officiis.* With English translation by Walter Miller. Cambridge, MA: Harvard University Press, 1990.

______. *On Duties.* Edited by Miriam T. Griffin and E. Margaret Atkins. Cambridge, UK: Cambridge University Press, 1991.

______. *Rhetorica ad Herennium.* With English translation by Harry Caplan. Cambridge, MA: Harvard University Press, 1989.

Secondary Sources

Achenbach, Thomas M. (1990). "Conceptualization of Developmental Psychopathology." In *Handbook of Developmental Psychopathology,* edited by M. Lewis and S. M. Miller, 3–14. New York: Plenum.

Ainsworth, Mary D., et al. (1978). *Patterns of Attachment: A Psychological Study of the Strange Situation.* Hillsdale, NJ: L. Erlbaum.

Albrecht, Pierre Yves, and Jean Zermatten (1991). *L'Archer blanc: De la dépendance à l'initiation.* Chapelle-sur-Moudon (CH): Ed. Ketty et Alexandre.

Aldous, Joan (1983). "Problematic Elements in the Relationships between Churches and Families." In W. V. D'Antonio and J. Aldous, ed., *Families and Religions: Conflict and Change in Modern Society*, 67–80. Beverly Hills, CA: Sage.

Allport, Gordon W. (1937/1961). *Pattern and Growth in Personality*. New York: Holt, Rinehart and Winston.

_______ (1950/1967). *The Individual and His Religion: A Psychological Interpretation*. New York: MacMillan.

Allport, Gordon W., and J. M. Ross (1967). "Personal Religious Orientation and Prejudice." *Journal of Personality and Social Psychology* 5: 432–43.

Anderson, E. (1991). "Neighborhood Effects on Teenage Pregnancy." In C. Jencks and P. E. Peterson, eds., *The Urban Underclass*, 375–98. Washington, DC: Brookings Institute.

Anderson, Kathryn Hoehn (1998). "The Relationship between Family Sense of Coherence and Family Quality of Life after Illness Diagnosis." In H. I. McCubbin et al., eds., *Stress, Coping, and Health in Families: Sense of Coherence and Resiliency*, 169–87. Thousand Oaks, CA: SAGE.

Annas, Julia (1993). *The Morality of Happiness*. New York: Oxford University Press.

Anscombe, G. E. M. (1981, orig. 1958). "Modern Moral Philosophy." In *Collected Philosophical Papers*. Vol. 3: 26–41. Oxford: Oxford University Press.

Anthony, E. J., and B. J. Cohler, eds. (1987). *The Invulnerable Child*. New York: Guilford Press.

Antonovsky, Aaron (1979). *Health, Stress and Coping: New Perspectives on Mental and Physical Well-Being*. San Francisco: Jossey-Bass, 1979.

_______ (1987). *Unraveling the Mystery of Health*. San Francisco: Jossey-Bass, 1987.

_______ (1998). "The Sense of Coherence: An Historical and Future Perspective." In H. I. McCubbin et al., eds., *Stress, Coping, and Health in Families: Sense of Coherence and Resiliency*, 3–20. Thousand Oaks, CA: SAGE.

Arnold, Magda. B. (1960). *Personality and Emotion*. New York: Colombia University Press.

Arnould, Jacques (1994). "René Dubos, Pionnier de l'écologie scientifique." *RSPT* 78: 81–94.

_______ (1996). "Le débat contemporain entre sociobiologie et théologie. Quelques éléments d'information pour une réflexion." *RSPT* 80: 221–42.

Ashley, Benedict M. (1961). "A Social Science Founded on a Unified Natural Science." In James Weisheipl, ed., *The Dignity of Sciences*. Washington, DC: Thomist Press.

_______ (1985). *Theologies of the Body: Humanist and Christian*. Braintree, MA: Pope John Center.

Augrain, Charles (1995). "Martyr." In *VTB*, 723–24.

Averill, James R. (1982). "A Constructivist View of Emotions." In R. Plutchik and H. Kelleman, eds., *Theories of Emotion*, 305–39. New York: Academic Press.

Averill, James R., and E. P. Nunely (1992). *Voyages of the Heart: Living an Emotionally Creative Life*. New York: Free Press.

Bahr, S., R. Hawks, and G. Wang (1993). "Family and Religious Influences on Adolescent Substance Abuse." *Youth and Society* 24: 443–65.

Bainbridge, William Sims (1992). "Crime, Delinquency, and Religion." In John F. Schumaker, ed., *Religion and Mental Health*, 199–210. New York: Oxford University Press.

Baird, R. M. (1985). "Meaning in Life: Discovered or Created?" *Journal of Religion and Health* 24: 117–24.

Baldwin, Alfred L., Clara Baldwin, and Robert E. Cole (1990). "Stress-Resistant Families and Stress-Resistant Children." In Jon Rolf et al., eds., *Risk and Protective Factors*, 257–80. Cambridge, UK: Cambridge University Press.

Bandura, Albert (1977). *Social Learning Theory*. Englewood Cliffs, NJ: Prentice-Hall.

_______ (1986). *Social Foundations of Thoughts and Action*. Englewood Cliffs, NJ: Prentice-Hall.

Barad, Judith (1991). "Aquinas on the Role of Emotions in Moral Judgment and Activity." *Thomist* 55: 394–413.

Barbour, Ian (1974). *Myth, Models, Paradigms.* New York: Harper and Row.

Bardy, Gustave (1953). "Cyprien (Saint)." In *DS* II.2: 2661–69.

Batson, C. Daniel, and W. Larry Ventis (1982). *The Religious Experience.* New York: Oxford University Press.

Bauer, Walter (1979). *A Greek-English Lexicon of the New Testament and Other Early Christian Literature (GELNT).* Chicago: University of Chicago Press.

Baumeister, Roy F., Laura Smart, and Joseph M. Boden (1996). "Relation of Threatened Egotism to Violence and Aggression: The Dark Side of High Self-Esteem." *Psychological Review* 103: 5–33.

Beattie, Melody (1987). *Codependent No More.* New York: Harper/Hazelden.

Bellah, Robert, et al. (1986). *Habits of the Heart: Individualism and Commitment in American Life.* New York: Perennial.

Benard, Bonnie (1987). "Protective Factor Research: What We Can Learn from Resilient Children." *Prevention Forum* 7, no. 3: 1–11.

Berger, Peter (1983). "On the Obsolescence of the Concept of Honor." In S. Hauerwas and A. MacIntyre, eds., *Revisions: Changing Perspectives in Moral Philosophy,* 172–81. Notre Dame: University of Notre Dame Press.

Berger, Peter L. (1997). *Redeeming Laughter: The Comic Dimension of Human Experience.* Berlin: Walter de Gruyter.

Berger, Peter L., and Thomas Luckmann (1966). *The Social Construction of Reality: A Treatise in the Sociology of Knowledge.* Garden City, NY: Doubleday.

Bernard, Charles-A. (1964). "Fruits du Saint-Esprit." *DS* V:1569–75.

Bjorck, Jeffrey P., and Lisa L. Klewicki (1997). "The Effects of Stressor Type on Projected Coping." *Journal of Traumatic Stress* 10, no. 3: 481–97.

Bloom, Martin (1996). "Primary Prevention and Resilience: Changing Paradigms and Changing Lives." In R. Hampton et al., eds., *Preventing Violence in America,* 78–114. London: Sage Publications.

Bodenmann, Guy, and Meinrad Perrez (1993). "Le stress et sa gestion en relations intimes: une approache multimodale." University of Fribourg: Institut de Psychologie.

Boone, James L. (1998). "The Evolution of Magnanimity: When Is It Better to Give than to Receive?" *Human Nature: An Interdisciplinary Biosocial Perspective* 9, no. 1: 1–21.

Boone, James L, and Karen Kessler. 1999. "More Status or More Children: Social Status, Fertility Reduction, and Long-Term Fitness." *Evolution and Human Behavior* 20: 257–77.

Booth, Tim, and Wendy Booth (1997). *Exceptional Childhoods, Unexceptional Children: Growing Up with Parents Who Have Learning Disabilities.* London: Family Policy Centre.

Bowlby, John (1969/1982). *Attachment and Loss.* Vol. 1: *Attachment.* New York: Basic Books.

_______ (1973). *Attachment and Loss.* Vol. 2: *Separation: Anxiety and Anger.* New York: Basic Books.

_______ (1988). "The Arrival of Developmental Psychiatry Has Sounded" (esp. "Continuity and Discontinuity: Vulnerability and Resilience"). *American Journal of Psychiatry* 145, no.1: 1–10.

Bowlin, John R. (1996). "Rorty and Aquinas on Courage and Contingency." *J Rel* 77: 402–20.

Brachtendorf, Johannes (1997). "Cicero and Augustine on the Passions." *Revue des Etudes Augustiniennes* 43: 289–308.

Bradford, John (1993). "Spiritual Dimensions of Resilience." Conference presentation for the International Catholic Child Bureau, Geneva, (3 November) 1993.

_______ (1994). "The Spiritual and Religious Rights of the Child." *Children Worldwide* 21(1): 16-21.

Braibant, Isabelle (1998). *La vertu de patience chex S. Thomas d'Aquin. Etude de la question 136 de la IIa IIae: sources et analyse.* Fribourg: Université de Fribourg.

Brantschen, J.-B. (1992). *Hoffnung für Zeit und Ewigkeit. Der Traum von wachen Christenmenschen.* Freiburg: Herder.

Breznitz, S. (1986). "The Effect of Hope on Coping with Stress." In M. Appley and R. Trumbull, eds., *Dynamics of Stress: Physiological and Social Perspectives*, 295–306. New York: Plenum Press.

Brooks, Jeffrey D. (1998). "Salutogenesis, Successful Aging, and the Advancement of Theory of Family Caregiving." In H. I. McCubbin et al. *Stress, Coping and Health in Families*, 227–48. Thousand Oaks, CA: Sage Publications.

Browning, Don S. (1987). *Religious Thought and the Modern Psychologies: A Critical Conversation in the Theology of Culture*. Philadelphia: Fortress Press.

______ (1999). "The Challenge and Limits of Psychology to Theological Ethics." *Annual of the Society of Christian Ethics* 19: 133–43.

Brugués, Jean-Louis (1984). "L'art de durer." *Communio* 9: 47–58.

______ (1991). *Dictionnaire de morale catholique*. Chambray: C.L.D.

______ (1995). *Précis de théologie morale générale. Tome 1: Méthodologie*. Paris: Mame.

Bujo, Bénézet (1984). *Die Begründung des Sittlichen: Zur Frage des Eudämonismus bei Thomas von Aquin*. Paderborn: F. Schöningh.

Bultmann, Rudolf (1963). "*ἐλπίς, ἐλπίζω*." In Kittel, ed., *TDNT* 2: 517–35.

Burhoe, Ralph Wendell (1986). "War, Peace and Religion's Biocultural Evolution." *Zygon* 21, no. 3: 439–72.

Buss, David (1994). *The Evolution of Desire: Strategies of Human Mating*. New York: Basic Books.

Byers, David M., ed. (1987). *Religion, Science, and the Search for Wisdom*. Washington, DC: USCC.

Cahill, Lisa Sowle (1980/1989). "Moral Methodology: A Case Study." *Chicago Studies* 19: 171–87. Reprinted in Hamel and Himes, eds., 1989, 551–62.

______ (1998). "Community versus Universals: A Misplaced Debate in Christian Ethics." *Annual: SCE* 18: 3–14.

Cahill, Lisa Sowle, and James E. Childress, eds. (1996). *Christian Ethics: Problems and Prospects*. Cleveland: Pilgrim Press.

Canto-Sperber, Monique (1996). *Dictionnaire d'éthique et de philosophie morale (DEPM)*. Paris: PUF.

______ (1996a). "Bonheur." In Canto-Sperber, ed., *DEPM*, 166–77.

______ (1996b). "Courage." In Canto-Sperber, ed., *DEPM*, 333–40.

Carr, Anne E. (1990). *Transforming Grace: Christian Tradition and Women's Experience*. San Francisco: Harper and Row.

Cates, Diane Fritz (1997). *Choosing to Feel: Virtue, Friendship and Compassion for Friends*. Notre Dame: University of Notre Dame Press.

Cessario, Romanus (1991). *The Moral Virtues and Theological Ethics*. Notre Dame: University of Notre Dame Press.

______ (1996). *Christian Faith and the Theological Life*. Washington, DC: Catholic University of America Press.

______ (2001). *Introduction to Moral Theology*. Washington, DC: Catholic University of America Press.

Chamberlain, Kerry, and Sheryl Zika (1992). "Religiosity, Meaning in Life, and Psychological Well-Being." In John F. Schumaker, ed., *Religion and Mental Health*, 138–48. New York: Oxford University Press.

Changeux, Jean-Pierre, and Paul Ricoeur (1998). *La nature et la règle: ce qui nous fait penser*. Paris: Ed. Odile Jacob.

Chapot, Fréderic (1999). "Tertullian." In Allan D. Fitzgerald, ed., *Augustine through the Ages: An Encyclopedia*, 822–24. Grand Rapids, MI: Wm. B. Eerdmans.

Chess, Stella, and Alexander Thomas (1992). "Interactions between Offspring and Parents in Development." In B. Tizzard and V. Varma, eds., *Vulnerability and Resilience in Human Development*, 72–87. London: J. Kingsley.

Cicchetti, Dante (1990). "A Historical Perspective on the Discipline of Developmental Psychopathology." In Jon Rolf et al., eds., *Risk and Protective Factors*, 2–28. Cambridge, UK: Cambridge University Press.

Cicchetti, Dante, and P. Hesse (1983). "Affect and Intellect: Piaget's Contributions to the Study of Infant Emotional Development." In R. Plutchik and H. Kellerman, eds., *Emotion: Research and Theory*, vol. 2, 115–69. New York: Academic Press.

Clarke, Anne M., and Alan D. B. Clarke (1992). "How Modifiable Is the Human Life Path?" *International Review of Research in Mental Retardation* 18: 137–57.

Coie, J. D., et al. (1993). "The Science of Prevention: A Conceptual Framework and Some Directions for a National Research Program." *American Psychologist* 48: 1013–22.

Coles, Robert (1990). *The Spiritual Life of Children*. Boston: Houghton Mifflin.

Comte, August (1875). *System of Positive Polity*. 2 vols. London: Longmans Green.

Comte-Sponville, André (1995). *Petit traité des grandes vertus*. Paris: PUF.

Congar, Yves-Marie (1974). "Le traité de la force dans la Somme Théologique de Saint Thomas d'Aquin." *Angelicum* 51: 331–48.

Consortium on the School-Based Promotion of Social Competence (1994). "The School-Based Promotion of Social Competence: Theory, Research Practice, and Policy." In Robert J. Haggerty et al., eds., *Stress, Risk, and Resilience*, 268–316. Cambridge, UK: Cambridge University Press.

Cottier, Georges (1980). "La foi et les sciences de l'homme." *Nova et Vetera* 3: 161–69.

Cowan, Philip A., Carolyn Pape Cowan, and Marc S. Schulz (1996). "Thinking about Risk and Resilience in Families." In Hetherington and Blechman, eds., *Stress, Coping, and Resiliency in Children and Families*, 1–38.

Crossin, John W. (1985). *What Are They Saying about Virtues?* New York: Paulist Press.

Cunningham, Stanley B. (1985). "The Courageous Villain: A Needless Paradox." *Modern Schoolman* 62: 97–110.

Curran, Charles E. (1971). *Catholic Moral Theology in Dialogue*. Notre Dame: Fides.

Curzer, Howard J. (1990). "A Great Philosopher's Not So Great Account of Great Virtue: Aristotle's Treatment of 'Greatness of Soul.'" *Canadian Journal of Philosophy* 20: 517–37.

_______ (1991). "Aristotle's Much Maligned *Megalopsuchos*." *Australasian Journal of Philosophy* 69, no. 2: 131–51.

Cyrulnik, Boris (1998). *Ces enfants qui tiennent le coup*. Revigny-sur-Ornain: Hommes et Perspectives.

_______ (1999). *Un merveilleux malheur*. Paris: Ed. Odile Jacob.

_______ (2001). *Les vilains petits canards*. Paris: Ed. Odile Jacob.

Cyrulnik, Boris, et al. (2000). "La Résilience en question." Joint text. Paris: Fondation pour l'Enfance.

Cyrulnik, Boris, et al. (2000). "La Résilience en question," Joint text. Paris: Fondation pour l'Enfance.

D'Antonio, William V. (1983). "Family Life, Religion, and Societal Values and Structures." In W. V. D'Antonio and J. Aldous, eds., *Families and Religions: Conflict and Change in Modern Society*, 81–108.

D'Antonio, William V., and J. Aldous, eds. (1983.) *Families and Religions: Conflict and Change in Modern Society*. Beverly Hills, CA: Sage.

D'Antonio, William V., and Mark J. Cavanaugh (1983). "Roman Catholicism and the Family." In W. V. D'Antonio and J. Aldous, eds., *Families and Religions: Conflict and Change in Modern Society*, 141–62.

Daly, Robert J., ed. (1984). *Christian Biblical Ethics. From Biblical Revelation to Contemporary Christian Praxis: Method and Content*. New York: Paulist Press.

Damasio, Antonio R. (1994). *Descartes' Error: Emotion, Reason, and the Human Brain*. New York: Grosset / Putman.

______ (1999a). *The Feeling of What Happens: Body and Emotion in the Making of Consciousness.* New York: Harcourt Bruce.

______ (1999b). "How the Brain Creates the Mind." *Scientific American,* December: 74–79.

Damon, William (1990). *The Moral Child: Nurturing Children's Natural Moral Growth.* New York: Free Press.

______ (1999). "The Moral Development of Children." *Scientific American,* August: 56–62.

Danieli, Yael (1994). "Résilience et espoir." *L'Enfance dans le Monde* 21: 47–49.

David, C. Clark, Robert S. Pynoos, and Ann E. Goebel (1994). "Mechanisms and Processes of Adolescent Bereavement." In Robert J. Haggerty et al., eds., *Stress, Risk, and Resilience in Children and Adolescents,* 100–46. Cambridge, UK: Cambridge University Press.

Dawkins, Richard (1976). *The Selfish Gene.* New York/Oxford: Oxford University Press.

______ (1995). *A River out of Eden: A Darwinian View of Life.* New York : Basic Books.

De Laubier, Patrick (1982). *Idées sociales. Essai sur l'origine des courants sociaux contemporains.* Fribourg: Editions Universitaires.

de Lubac, Henri (1964). *Exégèse médiévale.* Vol. 2. Paris: Aubier.

de Waal, Frans B. M. (1997). *Good Natured: The Origins of Right and Wrong in Humans and Other Animals.* Cambridge, MA: Harvard University Press.

______ (1999). "The End of Nature versus Nurture." *Scientific American,* December: 56–61.

Deferrari, Roy J. (1986). *A Latin-English Dictionary of St. Thomas Aquinas.* Boston: St. Paul Editions.

Delhaye, Philippe (1984). "Les morales de l'Esprit et de la nature dans les commentaires bibliques de saint Thomas." In L. J. Elders and K. Hedwig, eds., *The Ethics of St. Thomas Aquinas,* 226–53. Vatican: Libreria Ed. Vaticana.

Deman, Th. (1928). "Le 'Liber de bona fortuna' dans la théologie de saint Thomas d'Aquin." *RSPT* 17: 38–58.

DeMarco, Donald (1996). *The Heart of Virtue: Lessons from Life and Literature Illustrating the Beauty and Value of Moral Character.* San Francisco: Ignatius Press.

Dent, Nicolas J. H. (1981). "The Value of Courage." *Philosophy* 56: 574–77.

______ (1984). *The Moral Psychology of the Values.* Cambridge, UK: Cambridge University Press, 1984.

Diel, Paul (1947/1991). *Psychologie de la motivation.* Paris: Payot.

Dixsaut, Monique (1996). "Générosité et magnanimité." In M. Canto-Sperber, ed., *DEPM,* 595–99.

Donahue, M. J. (1985). "Intrinsic and Extrinsic Religiousness: Review and Meta-analysis." *Journal of Personality and Social Psychology* 48: 400–419.

Dougherty, R. J. (1999). "Natural Law." In Allan D. Fitzgerald, ed., *Augustine through the Ages: An Encyclopedia,* 582–84. Grand Rapids, MI: Wm. B. Eerdmans.

Dubos, René Jules (1959/1987). *Mirage of Health: Utopia, Progress and Biological Change.* New Brunswick: Rutgers University Press.

Dunn, Judy (1988). "Normative Life Events as Risk Factors in Childhood." In M. Rutter, ed., *Studies of Psychosocial Risk,* 227–44. Cambridge, UK: Cambridge University Press.

Durkheim, Emile (1982). *The Rules of Sociological Method.* Translated by W. D. Halls. New York: Free Press.

______ (1995). *The Elementary Forms of Religious Life.* Translated by Karen E. Fields. New York: The Free Press.

Durkin, Kevin (1995). *Developmental Social Psychology: From Infancy to Old Age.* Oxford: Blackwell.

Dyck, Andrew R. (1996). *A Commentary on Cicero, De Officiis.* Ann Arbor: University of Michigan Press.

Edwards, Jonathan (1987; original 1746). *Religious Affections.* New Haven: Yale University Press.

Eisen, George (1988). *Children at Play in the Holocaust: Games among the Shadows.* Amherst: University of Massachusetts Press.

Ekman, Paul (1992). "An Argument for Basic Emotions." *Cognition and Emotion* 6: 169–200.

Ellison, C., et al. (1989). "Does Religious Commitment Contribute to Individual Life Satisfaction?" *Social Forces* 86: 100–123.

Emery, Robert (1994). "Parental Divorce and Children's Well-being." In Haggerty et al., eds., *Stress, Risk, and Resilience in Children and Adolescents,* 64–99. Cambridge, UK: Cambridge University Press.

Erickson, R. C., R. Post, and A. Paige (1975). "Hope as a Psychiatric Variable." *Journal of Clinical Psychology* 31: 324–29.

Erikson, Erik H. (1950/1985). *Childhood and Society.* New York: W. W. Norton.

Eysenck, Michael W. (1982). *Attention and Arousal: Cognition and Performance.* New York: Springer-Verlag.

Felsman, J. Kirk, and George E. Vaillant (1987). "Resilient Children as Adults: A 40-year Study." In Anthony and Cohler, eds., *The Invulnerable Child,* 289–314.

Flew, Anthony (1978). "From Is to Ought." In A. L. Caplan, ed., *The Sociobiology Debate,* 142–62. New York: Harper and Row.

Foote, Philippa (1976). *Virtues and Vices and Other Essays in Moral Philosophy.* Berkeley: University of California Press.

Forschner, Maximilian (1983). "Courage." In Otfried Höffe, ed., *Dictionnaire de morale,* 33–34. Fribourg and Paris: Editions Universitaires Fribourg and Editions du Cerf.

Fowler, James (1974). "Toward a Developmental Perspective on Faith." *Religious Education* 69: 207–19.

_______ (1981). *Stages in Faith: The Psychology of Human Development and the Quest for Meaning.* San Francisco: Harper and Row.

_______ (1982). "Stages of Faith and Adults' Life Cycle." In Kenneth Stokes, ed., *Faith Development in the Adult Life Cycle,* 179–207. New York: W. H. Sadlier.

Frankl, Victor (1963/1984). *Man's Search for Meaning.* New York: WSP.

_______ (1967). *Psychotherapy and Existentialism.* New York: Simon and Schuster.

Freud, Sigmund (1922/1955). *Beyond the Pleasure Principle.* New York: Liveright.

_______ (1961). *Civilization and Its Discontents.* New York: W. W. Norton.

Fuchs, Josef (1980). "Is There a Christian Ethics." In C. Curran and R. McCormick, eds., *The Distinctiveness of Christian Ethics,* vol. 2, 3–19. New York: Paulist Press.

_______ (1993). *Moral Demands and Personal Obligations.* Translated by Brian McNeil. Washington, DC: Georgetown University Press.

Garbarino, James, and Claire Bedard (1996). "Spiritual Challenges to Children Facing Violent Trauma." *Childhood: A Global Journal of Children Facing Violent Trauma* 3: 467–78.

Garber, Judy, and Martin E. P. Seligman (1980). *Human Helplessness: Theory and Applications.* New York: Academic Press.

Garmezy, Norman (1976). *Vulnerable and Invulnerable Children: Theory, Research and Intervention. Master Lecture on Developmental Psychology.* Washington, DC: American Psychological Association (No. 1337).

_______ (1983). "Stressors of Childhood." In N. Garmezy and M. Rutter, eds., *Stress, Coping and Development in Children,* 43–84. New York: McGraw-Hill.

_______ (1985). "Stress Resistant Children: The Search for Protective Factors." In J. E. Stevenson, ed., *Recent Research in Developmental Psychopathology,* 213–33. Pergamon Press.

_______ (1990). "A Closing Note: Reflections on the Future." In Jon Rolf et al., eds., *Risk and Protective Factors,* 527–34.

(1994). "Reflections and Commentary on Risk, Resilience, and Development." In R. J. Haggerty et al., eds., *Stress, Risk, and Resilience in Children and Adolescents: Processes, Mechanisms, and Interventions,* 1 18. Cambridge, UK: Cambridge University Press.

Garmezy, Norman, and Ann Masten (1990). "The Adaptation of Children to a Stressful World: Mastery of Fear." In L. E. Arnold, ed., *Childhood Stress*, ch. 17. New York: Wiley International.

Gauthier, René-Antoine (1951). *Magnanimité: l'idéal de la grandeur dans la philosophie païenne et dans la théologie chrétienne*. Paris: J. Vrin.

Geach, Peter (1979, orig. 1977). *The Virtues*. Cambridge, UK: Cambridge University Press.

Geenan, C. G. (1952). "The Place of Tradition in the Theology of St. Thomas." *Thomist* 15: 110–135.

Geertz, Clifford (1968). *Observing Islam: Religious Development in Morocco and Indonesia*. New Haven: Yale University Press.

_______ (1973). *The Interpretation of Cultures: Selected Essays*. New York: Basic Books.

Gilligan, Carol (1982). *In a Different Voice: Psychological Theory and Women's Development*. Cambridge, MA: Harvard University Press.

_______ (1992). "Reply to Critics." In Mary Jeanne Larrabee, ed., *An Ethic of Care: Feminist and Interdisciplinary Perspectives*, 207–14. New York: Routledge.

Gillon, L.-B. (1959). "L'imitation du Christ et la morale de S. Thomas." *Angelicum* 36: 263–86.

Gilson, Etienne (1946). "La vertu de patience selon saint Thomas et saint Augustin." *Archives d'histoire doctrinale et littéraire du Moyen-âge* 15: 93–104.

Goleman, Daniel (1995). *Emotional Intelligence*. New York: Bantam Books.

_______ (1998). *Working with Emotional Intelligence*. New York: Bantam Books.

Gondreau, Paul (2002). *The Passions of Christ's Soul in the Theology of St. Thomas Aquinas*. Münster: Aschendorff Verlag.

Gore, Susan, and John Eckenrode (1994). "Context and Process in Research on Risk and Resilience." In R. J. Haggerty et al., eds., *Stress, Risk, and Resilience in Children and Adolescents*, 19–63.

Gould, Stephen Jay (1996). *The Mismeasure of Man*. Rev. ed. Paris: Odile Jacob.

_______ (1999). *The Rocks of Ages: Science and Religion in the Fulness of Life*. New York: Ballantine.

Greaves, Margaret (1964). *The Blazon of Honour: A Study in Renaissance Magnanimity*. London: Methuen.

Gregersen, Niels Henrik, and J. Wentzel Van Huyssteen (1998). *Rethinking Theology and Science: Six Models for the Current Dialogue*. Grand Rapids, MI: Wm. B. Eerdmans.

Griffin, Miriam T. (1991). "Introduction." In Cicero, *On Duties*, ix–xxviii. Edited by M. T. Griffin and E. M. Atkins. Cambridge, UK: Cambridge University Press, 1991.

Grotberg, Edith (1995). *A Guide to Promoting Resilience in Children*. The Hague: Bernard van Leer Foundation.

Grundmann, Walter (1967). "*μέγας, μεγαλεῖον*." In G. Kittel, ed., *TDNT* 4: 529–44.

Gula, Richard M. (1982). *What Are They Saying about Moral Norms?* New York: Paulist Press.

Gustafson, James M. (1971/1989). "The Relationship of Empirical Science to Moral Thought." *Catholic Theological Society of America* 26: 122–37. Reprinted in Hamel and Himes 1989, 428–38.

_______ (1981). *Ethics from a Theocentric Perspective*. Vol. 1: *Theology and Ethics*. Chicago: University of Chicago Press.

_______ (1994). *A Sense of the Divine: The Natural Environment from a Theocentric Perspective*. Cleveland: Pilgrim Press.

Haan, Norma (1989). "Coping with Moral Conflict as Resiliency." In T. Dugan and R. Coles, eds., *The Child in Our Times*, 23–44. New York: Brunner / Mazel.

Haggerty, Robert J., et al., eds. (1994). *Stress, Risk, and Resilience in Children and Adolescents: Processes, Mechanisms, and Interventions*. Cambridge, UK: Cambridge University Press.

Hall, Pamela M. (1994). *Narrative and the Natural Law: An Interpretation of Thomistic Ethics*. Notre Dame: University of Notre Dame Press.

Halper, Edward (1999). "The Unity of the Virtues in Aristotle." *Oxford Studies in Ancient Philosophy* 17: 115–43.

Hamburg, B. (1990). *Life Skills Training: Preventive Interventions for Young Adolescents.* New York: Carnegie Council on Adolescent Development.

Hamel, Ronald P., and Kenneth R. Himes (1989). *Introduction to Christian Ethics: A Reader.* New York: Paulist Press.

Hansen, Gary L. (1992). "Religion and Marital Adjustment." In John F. Schumaker, ed., *Religion and Mental Health,* 189–98. New York: Oxford University Press.

Harak, G. Simon (1993). *Virtuous Passions: The Formation of Christian Character.* New York: Paulist Press.

Hardie, W. F. R. (1978). "Magnanimity in Aristotle's Ethics." *Phronesis* 23: 63–79.

Häring, Bernhard (1992). *La théologie morale. Idées maîtresses.* Paris: Cerf.

Harter, S. (1983). "Developmental Perspectives on Self-System." In E. M. Hetherington, ed., *Socialization, personality, and social development.* Vol. 4: *Mussen's Handbook of Child Psychology,* 275–385. 4th ed. New York: Wiley.

Hauerwas, Stanley (1981). *Vision and Virtue.* Notre Dame: University of Notre Dame.

_______ (1993). "The Difference of Virtue and the Difference It Makes: Courage Exemplified." *Modern Theology* 9: 249–64.

Hauerwas, Stanley, and Charles Pinches (1997). *Christians among the Virtues: Theological Conversations with Ancient and Modern Ethics.* Notre Dame: University of Notre Dame Press.

Hay, Dale F. (1988). "Studying the Impact of Ordinary Life: A Developmental Model, Research Plan and Words of Caution." In M. Rutter, ed., *Studies of Psychosocial Risk,* 245–54.

Hellegouarc'h, J. (1963). *Le vocabulaire latin des relations et des partis politiques sous la République.* Paris: Société d'édition 'Les Belles Lettres.'

Hetherington, E. Mavis, and Elaine A. Blechman, eds. (1996). *Stress, Coping, and Resiliency in Children and Families.* Mahwah, NJ: Erlbaum.

Hill, Reuben (1949). *Families under Stress.* New York: Harper and Row.

Hittinger, Russell (1999). "Veritatis Splendor and the Theology of Natural Law." In J. A. DiNoia and R. Cessario, eds., *Veritatis Splendor and the Renewal of Moral Theology,* 97–127. Princeton: Scepter Publishers.

_______ (2003). *The First Grace: Rediscovering the Natural Law in the Post-Christian World.* Wilmington, DE: ISI Books.

Höffe, Otfried, ed. (1983). *Dictionnaire de morale.* Fribourg and Paris: Editions Universitaires de Fribourg and Editions du Cerf.

Hollenbach, David (1996). "Tradition, Historicity, and Truth in Theological Ethics." In L. S. Cahill and J. E. Childress, eds., *Christian Ethics: Problems and Prospects,* 61–75. Cleveland: Pilgrim Press.

Hood, Ralph W., et al. (1996). *The Psychology of Religion: An Empirical Approach.* 2nd ed. New York: Guilford Press.

Horner, David A. (1998). "What It Takes to Be Great: Aristotle and Aquinas on Magnanimity." *Faith and Philosophy* 15, no. 4: 415–44.

Hudson, Deal W., and Dennis Wm. Moran, eds. (1992). *The Future of Thomism.* Notre Dame: American Maritain Association / University of Notre Dame Press.

Hudson, W. D., et al. (1969). *The Is-Ought Question: A Collection of Papers on the Central Problem in Moral Philosophy.* London: MacMillan.

International Catholic Child Bureau (1994). "The Family and Child Resilience." Special ed. *Children Worldwide.* Geneva: BICE.

Jahoda, Marie (1958). *Current Concepts of Positive Mental Health.* New York: Basic Books.

James, William (1902). *The Varieties of Religious Experience: A Study in Human Nature.* London: Longmans, Green.

Jessor, R., and S. Jessor (1977). *Problem Behavior and Psychosocial Development: A Longitudinal Study of Youth.* New York: Academic Press.

Joachim, H. H. (1951). *Aristotle, the Nicomachean Ethics.* Oxford: Clarendon Press.

Jordan, Mark (1986a). "Aquinas' Construction of a Moral Account of the Passions." *FZPT* 33: 71–97.

_______ (1986b). *Ordering Wisdom.* Notre Dame: University of Notre Dame Press.

_______ (1994). "The *Pars moralis* of the *Summa theologiae* as *Scientia* and as *Ars.*" In Ingrid Craemer-Ruegenberg and Andreas Speer, eds., *Scientia und ars im Hoch- und Spätmittelalter, Miscellanea Mediaevalia* 22, 468–81. Berlin: Walter de Gruyter.

Jullien, J. (1983). "Les sciences humaines laissent-elles encore un avenir à la morale?" *NRT* 4: 481–97.

Jung, Carl (1933). *Modern Man in Search of a Soul.* New York: Harcourt, Brace and World.

Kaczor, Christopher (1998). "Double-Effect Reasoning from Jean Pierre Gury to Peter Knauer." *TS* 59: 297–316.

Kagan, Jerome (1979). *The Growth of the Child: Reflections on Human Development.* Stanford Terrace (UK): Harvester Press.

_______ (1994). *Galen's Prophesy.* New York: Basic Books.

Kagan, Jerome, et al. (1990). "A Temperamental Disposition to the State of Uncertainty." In Jon Rolf et al., eds., *Risk and Protective Factors,* 164–78. Cambridge, UK: Cambridge University Press.

Kahneman, Daniel, and Aaron Tversky (2003). "A Perspective on Judgment and Choice: Mapping Bounded Rationality." *American Psychologist* 58: 697–730.

Keenan, James (1992). "Distinguishing Charity as Goodness and Prudence as Rightness: a Key to Thomas's *Secunda Pars.*" *Thomist* 56: 407–26.

_______ (1994). *Goodness and Rightness in St. Thomas Aquinas's* Summa theologiae. Washington, DC: Georgetown University Press.

Kenny, Anthony (1993). *Aquinas on Mind.* London: Routledge.

Kent, Bonnie (1995). *The Virtues of the Will: The Transformation of Ethics in the Late Thirteenth Century.* Washington, DC: Catholic University of America Press.

King, M. B., and R. A. Hunt (1975). "Measuring the Religious Variable: A National Replication." *JSSR* 14: 13–22.

King, Peter (1999). "Aquinas on Passion." In E. Stump and S. MacDonald, eds., *Aquinas's Moral Theory: Essays in Honor of Norman Kretzmann,* 101–32. Ithaca, N.Y.: Cornell University Press.

Kittel, Gerhard (1964–1976). *Theological Dictionary of the New Testament.* Grand Rapids, MI: Wm. B. Eerdmans.

Kittel, Gerhard, and Gerhard van Rad (1964). "*δοξέω, δόξα.*" In G. Kittel, ed., *TDNT,* 2: 232–55.

Kohlberg, Lawrence (1971). "From Is to Ought." In T. Mischel, ed., *Cognitive Development and Epistemology,* 151–235. New York: Academic Press.

_______ (1976). "Moral Stages and Moralization: The Cognitive-Development Approach." In T. Lickona, ed., *Moral Development and Behavior,* 31–53. New York: Holt, Rinehart and Winston.

_______ (1980). "Stages of Moral Development as a Basis for Moral Education." In Brenda Munsey, ed., *Moral Development, Moral Education, and Kohlberg,* 15–98. Birmingham: Religious Education Press.

Kohlberg, Lawrence, J. Lacrosse, and D. Ricks (1972). "The Predictability of Adult Mental Health from Childhood Behavior." In B. B. Wolman, ed., *Manual of Child Psychopathology,* 1217–84. New York: McGraw-Hill.

Kopfensteiner, Thomas R. (1998). "The Role of the Sciences in Moral Reasoning." *Science et Esprit* 1: 79–97.

Kosman, L. A. (1980). "Being Properly Affected: Virtues and Feelings in Aristotle's Ethics." In A. O. Rorty, ed., *Essays on Aristotle's Ethics.* 103–16. Berkeley: University of California Press.

Krämer, Hans (1992). *Integrative Ethik*. Frankfurt: Suhrkamp Verlag.

Kuhn, Thomas S. (1970). *The Structure of Scientific Revolutions*. 2nd ed. Chicago: University of Chicago Press.

Labourdette, M.-Michel (1957). "Dons du Saint-Esprit, IV. Saint Thomas et la théologie thomiste." In *DS* III: 1610–35.

_______ (1961–62). *Force et Tempérance*. Scriptum for a course in Moral Theology. Toulouse.

Lacoste, Jean-Yves (1998). "Espérance." In J.-Y. Lacoste, ed., *DCT*, 400–404.

_______, ed. (1998). *Dictionnaire critique de théologie (DCT)*. Paris: PUF.

Larrabee, Mary Jeanne, ed. (1992). *An Ethic of Care: Feminist and Interdisciplinary Perspectives*. New York: Routledge.

Lazarus, Richard S. (1968). *Patterns of Adjustment and Human Effectiveness*. New York: McGraw-Hill.

_______ (1982). "Thoughts on the Relations between Emotion and Cognition." *American Psychologist* 37: 1019–24.

_______ (1991a). "Cognition and Motivation in Emotion." *American Psychologist* 46: 352–67.

_______ (1991b). "Progress on a Cognitive-Motivational Relational Theory of Emotion." *American Psychologist* 46: 819–34.

Lazarus, Richard S., and S. Folkman (1984). *Stress, Appraisal, and Coping*. New York: Springer.

Lazarus, Richard S., and Bernice N. Lazarus (1994). *Passion and Reason: Making Sense of Our Emotions*. Oxford: Oxford University Press.

Lebovici, Serge, René Diatkine, and Michel Soule, eds. (1998). *Nouveau traité de psychiatrie de l'enfant*. 4 vols. Paris: PUF.

Lee, T. W., E. A. Locke, and G. P. Latham (1989). "Goal Setting Theory and Job Performance." In L. A. Pervin, ed., *Goal Concepts in Personality and Social Psychology*, 291–326. Hillsdale, NJ: Erlbaum.

Leighton, Stephen (1980). "Aristotle and the Emotions." In A. O. Rortie, ed., *Essays on Aristotle's Rhetoric*, 203–37. Berkeley: University of California Press.

Leighton, Stephen R. (1988). "Aristotle's Courageous Passions." *Phronesis* 33: 76–99.

Léon-Dufour, Xavier (1975). *Dictionnaire du Nouveau Testament*. Paris: Ed. du Seuil.

_______, ed. (1995). *Vocabulaire de théologie biblique*. Paris: Ed. du Cerf.

Levin, J. S., and K. S. Markides (1986). "Religious Attendance and Subjective Health." *JSSR* 25: 31–38.

Lewis, Paul Allen (1991). *Rethinking Emotions and the Moral Life in Light of Thomas Aquinas and Jonathan Edwards*. Ph.D. diss., Duke University.

Long, A. A. (1995). "Cicero's Politics in *De Officiis*." In A. Laks and M. Schofield, eds., *Justice and Generosity*, 213–40. Cambridge, UK: Cambridge University Press.

Long, A. A., and D. N. Sedley. (1987). *The Hellenistic Philosophers*. 2 vols. Cambridge, UK: Cambridge University Press.

Lösel, Friedrich (1994). "Resilience in Childhood and Adolescence." *Children Worldwide*. Geneva: BICE.

Lösel, Friedrich, and T. Bliesener (1990). "Resilience in Adolescence: A Study on the Generalizability of Protective Factors." In K. Hurrelmann and F. Lösel, eds., *Health Hazards in Adolescence*. New York: Walter de Guyter.

Lottin, Odon (1942–60). *Psychologie et morale aux XIIe et XIIIe siècles*. 8 vols. Louvain: Abbaye Mont César.

Louth, Andrew (1998). "Martyre." In J.-Y. Lacoste, ed., *DCT*, 711–13.

Lumsden, Charles J., and Edward O. Wilson (1981). *Genes, Mind, and Culture: The Coevolutionary Process*. Cambridge, MA: Havard University Press.

Luthar, Suniya S. (2003). *Resilience and Vulnerability : Adaptation in the Context of Childhood Adversities*. Cambridge, UK: Cambridge University Press.

Luthar Suniya S., and Zigler E. (1991). "Vulnerability and Competence: A Review on Research on Resilience in Childhood." *American Journal of Orthopsychiatry* 61(1): 6–22.

MacIntyre, Alasdair (1966/1999). *A Short History of Ethics.* London and New York: Routledge and Kegan Paul.

_______ (1981/1985). *After Virtue: A Study in Moral Theory.* London: Duckworth.

_______ (1983). *Against the Self-Images of the Age: Essays on Ideology and Philosophy.* New York: Schocken Books.

_______ (1984). *Marxism and Christianity.* Notre Dame: University of Notre Dame Press.

_______ (1988). *Whose Justice? Which Rationality?* London: Duckworth.

_______ (1990). *Three Rival Versions of Moral Enquiry: Encyclopedia, Genealogy and Tradition.* Notre Dame: University of Notre Dame Press.

_______ (1994). "A Partial Response to My Critics." In J. Horton and S. Mendus, eds., *After MacIntyre: Critical Perspectives on the Work of Alasdair MacInytre,* 283–304. Notre Dame: University of Notre Dame.

_______ (1999). *Dependent Rational Animals: Why Human Beings Need the Virtues.* Paul Carus Lecture Series 20. Chicago: Open Court.

Macrobius, Ambrosius Theodosius (1994). *Commentarii in Somnium Scipionis.* Edited by Jacob Willis. Stutgard: Teubneri.

Maddi, Salvatore R., and Suzanne C. Kobasa (1984). *The Hardy Executive: Health under Stress.* Homewood, IL: Dow Jones-Irwin.

Manciaux, Michel (1995). "De la vulnérabilité à la résilience: du concept à l'action." Unpublished notes. Université de Nancy (France).

Manciaux, Michel, et al. (2001). "La résilience: état des lieux." In Michel Manciaux, ed., *La résilience: résister et se constuire,* 13–21. Geneva: Editions Médecine and Hygiène.

Mannoia, V. James (1980). *What is Science? An Introduction to the Structure and Methodology of Science.* Lanham: University Press of America.

Marcus, George E., and Michael M. J. Fischer (1986). *Anthropology as Cultural Critique: An Experimental Moment in the Human Sciences.* Chicago: University of Chicago Press.

Maslow, Abraham H. (1971/1987). *Motivation and Personality.* Revised by R. Fager, J. Fadiman, and D. McReynolds. New York: Harper and Row.

Masten, Ann S., K. M. Best, and N. Garmezy (1990). "Resilience and Development: Contributions from the Study of Children Who Overcome Adversity." *Development and Psychopathology* 2: 425–44.

Masten, Ann S., and N. Garmezy (1985). "Risk, Vulnerability and Protective Factors in Developmental Psychology." In B. B. Lahey, & A.E. Kazdin, eds., *Advances in Child Clinical Psychology,* 1–52. New York: Plenum Press.

Masten, Ann S., and Marie-Gabrielle Reed (2002). "Resilience in Development." In C. R. Snyder and S. J. Lopez, eds., *Handbook of Positive Psychology,* 74–88. Oxford: Oxford University Press.

Masten, Ann S., et al. (1990). "Competence under Stress: Risk and Protective Factors." In Jon Rolf, et al., eds., *Risk and Protective Factors,* 236–56.

Masters, Kevin S., and Allen E. Bergin (1992). "Religious Orientation and Mental Health." In John F. Schumaker, ed., *Religion and Mental Health,* 221–32. New York: Oxford University Press.

Mattison, William C., III (2001). "Examining the Role of the Emotions in the Moral Life." In Michael H. Barnes, ed., *Theology and the Social Sciences,* 277–292. New York: Orbis Books.

Maughan, Barbara (1988). "School Experiences as Risk / Protective Factors." In M. Rutter, ed., *Studies of Psychosocial Risk,* 200–220.

McCubbin, Hamilton I., et al. (1998). "Ethnicity, Schema, and Coherence: Appraisal Processes for Families in Crisis." In H. I. McCubbin et al., eds., *Stress, Coping, and Health in Families,* 41–67. Thousand Oaks, CA: SAGE.

McDermott, Timothy (1999). "Beginnings and Ends: Some Thoughts on Thomas Aquinas, Virtue and Emotions." *Studies in Christian Ethics* 12, no. 1: 35–47.

McGrady, Andrew G. (1994). "Metaphorical and Operational Aspects of Religious Thinking: Research with Irish Catholic Pupils (Part 2)." *British Journal of Religious Education* 17: 156–62.

McInerny, Daniel (1997). "'Divinity Must Live within Herself': Nussbaum and Aquinas on Transcending the Human." *International Philosophical Quarterly* 37, no. 1: 65–82.

McNamee, Maurice B. (1960). *Honor and the Epic Hero: A Study of the Shifting Concept of Magnanimity in Philosophy and Epic Poetry.* New York: Holt, Rinehart and Winston.

Meilaender, Gilbert (1984). *The Theory and Practice of Virtue.* Notre Dame: University of Notre Dame Press.

Meyer, Aleta L., and Linda Lausell (1996). "The Value of Including 'Higher Powers' in Efforts to Prevent Violence and Promote Optimal Outcomes in Adolescence." In R. Hampton et al., eds., *Preventing Violence in America,* 115–32. London: Sage Publications.

Michel, Bernard-François (1998). "Un modèle de résilience: les centenaires." In Boris Cyrulnik, ed., *Ces enfants qui tiennent le coup,* 91–108.

Moberg, Carol L., and Zanvil A. Cohn (1991). "René Jules Dubos." *Scientific American,* May: 32–38.

Morval, M., ed. (1986). *Stress et famille.* Montréal: Les Presses de l'Université de Montréal.

Munier, Charles (1991). "Tertullien." *DS* XV: 271–95.

Murphy, Lois Barclay (1987). "Further Reflections on Resilience." In E. J. Anthony and B. J. Cohler, eds., *The Invulnerable Child,* 84–105.

Murphy, Lois Barclay, and Alice E. Moriarty (1976). *Vulnerability, Coping and Growth: From Infancy to Adolescence.* New Haven: Yale University Press.

Murphy-O'Connor, Jerome (1990). "The Second Letter to the Corinthians." In R. Brown, ed., *New Jerome Biblical Commentary,* 816–29. New York: Prentice Hall.

Musick, Judith S., et al. (1987). "Maternal Factors Related to Vulnerability and Resiliency in Young Children at Risk." In E. J. Anthony and B. J. Cohler, eds., *The Invulnerable Child,* 229–52.

Myers, David G., and Ed Diener (1996). "The Pursuit of Happiness." *Scientific American,* May: 54–56.

Naroll, Raoul (1983). *The Moral Order: An Introduction to the Human Situation,* with the ed. assistance of Frada Naroll. Berkeley Hills and London: Sage.

Nef, Frédéric, and Jean-Yves Lacoste (1998). "Béatitude." In J-Y. Lacoste, ed., *DTC,* 148–53.

Nelson, Paul (1987). *Narrative and Morality: A Theological Inquiry.* University Park: Pennsylvania State University Press.

Nessan, Craig L. (1998). "Sex, Aggression, and Pain: Sociobiological Implications for Theological Anthropology." *Zygon* 33: 443–54.

Neyrey, Jerome H. (1998). *Honor and Shame in the Gospel of Matthew.* Louisville: Westminster John Knox Press.

Noble, H.-D. (1932). *Les Passions dans la vie morale.* 5th ed. Paris: Lethielleux.

Noonan, John T., Jr. (1993). "Development of Moral Doctrine." *TS* 54: 662–77.

Nussbaum, Martha C. (1988). "Non-Relative Virtues: An Aristotelian Approach." *Midwest Studies in Philosophy, Ethical Theory: Character and Virtue* 13: 32–53.

_______ (1994). *The Therapy of Desire: Theory and Practice in Hellenistic Ethics.* Princeton: Princeton University Press.

Nye, Rebecca, and David Hay (1996). "Identifying Children's Spirituality: How Do You Start without a Starting Point?" *British Journal of Religious Education* 18, no.3: 145–51.

O'Connell Higgins, Gina (1994). *Resilient Adults: Overcoming a Cruel Past.* San Francisco: Jossey-Bass.

O'Connor, Edward D. (1974). *The Gifts of the Holy Spirit (Summa theologiae, vol. 24, 1a2ae. 68–70).* English translation, introduction, notes, appendices, and glossary. London: Eyre and Spottiswoode.

Ockham, William (1942). *Tractatus de praedestinatione et de praescientia Dei et de futuris contingentibus*. Edited by Philotheus Boehner. St. Bonaventure, NY: Franciscan Institute.

O'Rourke, John J. (1968). "The Second Letter to the Corinthians." In R. E. Brown, J. A. Fitzmyer, and R. E. Murphy, eds., *The Jerome Biblical Commentary*, vol. 2, 276–90. Englewood, NJ: Prentice Hall.

Osborn, Albert F. (1990). "Resilient Children: A Longitudinal Study of High Achieving Socially Disadvantaged Children." *Early Child Development and Care* 62: 23–47.

______ (1993). "What Is the Value of the Concept of Resilience for Policy and Intervention?" Conference presentation for the International Catholic Child Bureau, Geneva, 3 November 1993.

______ (1994). "Resilience and Intervention Strategies." *Children Worldwide* Geneva: BICE, 21, no. 1: 12–15.

Osiek, Carolyn (1989). "The New Handmaid: The Bible and Social Sciences." *TS* 50: 260–78.

Osiek, Carolyn, and David L. Balch (1997). *Families in the New Testament World: Households and House Churches*. Louisville: Westminster John Knox Press.

Otto, Rudolf (1923). *The Idea of the Holy: An Inquiry into the Non-rational in the Idea of the Divine and Its Relation to the Rational*. Translated by John W. Harvey. London, New York: H. Milford, Oxford University Press.

Palmer, Richard E. (1969). *Hermeneutics: Interpretation Theory in Schleiermacher, Dilthey, Heidegger, and Gadamer*. Evanston: Northwestern University Press.

Pargament, K. I., et al. (1990). "God Help Me: (I) Religious Coping Efforts as Predictors of the Outcomes to Significant Negative Life Events." *American Journal of Community Psychology* 18: 793–824.

Parks, Sharon Daloz (1986). *The Critical Years: Young Adults and the Search for Meaning, Faith, and Commitment*. San Francisco: Harper Collins.

______ (1990). "Social Vision and Moral Courage: Mentoring a New Generation." *Cross-Currents* 40: 350–67.

______ (1993). "Professional Ethics, Moral Courage, and the Limits of Personal Virtue." In Barbara Darling-Smith, ed., *Can Virtue Be Taught?* 175–93.Notre Dame: University of Notre Dame Press.

Patterson, Joan M., and Ann W. Garwick (1998). "Theoretical Links: Family Meanings and Sense of Coherence." In H. I. McCubbin et al., eds., *Stress, Coping, and Health in Families*, 71–89. Thousand Oaks, CA: SAGE.

Pearson, Karl (1911). *The Grammer of Science*. London: Walter Scott.

Pelham, Brett W., (1991) "On the Benefits of Misery: Self-Serving Biases in the Depressive Self-Concept." *Journal of Personality and Social Psychology*. 61: 670-681.

Perrez, Meinrad (1992). "Cognitive Appraisals as Antecedents of Emotions and Coping: Analysed under Real Life Conditions. " *Scientific Report*, Nr. 91. University of Fribourg: Institut de Psychologie, 1992.

______ (1994a). "Cognitive Appraisals as Antecedents of Emotions and Coping Analyzed under Real Life Conditions." In D. Bartussek and M. Amelang, eds., *Fortschritte der Differentiellen Psychologie und Psychologischen Diagnostik*, 345–54. Gottingen: Hogrefe Verlag.

______ (1994b). "Stress and Coping with Stress in the Family." *Scientific Report* 111. Fribourg: Psychology Institute, University of Fribourg.

Perrez, Meinrad, and Michael Reicherts (1992a). *Stress, Coping, and Health. A Situation-Behavior Approach: Theory, Methods, Applications*. Seattle: Hogrefe and Huber.

______ (1992b). *Stress, Appraisal and Coping: A Situation-Oriented Approach to Coping Behavior*. Toronto: Hogrefe and Huber.

Persson, Per Eric (1970). *Sacra Doctrina: Reason and Revelation in Aquinas*. Translated by Ross McKenzie. Philadelphia: Fortress Press.

Pervin, L. A., ed. (1989). *Goal Concepts in Personality and Social Psychology*. Hillsdale, NJ: Erlbaum.

Peterson, Christopher, Steven F. Maier, and Martin E. P. Seligman (1993). *Learned Helplessness: A Theory for the Age of Personal Control.* New York: Oxford University Press.

Peterson, Christopher, and Martin E. P. Seligman. 2004. *Character Strengths and Virtues: A Handbook and Classification.* Oxford: Oxford University Press.

Petit, Christine, Marianne Lalou-Moatti, and Patrick Clervoy (1998). "Santé mentale. Risque. Vulnérabilité. Ressources." In Serge Lebovici et al., eds., *Nouveau traité de psychiatrie de l'enfant et de l'adolescent,* vol. 4, 3043–46. Paris: PUF.

Philibert, Paul J. (1975). "Lawrence Kohlberg's Use of Virtue in His Theory of Moral Development." *International Philosophical Quarterly* 15: 455–79.

_______ (1980). "Theological Guidance for Moral Development Research." In James Gaffney, ed., *Essays in Morality and Ethics,* 106–25. New York: Paulist.

_______ (1988). "Kohlberg and Fowler Revisited: An Interim Report on Moral Structuralism: A Review Essay." *Living Light* 24: 162–71.

Piaget, Jean (1965, orig. 1932). *The Moral Judgment of the Child.* New York: Free Press.

Pianta, Robert C., Byron Egeland, and L. Alan Sroufe (1990). "Maternal Stress and Children's Development: Prediction of School Outcomes and Identification of Protective Factors." In Jon Rolf et al., eds., *Risk and Protective Factors,* 215–35.

Pieper, Josef (1966, orig. 1949–59). *The Four Cardinal Virtues.* Notre Dame: University of Notre Dame Press.

_______ (1994, orig. 1967). *Hope and History.* Translated by D. Kipp. San Francisco: Ignatius.

_______ (1998, orig. 1958). *Happiness and Contemplation.* South Bend, IN: St. Augustine's Press.

Pilling, Doria (1992). "Escaping from a Bad Start." In B. Tizzard and V. Varma, eds., *Vulnerability and Resilience in Human Development,* 88–101. London: J. Kingsley.

Pinckaers, Servais-Théodore (1976). "Le désir naturel de voir Dieu." *Nova et Vetera* 51: 255–73.

_______ (1978a). *Le renouveau de la morale.* Paris: Téqui.

_______ (1978b). "Autonomie et hétéronomie selon saint Thomas d'Aquin." In *Dimensions éthiques de la liberté,* 104–23. Fribourg: Cerf.

_______ (1979). *Quête du bonheur.* 2nd ed. Paris: Téqui.

_______ (1984). "La béatitude dans l'éthique de saint Thomas." In L. J. Elders and K. Hedwig, eds., *The Ethics of St. Thomas Aquinas,* 80–94. Vatican: Libreria Ed. Vaticana.

_______ (1985). *Les sources de la morale chrétienne. Sa méthode, son contenu, son histoire.* Fribourg/Paris: Editions Universitaires / Cerf.

_______ (1989). "Autonomie du devoir et du bonheur? La question de l'eudémonisme." *Nova et Vetera* 64: 98–114.

_______ (1990). "Les passions et la morale." *RSPT* 74: 379–91.

_______ (1991). *La morale catholique.* Paris: Cerf / Fides.

_______ (1992). "Nature-surnature chez Saint Thomas d'Aquin." In *Ethique et natures,* 19–28. Geneva: Labor et Fides, 1992.

_______ (1993). "L'Enseignement de la théologie morale à Fribourg." In *Revue Thomiste* 93: 430–42.

_______ (1995a). *The Sources of Christian Ethics.* Translated by M. Th. Noble. Washington, DC: Catholic University of America Press. Orig. French 1985.

_______ (1995b). "The Use of Scripture and the Renewal of Moral Theology: the *Catechism* and *Veritatis Splendor.*" *Thomist* 59: 1–19.

_______ (1996). *La vie selon l'Esprit. Essai de théologie spirituelle selon saint Paul et saint Thomas d'Aquin.* Luxembourg: Editions Saint-Paul.

_______ (1997). "La parole de Dieu et la morale." *Revue d'éthique et de théologie morale, "Le Supplément"* 200: 21–38.

_______ (1998). "The Desire for Happiness as a Way to God." *Maynooth University Record:* 33–48.

_______ (1999). "The Recovery of the New Law in Moral Theology." *Irish Theological Quarterly* 64: 3–15.

_______ (2000a). "La Morale et l'Eglise, Corps du Christ." *Revue Thomiste* 100: 239–58.

_______ (2000b). "Human Freedom and Natural Law." In E. J. Furton and V. McLoud Dort, eds., *Ethical Principle in Catholic Health Care*, 41–43. Boston: National Catholic Bioethics Center.

_______ (2001a). *Le traité de la Béatitude*. Translation and notes on St. Thomas Aquinas' *Summa theologiae*, I-II qq. 1–5. Paris: Ed. du Cerf.

_______ (2001b). "Un Symposium de morale inconnu." *Nova et Vetera* (January/March): 19–34.

_______ (2001c). *A l'école de l'admiration*. Versailles: Ed. St. Paul.

_______ (2001d). *Morality: The Catholic View*. Preface by Alasdair MacIntyre. South Bend, IN: St. Augustine's Press.

_______ (2002). "The Sources of the Ethics of St. Thomas Aquinas." In S. J. Pope, ed., *The Ethics of Aquinas*. Washington, DC: Georgetown University Press.

_______ (2005). *The Pinckaers Reader: Renewing Thomistic Moral Theology*. Edited by J. Berkman and C. S. Titus. Translated by Mary-Thomas Noble et al. Washington, DC: Catholic University of America Press.

Pinckaers, Servais-Théodore, and C.-J. Pinto de Oliveira, eds. (1986). *Universalité et permanence des lois morales*. Paris/Fribourg: Cerf / Editions Universitaires.

Pinto de Oliveira, C.-J., ed. (1991). *Novitas et veritas vitae: aux sources du renouveau de la morale chrétienne*. Fribourg/Paris: Editions Universitaires Fribourg/Cerf.

Plato (1961). *Republic, Phaedo, Laches*. In *The Collected Dialogues of Plato*, ed. Edith Hamilton and Huntington Cairns. Princeton: Princeton University Press.

Polanyi, Michael (1958). *Personal Knowledge*. London: Routledge and Kegan Paul.

Pope, Stephen J. (1994). *The Evolution of Altruism and the Ordering of Love*. Washington, DC: Georgetown University Press.

_______ (1996). "Descriptive and Normative Uses of Evolutionary Theory." In L. S. Cahill and J. F. Childress, eds., *Christian Ethics: Problems and Prospects*, 166–82. Cleveland: Pilgrim Press.

_______ (1997). "Scientific and Natural Law Analysis of Homosexuality: A Methodological Study." *Journal of Religious Ethics* 25: 89–126.

_______ (1998a). "Sociobiology and Human Nature: A Perspective from Catholic Theology." *Zygon* 33, no. 2: 275–91.

_______ (1998b). "The Evolutionary Roots of Morality in Theological Perspective." *Zygon* 33, no. 4: 545–56.

Pope, Stephen J., ed. (2002). *The Ethics of Aquinas*. Washington, DC: Georgetown University Press.

Popper, Karl (1972). *Objective Knowledge: An Evolutionary Approach*. Oxford: Oxford University Press.

Porter, Jean (1990). *The Recovery of Virtue: The Relevance of Aquinas for Christian Ethics*. Louisville, KY: Westminster/John Knox Press.

_______ (1992). "The Subversion of Virtue: Acquired and Infused Virtues in the Summa theologiae." *Annual of the SCE* 11: 19–41.

_______ (1995). *Moral Action and Christian Ethics*. Cambridge, UK: Cambridge University Press.

_______ (1998a). "Vertus." In J.-Y. Lacoste, ed., *DCT*, 1218–20.

_______ (1998b). "Vertus permanentes et liées au temps: sagesse pratique, courage, et tempérance." *Concilium* 211: 79–90.

_______ (1999). *Natural Law and Divine Law: Reclaiming the Tradition for Christian Ethics*. Grand Rapids, MI: Wm. B. Eerdmanns.

_______ (2004). *Nature As Reason: A Thomistic Theory of the Natural Law.* Grand Rapids, MI: Wm. B. Eerdmans.

Post, Stephen G. (2006). *Altruism and Health.* Oxford: Oxford University Press.

Post, Stephen G., et al., eds. (2002). *Altruism and Altruistic Love: Science, Philosophy and Religion in Dialogue.* Oxford: Oxford University Press.

Post-White, Janice (1998). "The Role of Senses of Coherence in Mediating the Effects of Mental Imagery on Immune Function, Cancer Outcome, and Quality of Life." In H. McCubbin et al., eds., *Stress, Coping, and Health in Families: Sense of Coherence and Resiliency,* 279–91.

Prümmer, Dominicus M., ed. (1923). *Manuale theologiae moralis secundum principia S. Thomae Aquinatis.* 3 vols. Freiburg im Breisgau: Herder.

Puddefoot, John, C. (1998). "Sciences de la Nature." In J.-Y. Lacoste, ed., *DCT,* 1076–77.

Quetelet, L. A. (1848). *Du Système social et des lois qui le régissent.* Paris: Guillaumin.

Radke-Yarrow, Marian, and Tracy Sherman (1990). "Hard Growing: Children Who Survive." In Jon Rolf et al., eds., *Risk and Protective Factors,* 97–119.

Randall, John Herman, Jr. (1960). *Aristotle.* New York: Columbia University Press.

Reich, K. Helmut (1995). "From Either/Or to Both-And through Cognitive Development." *Thinking* 12, no. 2: 12–15.

Rhonheimer, Martin (2000). *Natural Law and Practical Reason: A Thomist View of Moral Autonomy.* Translated by G. Malsbary. New York: Fordham University Press.

Ricoeur, Paul (1981, orig. 1977). *The Rule of Metaphor: Multi-disciplinary Studies of the Creation of Meaning in Language.* Translated by R. Czerny. Toronto: University of Toronto Press.

Roberts, Robert C. "Emotions among the Virtues of the Christian Life." *Journal of Religious Ethics* 20 (1992): 37–68.

Robinson, Daniel N. (2002). *Praise and Blame: Moral Realism and Its Applications.* Princeton, NJ: Princeton University Press.

Roemer, Lizabeth, and Thomas Borkovec (1993). "Worry: Unwanted Cognitive Activity That Controls Unwanted Somatic Experience." In D. M. Wegner and J. W. Pennebaker, eds., *Handbook of Mental Control,* 220–38. Englewood Cliffs, NJ: Prentice-Hall.

Rogers, Carl (1961). *On Becoming a Person: A Therapist's View of Psychotherapy.* New York: Mariner Books.

Rolf, Jon, et al., eds. (1990). *Risk and Protective Factors in the Development of Psychopathology.* Cambridge, UK: Cambridge University Press.

Rorty, Richard (1982). *Consequences of Pragmaticism.* Brighton: Harvester Press.

Rose, Steven (1998). *Lifelines: Biology, Freedom, Determinism.* Oxford: Oxford University Press.

Rosenhan, David L., and Martin E. P. Seligman (1984). *Abnormal Psychology.* New York: R. S. Means.

Ross, W. D. (1959, orig. 1923). *Aristotle: A Complete Exposition of His Works and Thought.* 5th ed. New York: Meridian Books.

Rutter, Michael (1981). "Stress, Coping and Development: Some Issues and Questions." *Journal of Child Psychology and Psychiatry* 22: 323–56. Reprinted in N. Garmezy and M. Rutter, eds., *Stress, Coping, and Development in Children,* 1–42. New York: McGraw-Hill.

_______ (1985). "Resilience in the Face of Adversity: Protective Factors and Resistance to Psychiatric Disorders." *British Journal of Psychiatry* 147: 598–611.

_______ (1988). "Longitudinal Data in the Study of Causal Processes: Some Uses and Some Pitfalls." In M. Rutter, ed., *Studies of Psychosocial Risk: The Power of Longitudinal Data.* Cambridge, UK: Cambridge University Press.

_______ (1990). "Psychosocial Resilience and Protective Mechanisms." In Jon Rolf et al., eds., *Risk and Protective Factors,* 181–214.

_______ (1992). "Nature, Nurture and Psychopathology: A New Look at an Old Topic." In B. Tizzard and V. Varma, eds., *Vulnerability and Resilience in Human Development,* 21–38. London: J. Kingsley.

_______ (1994a). "Continuities, Transitions and Turning Points in Development." In M. Rutter and D. Hay, eds., *Development through Life: A Handbook for Clinicians.* Oxford: Blackwell Scientific.

_______ (1994b). "Stress Research: Accomplishments and Tasks Ahead." In R. J. Haggerty et al., eds., *Stress, Risk, and Resilience in Children and Adolescents: Processes, Mechanisms, and Interventions,* 354–85.

_______ (1998). "L'Enfant et la résilience." *Le Journal des Psychologues* 162 (November): 46–49.

Sabstad, Frode (1995). "Child Resilience and Religion in Relation to Humor Theory and Practice." Working paper, 17 October 1995.

Sagy, Shifra, and Aaron Antonovsky (1998). "The Family Sense of Coherence and Retirement Transition." In H. McCubbin et al., eds., *Stress, Coping, and Health in Families,* 207–26.

Salovey, Peter, and John D. Mayer (1985). "Emotional Intelligence." *Imagination, Cognition, and Personality* 9: 185–211.

Sameroff, Arnold J., and Ronald Seifer (1990). "Early Contributors to Developmental Risk." In Jon Rolf et al., eds., *Risk and Protective Factors,* 52–66.

Sameroff, Arnold J., Ronald Seifer, and C. Baldwin (1993). "Stability of Intelligence from Preschool to Adolescence: The Influence of Social and Family Risk Factors." *Child Development* 64: 80–97.

Sampley, J. P. (1995). "The Weak and the Strong: Paul's Careful and Crafty Rhetorical Strategy in Romans 14:1–15:13." In L. M. White and O. L. Yarbrough, eds., *The Social World of the First Christians,* 40–52. Philadelphia: Fortress Press.

Savage, Timothy (1996). *Power through Weakness: Paul's Understanding of the Christian Ministry in 2 Corinthians.* Cambridge, UK: Cambridge University Press.

Schaffer, H. Rudolph (1992). "Early Experience and the Parent-Child Relationship: Genetic and Environmental Interactions as Developmental Determinants." In B. Tizzard and V. Varma, eds., *Vulnerability and Resilience in Human Development,* 39–53. London: J. Kingsley.

Scheier, M. F., and C. S. Carver (1985). "Optimism, Coping, and Health: Assessment and Implications of Generalized Outcome Expectancies." *Health Psychology* 4: 219–47.

Schumacher, Bernard N. (2000). *Une philosophie de l'espérance. La pensée de Josef Pieper dans le contexte du débat contemporain sur l'espérance.* Fribourg/Paris: Eds Universitaires / Eds du Cerf.

Schumacher, Michele (2003). "Vers une nouvelle sacramentalité féministe du corps." In *Femmes dans le Christ, vers un nouveau féminisme,* sous la direction de Michele M. Schumacher, 295–336 (surtout 301–23, 333–36). Toulouse: Éditions du Carmel.

Schumaker, John F. (1992). "Introduction" and "Mental Health Consequences of Irreligion." In John F. Schumaker, ed., *Religion and Mental Health,* 3–30, 54–69. New York: Oxford University Press.

Schweiker, William (1996). "Understanding Moral Meanings: On Philosophical Hermeneutics and Theological Ethics." In L. S. Cahill and J. E. Childress, eds., *Christian Ethics: Problems and Prospects,* 76–92. Cleveland: Pilgrim Press.

Secrétan, Philibert (1993). "Courage et prudence." In *Initiation à la practique de la Théologie.* Vol. 4: *Ethique,* 295–317. 3rd ed. Paris: Cerf.

Seligman, Martin E. P. (1975). *Helplessness.* New York: W. H. Freeman.

_______ (1995). *The Optimistic Child.* New York: Harper Perennial.

_______ (1998, orig. 1991). *Learned Optimism.* New York: Pocket Books.

_______ (2002). "Positive Psychology, Positive Prevention, and Positive Theory." In C. R. Snyder and S. J. Lopez, eds., *Handbook of Positive Psychology,* 3–12. Oxford: Oxford University Press.

Seligman, Martin E. P., and M. Csikszentmihalyi (2000). "Positive Psychology: An Introduction." *American Psychologist* 55: 5–14.

Sharp, Ann Margaret, and Laurence Splitter (1995). *The Classroom Community of Inquiry.* Melbourne, Australia: ACER.

Sherman, Nancy (1997). *Making a Necessity of Virtue: Aristotle and Kant on Virtue.* Cambridge, UK: Cambridge University Press.

Sherwin, Michael S. (2005a). *"By Knowledge and by Love": Charity and Knowledge in the Moral Theology of St. Thomas Aquinas.* Washington, DC: Catholic University of America Press.

_______ (2005b). "In What Straits They Suffered: St. Thomas's Use of Aristotle to Transform Augustine's Critique of Earthly Happiness." *Nova et Vetera* 3: 321–34.

Shortz, Joianne L., and Everett L. Worthington (1994). "Young Adults' Recall of Religiosity, Attributions, and Coping in Parental Divorce." *JSSR* 33: 172–79.

Smoes, Etienne (1995). *Le courage chez les grecs, d'Homère à Aristote.* Bruxelles: Editions OUSIA.

Snyder, C. R., and Shane J. Lopez, eds. (2002). *Handbook of Positive Psychology.* Oxford: Oxford University Press.

Snyder, C. R., et al. (1991a). "The Will and the Ways: Development and Validation of an Individual-Difference Measure of Hope." *Journal of Personality and Social Psychology* 60: 570–85.

_______ (1991b). "Hope and Health." In C. R. Snyder and Donelson R. Forsyth, eds., *Handbook of Social and Clinical Psychology: The Health Perspective,* 285–305. New York: Pergamon Press.

Somme, Luc-Thomas (1999, 2000). "La magnanimité chez Aristote." *RT* 99 (1999): 700–735; 100 (2000): 62–78.

Sorabji, Richard (2002). *Emotion and Peace of Mind: From Stoic Agitation to Christian Temptation.* Gifford Lectures. Oxford: Oxford University Press.

Spangler, G. (1990). "Mother, Child, and Situational Correlates of Toddlers' Social Competence." *Infant Behavior and Development* 13: 405–19.

Spanneut, Michel (1982). "Le stoïcisme dans l'histoire de la patience chrétienne." *Mélanges de Science religieuse* 39, no. 3: 101–30.

_______ (1984a). "Influences stoïciennes sur la pensée morale de saint Thomas d'Aquin." In L. J. Elders and K. Hedwig, eds., *The Ethics of St. Thomas Aquinas,* 50–79. Vatican: Libreria Ed. Vaticana.

_______ (1984b). "Patience." In *DS* XII: 438–76.

Spicq, Ceslas (1970). *Théologie morale du Nouveau Testament.* Paris: Lecoffre.

_______ (1972). *Vie chrétienne et pérégrination selon le Nouveau Testament.* Lectio divina 71. Paris: Ed. du Cerf.

_______ (1991a). "*ὑπομένω, ὑπομονή.*" In *Lexique Théologique du Nouveau Testament,* 1554–61. Paris: Cerf.

_______ (1991b). *Lexique théologique du Nouveau Testament.* Fribourg: Editions Universitaires.

Spilka, B., P. Shaver, and L. A. Kirkpatrick (1985). "A General Attribution Theory for the Psychology of Religion." *JSSR* 24: 1–20.

Stark, Rodney, and William Sims Bainbridge (1985). *The Future of Religion: Secularization, Revival and Cult Formation.* Berkeley: University of California Press.

Sternberg, Robert J. (1985). *Beyond IQ: A Triarchic Theory of Human Intelligence.* Cambridge, UK: Cambridge University Press.

Stocker, Michael, and Elizabeth Hegeman (1996). *Valuing Emotions.* Cambridge, UK: Cambridge University Press.

Stotland, E. (1969). *The Psychology of Hope.* San Francisco: Jossey-Bass.

Stout, Jeffrey (1988). *Ethics after Babel: The Languages of Morals and Their Discontents.* Boston: Beacon Press.

Stroup, George W. (1984). *The Promise of Narrative Theology.* London: SCM Press.

Tertullian (1963). *Of Patience.* Translated by S. Thelwell. In *Ante-Nicene Fathers,* vol. 3, 707–17. Grand Rapids, MI: Wm. B. Eerdmans.

_______ (1984). *De la patience.* Translated and intro. by Jean-Claude Fredouille. Paris: Cerf.

Thomas, Alexander, and Stella Chess (1989). "Temperament and Personality." In G. A. Kohnstamm et al., eds., *Temperament in Childhood,* 249–62. Chichester: Wiley.

Thomas, Darwin L., and Craig Carver (1990). "Religion and Adolescent Social Competence." In T. P. Gullotta, G. R. Adams, and R. Montemayor, eds., *Developing Social Competency in Adolescence,* 195–219. Newbury Park, CA: Sage.

Thomson, J. A. K. (1953). *Ethics.* Penguin Classics.

Tillich, Paul (1954/2000). *The Courage to Be.* New Haven: Yale University Press.

Titus, Craig Steven (1990). *The Development of Virtue and "Connaturality" in Thomas Aquinas' Works.* Licentiate Thesis. University of Fribourg (CH).

Tomkiewicz, Stanislaw (2001). "Du bon usage de la résilience: quand la résilience se substitue à la fatalité." In Michel Manciaux, ed., *La résilience: résister et se constuire,* 229–39. Geneva: Editions Médecine and Hygiène.

Torrell, Jean-Pierre (1994). "S. Thomas d'Aquin et la science du Christ: une relecture des Questions 9–12 de la *Tertia Pars* de la *Somme de théologie.*" In S.-T. Bonino, ed., *Saint Thomas au XXe siècle,* 394–409. Paris: St. Paul.

_______ (1996). *Saint Thomas Aquinas: His Person and Work.* Vol. 1. Translated by Robert Royal. Washington: Catholic University of America Press.

_______ (1999). *Le Christ en ses mystères: La vie et l'oeuvre de Jésus selon saint Thomas d'Aquin.* Vol. 1. Paris: Desclée.

_______ (2003). *Saint Thomas Aquinas: Spiritual Master.* Vol. 2. Translated by Robert Royal. Washington: Catholic University of America Press.

Toulmin, Stephen (1967). "The Evolutionary Development of Natural Science." *American Scientific* 55: 456–71. Reprinted in W. H. Truit et al. eds., *Science, Technology, and Freedom,* 106–17. Boston: Houghton-Mifflin, 1974.

Tousignant, Michel (1997). "Refugees and Immigrants in Quebec." In I. Allisa and M. Tousignant, eds., *Ethnicity, Immigration and Psychopathology,* 57–70. Series Stress and Coping. New York: Plenum Press.

_______ (1998). "Ecologie sociale de la résilience." In B. Cyrulnik, ed., *Ces enfants qui tiennent le coup,* 61–72.

Turner, Stephen P. (1986). *The Search for a Methodology of Social Science: Durkheim, Weber, and the Nineteenth-Century Problem of Cause, Probability, and Action.* Dordrecht: D. Reidel.

van der Meersch, J. (1925). "Grace." In *DTC,* VI.2: 1554–1687.

Van Huyssteen, J. Wentzel (1998). *Duet or Duel? Theology and Science in a Postmodern World.* Harrisburg, PA: Trinity Press International.

_______ (1999). *The Shaping of Rationality: Toward Interdisciplinarity in Theology and Science.* Grand Rapids, MI: Wm. B. Eerdmans.

Vanistendael, Stefan (1995). *Growth in the Muddle of Life. Resilience: Building on people's strength.* 2nd ed. Geneva: Bureau International Catholique de l'Enfance.

_______ (2002). *Le réalisme de la foi: résilience et spiritualité.* Paris: Bureau International Catholique de l'Enfance.

Vanistendael, Stefan, and Jacques Lecomte (2000). *Le bonheur est toujours possible: construire la résilience.* Paris: Bayard.

Vansteenberghe, E. (1932). "Patience." In *DTC,* XI.2: 2247–51.

Verbeke, Gerard (1994). "L'éducation morale et les arts chez Aristote et Thomas d'Aquin." *Scientia und ars im Hoch- und Spätmittelarter (Miscellanea Mediaevalia),* vol. 22, 449–67. Berlin: de Gruyter.

Vitz, Paul C. (1997). "A Christian Theory of Personality." In R. C. Roberts and M. R. Talbot, eds., *Limning the Psyche: Explorations in Christian Psychology,* 20–40. Grand Rapids, MI: Wm. B. Eerdmans.

von Wright, G. H. (1963). *Varieties of Goodness.* London: Routledge and Kegan.

Waldstein, Michael M. (1994). "On Scripture in the *Summa Theologiae*." *Aquinas Review* 1: 73–94.

Wallace, William A. (1996). *The Modeling of Nature: Philosophy of Science and Philosophy of Nature in Synthesis*. Washington, DC: Catholic University of America Press.

Wallwork, Ernest (1999). "Psychodynamic Contributions to Religious Ethics: Toward Reconfiguring *Askesis*." *Annual of the Society of Christian Ethics* 19: 167–89.

Walsh, P. G. (1966). *Commentary on* Summa Theologicae. Vol. 42: *Courage*. Edited and translated by Anthony Ross and P. G. Walsh. London: Eyre and Spottiswoode.

Walton, Douglas N. (1986). *Courage: A Philosophical Investigation*. Berkeley: University of California Press.

Watt, Norman, et al. (1990). "Children's Adjustment to Parental Divorce: Self-Image, Social Relations, and School Performance." In Jon Rolf et al., eds., *Risk and Protective Factors*, 281–303.

Watts, Fraser N. (1997). "Psychological and Religious Perspectives on Emotion." *Zygon* 32: 243–60.

Watts, Fraser N., and Mark Williams (1988). *The Psychology of Religious Knowing*. Cambridge, UK: Cambridge University Press.

Weber, Edouard-Henri (1991). *La personne humaine au 13ème siècle. L'avènement chez les maîtres parisiens de l'acceptation moderne de l'homme*. Vol. 47. Bibliothéque Thomistique. Paris: Vrin.

Webster's Encyclopedic Unabridged Dictionary of the English Language (1989). New York: Portland House.

Werner, Emmy E. (1989). "Children of the Garden Island." *Scientific American* (April): 76–81.

Werner, Emmy E., and Ruth S. Smith (1986). *Vulnerable but Invincible: A Longitudinal Study of Resilient Children and Youth*. New York: Adams, Bannister, Cox.

_______ (1992). *High Risk Children from Birth to Adulthood*. Ithaca: Cornell University Press.

_______ (2001). *Journeys from Childhood to Midlife: Risk, Resilience, and Recovery*. Ithaca, NY: Cornell University Press.

Westberg, Daniel (1992). "The Relation of Law and Practical Reason in Aquinas." In Deal W. Hudson and Dennis Wm. Moran, eds., *The Future of Thomism*, 279–90. Notre Dame: American Maritain Association / University of Notre Dame Press.

Whitmore, Todd David (1999). "Will it Be Radical?: Countering the Catholic Theodramatics of 'Intimate' Rape." Conference delivered at the SCE annual convention, 9 January 1999.

Wills, Thomas Ashby, et al. (1996). "Family Support, Coping, and Competence." In E. M. Hetherington and E. A. Blechman, eds., *Stress, Coping, and Resiliency*, 107–33.

Wilson, Beverly J., and John M. Gottman (1996). "Attention—The Shuttle between Emotion and Cognition: Risk, Resiliency, and Physiological Bases." In E. M. Hetherington and E. A. Blechman, eds., *Stress, Coping, and Resiliency*, 189–228.

Wilson, Edward O. (1975/1978). *Sociobiology: The New Synthesis*. Cambridge, MA: Harvard University Press.

_______ (1987). "Religion and Evolutionary Theory." In David M. Byers, ed., *Religion, Science, and the Search for Wisdom*, 81–90. Washington, DC: USCC.

_______ (1998). *Consilience: The Unity of Knowledge*. New York: Knopf.

Winnicott, D. W. (1971). *Playing and Reality*. London: Tavistock.

_______ (1987). *The Child, The Family and the Outside World*. Reading, MA: Addison-Wesley.

Wolin, Steven, and Sybil Wolin (1993). *The Resilient Self: How Survivors of Troubled Families Rise Above Adversity*. New York: Villiard Books, 1993.

Woods, Walter J. (1998). *Walking with Faith: New Perspectives on the Sources and Shaping of Catholic Moral Life*. Collegeville, MN: Liturgical Press.

Yearly, Lee H. (1971). "The Nature-Grace Question in the Context of Fortitude." *Thomist* 35: 557–80.

_______ (1990). *Mencius and Aquinas: Theories of Virtues and Conceptions of Courage.* Albany: State University of New York Press.

Yule, William (1992). "Resilience and Vulnerability in Child Survivors of Disasters." In B. Tizzard and V. Varma, eds., *Vulnerability and Resilience in Human Development,* 182–98. London: J. Kingsley.

Zagar, Janko (1984). *Acting on Principles.* Lanham: University Press of America.

Index of Subjects

Index of Names

Resilience and the Virtue of Fortitude: Aquinas in Dialogue with the Psychosocial Sciences was designed and typeset in Jenson by Kachergis Book Design of Pittsboro, North Carolina. It was printed on 60-pound Natures Natural and bound by Thomson-Shore of Dexter, Michigan.